This book belongs to

"*The Bible Recap* is about to be your go-to resource for reading through the Bible in one year. Each day you will see the character of God through Scripture jump off the page, and your heart and relationship with God will be forever changed in the best ways possible."

—**JAMIE IVEY**, bestselling author and host of *The Happy Hour with Jamie Ivey* podcast

"Tara-Leigh gets me excited to read the Bible. Period. I have found a trusted guide to walk me into deeper understanding of the Scriptures. Humble, approachable, and wise, Tara-Leigh leads us into the larger narrative of the Bible with humor, truth, and accuracy."

—**MICHAEL DEAN MCDONALD**, director of global focus and strategic relationships, the Bible Project

"I have been a Bible reader for years, but Tara-Leigh has opened greater depth and understanding to my Bible engagement through *The Bible Recap*. This resource is one of my top recommendations for anyone looking to plunder the goodness of God's Word in bite-size portions. Read, discover, and enjoy!"

—**LAUREN MCAFEE**, ministry investments at Hobby Lobby Corporate and author of *Not What You Think*

"Tara-Leigh has the most insightful audio commentary of the Bible in the world! You better believe this book is an incredible resource. She's thoroughly done her homework and does an awesome job of presenting the reader with a helpful guide to the Bible. I've been a fan of hers for quite a while because she makes me a bigger fan of Jesus and His Word."

—**JONATHAN POKLUDA**, lead pastor, Harris Creek Baptist Church

"I have the greatest desire to read the Bible, but I often resist doing it because I need help understanding what I am reading, how it pertains to my life, and how I can grasp the character of God in Scripture. I am so thankful for *The Bible Recap*, first because it provides a reading plan, and second because it is has given me such a deep look into the narrative of Scripture and the presence of God. It has completely deepened my time with the Lord!"

—**LAUREN SCRUGGS KENNEDY**, *New York Times* bestselling author, lifestyle blogger, and founder of LSK, LSK Foundation, and Stranded

"Tara-Leigh's love for Christ and His church is poured over every single page of this book like perfume from a broken alabaster jar. As a companion to the Word itself, *The Bible Recap* works like a key to unlock room after room in God's hallway of mysteries. I am confident this will be a powerful resource for God seekers and God lovers for years to come."

—**LEE MCDERMENT**, Greenville campus pastor, NewSpring Church

"As a young believer I was taught to love good worship and good preaching, but no one taught me how to love (and understand) the Bible for myself. *The Bible Recap* has helped stir in me a love and a desire for God's Word, and I wish I had it earlier in my journey. I am making this my year of the Bible by joining my friend Tara-Leigh, and I encourage you to do the same!"

—**NICK HALL**, founder and chief communicator, Pulse

"Tara-Leigh approaches the Bible with humility, passion, and a deep desire to exalt God. With an approachable style and rich content, *The Bible Recap* will help you fall in love with God's Word and, ultimately, who it points to—Jesus Christ."

—**DAVID BOWDEN**, founder, Spoken Gospel

"Understanding the Bible is paramount in our lives, and Tara-Leigh Cobble is amazing at teaching others to understand the Bible and its truth. This is a must-read!"

—**CHERYL SCRUGGS**, biblical marriage counselor, podcast host, and coauthor of *I Do Again*

"I love *The Bible Recap* because it is eternally valuable and immediately practical! My family has truly appreciated this resource."

—**BRAD COOPER**, lead pastor, NewSpring Church

"Tara-Leigh is one of those people you could sit and discuss the Bible with for hours and walk away with your soul both satisfied and hungry for more. Now she's captured these chats in a format we can carry with us. *The Bible Recap* will not only give you a greater understanding of Scripture, but it's sure to enhance your love for the God who penned it."

—**DAVEY BLACKBURN**, author, speaker, and podcaster, Nothing is Wasted Ministries

"I am in awe of Tara-Leigh Cobble's passion and knack for teaching us all how to better understand God. Her fresh, quick, powerful teaching resonates with millions for a reason: It's good! She has created an engaging and easy-to-understand guide that strengthens your faith and leaves you feeling hopeful and excited about the Word of God."

—**VALORIE BURTON**, bestselling author of *Successful Women Think Differently* and CEO of the CaPP Institute

THE BIBLE RECAP

THE BIBLE RECAP

A ONE-YEAR GUIDE TO READING AND UNDERSTANDING THE ENTIRE BIBLE

TARA-LEIGH COBBLE

BETHANYHOUSE
a division of Baker Publishing Group
Minneapolis, Minnesota

Published by Bethany House Publishers
Minneapolis, Minnesota
BethanyHouse.com

Bethany House Publishers is a division of
Baker Publishing Group, Grand Rapids, Michigan

This edition published 2026

Printed in China

ISBN 978-0-7642-3703-4 (cloth edition)
ISBN 978-0-7642-4191-8 (personal size, blue)
ISBN 978-0-7642-4760-6 (personal size, pink)

Instances of italics in Scripture quotations are added by the author.

Cover design by Rob Williams, InsideOut Creative Arts, Inc.
The Bible Recap logo design by Landon Wade

The author is represented by Alive Literary Agency, www.aliveliterary.com.

Baker Publishing Group publications use paper produced from sustainable forestry practices and postconsumer waste whenever possible.

26 27 28 29 30 31 32   7 6 5 4 3 2 1

This book is dedicated to every person who has tried and failed countless times to read the Bible, who has almost given up on understanding God and His Word, and who is here, trying one more time—with equal parts hope, fear, and skepticism—to draw near to the God of the universe.

May you come to know and love Him more and to understand that despite all your failures, He has never given up on pursuing you with love to this very page.

> "And I am sure of this, that he who began a good work in you will bring it to completion at the day of Jesus Christ."
>
> —Philippians 1:6

Contents

A Letter from Tara-Leigh Cobble

For years I struggled with Bible reading even though I was in full-time ministry. Not only was Scripture challenging to understand, but the challenge also left me with a lack of desire. Every day I felt defeated before I even started, and many days I didn't start at all. Eventually, I learned I was making three primary mistakes that held me back from understanding and loving Scripture.

Mistake #1

My first major mistake was looking for myself. I viewed the Bible as a big to-do list, and if I checked all the right boxes, God would respond by fulfilling all my desires. I approached the Bible primarily to get my application points, feel like a good, moral person, and move on. Reading Scripture as a story about God—not me—felt unnatural at first, so I started asking myself a few questions to narrow my focus:

- What does God say or do in this passage?
- What does this reveal about what God loves?
- What does this reveal about what God hates?
- What does this reveal about what motivates God to do what He does?
- In all of that, what attributes of God are displayed?

The questions we ask of the Bible impact the wisdom we glean from it. Reading the Bible is not a means to self-help or an attempt to earn God's favor. It's an opportunity to behold the beauty of God and be drawn in by Him.

Mistake #2

My second major mistake stemmed from mistake #1. Since I was only looking for the steps I needed to take to appease God and have a perfect, joy-filled life, I hovered over the same passages of Scripture and disregarded the rest. There were so many old laws we no longer follow and passages about people with names I couldn't pronounce—those parts confused or bored me. But my standard approach had me dropping down in the middle of a movie and staying for five minutes, with no real idea of the story line or who the characters were, and hoping to understand it. Not only is it impossible to understand something when you handle it that way, but it's also impossible to love it.

To correct this mistake, I decided to read through Scripture chronologically, not front to back. I wanted to see the overall story line or metanarrative. I began each book by identifying who wrote it, when they wrote it, whom they wrote it to, and what style they wrote it in. The Bible has sixty-six individual books that together tell one story, but they're from a wide variety of vantage points and styles—narrative history, poetry, prophecy—and much to my initial dismay, the bulk of it is not promises or action points. Most of it serves to tell me a story about God and His unshakeable love for His people.

Reading the story in order and paying attention to the context helped me make sense of verses that appear to contradict each other. I also learned how to sift through the confusing passages to find God's character.

Mistake #3

My first two mistakes worked together to create my other major mistake: drawing conclusions about God before I'd read the whole Bible. Since I had primarily read Scripture for selfish reasons, I was impatient and didn't take time to read it all. That was a dangerous approach because I didn't have all the information. I was tempted to build a theology around one verse without knowing what other verses had to say. I was tempted to read every verse as a command, even if the verse was just describing what was happening. I wanted quick answers, and I didn't take the time to consider context or evaluate the verses against the rest of Scripture to see the fullness of God's revealed counsel.

The Bible is the story of God pursuing His people despite their sin. Bit by bit, we see Him giving them more information about who He is and who He is making them into. But it isn't all revealed at once, because they can't handle it all at once. He's patient with them, giving them baby steps. For instance, it's easy to read through parts of the Old Testament and conclude that God is angry and wants to kill anyone who disobeys Him. But when we zoom out and read the whole story, we see a through line of grace and mercy and rescue.

It required patience to hold my questions and conclusions with an open hand and continue to ask God to guide me in wisdom, knowledge, and understanding as I read each day. Some of the questions I had in Leviticus weren't answered until Hebrews. But all good relationships require patience, and they develop over time. It's worth holding some things with an open hand and waiting until God reveals more of Himself.

I spent years trying to build my life around a book I hadn't read about a God I didn't know. But now that I really know Him, I want to help others know Him better too!

By the way, I'm not an academic. I didn't go to seminary, and I'll only occasionally mention what the original Hebrew might mean, and even then, chances are I don't know how to pronounce it. I've learned much of what I know by studying and listening to a variety of scholars, so any wisdom you find in this book certainly didn't originate with me, but if you do happen to spot an error, it's likely mine.

Overall, my approach in this book will be less like a scholarly Bible commentary and more like an overview and a highlight reel rolled into one. What that means is, I'm less inclined to tell you about archaeological details and more inclined to point to the character of God as revealed in that day's reading. I want to help you learn how to find and see and know God and His character more than anything else. I don't care if you never know what year the temple was built and destroyed and rebuilt and redestroyed—those are great details to be aware of, but they will never serve you like the personal knowledge of God. They will never bring you joy or sustain you in trials. They will never draw you in to spend more time with God out of sheer joy and delight.

Here's what I'm imagining for you this year: Picture yourself being drawn to God and His character instead of feeling alienated by the God of the Old Testament. Imagine understanding the motives behind His actions instead of feeling confused or even frustrated by what He does. Picture yourself actually hearing from God in His Word directly and feeling closer to and more intimate with Him than you ever have before—just because you've committed to spending the first 1 percent of your day with Him. If all you gain from this is one new insight about God, that insight could change the rest of your life and your relationship with Him. And no matter how your circumstances change, I believe your joy will grow deeper and richer, because you will be spending time with Him—and He's where the joy is!

For the gospel,

Tara-Leigh

How to Use This Book

This book is arranged according to a one-year chronological plan, but you don't have to buy a chronological Bible. In fact, I encourage you not to because it's probably laid out differently than the plan we are doing. Each day's reading is listed at the top of each day in the book. Unlike a front-to-back plan (canonical), or plans that have you read from both the Old and New Testaments each day, the chronological plan takes you through the story of Scripture as it happened. Since Bibles aren't laid out in order, this plan will occasionally have you flipping back and forth a bit. You can go to thebiblerecap.com/start for a free printable calendar to chart your progress.

When it comes to Bible translations, it seems like everyone has a favorite among the many options. Some people prefer readability while others prefer precision. The ESV (English Standard Version) is what we'll be quoting primarily, and it has a great mix of both. While it's not necessarily the most readable translation, I've chosen it instead of other translations that are slightly easier to read because it is a "word-for-word" translation. The options that are slightly easier to read—like the New Living Translation or the New International Version—are often "phrase-for-phrase" translations. And some versions, like *The Message*, for instance, are best read as commentaries because they're more of a retelling than a translation.

Each day, you'll read the assigned chapters in the Bible. When something stands out at you as meaningful or encouraging, take note of it in your journal. When you're confused about something you read, write a question about it in your journal so you can research it later.

After you finish reading the day's Bible chapters, come back to this book to get a summary and highlight reel along with some explanations of the more confusing parts of the text. The Bible Recap team has also built a list of free resources for you on our website that correspond to the days of this plan: thebiblerecap.com/links. We'll include a footnote in the days that have resources so you'll know when to look for those.

Each day in this book ends with a section called Today's God Shot, which points to one place where God's attributes are on display in that day's reading. It's called a God Shot because it's a snapshot of God's character. I encourage you to look for your own God Shot each day too. He's on every page of Scripture, so keep your eyes peeled for things that reveal Him to you—what He says and does, what He loves and hates, and what motivates Him to do what He does.

As we move through these books, the tone and feel will change regularly. That's because some of these books are written in a wide range of literary genres, such as narrative history, poetry and wisdom literature, prophecy, and letter. They were written over several hundred years by dozens of different writers, but they all have a cohesive theme in the metanarrative. As you begin each new book, take time to research who wrote each book, to whom they wrote it, when they wrote it, and the literary style in which it was written. Those details may seem unimportant, but they set the scene for reading it as it was meant to be read, which is the only way to truly understand it—and that's our goal! Let's get started!

THE RECAPS AND CHRONOLOGICAL READING PLAN

GENESIS 1–3

Genesis is a book of the law; it's not a science book or a history book, though it does tell us a lot about history. While Scripture is 100 percent true, it isn't always 100 percent literal. It's important to hold our scientific conclusions or opinions with an open hand. It's even important to hold our questions with an open hand, because this book isn't necessarily here to answer them; it's here to reveal GOD. Today's reading is a good example. Some people believe the days of creation were prolonged periods of time lasting tens of thousands of years. This is called the day-age theory, and it's held by many old earth creationists. Most young earth creationists believe God created the earth in six literal days. What's clear in Scripture is that God is the Creator; none of this was an accident.

In 1:26, God refers to Himself in the plural form: "Let us make man in our image." All three persons of the Trinity are present and active at creation: God the Father, God the Son, and God the Spirit. The Father gives the creation commands, the Son does the manual labor of creation (John 1:3), and the Spirit hovers over creation, sustaining and approving of it. They work in tandem toward the same goal. It's important to note that Jesus doesn't just show up on the scene when He's born in a manger in the New Testament. Before God the Son took on the name Jesus, He resided in heaven with the Father. He's been here all along. In fact, we'll see Him a lot in the Old Testament. Be on the lookout for Him!

In 2:4, the word *Lord* is in all caps; this is different from when we see the word spelled *Lord* or *lord*. All lowercase *lord* can refer to anyone who is in charge, like your land*lord*. When it's capitalized as *Lord*, it means "Adonai," the Hebrew word for *Master*, which is a proper name of God, not just a general term. When you see all-caps *Lord*, it represents an ancient Hebrew spelling of YHWH. It has no vowels, so when we try to pronounce it, it sounds like "Yahweh" or "Jehovah." This is God's

For more information on today's reading, see thebiblerecap.com/links.

personal name. By telling us His name, He's showing us *right out of the gate* that He wants to be personal with His creation. He's not setting Himself apart as one not to be known or spoken to. He tells humankind His name! Despite that, it doesn't bring Him to our level. YHWH is still Lord (Master), after all.

Later, we see the fall of humankind in the sin of Adam and Eve. Because God is sovereign and isn't confined to time, nothing surprises Him. Their sin doesn't thwart His plan—His plan accounted for their sin. In 2:17 He tells them, "*In the day that you eat* of [the tree of the knowledge of good and evil] you shall surely die." He didn't say *if*; He said *when*; it implies certainty. The rest of Scripture supports this, letting us know that God wasn't relegated to plan B after they ate the fruit; it was always plan A.

When Eve questions God's goodness, she buys the lie that He's holding out on her and decides she'd make a better god. Adam is right there with her—and according to Romans 5, God holds him responsible for his role in this too. That's when the world was first fractured by sin, and it's still fracturing. Not only do we still believe and act on the same lies, but the curses pronounced over Adam and Eve still resonate in our world today. In 3:16–17, the curse states that pain will now surround childbirth and work and that sin will corrupt the relationship between husband and wife. There are a few views on what this corruption looks like, but suffice it to say that sin has impacted not only our relationships with God, creation, and ourselves, but also our relationships with each other.

TODAY'S GOD SHOT

God is our Creator and the Lord over everything, but despite His lordship and His perfection, He's merciful toward the sinners He's in relationship with. He said they'd die if they ate of the fruit, but He lets them live! He doesn't strike them down on the spot. Any time we see God hedge on His promises, it's always on the side of mercy. He doesn't break promises; He *exceeds* them. We see it again in 3:9–10, when they're hiding from Him and lying to Him. Before they even repent, He pursues them out of His great love. At the height of their sin, He continues to show them both mercy and discipline. It's such a gift to them and to us that He doesn't give up on pursuing us, because He's where the joy is!

GENESIS 4–7

Yesterday, when God finished creating, He declared it *very good*, but that's different from being perfect and complete. Imperfect man can't live up to God's standard of perfection, and that's evident in Cain's murder of Abel. This happened about 2,500 years before God gave Moses the Ten Commandments, but Cain still knew murder was wrong; he even feared other people killing him in response to it (4:14).

People often wonder whom Cain married. Adam and Eve had lots of children after Cain and Abel, so it's likely he married one of his sisters or nieces. The scientific reason incest isn't problematic here is that there's no genetic load yet. God doesn't ban incest until much later, and up until that point it serves as a tool to populate the earth. This doesn't mean God changed; it shows He has an orderly plan. Only He can know the point when genetic mutations will be a problem, so only He will know when incest has served its purpose and has crossed into dangerous territory.

The phrase *sons of God* (6:4) is one way Scripture refers to angels. The prevailing view of ancient Jews was that *sons of God* referred to fallen angels who, in this text, took human wives and had kids with them, creating a crossbreed of angels and humans known as Nephilim. Scripture says angels in heaven don't procreate, but that could be because (a) the angels in heaven are the elect angels who live under God's rule and don't rebel against Him, and/or (b) all angels referred to in Scripture are male, so they can't procreate among themselves. But if they procreated with human females, then theoretically this kind of crossbreeding would be possible. If that's the case, there's a strong chance the presence of the Nephilim contributes to the increasing wickedness on the earth.

Why would fallen angels do this? Here's a theory: The angels who lived in heaven with God knew His plan from before creation was to send God the Son to earth as a human named Jesus to redeem and restore everything; but then they rebelled against God and His kingdom, so they

For more information on today's reading, see thebiblerecap.com/links.

tried to thwart and counterfeit His plan to deceive His people. It's possible the enemy is trying to corrupt the human bloodline to prevent the birth of the Messiah by counterfeiting the supernatural-natural union. We don't have all the information here, so we hold this with an open hand. But if this *did* happen the way the ancient Jews understood it, it makes sense that God would wipe out the crossbreed population via the flood. And in this scenario, the only family whose bloodline hasn't been infiltrated by fallen angels is Noah's, so God preserves them. Regardless of what happened, God sets apart this family, these particular descendants of Adam, as the family He is in relationship with.

The ark God has Noah build is one-and-a-half football fields long, the width of a six-lane interstate, and as tall as a four-story building. Noah probably takes the tiniest of each kind of animal, and there are more breeds of animals now, but God certainly knows the ark is the perfect size to hold whatever He needs it to hold. It probably doesn't smell great, though.

Then God mentions the word *covenant* for the first time. He singles out Noah as the start of this covenant; He's continuing to work through this one family of people. Before the flood comes, He tells Noah this is only the beginning of their relationship—he's not going to die in the waters. If the timeline is spot-on, the flood happened 1,656 years after Adam was created.

TODAY'S GOD SHOT

God's sovereignty is on display here. Nothing can thwart His will. Nothing can keep Him from His plan to rescue the people He entered into relationship with. The enemy's attempts to thwart the bloodline of Christ don't prevail. God is even sovereign over weather and creation. He's at work in all things to restore fallen humanity in relationship with Himself. What incredible news—He's where the joy is!

GENESIS 8–11

In the aftermath of the flood, everything on earth has been destroyed except what's on the ark. Postflood, God establishes the covenant with Noah that He promised preflood. He engages with this family and promises to be faithful to them, despite how every other aspect of their world has shifted dramatically. Everyone they know is dead. The world is muddy and gross. They live in a new location. Everything has changed. Even their life-span will change. God gave them a heads-up in 6:3 not to expect lengthy life-spans anymore. The environment has changed dramatically, and they're a couple of millennia removed from the genetic perfection of Adam and Eve, so it makes sense that they'd drop to a general range of 120 years. Others say this timeline refers to the years between God's warning about the flood and the time of its fulfillment.

Despite the changes, God promises something that will *not* change. In His covenant, He promises never again to destroy the earth with a flood. Later in Scripture (2 Peter 3), He says He'll someday destroy the earth with fire but not with a flood. And in the same way that the earth existed after it was destroyed by water, it will still exist after it's destroyed with fire. In fact, in the eternal kingdom, all of those who have been adopted into God's family will reign with Christ on the re-created earth (Revelation 5).

This is interesting, especially as it pertains to the ultimate limits of damage to the earth and climate. God, who is sovereign over it all, promises there's a *limit* to that damage. There'll be seasons and harvests as long as the earth remains (8:22). However, His promise to sustain the earth doesn't negate His call to us to be good stewards of His gift of creation.

God calls Noah to join in on His plans. Noah plays an important role; there are only eight people on earth, and God will be sending the Messiah in about two thousand years. These eight people have a role to play in accomplishing His purposes (9:1); He tells them to be fruitful and multiply, to fill the earth. They partially obey, but they hedge on the “fill the earth” part. They multiply, but they prefer to stay put (11:4), pridefully rejecting His command. But God, being sovereign, works out His plan despite their resistance. He disperses them all over the face of the earth by dividing their languages. God always accomplishes His plans; we can’t thwart His will, despite our best sinful efforts. This is a comfort, not a threat; we can’t mess up His plan!

There are a lot of theories about 9:18–27. The general conclusion is that Ham—and possibly Ham’s son Canaan—does something blatantly contrary to God’s orders. This is long before the Ten Commandments, but there’s still an understanding of what’s right and wrong; it just hasn’t been written out yet. When Noah awakens, he curses Canaan and his descendants. One cursed line of descendants we’ll see throughout the Bible are the Canaanites. They are enemies of God’s people, but God does some really beautiful things by redeeming people outside of His clan, like Rahab the prostitute, who was a Canaanite but who is also listed in the lineage of Jesus. This shows us how God acts toward all of us whom He redeems. We are *all* enemies of God by birth. We are only children of God by adoption.

TODAY’S GOD SHOT

God did a lot of blessing in the first few chapters. It’s true that God is love, but it’s also an incomplete summary of His character. He doesn’t just dole out blessing. He’s much more complex than that. He’s a God who blesses *and* curses. And even still, He’s a God who blesses His enemies. That’s where we all started; for those of us who have been adopted into His family, He pursued us as His enemies and clothed us in the righteousness of Christ. This is reminiscent of when He pursued Adam and Eve, who were running from Him, and chased them down—not to punish them but to clothe them. He did that with us too. It’s evident every day on these pages that He’s where the joy is!

JOB 1–5

Today's reading lands us about four hundred years postflood, and we meet a man named Job. Initially, he sounds a lot like Noah; he's blameless and upright and fears God. In Noah's story, things got really dark, then there was some relief at the end, and we'll see the same pattern play out in Job's story.

After what we covered in Day 2, you may have noticed that 1:6 referred to angels as the "sons of God," including Satan, who, in his created form, is an angel. God initiates a conversation about Job with Satan. The word *satan* means "adversary, one who resists, accuser." Some scholars believe it's not necessarily a proper name that refers to one particular being, but that it's a general term referring to God's adversary, who, in this instance, is a fallen angel opposing God's reign.

Later in Scripture, there are references to a fallen angel named Lucifer, but there's reason to believe that the word *satan* doesn't always refer to Lucifer. There are many fallen angels who are God's adversaries. In fact, a lot of people believe Revelation 12 indicates that one-third of all the angels God created rebelled against Him and were cast from heaven, so there are a lot of satans.

After God initiates the conversation about Job with one of His enemies, the enemy concocts a plan to test Job, and God allows it. There's something noteworthy here: God doesn't create the plan for testing Job, but God allows it. He isn't the active agent in the evil perpetrated by Satan, but He's still sovereign over it. And in His mercy, He *limits* it. Satan is on a leash. He isn't allowed to take Job's life.

Satan attacks Job in a variety of ways. Job's losses come twice as acts of men (Sabeans and Chaldeans) and twice as acts of nature (fire from heaven and wind). God grants Satan the opportunity to influence both of those things: the acts of man and the acts of nature. For God to allow Satan to influence those things means that God Himself is the one who

For more information on today's reading, see thebiblerecap.com/links.

has control over those things, because you can't give someone influence over something that isn't in your domain.

Job's response is humble here. "In all this Job did not sin or charge God with wrong" (1:22). He acknowledges that everything comes from God's hand, and he receives it (2:10). He's handling his grief pretty well until three of his friends show up on the scene. They come to show him sympathy and comfort him, and they do a great job of that during the seven days when they sit in silence with him. The problem is when they start to speak. Maybe you've had friends like that. Or maybe you've *been* a friend like that.

There are some good lessons for us here in how to comfort someone who has experienced trauma or loss. Sitting with them in silence is a safe bet. But Job's friends start giving him bad counsel. We heard from the first one today, Eliphaz. He claims to have a word from God about what Job has done wrong (4:12–16). He insinuates that Job has brought this trouble on himself, but we know from the story that Eliphaz is wrong here. Tomorrow we'll see how Job responds to his opinionated friend.

TODAY'S GOD SHOT

God's sovereignty over evil should serve as a great comfort to His kids. God limits the actions of the enemy. And every action the enemy takes against Job serves God's greater purposes as we see them unfold in the rest of Job's story. This story gets dark, but it has a happy ending. Keep looking for God in the dark spots of this story, because He's where the joy is!

JOB 6–9

After losing everything, Job has to continue listening to and responding to bad advice from his three friends. In response to Eliphaz, Job defends himself. He's despairing, but he doesn't curse God. He knows this pain isn't the result of sinful actions. A couple of the questions counselors train you to ask yourself in relational difficulty are, "Where is my sin in this situation?" and "What can I take ownership of?" Those are important questions to ask, especially because we're often blind to our own sin. But there are times when life is just hard, or when you've been sinned against, and your troubles aren't the result of something you contributed. For instance, we'd never tell someone who had been raped or physically abused to think about what they did to deserve or cause that. It's not always true that our circumstances are the result of our choices; sometimes they're the result of our fallen world.

Much like Eliphaz, Bildad gives bad counsel. He tells Job he needs to repent. But chapter 1 told us that Job was blameless and upright and that these problems occurred *because of* his uprightness, not as the result of sin. Job's friends are attacking him in the midst of his grief, but they really think they're on the right track. They think they're helping him and that if they can just convince him to repent, all his troubles will subside. Stay tuned to see how that plays out.

Job replies to Bildad with a lot of truth about God. Job says he'll appeal for mercy to his accuser (9:15). Who is his accuser? While this could be a reference to God, it could also refer to Satan, whose name means "the accuser, the adversary." However, one of the other ways the Hebrew can be translated is "I must appeal for mercy to my judge." If that's what he's saying, then it seems he's referring to God.

Regardless of whether Job is referring to his accuser, Satan, or his judge, God, this is a good place to point out something about the word *mercy*. We often use the words *mercy* and *grace* interchangeably, but they actually mean very different things. They're like a pair of opposites that work together.

Mercy is when you don't get what you deserve. For fallen humanity, we all deserve hell. We've sinned against a holy God and tried to elevate ourselves to His rank. We deserve nothing but punishment. The fact that we're breathing right now is God's mercy toward us. Just like He showed mercy toward Adam and Eve when they sinned in the garden, He hasn't given us the immediate death we deserve for our rebellion.

On the other hand, grace is when you *get* what you *don't* deserve. It's everything over and above not being annihilated. It's the way food tastes delicious, it's the way music brings us joy, and mostly, it's the way we get to enter into a relationship with God despite our wickedness.

Job has done nothing wrong in this situation, but he's still a sinful, fallen human like the rest of us. He knows he deserves annihilation, but he also knows God might still show him mercy, because he knows God's character.

TODAY'S GOD SHOT

God's power is on display in Job's story. Job waxes about His power for several verses. God commands the sun, He does great things, He is wise in heart and mighty in strength. But this enormous God also steps down to be intimate with humankind, like Job says in 7:17, "What is man, that you make so much of him, and that you set your heart on him?" God created and is in charge of everything, but His heart isn't set on the mountains or on Orion or the Pleiades; it's set on humanity. What a shocking gift! He's where the joy is!

JOB 10–13

We've already heard from Eliphaz and Bildad, who gave their reasons for Job's life falling apart. Today we meet Job's third friend, Zophar. The hard part about listening to these guys and discerning what's applicable is that sometimes they do say true things; it's not all wrong. For example, when Zophar is talking about God, he says, "God exacts of you less than your guilt deserves" (11:6). This is true of *all* of us. We all deserve death, but He's merciful; He lets us live. We even get to live on His earth and breathe His air and eat His food—that's so much more than we deserve. That's His *grace*.

Zophar says a lot of things that are true about God. It's when he starts drawing conclusions about Job that things take a left turn. At this point, Job seems to be exhausted by the attacks from all three friends, and he starts getting sarcastic in his responses to them. He says, "No doubt you are the people, and wisdom will die with you" (12:2). Maybe he's been hoping that at least one of his friends will understand, but none of them gets it. They've all joined forces against him.

He offers some words of wisdom for those of us who want to comfort grieving friends. He says, "In the thought of one who is at ease there is contempt for misfortune; it is ready for those whose feet slip" (12:5). He's pointing out that those who aren't struggling don't understand those who are; and in fact, they have contempt for them, not compassion. Job is beginning to sense their contempt for him. Perhaps some of it is rooted in jealousy. It sounds crazy to be jealous of Job at this point, but he's a man who had everything and who was honorable. This period following the recent disasters might be the first time his friends have felt superior to him, and they jump at the chance to try to point out his sins.

In 12:9, Job acknowledges that God is the author of everything, even when He isn't the active agent in what's happening. God didn't commit these actions against Job, but if God could have stopped it and He

For more information on today's reading, see thebiblerecap.com/links.

didn't, doesn't it still kind of terminate on Him? This is a mysterious aspect of God's character; He's not the agent of evil, but it's a necessary part of the story He's writing. We'll talk more about this as we move through Scripture, so don't get hung up on it. In the meantime, resist the urge to reach conclusions about God based on what you think humans deserve—unless you're primarily recalling that we deserve nothing but hell and death. That kind of entitlement is a dangerous trap. Most, if not all, of our frustrations about God's actions are rooted in the lie that we deserve something.

The word *deserve* is saturated with the poison of entitlement. Companies use it in advertising to appeal to and feed our self-centeredness. Advertisers know how gullible we are when it comes to our comfort and pleasure. Because of God's mercy and grace, what His children are promised is that we *don't* get what we deserve—and that's a good thing.

TODAY'S GOD SHOT

"Though he slay me, I will hope in him" (13:15). Job knows the only place his hope is found. After all he's been through, even as a righteous man who is being wrongly called to account by his friends, he knows that the mercy of God is his only salvation. If you're in a dark place, dig deep into the story of Job. He gets it. Not only is God our hope in the darkest night, but ultimately, He's where the joy is!

JOB 14–16

Bad friend number one is back with his busted theology today. But before Eliphaz starts talking, Job has some good things to say. He says man's "days are determined." You know the phrase "your days are numbered"? If you've ever heard someone say that in conversation, they were probably using it as a threat: "Your days are numbered, buddy." But in the grand scheme of things, that's no threat; it's a promise and a comfort! Job said to God, "You have appointed [man's] limits that he cannot pass." God is sovereign over our life-span! Each day is appointed, and our lives will last the exact amount of time He has determined—no more, no less.

In the second half of chapter 14, Job grows melancholy while talking about his future, which makes sense given all he's been through. It's hard not to want to rush him to healing; it's hard to sit with him in his pain.

In chapter 15, Eliphaz speaks again. He's falsely accusing Job, misunderstanding his heart and his motives. He thinks Job's grief is a sign that he doesn't trust God. But those two things aren't mutually exclusive. After all, Jesus grieved and mourned, and He *is* God. It's hard to feel alone in your pain, but even harder to feel unknown in your pain.

In the ESV, chapter 16 is titled "Job Replies: Miserable Comforters Are You." Job shoots straight. He calls them out for being terrible friends. In 16:3, he even begs them to be silent and to stop advising him. "Shall windy words have an end? Or what provokes you that you answer?" We'd be wise to think carefully about when and how we advise others. God calls us to mourn with those who mourn, not to advise those who mourn—and certainly not to condemn them for their mourning.

Job has been acknowledging God's hand in all this. He recognizes that God plays a role in what's happening to him, albeit a passive one. But in 16:7, he begins to attribute the harm to God and to doubt His goodness. He believes God hates him. He blames God for all the things Satan did.

If you're in a dark place, this book is probably serving as a comfort to you. But if you're *not* in a dark place, be patient with Job. Don't engage with Job's story the same way his friends did; they wanted him to repent or change so they could get on with things. Suffering always lasts longer than we want it to. But sitting in someone else's suffering with them teaches us patience and compassion. And those are certainly the kinds of things we want others to display toward us when we're struggling. Let this book help you strengthen your patience and compassion muscles.

TODAY'S GOD SHOT

God—not the enemy—is sovereign over our life-span. This should serve as a great comfort, because God is trustworthy! Job recognizes that God is sovereign over his life and his family members' deaths (14:5). We've seen God's sovereignty over many things this week, and it's fitting that we notice all these separate areas, because *sovereign* really means that God is the supreme authority over all things, that everything is under His control. Notice if and when it feels offensive to you that He's in charge. Where do you want to be the god of your own life? Where do you feel like He's infringing on your rights with His sovereignty? Keep looking for Him in these pages, because He's where the joy is!

JOB 17–20

Today Job tells his friends, "My spirit is broken." Have you ever been there? Then Bildad, friend number two, speaks again; he's the one who told Job he needed to repent. Today he's doubling down with reminders that God punishes the wicked. This is a catch-22; it not only means Job's suffering was punishment for his wickedness, but that if he doesn't change his ways, more punishment is coming for him!

Job points to God's role *and* rescue in his troubles. He says, "He has walled up my way, so that I cannot pass, and he has set darkness upon my paths" (19:8), and yet he also says, "I know that my Redeemer lives, and at the last he will stand upon the earth" (19:25). This isn't just a hopeful statement—it's actually prophetic. It points not only to the first coming of Christ, which has already happened, but also to the second coming of Christ, which is yet to come. Even in his darkest moments, Job points out eternal truths about God.

Then Zophar, friend number three, speaks again. He claims a spirit spoke to him, and he believes it was a word from God. Eliphaz claimed the same thing when he first spoke (4:12–16). Zophar and Eliphaz presumably do this to add more weight to their words and force Job to listen and comply. But here's what's interesting: This "spirit" (or spirits) referenced in chapter 4 and chapter 20 never identifies itself. Scripture doesn't tell us who it is. Hold on to that thought as we continue reading, because you may reach some conclusions about who this spirit was.

The last part of Zophar's speech today reinforces the idea that he may be jealous of Job, because he accuses Job of being greedy and selfish. He says, "He has crushed and abandoned the poor; he has seized a house that he did not build. . . . He knew no contentment in his belly, he will not let anything in which he delights escape him" (20:19–20). But when we weigh Zophar's words about Job against God's words about Job, they don't align. These passages with Job's friends are examples of why we shouldn't take Scripture out of context. If you were to pull some of their quotes out of this section, you'd think Job was a terrible person. The statements are in Scripture, and Scripture is God's Word, but this passage is a personal quote within God's Word; it's God quoting someone else. We have to pay close attention to context, or we'll miss what's actually being communicated to us by God.

TODAY'S GOD SHOT

Job said, "I know that my Redeemer lives, and at the last he will stand upon the earth." So much of God's character is evident in this verse. First, we see the nature of God's relationship with Job even on his worst days. Job doesn't just call God a Redeemer or *the* Redeemer, but *my* Redeemer. It's personal, intimate. Second, we see that God is a redeemer! *To redeem* means "to buy back." Job has hope that this isn't the end of his story, even if it's the end of his life. Job trusts God will redeem this somehow. Third, we see that God is alive: My Redeemer lives. So many of Job's loved ones passed away, but not God. He knows that God is still with him and will be forever: "At the last he will stand upon the earth." Storing up truth about God, like we're doing as we read, is one way to make sure our feet are on solid ground when the storms come, because He's where the joy is!

JOB 21–23

Job's friends keep pointing out that all these bad things must be happening because he's acting wickedly. This kind of thinking is embedded in our nature: *If you do good things, God will give you what you want; if you do bad things, God will punish you*. When things don't go your way, do you ever wonder if God is punishing you? Or if you can't think of anything you've done wrong to earn this treatment from Him, you may start to wonder why He's not holding up His end of the bargain. If we're not careful, we find ourselves with the same mind-set of Job's friends, thinking if we walk uprightly with God, we can use that as bargaining chips to get what we want from Him. Job's story points out the error in our thinking, and it also points out the true wickedness that lies at the heart of our motives when we try to use God as a means to our desired end.

Job rebuts his friends' claims. "[The wicked] say to God, 'Depart from us! We do not desire the knowledge of your ways. What is the Almighty, that we should serve him?'" Then he marvels, "Behold, is not their prosperity in their hand?" (21:14–16). Wicked people do prosper; they amass fortunes and live their dream lives, all while cursing God. The reality Job brings to light here is that our lot in life isn't a good barometer for the state of our heart. Good things do happen to wicked people, and it doesn't seem fair.

But if we recall what we've learned about grace and mercy and what we deserve, we'll see just how much we *don't* want what's fair. In the grand scheme of things, don't you *want* God to call you out of your sin? Do you want to wander off into callousness, doing whatever you desire with no regard for God, like the wicked people Job describes here? It's His kindness that prompts us to repent. When God actually lets wicked people have their way, forgetting Him altogether, *that's* what punishment looks like, not the troubles we encounter. Those teach us to rely on God, and they serve to conform us to His image.

Eliphaz speaks again and implies that his words are straight from God, "Agree with God, and be at peace; thereby good will come to you" (22:21). Yikes, Eliphaz! That's pretty self-assured. There's no humility in his words.

Then Job laments the distance of God. He wants to plead his case before God. In the middle of his lament, he says, "Behold, I go forward, but he is not there, and backward, but I do not perceive him; on the left hand when he is working, I do not behold him" (23:8). Job trusts God is there, at work in the midst of it all, even though he doesn't perceive Him anywhere. He says, "He will complete what he appoints for me, and many such things are in his mind" (23:14). He's terrified of what those things might be. Maybe you've been there, expecting Him to do the worst, anticipating that because you hate cold weather, He's going to make you be a missionary in Siberia, because He's cruel like that. Despite his fear, Job still doesn't curse God. He continues to yield to Him and acknowledge His sovereignty. He says, "He is unchangeable and who can turn him back? What he desires, that he does." Job wrestles with his own lack of control while yielding to God's ultimate control over his life.

TODAY'S GOD SHOT

God is at work even when we can't see what's going on. He's still in control; He's still active. Even though we may have to wrestle with ourselves over fears of what may come, and we may have to surrender our desire to have all the answers, it's evident that He's at work. Job knows it too. "On the left hand when he is working, I do not behold him." And Job wants to talk to that God—maybe to get answers or maybe to try to make a point—but hopefully, a little of what's built into his desire to talk to God is the knowledge that God gets him when none of his friends do. God *knows* what's happening and isn't just guessing. Job trusts God despite it all. Deep down, Job knows that He's where the joy is!

JOB 24–28

Today Job wraps up his response to Eliphaz's third speech. He continues to point out that good things happen to the wicked and adds that bad things happen to the righteous. Job's reply may sound like a complaint, but he seems to be consoling himself with these details, reminding himself that his trials don't negate his status as a righteous man before God, while trying to convince his friends as well.

Job points out some really important things here. If we follow his friends' beliefs to their logical conclusion, we'd be likely to think that all those who are healthy and wealthy are living righteous lives and that the poor, sick, and needy are suffering because of their sin. There's no shortage of people who subscribe to this belief today. One of the dangers of this belief is that anytime there's a disaster—a fire or a flood or a terrorist attack—some very public people say it's God's judgment, *as if they know the mind of God*. They're guilty of the same reductionism as Job's friends. In Job's story, we're given a glimpse into God's motives since they're recorded in Scripture; but in everyday twenty-first-century life, we don't have access to that information. We'd be wise not to jump to conclusions about why hurricanes and mass murders happen where they do, because God's motives aren't always clearly revealed to us.

Bildad pushes back, saying not only is Job unrighteous, but that it's impossible for a man to be righteous at all. While there's some truth in this—that we can't be perfect—we can be declared righteous by God despite our actions because of the finished work of Christ. In Scripture, *righteousness* is often used as a kind of legal term; it's more of a decision and a declaration by the judge than the accumulated overview of our actions. For every one of us who is adopted into God's family, God the Judge has declared every one of us who is adopted into His family righteous—not because we tricked Him, and not because we get more things right than we get wrong, but because God the Son, Jesus, granted us His righteousness. It's a legal transaction; He traded our sinfulness, which we were in *full* possession of, for His righteousness. He took our death penalty and granted us His kingdom. If you want to talk about what's not fair, that's the best place to start. It's unfair in the most beautiful way imaginable!

Job has a reverence for God's mystery that his friends can't seem to grasp. He says heaven trembles at God's rebuke. This is reminiscent of Genesis 6 and the "sons of God" rebelling against Him. And again, Job prophesies about Jesus without even knowing it. "By his power, he stilled the sea." We know who did that (Mark 4:35–41)!

Job continues to maintain his integrity and even tells them that despite all their rebukes, he feels no conviction. "My heart does not reproach me for any of my days" (27:6). His conscience is clean before God and man. He's certain that this trial is not punishment from God. Job knows how to live in the tension—he can be angry and sad, yet not mistrust God's heart when things are falling apart.

Despite everything, Job points to God as the source of all wisdom. "Behold, the fear of the Lord, that is wisdom, and to turn away from evil is understanding." Many of Job's words and thoughts are echoed later by Solomon, the wisest man who ever lived. Job had a lot of wisdom too. He "fears God and turns away from evil." We already know Job is wise, and he's demonstrating it here through his knowledge of God.

TODAY'S GOD SHOT

Job points to God as the source of all wisdom. By fixing our eyes on Him, looking for Him, and reading His Word daily, we're tapping in to that source. So even as you may be realizing how little you know of God so far, it takes wisdom to realize that. By putting your eyes on His Word every day, you're growing in wisdom daily. He's fulfilling His promise to you—that those who seek Him with all their hearts will find Him. And the even better news for us all is He's not only where the wisdom is, but He's where the joy is!

JOB 29–31

Today as Job continues the speech he began yesterday, he shows us how much he longs for the past, specifically in the area of his relationship with God. He reflects on a time when he felt the nearness of God in a way he describes as friendship. He says, "The friendship of God was upon my tent." Knowing about someone, or even knowing someone, is different from having a friendship with them. And it's certainly different from saying you feel like their friendship dwells in your home with you.

Job also laments the loss of his reputation. People used to listen when he spoke and be in awe at his wisdom; now they won't stop advising him, and they think he's a fool. But his wisdom hasn't vanished; the only things that have changed are his circumstances. The people around him are assessing his wisdom and righteousness based on his life circumstances.

Previously Job's friends accused him of mistreating the poor, but here Job tells us about all the ways he has extended his hands to the needy and fought for justice. Now not only are his friends not fighting for him, but they're fighting against him. And because God revealed His vantage point to us in the first chapter of this book, we know which scenario is true; we know his friends are wrong.

This is the lowest point of Job's despair. All along he has been acknowledging that God is responsible for his circumstances—even though God isn't the active agent, He's still sovereign over it and has allowed it, so there's some truth in that. But Job didn't have all the information we have; God's motives were largely unknown to him. In chapter 30, Job seems to begin drawing his own conclusions about what his trials say about God's motives and character. He says, "You have turned cruel to me; with the might of your hand you persecute me."

After all this, Job's troubles make him question the character of God. Even though Job is righteous indeed, he has pride and entitlement in his heart. Job is innocent of the things his friends accuse him of, but God uses this trial to reveal these other things in his heart, things that couldn't have been revealed in any other way but through this trial. Now that these thoughts of Job's heart have surfaced, we're reaching the turning point of the story. God loves Job and doesn't want Job to think things about Him that aren't true—just like Job didn't want his friends to think things about him that weren't true. Has anyone ever misunderstood you? Don't you want to help them see the truth, especially if it's someone you love? God wants to help Job see the truth so that Job won't believe lies about Him anymore. God is always in the process of revealing Himself to His kids.

TODAY'S GOD SHOT

Job considers God his friend. Even though he doesn't feel God's nearness at the time, it's encouraging to know that it's even possible to have that level of intimacy with God. Friendship implies not just knowledge of a person, but trust of a person. You can only trust someone you know, and you can only know someone you *spend time with*. May our knowledge of God and our trust of God always be increasing, so that our friendship with God grows richer and deeper all the time. He's where the joy is!

JOB 32–34

For the first time in almost a week of reading, someone new shows up on the scene. This man, Elihu, is very angry—not only at Job but also at Job's three friends, because they're all a bit self-righteous. It sounds like he's been there all along (32:4), listening to the back-and-forth from everyone, but he's been holding his tongue. After listening to everyone talk, he realizes the three older men have nothing good to say, so he speaks up. Elihu points out that God—not time—is how a person gets wisdom; wisdom doesn't only come via time and life experience. Age doesn't always equal wisdom, and youth doesn't always equal foolishness. Elihu believes God has advanced his wisdom beyond his years; we'll have to wait a little longer to see if he's right.

First he rebukes Job's three friends and says they were never able to offer a proper rebuttal to Job. Then he rebukes Job, but he's a little gentler than the others. "My pressure will not be heavy upon you," he says. "I too was pinched off from a piece of clay." His approach is humbler than that of Job's other friends. He isn't spot-on though. He wrongly says Job claimed to be without transgression. However, Job offered sacrifices to God, which means he knows he isn't innocent before God. He knows that if he had to sit before God the Judge, there'd be claims against him.

Elihu says sometimes God brings hardship in the temporary in order to bring healing in the eternal: "Behold, God does all these things, twice, three times, with a man, to bring back his soul from the pit, that he may be lighted with the light of life" (33:29–30). It's true that God sometimes does things like that, but by adding this idea to his speech, Elihu starts to take on the same themes Job's friends presented. He's basically saying God let all this happen "to bring back Job's soul from the pit," or in more direct terms, so Job would turn from his sins. It's all starting to sound very familiar. He starts to accuse Job of walking with wicked men, of being foolish, and of sinning and rebelling against God. This is like a broken record.

Are you exhausted of the ways Job is misunderstood? Imagine you just lost your job and your home, your family was killed, God feels distant, and your friends rebuke you, but you have no idea what you might need to repent of. On top of that, you're covered in boils! In all our aches, Job's story reminds us that we're not alone. And he demonstrates how to ache well.

TODAY'S GOD SHOT

Much of what these men say about God is true; it's when they talk about Job that they get things wrong. Elihu points out that sometimes God allows us to struggle when it serves to turn our hearts from darkness to light. Maybe this seems cruel, but isn't that what all good parents do sometimes? A good parent lets their child suffer through swim lessons so they can enjoy trips to the pool. God knows how long the struggle will last, how painful the trial will be, and the strength we'll need to have on the other side of it. He's where the joy is!

JOB 35–37

Even though Elihu started off humble yesterday, he becomes more self-assured the longer he talks, growing harsher in his rebuke of Job, bordering on cruelty. Like the others, he claims to be speaking on God's behalf and even refers to himself as "perfect in knowledge." Wow.

Just like with Job's other friends, the hard part about sorting through Elihu's words is that a lot of what he says about God is true. For example, he says neither our sin nor our righteousness affects God's position or perfection. That's true. He tells Job that his righteousness can't be used for bartering with God. That's true too. But where Elihu goes wrong is in assuming that Job is *trying* to use his righteousness as a bartering tool.

He says godless people cherish anger, which is interesting because the first thing we ever read about Elihu was that he was angry. There are certainly good things to be angry about—God is angry at sin, for instance, and that's a righteous kind of anger. Being angry at sin and oppression aligns with godliness. But most of the reasons for our anger are selfish, which makes for *un*righteous anger. To "cherish" that kind of anger sounds awful! When we cherish anger, we grow increasingly self-righteous. We don't have a desire to forgive the person we're angry with. We start on a path toward bitterness, and our heart grows hard toward people and God. We become cynical and arrogant. While we don't know Elihu's heart, it seems like this could be the trajectory he's on here too, especially given that his argument keeps ramping up.

He repeats some of his earlier themes and says things about God like, "He delivers the afflicted by their affliction, and he opens their ear by adversity" (36:15). That's true. God does use adversity and affliction to draw people to Him. This trial that Satan meant for evil is one God used to purify Job and glorify Himself all the more.

Often, when life abounds with riches and comfort and ease, it's easy to feel like we don't need God. Only His mercy can open our eyes to the truth that those things don't ultimately satisfy. Dark times can make the light of the truth shine brighter. Even the thief who was crucified beside Jesus had a moment like this in his final hours. And on the other side of those trials, if we've really seen the true value and beauty of an intimate relationship with God, we'd surely say those struggles were worth it to know Him better. We'd echo the words of Philippians 3:8: "I count everything as loss because of the surpassing worth of knowing Christ Jesus my Lord." A quote often attributed to Charles Spurgeon puts it this way, "I have learned to kiss the wave that strikes me against the Rock of Ages." The phrase "Rock of Ages" is a reference to God. When all else is moveable, God our Rock has been unmoved throughout all the ages.

As Elihu wraps up, he praises God's glory and majesty, but in a way that's intended to crush Job; he uses poetry as a hammer. He closes by saying, "He does not regard any who are wise in their own conceit" (37:24). God does draw near to the humble, which means God is probably drawing near to Job in this, because Elihu has gone on for six chapters about how wrong Job is, and Job hasn't pushed back once. Maybe Job is staying silent out of humility, or maybe he's just too defeated to fight back.

TODAY'S GOD SHOT

"Whether for correction or for his land, or for love, he causes it to happen." This is God's providence—His protective care and His preparation for the future. He has His purposes, and they may remain a mystery to us, but we can trust He's at work. In His providence, He's attentive to every detail and He's intentional in working out His plan. Maybe it's a plan to correct the hearts of the wayward, maybe it's a plan to establish and bless His people, or maybe it's just an act of love far beyond our understanding. But we can rest knowing He's working in all things for His glory and our joy, and *especially* knowing that He's where the joy is!

JOB 38–39

Finally, God speaks! Sometimes when God has been silent, it doesn't even matter what He says, you're just happy to hear Him speak. God's words here are no exception—these chapters are a treasure.

First of all, you may remember what we learned about the word *Lord* on Day 1 in Genesis 1–3. When we see it in all caps, it's a reference to YHWH, which is often pronounced "Yahweh" or "Jehovah"; it's God's personal name. So right out of the gate today, God is interacting with Job on a deeply personal level. This flies in the face of what all Job's friends said would happen. They said Job would continue to get God's silence and that his consequences would increase all the more if he didn't repent. Well, he didn't repent. And yet God shows up here, speaking to him directly, intimately.

When God first starts speaking to Job, His words have nothing to do with Job's problems. He begins by establishing *who He is*. That's because everything else is secondary. He establishes Himself as the Creator and Commander of everything. He initiates, sustains, and fulfills everything in accordance with His plan. And He makes it clear that His attention doesn't just fall to the things we consider to be of utmost importance; in fact, He even ordains and orders the details of the food chain of the animal kingdom. The lion hunts at His command. He's the one who feeds the ravens. He tells the eagles where to build their nests. He's attentive to where birds build their homes of sticks and straw, so He's certainly attentive to what's happening to Job.

Speaking of straw, there's a possibility we encountered a prophecy about Jesus in Job 39:9: "Is the wild ox willing to serve you? Will he spend the night at your manger?" A few thousand years later, Jesus is born in a cave where the animals are kept at night, and Mary lays Him in a manger, which is a feeding trough for the animals. There's a good chance an ox keeps Jesus company that night. And of course, the sovereign God of the universe, who is outside of time, would know all those details before they played out, so it feels like He's dropping a little hint here.

Another thing you may remember is that earlier in this book, Job got sarcastic with his friends. In 38:21, God speaks to Job in his own language by using a little sarcasm as well. He's been asking Job all kinds of questions about the creation of the universe, and He says, "You know, for you were born then, and the number of your days is great!" He isn't calling Job old; He's calling Job out for not being eternal. It's almost like He's saying, "Listen, were you there? I don't remember seeing you there. Oh right . . . that's because I hadn't made you yet." God puts Job in his place, and rightfully so. He *invented* Job, the one who is questioning Him. So Job gets a bit of a subtle, firm rebuke here, but you know what he doesn't get? He doesn't get God's anger. God doesn't strike him dead. Instead, He patiently reminds Job of the truth.

TODAY'S GOD SHOT

God draws near to Job despite what everyone says. And God responds to Job's questions, even if He doesn't answer them. We *can* question God; after all, that's part of what happens in a relationship. He's not threatened by our questions, but He's also not required to give us any of the answers we're seeking. Job's story reminds us to hold our questions with humility and ask them with reverence. Even your questions are a place to remember who made you and remember who loves you. He's the God who hung the heavens and feeds the ravens. He's the God who draws near to Job even after Job questions Him. He's your Creator, He's your Father, and He's where the joy is!

JOB 40–42

Today Job gives a brief reply to God, which basically amounts to "I think I'll keep my mouth shut." God had asked Job to answer Him, and he didn't, so God pushes a little more: "Will you even put me in the wrong? Will you condemn me that you may be in the right?" (40:8). Sometimes we get so frustrated by our circumstances that we carry a subtle undercurrent of belief that God is cruel for letting us endure trials. That amounts to calling God a bad, unjust God; it's basically the belief that we'd make a better god, because if we were god, our plans would be flawless.

God points out Job's entitlement. Yes, Job glorified God, made sacrifices, and honored God with his life and actions, but he valued his righteous actions too highly, perhaps believing God owed him something. Finally, Job repents. Some versions say, "I despise myself," but the Hebrew word here also means "to withdraw or reject," so it's possible his statement is more like, "I withdraw from myself." The tone it carries is more about humility than shame. Shame feels like an accusation about who you are as a person, someone who is undeserving of love. Humility, on the other hand, is rightly viewing who you are as a person who is loved despite being undeserving. Humility is the narrow zone where you're not building yourself up or beating yourself up, because you realize *it's not about you*.

After Job repents, God rebukes his friends. We finally get official confirmation from God about how wrong those guys were. He says they haven't spoken of Him what is right. While a lot of what they said about God was true, some of it missed the mark. Remember how they said they were delivering the very words of God, how they were visited by a spirit who told them things? It's possible this connects back to chapter 1, where God addresses the "sons of God," a potential reference to angels, and in this case fallen angels. If Job's friends were telling the truth about being visited by spirits, those spirits were likely evil spirits, fallen angels masquerading as angels of light.

Whether Job's friends were lying or whether they were deceived by spirits and passed those deceptions on to Job, their statements weren't from God. In the midst of all the true things they said about God, their speech was peppered with lies about Him. That's one reason it's important for us to see Scripture's full view of God instead of plucking out one or two attributes we want to home in on to the exclusion of the others. God tells Job's friends to go to him and offer a burnt sacrifice. This practice requires them to seek Job's intercession, and God says Job will pray for them. God works to purify and humble them all, then He works to restore—not just relationships, but everything in Job's life. Job gets it all back in a double portion!

In the genealogies, something interesting happens. This is a rare moment when the females and not the males are named in the lineage. That's the opposite of what most ancient genealogies did. Not only do the women get named instead of the males, but they also get an inheritance along with the males, which was relatively unheard of in those days. This is a gesture of extreme generosity on Job's part, which also reveals a lot of humility. There will be plenty of moments where the ancient cultures ignore women, so if you're a woman, hold on to this moment for when you feel like Scripture overlooks you.

TODAY'S GOD SHOT

God's heart for restoration is so evident here. He not only restores Job's fortunes and his family, but He also restores Job's relationship with his friends. And most importantly, God restores Job's view of God and himself. He sets things right. If you've ever felt distant or alienated from God, you know how disorienting it is, how paralyzing it can be. And here's the God who draws near to the very people who viewed Him wrongly, misunderstood Him, told lies about Him, and accused Him of being cruel—and then He restores them in relationship with each other *and* Himself! Job probably values that a lot more than six thousand camels, because Job has finally figured out that He's where the joy is!

GENESIS 12–15

When we were last in Genesis, a man named Abram had just been born through the bloodline of Adam and Noah, via Noah's son Shem. According to the timeline Genesis marks out, Abram was born almost two thousand years after Adam, but only about three hundred years after the flood. Just like with Adam and Noah before him, God continues His unique relationship with this family through Abram. He tells Abram that He's going to bless him, so that he may *be* a blessing. This blessing doesn't terminate on Abram; it's ultimately about way more than him—it's about how the Messiah will be born through his bloodline. That's how this family will be a blessing to all the families of the earth! All this is way over Abram's head at this point; initially God just promises to bless him with land and possessions. But there's one problem: The land God promises him is currently inhabited by the Canaanites, enemies of God.

There's a famine, so Abram and his wife, Sarai, move to Egypt, and his nephew Lot goes with them, as do all their servants and animals and possessions. Abram is afraid the Egyptian pharaoh is going to steal Sarai and kill him, so Abram convinces her to pretend to be his sister—and she kind of is, because she's his half sister. Pharaoh does kidnap Sarai, and she's basically taken into his harem of wives. God is *not* okay with it. He has big plans for Sarai, so He brings the truth to light via some classic plagues in order to get Sarai released. By the way, she's about sixty-five years old, so apparently she and Jennifer Lopez share DNA.

They leave Egypt and go to the Negev, a desert region. God has blessed them with so much that there's not enough grass to feed all their animals. Abram and Lot decide to part ways, and Abram leaves the first choice of land up to Lot, who wastes zero time picking the land that looks most beautiful and fruitful. Unfortunately, it's also near all the wicked people. He sets up camp near the Dead Sea. Maybe you have some salt or lotion

For more information on today's reading, see thebiblerecap.com/links.

from his old neighborhood. War breaks out not long afterward, and Lot is kidnapped. When Abram finds out, he and the 318 warriors who live in his house chase them for over 150 miles until they catch up and get Lot and his people back.

Then we meet Melchizedek, king of Salem. He brings out bread and wine. He's priest of God Most High. Let's hover over this for a moment. His name means "King of Righteousness," and he's the king of a place called Salem, which means "peace." So he's King Righteousness of Peace. He brings out bread and wine—does that sound familiar? Also, he's a king *and* a priest, which are two roles that are rarely combined. Melchizedek is a picture of Jesus—an archetype, a model. We'll see him a few more times as we read through the Bible together, so remember his name.

Then God makes Abram a promise that he's going to have a son! (This is awesome, unless you're Eliezer of Damascus, the original heir to Abram's massive fortune.) Abram believes God, despite his advanced age. His belief in God's word is counted as righteousness—not his actions, not his sacrifices, but his belief. This is consistent with what the rest of Scripture teaches us as well. Even in the Old Testament, *faith* in God's word is what connects people to God, not obedience to the law. What happens next is pretty peculiar on the surface, but it's beautiful when we dig deeper. Even though Abram believes God, he asks God for confirmation. God tells him to cut animals in half, then a deep sleep falls on Abram. Then God shows up on the scene—not to miraculously hand Abram the promised child, but to make a covenant with him.

TODAY'S GOD SHOT

This odd scene of a firepot passing between the cut-up animals is an example of an ancient covenant-making ritual between a king and servant. Typically the servant walks between the cut-up animals as a way of saying, "I take the curse of this covenant, that I'll be cut in half like these animals if I don't fulfill my part of the covenant." But here, God shows up in the form of fire—which is typical of the presence of God in the Old Testament—and passes between the pieces Himself. The King is vowing to take the penalty on Himself. This is *unheard of*! He's a promise maker, and He's where the joy is!

GENESIS 16–18

Sarai is now at least seventy-five years old, and she still hasn't had a child like God promised. She does what many of us do when we feel like God is holding out on us: She takes matters into her own hands. In these days, servants and their children are considered possessions. Sometimes, like here, Scripture is descriptive, not prescriptive—it's telling us what *is* happening, not what *should* happen. It never condones treating people like possessions; it just acknowledges what's happening at the time. Sarai uses that cultural norm as her logic for making her servant have sex with her husband. Because then if Hagar has a child, Sarai will own it. Sarai is tired of waiting. She tries to take a shortcut, and her fear and impatience yield pain and division in their household. We never sin in a vacuum. Countless other scenarios and people laid the groundwork for this situation, but Sarai's sin impacted Hagar, Hagar's son Ishmael, Abram, and Sarai herself.

Sarai abuses Hagar, who flees to the wilderness—pregnant, abused, and alone. Then something very important happens. In Scripture the phrase "an angel of the Lord" refers to a messenger angel. But in this instance, 16:7 says "*the* angel of the LORD." Many scholars believe this distinction refers to the preincarnate Jesus—God the Son appearing on earth as a man *before* He was born as a human named Jesus. We'll see this throughout the Old Testament. Why do scholars think this is Jesus? We see two reasons today. First, in 16:10, He says, "*I* will surely multiply your offspring." Angels can't do that; they aren't in charge of life. Second, 16:13 says it was the LORD who had spoken to her. When God shows up on earth in a physical form like this (including His appearance as fire yesterday), it's called a *theophany*.

By the way, forget what you know about angels from Renaissance paintings—most of those artists hadn't read the Bible. That's why they gave us a blond-haired, blue-eyed Jesus, even though He's Jewish and likely wore a turban. They also gave us flying, haloed angels with two wings. No angels in Scripture have two wings; they actually have zero wings. Scripture depicts them as human males who were possibly large and imposing, especially since the maybe-related Nephilim were giants. If angels are giants, that could be why people are afraid when they show up, or it could be because they seem to materialize out of thin air. A few forms of created beings do have wings, but none of them are angels. For instance, cherubim have four wings and faces and seraphim have six wings—and all of those wings are covered with eyeballs. You'll never see that in a Renaissance painting!

God changes Abram's name to Abraham and orders him and all his male offspring to be circumcised. God also changes Sarai's name to Sarah and promises to bless her, even though we have no evidence of her repenting for mistreating Hagar. God clarifies that *Sarah* will be the birth mother, putting a stop to this loophole nonsense. Both Abraham and Sarah laugh at this promise; Abraham actually *falls on his face* and laughs.

Later, God and two other angels appear to Abraham. He's so awestruck that he bows in reverence and offers worship. He does not want God to leave; he wants to stay in God's presence. God says He plans to destroy the place where Lot lives, and Abraham begs Him to spare it. We end with a cliffhanger.

TODAY'S GOD SHOT

As far as loyalties are concerned, God has no reason to pay special attention to Hagar. His commitment is to a specific family that she doesn't belong to. But she has lived with that family, so she knows about God and what He's capable of. She even gives Him a name: El Roi—"The God who sees me." The preincarnate Christ shows up in the desert in the form of an angel man to comfort this slave woman and foretell the birth of her child. And yes, it might be kind of a downer because He also tells her that Ishmael and his offspring will become enemies of God's people, but in the moment she may be more focused on the fact that God sees her and speaks to her at all. He sees and He's merciful, and He's where the joy is!

GENESIS 19–21

Today two angel men come face-to-face with the brokenness and wickedness of humanity. The men of Sodom demand to have sex with them. This is similar to Genesis 6, but this time it's human *males*. Sodom is remembered for several types of sin, including homosexuality, but it's not fair to say this was *the* sin they were known for at the time. Ezekiel 16:49–50 says, "Behold, this was the guilt of your sister Sodom: she and her daughters had pride, excess of food, and prosperous ease, but did not aid the poor and needy. They were haughty and did an abomination before me. So I removed them, when I saw it." We definitely see this in the way they treat the angels; gang rape is horrific. Lot even responds wickedly to the men's wicked suggestion, offering them his virgin daughters. It's *unfathomable*. Many scholars think Lot is bluffing or expects his offer to be rejected. Regardless of what his intentions are, God's power intervenes: His angels strike the men with blindness, which seems like an appropriate penalty for their lust and greed.

God can't even find ten righteous men in Sodom; this is like Noah's days when only eight people survived. God destroys Sodom and its neighbor Gomorrah, but He's merciful to Lot and his daughters despite Lot's rebellious delays. Lot's wife dies when she disobeys the angels' commands and looks back longingly. It's shocking when God destroys entire cities or peoples, but here we get a glimpse into not only God's motives but also God's mercy. Lot and his daughters move to the mountains, and the daughters despair over their singleness. They take matters into their own hands, much like their great-aunt Sarah did with Hagar. Scripture hasn't yet forbidden incest, but there's still a lot of sin happening here. It mirrors the postflood scene between Noah and his son Ham, who was cursed for his actions.

Meanwhile, Abraham is on the move again. He's in King Abimelech's territory and gets flashbacks of Pharaoh stealing Sarah in Egypt. He goes back to his old tricks, pretending she's not his wife. Then Abimelech steals her. One major difference is Abimelech doesn't sleep with her, whereas we have reason to believe Pharaoh did, since he took her as a wife. Sarah's kidnapping could really put a wrench in God's plan for her to have Abe's son, so it's a good thing God's plans can't be stopped! God rescues them *again* by appearing to the king in a dream and telling him He kept him from sinning. Abe keeps making plans to protect himself and Sarah, but both times, his efforts get them into deeper trouble, and it's only God who gets them out.

Finally, the long-awaited Isaac is born. Even though his birth fulfills God's twenty-five-year-old promise, it throws fuel on the fire between Sarah and Hagar and the now fourteen-year-old Ishmael. One day Sarah hears Ishmael's mocking laughter toward Isaac, and she tells Abe to kick them out so that Isaac doesn't have to split his inheritance. God tells Abe to do whatever Sarah says. But God doesn't forget Hagar and Ishmael; He promises to make *two* nations from them. He promises Ishmael's line descendants, and He promises Isaac's line descendants *and* land. Hagar and Ishmael flee to the desert, where Ishmael almost dies, but the Angel of the Lord shows up, listens to their cries, and provides for them. Meanwhile, Abe wants ownership of a well, so he makes a treaty with some locals to acquire it.

TODAY'S GOD SHOT

When God tells Abraham to pray for King Abimelech, who stole his wife, we see God's heart of forgiveness. Remember how God had Job pray for the friends who wronged him? This is reminiscent of John 17:20, where Christ prayed for us, the ones whose sins are the reason for His death. Not only does God forgive, but He wants to display His heart of forgiveness to a broken world through us, His people. Even though *all* God's children are children by adoption, He still wants His kids to look like Him. He wants us to point others to His heart, because only then can they see that He's where the joy is!

GENESIS 22–24

God's call to offer Isaac as a sacrifice sounds completely out of character! Does God endorse human sacrifice? Nuance is important here. Abraham is called to *offer* Isaac as a sacrifice, not to sacrifice him; it's an offer God rejects. While Abe gets some of Scripture's toughest assignments, he doesn't hesitate to obey. He knows God isn't going to make him kill Isaac—or that if He does, He'll resurrect him. This is a huge faith, but it's not the size of our faith that makes things happen—it's the *plan of our God*. God's plan is to preserve Isaac and to test Abe. We often picture Isaac as a boy here, but Jewish historians say he's a teenager at the youngest, but more likely twenty-five to thirty. A boy can't carry all that wood up a mountain. And anyone strong enough to carry wood is strong enough to resist their elderly assassin, but Isaac doesn't resist. The wood is laid on him, just like it was laid on Christ. Isaac is a Christ type. This story points us toward something greater.

While he's on the altar, the Angel of the LORD (probably Jesus) hits the brakes. God provides a substitute, just like Abe said. Abe gives God a name when this happens. In Scripture, names are based on what you do—they represent your activity. Abe calls God "the LORD who provides." God's names reveal His character and actions. And where He provided is noteworthy too. It was "on the mount of the LORD." Most people believe this mountain is where Solomon builds the temple and that it's also on this short stretch of mountains that Jesus is crucified. "On the mount of the LORD it shall be provided" (22:14). And it was.

God reiterates His promise: "In your offspring shall all the nations of the earth be blessed." This foretells the birth of Jesus, who came to save people from every nation, even people who aren't descendants of Abe. When Sarah dies, Abe negotiates a burial spot for her in Canaan, the very land God promised him. This isn't just caves and fields and silver coins—it's significant.

Abe wants to make sure everything is in order for his death, so he makes an oath with his servant in a way that's customary at the time, by putting a hand under the thigh. The widely accepted meaning is that it's more likely the general thigh region—where one might swear on their offspring. Isaac is still single, and Abe knows he'll need to marry in order to fulfill the promise. Abe and Isaac live in the land of their enemies, the Canaanites, who aren't circumcised and don't live according to God's ways. But because it's the land God promised them, Abe has to stay put. There are zero women his son can marry there, because he has to make sure Isaac only marries someone who worships YHWH. You can see the conundrum.

His servant treks to Abe's homeland and heads straight for the well, where all the young women go to draw water. He asks God for help and direction, and *before he finishes praying*, the answer to his prayers appears. She's kind and helpful and, most importantly, is from Abe's clan, so they worship the same God. As she's leaving, her family prays the same blessing over her that God spoke over Isaac! Then, while forty-year-old Isaac is out meditating in the field, where he likely had also been working, he meets Rebekah, who had been working at the well. They're both walking out their calling, and God crosses their paths through a weird oath, a servant's prayer, and a bunch of camels.

TODAY'S GOD SHOT

God speaks to Abraham in specific yet vague ways like, "One of the mountains of which I shall tell you" and "The land that I will show you." Many of us want God to tell us the whole plan so we can do it, but the point is not just doing what God wants but doing it *with* God. It's kind of like this: Let's say you're going on a road trip to a friend's beach house and you have two options: (1) You ask a friend to tell you the destination, type it into your GPS, then wave good-bye as you head out on your own, or (2) you ask your friend to get in the car with you and show you the way there. We're on a journey with God as He leads us step by step. It's way more beautiful to enjoy the intimacy that comes in the constant interaction, because the beach house may be awesome, but *He's* where the joy is!

GENESIS 25–26

Abraham remarries after Sarah's death and has six more kids, for a grand total of eight. But his entire estate goes to Isaac, because Isaac is the child of God's promise. He's also the only child of Abe's first wife. Abe dies at 175 years old, and God appears to Isaac to reiterate His promise. Then right after God appears to him, Isaac starts lying! He manifests the sins of his father, calling his wife his sister—but this time, it isn't even *half*-true. Some scholars say this could also be the same King Abimelech who stole Sarah. In both stories, Abimelech demonstrates a higher view of God's holiness than Abe and Isaac do.

In response to Isaac's sin, God protects and blesses him—and quickly. Within a year, Isaac sows and reaps one hundredfold! Because of his success, Abimelech tries to get rid of him. Whenever this particular family starts to flourish, the people around them notice; they become jealous or afraid of them and want them dead and gone.

God appears to Isaac at Beersheba, the very first well his dad took possession of. God reiterates the promise that was originally for Abraham; it *must* extend through Isaac, because he's the child of the promise, the only child of Abraham and Sarah. Isaac and Rebekah have their first baby when he's sixty. She was barren for twenty years, but Isaac knows the God who grants life, so he intercedes on Rebekah's behalf and God answers with a yes. Sometimes God answers with a no, but all His answers to our prayers—yes, no, or wait—serve to establish His very good plans. In this instance, in order for God to fulfill His promise of many offspring to Isaac, God has to open Rebekah's womb. When He does, Rebekah is pregnant with twins.

Rebekah has a lot of questions about it all, and she takes her questions to God. His answer is perplexing, because His plan for these twins goes against the cultural norms. The younger son will rule instead of the older. Through a tangled mess of sin, part of which we saw today, God accomplishes His purposes to that end. Esau's impatience and Jacob's scheming add up to a transferred birthright, which is typically bestowed on the firstborn and signals inheritance and prominence. God flips the script with a bowl of stew. This promise transference to the younger child isn't just a one-off situation as far as God is concerned. It's actually a theme in Scripture. Here are two other examples we've seen so far: The offering of younger brother Abel was accepted, while firstborn Cain's wasn't, and younger brother Isaac got the promises that belonged to firstborn Ishmael. Scripture calls Jesus our older brother. If He's the firstborn and we're the younger siblings, He should get all the inheritance. But Romans 8 says we share in His inheritance!

Like his dad, Esau marries at forty. Some say sexual purity is an outdated idea because when the Bible was written, people got married at thirteen or fourteen. Maybe some did, but not according to the ages we have recorded. Esau marries two Hittite women. Not only does he marry two women (this is descriptive, not prescriptive), but both women are outside God's family. Jacob is committed to God's plan for this family, but Esau is indifferent or antagonistic. But rest assured, even his rebellion fits into the big picture.

TODAY'S GOD SHOT

God is no respecter of persons. He shows attention and favor to those who *aren't* in positions of honor, like sojourners and latter-born kids. This aspect of God's character extends far beyond birth order to those who have a mental illness or a physical uniqueness or are developmentally delayed. The God who made the human brain and body certainly isn't limited to the number of their functions we're currently aware of. There seems to be a special way God communicates with those in situations that seem less desirable or more impossible. He's endeared to the needy, the lowly—and that's all of us, really. The more we're aware of our need for Him, the more we'll delight in His nearness and provision, and the more our hearts remember that He's where the joy is!

GENESIS 27–29

The sins of Rebekah and Isaac play a role in God's unusual plans for Jacob. Rebekah tricks her husband into giving his blessing to her favorite son, Jacob, and Isaac goes against God's words by intending to bestow his blessing on the child God had not chosen for it. A blessing is different from an inheritance. It carries more of a spiritual significance than a financial one, and once it's given, it's irrevocable. Jacob isn't sinless here either, and he even refers to Yahweh as Isaac's God, not his own. In Isaac's blessing, he speaks the same ideas God used in 25:23. Isaac says, "Be lord over your brothers, and may your mother's sons bow down to you" (27:29). Decades earlier, God said, "The older shall serve the younger." But before you feel sorry for Esau, note his entitlement when denying responsibility for selling his birthright. He never grasps the weight of it. He threatens to kill Jacob, so Rebekah sends Jacob to live with her brother Laban in Haran, the Canaanite land. As he's leaving, Isaac warns him, "Don't marry a Canaanite. You have to marry someone in YHWH's family!"

On the way, he has a dream in which God connects Himself to earth via a ladder. Jesus refers to this and describes Himself as the ladder—the connection point between God and earth, a ladder God descended, *not* one man climbed (John 1:51). God reiterates two promises: He'll give this enemy land to Jacob's family, and He'll use them to bless all the families of the earth (through the birth of Jesus). Jacob isn't even married, but God promises him offspring. He's not perfect, but he's the one option for carrying out the lineage of God's promise. Jacob builds a pillar on the site; it sounds nice, but pillars typically are pagan structures erected by the Canaanites, not the people of God. Then he says, "If God keeps His promises, *then* I will yield to Him." He still doesn't really believe; YHWH isn't the God of Jacob yet.

When he makes it to the edge of Haran, he goes to the well like any smart man looking for a wife. He sees Rachel, a shepherdess, which isn't an uncommon job for a girl. In fact, some scholars say the shepherds that the angels appeared to on the night of Christ's birth were likely females—just another way Renaissance paintings may have misled us. Jacob is thrilled to know this beautiful girl is his first cousin, because he has to marry in the family. Her dad, Laban, agrees to let him marry her in exchange for seven years of work; but then Laban tricks him with a false identity (Leah), just like Jacob tricked his dad with a false identity. Because the consummation happens at night in a time predating electricity, Jacob doesn't discover the lie until after they've consummated the marriage. There's no turning back—kind of like with the blessing he received.

Jacob bargains for Rachel with another seven years. Laban's trick failed Jacob *and* Leah, because Jacob hates her; this word often describes a mortal enemy, someone you're *at war with*. But as we've seen before, God has a special affinity for the overlooked and unloved. He's generous and attentive to Leah. She has four sons, and the names of the first three reveal how much striving is in her heart, how much she just wants to be loved by Jacob. By the time she has her fourth son, she's beginning to see God as enough; but she'll have to relearn this lesson, so it's not quite tied up with a pretty bow.

TODAY'S GOD SHOT

We've already noted His sovereignty over the evil of the enemy, but here we see another layer of His sovereignty over evil: It's over the sins of man, the evil of our own hearts and actions. Ultimately, Rebekah's manipulation is a tool in God's hands to accomplish His desired outcome. Even sin bends to God's will—it can't thwart His plan. We've seen this since Day 1 in the garden. Romans 8:28 says even things that aren't good are still used for our good and for His glory! If you think you've train wrecked your life with a sin that you can't forgive yourself for, take heart. God is outside of time, and He knew all the things you'd do wrong as a human, a parent, a spouse, a friend, and He even knows all the sins you haven't committed yet—and *He's in this with you,* working through it all. He's with you, and He's where the joy is!

GENESIS 30–31

Rachel envies Leah's ability to have kids and puts pressure on Jacob to get her pregnant. He reminds her that only God can give life. She follows the ways of her ancestor Sarah, offering her maidservant to her husband, and she has two kids for them. Leah follows suit and gives him *her* maidservant, who also has two kids. Bitterness and jealousy are growing in the sisters' hearts, leading to manipulation and retaliation. The spirit of greed and comparison, plus their scarcity mentality, drives all their actions. This isn't love for God, and it isn't love for Jacob. It doesn't even seem like love for their children. It seems more like love for self that is manifesting in fear, idolatry, and self-promotion.

When Leah gets pregnant again, she thinks it's God's reward for sharing her servant with Jacob, but 30:17 just says God heard her cries. She didn't earn a baby through good behavior, especially since coercing your husband into infidelity isn't good behavior. She sinned and misunderstood God's ways, and still, God heard her desires and responded with a yes.

Jacob's favorite wife, Rachel, finally has her first child, Joseph. You can probably guess which of Jacob's kids is his favorite. He wraps up his fourteen years of service to Laban and asks to leave. He's not supposed to stay in Haran, because God has promised him the land of the Canaanites. Laban doesn't want him to leave, because he learns God has blessed him through Jacob's presence; Laban gets that information from a wicked source, but it's accurate. We have no indication that Laban worships YHWH, so it's no surprise that he seeks out divination. Jacob and Laban act like they're making a deal for Jacob to stay, but they're both still up to their old tricks, not to mention some weird livestock breeding techniques that Jacob borrows from local magicians. Despite his sin, God makes him animal-rich. But the problem is, God doesn't want him to stay there and just keep getting wealthier; He wants Jacob back in the land He promised him. Jacob finally packs up to go.

It's been about twenty years since Jacob left Canaan. As they're sneaking off, Rachel steals some of Laban's household gods—which likely refers to idols. We don't know why she wants these gods—maybe she worships them too or maybe she wants to sell them or maybe she wants her dad to stop worshipping them. It takes Laban three days to realize they're gone. On his way after them, God appears to him in a dream and warns him to keep his mouth shut. When he finally catches them, he acts nice at first. "I didn't even get to say good-bye!" Then he cuts to the chase: His household gods are gone. They search for the gods, which Rachel hides under a camel's saddle and a ruse about her period.

Laban tries to save face, setting up an agreement with Jacob. This passage is often taken out of context: "The LORD watch between you and me, when we are out of one another's sight" (31:49). It sounds endearing, but given the history between them, it's more like he's saying, "I don't trust you. So remember that God sees you even when I can't. Don't do anything sketchy." They set up two witnesses for their treaty: a stone pillar and a heap of stones. These tend to be pagan practices, even though they both invoke God's name. Some scholars say Jacob's singular pillar represents his monotheistic worship of God—the one true God, YHWH—whereas Laban's pile of rocks represents his polytheism, the worship of *many* gods.

TODAY'S GOD SHOT

Remember when Leah manipulated Rachel and Jacob in order to sleep with Jacob, then praised God for her pregnancy? Remember how Jacob manipulated the breeding processes and praised God for his abundance? Maybe your sense of right and wrong is starting to kick in. But let's look past that to see what we can see about God here: He is kind to sinners. That's good news because *that's all of us*. Luke 6:35 says, "He is kind to the ungrateful and the evil." Does God hate sin and injustice and ingratitude? Absolutely. But today we see His mercy. Today we see His kindness and His provision for the flawed kids He's adopted into His family. We've been adopted by a kind Father. He's where the joy is!

GENESIS 32–34

Jacob fears how things will go if he encounters his brother on their trip to Canaan. He gets word that Esau is coming and has four hundred guys with him. *Uh-oh*. Jacob divides things so that if Esau attacks, he can't take it all. He may be driven by fear, but in 32:9, Jacob addresses God by His name for the first time. He's humbled and praises God for providing. In the midst of fearing the worst, he recalls God's words and appeals to Him with reminders of His promises. He sends a present ahead to Esau to appease him, then sends his wives and kids ahead of him and spends the night alone.

During the night he wrestles with God—and this doesn't appear to be a metaphor or a vision, mainly because he leaves with an injury. This is another theophany, an appearance of God on earth. They wrestle all night, and as the sun is rising, Jacob tells Him he won't let go until He blesses him. He replies, "What is your name?" God always asks questions He knows the answer to; those are literally the only kinds of questions God can ask. The man's response clues us in that He's God: First, He affirms that Jacob not only wrestled with men, but also with God, and second, He changes Jacob's name, which is a big God move. Sometimes, when God is revealing a new assignment or direction for someone's life, He renames them. Jacob is called Israel; it's the first time we see this word in Scripture. The name eventually refers not only to this one man, but to his descendants too. Jacob leaves renamed and limping. This is his moment of transformation—encountering God face-to-face like his dad and granddad did. His faith is becoming his own.

They eventually run into Esau, who seems excited to see him. Their nice chat makes it hard to tell whether they're being kind or they still don't trust each other. Jacob's position becomes clear when he agrees to follow Esau but then goes a different direction. Esau goes south, and Jacob goes west, toward Canaan. He follows God, not Esau. He buys land and commemorates the occasion. But for the first time, he doesn't build a pillar; he builds an altar. Not a Canaanite memorial, not a pagan ritual—an altar. He names it "God, the God of Israel," honoring the God who drew near to him, wrestled with him, injured him, and protected him all at once!

What happens next is horrific. Dinah, Jacob's only daughter, is enchanted with the pagan land of Shechem. A guy named Shechem lives there, and his dad has a lot of status. Shechem falls in love with Dinah—or at least her appearance—and rapes her. He wants to marry her and has his dad negotiate with Jacob. Jacob and his sons are outraged, and rightly so. Rape is taken seriously among their people, but Jacob sits by passively while his sons make a plan. They do it in much the same way Jacob makes plans—which is to say, sneakily. They plan to kill all the men of Shechem in retaliation. They say the men all have to be circumcised—a kind of forced, false conversion. Shechem and his dad agree on behalf of everyone in town.

After the men are circumcised, Simeon and Levi, two of Dinah's full brothers in their blended family, enter the town, kill all the males, and rescue Dinah. Jacob disapproves, but mostly because he fears retaliation. God never endorses their actions; in fact, we'll see more about God's response to this later.

TODAY'S GOD SHOT

God changes hearts, though difficult circumstances are often His tool of choice. But often that's the most effective tool. He uses a scary situation to humble Jacob when he's about to see Esau. When Jacob is humbled and alone, God draws near to him, wrestles with him, renames him, and changes him. And Jacob goes from being the man who erects pillars to the man who builds altars! But rest assured, he's still a work in progress; he still lies and manipulates, and even his response to the slaughter is still self-focused. But God never gives up on him; God will complete the work He started in him. And it seems like Jacob is starting to *want* to grow in that direction, to become the new man with the new name, the man whose actions reveal his trust in God, the man who knows that He's where the joy is!

GENESIS 35–37

As Jacob-Israel and his family prepare to leave Shechem, he tells his family that they're *only* going to worship YHWH and buries all their gods. As they pass through the land, God makes the locals afraid of them; He creates terror in the hearts of those who oppose Him in order to protect His people. This is the only place in Scripture where this Hebrew word for *terror* is used. Often when we refer to the fear of God, it carries a connotation of reverence and awe, but this particular word indicates only sheer terror.

God calls Jacob to settle in Bethel, home of his famous ladder dream. Back then, Jacob set up a pagan pillar, but he's a new man with a new heart so he replaces the pillar with an altar. Jacob tears down the old things that dishonor God and puts up new things that honor Him and point to Him. Then God changes Jacob's name. We've already seen this, so why is this story here? Is it just repeated for emphasis? Possibly.

Maybe you're also wondering why God keeps switching back and forth between the names Jacob and Israel, especially after He's changed his name at least once. Some scholars think this is for the sake of clarity, since by the time Genesis was written, the name Israel represented far more than just Jacob. Others say the switching back and forth is a subtle way of indicating the direction in which Jacob-Israel's heart is focused at the time: Jacob is the old man, who looks to himself, but Israel is the new man, who looks to God.

When they leave Bethel and head to Ephrath, Rachel has a baby, Benjamin, but she dies in labor. Jacob puts a pillar over her tomb, but don't let that pillar alarm you—it's a memorial stone for a human, not a pagan worship site for a false god. Then Jacob goes to see his dad, Isaac, whom he hasn't seen since he tricked him decades ago, and shortly afterward, Isaac dies.

For more information on today's reading, see thebiblerecap.com/links.

Joseph, the firstborn child of Rachel, has been Jacob's pride and joy, which puts him several notches above his brothers. It's no surprise that Joseph and his brothers don't have a great relationship. Throwing fuel on the fire, Jacob makes Joseph a fancy robe—and it's up for debate, but the Hebrew word here probably describes a long robe with long sleeves, *not* a multicolored robe. Then Joseph has a dream that his brothers worship him. In a move that's either foolish or arrogant, or possibly both, Joseph tells his brothers the dream and they hate him even more for it. They conspire to kill him, but his oldest brother, Reuben, pipes up and saves his life. In 35:22, we learn that Reuben slept with one of Jacob's concubines (basically his stepmother) and that Jacob found out about it. Some people believe Reuben is now trying to win back his dad's favor, but others think he just has mercy on Joseph.

Joseph's brothers sell him to the Ishmaelites, descendants of Ishmael. They're semiclose blood relatives, but they don't worship YHWH. They're also called Midianites, another line from Abraham. Since they go by both names, it's likely there may have been intermarriage or a partnership between the two groups. They buy Joseph and take him south to Egypt and sell him as a slave to Potiphar, a high-ranking man under Pharaoh, the Egyptian king. Meanwhile Joseph's brothers send his robe, covered in a goat's blood, back to Jacob, who is inconsolable. This scene is reminiscent of the time Jacob deceived *his* father using a stolen cloak and a slaughtered goat.

TODAY'S GOD SHOT

When Reuben tries to convince the brothers not to kill Joseph, his hope is that he might "restore him to his father" (37:22). Reuben, the older brother, acts on behalf of the one who has gotten himself into big trouble. He saves his life that he might restore him to his father. Jesus, our older brother, acts on behalf of us, and because of His saving actions, our lives are spared that we might be restored to our Father! Today, Reuben shows us a picture of Jesus—an imperfect one, for sure, but he points us to the great saving hand of God in a world where we can't save ourselves. Jesus takes action to restore us to the Father, and He's where the joy is!

GENESIS 38–40

Joseph's half brother Judah marries a Canaanite and has three sons. He arranges a marriage between son number one and a woman named Tamar, but son number one is wicked so God kills him. God is just *and* merciful; and in this instance, He leans into His justice. Then Judah gives Tamar to son number two, because the lack of a husband and children is basically a death sentence. But son number two isn't having it, so he gets sneaky to make sure she doesn't get pregnant. God's protection of Tamar kicks in, and He kills son number two. Son number three is still a child, so Judah tells Tamar to stick around until he's old enough to marry. But Tamar fears she'll never have kids. For the descendants of Abraham, kids are the sign of God's blessing, because that's what He promised Abe; not to have kids was shameful for anyone in his line. So she takes matters into her own hands. We've seen this before, and it never goes well.

She veils herself and sits at the side of the road. Some scholars say she intentionally dresses like a prostitute, but others say she veils herself as a reminder to Judah that she's supposed to be a bride. Either way, he mistakes her for a prostitute, and she goes along with it, then asks for collateral until his payment arrives. He gives her three personal items. When word gets out that she's pregnant, he orders her death, then she pulls out the stash of his stuff. He's deeply humbled, and her life is spared, and then she gives birth to twins.

Meanwhile, Joseph is still in captivity. But he's not alone! Four times Scripture says, "The LORD was with Joseph." God's nearness and blessing made Potiphar take notice and put Joseph over more things. This falls right in line with the promises God made to the patriarchs (which is what we call the fathers of our faith who are from this particular family): God promised to bless those who bless them and curse those who curse them, and He's fulfilling this promise with Joseph.

Joseph is easy on the eyes, so Potiphar's wife launches a seduction campaign, but he remains honorable. He knows it's a sin against Potiphar and her and himself, but mainly *against God*. Her seduction plans fail, so she forces herself on him, but he escapes. She takes revenge, using the clothes she tore off him to accuse him of trying to attack her. This is the second time Joseph is wronged by someone who uses his clothes to lie about him. In her lie, she refers to Joseph as a Hebrew—this is a subtle prejudiced dig; she's leaning on the cultural tension between her people and Joseph's people, whom the Egyptians are enslaving.

Despite Joseph's loyalty to Potiphar, he puts Joseph in prison. There's not even a trial, because he's a Hebrew slave in Egypt and has no rights. But because God is with him, Joseph gains favor even in prison. Then two new prisoners show up: the king's cupbearer and chief baker. They have terrible dreams and want someone to interpret. They view dreams as messages from God, and Joseph knows only God can provide an accurate interpretation for any messages He sends. Since God is with him, he steps up in confidence. The cupbearer's dream means he'll be restored to his position in three days. Joseph asks him to put in a good word for him. The chief baker's dream means he'll be killed in three days. The king's birthday is in three days, and everything happens just as God said and Joseph interpreted, but the real letdown is that the cupbearer forgets about Joseph.

TODAY'S GOD SHOT

This story of Tamar and Judah is filled with sin, but despite the ways people are unfaithful to God, He remains faithful to His promise to their family. Matthew 1 lists Judah, Tamar, and their son Perez in the lineage of Jesus! While Scripture never endorses most of what happens in Genesis 38, God is working in all that mess to bring about the birth of the very one who redeems us from sins like these. Jesus comes from the line of Judah, which is why one of His names is the Lion of Judah. Judah is a broken man. Tamar is a broken woman. But even though we are broken and unfaithful, He continues to be faithful to every promise He has made. He's a promise keeper, and He's where the joy is!

GENESIS 41–42

Today Pharaoh has a pair of odd dreams and calls for his magicians to interpret. These aren't David Blaine–type magicians; they're more like spiritual mediums who interpret signs and omens. Scripture repeatedly warns against consulting mediums and spiritists, but Pharaoh doesn't know YHWH. His magician-mediums fail, which is all part of God's plan to refresh the cupbearer's memory. It's been a couple of years, but the cupbearer remembers a prisoner who interprets dreams. Pharaoh calls for Joseph, and they give him a quick shave, because Egyptians love a bald head.

Joseph makes it clear that interpretation isn't a skill he possesses—it's a gift from God. Then he interprets the dreams: There will be seven years of abundance in Egypt, then seven years of famine in the region, and it will happen soon. Then Joseph says that because this is happening soon, Pharaoh should put someone in charge of prep. Pharaoh decides that since Joseph is discerning and wise, he should be the one in charge of everything. Pharaoh gives him new clothes, a fancy ride, and a gold chain and puts his signet ring on him. By this time, Joseph is thirty. He suffered in slavery and prison for thirteen years, but God has brought him to a place of abundance. Pharaoh arranges for him to marry a woman from a prominent local family. While he's busy doomsday prepping, he also fathers two children, Manasseh and Ephraim; both of their names signify his gratitude.

When the seven years of abundance end, Joseph is thirty-seven. It's been twenty years since his brothers sold him. Cut to Jacob in Canaan with his eleven sons during the famine. They hear that Egypt is selling grain, so the ten older brothers make the trek, but Dad keeps Benjamin at home to protect him. Joseph and Ben are Jacob's only children by Rachel, the wife he loved. Obviously, Jacob is going to be especially protective of Ben, because he thinks Joseph is dead, so Ben is ostensibly his only living child from his favorite wife.

Imagine being Joseph, and one day your traitor brothers bow to you, fulfilling the prophetic dream you had twenty years earlier. He recognizes them but plays it cool. He even speaks to them through an interpreter so they won't know he speaks Hebrew. He's pretty mean at first, even accusing them of being spies. Initially, it's hard to tell if he's being vindictive or if he has other motives at play here. He says they have to prove they aren't spies by bringing back their youngest brother. This could be a test of their sincerity, but it's more likely he just wants to see Ben, who's roughly twenty years old now. He imprisons them briefly and says he'll keep one brother, Simeon, as a hostage while they make the trip to get Ben. The brothers panic. Their confinement makes them introspective; they confess their guilt and regret to each other—and they do it in front of Joseph in a language they don't know he understands. Can you imagine? Joseph steps away and weeps.

They head home, and Joseph gives them free grain by sneaking their money back into their bags. This may be a test or an act of generosity or both, but the brothers receive it as neither. They think it's God's judgment. They panic. They tell Jacob that they have to bring Benjamin back in order for Simeon to be released, but Jacob refuses.

TODAY'S GOD SHOT

God's abundant generosity shows up not only in Joseph's life, but also in His provision for His enemies. In Egypt, a land that doesn't honor Him, a land whose very name represents His enemies throughout Scripture, He sends one of His people to warn them about a famine and make a way to feed them. And then there's His generosity to Joseph's brothers. They not only get grain, but they get it for free! What appears to be tragic and prompts fear in them is actually a *double portion* from God. Maybe you're in the famine right now, and there's no end in sight. You don't have the benefit of a seven-year timeline, and God doesn't seem to be generous. Be encouraged by Joseph's story. I'm sure being in power is great and having your own chariot is awesome. But even in the pit and the prison, Joseph knew that a *very real* sense of joy was possible, because God was with him, and He's where the joy is!

GENESIS 43–45

When Jacob and his family finish off their grain supply, Jacob agrees to let Ben go with his other sons for more food because Judah agrees to take the blame if anything happens. When they arrive, Joseph sees Ben and orders them to his home. He's planning a feast, but they think they're in trouble. In their panic, they try to explain things to his servant, but he already knows because he is in on it. In front of all eleven brothers, Joseph offers Ben a special blessing, then seats them in precise birth order. There are eleven brothers, many very close in age, so what are the chances that some guy from Egypt could accurately seat them oldest to youngest? They look at each other in shock, eyes wide. Then Joseph shows Ben more favor, giving him *five times* the portions. Maybe he wants to bless Ben, his only full brother, or maybe he's testing the brothers. Will they still be jealous when the youngest gets honored? Or have they learned from their sins?

They head back to Canaan, and Joseph repeats the money-in-the-bag trick, with the added bonus of putting his silver cup in Ben's bag. But this time they don't discover it on their own—Joseph sends his squad to accuse them of theft. The squad opens the bags one by one, oldest to youngest, to heighten the suspense, and finds the cup in Ben's bag. Will they turn on their brother like they did before? Judah knows he'll have to take the fall for this, which means he'll either die or become an Egyptian slave for life. They all head back into the city again to face the music, and Joseph confronts them.

Joseph briefly mentions he can practice divination. This could be an empty threat to throw them off, or it could mean he does practice divination, since that's a common practice in Egypt (though that doesn't mean God approves of it), or it could refer to his ability to discern truth through divine intervention and discernment, like with dream interpretations. Divination hasn't been forbidden by God yet, but it's still disrespectful at best and wicked at worst to seek answers and guidance from spirits instead of God. Many scholars think Joseph was bluffing, like interrogators do when they're trying to get a suspect to confess.

But they can't confess, because they're innocent—at least of cup stealing. Judah says they do have guilt. For ten of them, it's the guilt of Joseph's presumed death. As for Ben, it's possible Judah thinks he *did* steal the cup. Judah gives a beautiful speech that shows how God has humbled him and brought repentance—from his part in selling Joseph, to losing his wife and two of his sons, to having his own hypocrisy revealed when he slept with Tamar. This is the guy who originally suggested they sell Joseph into slavery, and now he's offering himself in Ben's place! This is a picture of Christ, and it's fitting, because Christ, the older brother, offers Himself for the guilt of us, the younger brother.

At the end of Judah's speech, Joseph can't fake it anymore and tells them he's their brother. He speaks in Hebrew, without an interpreter. He tries to calm their fears, but he can't calm their shock. It's like they're seeing a ghost. He tells them to move to Egypt so they can escape the famine. Pharaoh offers to provide everything for them—the best of the land. Jacob is dumbfounded when his sons bring this news, but when the caravan arrives, it confirms what they've said.

TODAY'S GOD SHOT

God invites us into freedoms that only come from knowing and trusting Him. In 45:5–8, Joseph leans on God's sovereignty to put his brothers' regrets to death. They haven't derailed God's plans or promises with their sins. God is at work *in all things*—that not only helps us forgive those who repent for sinning against us, but it also calls us to forgive ourselves. God has forgiven us, and we can't sin ourselves out of His plan! Joseph wants that freedom for his brothers. He doesn't want them to carry guilt over their sins against him; it all serves to work out God's plan for good. God brought Joseph out of literal bondage into freedom, He brought Joseph's brothers out of emotional bondage into freedom, and He has brought all His adopted children out of spiritual bondage into freedom. He is freedom, and He's where the joy is!

GENESIS 46–47

Jacob packs up his stuff for the 450-mile journey to Egypt. He stops in Beersheba to offer a sacrifice to God. Both his father, Isaac, and his grandfather Abraham had lived there, so this may be a nostalgic farewell to his homeland; he expects to die in Egypt. While he's in Beersheba, he has a vision in which God confirms he's supposed to go to Egypt. This is noteworthy, because Egypt is generally regarded as a terrible place for Hebrews to go; Egyptians are enemies of God's people. But God comforts Jacob and promises to be with him.

When it comes to God's presence, there's a difference between His general presence everywhere, which is called omnipresence, and His special presence, which is called manifest presence. Saying, "God is everywhere" is different from saying, "God is here." Even if God hadn't made this promise to Jacob, we could easily conclude that God is in Egypt. But when God promises to be with Jacob in Egypt, that's a nod to His manifest presence. It's kind of like the filters on Instagram that increase saturation. You didn't invent the red in your picture; it was already there. But when you dial up the saturation, it pops—it's more noticeable, more *manifest*.

Skip ahead a few thousand years, and we now have access to God the Spirit, who dwells in all believers, and we carry Him wherever we go. But this was not the case back then—God's special presence was a unique thing. That's why David prayed, "Do not take your Holy Spirit from me," because that was a real possibility he was concerned about. But today, for those who have His Spirit (which is all of His adopted children), that prayer is a moot point. He has filled us with His Spirit and promises to stay with us forever!

God promises to make Jacob into a great nation *while they're in Egypt*. They start out as seventy people, but it won't stay that way for long. When they arrive, Joseph tells them what to say to Pharaoh. He wants to make sure they have access to an outlying area called Goshen, a place with fertile land for their animals. Since Egyptians have a unique disdain for shepherds and prefer to keep them at a distance, Joseph wants to make sure Pharaoh knows they're shepherds. Pharaoh agrees to let them live in Goshen. Then when he meets Jacob, we see how much humility God has developed in Jacob over time. Remember how he manipulated things to get what he wanted from both his father *and* his father-in-law? Remember the scarcity mentality that drove him to half-truths and self-protection? He recognizes it now. He says, "Few and evil have been the days of the years of my life." He's humbled.

Joseph's family thrives in Egypt even as the famine gets worse. He makes a few business arrangements to provide for the people—he buys their livestock, then their land, then even their service in exchange for seeds, provided they give Pharaoh 20 percent of what they grow. Some say he's exploiting the people, but the people themselves seem to be grateful. At the very least, this shows the magnitude of the famine.

After the famine has been over for a decade, Jacob and his family still live in Egypt for some reason. In preparation for his death, Jacob asks Joseph to make him an under-the-thigh promise. He's asking Joseph to swear on Jacob's offspring—which includes Joseph himself—that Joseph won't leave his bones in Egypt. God promised to bring Jacob out of Egypt, and this is how Jacob ensures that will happen. He believes God's promises will be fulfilled for him, whether he's dead or alive.

TODAY'S GOD SHOT

In the land of their enemies, during a famine, God provides for His people. He has a plan and a promise to bring the Messiah through their bloodline, so it's imperative that they flourish. And there's no true flourishing apart from the presence of God. People can certainly accumulate things and be happy without God; wicked people can and do succeed. But they don't flourish—not in the deepest sense. They build temporary castles and seek fleeting pleasures. But their souls don't thrive like the people who draw near to God's presence—the people who know He's where the joy is!

GENESIS 48–50

Jacob recounts God's promises to give him many offspring and give them the land of Canaan. He refers to God as God Almighty. God's names represent His character. They tell us who He is and what He does. We'll continue to collect more names of God throughout Scripture.

Joseph asks his father to bless his sons before he dies. During the process, Jacob formally adopts Joseph's children as his own—he'd been robbed of having Joseph around as a young boy, but he's spent many years with Joseph's kids. He compares Joseph's two oldest kids to his own two oldest kids, Reuben and Simeon. This is actually a generous move, a way of establishing that these two boys will receive an inheritance from him along with Joseph's brothers—they'll be heirs to the land and the promise.

Joseph brings the boys to Jacob and positions the oldest in front of Jacob's right hand, which is considered to be the hand of blessing and power, and the youngest in front of Jacob's left hand. But Jacob crosses his hands, putting his right hand on the head of the youngest. Jacob is going blind, so Joseph thinks maybe he can't see what he's doing, but it's intentional. He blesses both boys but passes the ruling power to the younger brother, Ephraim, continuing God's theme of doing the unexpected and passing the blessing to the undeserving. Manasseh will become a people, but Ephraim will become a multitude.

Jacob gathers his sons to give his final blessing. He retracts the preeminence of Reuben, the oldest, who slept with his concubine. The birthright also passes over Simeon and Levi, his second and third sons. They're the ones who killed the men of Shechem in retaliation for raping their sister Dinah. Instead, this blessing lands on the fourth son, Judah. But make no mistake—it wasn't because Judah was perfect. After all, he's the one who slept with his daughter-in-law Tamar. But his sin didn't threaten the family unit like the actions of the other three did. Judah gets preeminence. He fathered Perez, who is listed in the lineage of Jesus. And by the way, Perez isn't the firstborn either. This law of primogeniture keeps getting overturned. All of this paints the picture of Christ, our older brother, laying down His rights and privileges to share His inheritance with us.

Jacob gives Joseph a distinct blessing that sets his descendants apart. More on that in the days to come. Then we encounter the phrase *the twelve tribes of Israel*. Jacob is Israel, and these are his twelve sons. They'll all have many offspring, and each man's offspring belong to his tribe.

After Jacob dies, Joseph's brothers begin to fear him, thinking he'd been faking it until their dad died but that he'll retaliate now. They say Jacob wanted Joseph to forgive them. Maybe their story is true, but Joseph has already forgiven them. His heart is free of bitterness, so he reminds them not of what they did or even of how he has forgiven them, but of who *God* is. God is the one who went before all of them and made a way—a very difficult way, no doubt, but a way nonetheless—for them all to be alive and cared for.

In Joseph's final days, he echoes the same desires of his father; he doesn't want to be buried in Egypt. He knows God's promise to give them the land of Canaan will be fulfilled, and he says, "When that day comes, don't leave my bones behind." He trusts in God's word.

TODAY'S GOD SHOT

In Jacob's blessing to Judah, we see some "Lion of Judah" prophecies about Jesus. Micah 5:2 says the coming ruler of Israel, who is from the tribe of Judah, will be born in Bethlehem. Jacob's blessing says, "He has washed his garments in wine and his vesture in the blood of grapes" (49:11). Wine is the appointed symbol of Christ's blood, and this verse also echoes Revelation 19:13, which says, "He is clothed in a robe dipped in blood." Images and prophecies of Christ are abundant in the Old Testament—no one could have invented them all in such a way that they'd so perfectly line up with Christ's coming. Some say there are more than four hundred. But this picture today of Jacob blessing Judah—receive that for yourself, because through Judah, you have been blessed. You've received the promise of the coming Messiah, who reigns forever, and the scepter shall not depart from Him. He's our King Jesus, and He's where the joy is!

EXODUS 1–3

In Genesis 15:13–14, God told Abe, "Your offspring will be sojourners in a land that is not theirs and will be servants there, and they will be afflicted for four hundred years. But I will bring judgment on the nation that they serve, and . . . they shall come out with great possessions." It's currently four hundred years after Genesis ended, and the seventy people who went into Egypt during the famine stuck around and had a bunch of kids. Joseph is dead and gone, and so is the pharaoh who treated them well. There's a new king, and the prejudice against Hebrews has kicked into high gear. Fear and self-preservation feed racism and tribalism, and that's what happens to Pharaoh. He imagines a hypothetical future war with an unnamed army and worries the descendants of Israel will join the unnamed army in a fight against him!

Since he feels threatened, he forces the Israelites to work and makes things hard on them—because if they work long days in the hot sun, they won't have the energy to fight in the hypothetical war. But even under his oppression, they thrive. One important note: In Scripture, slavery and forced labor are often different categories. Slavery was often a mutual agreement for a prearranged period of time in order to pay off debt, and slaves were treated like family; slavery in the Bible was often far more civil than more recent slavery, such as the American enslavement of other people groups, for example. However, what the Hebrews endure here is forced labor, even though it's sometimes referred to as slavery. Forced labor in Scripture is much closer to our modern understanding of slavery.

Pharaoh's oppression doesn't make a dent in their population, so he orders the Hebrew midwives to kill male Hebrews at birth, but they disobey. They're praised and rewarded by God for fearing Him. It may bother you that they're honored, since they lied and disobeyed the king, but when they were put in a position to be either liars or murderers, they were discerning enough to choose wisely.

For more information on today's reading, see thebiblerecap.com/links.

Pharaoh pushes back; he makes his plan a national order. One Hebrew mom hides her baby for three months, then sends him off in a basket on the Nile. When Pharaoh's daughter finds him, his sister makes an arrangement where the baby gets to live and the mom gets paid to nurse him. Pharaoh's daughter takes him back and becomes his second mom, renaming him Moses. He grows up in Pharaoh's house but knows he's a Hebrew. When he's forty, he sees an Egyptian beating a Hebrew and murders the Egyptian, but then he gets called out by another Hebrew. Pharaoh finds out and wants to kill him, so Moses flees three hundred miles to Midian. His first stop is the well, where he meets the daughters of the local priest and is kind to them. Their dad invites him to dinner *and* to marry his daughter Zipporah.

Meanwhile, Pharaoh number two dies. The Hebrews beg God for rescue; He hears and is moved to action. He promised them four hundred years of oppression, and His timeline is finally wrapping up. The Angel of the LORD shows up to Moses; this time He's a fire, and the fire is on a bush. God calls him by name and tells Moses that the plan to rescue His people includes *him* as the leader. Moses makes excuses for why he's a bad choice; it's hard to tell if his rebuttals are born out of insecurity or disobedience, but regardless, neither gets traction with God. God reminds him, "I AM sent you." I AM is an ancient name for God that means "I have always been what I will always be," or, more succinctly, "the self-existent One." No one created God; He has always existed and always will. And God says that despite all the things that will appear to be setbacks along the way, His plan will succeed.

TODAY'S GOD SHOT

God uses broken people. Moses is raised in the home of a wicked, paranoid bigot who wants him dead. He murders a man and goes on the lam. He's either insecure or disobedient or both. But he is the man God appoints over His people. If you've had a crazy life, or if you're a parent who worries that your mistakes have ruined everything for your child—take heart. God has nothing but sinners to work with, and He seems to specialize in using the unlikely. He calls to those furthest from Him, and He draws them near. That's the best news for all of us, because He's where the joy is!

EXODUS 4–6

Today God gives Moses some signs he can use to prove himself in Egypt, but Moses gives more excuses and rebuttals. He has some good points, but God is unmoved. God patiently responds to each of his concerns, never hedging on His plan, despite the fact that Moses is completely ill suited for this calling. Exhibit A: When Moses throws the staff on the ground and it becomes a snake, he runs from it! The guy who is afraid of a reptile probably shouldn't go toe-to-toe with a dictator.

But God reassures him. Not with a promise that everything will go perfectly, but with these words: "I will be with your mouth and teach you what you shall speak"—I will send a helper (4:12, 14). Moses doubts himself, but God reminds him whom he's talking to. Questioning God's calling is an insult to the God who made him. All of Moses' excuses are identity issues; given the environment he grew up in, it'd be shocking if he didn't have identity issues. At this point, it doesn't seem like he really knows or believes God, which means he can't really know who *he* is either. God gets angry at his final excuse because his hesitation is an affront to God's wisdom in calling him. His fears and insecurities are an attack on God's character, but God doesn't lean into this offense. He leans into patience and compassion. He provides for Aaron, Moses' older brother, to go with him. But God does not promise an easy journey. He tells Moses, "You're going to ask Pharaoh for something, and I'm going to harden his heart so that he says no." That's a tough assignment! But yesterday God promised He'd compel Pharaoh to submit eventually.

On the way to Egypt, God gets angry and seeks to kill someone, but it's unclear who or why. Most scholars believe the reason for God's anger is that Moses' son Gershom hasn't been circumcised, and most think God's anger is directed toward Moses. Not circumcising his son is a violation of the covenant, and this is especially important given that Gershom is about to be in the midst of a powerful enemy culture; he must be set apart. So Zipporah to the rescue! She circumcises Gershom, then touches the foreskin to Moses' feet. But one caveat: The Hebrew word for *feet* is occasionally used as a euphemism for genitals. By the way, if it *was* Moses God sought to kill, then this is the second time his life has been saved through the help of a woman. And if it was Gershom God sought to kill, then this is an interesting foreshadowing of killing the firstborn son of those who don't live under God's protective covering. More on that in the days ahead.

God sends Moses' older brother Aaron to help him. In Egypt, Aaron gives a speech to the Israelites, Moses demonstrates the signs from God, and the people are thrilled. But when Moses and Aaron approach Pharaoh, he denies their request. So they ask again. This time, he not only says no but cracks down even harder on the Israelite slaves, who blame Moses for it. Moses obeys God's commands, but things get worse.

God has Moses tell the Israelites about His promises, but they don't believe him. Their short-lived enthusiasm was crushed by the increased workload. Life is too hard for them to be hopeful. Moses is connected to this people, and we see it in the genealogy; after Scripture makes this connection, Moses doesn't doubt God's power anymore. He begins to find confidence and freedom in God, despite his shortcomings.

TODAY'S GOD SHOT

God shows compassion in His response to a hesitant, doubtful Moses. God knows his story; He knows his brokenness. Later, we see God's compassion again when Moses goes back to the Israelites the second time, after their workload has been increased and their former excitement has turned to despair. They can't muster any kind of faith on their own. Heartache and oppression have stolen their ability to hope and trust in the words of God. He knows they have no strength to fight, so He sends someone to fight for them. He sends someone who has received His compassion, who can demonstrate it to them. He sends a conduit of hope and freedom to a people who are hopeless and have never known freedom. He's compassionate, He's attentive, and He's where the joy is!

EXODUS 7–9

God reminds Moses and Aaron that Pharaoh won't listen; He's going to harden Pharaoh's heart against their request. This reveals that God is sovereign over hearts. If you're new to this idea or it troubles you, resist the urge to read into His motives or draw conclusions about Him based on this. For now, let's just notice that He has the power to change hearts. God also mentions several times that He's doing all this so that Israel will know He is the LORD. The word *know* doesn't just refer to a cognizant assent to this reality; it has more to do with a person's posture in response to the truth. God wants them to believe it in their bones, not just acknowledge it as a fact. He wants their lives to reflect it. The plagues will serve this same purpose for the Egyptians—for them to know that He is the LORD. Unfortunately, it's possible to know YHWH is the LORD and still not yield to Him. Remember the "sons of God," including the satan, the accuser? Most scholars believe they lived in heaven with God before their fall, serving Him. Who would know the truth more than they would? They know the truth but don't yield to God as their Lord.

Moses and Aaron warn Pharaoh that God will act with power if he continues to rebel and His acts will serve as judgment on Egypt. They perform the signs God gave them, but Pharaoh isn't impressed, because his magicians can do similar tricks. The enemy loves to counterfeit God's work, but the enemy can't stop God's work. Their snake staffs are swallowed up by Aaron's, and Pharaoh's heart is hardened, as the LORD had said. After the snake sign, the plagues begin. These plagues aren't just about inducing pain; each one is a direct attack on one or more of the false gods worshipped by the polytheistic Egyptians. They even worship Pharaoh, and these plagues reveal that YHWH is greater than Pharaoh. This whole series of events shows how all of Egypt's false gods fail them.

For more information on today's reading, see thebiblerecap.com/links.

After God displays power over the Nile River by turning it to blood, the local magicians do the same thing; again, Pharaoh is unmoved. His heart remains hard, as the LORD had said. The magicians replicate the frog plague too. Interestingly, they can't ever *solve* the problem—they can only make it worse. "Oh, God sent a bunch of frogs to overwhelm the land? We can't make them disappear, but we can add more!" Nobody needs that, you guys! In the midst of all this, Pharaoh promises to yield, but the minute the frogs vanish, so do his promises. Pharaoh hardens his heart. Same story with the gnats. Pharaoh's heart is hardened, as the LORD had said.

Then God does a plague with a twist. He calls the Egyptians "Pharaoh's people" and the Israelites "My people" as a reminder that Israelites are the only people He's in covenant with. He'll send flies, but they won't attack Goshen, where His people live. Despite this evidence of God's power in being location specific, Pharaoh hardens his heart. Then we have livestock and boils and hail. Hail is the first plague where human lives are threatened. God explicitly tells Pharaoh how to avoid it, but he hardens his heart. Things are going exactly as God said they would. Pharaoh even asks Moses to pray to God on his behalf, but still he never repents. His heart is always hard.

TODAY'S GOD SHOT

God's patience is so evident in these chapters. In 9:15–16, He says to Pharaoh, "By now I could have put out my hand and struck you and your people with pestilence, and you would have been cut off from the earth. But for this purpose I have raised you up, to show you My power, so that My name may be proclaimed in all the earth." He has patience toward sinners. Step by step, He's working out His plan. His patience with Pharaoh is probably frustrating to Moses and the Israelites, and even to the Egyptians. They were probably thinking, *Let them go already, Pharaoh!* We're often far less patient with God than He is with *everything*. We try to rush His plan, and we mistrust His heart. Still, He's with us in the struggle and the waiting, which means there can be joy even in those moments. Because He's where the joy is!

EXODUS 10–12

Today God opens with, "I have hardened his heart and the heart of his servants, that I may show these signs of mine among them . . . that you may know that I am the LORD." What a weighty paragraph! It almost sounds like part of God's plan is to harden Pharaoh's heart against His plan. He uses the wicked as a tool to advance His plan and bless His kids. This truth is difficult and mysterious, and it's okay not to understand it fully yet, or maybe ever. But we can't cut it out of Scripture; we have to see how it fits in. We've seen several places where God hardened Pharaoh's heart, a few that say "his heart was hardened," and a few that attribute the hardening to Pharaoh himself. But interestingly, Pharaoh's hardening of his own heart is almost always followed with the statement "as the LORD had said."

It can feel threatening to realize God is bigger than our hearts, that He can shape them for His own purposes. It's important not to let fear drive that thought. The enemy of your soul wants you to view God's power through a lens that pushes you away from Him instead of drawing you in. Instead, think of how comforting it is to know a God that powerful! You probably know and love people who are far from God, people you've prayed for and cried for, people who have told you they never want to hear another word about God again. He can soften their hearts and turn them on their heels. That's what He did with the apostle Paul, who wasn't just *not* seeking God, but who was actively at war against God and His people. For God to be sovereign over sins and hearts means no one is beyond His reach and it's never too late. What a comfort!

Pharaoh's resolve begins to weaken, but instead of obeying he asks for a compromise, and God turns it down. Locusts and darkness come, but still no repentance. Then God sends what He knows is the final plague. Moses has the Israelites ask the Egyptians for their valuables. He tells them to sacrifice a lamb and sprinkle its blood on the left side, right side, and top of their doorways, marking their homes and families by the blood of a sacrifice. Interestingly, because of the blood that drips to the ground from the top of the doorway, this forms the shape of a cross. God says to eat dinner quickly—don't even make bread that rises—and stay fully dressed.

He says He has planned a dinner party to celebrate what He's about to do. He's already telling them how to commemorate His deliverance before He fulfills it. Jewish people around the world still celebrate this event, and the Hebrew calendar is built around it. It's called Passover because God passes over the houses marked with blood, keeping them all alive. The destroying angel comes for Egypt, though. His identity is questionable, but most signs point to it being a theophany, specifically a Christophany, an appearance of Christ. After the angel (maybe Jesus) passes through, the Egyptians drive the Israelites out just like God promised, and the Israelites leave with fistfuls of jewelry and fine clothing just like God promised.

In the middle of the night, two to three million Israelites flee Egypt. Some non-Israelites join them, and we find out later that some Egyptians went too. God says to treat them like family as long as they're circumcised. They've been in Egypt for 430 years, but don't worry, God isn't 30 years late—for two possible reasons: 400 years could be a generality and not a down-to-the-minute timeline, or the first 30 years may have included the time when Joseph first moved his family there, before the second pharaoh enslaved them.

TODAY'S GOD SHOT

God spares the lives of the Israelites, but He also causes the pain of the Egyptians, and to secure our freedom, He sacrificed His own firstborn Son. We could never pay our sin debt, even with His help. We don't need Him to help us; we need His utter and complete rescue. And He gives it! Through the plan He initiated to sacrifice His Son, He also initiated a relationship with us and saved us from ourselves. We need an initiator—God the Father. And we need a mediator—God the Son. And we need someone to sustain and fulfill His work in us—God the Spirit. The plan He initiates, sustains, and fulfills is the only way we can be united with Him. And *thank God*, because He's where the joy is!

EXODUS 13–15

God wants to make sure this exodus experience sticks with His people, so He plans an annual party. In addition to Passover dinner, He orders the seven-day Feast of Unleavened Bread. Remembering and celebrating will help them keep God at the forefront of their minds. Remembering and celebrating helps them pass this story on to their children. Our hearts are fickle: When things go well, we forget God; when things go poorly, we doubt God. But remembering and celebrating will help the Israelites live according to God's character. He says this will all be "as a sign to you on your hand and as a memorial between your eyes." They take this literally. If you go to Jerusalem, you'll see people with small leather boxes tied on their foreheads or strapped around their arms and hands. These are phylacteries, and they hold Scripture; it's one way they aim to remember God's Word.

The Israelites know God has appointed Moses as their mediator, so the way they respond to Moses shows how they're responding to God in their hearts. Moses is under no illusion that he's in charge. He's God's representative, but God is their primary leader. Right out of the gate, God leads them the long way around—but He does it for their protection and their good. He knows their faith is brand-new and isn't strong enough to face the horrors of war. The Angel of the LORD leads them, and God also leads them via a cloud during the day and a fire at night—perhaps with the Angel out front and the cloud or fire overhead.

A cloud can shield you from the blistering desert sun and provide water at times, and a fire at night can light your way or keep you warm or drive away coyotes. With the Angel of the LORD and the fire and cloud, this may be a double theophany. Based on what we see throughout Scripture, it's possible that the fire and cloud are the presence of God the Father and the Angel is the presence of God the Son.

God gives Moses advance warning that Pharaoh is heading their way—in fact, He says to set up camp in their path! By now Moses trusts God, but the Israelites have just met God and Moses, so they aren't even close to trusting them yet. When they see the army, they fear the chariots more than they trust God. They blame Moses for their trouble and get nostalgic about their past. They've already forgotten the thing God wants them to remember, and it's basically week one. Despite their unbelief, God delivers them through the sea, killing Pharaoh's army. They sing the first worship song in Scripture—all about God's deliverance, how He's a warrior who fights for Israel. Miriam the prophetess leads the refrain; she's Moses' sister and possibly the one who helped save his life when he was a baby in a basket. Prior to the arrival of Moses and Aaron on the scene, Miriam had likely been in captivity in Egypt—she was probably one of the people they rescued.

After they finish worshipping God and His powers of deliverance, they're thirsty and grumble against Moses about the taste of the water. From worshipping to complaining in five seconds. God provides better water and says if they obey Him, He'll spare them from the diseases He put on the Egyptians. Then, the One who can both give and withhold disease calls Himself their healer. He's sovereign over both disease and health. Finally, they reach an oasis, and we end with a happy scene. Enjoy that for the next twenty-four hours. It doesn't last long.

TODAY'S GOD SHOT

There is no love without wrath. If you truly love something, you'll hate whatever threatens it. Out of God's great love for Israel, He fights for them. And when God makes war, He wins. He has solutions we can't even conceive of—who would even think to pray for a path through the sea? That military strategy doesn't exist. But our warrior God wages His own kind of warfare. He fights for us against all the things that threaten our relationship. And if we're honest with ourselves, we're often our own worst enemy. Our flesh is more present and more persistent than any outside enemy, so that means sometimes He fights *against* us while He's fighting for us. He knows better than we do. He loves better than we do. He helps eradicate the things that distract our hearts from Him to help us remember that He's where the joy is!

EXODUS 16–18

Just forty-five days after God's miraculous deliverance, the Israelites are grumbling and wishing they were back in Egypt, where the food was better. But all their complaints against Moses are actually complaints against God. Complaining reveals our view of God and His provision. God hears their grumbling, but He doesn't punish them for mistrusting Him. Instead, He promises food and makes Himself known in the cloud—in case they'd forgotten that it's not just a regular cloud they're dealing with. He promises to give them bread in the morning and meat in the evening. This manna seems to serve a threefold purpose: It serves a practical purpose by feeding the people, it serves an eternal purpose by glorifying God and showing His power, and it serves a spiritual purpose by testing the people and training them to trust God.

He says to gather manna every day except the Sabbath, which is the Hebrew name for the seventh day of the week—what we call Saturday. God is testing for potential pitfalls in their thought life: *Will I have a scarcity mentality and try to hoard the manna, or will I trust it will be there again tomorrow? Am I willing to work twice as hard gathering on Friday in order to rest on Saturday? Will the food I gather on Friday be enough to carry me through Sunday morning? Will God keep His promise to provide for me if I stop to rest as He has commanded?* God hasn't given them the Ten Commandments yet, but He's been hinting at this idea of resting on the Sabbath since creation, and He points to it again here. If they trust that He controls the forces of nature, they'll respond by obeying.

When they move to a new site with no water, God has Moses strike a rock with his staff and water pours out. Provision! Then we see His protection when an invading army attacks them out of nowhere. Moses appoints Joshua to put together a last-minute army so they can fight back against the Amalekites, distant relatives via Esau's line. During the war, Moses stands on top of the mountain and holds up his hands and his staff, and as long as he does that, the Israelites are winning. But when he lowers them, they're losing. Aaron and Hur prop up his arms until Joshua and his army win at sundown. God promises to destroy the Amalekites for attacking His people, and guess what—they don't exist anymore. We never see them after 1 Chronicles, except for a brief mention in the Psalms.

After the battle, Moses builds an altar and gives God a new name: The LORD Is My Banner. A banner is a visible identifier on display. Banners commemorate a victory for the winning team. A flag is a kind of banner. *The LORD Is My Banner* means a lot of things: "God is victorious," "I want to honor God's victory," "I want to remind myself what God has done," "I want everyone to know I belong to God." Giving God this name is an act of worship, and it's also a personal statement Moses is making about his own identity.

One day Moses' father-in-law, Jethro, steps in with some advice: Delegate tasks to trustworthy, tiered leadership. Moses could've said, "Uh, thanks, Jethro, but I've got a direct line to YHWH, so if I need advice, I think I know who to ask." But he doesn't. He's humble and knows good wisdom when he hears it. Could God have given Moses this counsel directly? Of course. But sometimes God uses others as His mouthpiece.

TODAY'S GOD SHOT

God commands His people to rest and trust Him to provide. They've been slaves with no days off, so it feels unnatural to them not to strive and work. But this is just one more way God shows them that He's a better God than Pharaoh. Pharaoh commanded them to work, but God commands them to rest. He knows our human nature longs to earn things, to feel accomplished. But the very nature of His relationship with us is that we're the recipients, not the earners, not the doers. He is the doer, and He says it is done! Hebrews 4:9 calls Jesus "our Sabbath rest"; His finished work on the cross frees us from trying to earn His approval and favor. We have nothing to offer anyway. It is said that when Martin Luther was asked what he contributed to his salvation, he replied, "Sin and resistance." God Himself has done all that He requires of us. May we learn how to rest in Him, because He's where the joy is!

EXODUS 19–21

Seven weeks after leaving Egypt, the Israelites get to Mount Sinai, also called the mountain of God. God says He wants to meet with them so they need to consecrate themselves. This is what He told them to do for the firstborns—to set them apart and prepare them to encounter God. Consecration usually involves a bath and clean clothes. Moses says to abstain from sex too—not because women are evil, but because seminal fluids and blood are symbols of life and death. To be depleted of either of those things points to the depletion of life, which isn't fitting for the presence of the Giver of life. Also, they can't get close to the mountain or they'll die. If someone does die, no one's allowed to touch that person because it'll transfer both their death sentence and the power of God. Bottom line: God's power isn't hypothetical.

A storm and a trumpet blast signal God's arrival. He descends as fire, covering Sinai in smoke. Then there's an earthquake. In the midst of the storm, fire, smoke, earthquake, and ever-increasing trumpet sound, God tells Moses to come closer, to climb the mountain no one's allowed to touch, because God has a few things to tell him. Namely, the Ten Commandments. God is talking to Moses, but the people overhear. God uses His personal name with them and points to His love for them: "I am YHWH, your God . . . I brought you out of slavery." He enters with relationship, *before* telling them His laws. Then He gives the ten "words"—that's what they're called in Hebrew. The first five words are vertical—how to honor God, and the last five words are horizontal—how to honor others. Here are some things worth noting:

The second word, about idols and graven images, reveals our natural inclination to worship things. Everyone worships something. Mostly we worship what we see regularly. The challenge for our idolatrous hearts is that YHWH has no physical form. In order to worship Him, we have to move beyond our human nature, which means setting aside the created

---

For more information on today's reading, see thebiblerecap.com/links.

things we can see with our eyes. Even though God does appropriate a physical form from time to time, like in theophanies, He's not attached to or confined to that form. And when God says He's jealous, it's not like our jealousy and envy. The word used here is used only in reference to God. Its meaning is more like "protective" or "zealous." He's protective of and zealous for His relationship with us. It's an act of love.

In the third word, we see how seriously God takes His name. There are lots of layers here, but let's focus on three: (1) As people who have taken His name, we're called to live in ways that show we belong to Him, (2) this prohibits any kind of insincere or frivolous use of His name because it suggests we're not taking it seriously, and (3) God takes personal offense to anything that diminishes His personhood or character. His names represent His character and His actions. Taking God's name in vain could also correspond to doubting that He is who He says He is.

Chapter 21 gives a general outline for how to live in civil society and treat others well. It reveals God's desire to protect and respect life, including life in the womb, because all life points to its Giver.

TODAY'S GOD SHOT

When the people see God's power and are afraid, Moses says something that seems contradictory at first: "Do not fear, for God has come to test you, that the fear of him may be before you, that you may not sin" (20:20). So should we be afraid or not? There's a crucial distinction to make between the two uses of the word *fear*. The fear in "do not fear" carries the idea of dread—this kind of fear drives us *away* from God; it's sin adjacent. But Moses uses a different word when he refers to fearing God; it carries the idea of reverence and awe—it's joy adjacent, and it has the effect of drawing us *to* God. The fear of God is composed primarily of delight and awe, moving us toward God. It's like what we feel at the Grand Canyon—we take long trips to go stand on the edge with our eyes and mouths open wide, overwhelmed with beauty, yet knowing it could kill us. Moses says that's the kind of fear that keeps us from sinning against God. I like the kind of fear that draws me closer to God, because He's where the joy is!

EXODUS 22–24

God talks more about the laws for restitution, directing His people toward a civil, just society that treats others with respect and honors life. He unpacks specific implications of the Ten Commandments. For instance, a thief often has to pay back more than he stole, so the consequences serve as deterrents. These laws may feel intimidating if you're the one committing the sin, but if you're the victim, it's easier to appreciate why God established these laws. He protects female virgins by threatening several years' wages from the men who take advantage of them. This isn't referring to rape; Deuteronomy 22:25 says the penalty for rape is death. This law refers to seduction that leads to consensual sex.

God also forbids charging interest; most interest rates in those days started at 25 percent. But guess who borrows money? The needy. God says it's cruel to increase the burden of one of His needy kids. Instead, He emphasizes compassion toward the poor. He says to care for sojourners, widows, and orphans. He shows special attention to the most vulnerable. He teaches His people to love each other and not exploit each other. They have a lot to unlearn about behavior—they've been oppressed, they've lived with a scarcity mentality. So He reminds them to be compassionate because He is compassionate, to be openhanded because He's their provider.

Then He addresses sorcery, like the divination we've seen before. God takes it seriously; it's punishable by death. These practices engage with spirits for guidance and power—spirits who aren't on God's team. When people seek answers from the enemy instead of God, it's not only idolatry, it's treason against the kingdom of light. God orders death for anyone who practices this or lures people into their web of wickedness. He aims to protect His people from the enemy's subtle deceptions.

He's also attentive to the enemy's tactics when it comes to the land He's giving His kids. He says to break the stone pillars the pagans have

---

For more information on today's reading, see thebiblerecap.com/links.

set up and drive out anyone who worships other gods. In fact, He'll even do some of that driving out on His own. It's important to note that this distinction has nothing to do with race, but it has everything to do with idolatry. We know this because sojourners are welcomed, but not those who worship other gods. God is preserving this family for the birth of the Messiah. There are lots of people who say they worship God but who also acknowledge the power and validity of other gods. This is called *monolatry*, a hybrid of monotheism and idolatry. While He never denies other gods exist, and in fact, He seems to indicate in the first commandment that they do, He continues to point out that Israel's loyalty must be to Him alone. All other gods are false gods, lesser gods, demon gods, idols—and they're impotent before YHWH. Monotheism affirms that YHWH is the one true God.

He ordains three feasts that serve as reminders of His provision. We've seen the Feast of Unleavened Bread before, and today we see the Feast of Harvest and the Feast of Ingathering. These are both feasts of thanks and trust. They celebrate God's provision at the start and end of the harvest season, and their feasting shows they trust God to keep providing for them in the future.

When the people enter into this covenant with God at Mount Sinai, agreeing to do all He says, Moses offers a sacrifice and throws blood on them. While this sounds disturbing, it's likely a symbol that they're tied to the covenant, much like when God had Abraham split the animals in half and then passed between them. Also, being sprinkled with blood often symbolizes being purified and atoned for—it actually foreshadows Christ's death covering us. Then Moses ascends the mountain.

TODAY'S GOD SHOT

God is so protective of His people, but He also commands them to show kindness to those they consider enemies or those who hate them. This is the whole reason we're in a relationship with Him to begin with! We all started out as His enemies, and this is how He has treated us—with mercy and compassion, stepping into our need despite the fact that we've waged war against Him with our sin and rebellion. He is a God who pursues His enemies and turns them into His family. He's where the joy is!

EXODUS 25–27

If you're into home renovation shows or architecture, today's reading should've been right up your alley. It includes all kinds of furniture and construction details. We have a bunch of former slaves living in the desert, and God wants them to build a portable tabernacle where He can dwell with them in the midst of the wilderness. He tells them to use all kinds of precious metals and fabrics for this tabernacle. Where would they get all this stuff? From plundering the Egyptians! It turns out the things God blessed them with are used for His glory. The blessings don't terminate on them—they serve a much bigger purpose.

You may feel like this information is boring and wonder why we have to read about all these details, or maybe you wish God would be this detailed with communicating His plans for your life. Perhaps you even have both of those thoughts. Hang in there through these details and be encouraged that our God is a God of detail. We want and need Him to be.

Let's touch on a few noteworthy things. First, the construction metals get more precious the closer they get to the Most Holy Place, where God dwells: gold inside, silver outside, bronze furthest out. Second, the ark of the covenant (also called the ark of the testimony) is almost four feet long, a little more than two feet wide, and a little more than two feet high. Humans aren't supposed to touch it after it's constructed. Just like when they couldn't touch Mount Sinai, God is protecting them from His power, because they can't survive coming into contact with it. When they have to pack up and relocate the tabernacle as they move around in the wilderness, God says to carry it with gold-covered wooden poles over their shoulders.

The lid of the ark is called the mercy seat, and it has two cherubim on it. If you've seen a drawing of a cherub, it probably looked like a naked baby with wings. As always, forget what you know from Renaissance

---

For more information on today's reading, see thebiblerecap.com/links.

art and Precious Moments figurines. We talked about cherubim not long ago—they have four wings covered in eyes, and they likely have the form of a man, but they have four faces. They most often appear as guardians of holy places, like the garden of Eden. If your job is to guard a holy place, it's helpful to have four faces so you can look in every direction at all times. The mercy seat is made of pure gold and the cherubim are positioned on opposite ends. This is God's resting place, essentially God's throne on earth. God says, "There I will meet with you." The Hebrew word for *meet* also means "betroth," and the term *mercy seat* is related to the word that means "to make atonement." The mercy seat descriptions are similar to what we see with the angels who appear in Jesus's tomb after His resurrection in John 20:12. They were positioned in the same way, at opposite ends of Jesus's burial spot.

The golden lampstand is still a part of Jewish culture. The word *menorah* is Hebrew for "lampstand." It's a symbol of God's presence, so people began keeping them in their homes as a reminder of Him. The standard menorah has six branches and seven lamps, but there are also special types of menorahs used for Hanukkah; those have nine branches and are called hanukkiahs.

TODAY'S GOD SHOT

There's so much beauty in the fact that God wants to dwell with His people. These people have sinned against Him and doubted Him, and they keep forgetting all He's done for them. Yet He wants to be near to them always. There's a lot of detail in this section, but one interesting thing is that the layout of the tabernacle parallels a lot of what we saw in Eden: There's an east-facing entrance, there are cherubim guards, the burning lampstand symbolizes the Tree of Life, and the testimony (the law) symbolizes the Tree of Knowledge of Good and Evil. So when God starts telling them these details and says He'll come there to dwell with them, it's a step toward restoring paradise and all that was lost in the garden of Eden. We won't see the fulfillment of this until Christ returns and we have a new heaven and a new earth. But here in Exodus, we see God advancing in that direction to dwell with His people forever. I can't think of anything better, because He's where the joy is!

EXODUS 28–29

If this section is challenging, persevere! It sets us up to learn more about God and His story. In passages like this, don't try to remember all the details; just try to come away with an overall idea of the purpose of it all. Try seeing what ties these details together, then ask yourself what those things reveal to you about God. For instance, why would He pay this kind of attention to detail? And why would He include those details in a book that would long outlive the use of these things? Whatever these difficult passages show us about Him is still in effect, even if the offerings and sacrifices and garments are long gone.

Remember the sons of Jacob, the twelve tribes of Israel? In Exodus 2:1, we learned that Moses and Aaron are from the tribe of Levi. Levi was one of the two brothers who killed the men of Shechem to avenge their sister Dinah's rape. Yet here we are, with Levi's descendants being appointed as priests unto God. Talk about redemption! Levi's descendants are called Levites, and the book we'll read next, Leviticus, is all about their work. God addresses His plans for Aaron and his offspring in their roles as priests. He pays a lot of attention to their priestly attire, but it's not just clothes we're dealing with here—it's more like sacred equipment. Think of a police officer's utility belt or a football player's pads. These garments serve a function. They're listed along with all the tabernacle details and equipment, and they're explicitly designed for use in the sanctuary by active priests, so it's not like they wear this stuff to the camel races on Tuesdays. These garments are also intended "for glory and for beauty." They display God's splendor and attention to detail, and He specifically gifted people to make them—that's how serious He is about this.

The high priest is a foreshadowing of Christ, connecting God and man, so his clothes are supposed to indicate his role as a mediator. His attire symbolically represents the people while he's in the presence of God—hence the names of the tribes on the shoulder pieces and the twelve stones of the ephod—and symbolically represents God to the people. Then there's the Urim and Thummim. We don't really know what these are, except that they're part of the ephod and they seem to be tools used for discerning God's will. Some say they're like dice. It's possible that the Urim, which seems to be the primary device they use, gives off some kind of supernatural light, because its name is closely related to the Hebrew word for light.

Even the bells on the hem of the robe serve a purpose. The priest has a lot of duties, and all that movement keeps those bells ringing. If the priest falls dead while performing his tasks, the bells go silent. This is important because the priest has to enter the Most Holy Place alone and surveillance cameras don't exist yet.

The priests go through an intense seven-day ordination and consecration ceremony, where blood is sprinkled on their right ear, right thumb, and right big toe. We know that blood symbolizes purification in these ceremonies, but why do they put it on those spots? Since their priestly garments cover most of their skin, the blood is placed on some of the only exposed skin and at their farthest exposed extremities: head, finger, toe. Making these marks of purification on these three spots likely symbolizes that their whole body has been purified. Then they have to make offerings of costly animals without defect.

TODAY'S GOD SHOT

The ordination ceremony and sacrifices point to God's holiness. *Holy* means "set apart." God also establishes the altar and sacrifices as holy, set apart for sacred use by the Divine. And even though holiness by definition indicates separation, God ends today's reading with these words: "I will meet with you, to speak to you there. There I will meet with the people of Israel. . . . I will dwell among the people of Israel and be their God." In His holiness, in His set-apartness, He makes a way to draw near. Nothing will stop Him from being with His people—not His holiness, not their sin, nothing. To be pursued by Him is the best gift, because He's where the joy is!

EXODUS 30–32

As we read about offerings and sacrifices, don't try to remember or understand it all; just keep looking for what it shows us about God. It reveals that He wants a relationship with us. It reveals that our sins need to be atoned for and He made a plan to accomplish that.

God unloads a bunch of details to Moses and Joshua, including a onetime census tax of half a shekel, roughly three dollars today. One of the problems with a census is that people can be arrogant about numbers. So God attaches a reminder to this tax that this census isn't about their population—it's a reminder that they owe Him their lives. He's pointing their gaze to His goodness in sparing their lives, pardoning their sins, and providing them with a place to meet with Him.

The phrase "cleanliness is next to godliness" is not in the Bible, but if it were, it'd be in Exodus 30 amid the hygiene rituals. Cleanliness is about purity, and purity is a big deal when it comes to drawing near to a set-apart God. Even the priests have to make sure they're clean, washing their hands and feet in a bronze basin so they won't die. This foreshadows a time when Jesus knelt down and washed the feet of His disciples. He must wash us clean so we won't die, so we can draw near to God.

God chooses two craftsmen for the tabernacle tasks, and His Spirit fills them. That's a big deal because God the Spirit is traveling around a lot in the Old Testament. He comes to empower people for specific tasks, then He moves on. He empowers Bezalel with ability, intelligence, knowledge, and craftsmanship—to be used for His glory, building the things He wants in His tabernacle. Whatever God requires of us, He equips us for; He gives us all we need for the assignment.

But He doesn't just initiate work; He initiates rest. He tells Moses the Sabbath is a sign between them, which elevates it to the level of circumcision, like in God's covenant with Abraham. In fact, this conversation is called the Sinai Covenant. The Sabbath is "holy to the Lord," and He calls them to honor it each week. This is a much higher requirement than a onetime event like circumcision; it's a regularly recurring reminder of who God is to them.

When Moses has been on Sinai for six weeks, the people grow impatient. They're itching for something to worship, so they ask Aaron to make them a god, and he complies. Perhaps he's jealous of Moses and wants to usurp his leadership. This is the man God appointed as high priest, and here he is, melting down earrings to make a cow. The people attribute their deliverance from Egypt to this thing that, moments earlier, was in their ears and on their fingers. Meanwhile, God fills Moses in. He says He wants to destroy them and start fresh, but Moses appeals to Him based on His irrevocable promises and His unchanging character. Did God really plan to kill them? It's more likely that this was a test for Moses, an opportunity for *him* to be reminded of God's promises and character, because he's going to need to remember them in the days ahead.

When Moses sees the mayhem, he breaks the tablets, destroys the calf, and rebukes the people. Meanwhile, Aaron is dodgy, shifting blame. Moses asks the people if their hearts are with God or not. The Levites are all in, but Moses commands death for anyone who isn't. Three thousand people die that day, whether by sword or by plague. Some theologians believe that the "plague" the Lord sent in 32:35 refers to those who died by the swords of the sons of Levi in 32:28. Either way, compared to the three million who went along with the golden-calf plan, three thousand who are unrepentant and die is a small number. This may seem harsh, but these are the people of the covenant, the people the Messiah will be born through, and now three thousand of them are unapologetically worshipping their jewelry. It's merciful that God lets the other 2,997,000 live.

TODAY'S GOD SHOT

The people call God's timing a delay, but He says they turned aside quickly. What they perceive as a delay, He calls quick. They're worshipping a golden calf while He's making plans to draw near to them, agreeing to spare their lives. How often do we doubt His timing and take matters into our own hands? How often do we find something else to worship when it seems He's forgotten us? May we trust His timing, even in His so-called delays. He has spared our lives since breath number one, and He made plans to wash us clean and save us. His nearness is our greatest good, because He's where the joy is!

EXODUS 33–35

God and Moses spend time together regularly, meeting face-to-face. But God the Father is spirit, so He doesn't have a face, technically. Scripture often anthropomorphizes God, explaining Him in human terms we can grasp. So don't imagine God with an actual face. That's just Scripture's way of showing us the level of accessibility and intimacy Moses has with Him.

Today God sends the Israelites away from His mountain, toward Canaan, the promised land. He says He won't personally be going with them, but He'll send His angel. If this particular angel is *the* Angel of the LORD, then it sounds like God the Son will be accompanying them but not God the Father. He wants to consume them because of how they've broken the covenant with Him. They're a stiff-necked people, stubborn and rebellious, and He's furious with them. It's not always fitting to compare human emotions with God's emotions—that can get us off track sometimes—but at the risk of that, it may be helpful to recall how you felt if someone broke a covenant with you. Was your initial reaction something like burning anger in response to the pain of it all? Regardless, Moses isn't okay with God's response. He reminds God of His promises to him and that these are His people, appealing again to God's promises and heart. Moses knows they're all helpless without God, so he wants to make certain God will go with them. In fact, he says the very reason God should go with them is *because* they're a stiff-necked people, which makes them especially in need of His presence and guidance.

Then Moses asks God to show him His glory. Again we see a lot of anthropomorphizing, so don't imagine the Father with an actual body. These are metaphors. He tells Moses a few more things about Himself, saying, "I will be gracious to whom I will be gracious, and will show mercy on whom I will show mercy" (33:19). This is fitting, especially if you recall what we've said about grace and mercy and what we deserve. Mercy is not getting what you deserve, and grace is getting what you don't deserve. God doles out mercy and grace to whomever He wants, whenever He wants, and right now, He's choosing to show mercy to a bunch of people who just broke their covenant with Him.

God says they're going to remake the tablets Moses broke, then tells him even more about Himself in 34:6–7: He's merciful, gracious, slow to anger, abounding in steadfast love and faithfulness, keeping steadfast love for thousands, forgiving iniquity and transgression and sin—these are all things we've seen from Him, and they all sound amazing. Then He says He won't clear the guilty and reminds Moses that sins have generational consequences. In the scope of God's character, even the harsh is good and necessary. We *want* a God who punishes the guilty. No one would trust a judge who didn't do that. He'd be impeached. God is both loving and just, and those two things are not at odds. When He says, "keeping steadfast love for thousands," many scholars believe this actually translates to "keeping steadfast love for a thousand generations." If that's true, and we compare it to the effects of sinfulness on the generations, which extends to the third and fourth generations, then God's steadfast love is carried out approximately three hundred times as long. He leans heavily on mercy and grace.

When Moses comes back down from the mountain, his face is radiant from being in God's presence, so he has to wear a veil because people are afraid to look at him. Then God has Moses revisit the laws of their society, and He also sets out an optional donation for the tabernacle, and "everyone whose heart stirred him" donated (35:21). How do hearts get stirred? Who does that?

TODAY'S GOD SHOT

In 33:16, Moses says, "Is it not in your going with us, so that we are distinct, I and your people, from every other people on the face of the earth?" God is the one who gives us our identity. Through His children, He makes Himself and His goodness known throughout the earth. He shines light in the dark, He gives hope to the lost, He shows kindness to the harsh, He brings patience to the frantic. He is our identity, He is what's noteworthy about us, and He's where the joy is!

EXODUS 36–38

Yesterday we left off with Moses telling the people what was needed to build the tabernacle, where God would dwell in their midst, and God said anyone who wanted to could contribute. Today we open with God putting intelligence and skill into the craftsmen so they can build the sanctuary just like He wants it. Many people bring donations, and they're dropping things off every morning. They're spring-cleaning their tents like crazy—so much so that Moses has to tell them to stop. God overprovides here. This reveals that they seem to be truly repentant. Romans 2:4 says God's kindness leads us to repentance, and He has certainly been kind to them in sparing their lives after that golden calf debacle and in renewing His covenant with them.

Some of today's lengthy passages may seem redundant, since we just read about this a few days ago. The point of this repetition is to highlight that the people who just rebelled against God are actually following God's instructions to the letter. Don't miss that! We'll have plenty of opportunities to be frustrated with their sins, so let's just take a moment to enjoy and appreciate this rare moment of obedience. It might be boring, but it's glorifying to God nonetheless.

There are often meaningful details we fail to notice in passages that feel dry. For instance, each of these pieces of furniture and even the way they're arranged in the tabernacle paint a divine picture for us. Some scholars say the furniture was actually laid out in the shape of a cross. All of this—the tabernacle and its furnishings and all the rituals associated with it—is all just a shadow of the good things to come, according to Hebrews 9:1–10:18. This is a foreshadowing of Christ.

Each piece of furniture symbolizes some aspect of our relationship with God. The brazen altar, which is the first piece we encounter outside, represents the sacrifice of Christ. The bronze laver, which is the washbasin, represents being washed clean. The table of showbread represents feasting on the Word. The altar of incense represents prayer. The menorah, or candlestick, represents the light of the Holy Spirit constantly aflame in us. And of course, the ark of the covenant and the mercy seat, where God dwells, represent His presence with us. They also parallel the six days of creation followed by a day of rest. There are seven pieces of furniture, six of which are work related, and the seventh and final piece is the mercy seat, on which God's presence rests, much like He rested on the seventh day. When you're reading about these pieces, try to remember not just their function but what they symbolize as well.

This tabernacle and God's presence are worth it all to the Israelites. They donate their plunder, they melt down their shekels, they weave fabrics and craft curtain rods, all so YHWH can dwell in the midst of them. Surely you recognize yourself in these people a little bit. You've probably had moments of rebellion and golden-calf parties, and you've probably also had moments when you would've given away all your best possessions if it meant the nearness of God. Based on the way you're spending time in His Word right now, you're probably closer to the second place than the first. You're here reading and even recapping what many would consider to be a very dry passage of Scripture. It reveals a lot about what God's doing with that lampstand in your heart, that continual fire of the Spirit, burning even when you can't detect it.

TODAY'S GOD SHOT

He is here with us, drawing us near even on the days when there seems to be nothing flashy about Him, even in the spaces that feel routine or humdrum. He's in the ritual, and He's in the ordinary. There will probably be days when the priests are mixing the incense and slaughtering the animals that they don't feel any closer to God than they did beforehand. They may wonder if it is really even doing anything. But they keep at it, trusting beyond their own understanding that doing these things over and over really does serve some kind of purpose, even when they can't see it. They trust His Word, and I hope you do too. Drawing near to God, bit by bit, will always be worth the slow days, because He's where the joy is!

EXODUS 39–40

When everything for the tabernacle has been created according to God's plan and presented to Moses, we see another parallel of creation. After God finished creating humankind, He blessed them. Today, we see that's true of the tabernacle too—the place where He came to dwell with humankind. When Moses sees the pieces of the tabernacle completed as God commanded, he blesses them. These parallels are intentional; the tabernacle is a step in the direction of God restoring what was broken in the garden of Eden 2,700 years earlier. God is camping out with a bunch of sinners, because He just can't stay away from His people.

Moses has all these tabernacle pieces, and it's his job to assemble it all, like ancient IKEA furniture. God has him anoint the furniture with oil and consecrate it. All this furniture is just wood and metal, stuff God created that had been owned by the wicked Egyptians and then plundered by the Israelites and that had a near miss with being part of the golden calf. There's nothing special about these things. But they're in God's sanctuary, and He said to *make* them holy, to set them apart for sacred use. So how is Moses supposed to do that? By putting oil on them. How does putting oil on something make it holy? In Scripture, oil symbolizes the Holy Spirit, so this furniture is being symbolically dedicated to God, establishing its purpose in serving Him.

After he consecrates the furniture, Moses brings in Aaron and his sons, washes them, puts the priestly garments on them, and anoints them. Then something important happens: God establishes the line of Aaron as the family of priests to serve before Him throughout their generations. If you're only familiar with Catholic priests, for instance, you may think that means this family line of priests will only last two generations, since Aaron and his sons obviously can't marry. But that's not what we see in the priesthood here; this line will continue on. There's no requirement of celibacy or singleness here. In fact, these specific people have been encouraged to multiply.

This all happens one year after they left Egypt, when they're a little more than a week away from celebrating their first Passover in the wilderness. This will actually be the second Passover, since the first one was in Egypt. This tabernacle is a great anniversary present, and it'll be a beautiful reminder when they celebrate Passover for the first time as free people. We'll get to that part soon! The next couple of books we read aren't going to be as story-driven as these first three have been. We do continue in this same storyline, with this same family, but it'll be less of a narrative for a bit. Don't give up. There's good stuff for us in the days ahead! Ask God for wisdom, ask Him to open your eyes, and you'll get something out of it you've never seen before.

Hopefully you've grown close enough to some of these people to care about what their lives are like in the next few books, even in the dry spots. When we started this book two weeks ago, they were slaves in Egypt. Put yourself in their shoes: You're a freed slave living in the wilderness with three million other freed slaves, a guy with a shiny face and who wears a veil is in charge of everything, and you're being led by a God who lives in a cloud. Whenever the cloud moves, you pack up your tent and your family follows the cloud, because you've come to realize it contains the presence and glory of the God who loves you. You complain about His plan, but He drowns an army to save you. You doubt Him, but He's still giving you manna six days a week. You sinned against Him, but He doesn't kill you. And still He's there, in your midst. What's this going to be like? When is God going to lead you into the land He promised to give you? He seems to be good, but how do you draw near to His goodness? Can you? We'll look at that in the days ahead.

TODAY'S GOD SHOT

In 40:35, we see that "Moses was not able to enter the tent of meeting because the cloud settled on it, and the glory of the Lord filled the tabernacle." There is density to the presence of God here, and this cloud *fills* the tabernacle. Every square inch, it seems. His glory is dense, His presence is undeniable, and He's where the joy is!

LEVITICUS 1–4

Leviticus is about a perfect, holy God who wants to draw near to His depraved, sinful people. It walks us through the messy process that makes that possible. There are many components, so set your mind to press through on days when it's not easy. First, who are the Levites? They're the descendants of Levi, one of the sons of Jacob and tribes of Israel. Yesterday God appointed them to be priests in the tabernacle. This book outlines things pertaining to these mediators between the holy God and His sinful people to make this relationship function. Almost everything we read in Leviticus is God talking to Moses. These are His words and ways.

There are three primary states of a person or thing: unclean, clean, and holy. God is always holy, and the people are generally unclean. God sets out rituals and laws to get them from the unclean state to the clean or even holy state. First, God establishes five types of ritual offerings: burnt, grain, peace, sin, and guilt. You may wonder why this barbaric stuff has to happen at all. Remember how in the garden of Eden God told Adam and Eve about the connection between sin and death? God spared their lives, but something had to die in their place. In that instance, God killed an animal to clothe them. And here we see many animals will have to die, because we've got three million sinners living in the desert together. So God sets up the sacrificial system so animals can die instead of people to make atonement for their sins.

Atonement means "to cover." The animal's death is a temporary covering for their sin. While animal sacrifice can be hard to stomach, it's important that we're never angrier at God's provision for covering our sin than at our sin itself. Sin demands death (Hebrews 9:22). God knows that this plan is temporary. It's a Band-Aid, not a cure. This foreshadows the real solution that will come in the form of Jesus and His death on the cross. But for now, we've got this system. And learning about it should increase our gratitude that we live after this has been done away with!

For more information on today's reading, see thebiblerecap.com/links.

Another thing we see taking place here is not only God's provision of a blood sacrifice, but also God's provision of food for the priests. Since their job involves mediating between God and the people, they can't be out raising food and farming. If they're going to obey His calling on their lives, they'll have to trust Him to feed them. Fortunately He has a plan, and it involves other people bringing them food all the time, via an offering—and God calls that offering most holy.

All offerings must be made with "the salt of the covenant with your God" (2:13). Salt implies preservation, and it symbolizes the preservation of their covenant with God. Fat represents the best part of the animal, so God keeps that for Himself. "All the fat is the LORD's"—that verse belongs on a T-shirt. Even unintentional sin requires a sacrifice, because sin is sin regardless of motive. And the higher your position, the more valuable the sacrifice required. Leadership comes with added weight and responsibility. If a priest sins against the congregation or leads the congregation into sin, he has to sprinkle the blood of his offering in front of the veil of the sanctuary, which separates the holiest part of the tabernacle from everything else inside. It holds the mercy seat and the ark of the covenant, the representation of God's throne on earth. His dwelling place. No one can enter that area except the high priest, and he can only go in one day each year. When regular people sin, the blood is thrown on the sides of the altar in the outer court. But when priests sin or the whole congregation sins, the blood is brought from the outer court through the tabernacle into the Holy Place and sprinkled in front of the veil of the Most Holy Place, because sins defile the whole tabernacle.

TODAY'S GOD SHOT

It must feel weighty to carry blood to God's doorstep. Surely it reminds the priests that God spared them via sprinkled blood on their own doorways just a year ago. They aren't far removed from hearing the screams of the Egyptian families in the night and fleeing as God rescued them. And now they stand in front of His earthly throne, deeply aware of their sin and His goodness. He's merciful, He provides a sacrifice, and He's where the joy is!

LEVITICUS 5–7

Tomorrow we'll get a break from sacrificial instructions and hear from some humans, but today God continues with laws for sin offerings. He shows them the distinction between committing a sin versus doing something that makes a person unclean. Being unclean isn't a sin, so it doesn't require an offering or sacrifice—it just requires them to be purified, take a bath, or spend time in isolation. This law almost always relates to something hygienic. We do things like this today, quarantining people when they're contagious. These hygiene regulations are especially helpful in a culture that predates modern science. For instance, it's a good idea not to touch dead bodies or eat meat after a certain period of time has passed.

Not all the cleanliness laws are straightforward and scientifically logical, but some are. For instance, some of the cleanliness laws relate to blood. While this may be hygienic, it's probably more symbolic. Blood can be a confusing symbol in the Old Testament—it symbolizes life *and* death. Life is a positive symbol, but when blood leaves the body, it symbolizes death and serves as a reminder of the fall, which makes a person unclean. God is in the process of re-creating Eden, so the unclean things have to be distanced. Being unclean isn't intended to be a permanent situation or a symbol of shame; everyone is unclean at some point. It isn't sinful or terminal. We see the phrase "that person shall be cut off from his people" four times today, and it's always in regard to someone who disrespects the sacrificial laws. Some scholars think this refers to isolating that person from the group, while others say it indicates premature death. Either way, God makes it clear that His sacrificial laws are to be honored.

As opposed to uncleanness, sin does require a sacrifice. God is also attentive to the needs of the poor when it comes to the sacrifices He requires of them. In many of these sacrifices, the wealthy are required to give a domestic animal from the flock, one without blemish, the best of the best. But the poor don't have animals, much less *perfect* animals, so He says they can bring birds, and if they can't afford birds, they can bring flour. And in that case, they don't even have to put the costly things like oil and frankincense on it. God meets His people where they are, poverty and all.

Sins of omission require the same sacrifice as sins of commission. A sin of omission is when we fail to do something we're supposed to do, like today's mention of failing to give testimony in a case where justice needs to be carried out. A sin of commission is when we do something God has ordered us not to do. In 6:1–7, God shows His heart in what's required of us when we sin against someone else. These sacrificial laws are Old Testament laws that no longer apply to us because Christ has offered the final sacrifice, but the heart behind all this remains. Sin against someone else requires the Israelites not only to offer something to God but also to the person they sin against.

TODAY'S GOD SHOT

Many Christians think God can't be in the presence of sin. One verse, Habakkuk 1:13, seems to point to that, but it's taken out of context. On the contrary, what we see here and elsewhere in Scripture is that God tells people to come to His courts when they sin and to offer their sacrifices there. He tells them to come nearer when they sin! From the beginning of humanity, sinners have been running from God, trying to hide, and He's been pursuing us, telling us to draw near. Not only can God be in the presence of sin, but He can't avoid it. It's everywhere. And in the first chapter of Job, the "sons of God" and Satan came to speak to God in what appears to be His throne room. Evil doesn't scare or threaten Him. Everything that isn't God is less than perfect, so He's used to it. He isn't corrupted by the presence of sin. If He were, He'd have to stay quarantined Himself, away from all of us forever. Instead, our God intentionally builds His home in the midst of sin. He knows sinners can't fix themselves. He's not afraid of you. He's not afraid of your sin. He paid for it because He wants to be near to you, and He's where the joy is!

LEVITICUS 8–10

Today we read about anointing, consecrating, and ordaining. *To anoint* is to apply oil to something. *To consecrate* is to set it apart for sacred use. And *to ordain* is to establish. Moses anoints, consecrates, and ordains Aaron and his four sons in a seven-day process in which Aaron offers the very first sacrifice on the altar. On day eight, we have the first official tabernacle service, and Aaron and his sons offer more sacrifices on the altar. Aaron's first job as high priest is to make atonement—or covering—for himself and then for the people. The order here is important: It starts with atoning for sin through the sin offering, then it moves to petitions and praises in the burnt offering, then to communion and fellowship in the peace offering. Aaron blesses the people, then he and Moses both bless the people, and then comes the biggest blessing of all: The glory of the LORD appears to all the people. Fire comes down and consumes the offering, and the people fall on their faces and worship. Praise is the proper response to all of God's actions.

Then Aaron's two oldest sons decide to completely ignore God's commands and do their own thing. Nadab and Abihu offer incense in a way that is not consistent with God's rules. Perhaps they offer something other than God's special incense, or they offer it at a time that isn't authorized, or they're drunk when they offer it, or most likely, they offer it *at all* instead of Aaron doing it. God sends fire down to kill them on the spot. Their actions are arrogant rebellion, and God demonstrates right out of the gate that He won't stand for it. Also, in keeping with a theme we've seen God establishing, the two oldest sons are passed over here.

Moses has two of Aaron's cousins dispose of their bodies, since Aaron can't touch a dead body or he'll be unclean. Then Moses tells two of Aaron's other sons not to perform the traditional grief practices in response to their deaths. Others can grieve respectfully, but not them. In the midst of this, God speaks to Aaron directly, which is a rare occurrence but is really sweet considering he just lost two of his sons. God gives him specific orders about the way he and the other priests are supposed to be set apart. First, they have to avoid drinking on the job. The fact that this is the first command is one of the reasons some scholars think Nadab and Abihu were drunk when they made the offering. Priests are supposed to protect the sacred space of the tabernacle and distinguish between clean and unclean. They're also called to teach everyone else what God has revealed to Moses. Teaching is one of their main jobs.

Moses orders the two remaining sons to make an offering and then eat it as a gift of provision from God. But they don't eat it, and Moses is furious. These were the people who were supposed to be teaching others to obey the things God told Moses, and they can't even obey those things themselves. Moses may be afraid God will strike down Aaron's two other sons as well, and then the priesthood will be done forever once Aaron dies. How will God keep His promise if He kills all four of Aaron's sons on the same day? Moses is stressed out!

TODAY'S GOD SHOT

God's character is evident in Moses' response to Aaron. Aaron appeals to Moses, reminding him that he *does* revere God's holiness but that eating the offering would've been inappropriate today given how it's been so painful. And Moses relents. This is reminiscent of how Moses appeals to God about things and God leans into compassion instead of being strict. Maybe all this time Moses has been spending with God has rubbed off on him. Have you seen that happening in your own life since we started this trip through Scripture? Have you found yourself growing in patience and kindness and compassion? Do you have more joy in reading His Word than you did before we started Day 1? There's a good chance the answer is yes. Because you're here today, in the midst of Levitical law, delighting in Him. You know He's where the joy is!

LEVITICUS 11–13

Today we enter into a section of laws that pertain to cleanness and uncleanness. God gives instructions on what to eat and avoid. If you felt like this had echoes of Eden in it ("You can eat all this, but don't eat that"), you're spot-on. What God started in the garden is being re-created in the wilderness. There are various theories on why specific animals are forbidden: hygiene, deviation from the norm, affiliation with Canaanite culture. But we don't really know. Keeping these food laws is one part of what is referred to in Jewish culture as "keeping kosher." There are lots of other aspects of keeping kosher, but dietary law is one of the biggest ones. Some say the saddest part of today's reading is 11:7: no bacon. In fact, one of the ways modern archaeologists can tell when and where ancient Jews lived in Israel is that there are no pig bones in that layer of soil. Pigs were a wildly popular food among the Canaanites, so there are pig bones all over pagan country. But not where God's people lived.

They're also not allowed to eat anything that dies on its own; it has to be killed. This is probably because if it dies on its own, it might have a disease. By the way, the word *detestable* that we see repeated here only appears twice outside the book of Leviticus, and one of those times is in reference to idols. So there seems to be a correlation here with turning away from God.

In chapter 12 there are laws for women who have given birth and how they go about being clean afterward. A female child makes a woman unclean for twice as long as a male child does, and this is probably because she's giving birth to someone else who will bleed and give birth. One thing of note in this chapter is that God makes the sacrifice more affordable for the poor. And guess who were poor—Jesus's parents, Mary and Joseph. How do we know? Because in Luke 2:22–24, as they aim to keep this law after Jesus is born, they don't bring a lamb. They bring the bird offering of the poor—two turtledoves or two pigeons.

Leviticus 13 can be hard to stomach, but it's important. Moses is a shepherd, not a doctor, so he needs God to share all these nuanced specifics with him so he can care for the people well when they're sick. By the way, leprosy as we know it today likely didn't exist back then. The word *leprosy* in Scripture is used as a blanket term for a variety of skin conditions. When someone has any of these skin conditions, they're considered unclean, and they go live outside the camp until they're clean to avoid spreading it and to avoid defiling the holiness of God's tabernacle. This doesn't mean they're condemned or shamed or unloved. And all the while, God's mediator, the priest, is keeping an eye on them. In doing this, the priest is serving God by keeping things holy, he's serving the healthy people by protecting them, and he's serving the unclean people by keeping watch on them and making sure they follow God's rules.

TODAY'S GOD SHOT

God says all these laws are a part of what it means to obey Him. He says, "I am the LORD your God"—He starts with relationship—then He continues, "Consecrate yourselves therefore and be holy, for I am holy" (11:44). He repeats this almost verbatim in the following verse, and God's repetition should always catch our attention. One interesting aspect of the word *consecrate*, which means "to set apart for sacred use," is that it's like the verb form of the adjective *holy*. In Hebrew, consecrate is *qadash* and holy is *qadosh*. So God is basically repeating Himself within this one statement, even before He repeats it in the next verse. It's like He's saying, "Set yourselves apart for sacred use. Be set apart as I am set apart." God tells them to imitate His character. He has initiated this process by showing us who He is—we don't have to become something He hasn't first shown us and been to us. If being set apart means being set apart *with Him*, then let's get our consecration on, because He's where the joy is!

LEVITICUS 14–15

While these laws may seem very detailed and frustrating to read through, don't lose sight of the point of it all: God is perfect and holy, and we are not. And there are many ways we're not. Some are sinful, while others are just because we live in a broken world and sometimes houses in a broken world get mold. But even that mold serves as a reminder of the fall, and it has to be atoned for. It has to be covered.

There are lots of offerings. The leprous person brings an offering when they're healed, but people also bring an offering for their house when the house is purified. With any of the various discharges, there's an offering. Reproduction and all its affiliated fluids are not gross or sinful—God ordained them. But even the best parts of God's plans have a kind of brokenness attached to them now. We saw this in the curses God laid out for Adam and Eve. Man's work, which brings him joy, would have new levels of struggle attached to it. Women's childbearing and relationships with their husbands, which are often sources of joy for them as well, would have new challenges. These things we try to find our identities and joy in prove less than perfect, forcing us to look back to God, our Creator, for true acceptance and love and joy.

In 14:34, God is clear on the fact that He's in charge of putting leprosy where it shows up. Some people like to attribute all disease and struggle to the enemy, but God is sovereign over even the enemy's work. In the midst of all this heavy stuff, God gives Moses a reminder that they aren't going to be living in tents in the wilderness forever. God goes ahead and tells Moses how to handle it if and when there's leprosy in their actual houses in the land of Canaan someday, when they finally get there. God's giving a fun reminder that someday they'll be in Canaan and they'll have houses! Those houses might have mold, though, so even Canaan isn't perfect.

With all these sacrifices and offerings, let's look at three important aspects at the heart of it all. First, it's about giving something that costs you: animals, food, oil. Second, it's about the element of substitution.

Something else is covering the debt for your sins. When they perform these sacrifices, they're essentially saying that the things being done to this animal are what they actually deserve themselves. Third, it's about drawing near. The heart of sacrificial offerings is to be able to draw near to God. Remember that He has them do these sacrifices at the entrance of His temple, not out in the middle of nowhere, not in the wilderness or far away from His manifest presence. Sinners are called to draw near.

In 14:3–4, we see the leprous man getting healed and then going to be cleansed. Those who are healed must then be cleansed. This paints a picture of justification and sanctification. *Justification* is when God the Judge declares us righteous, even though we're sinners, because of what Christ did on our behalf. It's a judicial term, a legal standing. *Sanctification* is the process of God cleaning us up to look more like Him. It's a relational act in which He purifies us, and it's a lifelong process. Those who are healed are then cleansed, and those who are justified are then sanctified.

TODAY'S GOD SHOT

In 14:3–4 God says, "If the case of leprous disease is healed in the leprous person, the priest shall command them to take for him who is to be cleansed two live clean birds and cedarwood and scarlet yarn and hyssop." This phrase seems confusing: "The priest shall command them to take for him who is to be cleansed." Who is the priest commanding to do this, to get the necessary components for the sacrifice? This likely refers to the high priest commanding other priests to get what's required for the leprous man, because he can't get it for himself. Anything he touches will become unclean and unfit for sacrifice if he gets it for himself. God knows we can't clean ourselves up. We can't heal ourselves. So He provides everything we need for healing and cleansing and even arranges for it to be brought to us. Here in the midst of laws about skin disease, we see what a great, generous God we serve. Truly, He's where the joy is!

LEVITICUS 16–18

The Day of Atonement (also known as Yom Kippur) is the "day of covering for sins" and purging impurity, and the people are called to fast and rest. It's also the only day when the high priest enters the Most Holy Place. Why does Aaron get to go in on this particular day? He's presenting annual sacrifices that cover the sins of the priests and the people. Since even the tabernacle itself is impacted by their sin, the sacrifices have to take place at the very heart of the tabernacle. But God's presence and glory are at their highest levels of intensity there, so he has to create incense smoke to cloud his eyes from seeing God's glory or he'll die. He even has ceremonial garments for this one day.

The sins of the priests are atoned for first in the ceremony, then the sins of the people. For this part, there are two goats; one is appointed for the LORD, and one is appointed for Azazel. *Azazel* could mean one of two things—it could mean "the goat that goes away," or it could be a proper noun referring to a goat demon associated with the angels that fell in Genesis 6. We will continue to see the connections between fallen angels and demonic spirits. By designating this goat for Azazel, they're symbolically sending the sins out of Israel's camp and into pagan territory. When the people confess their sins aloud, they're symbolically transferred to the Azazel, and it escapes into the wilderness. At the risk of telling you something you already know, this is the scapegoat. This is a picture of Christ, who bore all our sins. He was our scapegoat. The other goat also symbolizes Christ, the one sacrificed to the LORD.

God issues a command about sacrifices specifically because they're sacrificing to other gods. He calls these gods demons. There's ongoing idolatry among the people despite YHWH's living in their midst. He has provided a way to atone for their sins, but they're not only ignoring it, they're *despising it* by relying on other gods and turning to pagan demon-gods. The pagans believe consuming blood makes you stronger because you're absorbing the life-force, but God makes it clear that the blood of animals has one function for them: to make atonement for their sins before Him.

Then God addresses sexual purity and cleanliness, but it's not just about hygiene; it's about righteous actions too. He takes this so seriously that He devotes a whole chapter to it. As per usual, He starts out with relationship, reminding them who He is to them, then He lets them know how to be pure when it comes to sex. Abiding by His rules is the way to truly live and find freedom and flourish. By the way, God doesn't necessarily describe ideal scenarios here—He just lays out the bare minimum for living ethically in society together. The first thing He does is put a restriction on incest. We're up to three million people at this point, so there are plenty of options for marriage that aren't your aunt—it's time to think outside the tent. He prohibits offering children to Molech, a Canaanite god of child sacrifice. He prohibits adultery, homosexuality, and bestiality, and He hints at bigamy as well. These actions ignore the order He established in creation, so they're an affront to Him as Creator. These are His people, and they should be marked by holiness and order in the midst of pagan perversion.

TODAY'S GOD SHOT

The Day of Atonement points us forward to Christ. Hebrews 9:11–14 summarizes it: "When Christ appeared as a high priest of the good things that have come, then through the greater and more perfect tent (not made with hands, that is, not of this creation), he entered once for all into the holy places, not by means of the blood of goats and calves but by means of his own blood, thus securing an eternal redemption. For if the blood of goats and bulls, and the sprinkling of defiled persons with the ashes of a heifer, sanctify for the purification of the flesh, how much more will the blood of Christ, who through the eternal Spirit offered himself without blemish to God, purify our conscience from dead works to serve the living God." Jesus paid the price to cover our sins, not just for a year but forever! He's where the joy is!

LEVITICUS 19–21

God continues describing how to build a stable society, explaining holiness and cleanliness, vertical laws and horizontal laws. Then He dives into application of horizontal laws and loving your neighbor as yourself, which really serves to reveal His heart: He provides for the poor via the surplus of the rich (this law is one of the ways God brings Ruth and Boaz together), He speaks against injuring and abusing people in the areas of their weakness, He says not to be ruled by selfish emotions but to be reasonable and to communicate openly. He emphasizes the importance of the heart behind our actions.

Then He addresses honoring Him in the vertical laws. This is a challenging section to parse; we can't throw it all out—we can't assume that since Jesus came and fulfilled the law, God is okay with making daughters into prostitutes or sacrificing children to Molech. Even back then this required discernment. For instance, could you make your son a prostitute? Could you sacrifice your children to a different false god? They had to get to the heart of the commands to see how to apply them. How do we discern how to still honor God in these laws today? There are three basic types of laws here: civil (society's behaviors and punishments), ceremonial (cleanliness, sacrifices, etc.), and moral (things God declares right or wrong, like in the Ten Commandments).

For ancient Israel, all three types of laws applied. They were in a unique situation—they were a religious group that functioned as a nation, so all their laws overlapped. There was no separation of church and state. But today God's people are from many nations, so the civil laws He set out for Israel as a nation no longer apply; some of the principles of the laws still apply, but the ways they're walked out vary widely. The ceremonial laws were fulfilled in Christ, so we no longer need them. There are no more sacrifices, because He was the final and complete sacrifice covering all our sins, past, present, and future. While

---

For more information on today's reading, see thebiblerecap.com/links.

the moral laws were also fulfilled in Christ, they reflect God's character, so they're not going anywhere—God's character is the same, no matter your nationality, and it never changes. Jesus not only emphasizes the moral laws but also digs deeper, pointing out that the heart behind our actions matters too, not just the action itself.

All that to say, since rules like not wearing blended garments or getting tattoos were about staying ceremonially clean and being set apart from the pagan nations, those laws no longer apply. Jesus fulfilled the ceremonial and civil requirements. If you don't know what kind of law you're dealing with or whether it still applies, look for God's motive and heart in it. Here's an example: "If a man commits adultery with the wife of his neighbor, both the adulterer and the adulteress shall surely be put to death" (20:10). What kind of law is this? On the surface, it's a civil law because it doles out a specific punishment to be enacted. However, we know from the moral law that God hates adultery. So we keep the heart of it, the moral aspect—to not commit adultery—because it's clear how much God hates it, but we lose the civil punishments, meaning we don't kill adulterers. The reason God commanded that in ancient Israel was likely to preserve them for the birth of the Messiah in the midst of a strong pagan culture.

Priests must be especially set apart, more than the people. Levites with birth defects can receive the bread but not offer it. This isn't meant to point out the priests' flaws but to point out God's perfection. There are even rules like this for the priests who don't have birth defects; they have to wear certain things, enter at certain times, and so forth. No priest gets a pass on honoring God's perfection and holiness.

TODAY'S GOD SHOT

In 21:15 God says, "I am the LORD who sanctifies him." He's the one who cleans us up. There's a great distance between His holiness and our uncleanness, but take heart—His Spirit sanctifies us! After reading all these laws, it's an encouraging reminder: He has done all He requires for your salvation, and He is at work in you for your sanctification. He's with you, and He's where the joy is!

LEVITICUS 22–23

Today God continues with His laws for His people, but what's underneath the laws is what's most important. One of the truths underneath much of what we read today is that God wants His people to be clean, and He keeps reminding them that He's the one who makes them clean. He gives repeated reminders of both His holiness and His rescue.

There's also His love for celebration and remembrance. He gives directions for seven feasts and explains their significance. First, God reminds them *again* about a weekly feast, the Sabbath, plus six annual feasts. Several of these feasts have a few different names. You probably recognize Passover, which is also called the Feast of Unleavened Bread. The Feast of Firstfruits is also called the Feast of Harvest, and the Feast of Booths is also called the Feast of Ingathering. The feast we read about most recently is the Day of Atonement. One unique thing about the Day of Atonement is that it's called a feast but they're actually fasting on this day. That's part of what it means when it says, "They afflicted themselves." This is the holiest and most solemn day of the year. Instead of eating, they offer their food to God. On all the other feast days, they're not allowed to do any regular work, but they're allowed to do the work of offering sacrifices and preparing meals. The Day of Atonement, however, calls for zero work. This is still a celebration of provision, but a very different kind of celebration and a very different kind of provision.

There are only two feasts in this section that we haven't seen before. The Feast of Weeks, which is also called Pentecost because it means "fiftieth," occurs on the fiftieth day after Passover. It's called the Feast of Weeks because fifty days is seven weeks and a day, so it's basically a week of weeks, seven weeks. At this feast, something unique happens. It's the only feast where leavened bread makes an appearance. There's some rich symbolism here throughout the feasts. The unleavened loaf

For more information on today's reading, see thebiblerecap.com/links.

represents the Israelites, and the leavened loaf foreshadows the day when the Gentiles, non-Jews, will be brought into God's family.

The Feast of Trumpets is also known as Rosh Hashanah, the Jewish New Year, but at this time it signals ten days' notice for the Day of Atonement. The Israelites refer to this time of repentance as the Days of Awe. This points us back to what we learned not long ago: The fear of God, which consists primarily of delight and awe, draws us nearer to Him and serves to produce righteousness in us. Their days of repentance and awe lead up to the Day of Atonement, when they're purified.

Some people find it troublesome that God only accepts the best sacrifice. It seems unloving, perhaps because we know deep down that we aren't a good sacrifice. We're blemished and blind and scabbed and crushed, and it feels like God will reject us. It's hard to face the reality that we aren't enough. But God's message doesn't stop there! Jesus bridged the gap between our imperfection and God's requirements.

TODAY'S GOD SHOT

All these requirements of perfection are supposed to be weighty. The law is intended to remind us how impossible all of this is. It shows us God's perfection and our great need. Romans 5:20 says, "The law came in to increase the trespass, but where sin increased, grace abounded all the more." For every one of your sins, grace abounds. For every one of your imperfections, grace abounds. Romans 5:21 continues, saying, "So that, as sin reigned in death, grace also might reign through righteousness leading to eternal life *through Jesus Christ our Lord*." We're tempted to fix our eyes on ourselves and aim for perfection, but when we do that, we miss the fact that He has provided the perfect sacrifice in our place! How beautiful is it that He still wants to be near us even though we're imperfect? Praise God for providing the perfect sacrifice: Jesus Christ our Lord. He's where the joy is!

LEVITICUS 24–25

God continues explaining how the people should live in society together, since this is not only the first time they've had a chance to be free people but also the first time they've really interacted with God. They've only known Him for about a year at this point, and they're still learning to trust Him. His instructions cover a lot of territory, including the maintenance of the tabernacle, caring for the poor, and Jubilee. He also tells Israel how to handle blasphemers. A man curses the name of God, and God orders him to be stoned. Since this illustration involved a half-Egyptian man, it likely served to show that the same rules apply to foreigners living among them. And the death sentence he explains here serves as a reminder that the Israelites are in a unique situation—they're a nation-state set apart as God's people. This man got what he deserved, since we all deserve death and separation from God. If we're alive, we're living on mercy.

The blasphemer's story is immediately followed by a verse that says, "Whoever takes a human life shall surely be put to death" (24:17). This is an illustration of how killing is different from murder. Otherwise, the person who put a murderer to death would be a murderer, and someone would have to murder him, and then the chain reaction would continue until all God's people were dead. God establishes killing and murder as two different things and puts the power to kill in the hands of the judges. At least that's whom most commentators believe these instructions are for, in part because they're followed by instructions that seem to be guidance for judicial rulings. For instance, a judge would order repayment for what was stolen; Scripture isn't saying the victim should go take it for himself. God outlines order and civility and sets up some deterrents to sinning against others.

Then He continues with a new kind of Sabbath command, a command to let the fields rest on the seventh year, just like the people themselves. Seven symbolizes completion and perfection, so we'll continue to see God reiterate that. Then He sets out the plan for Jubilee, which will happen on the year after seven "weeks of years." Based on what we talked about yesterday, you probably already know what this means. Seven weeks of years would mean seven times seven, which is forty-nine, so the year after that is the fiftieth year, the Year of Jubilee. This pattern mirrors exactly what we saw yesterday with the fifty days between the feasts of Passover and Pentecost. The people also don't work the land during this year, so it has two back-to-back years off, the Sabbath year and the Jubilee year. You really have to trust God for His provision to let the land rest for two years, because your food has to last until the third year's harvest comes in. Sabbath requires faith. But God promises He'll give an abundant harvest in the year before this break.

In the Year of Jubilee, debts are canceled and people who sold themselves into service to pay off debt are set free. He calls the people to be kind to those in need and to help others get on their feet. Jubilee is a reminder that they're *all* God's servants and that He provides for them all.

TODAY'S GOD SHOT

There's a lot of joy and freedom in today's chapters, particularly in the picture of God as the one who defends the poor, provides for the needy, and calls the rich to be helpers by sharing and redeeming others out of debt. He loves freedom, rest, provision, and the poor. He basically reminds them, "When I came to rescue you, you had nothing. I'm the one who gave you everything you have. So don't be stingy with it—that doesn't mirror My heart." When we recall God's generosity and unwavering provision, we can live openhandedly. The accumulation of things will never make us happy, and it can never provide safety for us. Only He can do that. He's where the joy is!

LEVITICUS 26–27

As God wraps up this covenant conversation with Moses on Mount Sinai during visit 2.0, He does something that's pretty standard for a covenant agreement: He sets out the expectations for blessings and curses based on whether the covenant is kept or broken. This is a standard arrangement for covenants, listing footnotes at the end. If Israel remains faithful to God's laws and keeps His Sabbath, He'll bless them in obvious ways with peace, abundance, and security. While they'll still have enemies, they'll have victory over them. But if they don't stay faithful to Him, five phases of curses will follow their rebellion. If at any point they repent, He won't execute the next phase. The phases increase in intensity as they progress, with the final phase being exile and scattering from the land He promised to give them. Other terrible things come along with this too: hearts full of fear and paranoia, defeat at the hands of foreign armies, and a lack of food so pronounced that it leads to cannibalism. God says He'll make their heavens like iron and their earth like bronze, meaning the sky won't rain and the ground will be too hard to plant food. In that setting most of them would die, never returning from exile. And as a result of their sins, their kids would be raised up in the lands of foreign enemies, just like they had been.

If they break the covenant, these curses are intended to wake them up and prompt repentance. *To repent* means "to turn away from our sins and *toward* God." God is working out discipline, not punishment. Discipline is the act of any loving Father whose child is walking in rebellion. If this weren't discipline—if He were casting off these people altogether—He wouldn't be outlining the chance for repentance and redemption.

In chapter 26, YHWH makes vows to the people, and in chapter 27 we see the people's vows to Him. Each person is supposed to either serve in the sanctuary or make a financial vow; Levites serve, and the other tribes pay the vow. This ensures that everyone has an investment in the work of the sanctuary. No one sits on the bench; everybody participates. The vow values are adjusted based on what that person would contribute with physical labor. This shows us God's detailed care for people and their life circumstances. He says, "The priest shall value him according to what the vower can afford" (27:8). Wealthier people can vow their animals or houses or land to God too. If they give land, though, it reverts to the owner in the Year of Jubilee. It's less like selling and more like a lease that ends in the Jubilee year. They aren't allowed to exchange land long-term; it always reverts back to the person, family, or tribe God originally intended. He decides who gets what land, and they can't amend His plan. They don't actually have this land yet, but He's telling them in advance how to plan for what He will do when they're out of the desert and in the land He has promised.

Today the word *tithe* shows up for perhaps the first time in Scripture, depending on which Bible translation you use, and the word literally means "one tenth." It's a donation of 10 percent of their income to the sanctuary, even if that income is in the form of food or animals. This tithe helps provide for the Levites, since they're doing the hard work of helping people draw near to God, and for sanctuary maintenance.

TODAY'S GOD SHOT

When God tells them how He'll respond if they break the covenant and then repent, that's not a standard part of ancient covenants. A broken covenant usually means an *ended* covenant, but God isn't letting go. He's providing an opportunity for them to turn back, showing them next-level mercy. Even when they rebel, if they humble themselves and repent, God forgives. He won't break His covenant with them; He'll keep it and be their God. He keeps leaving the light on for them. With God, it's impossible to be too far gone. Whatever means He may or may not use to prompt repentance and discipline, He's working for our good and for our joy, to draw us back to Himself. What a merciful God. He's where the joy is!

NUMBERS 1–2

In Hebrew, this book is called In the Wilderness. If you don't love actual numbers, just know that while this book does contain them, it also contains some of Scripture's most underrated stories. But rest assured, we'll learn something about God even on the days of numbers and names.

This is the fourth book in the Torah, also called the books of the Law, the books of Moses, or the Pentateuch. This book continues with the story of the family we've been following for 2,700 years, since Adam on Day 1. Adam eventually led to Noah, and then God wiped out the earth's population except for the eight people in Noah's family, and they started over with a clean slate. Through Noah's second son, Shem, we eventually got to Abraham, and God promised to make him the father of many nations through his second son, Isaac. That promise continued on through Isaac's second son, Jacob. Jacob had twelve sons, and ten of them sold one of them, Joseph, into slavery. But God loved those twelve brothers and promised to give them the land of Canaan where their enemies lived. This one brother's enslavement took a turn for the good, but it resulted in all his family and their descendants being in slavery in Egypt for four hundred years. Just thirteen months ago, God rescued them out of Egyptian slavery through the hand of Moses and his older brother, Aaron. Moses just spent forty (more) days on Mount Sinai, where God passed down laws for these twelve tribes of people who are descendants of those twelve brothers we met almost five centuries ago.

Today God and Moses meet up to talk again, and God tells Moses to take a census of all the men aged twenty and up from these twelve tribes. This is the kind of thing someone might do in preparation for war, counting their soldiers. Given what we know so far, whom do you think God might be preparing them to fight against? Judah's tribe is the largest of the twelve by far, twice the size of some of the other tribes. Remember back in Genesis 49:8–12 when Jacob-Israel was dying and he

---

For more information on today's reading, see thebiblerecap.com/links.

prophesied a blessing over each of his sons? What we learn today about the size and preeminence of the tribe of Judah aligns perfectly with what Jacob-Israel said about Judah on that day over four hundred years ago.

With Joseph, the numbers split into the lines of his sons Ephraim and Manasseh because Jacob-Israel adopted them and blessed them as his own heirs. So it seems there are now thirteen clans, which could throw everything off. But not to worry—God has a plan for it all, and we'll see that unfold in the days ahead. God tells Moses not to count the Levite tribe because their jobs and lives center around the tabernacle. They work there, live around its perimeter, care for and protect it, protect others from dying by coming in contact with its holiness, disassemble it, carry it through the desert every time they move, and reassemble it in the new location. Their tribe of the original twelve is set apart.

God gives orders on how to arrange the tribes in camps around the tabernacle. This is a brand-new structure, and it's supposed to be in their midst, in the very heart of the encampment. The inner rectangle is the Levites and the outer rectangle has three tribes on each side, dividing them into four groups. God also gives their marching orders—group by group, tribe by tribe—for when they move through the desert.

TODAY'S GOD SHOT

In the census, we see God is at work, building their trust in Him and His promises. Think of all they've been through since God first promised Abraham that He would increase his offspring. Finally, here they are, likely numbering into the millions. This is evidence of God fulfilling His promises. We've seen so much sin in their story line, but they can't manipulate their way out of His plan, fear their way out of His plan, murder their way out of His plan, or in any way escape God's good plan for their good and His glory. They're in it—*this is the plan*. It's mountaintops somedays and pits and prisons other days. But on every kind of day, He's where the joy is!

NUMBERS 3–4

Now that Moses has instructions about how to build a society and the people know how to set up camp, God focuses on the service of the newly built tabernacle in the wilderness. God establishes Aaron and his two living sons, Eleazar and Ithamar, as the heads of the tabernacle. The other people from their tribe, the Levites, are there to help serve them and help them serve.

To establish these roles with order, God calls for three different censuses. The first is directly related to something God has been working out for a while. Typically the firstborn of each family is consecrated and set apart for service to the Lord, but here God refers to the Levites as His firstborn among Israel: "I have taken the Levites from among the people of Israel instead of every firstborn who opens the womb among the people of Israel" (3:12). He's making a trade here: Levites in exchange for firstborns. Each of the male Levites serves as a representative of each of the firstborns from the other tribes. To make sure each firstborn of Israel is replaced by a male Levite, the firstborns have to be counted too, so Moses does census number two. The numbers are fairly close, but not exact—they're still 273 Levites short. So God sets up a process where those 273 Israelite families who aren't represented by a Levite can give the tabernacle five shekels instead. That way, even though the family can't benefit the tabernacle through the service of a son, they can benefit it through the donation of their money.

During that process, we meet three clans in the Levite tribe: Gershonites, Kohathites, and Merarites. These are the descendants of Levi's three sons. Each clan has a specific assignment in caring for the tabernacle. The Gershonites deal with the curtains and coverings and fabric-related elements. The Merarites handle the structural elements like poles and pillars and tent pegs. The Kohathites are in charge of guarding the holy vessels, such as the ark and lampstand. Whenever it's time to pack up

---

For more information on today's reading, see thebiblerecap.com/links.

camp and move on, Aaron and his sons pack up the holy vessels, then the Kohathites carry the elements to the new location. The Kohathites likely have this assignment since they're the guards of the holy vessels, and this is an especially important time to guard them, given that the vessels might be more vulnerable to enemies as they travel. The Kohathites arguably have the most important role of these three clans. Moses and Aaron belong to the clan of the Kohathites, the ones of the highest position (Exodus 6:16–25). And in keeping with a theme we've been noticing, Kohath was the second-born son of Levi, and Moses was the second-born son of his father. Aaron was the firstborn, and that's possibly one reason Moses and Aaron have ongoing tension through the years, most recently with the golden calf incident.

Census number three tallies men aged thirty to fifty who can carry items when the tabernacle is transported to a new spot. Heavier items will be carried on oxcarts, but some things will be carried on poles. You may have noticed that the Levites are significantly smaller in number than all the other tribes. In many cultures, minorities are disregarded, but here God gives them a position of incredible honor, putting them in closest proximity to Himself, appointing them to guard His tabernacle and serve as mediators between Him and His people.

TODAY'S GOD SHOT

So just as the largest tribe, Judah, has a position of honor, so does the smallest tribe, the Levites. In God's economy, both the greatest and the least are welcomed in and bestowed with honor and a place in which to serve His kingdom. Ministering to people is one way of serving, and doing the less glamorous heavy lifting is another. In order for the tabernacle to function well and for all the people of Israel to be blessed, both types of service are necessary. People who serve visibly often get more praise and attention, but they can't do what they do without someone behind the scenes. You may think all you do at your church is stack chairs, park cars, or serve in the nursery, but everyone who serves the church has a vital role, appointed by God for the service and upbuilding of His people. No one is invisible to God, so "serve the LORD with gladness" (Psalm 100:2). He's where the joy is!

NUMBERS 5–6

Yesterday God focused on the role of Levites in serving the tabernacle, and today He addresses the rest of the tribes, making sure they're living the set-apart lives of purity and holiness that He called them to when He made a covenant with them. In dealing with impurity, He starts with the most obvious kind: external impurity. He orders them to put the people with skin diseases outside the camp, along with anyone who has come into contact with a dead body. This doesn't mean they're no longer His people or that they're homeless. They just have to be quarantined so they don't defile the tabernacle.

Then He addresses internal impurity, including sins committed against God or others. He calls for confession, repentance, and legal restitution accordingly. Then we hit a challenging section. God's words on adultery or suspected adultery are ultimately a call for marital purity, and He tells them how to handle the *suspicion* of adultery. We already know that the penalty for adultery is death (Deuteronomy 22:22), but it's unlikely that someone would confess adultery outright since it gets the death penalty. So they need a way to handle suspected adultery in order to avoid killing people who are falsely accused.

God addresses a hypothetical scenario in which a man suspects his wife of infidelity. The woman is held to account instead of the man, and two potential reasons are that (1) her husband might have no idea who she cheated with, and (2) if she gets pregnant, it could potentially prove she's lying. In this very odd ceremony to test her for adultery, God volunteers to testify as a witness since there are no other witnesses. He's the only person who could pull off this kind of thing. He's omniscient, which means He knows everything, His presence is everywhere, and He sees everything, so He definitely was a witness to whatever did or didn't happen. Not only that, but He's the only one who has the power to pull off the corresponding consequences—He's the giver of life, so He controls the outcome of any potential pregnancy here.

The meanings of these curses are unclear. Some scholars think they mean pregnancy or the appearance of pregnancy because of the womb swelling. Others think they mean miscarriage or infertility because of the phrase "her thigh shall fall away." And in case there's any confusion, 5:31 isn't referring to the male adulterer being free from iniquity; it likely refers to the husband, since he's the most recent man mentioned in the text. We already know God holds *both* adulterers responsible (Deuteronomy 22:22). This process of addressing suspicion likely protects an innocent woman from the wrath of her husband and their community. And for the guilty woman, she bears the curse but still receives God's mercy, because she doesn't get the death penalty she deserves under the law. There's no equivalent test for a woman who suspects her husband of committing adultery. That's likely because in the ancient Near East women just accepted it. We've even seen at least three instances where a woman gives her husband to another woman. Men having multiple wives was so common that women might not have known to expect more from their husbands, despite God's high view of marriage.

Then we read about Nazirite vows. John the Baptist, Samson, and Samuel were all lifelong Nazirites, but the vow was usually taken for a prearranged period of time. Most of the rules for being a Nazirite overlap with the requirements for a priest but some actually *exceed* them. For example, priests aren't allowed to drink on the job, but Nazirites aren't allowed to drink at all. They can't even have grapes or grape seeds! The point of the vow is for them to be visibly and morally distinct in ways that show they're set apart for God's work.

TODAY'S GOD SHOT

We end today with God's blessing for the people. He *wants* to bless. He actually *commands* His servants to bless His people. May this bless you too: "The Lord bless you and keep you; the Lord make his face to shine upon you and be gracious to you; the Lord lift up his countenance upon you and give you peace" (6:24–26). And may He also give you deep, abiding, fear-dispelling, chaos-calming, circumstance-defying joy. Because He's where the joy is!

NUMBERS 7

We are about to wrap up two months of reading the Bible. So far you've spent an estimated twelve hours reading the Bible, and you're still with it even in the trenches of Numbers, so it seems like you're in this for the long haul. May God keep drawing you in to read His Word!

We opened up our longest and most repetitive chapter yet with some offerings for the Levites initiated by the heads of the other tribes. They gave the Gershonites and the Merarites oxcarts to use as their tabernacle luggage, but the Kohathites didn't get any oxcarts, because they have to carry things on their shoulders according to the text. This is a reference to the poles we've already read and talked about, which go over their shoulders. Pairs of men walk with the poles resting on their shoulders, and the items are carried on top of the poles. This allows them to transport holy items that can't be touched in a way that keeps them under their close watch and control. Understanding the way this works will help us better grasp something we'll encounter in the future.

After they give the oxcarts and the oxen, they set up a dedication ceremony and God establishes the offerings that will come from each tribe during that process. Each tribe is assigned one day out of the twelve days of ceremony when its leaders will bring their offerings to the tabernacle.

Starting with Judah on day one, they work their way around the encampment clockwise. Each of the tribes, regardless of size, brings the Levites the same contribution to show that each tribe fully supports them. The Levites can't do this on their own; they need help from the people. In God's economy, everyone benefits by everyone contributing. When everyone works together, giving from what God has abundantly provided for them, then God's tabernacle is taken care of and God's leaders are taken care of. Not only that, but the hearts of the contributors are blessed and conformed to the image of the generous God who blessed them. This process isn't just about practical provision and order; it's about spiritual engagement at a heart level.

In total, they give 12 silver plates with a total weight of over 1,500 shekels, 12 silver basins with a total weight of over 800 shekels, 12 golden dishes weighing 120 shekels, oil and flour and incense, 6 carts, and 264 animals. These offerings serve not only to bless the Levites but also to bless all the people. They also help connect the hearts of the tribes to the Levites and what they're doing, which ultimately connects the people back to God. Jesus says heart follows treasure (Matthew 6:21), so when all the tribes give these things to this one tribe that is serving them, it helps them engage with the reality of what the Levites are doing on their behalf. God is efficient. He uses the gift of one to bless the whole, and He also uses our giving as a two-way highway by which we receive blessings in return. By the way, that doesn't necessarily mean financial blessing or getting all your prayers answered with a yes—it means the real and lasting treasure of His nearness and the beauty of mirroring Him to the world around us.

TODAY'S GOD SHOT

At the end of this twelve-day dedication period, Moses goes into the tabernacle to hear the Lord speak to him. This is the culmination of the previous eighty-eight verses—they're all building up to this. All the animals and ceremony and silver basins . . . none of it would mean anything if this moment at the end weren't happening: A holy God is drawing near to speak to sinful humans. Whether you're able to give a golden bowl or nothing at all, may your heart be knit closer to the Lord through the time you're spending in His Word. May you see it even more clearly after these two months: He's where the joy is!

NUMBERS 8–10

Today God gives Moses orders to purify the Levites. Their position of leadership requires them to undergo an even more thorough cleansing process than the people undergo. God reiterates His plan for the Levites and their position as His firstborn among Israel, who is also His firstborn, so they're the firstborn of the firstborn. The people put their hands on them, which is usually what they do to an animal before sacrificing it. They're symbolically offering the Levites up as something they're giving back to God. This symbol is repeated, but in a different way, when the Levites are given as a wave offering. Whatever item is waved in a wave offering always belongs to God afterward.

We're a year past Egyptian slavery, which means it's time to celebrate the Passover. God gives instructions about it, requiring everyone to participate, but also requiring everyone to be clean in order to participate. A few guys aren't clean, so they're frustrated with God that they can't celebrate the anniversary of His rescue. They talk to Moses about it, Moses talks to God about it, and God says, "You can celebrate it—you just have to wait a month." There are big consequences, possibly death or excommunication, if you opt out of the celebration altogether, because you can imagine what that might reveal about your heart toward God. God even opens up this celebration to the outsiders living among them, including the Egyptians who fled with them. God is so welcoming and hospitable!

They celebrate the second Passover in the wilderness of Sinai, then they begin a new season in their lives as God's people: moving through the wilderness. They're on their way to Canaan, the promised land. By most estimates, it's roughly an eleven-day journey from Egypt to Canaan. So why have they already been out here for a year? Have you ever heard someone say, "The Israelites were lost in the wilderness"? They aren't lost at all. They're following God, guided by His pillar of fire and cloud. They camp where God camps, stay as long as God stays, and follow God wherever He leads them next. This is an act of submission and trust and probably even desperation. To not break free and escape to the hills when times get tough, you must know you're absolutely dependent on Him for everything.

As they prepare to leave, God sets up two trumpeters with a series of different ringtones to communicate specific things to the people. Some call the people to celebrate, and some are used as a cry for help to God. Once all this is in place, they set out. After nearly a year in the wilderness of Sinai, they pack up the brand-new, recently assembled and consecrated tabernacle and get in their marching formation designed by God. Even the order that the clans of Levites arrive in is designed with efficiency in mind.

TODAY'S GOD SHOT

God consecrates the Levites for Himself, which gives us a fraction of visibility into the mind of God. He says He consecrated the Levites on the day He struck down all the firstborn sons of Egypt. Do you know what the Levites had done to catch His attention so that He'd bestow this great honor on them? By the way, this was before the golden calf moment when they killed three thousand of the idolaters in their camp, so it wasn't that (according to Exodus 32:29, that was the day He *ordained* them, but not the day He consecrated them for ordination). When God struck down the firstborn sons of Egypt, the only thing the Levites or any of the Israelite slaves had done, as far as we know, was doubt God. They've done nothing to be set apart like this. This is just God's generous, merciful plan, and He's been working it out all along. He says *He* consecrated them—He made them holy for Himself. He took a bunch of doubters and turned them into people who live and serve in closest proximity to Him. Even doubters are invited to draw near and see that He's where the joy is!

NUMBERS 11–13

We opened today with grumbling, and it seems to be unwarranted, because God is angry and sends a fire around the edge of the camp. Then they start grumbling again about food. Their complaints aren't related to an unmet need; God has given them manna. This isn't desperation—this is entitlement. God provides for them, but they don't think it's sufficient. They long for Egypt, forgetting that whatever God calls you to endure *with Him* is better than any kind of abundance *without Him*. It's not like they had abundance in Egypt anyway! They're romanticizing the past, and God calls it a rejection of Him.

Moses is stressed out by their crying and takes his frustration out on God. But God isn't his problem—the people are his problem. God's solution involves a delegation of responsibility and a distribution of God's Spirit. When God the Spirit moves among them, they prophesy. At the very least, prophecy is truth telling. Moses says he wishes all God's people were prophets. It's better to be a truth teller than an entitled complainer. Up to this point, Moses has been the only one communicating the words of God to the people, but here, others are doing it too. This brief moment of prophecy helps establish trust, and now these leaders in the camp show evidence of being connected to God too. Moses is thrilled to share authority with these leaders, even though God maintains that He and Moses have a distinct relationship.

God says He'll send the meat the people want. In fact, He'll send so much they'll regret asking. He brings a wind that blows so much quail into the area that their dead bodies pile three feet high. Those who gather the least amounts of quail get more than one thousand two-liter bottles! He also strikes some people with a plague directly related to their mistrust of His heart. God is *just* in whom He strikes down; He knows hearts and sees everything. They give the place a name that translates to "graves of craving."

After this, Moses gets hit with family drama. Miriam and Aaron push back on his leadership and make prejudiced remarks against his

Ethiopian wife. Moses doesn't fight back. Maybe he trusts God to act, or maybe he's just too emotionally exhausted to deal with it. But God rebukes Miriam and Aaron. He strikes Miriam with leprosy—which probably means she's the one who stirred up the sibling rivalry—and Moses asks God to heal her. God does, but He puts her in time-out for a week, so she has to get clean outside the camp. But even these consequences doled out by God are a means of restoration, not just punishment. The entire camp is impacted by Miriam's sin of gossip and slander. They have to wait another week before they can set out again.

God tells Moses to send twelve spies—a leader from each tribe—to scout out the land He promised them. After forty days of spying out Canaan and seeing how amazing and fertile it is, only two of the leaders believe God's promise that they can take the land: Caleb from the tribe of Judah, the largest tribe, and Joshua from the tribe of Ephraim, possibly the smallest of the non-Levite tribes. The greatest and the least. The other ten leaders doubt God's word. This is a game changer. When leaders are afraid and don't trust God, followers won't either.

The doubting spies report seeing Nephilim in the land. But how can they show up again here if God wiped them all out during the flood? Here are three theories: (1) More fallen angels are up to the same tricks, (2) the legend of the Nephilim is carried down through generations and has become a term they use to refer to any particularly large people, and (3) since the ten spies who doubt are so afraid, they're likely exaggerating to scare the people out of taking the land. Their report of Nephilim is never confirmed by God, Joshua, or Caleb, so it's likely just fear talking.

TODAY'S GOD SHOT

It's beautiful to see the three distinct persons of our one unified God all represented in the camp in various ways: God the Father dwelling in the Most Holy Place, God the Spirit resting on Moses and the others He chose, and—likely but not certain—God the Son appearing as the pillar of cloud and fire. Even in the midst of His people's grumbling, God is with them. And He's where the joy is!

NUMBERS 14–15; PSALM 90

Today the people respond to the spies' report. Because ten of the leaders are fearful, the whole camp is thrown into chaos. They try to usurp God's authority by choosing a leader other than the one God appointed and by going where God isn't leading: back to Egypt. "Going back to Egypt" becomes a metaphor for doubting and turning away from God. If we don't bring our doubts *to* God, they will drive us *from* God. The Israelites' doubt turns to fear, which prompts rebellion. Moses and Aaron fall on their faces, and Joshua and Caleb tear their clothes in grief and try to rally the people to trust God. But their speech fails, and the people want to stone them.

Fortunately, during the riot, God shows up. But He does not have good news. He wants to kill everyone and start over with Moses. Moses pleads with God to protect His name in front of the Egyptians, even arguing on behalf of the people at his own expense. He stands on God's promises and character, quoting God back to God. God relents, but not without giving consequences for the people's disbelief. The ten spies who doubted Him and made everyone panic die of a plague. And all the men who would prefer to die in the wilderness? God says He'll give them what they asked for. In fact, they'll all stay in the desert for forty years, long enough that everyone over the age of twenty, except Caleb and Joshua and their descendants, will die. Their deaths will be the result of plagues and judgments that come because of their consistent rebellion. None of those whose hearts rebelled against God will see the promised land.

Then God warns them that enemies are nearby and says to pack up and head south. But the people don't like His consequences, so they say, "On second thought, we'll go take the land after all!" They ignore God's directions and head north. As expected, they lose the battle. Their hearts are revealed: They want God's gifts more than they want God Himself. They're attempting to claim God's promises without His power or His

---

For more information on today's reading, see thebiblerecap.com/links.

presence. They're willing to disobey Him to get what they want. Notice that while they didn't believe His promise to give them Canaan, they believed His promise to kill them in the wilderness. Why is it so much easier to trust His wrath than His grace?

When they set up camp in a new place, God fills them in on more laws. Some are for unintentional sins, which still require an offering. But the laws for intentional, defiant sins committed "with a high hand" require more severe punishment. All sins are equal in their ability to make us unrighteous, and for those who are God's children, all sins are equally *paid for in full* by Christ's death. But other than that, we've seen that some sins are far more offensive and wicked than others, and God even weighs motives.

God reminds them again of the importance of the Sabbath. It seems small, but those little steps away from trusting God add up. By letting things like the Sabbath slide, they end up making golden calves and believing fearful spies. The Sabbath reminds them who God is; it's an act of trust. If we don't remind ourselves who God is, we risk becoming people who die in the wilderness, being near Him but missing out on the joy and peace of honoring and trusting Him. To help remind them of Him and His ways, He has them wear blue tassels on their clothes. Jesus was a law-abiding Jew who perfectly kept these laws, which means He wore these blue tassels. When we read about people touching the hem or fringe of His garment in Matthew 9:20–22 and 14:36, this is what it refers to!

Moses writes a psalm in response to all this tragedy. As a result of the people's sin, he'll suffer too. He had no idea what he was getting into when God called him. He probably imagined a two-week trek, not forty years. So he entreats God's favor. "Make us glad for as many days as you have afflicted us, and for as many years as we have seen evil" (Psalm 90:15).

TODAY'S GOD SHOT

After the rebellion God could've come out swinging, but He opens with, "When you come into the land you are to inhabit, which I am giving you." Despite all their sin, He reminds them that He hasn't changed His mind. He keeps His promise. They're still His people. What mercy. What integrity. What forgiveness. Even in the desert for forty years, He's where the joy is!

NUMBERS 16–17

Korah was a Kohathite, a guard of the holy vessels. He and three Reubenites, his next-door neighbors in the camp, conspire against Moses and Aaron. Even as a Kohathite, Korah is dissatisfied with his calling—he wants more power and influence. He rallies 250 people in a military coup, perhaps hoping that by raising up another leader they can avoid the thirty-eight more years of consequence God handed down yesterday. Korah argues that, as God's chosen family, they've all been set apart, so they all should be able to do the things Moses and Aaron do. They are disrespecting God's appointment of leadership.

Moses accuses Korah of being entitled and ungrateful and then proposes a challenge to Korah's crew: "Okay, rebels, come offer your incense and see how it goes." Two rebels refuse his request, but not because they realize they've overstepped; instead, they're saying, "You're not the boss of me." They falsely accuse Moses of bringing them out of "a land flowing with milk and honey." Moses brought them out of slavery, whereas "the land flowing with milk and honey" is God's language for Canaan. Once again, they're romanticizing the past. Then they accuse Moses of appointing himself as ruler over them, as if it weren't evident God made that appointment. Moses is used to being accused and knows how to handle it. He doesn't throw his weight around and order them to be stoned for their rebellion. Instead, He takes it to God and lets God sort it out—he's humble. But God Himself has no reason to be humble; humility is a posture we adopt in response to God. God is ready to kill them, but once again, Moses pleads for their lives. Then he and the leaders *and God* head over to the tents of the two men who refused to show their faces, and Moses basically says, "We're about to see who God is. If you guys die by natural causes, then I was wrong and I'll admit it. But if God opens up a sinkhole and swallows you right now, then we'll all know you were wrong." Then *sinkhole*. They go down to Sheol, which is the Old Testament phrase for "the grave" or "the realm of the dead."

God consumes the 250 others who unlawfully offered incense, and then Aaron's oldest living son, Eleazer, gathers their bronze incense holders and beats them into a covering for the altar to serve as a reminder of God's holiness. Surely all is well now, right? Nope. They wake with brand-new rebellion in their hearts, accusing Moses of killing the people, as if he had the power to command sinkholes and fires apart from God. At this point God's ready to kill everyone again, but Moses has an idea to appease Him. He has Aaron take incense out and let its holy fragrance cover the people, in an act of making atonement for their sins. Some people were already dead, but this stopped death and the plague. This is the beginning of the fulfillment of God's word that He would kill them all before the next generation can enter Canaan. He's keeping His promise in response to their unbelief, idolatry, self-exaltation, and rebellion against the kingdom of light.

In case they still doubt, He sets up one more scenario to establish Aaron as the high priest. He orders the tribal leaders to write their names on their staffs, Moses puts them all in the Most Holy Place, where they stay overnight, and in the morning, the one with Aaron's name has sprouted an almond flower! Those don't bloom overnight. The people repent and acknowledge this as a miracle of God, marking Aaron as unique among the chiefs of all the tribes. God has Moses store Aaron's staff in the ark of the covenant as a reminder to future generations.

TODAY'S GOD SHOT

When Aaron takes the incense and stands between the living and the dead, appealing for God's mercy, it's risky for him. As the high priest he isn't supposed to be near dead bodies at all. He could be struck dead. But he risks his life to stop the plague and save people from death through this offering to God. This shows us a picture of Jesus, our great High Priest, who intervened, not just risking death, but facing it and *defeating it* on our behalf. His death makes us alive! He's where the joy is!

NUMBERS 18–20

Yesterday, God validated Aaron's role as high priest, and today He addresses Aaron directly. This is rare; He usually has Moses pass things along to Aaron, but there are a few times He speaks directly to Aaron. He talks about how the priests and the Levites are supposed to care for the tabernacle. The priests—Aaron and his two sons—will guard the tabernacle on the inside near the holy vessels, and the Levites will guard it on the outside. If a Levite passes into the part reserved for the priests, they'll both die. God says all this in an effort to spare them the wrath He has to pour out when they rebel. God also unpacks something He's hinted at before: The Levites will have no inheritance among the people of Israel—no land or cattle, nothing to bank their futures on apart from His promise to provide. The other twelve tribes bring a tithe of their income to the Levites, and the Levites give a tithe back to God, who directs it to the priest. This is God's plan to provide for everyone.

Chapter 19 gives us laws pertaining to death. This is timely, not just because of all the death that has happened in the camp recently, but also because roughly two million people will die in the camp over the next thirty-eight years. They need to know how to handle it. Those thirty-eight years pass between chapters 19 and 20, and a lot of sad things happen in this chapter as we prepare to finish out their time. First, Miriam dies. She was a prophetess and the most highly regarded woman among the tribes. After her death, the people come to another spot where there's no water, and they complain again. For most of these grumblers, it's likely their first time complaining. The older generation has mostly died off. Even though they've inherited their parents' grumbling and they long for an Egypt they barely knew, their complaint is real—there is no water. So God tells Moses and Aaron how to handle it: Go get the staff (likely Aaron's staff), take all the people to the rock, then while they're all watching, speak to the rock and tell it to release water. Easy peasy, right?

They gather the people by the rock, and Moses tells all the rebels to pay close attention. But then *he* becomes a rebel, because he strikes the rock, twice, instead of speaking to it. As a leader of the people, he lets his anger, frustration, and exhaustion take the wheel. He's 120 years old, and it seems like this younger generation is repeating the errors of their parents. Moses disregards God's words—either casually or blatantly. Maybe he even reasoned that this was what he did before and it worked. When they were in this situation in Exodus 17, God told him to strike the rock. But the instructions are different this time, and Moses hedges. God still gives them water, but Moses' disobedience and unbelief cost him dearly. God shows His goodness by being kind to sinners who rebel against Him, but there are consequences even for slight disobedience. As a result, Aaron and Moses are prohibited from entering Canaan too.

As they make their journey to Canaan, they pass through Edom, the land of Esau's descendants. The Edomites are the Israelites' closest relatives. Moses has messengers ask the king of Edom if they can pass through, but he says no. It's a reasonable response. With that many people passing through, even on a highway instead of through fields, they'd deplete a lot of the natural resources the Edomites need to live. So Israel has to take a longer way around. Then, when Aaron dies, he's succeeded as high priest by his son Eleazer.

TODAY'S GOD SHOT

God's character is so consistent. Over and over, we see how He makes His rules and His people disobey Him, and while they have to deal with the consequences of their sins, He's ultimately so merciful. From clothing Adam and Eve while banishing them from the garden, to letting Moses lead the people but banishing him from Canaan, God calls sinners into His family and then works with what He's got. His mercy is such a comfort when we know the wickedness of our hearts. But the bits of wisdom He's given us are enough for us to know He's where the joy is!

NUMBERS 21–22

The Israelites are closing in on the promised land, carefully routing around Edom, since the king denied them passage. Unfortunately, they run into another king who pounces on them and takes captives. Going on the defense, Israel asks God for help and promises to destroy the pagan Canaanite cities if God helps them win. And He does! Then they hit another food and water shortage. Instead of asking God to help, like they know He can, they complain about Moses and God. They don't complain *to* Moses—just about him. They take their problems to everyone except the people who can solve them. Even though they're not talking to God, He hears. He sends snakes to kill them, continuing with His plan to wipe out the older generation. When they confess and repent, Moses prays for them and God shows mercy.

God tells Moses to make a fiery serpent and put it on a pole, and if anyone is bitten, they can look at the serpent and live. This seems like God is ordering Moses to break the second commandment, doesn't it? How is crafting a serpent any different from crafting a calf? The distinction is that they aren't worshipping the serpent. It's a sign of God's provision and rescue, pointing back to Him. Eventually, we see that it does become an idol for the people; they begin to worship it and make offerings to it, and it has to be destroyed in 2 Kings 18:4. In the second commandment, the "creating an image" part doesn't seem to be the issue so much as the "bowing down to it." That commandment is about the *heart* toward the item—whether it takes their eyes off God.

Next, Israel needs to pass through the lands of the Amorites and of Bashan, but their kings refuse and attack. The Israelites fight back, and God gives them victory and a lot of land. Word of their victory spreads, and the Moabites get nervous. The Amorites recently beat them in a war, so if someone can beat the Amorites, that's terrifying. King Balak of Moab gets an idea: He'll hire a guy named Balaam to cast a spell on them. He fears their power, and his fear prompts control, and then when his efforts are thwarted, he leans into manipulation. Balak sends more people to Balaam. It's unclear if Balaam is a prophet, diviner, pagan, worshipper of YHWH, or some combo. He's not an Israelite, but he could be a believing foreigner, like some of the sojourners who live among the Israelites, because he refers to YHWH as "my God." Regardless, God says, "Nope, you're not cursing the Israelites, because I've blessed them." So Balaam turns them down.

When they come back again, God gives Balaam permission to go but reminds him to obey. Then God gets angry when he goes. Why? He just said he could go! Balaam's heart seems to be set on money more than obedience—and of course, only God would know for sure. It seems He's angry not because of his actions but because of his *motive*. Balaam sets out on his journey, then the Angel of the Lord shows up (likely Jesus), but He's only visible to Balaam's donkey. God has power over what we see; He can hide and reveal things at will. When God opens Balaam's eyes so he can see the Angel too, he falls down, repents, and offers to turn back if it's evil in God's eyes. God's anger seems to be about Balaam's heart, not his actions. If Balaam had continued on this trip with money as his motive, it's possible the offer of more money would've swayed him and led him to curse Israel instead of bless them like God commanded. This is all part of God's plan; He doesn't change the course of the journey—Balaam just needs rebuking along the way. He needs his heart to be aligned with God's mission.

TODAY'S GOD SHOT

The serpent on the pole points us to something greater. It's symbolic of the way both Eden's serpent and Christ's cross affect us. It summarizes the fall and redemption, foreshadowing future redemption through Christ. Jesus references this in John 3:14–15. "As Moses lifted up the serpent in the wilderness, so must the Son of Man be lifted up, that whoever believes in Him may have eternal life." That fiery serpent on a pole can only save people from physical death, offering temporary rescue, but Jesus saves us from spiritual death, giving eternal rescue. He's where the joy is!

NUMBERS 23–25

The Canaanites believe you can speak things into existence, so King Balak hires Balaam to curse the Israelites. But God gives Balaam a word to speak about Israel, and much to King Balak's dismay, it's a blessing. So the king says, "Let's take a look at them from a different angle. Maybe you'll see something worth cursing then." But the same thing happens; Balaam can only pronounce blessing. His words don't have the power to undo what God has done. Nothing is weightier than God's will. Not only does Balaam know that now, but through this experience he abandons his sorcery and learns to seek God's face instead. The Spirit of God is empowering his words now—not evil spirits. Unfortunately, it's only temporary.

King Balak still isn't satisfied so he says, "Let's try this again, but this time don't say anything good or bad." Again, Balaam speaks blessing, and in fact, his words are terrifying to Balak, because they paint him as a future victim. "He shall eat up the nations, his adversaries, and shall break their bones in pieces" (24:8). This third blessing closes with the words God spoke to Abraham seven hundred years earlier: "Blessed are those who bless you and cursed are those who curse you." This ultimately means God is pronouncing a curse on King Balak; the thing he aimed for turned back on him. Balak is furious but also helpless. He's bargained, manipulated, stalled, and threatened. For all his mountain climbing, altar building, and animal sacrificing, Balak can't budge God's plan. For all it costs in frustration and effort, striving still only results in the preordained will of God.

After getting stiffed for his work, Balaam gives a final oracle about Israel, highlighting some future military victories. Meanwhile, the people are up to idolatry, naturally. The men are led astray by the pagan women and worship their false gods, specifically Baal. We find out later that Balaam is behind all this, scheming and advising Balak to use these women to entice the Israelites into idolatry, probably in an effort to cause Israel to lose their blessing. Money is likely involved, because the enemy is tricky. He knows what Balaam wants, and he uses our desires against us. Even though Balaam is behind this, Israel is still responsible for yielding. God's response to their idolatry is to have the chiefs killed first. Then He orders the judges to kill the covenant breakers. They're about to enter the promised land, and God doesn't want them to bring this impurity in. One man, the son of a chief, brings the daughter of a Midianite chief—the enemy—into his tent in front of everyone. This definitely counts as "sinning with a high hand"—belligerent, arrogant, shameless sin.

As a result, God sends another plague. People are dying left and right. Phinehas, Aaron's grandson, probably remembers what his grandpa did when this happened before, how he intervened, bringing out incense and stopping the plague. So Phinehas takes a spear and stabs them both, and the plague stops. But not before twenty-four thousand people die as a result of the idolatry. God honors Phinehas for his righteous anger, for his high view of God's holiness. God commands Israel to strike down the Midianites. Israel can't be left alone for a minute, or their hearts turn to false gods. YHWH wants more for them.

TODAY'S GOD SHOT

When God talks about Israel through the words of Balaam, it sounds like He's wearing rose-colored glasses. He says things like, "He has not beheld misfortune in Jacob, nor has he seen trouble in Israel" (23:21). The word for *misfortune* is almost always translated as "iniquity, unrighteousness, or wickedness," and the word *trouble* has similar possible translations. So this verse could also read: "He has not beheld iniquity in Jacob, nor has he seen wickedness in Israel." God *has* seen these things in them. Remember all the times He wanted to kill them? So what is He talking about? This is what love sees. Even one thousand–plus years prior to Jesus's death, His future blood paid for their present sins. God can pronounce these things as true, because to Him, they already are! He's outside of time and sees their sins are paid for. Even in our sin, He sees our redemption. He's where the joy is!

NUMBERS 26–27

Yesterday closed with a plague, and today opened with God talking to Moses and Eleazer, the new high priest since the death of his father, Aaron. God tells them to take a census. Why do we need another census? It's been thirty-eight years since the last one, and there have been lots of deaths and births. They need updated numbers since they're about to enter the promised land, and the leaders also need to verify that there are no people remaining from the first census—other than Caleb and Joshua and their families. That's one of the prerequisites for entering the promised land; all the old generation has to die off first. At the end of the census, they confirm this.

God tells Moses and Eleazar how to divide the land He's giving them. He says to give larger plots of land to larger tribes and smaller plots of land to smaller tribes. He reiterates that the Levites will be given no inheritance of the land because God Himself is their inheritance.

In chapter 27 we see a unique situation. Zelophehad had no sons to give his inheritance to before he died, so his five daughters approach Moses and Eleazer for consideration. But before they approach them, they've had to argue their case to four other judges, as outlined in Exodus 18. Remember how Moses' father-in-law, Jethro, told him to appoint judges over the people to handle things and that only the biggest problems that the judges couldn't solve should be brought to Moses? That's how these five women get there. They make their case and ask for land. Moses takes this request to God, and God says they're right. He orders Moses to give them what would've belonged to their father. Not only that, but God makes this a new law. The request of these five women and their persistence show they truly believed God when He said He was giving the Israelites the land—and they don't want to be left out!

Then God pulls Moses aside and lets him know that he's about to die, just like God promised. God says Moses will get to see the promised land from the top of the mountain before his death. God will reveal the promise fulfilled, but Moses won't get to enter it. Don't feel too sorry for him, though—he won't be missing it where he's headed. Then, despite how horrible these people have been to Moses over the past forty years, he pleads with God to appoint a new leader for them so they won't be like sheep without a shepherd. God tells Moses to commission Joshua, his assistant, for this role. And in front of Eleazer, the high priest, Moses lays his hands on Joshua and establishes him as his successor.

TODAY'S GOD SHOT

God's response to the five daughters of Zelophehad shows us not only His great compassion and generosity, but also His reasonableness. How comforting that our God strikes the perfect balance between the emotional aspects of His nature and the practical, logical aspects of His nature. And it makes sense, because *of course* He's where the truth is, but also, He's where the joy is!

NUMBERS 28–30

Today God outlines laws, feasts, and the religious calendar they'll follow once they're in the land. They'll be spread out at that point, not gathered in one encampment, so He's getting the word out in advance. Other than the Day of Atonement, every day of the year is to be bookended with worship—a sacrifice at twilight and in the morning. In ancient Jewish culture, the day starts at sunset. We first saw this in the flow of Genesis 1, which says, "There was evening and there was morning, the first day. . . . There was evening and there was morning, the second day."

As we continue getting to know this family, this cultural distinction will be important. It's why their Sabbath rest begins at sunset on Friday and ends at sundown on Saturday. If you're ever in Jerusalem on a Friday, you'll see people rushing around trying to get things done before sunset. After the Sabbath begins, there's no traffic on the streets, stores and restaurants are closed, and the city rests. When the sun sets again, people dance and celebrate in the streets, stores open back up, music pours out of windows, and the city comes alive again. They still live out this ancient principle handed down by God. The reason we're covering this at length is because God brings it up again today. We can hardly get through a section of laws without Him saying, "Don't forget: Rest one day each week." The Sabbath isn't just a day for doing nothing—it's a day for reconnecting with Him. He commands *twice* the number of sacrifices on the Sabbath as on any other day. Sacrificing isn't considered regular work; it's regarded as worship.

All these sacrifices seem extravagant—they're killing their food and source of income in mass quantities. But by requiring sacrifices, God reinforces that He has a plan for provision. He provides all He requires. Even though we no longer offer sacrifices, we still need to be reminded that He's providing for us. There are two things in our lives that serve this purpose: giving to the church (which some call tithing) and Sabbath. There are 168 hours in each week. If you sleep seven to eight hours a night on average, that means you're awake for sixteen to seventeen hours each day. So by taking one of those sixteen-to-seventeen-hour days and setting it aside for rest, you're giving back 10 percent of your time. It's like tithing with our time, not just our money. By giving back a portion of both, we demonstrate our trust in the God who provides for us and sustains us.

Chapter 30 requires a bit of unpacking. Sometimes, when people were in dire straits, they made a vow to God. Such a vow often involved sacrificing something of financial value, and it was a vow *on their life*. A modern version might be something like, "God, if You'll just give me a child, I'll start going to church again." When a man made a vow like this to God, there were no outs. If you're a man, that may frustrate you, because a woman might have a "get out of jail free card"—a man in her life could let her off the hook, if he renounced her vow. Women may have felt disrespected when that happened, but ultimately it was a protective measure for them, releasing them from vows they might not have been able to keep, but made in moments of desperation. The heart behind this law is to help and protect, not restrict. The text doesn't say, "Women can't make vows, because God doesn't take women seriously." Women did make vows—important ones. This option also protected the man of her household, who might have suffered financially if she had fulfilled her vow. Even though these laws aren't in effect today, many of us still have people in our lives who serve these kinds of vow-cancelling roles, people who see our blind spots and ask us to reconsider, people who will catch us before we make foolish decisions.

TODAY'S GOD SHOT

Out of all the Ten Commandments, there are two He keeps repeating: You shall have no other gods before Me, and *rest*. What other god commands rest? Most of our idols demand more from us—more striving, more trying, more doing. He says, "Nope. Not My people. The people of false gods run themselves ragged. But My people are provided for even when they take a day off to spend with Me." He's where the rest is, and He's where the joy is!

NUMBERS 31–32

God gives Moses his final assignment: Kill the Midianites. They're the ones who led His people astray. Moses rallies twelve thousand men, and they kill all the Midianite men, including Balaam, who advised King Balak on how to tempt the Israelites using the wiles of the Midianite women. The warriors bring the women and children back to the encampment, which is what they typically do after winning a battle. But this isn't just any battle. This is a battle that's primary cause *is* these women. So Moses orders the death of all the women who aren't virgins—the women who prompted the idolatry and the loss of twenty-four thousand lives. It's possible some of the soldiers brought back the very women who led them astray. And even if they *aren't* the same women, this is still trouble waiting to happen. The husbands of these idol-worshipping women are all dead now, so the widows will likely seek out new husbands from among the Israelites, which would create the same problem all over again. By ordering them to be put to death, Moses safeguards against another possible outbreak of idolatry and plague.

The warriors purify themselves and their plunder, then God tells them how to divide it between warriors, civilians, priests, and His portion. They also took thirty-two thousand virgin women from the land. These virgins—likely young women or girls—will be absorbed into the Israelite community and will eventually be allowed to marry Israelites if they turn to God. The portion of these women who are the Lord's tribute likely serve in the sanctuary.

Afterward, the Israelites count their men and find that not a single one died in battle! Then, because they took a census, they need to make a ransom payment based on the lives God brought safely back from war, so they offer up gold from their plunder—roughly five hundred pounds of it.

Next we see some land distribution. The Jordan River runs north to south. God's allotment of land for the twelve tribes is a sliver west of

---

For more information on today's reading, see thebiblerecap.com/links.

the Jordan River, east of the Mediterranean Sea. It's long and narrow, roughly the size of New Jersey. The Israelites are currently on the east side of the Jordan River, not in the promised land. They're in the land they won in Numbers 21. It's fertile land, and two of the agricultural tribes, Reuben and Gad, love it. They want to stay, even though this isn't the land God promised them. They ask Moses about it, and he is *not having it*. He thinks either they don't believe God's promise to give them the land of Canaan or they're afraid to fight the Canaanites when they do get there. He's having flashbacks from when the ten spies doubted. But they promise to cross the Jordan River along with everyone and fight for Canaan if they can just come back to this land when it's all said and done. Moses agrees but warns them that if they break their promise, they won't get the land. His response implies they've made a vow to God.

Reuben and Gad settle there, and so does the half-tribe of Manasseh. This is the first time we see the term *half-tribe*. At some point, the people of Manasseh divided. Half-Manasseh will settle east of the Jordan, outside of the promised land, along with Reuben and Gad. They're called the Transjordan tribes, since they're across the Jordan. The promised land has always been about a specific plot of land, so this may or may not be a problem. Scholars have different views on it, which mostly boil down to these two: (1) This isn't the land that God allotted them, so it's not holy land, and (2) land won in a holy war also belongs to God, so it's equally honorable for them to live there.

TODAY'S GOD SHOT

God takes our fidelity to Him seriously. Moses commands that Israel's temptations be eradicated. John Owen said, "Be killing sin, or it will be killing you."* Do we treat our temptations the way Moses does, like they're a predator out to destroy us? Or do we try to tame them and keep them for ourselves like the soldiers did? God is so vigilant for our hearts, and He knows it's not easy to be strong. He wants temptations eradicated if they might lead us to forget our deepest joy is found in Him. May God's Spirit always help us remember He's where the joy is!

*John Owen, *The Mortification of Sin* (Fear, Scotland: Christian Focus Publications, 1996), 28.

NUMBERS 33–34

Today Moses recounts all the places where they've camped. If you've ever doubted that the Bible is for real, this list should help settle it for you. No author would make up these kinds of details in hopes of good book sales. And no one who is trying to sound impressive about his leadership skills would tell you every step of how an eleven-day journey took him forty years.

At the end of chapter 33, we get directions from God. He tells Moses to instruct the people about some important business they need to attend to when they cross the Jordan. They need to drive out the people who live there—all of them. And they need to tear down their altars and their idols. Because if they don't get rid of everything, some of it will come back to haunt them, and on top of that, God will punish them, a double whammy. This isn't necessarily a command to kill the enemy—just to drive them out. God knows how easily the hearts of His people are led astray when temptations come.

In chapter 34, God gives the boundaries of the promised land for the first time. Until now we've known it generically as Canaan or the promised land. There are a few places you may know of that are used as markers in this layout, but the text refers to them by names that are likely unfamiliar. Let's walk through them: *the Salt Sea* refers to the Dead Sea, because while a normal ocean is 3.5 percent salt, the Dead Sea is 33.7 percent salt. It's ten times as salty. That's why you float. The salt concentration is also the reason nothing can live in the Dead Sea, which is how it got its modern name. But interestingly, Ezekiel 47 and Zechariah 14 prophesy about a day when there will be freshwater in the Dead Sea and it'll be filled with fish. So float while you can!

The Great Sea is the Mediterranean Sea. And *the Sea of Chinnereth* is the Sea of Galilee, where Jesus spent most of His three years of ministry. Keep in mind that some of these boundaries are estimates or generalities.

For more information on today's reading, see thebiblerecap.com/links.

It's hard to tell where the lines fall sometimes. On top of that, the Israelites didn't occupy all the land they were promised, and they occupied some land they weren't promised, like where the Transjordan tribes settled in yesterday's reading. So nine and a half tribes settle in what was originally known as the promised land, and two and a half tribes settle in the bonus land.

TODAY'S GOD SHOT

YHWH is superior to all other gods. At the very beginning of all of Moses' recapping, Scripture says, "The people of Israel went out triumphantly in the sight of all the Egyptians, while the Egyptians were burying all their firstborn whom the LORD had struck down among them. On their gods also the LORD executed judgments" (33:3–4). God defeats His enemies, including other gods. YHWH never denies that there are other gods; He just indicates that He's superior to them—that's the core belief of monotheism. He's the King of kings and Lord of lords—and He's also the God of gods. In the Ten Commandments He says, "You shall have no other gods before me." He doesn't say, "You shall acknowledge that no other gods exist." Instead, He says no other gods should get our affection and attention. There are two angles to this. First, anything we worship can be a false god or idol to us. And second, there are other spirit beings, demonic enemy forces that head up other world religions. They are *demon* gods. We've seen the demon god Baal in our reading. We've seen the demon god Molech. These are the demon gods of other religions. They're not equal to God, and in no way are they a threat to Him. YHWH is the one true God, and He sends other gods running. He shows them their limitations. He shows them His wrath. And He shows us, His kids, His great, protective love. He's where the joy is!

NUMBERS 35–36

While the Levites don't get to inherit land, they still need a place to live and keep their things. God's plan for this is to have each tribe donate a bit of the perimeter of their land to the Levites—forty-eight villages in total. The land isn't used only to house the Levites; it's also used to set up six sites known as cities of refuge, places for accidental murderers to live. The Levites are in charge of running the cities of refuge to keep the land clean from murder. It's one of their roles in service to the people, so it's fitting that the tribes donated land for this cause.

God sets out standards for what constitutes being a murderer versus being a manslayer, and it involves weighing the killer's motives. That's a tough thing to do, since we can't see people's hearts like God can. So God establishes a few things that tend to reveal motives: Was this person known to hate the person he killed? Did he use a tool that would be certain to cause death? If so, then the "avenger of blood" is supposed to avenge the murder, provided there were two witnesses to the murder. The role of avenger of blood goes to the closest male relative—it's his job to put the murderer to death. One problem that might arise is the closest male relative might want to seek revenge even if the death was accidental. That's where cities of refuge come in. Those who accidentally kill someone can go live in a city of refuge, where they'll be safe from the avenger of blood. But if they leave the city of refuge, all bets are off—the avenger can kill them. These cities aren't like prisons; they're more like the witness protection program. The killers have to stay there until the high priest dies. The premise behind this law is that only death can atone for sin and death, even accidental sin or death, and since the manslayer won't be put to death, the high priest's death is viewed as atonement for the wrongful death that happened on his watch.

As they continue planning their land divisions, some of the people of Manasseh's tribe realize that the five daughters of Zelophehad, who are a part of their tribe, might lose their tribe's inheritance if they happen to marry people outside of their tribe, because then their husbands' tribes would get ownership of the land. That would defeat the purpose of the new rule established back in Numbers 27. Ownership of land is a big deal because it's handed down by God, so they need a way to maintain the property according to God's commands. Moses talks to God about it, then fills the people in on the verdict: The people who were concerned about this are right and there does need to be a plan in place for this. The daughters of Zelophehad should marry within their own tribe, then everything will stay in place as God planned. And good news—they all married within the tribe. The book ends on a happy note: Everyone will be provided for in God's plan for His people.

TODAY'S GOD SHOT

In some scenarios God gives instructions beforehand, like with the cities of refuge. In other scenarios, they have to approach God with special cases, like with the daughters of Zelophehad. Some rules are established at the onset, and some are established as they progress. In these instances we see how accessible God is when we need direction and help. He doesn't say, "Figure it out on your own. I gave you a brain!" or "I'm too busy!" or "I've already told you all the important things. I don't care what you do with these little situations." He enters into the details, the seemingly small things. Out of three million people, He pays attention to these five women. He writes a new law addressing their situation. He cares.

That's one of the ways He keeps us near. With each new need, He embeds us a little deeper into this relationship, reminding us that our ultimate, constant need is for Him, His wisdom, and His guidance. We should rejoice that He keeps us coming to Him for direction, because He's where the joy is!

DEUTERONOMY 1–2

Of all the Old Testament books quoted in the New Testament, Deuteronomy ranks third, and it's one of the most quoted by Jesus. *Deuteronomy* means "second law." We'll revisit some old laws as well as see their practical applications. In many ways, Deuteronomy serves to recap everything we've read so far—it skims the surface of things that'll be familiar. This refresher is perfectly timed for us, because after Deuteronomy we'll move into some narrative portions with lots of new characters. When we read something familiar, try to lean into these two challenges: First, resist the potential frustration that might come from it. Be grateful you're recalling things you've already read! Second, even in the familiar stories, try to learn something new. Ask Him to give you wisdom to see something you've never noticed before.

These thirty-four chapters are a kind of motivational sermon by Moses before his death. They're his final words to the people he's spent forty years serving. He's loved them, sacrificed for them, fought for them, rebuked them—and soon he won't be there to guide them anymore. While he trusts God to fulfill His promises to them, he also knows the Israelites well and seems nervous that they'll go astray. When the Sinai covenant between God and the Israelites was set in place, it was established with the parents of the people in the wilderness today. Their parents didn't do a great job of keeping the covenant, so Moses sets up a covenant renewal. He wants to remind them that God promised them this land and that this covenant requires things of them as well.

Today he goes over highlights of their time in the desert since leaving Egypt—all God has done for them and all the things that've gone wrong because of their sins. He recounts the time they *almost* entered the promised land thirty-eight years earlier, but the spies were afraid and their fear was contagious. Fear magnifies the enemy and diminishes our perception of God. They grumbled against God, thinking He hated them. This is

---

For more information on today's reading, see thebiblerecap.com/links.

one example of what it means to take God's name in vain—His name is inextricably linked to His character, and when we disbelieve His character, we take His name in vain. God promised to spend thirty-eight years killing off their unbelief, then they tried to avoid those consequences by taking the land without God's blessing and command. This is a timely reminder for them as they're about to encounter land He is not giving them. God says if they act entitled just because they're His kids and try to take the land He allotted for Esau and Lot, things will *not* go well. He doesn't bless all our actions simply because we're His kids and we have a dream in our hearts. His plan still prevails, and we find our greatest joy in following Him, instead of our own plans.

Moses encourages them about upcoming battles. They're most afraid of the giants in the land, some of whom have already been driven out by Esau's people. The giants go by a lot of names—Emim, Rephaim, Anakim, Zamzummim—all of whom appear to be related to the Nephilim (Genesis 6). *Rephaim* is the Hebrew word used in Isaiah 26:14 to refer to the spirits of the dead, so it seems like there are some supernatural, evil things happening with these giants, which is likely another reason the Israelites are terrified of them. If these giants *are* related to fallen angels somehow, then of course the enemy would want to occupy the land God promised to His people, and of course he'd try to thwart and counterfeit God's plan.

TODAY'S GOD SHOT

God is generous, even to those who aren't His kids! He blessed Esau even though the blessing came through his brother, Jacob. He blessed Lot even though he wasn't a descendant of Abraham. God doles out promises and blessings as He wills, and they aren't limited to His kids. As His adopted children, we can still rejoice when He blesses others—it displays His abundant generosity and common grace. *Common grace* is when God's goodness is displayed to all of humanity, not just His children. Maybe He's enticing them in! And for those of us adopted into His family, we find our greatest comfort in having an eternal relationship with Him. Temporary blessings like land and possessions might bring some level of happiness, but we know *He's where the joy is*!

DEUTERONOMY 3–4

Moses continues recounting the history of the Israelites to the younger generation, making sure they remember where they came from. Yesterday he covered things their parents endured, but today he's touching on things they've lived through personally. He begins by recounting their victories over King Og of Bashan and King Sihon of the Amorites. The cities of Bashan were "fortified with high walls, gates, and bars," but God granted them victory. God is bigger than what keeps us from what He has called us to. We also learn that King Og was a Rephaite—a giant, perhaps of demonic origin—and Israel defeated him. He had a bed that was thirteen and a half feet long and six feet wide, and it was made of iron because apparently, that was the only thing strong enough to hold him. If he was as tall as his bed was long, he would dwarf Shaquille O'Neal. He'd be almost twice his height! After Israel defeated Kings Og and Sihon, they acquired the Transjordan land that God gave to the two and a half tribes: Reuben, Gad, and the half-tribe of Manasseh.

Remember how Moses repeatedly appealed to God to retract punishment for the Israelites, and God did? Moses also appeals to God to retract the punishment for striking the rock twice when God told him to speak to it. We don't know why God doesn't, but it could be because He holds leaders to a higher standard. We've also seen Moses reframing this incident in a way that paints him as innocent and passes the blame off on the people. We saw it yesterday in Deuteronomy 1:37, and we see it again today in 3:26 and 4:21 when he says, "The Lord was angry with me because of you [and would not listen to me]." So that could be why God doesn't relent. He tells Moses to appoint, encourage, and strengthen Joshua for the task ahead of him, because Joshua will be the one who takes the people into the promised land. This was probably an emotionally trying task for Moses. Appointing Joshua is a pretty straightforward job, but encouraging and strengthening him has some emotion involved in it. Moses has to set aside his own desires yet again—it's one of his final roles as a leader.

Then Moses turns from focusing on their past to focusing on their future. He calls them to obey God's laws and be set apart in the midst of wicked nations so that their distinctness points to God. He calls them to practice remembering what God has done, and in 4:9 he says, "Keep your soul diligently." He also points out that their habitation of the land is contingent on worshipping YHWH alone. He warns them over and over not to create idols—repeating it at length and giving lots of examples of what forms idols might take in their lives: men, women, animals, fish, sun, moon, stars. He follows it with a warning about what will happen if they *do* fall into idolatry: They'll die or be scattered out of the land, into exile, where they'll worship the gods they sought out, who will be impotent to help them. But even if this worst-case scenario happens—even if they sin by way of idolatry and are driven into exile—God won't reject them as His people. In fact, He promises to turn their hearts back to Him!

Deuteronomy 4:32–40 gives a pep rally–like call to remember all God has done and praise Him for it. Then Moses establishes three cities of refuge in the Transjordan areas of land that are already set aside for Reuben, Gad, and the half-tribe of Manasseh.

TODAY'S GOD SHOT

God is so patient with our tiny faith, growing it to be stronger over time as we see His character proven over and over. As He tells the Israelites about the giants and the battles they'll face, He reminds them that He's already given them victory in other battles and over at least one giant so far. He doesn't force them to go from zero to one hundred without getting to know Him first; He gives them training wheels. He's patient with us while we learn His character. And as we learn it, we find out more and more that trusting Him is where the joy is, because *He's* where the joy is!

DEUTERONOMY 5–7

Today Moses says God's covenant is not with their fathers—it's with them. Of course it's with their fathers too, but he's emphasizing that they have their own relationship with God; it's not lesser or secondhand. While God technically didn't rescue these people out of Egyptian slavery, still He did—because if He hadn't rescued their parents, they'd be in slavery too.

In chapter 6, we see the beginning of a prayer called *the Shema*, which means "hear." Religious Jews pray this prayer twice a day, morning and evening, and often cover their eyes with their right hand to increase their focus. You may recognize part of this prayer from where Jesus quotes it. Jesus also says, "Love the LORD your God with all your *mind*." Ancient Hebrew conflates the words for heart and mind, so the meaning is included here. But in Aramaic, which Jesus speaks, the words for heart and mind are different, so He adds that to the quote to fill out the original meaning.

The Shema says God's words should fill our hearts, mouths, minds, and lives. When we're sitting, walking, lying down, or waking, we should be mindful of God. His Word should be on our hands and eyes. Some religious Jews do this literally via phylacteries, but if you're taking it figuratively, it could mean God's Word should be the framework for how you see the world and live. The Shema also says God's words should be on our homes and on our gates. Some religious Jews put Scripture on their doorposts in a small scroll box called a mezuzah, but you might figuratively keep the spirit of this law by having reminders of God in your home, by building your home around God and His Word. Remembering is vital. Because of the covenant Israel has with God, their nation-state has consequences if they fail to keep it. YHWH wants their allegiance in action *and* in thought; this is the primary theme of Deuteronomy. Today and tomorrow, Moses warns against three specific thoughts. In 7:17–18, he warns them not to be afraid of God's plan or think of it as impossible. Each time he warns them against a specific thought, he reminds them that the way to avoid letting that thought take over is to remember who God is and to recall what He's done for them.

He anticipates a day when they'll have kids of their own who ask, "Why do we have to do all these things?" It's like he's preparing them to answer: "God rescued us out of slavery and provided for us in miraculous ways, and that God who loves us commanded these things, and they're *for our good always*." They must completely drive out all their enemies and not intermarry with them or pity them. If some or all of the people they'll be dealing with *do* happen to be the crossbreed between humans and fallen angels, you can see all the more why this would be important. But even if they aren't, this is still God's way of accomplishing many aspects of His plan. He's punishing the wicked nations for their rebellion and using Israel as a tool to accomplish that justice, He's ensuring the line of the Messiah stays intact, and He's protecting the hearts of His people from lesser gods. Moses says to destroy all signs of idolatry in the land, because things won't go well if they don't. God's plan is to drive out the enemy little by little. When they grow impatient, He wants them to remember that He has a process in mind. He's in this for the long haul.

Moses basically says, "God chose us before we were even a people. He *invented* the Israelites. He didn't choose us because we were a massive, powerful nation and would make Him look awesome if He picked us for His team. There were zero of us and we had zero to offer Him, but He set His love on us and grew us into the nation we are today."

TODAY'S GOD SHOT

God gives them cities they didn't build, houses they didn't fill, cisterns they didn't dig, and vineyards they didn't plant. He's incredibly generous, but He also wants them to remember who gave this to them! He doesn't want their hearts to turn away to other gods when they get these blessings from Him, when they're no longer living in tents in the desert with a fire-cloud to guide them. He wants to remind them of the *relationship* He's in with them. He's after our hearts, He's after our joy, and He's where the joy is!

DEUTERONOMY 8–10

Today Moses continues his speech to the new generation of Israelites before they enter the promised land. The wilderness was a test to refine them, and the promised land will be a test too. It's not a place where they can kick back and do whatever they want—they won't retain the land unless they respond to God's covenant promise by worshipping Him alone. The land is a step in God's process to restore fallen humanity in relationship with Him. He knows how this step will turn out—He's not testing them for His sake, He's testing them for their sake. This generation had to endure the wilderness as a result of their parents' sins, but they haven't encountered their own consequences yet. For them, the thirty-eight years were discipline and training, learning how to endure hardship and trust God. The distinction between punishment and discipline is important. We'll be disciplined by Him, but we'll never see His wrath or punishment. *Never.* Jesus absorbed it all on the cross! We deserve punishment, but Christ took what we deserve and gave us what we could never earn: eternal love and adoption into God's family forever.

Yesterday Moses warned against one kind of wrong thinking, and he warns against two more today. First, he says, "Beware lest you say in your heart, 'My power and the might of my hands have gotten me this wealth'" (8:17). This is a warning against pride in their own efforts. In his third warning he says, "Do not say in your heart, after the LORD your God has thrust them out before you, 'It is because of my righteousness that the LORD has brought me in to possess this land'" (9:4). This warning is also against pride, specifically in their own righteousness. Yesterday he warned against fear and today he warns twice against pride. Pride makes us forget God just as much as fear does. In a society that builds us up and tells us we deserve whatever we want, we'd do well to heed these warnings. Both kinds of wrong thinking, fear and pride, are rooted in forgetting God and fixing our eyes on ourselves or our enemies. We fight these lies by remembering who God is and what He has done.

God doesn't give them land because they're righteous, but because the other nations are unrighteous. We can't earn His blessings; they're a gift—freely given to the undeserving. This is both humbling and comforting. We can stop striving for His approval, because it's been granted to us in Christ! God blesses us because of His goodness, not ours. In fact, right after Moses warns them against thinking it's because of their goodness, he gives them a lengthy reminder of exactly how not good they really are by going over five stories of their rebellion in the wilderness. God doesn't just want their obedience, though; He wants their affection and relationship. Moses reminds them that God's rules aren't about diminishing their joy and freedom but about *increasing* it. Moses uses a peculiar turn of phrase when describing how all this plays out. In 10:16 he says, "Circumcise your heart." Circumcision serves as a physical sign of the covenant between them, but the word *heart* indicates a full transformation and commitment—spiritual, emotional, and mental.

One way they can show the love they've received from God is by caring for those who have no physical land or inheritance. Their unique nation-state community is to care for the vulnerable. God made this same kind of provision for the Levites, who also have no land inheritance. He's attentive and thoughtful toward everyone.

TODAY'S GOD SHOT

"Behold, to the LORD your God belong heaven and the heaven of heavens, the earth with all that is in it. Yet the LORD set his heart in love on your fathers and chose their offspring after them, you above all peoples" (10:14–15). God owns everything, yet He set His heart on us. Not only is it *not* because of any good works or righteousness, but it's despite the fact that we lack those things. That kind of love is magnetic! If we remember who we are and who He is, we can't help but be drawn to Him. He's where the joy is!

DEUTERONOMY 11–13

Today God opens with a command to love Him. Love indicates emotion; it's action adjacent but emotion specific. How do you command a feeling? It's impossible to fully love something or someone we don't know, and we can only know what we pay attention to. Moses also tells them to pay attention to their hearts, because they'll be enticed into idolatry if they're not vigilant. If they stay faithful to God, no nation will overtake them; God has already proven He can defeat bigger armies. Then Moses sets up an interesting image; he says to choose between blessing and cursing, represented by two mountains—Mount Gerizim (blessing) and Mount Ebal (cursing). They'll perform the ceremony for this later, so put a pin in it for now.

God says to remember His Word when they sit, walk, lie down, and stand—those things happen *several* times a day. He reminds them to destroy pagan worship paraphernalia, including Asherim, which are wooden poles featuring Ashera idols. Ashera is a fertility goddess of the Canaanites—they worship fertility, and based on what we've seen from the Israelites, they seem to as well, so this goddess presents a real temptation for them. God says to destroy the Asherim and "high places," which are pagan worship sites usually found on hills or mountaintops or under distinct trees.

There'll be a major shift in how some laws and sacrifices work once they get into the promised land. First, there'll be one specific spot where God will make His dwelling place. It'll be in the middle of the whole land, which is roughly the size of New Jersey. While Levites will be appointed to live among each tribe, God's tabernacle is the only place where they can offer burnt offerings. All the Israelites will travel to that one spot, even if their land allotment is far away; when they go, they'll worship God and make their sacrifices there. Also, when they enter Canaan, they can eat meat anytime they want, and even unclean people can eat meat. This implies that up until this point, the only meat anyone could eat was meat offered to God. And since having that offering come into contact with an unclean person would make it unclean, then unclean people had to be vegetarians by default. With this new situation unfolding in which they have to travel long distances to make sacrifices, God is basically saying, "You can eat meat in your own land anytime you want. It doesn't have to be sacrificed to Me first."

Moses warns them not to add to or subtract from God's commands. He warns about people who will mingle truth with lies as a means of enticing them little by little, giving the example of a false prophet or a diviner who provides some correct insights and then uses that wow factor to lure people away from YHWH. Just because someone speaks truth, that doesn't make them a prophet of YHWH. Even a false prophet can be right, but that doesn't mean we should follow them or seek truth from them. False prophets and diviners get the death penalty—not only because that's what the covenant requires for those who break the first commandment, but also as a means of protecting their covenant community from further spread of the lies. God also demands they be allegiant to Him over strangers and even over friends and family members who try to lure them into apostasy. These are intense preventive measures, but these laws are supposed to deter people from rebelling or enticing others into rebellion, and they're a necessary step in God's plan to restore humanity in relationship with Him. This is meant to protect *everyone*.

TODAY'S GOD SHOT

Three times today (12:7, 12, 18), God says something like, "You shall bring your burnt offerings and sacrifices . . . and there you shall rejoice." When people make sacrifices to false gods, it's to appease them or entice them to give them what they want. It's an attempt at initiating some kind of response. But with YHWH, our offerings are a response to His initiation. It's not about appeasing Him; it's about rejoicing in His provision and relationship. What a contrast to every other god! All those pagan worshippers are missing out on the rejoicing, because they're missing YHWH, and *He's* where the joy is!

DEUTERONOMY 14–16

Moses is still giving his final speech to the Israelites before he dies and they enter the promised land. He starts with some peculiar commands about haircuts. One way pagans grieve is by shaving their heads, so Moses outlaws that since it's pagan adjacent. God gave this law to the priests in Leviticus 21:5, but here Moses gives it to all Israelites; they're supposed to look different from and live differently from their neighbors. Pagans also cut themselves as a part of their ritual mourning practices, so Moses forbids that too.

He covers dietary laws, many of which we've seen before. One that carries a lot of weight in keeping kosher is the command not to boil a goat in its mother's milk. When rabbis debate how to apply these laws, they often extend the boundaries of what is unacceptable to make sure they don't come close to breaking the actual law. They call it "building a fence around the law." This law's "fence" forbids mixing milk and meat, so these two things aren't served at the same meal for kosher-keeping Jews. Kosher households won't even use the same plates for meat and dairy, and if you're a wealthy kosher family, you have two separate kitchens. While the heart behind this can be good, we'll see how people begin to treat these man-made fences like they're actually part of God's law.

God sets out commands about how to feel and think, not just how to act. In 15:9–10 He says, "Take care lest there be an unworthy thought in your heart" and "Your heart shall not be grudging when you give to him." He has always been after our hearts, not just our obedience. Laws for the sabbatical year display God's heart for the poor. Debts are forgiven and servants are released from their contracts. God says if they're faithful to His commands, there'll always be enough to go around; the poor will be cared for by the surplus of the wealthy. He'll bless them so much that other nations will borrow from them and they'll never have to borrow. This will keep them free from financial attachments to pagan nations that might result in enslavement.

Even though the word *slave* is used in Scripture, this arrangement for debtors is different from the Atlantic slave trade, for instance. Remember how Jacob agreed to serve his father-in-law, Laban, for seven years in exchange for a wife? That's the kind of arrangement we see in Scripture, working to pay off debt. Jacob worked off the bride price, and then voluntarily stayed with Laban after his debt was paid, and then he asked Laban to bless him with some animals when he left. This gives us a good picture of what slave relationships were like. If a slave likes his boss, he can stay with him forever and be absorbed into the family; they mark this decision by piercing his ear. In the arrangement for the Sabbath year release of these servants, God commands that they not only be released but also blessed and provided for.

Moses covers some of the festal calendars again. He reiterates a lot of these laws now, because the way they do things will shift once they're spread out in the promised land. There the festivals will require them to travel to the centrally located tabernacle. God calls them to remember where they came from and what He has done for them; it'll keep them humble and grateful.

TODAY'S GOD SHOT

The exodus is to Jews what the resurrection is to Christians—it's the most important thing in their history. They look back at the exodus to remember who they are, just as we look back at the resurrection to remind us who we are. But we also get to look *forward* to the return of the resurrected Christ. We live in the time period theologians call "the already but not yet"—the time between the first coming and the final coming of the Messiah. The best way for us to stay humble and worshipful is to remember these things too. It also helps us stay joyful. When Moses talks about the Feast of Booths, he says, "You shall *rejoice* in your feast" and "The LORD your God will bless you in all your produce and in all the work of your hands so that you will be *altogether joyful*." God is after our joy! In Psalm 16:11 David says, "In your presence there is fullness of joy." And David is right. He's where the joy is!

DEUTERONOMY 17–20

Moses has been giving laws for how things will shift once they're no longer camping in the desert. Today he gives laws about worship. They're entering foreign territory where pagan gods are revered. If anyone worships other gods, there'll be a trial involving at least two witnesses before the death penalty is given. And the witnesses will carry out justice. If they're lying, then they'll be guilty of murder. And because these situations can be complex and challenging, God sets up a court of appeals made up of judges and priests to handle the more difficult matters.

Moses predicts there'll be a day when they look around and think, *All these other nations have kings—we want one too!* When the time comes, it will be important for their kings not to be drawn to wealth, horses, or women. The prohibition against accumulating these is supposed to keep them humble, trusting in God for their provision and protection. Wealth can lead a person's heart astray. Horses represent power, which is usually about military prowess. And acquiring foreign wives is often a way of making political alliances with other nations, which are all pagan, which also means the women might lead their hearts astray. The king needs to have his own book with God's laws written in it so he can read it daily for the rest of his life. His heart is at stake—power has a way of corrupting people and leading them off the path of righteousness. But reading God's Word daily will keep him upright and humble.

God promises to raise up a new prophet from among them—someone who hears from Him and speaks His words to them. This is why it's such a slap in God's face for them to seek answers from mediums or fortune-tellers—not only are those people wicked, but the Israelites themselves already have access to God and His counsel. God will hold the prophet accountable for what he says, and He'll hold the people accountable to listen to him.

Military endeavors for this particular nation-state are unique, because God is their commander in chief. He says not to fear large armies; in fact, He's already defeated large armies on their behalf. God is always the bigger army, always the majority. Because of that, He doesn't mind at all if their army is smaller. He tells the officers to spread the news: "Are you a young soldier with a new wife or a house or a garden? Go home and enjoy! You don't have to go to war with us. We'll be fine without you. Are you afraid? You're free to go! Fear is communicable, so we only want people here who trust in God and His promises."

God gives different commands for how to deal with cities outside the promised land versus inside: Approach those outside the land with peace. If they return the peace, take the city peaceably. If they don't comply, kill the men and take everyone and everything as plunder. For cities inside the land, God is accomplishing at least three things through His processes: He's fulfilling His promise of land to Israel, He's aiming to wipe out the signs of idolatry so they don't tempt the Israelites, and He's using Israel as a means of enacting justice on the wicked nations. He tells Israel to completely wipe out the current inhabitants. On the surface, it's hard to see this as a good and just command from God, but as we continue reading, we'll begin to see the wisdom in His instructions.

TODAY'S GOD SHOT

Three times today Moses said, "Purge the evil from your midst." This indicates capital punishment. Paul uses a similar phrase in 1 Corinthians 5:13 when giving instructions about people walking in blatant rebellion within the church. He tells the church to purge the evil person from among them. But in Paul's letter, it's not a call for capital punishment—it's a command to disassociate in hopes that the consequences might awaken the person to the reality of their sin, prompting repentance. In the long arc of God's storyline, we see how much He leans into grace toward His kids, because Christ received our punishment. He gives so many second chances, so much time to repent. Despite the fact that we deserve to be purged in the original sense, He's patient with us when we sin against Him and question His heart. Even when we don't believe it or remember it, He's where the joy is!

DEUTERONOMY 21–23

Moses continues his farewell speech today, covering a wide variety of laws. We'll look at a few of the most perplexing ones, most of which pertain to relationships between men and women. But before we get there, let's make sure we have the proper framework for what we're encountering. God isn't setting up a utopian society where everything is ideal. He's meeting them where they are and giving them a foundation for a functional society in which people are treated with at least the bare-minimum level of respect. When God addresses something like having multiple wives, it doesn't mean He's putting His seal of approval on it—it means He's acknowledging that it happens and He's giving them honorable ways to respond to an imperfect, sinful situation. We'll hit some challenging passages today, and it's important for us to remember not to overlay our cultural experiences onto theirs.

The first tough segment involves marrying female captives. For anyone in Western society today, this idea is really cringe inducing. One of the things we have to remember about this society is that marriage rarely fits with our modern view of love. It was uncommon for people to marry for love. Women often married for provision. In this text, the Israelites would've conquered a city, killed all the men, and taken the women and children alive. Some of these women would be absorbed into the society, but if a man found a woman he wanted to marry, she likely wouldn't object. The law God sets out here honors the woman by giving her a thirty-day period to mourn and grieve all she's lost before marrying the Israelite man. If things in the marriage go poorly, God protects the woman by requiring the man to treat her with honor, not like she's his property. Don't miss God's heart in this—even though so much of this seems archaic, we can still see God's plan to provide for the woman through the man and to protect her if the man fails to honor her well.

Other laws pertain to ensuring a woman's virginity. One of the many detrimental aspects of sexual infidelity is that it has the potential to threaten the tribe's economy and God's allotted land inheritance. Moses also sets standards for determining whether a woman has been raped or not. The portions saying, "If it happened in the country" and "if it happened in the city" have the potential to be confusing, but here's the premise behind them: If the encounter happened in the country, even if she screamed, no one would've been there to hear her, so she's given the benefit of the doubt. If it happened in the city, people would be around to hear her screams of objection. God's heart is for justice here, and He's setting up rules that can help people make determinations about what really happened on a case-by-case basis.

Another potentially confusing section is in the laws about not mixing different things together: seeds in a field, animals for plowing, fabrics in a garment. While we don't know all the reasons behind these laws, scholars suggest it's to remind the Israelites of the importance of being set apart from nations that don't follow YHWH. These laws may be little daily reminders that they're called to be separate.

TODAY'S GOD SHOT

The law about a man who is punished by being hung on a tree says, "His body shall not remain all night on the tree, but you shall bury him the same day, for a hanged man is cursed." Paul references this in Galatians 3:13: "Christ redeemed us from the curse of the law by becoming a curse for us—for it is written, 'Cursed is everyone who is hanged on a tree.'" Christ took the curse for us. Later in today's reading, Moses says, "The LORD your God turned the curse into a blessing for you, because the LORD your God loved you." This refers back to King Balak's efforts to get Balaam to curse the Israelites in Numbers 22–24. God reverses our future: He takes the thing we deserve—what we've fully earned, the curse—and absorbs it Himself through His death on the cross so that we might receive the blessing, just like the Israelites did. The God who turns our curse to a blessing is a God worth worshipping forever! He's where the joy is!

DEUTERONOMY 24–27

In Moses' final speech, we encounter a wide variety of laws, including the only law about divorce in the Old Testament, and it's *very* specific. The cultural practices of the day help us see more of what this law is about, but it's still not entirely clear. Some believe this practice protects the first husband from an adulterous wife, while others believe it protects the wife from a greedy husband. Since the first husband got the bride's dowry, and she inherited her second husband's property when he died, this law prevents the first husband from exploiting her for financial gain. One way or another, this law serves as a means of protection. Other laws show us how God is protective of all human life: He disapproves of slavery as we know it, and kidnapping is forbidden and is punished by death.

We also see lots of measures to protect the poor: Return the coat of a poor person if they offer it as collateral; don't take their millstones as collateral, because they need those to grind food; pay the poor servants when they need it (which usually means the same day they do their work, because they don't have any savings stored up to live on); remember those without land (they're usually the poorest and most vulnerable).

Verse 3 of chapter 25 limits punishment of a guilty man to forty lashes. Over time the Jews reduced it to thirty-nine, in case of miscounting. They "built a fence around the law" to make sure they didn't accidentally give a man forty-one lashes. So the law given by God sets a limit of forty lashes, but the law as amended by the rabbis puts the limit at thirty-nine. Paul says he endured this beating of thirty-nine lashes *five times* (2 Corinthians 11:24).

The law in 25:5–10 pertains to Levirate marriage, and it has a lot of moving parts to consider: keeping the allotment of land and inheritance, protection from marrying outsiders, and aiming to provide for widows while also protecting them from marrying unwilling men who'd likely mistreat them. This is a lot like what happens between Boaz and Ruth in the book of Ruth, where Boaz acts as the kinsman redeemer. This is actually our second nod to Ruth and Boaz today. The first was when we read about the law to leave some of the harvest behind so the poor can go in and reap (24:19–22). That's what poor Ruth was doing in wealthy Boaz's field when they met. While Levirate marriage served to protect a woman and her potential offspring, the very specific law immediately after it served to protect a man and his potential offspring (25:11–12).

Today God also tells the Israelites to remember what happened between them and the Amalekites. This is not a "forgive and forget" situation, in part because Amalek was unrepentant. If Amalek had stopped and said, "You're right—YHWH is the one true God, and we were wrong to go against His people," then things likely would've been different. But they didn't repent; they're bent on destroying Israel.

Moses gives a few instructions for when they enter into the promised land, which is in the near future. He says six tribes will climb Mount Gerizim and six will climb Mount Ebal while the Levite priests declare the curses. There God will demonstrate the blessings and curses of the covenant. One of the curses foreshadows Judas Iscariot's betrayal of Jesus. It says, "Cursed be anyone who takes a bribe to shed innocent blood." Christ was innocent of *all* sin, and Judas betrayed Him for thirty pieces of silver.

TODAY'S GOD SHOT

Verses 18–19 of chapter 26 say, "You are a people for his treasured possession. . . . He will set you in praise and in fame and in honor high above all nations that he has made." He calls Israel His treasured possession, above all the nations He made. He treasures Israel and He possesses Israel. He's put His name on them. How beautiful to be treasured, possessed, and loved infinitely by an infinitely lovable God. He's where the joy is!

DEUTERONOMY 28–29

As Moses reviews the blessings and curses of the covenant, he reminds the people that blessings await them if they obey God. Not only will He give them victory in battle, but He'll *command His blessing* on them. Wow. Blessings go where God tells them to go! And He promises to give the things only He can give: life, growth, and rain. When He does, people around them will take notice that there seems to be a unique blessing on the nation-state of Israel. God's protection and provision will cause the other nations to fear the Israelites; nothing is more terrifying than when your enemy is thriving. When Israel thrives, they'll lend to their neighbors in need, and these neighbors are not their friends. These surrounding nations oppose Israel and reject YHWH. This abundance and blessing will follow Israel if they follow God.

If they don't follow God, curses will come. And they sound terrible! Covenant curses are typically the complete reversal of blessing. For example, the blessing makes them victorious over their enemies, who scatter in seven directions, but the curse makes them lose to their enemies while *they* scatter in seven directions. That's how covenants were typically written, and it's one reason some of this might seem extra harsh. But this is more a demonstration of covenant than of character. Take 28:63, for instance: "As the LORD took delight in doing you good and multiplying you, so the LORD will take delight in bringing ruin upon you and destroying you." This is typical covenant language, and it's the opposite of what we've seen about God's character in how He regards His people. He doesn't delight in harming them.

We heard some harsh words from Moses, but this conversation isn't over yet, and we have to remember what we've learned about God in other conversations. Resist the urge to isolate this text and build theology around something taken out of the greater context. For example, in Leviticus 26:44–45 God said He'll be faithful even when they're faithless; He'll pursue them when they go astray. We've seen that God only sends the bad in order to bring about good in the end. And we've seen that we don't want a God who lets us rebel without consequence—we want a God who calls us back to Him when we stray. That's exactly the kind of God YHWH is—a God of discipline and protection. His discipline protects us from the far greater harm we'd bring on ourselves and others if we continued in rebellion unchecked.

As Moses wraps up the blessings and curses, he urges the Israelites to keep this covenant. God isn't just making a covenant with the leaders—it's with everyone, from the greatest to the least, including foreigners and sojourners living among them, and even the Israelites yet to be born. Moses warns everyone against thinking they might be the exception to the rule. He warns against an unrepentant heart and against presuming upon God's grace. He encourages them to do what God has shown them (the revealed things) and trust God with the rest (the secret things). But Moses also knows these people well, and he knows they'll rebel. He says, "To this day the LORD has not given you a heart to understand or eyes to see or ears to hear" (29:4). Many scholars even say that's probably why he spends so much more time going over the curses than the blessings—because it's so heavy on his heart, so he's imploring them to obey. But, spoiler alert, they don't. Moses knows this, and God knows this, yet God still chose them to be His people, knowing all the ways their hearts would rebel against Him.

TODAY'S GOD SHOT

God reveals things to His people but also keeps some things hidden. "The secret things belong to the LORD our God, but the things that are revealed belong to us and to our children forever, that we may do all the words of this law" (29:29). What He tells us is for our obedience and our joy, but so is what He hides from us. It's good that we don't know everything. It's good that we have to walk in step with Him, trusting His goodness. Regardless of what we know or don't know, He's working for our good. And one thing we do know is that He's where the joy is!

DEUTERONOMY 30–31

Moses has good and bad news for the Israelites today: "You're going to break this covenant. God knows it, I know it, you know it—so here's what you need to do when that happens: *Repent*. Turn back to God. He won't abandon you. He'll restore everything you lost when you turned away from Him." When they sin and are carried into captivity, God will use those circumstances to change their hearts (30:6), then they'll turn to Him and begin to obey Him. When God gives someone a new heart, their desires change. The Hebrew word for *heart* combines the words we use for *heart* and *mind*; it's where desire and will overlap, and it's what drives our actions. Without a new heart, it's impossible to please God. Only when He changes our hearts will we respond to Him rightly, because He doesn't just want to be obeyed—He wants to be known and loved.

Moses wants them to experience not just the land God promised, but also the life that's only found in relationship with God. Moses doesn't get to enter the promised land, so he can only speak on the experience of knowing God. Since the day he met God, his assignment has been to live in the desert with sinners. But because he knows God, this experience contains a surprising peace and an irreplaceable intimacy. Even without the earthly benefit of land, his relationship with God is joy inducing. He wants this joy and freedom for the Israelites too.

When he tells them he's about to die, it's probably terrifying for them—he's the only leader they've ever known. He probably wants to calm their fears, because he knows firsthand how much fear can lead to rebellion, so he starts by reminding them that *God* is their leader. God Himself will go before them into the promised land. He'll fight against the nations that live there, and He'll win. Then Moses calls Joshua up front and tells him not to fear too. In both instances, he doesn't tell them to think about how awesome they are or to believe in their dreams. Instead, he says to *remember the nearness of God*—that's what Moses offers as the antidote to fear.

After he commissions Joshua for his role as leader, he says they should read the law aloud—all of it—every seven years during the Feast of Booths, which will take place in the city where God establishes the tabernacle. All the Israelites, and even the sojourners living among them, will travel there once every seven years, and they'll be reminded of all the laws. Then God calls a meeting with Moses and Joshua. God doesn't have great news: "Moses, you're about to die. Joshua, you're about to lead these people. And guess what—they're about to rebel." This is similar to when God first called Moses to talk to Pharaoh about releasing the Israelites. God basically said, "Go ask Pharaoh to do this specific thing. By the way, I'm going to harden his heart so that he says no to what I'm telling you to ask him to do." It says a lot about their trust in God that they do these things after He tells them they'll fail first. It's easy to think that if God tells us to do something, it's guaranteed to succeed. God says He'll bless the people with plenty, and then they'll get comfortable in their easy lives and break the covenant. They rebelled in the lack of the wilderness, and they'll rebel in the abundance of the promised land. God will be angry with them, and they'll be devoured. Instead of remembering what Moses just said to them and repenting of their idolatry, they'll question God's love and presence. God commissions Joshua and reminds him, "I'll be with you." Joshua will need that reminder soon when his mentor dies and everything goes south with the people he's leading.

TODAY'S GOD SHOT

God knows how much betrayal He'll endure, how He'll be doubted, forgotten, and falsely accused of abandonment, but still His love persists. Knowing the future—especially a future like that—could easily threaten a lesser love. But not YHWH's love. He enters in with full knowledge of the pain He'll endure, knowing we will not be worth it, and still He doesn't let go. We can't change His mind or talk Him out of His choice to set His heart on us. No one else loves like Him—He's where the joy is!

DEUTERONOMY 32–34; PSALM 91

Today we finished reading the Torah! Yesterday as we wrapped up, God told Moses to write a song about the Israelites' past, present, and future. It calls Israel to pay attention to God's greatness, then it uses some poetic devices—similes, metaphors, personification, anthropomorphizing, hyperbole—so don't panic when you read phrases like, "They are no longer His children, because they are blemished; they are a crooked and twisted generation" (32:5). God has *not* cast them off forever; this is hyperbole emphasizing the weight of what has happened. The rest of the context helps clarify these terrifying verses. Any time Israel rejects God, He begins to integrate other nations into His family. Part of His plan involves sending Israel into disaster, but He's measured in all of it, never wanting the enemy to get credit for their victory over Israel. The only way to gain victory over God's people is if God allows it. But He'll have compassion on Israel in their weakness and bring justice.

The word *Jeshurun* that appears three times in this song is a reference to the Israelites. It means "upright ones," and it's used ironically here, since they aren't upright. This is the song God wants the people to remember when they're at the beginning of this story, *before* they fall away into apostasy. If they refuse to listen at that point, then He wants them to remember it when they're halfway through the story it tells. He wants them to know He's still there, loving them.

After Moses sings his song, God tells him which mountain to die on. From the top of that mountain, he'll see the promised land. Then he offers a final blessing to eleven of the twelve tribes. Simeon's tribe isn't mentioned here, but Moses likely didn't forget them. It is probably a prophetic move on his part, giving us an indication of what God has in store. The Simeonites will eventually be dispersed, and the tribe of Judah will absorb them. Jacob prophesied along these same lines back in Genesis 49:7.

After Moses blesses them, he goes up to the mountain, sees the promised land, and dies, old and strong. Then we see something strange and beautiful: God buries Moses—not on Mount Nebo, where he died, but in the valley in a spot no one knows. This probably serves to prevent them from building a shrine on his grave, which could lead to idolatry. Israel mourns for him for thirty days, and their new leader, Joshua, is filled with the spirit of wisdom to lead them.

As for Psalm 91, one of the psalmists set Moses' words to music so they could be sung and remembered. It's a sweet reminder for the Israelites of who God is and what He has brought them through.

TODAY'S GOD SHOT

Psalm 91:14 says, "Because he holds fast to me in love, I will deliver him; I will protect him, because he knows my name." These words are potent. The word for *holds fast* in the phrase "he holds fast to me" indicates a longing and desire. The word for *know* in the phrase "he knows my name" is the same word used to say things like "Adam knew his wife"; it indicates intimate knowledge. And since name indicates character, then for God to say, "He knows my name" is like saying, "He is intimately acquainted with who I truly am." There's a good chance that's what's happening here as you read His Word. Your heart is being knit to Him in deeper ways. You probably find yourself *wanting* to read your Bible sometimes, and maybe that feeling has taken you by surprise. Maybe it's altogether new and unfamiliar to you. Through this, He's teaching you to hold fast to Him. He's showing you who He is, teaching you to know His name. There's deliverance and protection for us in this—deliverance from the world and from ourselves, deliverance into greater freedom and joy and into Him—because He's where the joy is!

JOSHUA 1–4

Today we step into the first of the history books, and while they do reveal history, their primary goal is to reveal God. Keep looking for Him! Both God and the Israelites tell their new leader, Joshua, to be strong and courageous. As they prepare to enter Canaan, he reminds the Transjordan tribes that they still have to cross the Jordan and fight for the land like all the other tribes, and then they can come back east and live in the pasturelands they asked God for in Numbers 32.

Joshua sends two spies to Jericho, the first city across the promised land's border. It likely has a double wall, and it's common for poor people like Rahab to build their homes in the narrow space between the two walls. The spies have two main goals here: Stay safe and get a good view of the city's layout. What better place to accomplish both goals than a rooftop on the edge of the city? Some scholars think they're at Rahab's house for reasons that aren't honorable, but others say it's a locationally strategic move. Some historical texts suggest Rahab also ran a hotel of sorts, so that could be why they're there. Scripture doesn't give any reason to think they have ill intentions, and we know Scripture isn't afraid to tell ugly truths.

Even though Rahab is a Canaanite prostitute, she fears YHWH. She seems to have a real faith in Him and knows what He's capable of. She's heard stories of what He did hundreds of miles away, forty years earlier—how He led them across the Red Sea on dry land. She's praised twice in Scripture for living out her faith (Hebrews 11:31; James 2:25), and she's included in the genealogy of Jesus! Her knowledge of YHWH prompts radical loyalty to Him. She hides the spies and lies to the king's men about their location.

They make a deal with her for saving their lives: When they conquer Jericho, she'll throw a red rope out the window so they can easily identify her home and spare her family. Remember this moment. We'll

---

For more information on today's reading, see thebiblerecap.com/links.

encounter lots of wartime language where God tells Israel to destroy all the people in the land of Canaan, and it's important for us to remember that God is *not* calling for genocide or ethnic cleansing. This has nothing to do with their ethnicity and everything to do with the fact that they're idolaters who participate in atrocities like child sacrifice. God is bringing judgment on their sins, but He's always willing to spare the repentant. *Anytime* someone repents, they're kept alive and welcomed among the Israelites. God isn't calling for the wholesale slaughter of Canaanites; the text shows us obvious exceptions, and Rahab and her family are among them.

These spies believe God's promise. They say, "*When* the LORD gives us the land we will deal kindly and faithfully with you" (2:14). Not only do they believe God will bless them as He said, but they're already planning on paying that blessing forward. When they give Joshua the good news, he rallies everyone to cross into the promised land. They come to a river, but this isn't their first river-crossing rodeo. The last time they had to cross a body of water, God stopped the water before they entered. But this time the water doesn't stop until they step into it. Walking with God requires increasing amounts of obedience and trust. As they cross over, God calls them a nation for the first time, fulfilling His promise from Genesis 12:2, then He has them set up twelve stones, one for each tribe. These stones serve as a reminder for them, their children, and all the peoples of the earth (4:24). The miracle of God's provision for Israel is an invitation to all people to know and fear Him.

TODAY'S GOD SHOT

God repeatedly tells Joshua to be strong and courageous. But every time God gives this command, He precedes or follows it with the promise that He'll be with him. Strength and courage aren't things we muster on our own; it's not just a mental pep rally or a mindset we meditate our way into. True strength and courage come through being mindful of God's presence in our lives. He never asks us to do things on our own; His nearness is what equips us to obey. He never asks us to be our own strength or provision—He provides all He requires of us. He's where the strength is. He's where the courage is. And He's where the joy is!

JOSHUA 5–8

The Israelites just set foot in the promised land for the first time, as a *nation*. Their enemies still live there, and the first city they plan to take is Jericho, but God wants them fully prepared. In God's economy, preparing for battle has very little to do with sharpening your weapons and everything to do with readying your heart. First they circumcise all Israelite males, then they celebrate Passover. Their hearts need to remember Passover—it reinforces their faith. Then the next day, the manna ceases. This is incredible. This is God's precise provision on display. He gave them miracle food six days a week for forty years—it even followed them into the promised land—and it stops the day after they have access to local food. God's provision has no gaps!

Then Joshua has a strange encounter with a man holding a sword. This is scary—they're in enemy territory. Joshua asks if he's an Israelite or a Canaanite, and the man basically says, "Nope. I'm God." Some people say God refuses to take sides in the battle, since He doesn't give Joshua a straight answer, but we know from the surrounding text that God has aligned Himself with the Israelites. God's reply suggests that Israel is on *His* side more than that He's on Israel's side. How do we know this is God? First, He receives worship. God's elect angels don't let people worship them; they reject it because they know they don't deserve it. Second, the Angel of YHWH tells Joshua to take off his shoes, which is reminiscent of the burning bush encounter. Angels don't make things holy; only God can do that.

God tells Joshua that Jericho is theirs for the taking, because He's giving it to them. But He gives odd instructions on how to accomplish this: March around the city with the ark, blowing trumpets, once a day for six days, then on day seven, march around *seven* times; on that seventh trip, have all the people shout, then the walls will fall and they'll have an opening to go in and devote everything to destruction except for Rahab's family. The two spies are in charge of saving her. They defeat Jericho with zero military strategy, and Joshua pronounces a curse on anyone who rebuilds it. By the way, it's been rebuilt, so remember this curse.

Joshua forbids the soldiers to take plunder; it's devoted to God like a firstfruits offering. But a guy named Achan secretly takes plunder valued at the amount of a worker's lifelong income. Meanwhile, Joshua sends his people to go take another city, Ai, but doesn't consult God first. Not only do they lose, but thirty-six men die in the process. Joshua grieves and begins to doubt God, thinking God betrayed them. He appeals to God, but God points the finger back at the Israelites; He views them as a unit, so one man's sin impacts the whole. Achan is personally responsible for his spiritual adultery, but the whole community is affected. Since Achan's sin represents spiritual adultery against God, it requires the death penalty. Achan is from the most esteemed tribe, but he's rejected from the people of Israel because his heart isn't devoted to YHWH. This is important. Through Rahab and Achan we're already seeing that being a part of God's people, the Israelites, has nothing to do with race or genes, and it has everything to do with the heart. God's family is made up of people with new hearts, not similar DNA.

God tells them to go back and conquer Ai and says they can keep its livestock and plunder for themselves, and then they must set it on fire. This is God's judgment on its inhabitants for their wickedness. Then Joshua builds an altar to God and follows God's instructions, speaking the curses from Mount Ebal and the blessings from Mount Gerizim (Deuteronomy 11), and then renews the covenant with the people.

TODAY'S GOD SHOT

As they took their first six trips around Jericho, they probably thought all the walking was a waste of time. Maybe you feel like that some days in our reading plan or in prayer—but He's doing something. Sometimes what God does in our hearts through obedience is beyond our capacity to understand. He's at work, even on the "nothing" days, when obedience feels like we're walking in circles. Listening to Him is the best place to be, even when we don't fully understand, because He's where the joy is!

JOSHUA 9–11

In Deuteronomy 20:10–18 God gave different instructions on how the Israelites were to handle cities outside the promised land versus cities inside it. For cities outside Canaan, they should greet them with peace and kill only males who oppose them. For cities inside Canaan, they should operate by a principle called *cherem*, under which everything is dedicated to YHWH and devoted to destruction. God uses this to serve multiple purposes, including judgment and provision. The Gibeonites (also called Hivites) learn of this strategy and pretend to live outside Canaan to get the more lenient treatment. They ask Israel to enter a protective covenant, and Joshua agrees without asking God, accidentally making a covenant with his enemies. The Israelites find out they've been deceived and want to destroy the Gibeonites. But Israel's leaders say they have to keep their covenant and suffer the consequences of this sinful decision. So instead of killing the Gibeonites, they assign them to manual labor in the service of the temple. Even God's enemies who have deceived God's people end up serving God's purposes and glory.

Some local kings hear about this and declare war on Gibeon for making peace with the Israelites. The Gibeonites panic and beg Israel for help. Joshua seeks God, who says, "Do not fear, for I have given them into your hands. Not a man of them shall stand before you" (10:8). He uses miraculous tactics—confusion, hailstones, cosmic events—and wins the war for Israel. Joshua knows how to proceed because he listens to and believes God. He quotes God's words to His people as the battle ends. They defeat six more cities in southern Canaan, so the northern kings start to get nervous. God tells Joshua that the next day He'll give all of them to Israel in battle, and He does! Joshua is starting to listen carefully to God, and because of God's unique covenant with this nation-state, they continue to see victory in battle when they obey. Joshua begins to display thorough and persistent obedience.

They also defeat the Anakim, who are always a reminder that there's likely more going on than meets the eye. The Israelites are destroying a lot of people, but it's possible that these people are the enemy's attempt to wipe out the Messiah's bloodline by interbreeding with humans. It's what the ancient Jews believed, and it's been a thread through the books we've read, so we don't want to dismiss the possibility.

God hardened the enemy's hearts (11:20). This isn't an easy phrase, but we can't cut it out of Scripture. In Exodus 33:19, God told Moses, "I will be gracious to whom I will be gracious, and will show mercy on whom I will show mercy." This may chafe against our sense of justice or make us feel like God isn't fair. It's important to remember we're all sinners who deserve death and separation from God. For those of us who *don't* get that, we're the ones for whom things aren't fair—we do not get what we deserve. There's a mystery here that we won't understand on this side of eternity—it's okay to have a hard time with it, to wrestle and question, to hold it with an open hand and ask God to reveal Himself. The enemy of your soul wants nothing more than for you to mistrust God's heart. Hopefully you've seen enough of His heart by now to trust Him even when there are parts of Him you don't understand. There's a 100 percent chance you won't always like what God does, because He's God and you aren't. As Tim Keller said, "If your god never disagrees with you, you might be worshipping an idealized version of yourself."*

TODAY'S GOD SHOT

Joshua set his heart to obey God, but God didn't grant him an immediate victory. In fact, God lengthened his day. Joshua asked for something impossible and God granted it, but it didn't come the easy way. He had to fight longer. Even when it feels like God is lengthening our days, He's still working on our behalf. We can ask Him for impossible things, and we can trust Him and praise Him even when His answer is no or His yes takes longer than we would prefer. Because ultimately His *answers* aren't what we're after—we're after *Him*, because He's where the joy is!

*Timothy Keller, Facebook, May 15, 2014, https://www.facebook.com/TimKellerNYC/posts/if-your-god-never-disagrees-with-you-you-might-just-be-worshiping-an-idealized-v/754367937936428/.

JOSHUA 12–15

Yesterday the Israelites won a lot of wars and took a lot of land, so today we open with a summary of what land they've acquired and unfamiliar boundaries that seem unimportant. However, they were deeply important to the people at the time, and these lists have served our faith historically and archaeologically. Hang in there during these dry spots; they serve a greater purpose than entertainment.

The land they conquered when Moses was still alive is the area east of the Jordan River where the two and a half Transjordan tribes live (Gad, Reuben, and half of the tribe of Manasseh). Unfortunately, the Transjordan tribes didn't drive out all the people who lived there. We'll continue to see how this act of disobedience causes them trouble through the years. When we cross the Jordan River heading west into the promised land, we see the areas conquered by Joshua. After all this conquering, Joshua is pretty old, but God says He's not done with him. There's still more land to take, so he's not going to die yet. But God will do the heavy lifting for them and drive out the inhabitants Himself, then Joshua will give the land to the remaining nine and a half tribes. The final tribe, the Levites, have God Himself as their inheritance, and they'll be spread out to live among each of the tribes.

Then we have an encounter with Caleb; he's the other spy who, along with Joshua, believed God forty-five years earlier when they spied out this land. He's talking to Joshua about what they endured and what God promised to them. He recalls following God in the face of fear, and he's ready to do it again. Even at the age of eighty-five, he wants to go fight against the Anakim—the giants in the land—and he succeeds with Joshua's blessing and God's direction!

Judah is the largest tribe by far, so they get the largest plot of land. Almost everything they get is desert, but on the bright side, it edges in on Jerusalem. They also get the mineral-rich soil of the Dead Sea. By the way, anytime the word *Negeb* appears, it refers to the desert. Since Caleb is part of the tribe of Judah, his inheritance falls within their allotment. There's one plot of land promised to him that he asks for help with, and he promises that whoever conquers that city will get to marry his daughter. It probably would've been considered an honor to be the grand prize for the warrior who conquered the most difficult city in the land. His nephew Othniel conquers it, and Caleb's daughter makes one request. Since her portion includes the desert, she also wants two springs of water (smart woman!) and her dad gives them to her.

TODAY'S GOD SHOT

Joshua 13:13 says the Transjordan tribes did not drive out the people of the land, which suggests that they didn't even try. Then 15:63 says, "But the Jebusites, the inhabitants of Jerusalem, the people of Judah *could not* drive out, so the Jebusites dwell with the people of Judah at Jerusalem to this day." *Could not*—meaning they tried and they failed. Why? If God was with them, why couldn't they just believe in themselves and make it happen? Why couldn't they recall God's promises to them and hold Him to His words? God will not be manipulated by our mantras. He made a very specific agreement with them about how the land would be taken, and it involves obedience. They can't just show up with their entitlement and expect God to give them what they want, *even when it's what He promised them personally and directly*. This unique relationship their nation-state has with God means they have to walk in accordance with the covenant they made. And it seems something is off here—some sin keeps them from acquiring the land. Does that mean God failed them? No, the story isn't over yet. He's at work even in these so-called delays to shape their hearts, to do them good, to defeat their enemies despite their present failure. He's with them when they sin and fail. And He's with you when you sin and fail. Even in failure, trust can grow, faith can be strengthened, and joy can be found—because He's where the joy is!

JOSHUA 16–18

Today we encounter all the drama surrounding land allotments. The allotment for Joseph's descendants takes us back to the day when his dad, Jacob, formally adopted his sons, Ephraim and Manasseh. With that exchange, they received the right to Joseph's inheritance from Jacob, which means they're tribal leaders and landowners. At some point, the tribe of Manasseh split in half and became two half-tribes. Half of them wanted to live east of the Jordan River (Transjordan), so we'll call them East Manasseh. The other half inherited part of the original promised land across the Jordan, so we'll call them West Manasseh. But a problem crops up during the division process for the land when West Manasseh gets lumped in with Ephraim, and they complain about it. They want to go their own way and get land that suits the size of their tribe.

Joshua agrees to their request for division and says they're responsible for clearing the land and driving out the people in it. But we're starting to see a theme in that most of the tribes aren't driving out the Canaanites like God repeatedly commanded them to.

In other land allotment news, the daughters of Zelophehad approach Joshua and Eleazar, giving them a little nudge about the land God promised them, and the new leaders follow God's orders, allotting the land to them.

All the tribes gather in Shiloh, where they set up the tabernacle. This is the first place in the promised land where the tabernacle is erected. There are still seven tribes waiting to find out which land they'll be living in, and they're probably getting antsy. Joshua sends three men from each of those tribes on a mission to check out the remaining territory and report back to him. When they return, he divvies up the land accordingly. Benjamin and Judah both have detailed land allotments, likely because both tribes have special prominence. Benjamin and Judah get the

For more information on today's reading, see thebiblerecap.com/links.

land that borders Jerusalem to the north and south, respectively. This is important because Jerusalem will become the capital, the place where God will establish His tabernacle permanently. That's one reason it's a big deal that they haven't driven out the Jebusites who currently live there. But to their credit, Jerusalem is a hard city to take; it's on a hill surrounded by three deep valleys, so the people in the city always have a military advantage.

TODAY'S GOD SHOT

Jerusalem is surrounded by three valleys that converge to form an interesting shape. It looks like a sideways number three (or if you're a Trekkie, it looks like the Vulcan salute). To an Israelite, it's clearly the Hebrew letter *shin*, which is regarded as a sacred letter among the Jews. Why would they show honor to a letter? *Shin* is the first letter of the word *Shaddai*, which means "God Almighty"—it's how God identifies Himself to Abraham in Genesis 17. The Israelites regard this letter as God's initial. They stamp it on their mezuzahs, which adorn the doorposts of their homes (Deuteronomy 6:6–9).

In Deuteronomy 12, God said three times that His chosen place of worship where the tabernacle would be located was a place where He would put His name. In 2 Chronicles 6:6, He says, "I have chosen Jerusalem that my name may be there." Could He be speaking only figuratively and spiritually? Sure. But given the topography of Jerusalem, there's reason to believe He is also speaking literally. If you have a topographical view of the city of Jerusalem, it looks like God stamped His initial on it, monogrammed it with the letter *shin*. You monogram things you own, things you want to be identified with.

Long before aerial photos existed, God chose a city marked with the letter His people would regard as His initial. He comes down to dwell with them there—the people marked by His name in the city marked by His name. And here we are today, thousands of years later, marked by the same name, the people He has chosen to adopt into His family despite our sins and shortcomings. He's where the *shin* is, and He is where the joy is!

JOSHUA 19–21

Today we continue looking at the land allotments for the tribes. They've been waiting forty years for this; they've been fighting for this, quite literally. These assignments are where they'll build their lives and raise their families. And for the Israelites, this isn't a temporary placement—this land is marked out to be the home of their tribe forever, provided they keep up their end of the covenant they made with God. Since many of the ways these places are referred to in Scripture mean nothing to us, I'll offer a short description of each place we see today. Imagine you're one of the seven tribes who hasn't gotten their land yet, and you're waiting to find out where your family will live.

Simeon gets assigned land in the middle of Judah's plot of desert in the south. Zebulun gets a tiny plot in the north—it's the smallest plot besides Benjamin's, but it's a lush, green area with lots of plants and flowers. If you look at a map, you may notice that Zebulun gets the city of Bethlehem, but that's a different Bethlehem from the one where Jesus was born. There are two Bethlehems in the promised land, and He was born in the one just outside Jerusalem. Issachar also gets a small, fertile area near the Sea of Galilee and the Jordan River.

Asher gets the Mediterranean coastline to the north, some of which belongs to the Lebanon of today. Naphtali gets the mountainous north, including a mountain range that reaches over nine thousand feet high. You can ski there if you visit Israel in the winter. The people from the tribe of Dan get a gorgeous coastline area near a major port city called Joppa, which is adjacent to modern-day Tel Aviv. But Dan loses this land later, and they relocate to a part of Naphtali's plot in the north. (Stay tuned to find out how and why that happens.) The plot of land where they eventually relocate to is a gorgeous nature preserve today, covered with trees and rivers and wildlife. Both of the places where Dan lives are prime locations, but they're kind of a terrible tribe, as we'll see later.

Since Joshua was one of the two spies who believed God forty-five years earlier, he gets to choose where he wants to live. Like a gentleman, he lets everyone else get their land first. He chooses a hilly area in Ephraim's land, just north of Jerusalem, in a somewhat isolated area. He knows his years are drawing to a close, so he chooses a good spot for quiet and solitude.

The topographic diversity of this little nation is shocking. It may only be the size of New Jersey, but it covers a wide range of climates and altitudes—from snowcapped Mount Hermon to the lowest spot on earth, the Dead Sea, which is 1,400 feet below sea level. Land allotment determines nearly everything about the lives of the Israelites: their climate and scenery, the food available to them, their job opportunities, and how far they have to travel to get to the tabernacle in Jerusalem, their future capital. Life for a Simeonite in the southern desert would be the opposite of life for a Benjamite who lives in a city in the mountains of Jerusalem, or for a Naphtalite who wakes up to flowers and palm trees along the Sea of Galilee, or for a Manassite who watches the sunset over the Mediterranean Sea every night.

After the land is distributed, it's time to set up the cities of refuge, the areas where a manslayer (someone who accidentally kills someone) can live without fear of retribution. Cities of refuge are less like prisons and more like safe houses, but the manslayer isn't allowed to leave until the high priest dies. God intentionally spreads the cities of refuge throughout the tribes so that a manslayer will have a good chance of reaching one of them before someone tries to retaliate. God thinks of everything! The Levites are also distributed among the tribes, kind of like local pastors.

TODAY'S GOD SHOT

God shows us so much of His character in accomplishing all this for the Israelites. Not just generosity and faithfulness, but strength, power, and persistent love. Forgiveness and grace and mercy. God ushered them into this promised land, despite themselves. He has given them everything they need, but most important of all is Himself—because He's where the joy is!

JOSHUA 22–24

Now that the land has been sufficiently conquered, the Transjordan tribes have fulfilled their promise to fight for the land with the other tribes. Joshua affirms them, reminds them to be loyal to YHWH, and sends them home across the Jordan River to the east. On the way, they build a huge structure on the west side of the Jordan River. When the western tribes hear about it, they're ready to fight. You can't just go building altars wherever you want! This seems to be in direct defiance of YHWH's commands. They send a delegation headed up by Phinehas, son of Eleazar the high priest, and they accuse the Transjordan tribes of turning away from God. The western tribes fear God's judgment on all of Israel because of this rebellion. They ask for an explanation and offer the Transjordan tribes a gracious option for repentance: "Come live with us on the western side of the river instead of turning away from God."

But the Transjordan tribes clear things up quickly. It turns out they aren't rebelling against God or setting up an altar for worship. The structure is a monument to show the relationship between them and the western tribes, connecting them. They were afraid that in the future, the western tribes would disown them and their kids, so they wanted something to serve as a sign of their relationship. The western tribes are reasonable; they're satisfied with this explanation, so they head back home, breathing a sigh of relief. The last thing they want is to lose the land they just got settled in.

As Joshua nears death, he calls all the leaders of Israel for a pep talk. God is the one who accomplished these good things for them, and there's still work to do, namely, driving out the lingering Canaanites. Moses was very nervous about the Israelites turning away from God to worship the pagan gods, and here Joshua has the same concerns. God has equipped them with all they need to obey Him; they *can* drive out the people, because God has promised them that land, so they need to do it. Joshua warns against idolatry and intermarriage with those who don't worship YHWH. If they fail to honor God in this, it breaks the covenant and He'll take the land away. God has blessed them, but harm will come to them if they turn away from Him.

In chapter 24, Joshua walks them through their history, beginning with Abraham's father, Terah. They all started out worshipping other gods. There was no such thing as an Israelite until God invented them. God grew them, rescued them, blessed them, fought for them, and fulfilled His promises to them. Then he says, "You can serve YHWH, or you can serve these other gods. What'll it be?" The people respond with a hearty promise that they'll follow YHWH. Joshua reminds them that they aren't capable of keeping that promise on their own, but they say they'll totally do it.

Joshua is buried in the promised land. Then the bones of Joseph, which had sat in Egypt for a few hundred years, and which they've been lugging around the wilderness and all through the promised land, finally find a resting place in a spot Joseph's dad bought hundreds of years earlier. And it happens to be in the plot of land God apportioned for the tribes of Joseph. Full circle. We've been waiting for this since Genesis 50:25! Eleazar the high priest dies next. Since the priesthood is handed down generationally, his son Phinehas is primed to be the next high priest. But this signals the end of an era for the Israelites—their current leader and high priest are dying on the same page.

TODAY'S GOD SHOT

For the first time since God called Abraham, the people are living in at least partial fulfillment of all three of the promises He made to them: They've become a great nation, they have a blessed relationship with YHWH, and they're living in the promised land. Verse 14 of chapter 23 says, "You know in your hearts and souls, all of you, that not one word has failed of all the good things that the LORD your God promised concerning you. All have come to pass for you; not one of them has failed." God hasn't failed. He wasn't failing them in the desert when these things hadn't yet been fulfilled, and He isn't failing them now. He's failproof, and He's where the joy is!

JUDGES 1–2

Judges is full of bloody and wicked stories. It also requires us to reframe our understanding of the word *judge*—these aren't courtroom judges. They're civil and military leaders, and they're more like a hands-on president who enacts laws and commands the army. Israel is a theocratic nation-state. That means *God* rules the country—not a king or a president—so there's no separation of church and state. This kind of system may sound like a great idea, but having God as your leader doesn't mean people actually follow Him. The human heart doesn't respond to laws; it responds to what it loves. And if you don't love God, you'll find His rules repugnant and irrational, and you'll rebel against Him.

Even though they're in the promised land, they haven't conquered the land completely; there are pockets of Canaanites everywhere because they failed to obey God's covenant. He warned them repeatedly about the consequences: The Canaanites will become a snare and lead Israel into apostasy, then they'll be oppressed and dragged away. Today we set out for a long ride on the Apostasy Express—it runs in this loop: Israel sins; falls into oppression; cries out to God, who delivers them; then repents and enjoys peace for a while, before again deciding they like sin more than peace.

The Israelites are enticed by the Canaanites' sophistication. After all, their parents lived in Egypt as slaves, they came from nothing, and they've spent their entire lives in tents in the desert. Now they're in cities with art, architecture, literature, and ports of trade. And it seems like the way the Canaanites acquired this lifestyle was by worshipping their gods, which involved sex with the so-called sacred prostitutes at Baal's temple. The Israelites make concession after concession until their hearts fully turn from God.

In the beginning of Judges, Israel starts out strong after Joshua's death by inquiring of God. They want to eradicate the Canaanites like

For more information on today's reading, see thebiblerecap.com/links.

God commanded. God appoints Judah to lead the charge, and Judah asks Simeon's tribe for help. They have some early success, even in Jerusalem, but it's short-lived. They hedge on full obedience, allowing some Canaanites to remain in the land. In fact, nine of the nine and a half tribes in the original promised land still have Canaanites living there. The only exception is Issachar. The other tribes also keep some Canaanites alive as slaves, which is expressly forbidden by God. God shows up as the Angel of the LORD to rebuke them and tell them the consequences of their actions: The Canaanites will be a thorn in their flesh, and they'll fall into idolatry. They're devastated, and they weep and offer sacrifices to God, but their repentance is short-lived.

Today's reading gave us two flashbacks from the book of Joshua: the death of Joshua and the allotment of springs to Caleb's daughter. The flashback to Joshua's death is a reminder of a time when Israel was following God more closely. But even that great generation failed as leaders, because they didn't appoint new leaders. And they didn't tell God's story to the following generation. The people began worshipping the gods of Baal and Ashtaroth, male and female gods of the Canaanites. God is furious and brings on the very thing He promised: discipline via plundering and conquering. God raises up judges from among them to help lead them, but they reject these leaders and YHWH Himself and continue in wickedness. God promises not to drive out their enemies, since they've broken the covenant, and it will serve as a test to them. Will they repent? Will they turn back to Him?

TODAY'S GOD SHOT

Much of God's character shines in this text: His faithfulness to His covenant with the people—which includes blessings for obedience *and* curses for rebellion—His patience with them, His willingness to forgive, His compassion toward them. But above all, we see how much He loves them. He's not just trying to force obedience without relationship. He's after their hearts. Nothing changes unless hearts change. Yesterday Joshua told the people to incline their hearts toward God, and today we see that His heart is inclined toward them as well. His love for us prompts our hearts to love Him back, because *He's* where the joy is!

JUDGES 3–5

Today we met Israel's first four judges, all of whom are fairly good in the role. We also find out that God left a handful of Canaanite leaders in the land as a test for the Israelites. They've forgotten God and are worshipping the Baals and the Asheroth. God sells them into slavery, like He warned them He'd do when this happened. After eight years, they cry out to God and He raises up Othniel, the first judge and military leader, to save them. God gives him victory, and they have peace for forty years—until the Israelites decide they prefer sin over peace and rebel again. God strengthens their enemy—King Eglon of Moab—against them, and he gathers allies to attack Israel and take back Jericho, Israel's first conquest in the promised land. They make the Israelites their servants for eighteen years. When the Israelites cry out to God for rescue, He appoints the second judge, Ehud. He's from the tribe of Benjamin, which means "son of the right hand," but this left-handed warrior leads them in giving King Eglon a gift as a ruse to stab him; then they kill ten thousand Moabites, take back the land, and have peace for eighty years.

We only get one sentence on the third judge, Shamgar. Both his name and his family of origin suggest he's a native Canaanite who turned to worship YHWH. He leads them in victory over the Philistines. Then the people sin again, and God sells them into slavery for twenty years under King Jabin. This situation seems impossible to the people because Jabin and his military commander, Sisera, have access to nine hundred iron chariots and live in flat areas. If you have chariots, you want to fight on flat land. If you don't have chariots, you want to fight in the hills so you can beat the chariots. That the Canaanites have chariots and flat land doesn't bode well for the Israelites. The Israelites are worshipping Canaanite gods, who are worthless to save them; they have no hope but YHWH, so they cry out to Him. So God raises up Deborah, the judge who honors Him most and sticks closest to His commands.

She's a wise, bold, level-headed prophet who keeps her word and fears God. She's the only judge we'll encounter who presides over legal cases. The one traditional role she doesn't fulfill is the role of military leader. She says God appointed Barak for that position. He agrees but refuses to go to battle without her, even though she lets him know that a woman will be praised for the victory.

Deborah sends Barak into battle against Sisera and his nine hundred chariots with God's blessing. The Israelites kill a lot of Canaanites, but Sisera escapes on foot and goes to the tent of Heber the Kenite. Heber has a peaceful relationship with Sisera's king, so they're on decent terms, which may explain why Sisera goes to his tent. But there are at least two other odd dynamics here. First, Heber is a Kenite, not an Israelite, but those two peoples are closely related and have a peaceful relationship. The Kenites even settled in the land with the Israelites. So Sisera is showing up to a place where he is both a friend *and* an enemy. Second, Sisera actually goes to Heber's *wife's* tent. Wives often have separate tents from their husbands. It's a potentially awkward situation—but not for long, because she drives a tent peg through his temple, fulfilling Deborah's prophecy. Once again, God and His people gain victory over the enemy, and they have peace for forty years.

TODAY'S GOD SHOT

God chooses and appoints unlikely leaders: a left-handed man from a right-handed tribe, a Canaanite to lead the Israelites, and a woman. God uses the unlikely, not to pump up their self-esteem or give them bragging rights in front of the haters—that's prideful at worst and fleeting at best—but to reveal Himself at work, to reveal His heart for the overlooked. It's not even that He "sees potential" in these unlikely leaders, because it's not potential—it's a *reality*, and He created it, so He gets the credit and praise. We love stories of underdog champions and unlikely leaders; they bring Him glory, and they bring us joy, because they point to Him, and He's where the joy is!

JUDGES 6–7

Forty years after Deborah, the Israelites fall into sin again and are so oppressed by the Midianites that they hide in caves, and the Midianites eat all their food supply. After seven years, the Israelites cry out to God. Maybe they expect Him to send another judge, a military leader to rescue them. But God doesn't owe them that, and He knows they need something different at this point. He sends a prophet, someone to speak truth and call out their sin.

Meanwhile, a man named Gideon is beating out wheat in a winepress—which is an unusual place to do that, but it's because he's hiding the wheat from the Midianite food stealers. The Angel of the Lord shows up (likely God the Son). It seems God the Father also shows up here, disembodied. The Angel tells Gideon that God is with him, and Gideon basically says, "Oh really? God is with me? That's funny, because my life is a disaster. I actually feel pretty forsaken and forgotten by Him." Gideon questions the presence of God *to* the very presence of God!

God tells Gideon to deliver Israel from oppression, but Gideon pushes back. He's from the weakest clan in his tribe, and he's the least important person in that clan. God promises to be with him, but Gideon is skeptical. He offers God food and asks for a sign, then God the Son cooks the food with His staff and disappears. Wow! Gideon realizes whom he's dealing with and panics, but God tells him to receive His peace. Gideon builds an altar and calls it The Lord Is Peace.

God orders him to tear down his dad's pagan altars and idols and build an altar to God and offer a sacrifice to God. He obeys God but does it in the middle of the night to avoid getting caught. When he does get caught, the local men plan to kill him, but his dad stands up for him. In all of this, God is preparing them for war by ridding them of idols and calling them to worship Him.

Meanwhile the Israelites' enemies are stacking up against them. God's Spirit clothes Gideon, and his clan decides to follow him. Gideon's fear is always with him, so he decides to test God's plan by asking Him for a sign. Twice. He knows Mosaic law forbids this, and God already gave him orders face-to-face, so this is doubly disappointing. But God is patient—He knows the man He appointed for this task is given to fear. He doesn't rebuke or punish him for acting faithlessly. After God's double confirmation, Gideon and thirty-two thousand men set out for war. But God says the army is too big. He has Gideon send home anyone who is afraid *and* anyone who drinks water a certain way that seems to indicate they might be easier to attack. Gideon is left with three hundred men, 1 percent of his original army. God decreases the army so He can increase His glory. Gideon is probably extra afraid now, but God still doesn't rebuke him. Instead, He offers even more confirmation. He sends him to spy on the Midianites so he can hear what they say, because of course, God knows what they'll say. God gave a Midianite soldier a dream, God prompts another soldier to interpret it, and God arranges the timing of that conversation to happen at the very time and place where Gideon approaches the camp. The dream's interpretation is that Israel will defeat Midian.

So Gideon preps his soldiers with their weapons, right? No. He gets jars, candles, and trumpets for his soldiers, stationing them around the camp, and at ten o'clock, they make noise. The Midianites flee, and God turns their swords against each other. Gideon calls on people from other tribes to capture and kill the Midianites who had survived, and in tomorrow's reading we find out that 120,000 Midianites died in this battle.

TODAY'S GOD SHOT

Gideon doubts God a *lot*, and God never gets angry with him for it. God meets him in his questions. He's never impatient with Gideon's doubts and fears. He comes alongside him to embolden him, knowing that what Gideon needs to hear most isn't "You're awesome. You've got this. Believe in yourself! You may be the least in your family, but it's just because they're jealous of you." No. Gideon needs to hear *who God is*. God doesn't counter Gideon's doubt by puffing him up with positive self-talk; He says, "I am with you." And He's with you. And He's where the joy is!

JUDGES 8–9

Yesterday Israel's fearful fifth judge, Gideon, defeated the Midianites, but now the tribe of Ephraim is mad they weren't invited to the war, because they pride themselves on being warriors. They calm down when Gideon praises their prior military victories. Then he crosses the Jordan River in pursuit of two Midianite kings so they can finish off the war. He asks East Manasseh to feed his army. He's from West Manasseh, so these guys are technically from the same tribe, but they offer no support so he promises to destroy their town. Then he heads to Gad, the neighboring tribe to the south. They deny him food too, so he promises to destroy their tower. His anger is warranted, because these fellow Israelites are supposed to offer help, especially in war efforts. But Gideon's response seems a bit extreme, like he's operating out of insecurity.

He finally kills the two Midianite kings and steals their crescent ornaments, then returns to fulfill his threats to East Manasseh and Gad. Today's conquests feel different from yesterday's, likely because there's no mention of God. Gideon seems to be acting on his own impulses. When Israel tries to make him king, he says, "No, not me! God is your king," but immediately asks for all their gold jewelry. That's when things start to feel a little too familiar. He makes himself a golden ephod. Only the high priest is allowed to wear the ephod, so this violates God's commands and is an act of extreme arrogance.

Insecurity and arrogance are different sides of the same pride coin. Yesterday the coin was tails up—Gideon was full of fear and self-doubt. But today the coin has flipped heads up and he's full of himself. His time as Israel's judge has never been about God—it hasn't even been about *Israel*—it's always been about Gideon. And it shows. The people whore after his ephod, which may *feel* less sinful than worshipping pagan gods because it's YHWH adjacent, but it's not; it's still idolatry.

He has a lot of wives, concubines, and kids, and he names one son Abimelech, which means "my father is king." All his talk about God being king is just lip service; he wants to be king, and they seem to view him as king, but it's never ordained by God. Abimelech is divisive and scheming, trying to take over his dad's role even though other sons are in line before him. But the locals love his confidence. They give him money from the pagan temple, and he uses it to hire his sketchy entourage. He kills Gideon's other sons on one stone, possibly an altar, which likely means he's sacrificing them to Baal. In the midst of this mass murder, his youngest brother, Jotham, escapes.

The Shechemite leaders make him "king," but it isn't real. Jotham goes to the top of Mount Gerizim and tells them a parable to illustrate that Abimelech isn't a worthy king and he'll be destructive. Ultimately this is a prophetic curse, uttered from the mount of blessing. After he warns them, he flees. They don't listen, but Jotham leaves the consequences to God. God sends an evil spirit that causes division between Abimelech and his people, showing that even evil bends to God's will. Meanwhile, the Shechemites start to look for Abimelech's replacement, which leads to more fighting. The Shechemites set up an ambush, but Abimelech kills them and destroys the city altogether—even though he lives there! Some flee to a military stronghold, but he burns it down. Jotham prophesied this very thing. Now Abimelech needs a new place to live, so he goes to conquer Thebez, but a woman throws a stone, mortally wounding him. He has a man finish the job in a failed attempt to preserve his legacy. His manipulation never ceased.

TODAY'S GOD SHOT

God's justice is on display with Abimelech—he kills all his brothers on a stone, then dies by a stone. God's wrath and justice are *adjacent* to His love, not in contrast to it. When we love something, we have wrath toward anything that threatens it. We want to defend and protect it. When it comes to His name and His people, YHWH is vigilantly protective. Even in the midst of their wickedness and waywardness, He's still enacting justice to purify them and protect them from evil. In love and in justice, He's where the joy is!

JUDGES 10–12

Today we continue Israel's downward spiral with six bad judges. The Israelites are falling into apostasy again, worshipping seven groupings of other gods. They'll worship anything, it seems. God grows angry and sells them into the hands of two people groups, the Philistines and the Ammonites. They oppress them on the east side of the Jordan River and fight against them on the west side. Finally, Israel repents. But this time, God says things are going to happen differently. He's not going to raise up a judge to save them like He's done in the past. He says to cry out to those other gods for help instead. Their response to Him suggests that they really do get it this time—they agree that they don't deserve saving and they accept His words, while still begging Him for mercy and help. They know He's their only hope. Then they forsake their idols and worship YHWH.

Meanwhile the Ammonites in the Transjordan want war with Israel. The Israelites try to rally a sergeant for their army so they can fight, but instead of asking God for direction, they ask each other. They hastily appoint Jephthah, who is a lot like Abimelech. For being an outlaw and an outcast, he's pretty reasonable when he tries to negotiate with the Ammonite king. The king is angry because Israel took some land from him, but Jephthah explains why he's wrong: "We took it from someone else, not you, because you didn't own it when we conquered it. Besides, YHWH is the one who gave it to us, so you can't have it." The Ammonite king won't be reasoned with, and Jephthah knows he has a war on his hands.

God's Spirit travels with him as he passes through the land, protecting him. Even though he wasn't appointed by God as judge over His people, he has that role nonetheless, and God comes to help him. But Jephthah is hasty and makes a vow to God in an effort to win the war. If God grants victory, he'll sacrifice whatever comes out of his house first. He was probably expecting an animal, but this vow is foolish for a few reasons. First, God promised Israel victory if they kept His laws. *That's* the way to victory, not hasty vows. Second, when Jephthah's daughter comes out, that's the moment to cancel the vow and make a sin offering to God instead (Leviticus 5:4–6). When he says he can't take back his vow, he's wrong. Third, human sacrifice is strictly forbidden in at least four places in the books of the law. What Jephthah says is inconsistent with what God has said.

One caveat: Many people believe Jephthah didn't sacrifice his daughter but that he just consigned her to live as a single woman for the rest of her life. This would've saved him from the agony of murdering his daughter while leaving him with one consistent consequence. Whether she dies or lives as a single woman, his name dies with him since she's his only child. And regardless of which it is, she laments her lot in life. Lament is fitting; she even carves out time for it, and she does it in community, not alone.

Ephraim, the little tribe that's always looking for a fight, is mad that Jephthah didn't call them to fight with him, but he says he did. They threaten to burn his house down, so he fights them. They hurl insults and try to trick each other. The Ephraimites try to pose as Gileadites, but their accents give them away. This is the first internal battle between the tribes of Israel, and it's a sign that things are going downhill quickly.

TODAY'S GOD SHOT

"He became impatient over the misery of Israel" (10:16). What a tenderhearted God. God aches alongside us. He wants what is best for us even more than we do! When the Israelites keep choosing sin, He lets them hit rock bottom, but all the while His heart aches over their rebellion. He grieves when His kids are in misery, and He draws near. Psalm 34:18 says, "The Lord is near to the brokenhearted and saves the crushed in spirit." If you feel like the Israelites, miserable from your own rebellion, or if you feel like Jephthah's daughter, mourning your life circumstances, may you feel the nearness of the Lord in your brokenhearted state, and may your spirit feel somehow less crushed as you remember His great salvation. He is with you, and He's where the joy is!

JUDGES 13–15

Despite Samson's superhero image, he's probably the wickedest of all the judges. The Israelites have fallen into sin again and are oppressed by the Philistines for forty years. Then the Angel of the Lord (likely Jesus) shows up to tell the barren wife of Manoah that she'll have a son who'll help rescue Israel; He orders her to raise him under the Nazirite vow, which means no alcohol, no haircuts, and no touching dead things. God assigns Samson this vow for life, and it starts in the womb, so even his mom has to follow it during pregnancy.

Manoah and his wife seem to believe this prophecy; when they reference it, they say, "When this happens," not "If." They beg God for instructions and advice, offer a burnt offering, and worship God as "the one who works wonders." After Samson is born, God the Spirit begins prompting him about his calling. The first decision he makes—demanding to marry a certain Philistine—seems to be wicked and foolish, but underneath the demand is a plan set in motion by God. Samson is secretive, operating fairly independently, so even his parents don't know he's making an inroad to overthrow Israel's oppressors.

He also secretly kills a lion with his bare hands via the help of the Spirit. He keeps it a secret likely because it almost certainly violates the Nazirite vow about dead things. Not only does he touch a dead lion when he kills it, but he also touches it days later when he scoops honey out of its carcass. We begin seeing that he's prideful and entitled, driven by lust and impulsive desires, and he makes foolish decisions. He also breaks every rule of his Nazirite vow. His pride rears its head at his wedding feast, which almost certainly involved alcohol he wasn't supposed to drink but likely did. He taunts thirty Philistines with a riddle. When they can't solve it, they coerce his wife into getting the answer from him. Here we see his first sign of weakness: women. When the guys tell him the answer to his riddle, he's furious and embarrassed. He lost the bet and was betrayed by his new wife during his own wedding feast. So he goes to another Philistine town, kills thirty men, takes their clothes—which certainly involves touching their dead bodies—and then gives those clothes to the men who explained the riddle. One strange part of this text is that God the Spirit equips him for this task.

Later, when he returns and tries to consummate the marriage, his father-in-law tells him he's given his new bride to his best man, but he offers to let him marry her sister instead. Samson is enraged. He catches three hundred foxes, ties their tails together in pairs, lights them on fire, then sends them into a field to burn all the crops. The Philistines get revenge by burning his wife and father-in-law to death. Samson either kills more Philistines or beats them up in retaliation—the text isn't clear. They go back and forth until the tribe of Judah decides to capture Samson—*their own judge*—and turn him over to the Philistines as a bribe. While they're making the exchange, Samson breaks free and kills a thousand men, presumably Philistines, with a donkey's jawbone—which is touching the dead again.

One of the things you may have noticed is that the other judges fought with armies, but Samson didn't. Samson *was* the army. Every Philistine who died on his watch died by his hand. He's not a leader at all; he's a solitary vigilante. It's hard not to be impressed by him, though, and we definitely see God at work initiating and sustaining Samson's calling, but it can be a challenging text to work through theologically.

TODAY'S GOD SHOT

In God's complexity, He empowers sinful people with wicked motives to accomplish His righteous plan. He uses Samson's pride and rage to defeat Israel's enemy. When God's Spirit empowers Samson to do something, He's not endorsing Samson's sin, but sometimes He's using Samson's sinfulness to defeat a greater enemy. Any time God uses sinners (i.e., any of us), something is bound to be off track in us, but praise God, our sinful motives and actions aren't big enough to ruin His plan. He factored all that in! He uses us despite ourselves and even brings us joy in the process. He's where the joy is!

JUDGES 16–18

Today Samson visits a prostitute in Gaza, a Philistine city, so this is wicked on multiple levels. The locals plan to ambush him, but he leaves early and takes part of the city gate with him! Then he falls for a Philistine named Delilah, but the feeling isn't mutual—she's just a hired covert agent. The Philistine lords pay her 5,500 pieces of silver to find out the secret of his strength. Their curiosity suggests he isn't muscular—otherwise, they'd *know* where his strength comes from. But if he is, in fact, scrawny, then his feats of strength serve to glorify God, not his own body.

We learn a lot about him today: He's a deep sleeper, he has seven locks, either he's blinded by lust or he's arrogant and assumes he can't be overpowered (or both), and he does not learn from his mistakes. Delilah tries three times to find out where his strength comes from, and either he doesn't trust her or he's just being sneaky as usual. He lies repeatedly. When he finally explains that he's under a vow to God, he refers to God by His generic name, Elohim, not His personal name, YHWH. This shows us how he views God; it's the difference between knowing God and knowing *about* God.

He doesn't seem to take God's call on his life seriously. His disobedience leaves him vulnerable. Delilah gets her money and has a man shave his head, and the Spirit leaves him—at this point in history, this is possible because God the Spirit doesn't indwell people yet. The enemy overtakes Samson, and he's stripped of every aspect of his identity: his locks, his strength, and the Spirit. The Philistines' punishments are fitting because they correspond to his two major areas of sin. They gouge out his eyes, a major weakness for him, and they force him to do a woman's work, grinding at the mill, which has to be an affront to his pride. Without God, he doesn't even have the strength to do a man's work.

But as his hair grows back, so does his strength. They bring him out at a pagan festival as entertainment, which often involves taunting or beating a prisoner. It probably doesn't involve feats of strength, because as far as they know, he's weak. He cries out to God, *calling Him YHWH*, and asks for strength. Could it be that he's repentant? God gives him strength, and he pushes over two load-bearing pillars, destroying the pagan temple and killing everyone, including himself.

Then we see sheer anarchy in Israel. Micah, an Ephraimite, steals from his mom and then confesses, and she builds an idol to YHWH in response. This is the first of many instances where people show both a lack of awareness of God's laws *and* a total disregard for the ones they do know. Without leaders, people self-govern, but it's usually too subjective to be righteous. Micah sets up a temple in his house and ordains his son (who is not a Levite) as a priest; this secondary holy site is wicked and defiant. When he meets a Levite named Jonathan, who is appointed to live among Judah, Micah realizes this is his chance to have an actual Levite priest, and he tries to use God for selfish gain. He also makes his own ephod. It's good that he wants to know God's will, but he goes about it in ways that dishonor God. He's more interested in getting answers and being powerful than in drawing near to God.

The tribe of Dan never drove out the Canaanites, so they're looking for a new home. They ask Jonathan if it's okay to abandon the land God allotted. He gives them hopeful but wicked counsel, so they head to a town called Laish and kill unsuspecting people in a land *not* allotted to them before asking Jonathan to be their unauthorized priest in their unauthorized land.

TODAY'S GOD SHOT

Samson doesn't call God by His name until the end, and God meets this blind, rebellious prisoner in his hour of need. He doesn't say, "No, you've messed up too many times." God shows up with a yes to Samson's prayer and uses his tragic story as one of the steps toward setting His people free from oppression. He wants intimacy with us. Even in prisons and on death beds, He's ready to come closer. And that's good news for us whether we're in dire straits or in a place of abundance, because He's where the joy is!

JUDGES 19–21

Israel is living in total anarchy, which is beyond evident in today's reading. A Levite has a concubine, which is basically a household servant with fewer rights and less permanency than a wife and whose main job is to sleep with the boss and have his kids. She wants to leave this arrangement, but he goes to win her back. He meets her dad, who invites them to stay with him, but by day five the Levite is ready to head home. On the way, his servant suggests spending the night in a Canaanite city, but the Levite wants to keep moving until they hit an Israelite area. They stop in Gibeah among the tribe of Benjamin, and an old man urges them to stay at his place. The local leaders show up and demand to have sex with the Levite, but the old man offers his virgin daughter and the Levite's concubine instead. The locals don't like this offer, but the Levite saves himself by sending his concubine to them. God never endorses this—this is all the result of God's people turning away from Him.

The men rape her and beat her to death. The Levite doesn't even seem to be moved by her fate. It's heartbreaking and infuriating all at once. He takes her home, dismembers her, then sends pieces of her body throughout Israel, probably one piece to each tribe. Most scholars think he does this to prove that his story is true and that the Benjamites are guilty. In response, the men of fighting age from all the tribes except Benjamin gather. (The phrase *from Dan to Beersheba* refers to all of Israel, because the new city Dan just conquered is in the far north and Beersheba is in the far south.) Even the two and a half Transjordan tribes come. Nearly half a million men from eleven tribes gather to talk about what the Benjamites have done to the concubine. The Levite tells the story, conveniently leaving out the role he played, and asks what should happen in response to this abomination. They decide to confront the city of Gibeah.

First, they try to reason with the locals, asking them to bring out the men responsible so they can enforce the death penalty. But the town won't give them up; they protect their wicked leaders and refuse to hold them accountable. As a result, the Benjamites go to war against the rest of Israel. This is their first civil war. They fight for three days, and every day Israel asks God for guidance, He gives it, and they obey. They can't figure out why they're losing, since they're being obedient to God. But on days one and two God doesn't promise victory; He just tells them what to do. Obedience doesn't guarantee our desired outcome. Sometimes its purpose is to teach us faithfulness to God instead of our desires. On day three God says they'll win, and they defeat all the men of Benjamin except six hundred who hide.

Israel burns Gibeah, treating it like a Canaanite city. God never commands this, but they do it. While they're gathered, mourning and offering sacrifices to God, two things happen almost simultaneously: They're trying to figure out how to keep the tribe of Benjamin from disappearing altogether, and they realize there's a clan who didn't respond to the call to come fight, Jabesh-Gilead. *Without consulting God*, Israel puts together their most efficient plan: They send men to kill everyone in Jabesh-Gilead except female virgins, then bring back four hundred virgins to give to the six hundred surviving Benjamites. But since they're still two hundred women short, they hatch a plan for the Benjamites to kidnap some women while they're dancing at a festival. This passage is *descriptive*, not *prescriptive*. This is man's wicked plan to fix the circumstances they're in because of sin. When we fail to consult God and lean on our own understanding, we almost always make a bigger mess.

TODAY'S GOD SHOT

There wasn't much joy in today's reading, because there wasn't much God. The last line reminds us that "everyone did what was right in his own eyes," and the book ends with their wickedness increasing. Where God isn't feared and honored, where people do as they please and follow their own desires, there may be a temporary solution or a fulfillment of desires, but there isn't deep, lasting, sustaining joy. Because that isn't found in following every longing of our hearts—it's found in HIM. He's where the joy is!

RUTH 1–4

Ruth's story takes place during the time of the judges, when all kinds of wickedness is filling the land of Israel. The book opens with a married couple, Elimelech and Naomi, leaving their hometown to escape a famine. They settle in pagan Moab, across the Jordan River. After they and their two sons get to Moab, the sons do the very thing Moses warned them against. They marry women who worship other gods. Eventually, Elimelech and his sons die, leaving Naomi and her Moabite daughters-in-law to fend for themselves. Naomi is in dire straits—as a widow with no offspring, there's no way for her to be provided for, especially not in a foreign land that has no rules for providing for widows like Israel does. Fortunately, she gets word that the famine is over, so she packs her bags. She tells her pagan daughters-in-law to go back home, where they can start over.

Orpah goes home, but Ruth makes a shocking decision: She attaches herself to a destitute, depressed widow and leaves her country to move to a foreign land. As she's making this commitment to Naomi, Ruth invokes an oath to God and refers to Him as YHWH. This lets us know that something has happened in her heart; her allegiance has transferred from her pagan gods to Naomi's God.

They make it back to Bethlehem, but Naomi is bitter; she thinks God is mistreating her. She has no idea what's in store. Even as she complains, God's blessings are on their way, and every detail of timing and placement is orchestrated for her good. She sends Ruth to work in the field of a relative, relying on God's law that the Israelites must not reap the perimeters of their fields so the poor and sojourners can gather along the edges (Leviticus 19:9–10). Naomi's relative landowner, Boaz, sees Ruth working and asks about her. He's way out of her league; she's a foreign widow, and he's a wealthy leader in the community. But her work ethic and kindness catch his eye; her beauty may be implied, but Boaz only

For more information on today's reading, see thebiblerecap.com/links.

ever praises her character. He says her reputation of love, humility, and grace precedes her, and he treats her with an extra dose of generosity, even more than the law requires.

Naomi realizes there's potential and plays matchmaker. She tells Ruth to stop dressing like a widow and sends her to see Boaz at night. There's a lot of ambiguity here. Maybe she uncovers his feet so they'll get cold and it'll wake him up, but some scholars point out that the word *feet* is often a euphemism for a man's private parts. It's possible Naomi sent Ruth to seduce Boaz, but given the way Scripture continues to describe them both as upright and virtuous, we should likely conclude that they refrain from anything inappropriate. In fact, Boaz calls Ruth a worthy woman—the phrase used in Proverbs 31:10 in reference to a virtuous woman or an excellent wife.

Ruth basically proposes marriage to Boaz. He's interested but says there's a problem. According to the laws of Levirate marriage, someone else has the right of first refusal. Boaz makes an oath that if the man who is a closer relative says no, he'll marry her. Then he gives her more food and sends her home, promising to find a solution. He goes to the local gathering spot and fills the other guy in. That guy isn't interested, because whoever redeems a widow is responsible for giving her an heir, and this guy doesn't want to diminish his kids' inheritance by having more offspring. Boaz marries Ruth, they have a child, and everyone is thrilled!

TODAY'S GOD SHOT

This family displays God's heart to bring in the outsider. Boaz's mom is Rahab, the Canaanite prostitute who left her pagan life to follow YHWH. This son of an outsider marries an outsider and becomes the great-grandfather of King David. All these people are in the genealogy of Jesus! This story isn't just a fairy tale about the single girl getting married and finally having babies—it's about God working through loss, depression, longing, and famine to advance His plan to redeem His people, even as the Israelites spiral into wickedness more every day. Hang in there, Israel. Your king is coming. An earthly one first, then a divine one. And He's where the joy is!

1 SAMUEL 1–3

It's roughly 1050 BC, and the Israelites have been doing whatever they want. Things have grown continually worse in the promised land, and they're sure their problems would be solved if only they had a king. Elkanah and Hannah are a married couple from Levi, the tribe of priests, and Hannah is barren. Elkanah has a second wife, Peninnah, who isn't barren, but he loves Hannah more. Each year when they go to offer sacrifices at the tabernacle, Peninnah bullies Hannah. It's customary for each wife to have her own tent, so these trips may be the rare occasions when they interact.

Elkanah sees that Hannah is crushed, and in 1:8 he says something that goes against everything their culture values: "Am I not more to you than ten sons?" Ten sons would give him incredible prestige, so it's remarkable that he says their love is more valuable. But his sentiments don't comfort Hannah. After dinner, she goes to the tabernacle to cry out to God. She vows that if He'll give her a son, she'll set him apart as a lifelong Nazirite, like Samson. It's such a passionate prayer that the priest, Eli, thinks she's drunk. She explains her situation, and he leaves her with encouraging words that cheer her up. He blesses her and sort of prophesies that God will answer her prayer with a yes.

Soon after that, Hannah becomes pregnant with Samuel. True to her vow, she takes him back to God's house, offers an extravagant sacrifice, seeks out Eli the priest, and lets him know, "I'm the woman who asked God for a child. He said yes! And here's the child. I'm bringing him to you because his life is dedicated to serving God." Eli commits to raising Samuel in God's house, then Hannah worships God with a song. The song has three important themes we'll see demonstrated as we keep reading: God values humility and opposes pride, God is at work among His people despite all the chaos around them, and God will anoint and strengthen a future king.

For more information on today's reading, see thebiblerecap.com/links.

Eli raises Samuel but also has two sons, Phinehas and Hophni, who are horrible. They're priests, but "they did not know the LORD" (2:12). Scripture calls them "worthless men," *men of Belial* in Hebrew (or "a child of the devil"). They help themselves to more than the law allows, sometimes taking it by brute force; they take for themselves first instead of offering to God first; and they're sexually promiscuous. This isn't just casual disregard for God and His laws—it's contempt. They actually hate God's laws. Meanwhile, Samuel serves humbly. Eli has the authority to remove his sons from power, and God has even given him Samuel as an alternative, but all Eli does is rebuke them. Nothing changes. Since Eli won't remove them, God does. He sends a prophet to rebuke Eli and tell him everyone in his family will die young, including both sons, who will die on the same day. Only one man in his family will survive. God isn't breaking His promise to the Levites; the covenant He established with them has always been contingent upon their obedience. *They* broke it.

While Samuel serves in the tabernacle, God speaks to him audibly, but he has no idea what's going on. He hasn't even met God yet, so this is confusing; it's easy to see why he thinks Eli was the one talking to him. Eli eventually figures out that it's God and coaches Samuel on how to respond. God echoes His words to the prophet—Eli's family sinned with a high hand (Numbers 15:30–31) and they'll be cut off from God. Samuel is nervous to tell Eli the news, but he spills the beans when Eli threatens him. Eli surrenders to God's plan, saying, "It is the LORD. Let him do what seems good to him" (3:18). Samuel continues to serve and hear from God, and all his prophecies are fulfilled.

TODAY'S GOD SHOT

Hannah is the only female Scripture ever records as going to the tabernacle. She has real intimacy with God. She takes her pain to Him. This stands in stark contrast to Rachel (who was also barren) when she yelled at Jacob, "Give me children, or I shall die!" (Genesis 30:1). Hannah takes her problem to the one who can solve it, and she knows He can be trusted to care for her heart, regardless of the outcome. Hannah goes to God, because she knows He's where the joy is!

1 SAMUEL 4–8

Israel loses a battle with the Philistines and attributes the loss to God. But instead of consulting Him, they think they just need a lucky charm: the ark of the covenant. Eli's wicked sons help carry it off to battle, but Israel loses. A messenger tells Eli, "We lost the battle, your sons are dead, and the ark was captured." Eli knew his sons would die on the same day, so while it's heartbreaking, it's no surprise. However, the stolen ark is an unexpected tragedy for the entire nation. Eli dies when he hears the news.

The Philistines think they've defeated YHWH, since they captured what they *think* is Him. They've conflated God with the golden box that serves as His earthly throne. They put the ark in their pagan temple alongside the god they worship, Dagon. Then YHWH does something humorous and weighty. He repeatedly knocks Dagon facedown in front of the ark, a posture of worship, and even severs its hands and head! YHWH continues to afflict the Philistines wherever the ark goes—some get tumors, some die. They're distraught and want to return the ark to Israel, so they ask their priests and diviners for advice. They suggest sending a guilt offering to appease the Israelite God and to send it all on a cart pulled by milk cows. Why milk cows? Because they're untrained and have calves to feed, so their natural instincts mean they'll go home to their calves. But if they go against their natural instincts, then something supernatural is taking place, proving Israel's God must be in charge of all that's going on.

The cows go straight off into the distance. When they and the ark arrive at Beth-Shemesh in Judah, the Israelites offer the cows as a burnt offering to God. That sounds nice, but only male animals can be used for offerings (Leviticus 1:3). Also, seventy people look at the ark, violating God's law to shield it from view (Numbers 4:5–6). The Levites should know these things, so they're either ignoring God's laws or are ignorant of them—but even unintentional sin is still sin. God strikes them down, terrifying the people of Beth-Shemesh. They ask their neighbors in Kiriath-Jearim to take the ark, and they keep it for twenty years. The fact that it doesn't get returned to the tabernacle in Shiloh means Shiloh was likely destroyed by the Philistines, who probably rule over Israel at this point. As they often do when they're oppressed, the Israelites begin to repent.

By now, Samuel is their chief leader; he's their prophet, priest, and judge. He encourages them to fully repent and worship only YHWH—then God will deliver them from the Philistines. They fast, pray, make sacrifices, and repent. When the Philistines draw near to attack, Israel is afraid. Despite their shaky faith, God grants victory. Samuel raises a memorial stone to say, "Till now the LORD has helped us." They beat the Philistines. Samuel keeps watch to make sure everything keeps running according to God's commands. Two people who aren't obeying God are his sons, whom he set up as judges to preside over cases. They take bribes and disregard justice. The locals warn Samuel that things will go off the rails if he doesn't intervene. He's old, and his sons aren't fit to lead Israel when he dies. The people want a king like other nations have. God has made provision for a king, but He hasn't *called* for it. He says the people are rejecting Him but tells Samuel to give them what they want. Samuel warns them that it won't go well for them. This king will disregard God's commands in Deuteronomy 17:14–20, they'll beg God for help, and He won't send it. But Israel doesn't heed the warning.

TODAY'S GOD SHOT

God has set this nation apart to be different so other nations will recognize His glory. But anytime that starts to happen, Israel wants a different plan. The Philistines recognized His power, but the people of Beth-Shemesh don't and send the ark away! YHWH leads them, but they want a king as leader so they can be like other nations. They keep rejecting the very thing that makes them unique. He is their identity, but they just want to fit in and be respected. They're driven more by fear of man than by love of God. But man's approval is fleeting, so may this truth inform all our motives: He's where the joy is!

1 SAMUEL 9–12

God tells Samuel to appoint Israel's first king and arranges the circumstances of their meeting perfectly: He gets some donkeys lost, He puts an idea in the servant's head and a silver coin in his pocket, He stations girls at a well at what was probably an unusual time of day to be there, and He has it all line up not only with Samuel's arrival, but with the feast and with the future king's arrival too. *Whew!*

The new king is a Benjamite, the tribe that was almost completely wiped out not long ago. Apart from his appearance, Saul is an unlikely candidate for king. He's tall and handsome (and probably dark, because this *is* the Middle East, after all). Samuel invites him to the feast and gives him the most desirable piece of meat, which is reserved for the priest. He invites Saul to sleep on the roof, the most desirable sleeping spot because of the breeze. And as he walks Saul out of the city, he anoints him in the street by pouring oil on his head and says, "God has a plan for you to rescue His people. In case you don't believe me, here are three separate things that will happen on your way home." He tells Saul to go to Gilgal and wait for him for seven days, then he'll give him instructions on what to do.

All Samuel's prophecies come true on Saul's trip home, including the prophecy that God the Spirit would rush upon him and that Saul himself would prophesy. In the Old Testament, God the Spirit works this way, showing up to empower someone for a specific task or calling—this means God is with Saul to enable him to accomplish his task. And there's a noticeable change to those who knew him beforehand that can only be attributed to God's presence in his life.

Samuel calls everyone to gather. He privately anointed Saul but knows it's helpful for the people to see that he's God's choice, not just his, especially since Saul is from a tribe of ill repute. Samuel proceeds with the typical lot casting, and Saul is drawn, but they can't find him! God points out that he's hiding by the luggage. Saul appears fearful and reluctant—

he's not off to a great start. But when Samuel brings him out, most people approve. Samuel writes down the details of kingship for him.

Ammonite King Nahash is oppressing some Israelites, and when word gets back to Saul, God the Spirit rushes on him to equip him for action. Filled with righteous anger, he cuts up oxen and sends the pieces to all the tribes with word that they're required to come fight. And they win! Saul has an incredible first victory—it's the one shining moment in his kingship. He even shows grace to those who initially opposed his reign when others want to kill them. He wins the people over, and they renew his kingship.

Meanwhile, Samuel has retired as a judge, but he's still a prophet. He gives the people a chance to point out any of his errors, but Scripture regards him as honorable and the people confirm that. Like all the good leaders before him, he reminds them of all God has done for them and implores them to obey God. If they do, things will go well; if they rebel, things won't. Then he basically says, "When you asked for a king, you sinned. If I'm right, God will make it rain right now—on a clear day when you'd normally be harvesting your crops." *And it rains.* They beg Samuel to pray for them, and he says it's not too late for them. Even though they sinned, they can still turn to God. He hasn't cast them off.

TODAY'S GOD SHOT

In 12:22, Samuel says, "It has pleased the LORD to make you a people for himself." That's unbelievable! He actually delights in them, in us. After everything He's done for them, they've rejected Him as king, and still, He's so pleased that He chose them. He knew what He was getting into, adopting a bunch of sinners into His family and giving them a seat at His table. He knew they'd spill the food and stain the carpet and steal the wine goblet. And still, He knows He's sending the Redeemer to pay for all of it. He knows every wrong you've ever done and ever will do, and still, He's pleased to call you His child. No matter what regrets are in your past, no matter what sins you have yet to commit, Christ has paid the price for all the sins of all God's kids. He's where the joy is!

1 SAMUEL 13–14

Saul's son Jonathan is winning battles against the Philistines, but when they come back to retaliate, they bring many thousands of warriors and chariots, and the Israelites flee to the Transjordan. Remember yesterday when Samuel told Saul to wait for him at Gilgal for seven days? That almost certainly corresponds directly to what happens today. Saul is at Gilgal, much of his army is gone, and Philistines are breathing down his neck. He must feel panicked! But this is Israel, a nation-state of God's people, and their leaders are supposed to make decisions by consulting with God. Specifically, Saul is supposed to wait to hear from Israel's prophet Samuel, but it's been seven days and Saul is losing control of the people, so he does what only the priest is allowed to do: He offers a burnt offering to God.

As soon as he finishes, Samuel appears. Saul's impatience costs him dearly. He took matters into his own hands, disobeying not only the prophet of God but the law of God. He doesn't repent of his actions. He justifies them. God holds Israel's leaders to a high standard—they're supposed to be the first followers, not the decision makers. Saul shows he doesn't have what it takes to lead Israel well. This sin costs him the kingdom; God is raising up his replacement.

Meanwhile he still has the Philistines on his back. His army is tiny compared to theirs, and they have metal weapons. But Jonathan and his servant plan a sneak attack on the Philistines. While Saul is marked by fear, Jonathan is marked by zeal, courage, and trust in God. He and his servant kill twenty Philistines. Saul's men see the ruckus and do a head count to see who is fighting the Philistines. Saul demands for the ark (or maybe the ephod, according to some texts) to be brought in, because he wants to ask God a question. The priest tries to inquire of God for him, but Saul shuts him down. Instead of waiting for God's answer, he acts of his own volition again and goes to battle. Again Saul shows he's unfit to be Israel's king; instead of being directed by God's words, he's driven by his own impulses and fears. In the middle of the battle, he's impulsive again, making a vow to God and cursing anyone who eats food before sunset. It's a foolish move because soldiers fight better if they have sustenance, and not everyone is around to hear the vow, including Jonathan, who eats some honey.

They defeat the Philistines, the sun sets, and they're so hungry that they slaughter the animals and eat them quickly, before draining their blood. This violates God's command not to eat blood, because it represents life (Deuteronomy 12:15–16). Saul intervenes to try to solve the problem, then after they eat he builds an altar to God. It's an encouraging moment, but it's short-lived. In the next sentence he starts making decisions on his own again and plans to plunder the Philistine camp. The priest says they should stay put. Then Saul inquires of God—which is a great move—but God doesn't respond. Saul assumes God's silence means there's some kind of sin they need to deal with, so he casts lots to find out what's happening. Jonathan confesses to tasting honey and volunteers to die. He's repentant for his unintentional sin, demonstrating his integrity and trust in God's sovereignty. Saul is ready to go through with it, but the people stop him. They know God has used Jonathan and that Saul's vow was foolish and wicked. It's still a vow that God takes seriously, but the right thing to do is to not keep the vow and deal with the lesser sin of breaking it. Despite his wickedness, Saul continues to win battles and save Israel as God promised.

TODAY'S GOD SHOT

God is sovereign over timing. The tiny detail of Samuel's showing up right after Saul finishes offering the sacrifices and even the timing of Samuel's delay—it all figures into God's plan for Saul's successor. God uses even Saul's fear and impatience to move His plan forward, bending sin and rebellion to serve His ultimate will. This is such a great comfort to us—that nothing can ruin His plan and that He's active in every tick of the clock. David says it like this, "My times are in your hand" (Psalm 31:15). He owns every moment, and He's where the joy is!

1 SAMUEL 15–17

The Amalekites were the first to attack Israel in the wilderness. God commanded Israel to completely wipe them out, but that still hasn't happened so Samuel charges Saul with the task. Saul and his army win the battle, but he keeps the king—and lots of animals—alive. Saul's obedience is far from thorough, further proving he's unfit to be king. God talks to Samuel about Saul, and some translations say God regrets making Saul king. But 15:29 says God can't regret things. So which is it? The word is also translated "to be grieved," so it's possible this means God was grieved over making Saul king. God isn't saying He chose poorly; He's said all along how this choice would go for Israel, and now He's saying it went exactly like He said, and He's grieved over it.

When Samuel goes to confront Saul, he sees that Saul has set up a monument to himself, not God. As Saul brags about his obedience, two noteworthy things happen: (1) Saul refers to YHWH as "your God," not "my God" or "our God," and (2) Samuel hears animals. He confronts Saul, but Saul doesn't repent; he tells a series of lies about why the animals are there: "I obeyed. . . . I disobeyed but it was for a good reason. . . . The people were actually the ones who disobeyed." Samuel shuts him down. Any time Saul does his own thing, it's as bad as if he were following a false god—he has become his own god. He rejected YHWH, so YHWH rejects him as leader of His people. God has raised up a new king. When Saul hears this, he confesses. He feels the pinch, but he seems to respond only to consequences. Samuel has to finish Saul's job for him, killing the Amalekite king. But Samuel has a hard time with it all, like he feels responsible for Saul's failure. God says it'll all work out and that Samuel will play a part in that, because he'll anoint the new king!

Samuel goes to meet Jesse and his sons, but God says no to them all, even the tall one! God says the choice is about character and integrity, not inseam. He gives the thumbs-up to David, who's been out working on the family farm. Samuel privately anoints him as king. Then God the Spirit leaves Saul and comes to David, showing up as He does in the

Old Testament to equip and empower a person for a specific task. Since Saul's time on the throne is ending and David is being raised up, this is a natural transition of the Spirit's location and power. After He leaves Saul, God sends a harmful spirit to him. While God is never the active agent of evil, He does use the work of evil spirits to His own ends.

Saul's men see he's not doing well and suggest hiring a musician, namely David. When David plays, the harmful spirit leaves. Meanwhile the Philistines are back, trying to get more land. This war is different: Each side picks their strongest man, and the winner takes all. The Philistines have a giant named Goliath, whom no one wants to face, not even David's brothers, who are on the sidelines. One day David's dad asks him to take lunch to his brothers, and he arrives just as Goliath mocks Israel. When David asks about the winner's reward, Saul tries to shut him down, but David pushes back and Saul concedes. Goliath's armor alone probably outweighs David, but David rejects armor and goes with what he knows, a sling and a powerful battle cry. He stands in stark contrast to Saul, who is consumed by fear. David kills Goliath with one swing of a slingshot, decapitates him, and keeps his skull as a trophy. Then Saul takes more interest in David, wanting to know all about him. It may sound great for the king to attach himself to you, but it's probably not as great if he's tormented by a demon!

TODAY'S GOD SHOT

God's emotions are evident today, like when He's grieved over making Saul king. Even though He knows everything and is outside of time, He's still *in time* as well. He's in each moment with us. He hates that things are happening the way they are with Saul, even though He set it in motion and knows it will all work out smoothly in the end. The fact that He has emotions—that He's not removed and distant and unaffected—invites us to draw nearer to Him in each moment. He not only sits with us in our pain, but He's also where we access comfort and joy—because He's where the joy is!

1 SAMUEL 18–20; PSALMS 11, 59

Now that David is a local hero, Saul is *very* interested in knowing more about him. Jonathan is impressed by David too. Their society operates under the tradition of primogeniture, where the firstborn takes over the father's position eventually, but it's not a rule. Jonathan probably assumed he'd succeed his father as king, but today he gives David some gifts and they seem to indicate that he thinks David should be king instead of him. The local women praise David too and credit him with winning the war. Normally this credit would go to the king, so when it goes to David, Saul feels threatened. When Saul gets a visit from a demon, he tries to kill David twice, and he'll try at least fourteen more times. But God thwarts all of Saul's plans. Saul fears David because God is with David, not him. Saul has no concern for God's glory or what's best for the nation—he only seeks to serve himself. Self-focus is like fertilizer on fear.

Saul's plan B is to get David killed in war; but David succeeds, and everyone loves him even more. Saul moves to plan C: luring David into marrying his daughter Michal. This was supposed to be one of the prizes for killing Goliath, but apparently Saul defaulted on that and now he's requiring one hundred more Philistines be killed in order for David to marry Michal, hoping David will be killed in the process. But David doubles down, killing two hundred. Saul's efforts to destroy David only build him up. Saul may hope that Michal will lead David away from YHWH, because she practices idolatry (19:13).

Plan D is to get Jonathan and his servants to kill David. But Jon isn't on board. He tries to reason with Saul, and Saul pretends to concede. Jon tells David all is well, so David comes back to work for Saul. After David wins another war, Saul throws another spear at him. His demon always shows up after David has a great victory on God's terms: being anointed as king, killing Goliath, defeating the Philistines. David runs, and Saul sends assassins to David's house, but his wife, Michal, hatches a plot to save him and lies to the assassins while David runs to Samuel's house. Saul sends three teams of assassins there and even ends up going himself. But the joke's on him, because God sidetracks them all with praise and prophecy. God is sovereign, even over the efforts of an evil king. Saul is humbled.

Jon still believes his dad's promise not to kill David, but they make a plan for David to escape if Saul is, in fact, still after his life. David promises Jon he'll show favor to him and his family regardless. When there's a feast that David is expected to attend, he doesn't show up, and Saul gets suspicious. Jon lies about David's whereabouts, and just like with Michal's, it's a lie to protect a human life, which seems to be the more honorable option. But Saul doesn't believe him, and he threatens to take the kingdom away from Jon. But God has already told Saul that the kingdom has been appointed to someone else, so it's not Saul's to give. Then Saul attempts to murder his own son, the heir apparent. Now Jon knows his dad has been lying to him and David wasn't just paranoid. Jon commences with their plan for David's escape. They part ways with tears, blessings, and the holy kiss that serves as an ancient Near Eastern greeting. Then we read two psalms David wrote during or about all this.

In Psalm 11, David trusts God in the midst of the attacks on his life and doesn't doubt God's love, despite the testing he's enduring. He declares his innocence in regard to his enemies' attacks. In Psalm 59, he recounts God's past faithfulness, reminding himself who God *is* in the present and *will be* in the future. He preaches the truth to himself.

TODAY'S GOD SHOT

In Psalm 59:8, David talks about his enemies, who are also God's enemies, and says, "You, O Lord, laugh at them." The only circumstance in which Scripture mentions God laughing is at His enemies. His laughter at them should be a comfort to His kids, because it serves as a reminder that He's not worried. He has defeated His and our enemies. He's protecting us and defending His name at the same time. God laughs at His enemies because their plans will never succeed against Him. He's victorious, He's protective, and He's where the joy is!

1 SAMUEL 21–24

As a fugitive, David stops in Nob because he needs food and weapons. Ahimelech the priest seems suspicious, and David lies to protect his own life. This is less like Rahab's lie to protect the spies and more like Abraham's lie that Sarah was his sister—it's about saving himself, not others, and it suggests he doesn't believe God's promise to make him king. He breaks another law by eating the holy bread, which is only for priests; Ahimelech makes a concession here—people over process—and it's hard to know how to feel about it at the time. However, Jesus refers to this rule bending as a reminder that inherent in the law is the spirit of the law, which is that God values mercy over law (Matthew 12:1–8).

Doeg the Edomite is there too, probably as a prisoner of war. He watches closely, maybe thinking any information he gains can serve as his ticket to freedom. He sees David take Goliath's sword and flee to enemy territory, Philly-ville, to escape Saul. David meets Achish, lord of the city of Gath, who recognizes him. David may have wanted to offer himself as a mercenary, but the Gath locals are suspicious of him so he acts insane and flees back to Judah. He and his family live in a cave; their lives may be at stake too because of him. He assembles a ragtag bunch of outcast followers: four hundred men in distress, in debt, bitter, and discontent. They head east to Moab across the Jordan, and David drops his parents off; they're old and unfit for life on the lam. Moabites and Israelites are enemies, but David's great-grandmother Ruth was a Moabite, so he has roots in the land. Also, he and the Moabites now share a common enemy: Saul. He heads back west across the Jordan and stays at a stronghold in the desert until a prophet warns him to leave and he moves to a forest.

Saul gets suspicious that all his servants and troops have betrayed him, so Doeg the Edomite seizes the opportunity to prove he's no traitor and spills the beans. Saul summons Ahimelech and the priests from Nob and accuses him, but he pleads innocent and ignorant. Still, Saul orders Doeg to kill them all, and eighty-five priests die. Saul's army kills everyone in Nob too, including animals—but Ahimelech's son Abiathar escapes and fills David in. David pledges loyalty to him, and Abiathar becomes his priest for life.

Meanwhile, Keilah in Judah is attacked by the Philistines, so David consults with God, who promises and grants victory. Saul gets word of David's whereabouts and tries to chase him, but God gives David the inside scoop, so Saul can't find them. Next, David and his crew go to the wilderness of Ziph, and Jonathan shows up and acknowledges that both he and his father know David is Israel's next king. Meanwhile, some people from Ziph tip Saul off that David is there. Saul heads that way, but as soon as David is within sight, Saul gets word that the Philistines have attacked, and he has to rush back to war. Foiled again! You'll never get what God won't give.

Next David moves to an oasis called Engedi. When Saul comes to find him, he brings three thousand men. While David and his guys are in a cave, Saul comes in to relieve himself. David's men quote God's promises as a reason for him to take action, but we don't actually see that God said these things to David, so it's possible they're inventing promises or misapplying something they've heard. David wisely resists their words. His trust in God enables him to wait well. David cuts off part of Saul's robe, which lets him prove his intentions to Saul (see 1 Samuel 15:27–28).

David has no faith in the king, but he shows respect for the king and faith in God all at once. He trusts God's sovereignty over even the length of this wicked ruler's reign. He knows it will come to an end in God's perfect timing.

TODAY'S GOD SHOT

God has incredible timing. From a surprise attack by the Philistines that pulls Saul away at the last minute to Saul's need to relieve himself just as he approaches the very cave where David is hiding, everything we saw today was so perfectly timed that it almost read like choreography. God invites us into this dance with Him in which He guides His kids, always making a way to fulfill His plans no matter what attacks the enemy has in mind. He leads us so well, and He's where the joy is!

PSALMS 7, 27, 31, 34, 52

Today we read several psalms David wrote during or in response to his time as a fugitive.

Psalm 7 is a lament. As a refugee, David declares that God is his refuge. He may be on the run, but he maintains his innocence, much like Job did. He invites God to let his enemies punish him if he's guilty. And if he's innocent, then those who falsely accuse him are the guilty ones, so he asks God to punish them. He knows God is a God of justice, and he appeals to Him on that level. Near the end, he makes some general references to the terms of God's covenant with Israel in regard to sin and repentance and asks God to turn the acts of the wicked back on them as a part of His plan to bring restoration on earth.

Psalm 27 is also a song of lament and of confidence in God. David calls God his light, his salvation, his stronghold. He may have even written this while he was in the stronghold in the wilderness. Despite having a safe place to live, what he really wants is God's nearness. In 27:5, when he says, "He will conceal me under the cover of his tent," the word for *tent* is the same word used for the Tent of Meeting, where God's special presence dwelled. Instead of dwelling in the stronghold, he wants to dwell in God's tent. Then David says he'll offer sacrifices and shouts of joy. These are probably the same shouts of victory Israel gave when they defeated Jericho. It's like he's recounting God's relationship with Israel through the years, remembering who God is before petitioning God for help. He believes he'll see God's goodness in *this* life, not just in eternity. He has God's promise of his kingship to cling to, so he believes God even when his life appears to be at stake. He preaches the truth to himself again, telling his heart to be strong and courageous and to wait for the Lord.

By now, at Psalm 31, you may be seeing a pattern in how these laments tend to go. He starts with praise, brings his complaints and requests, and ends with praise again. By bookending his laments with praise, he's surrounding his needs with reminders of who God is. He calls God a stronghold again, a rock of refuge. Some scholars believe he lived at

Masada when he wrote this—it fits a lot of his imagery. Masada is a huge rock in the wilderness where King Herod will later build his desert fortress.

On the cross, Jesus quoted verse 5: "Into your hand I commit my spirit." David trusts God with his life. That trust comes from personal experience and from remembering God's covenant with His people.

David says, "My strength fails because of my iniquity" (31:10). Maybe he wonders if he's done something to bring this on himself, or maybe he's mourning over the deaths he caused by lying to Ahimelech. Even though that lie wasn't the cause of his distress, it was a sinful response in the midst of his distress. David felt like God cut him off, but now he realizes that was just his fear speaking. God rescued him in His own time.

Psalm 34 is one of thanksgiving. David praises God for delivering him and invites others to trust God too. He reminds the listener that looking to God delivers us from fears—not necessarily from the things we fear, but from the fear itself. In verse 13 he says, "Keep your tongue from evil and your lips from speaking deceit." Maybe David is preaching to himself here regarding the way he lied to Ahimelech. God attends to the righteous, and even though their lives won't be trouble-free, He's in the habit of delivering His kids. The righteous and the wicked will both have trouble, but the righteous are promised a different ending.

Psalm 52 has harsh words for Saul and possibly for Doeg the Edomite, but it also emphasizes God's justice and faithfulness as opposed to David's desire for revenge. He trusts his relationship with God to be all he needs in the midst of trouble.

TODAY'S GOD SHOT

Psalm 34:5 says, "Those who look to him are radiant, and their faces shall never be ashamed." You're looking to Him. He's changing and expanding your understanding of Him. You're carrying with you a new light and hope that's brighter than it was 105 days ago. Surely there's a new radiance to you because you're fixing your eyes on Him, and He's where the joy is!

PSALMS 56, 120, 140–142

Through more songs, David responds to God in light of his circumstances. And as a refresher, he's been promised the throne, but the current king has been hunting him down until recently, and he's living in the desert. Most of these psalms have some lament woven into them, but they also contain lots of hope.

In Psalm 56, David reminds himself of what is eternal, and he fixes his eyes on that—on God—in the midst of his troubles. It's easy to think God is distant or unfeeling when we endure trials, but David knows that's not true. God has kept count of his tossings, stored his tears in a bottle, and recorded all of this in detail in His book. God knows and God sees. He's not distant. David knows God is for him, despite what his circumstances say.

Psalm 120 is different from most laments, since it's short and doesn't end with hope or praise. It's his honest thoughts, his heart's cry to God, unpolished and seemingly incomplete, yet it's preserved in Scripture. It probably mirrors our prayers more closely than many of the other psalms he wrote. This psalm serves as a reminder that God invites us into conversation even when our prayers are unpolished and our hearts are in disarray.

Psalm 140 is another unusual psalm. David begs for deliverance from the words, hands, and plans of evil men. He asks God to be attentive and praises Him for being his covering: "Oh LORD, my Lord, the strength of my salvation, you have covered my head in the day of battle" (140:7). This is reminiscent of the helmet of salvation Paul references in Ephesians 6:17. With God as his covering, David has protection *and* salvation. And that's our only hope as well—Christ as our covering. David asks God to thwart the plans of the wicked, acknowledging God's sovereign control over the plans of man. When he prays for the destruction of his enemies, it may be hard to stomach, but these are God's enemies too, not just David's. David knows God is a God of justice and that the righteous will praise Him for His actions on their behalf.

He continues in Psalm 141 with a request for God to listen and act quickly. He's not near the tabernacle—he's in the wilderness—so he can't be there for sacrifices and incense burning. All he's got to offer are his prayers and his hands in praise, so he asks God to accept those offerings. He also asks God to guard his heart and his words. He knows how the human heart can easily be led astray, so even more than he asks God to protect him from his enemies, he asks God to grant him personal integrity. He wants to surround himself with the righteous, and he longs for accountability. If you've ever been without strong Christian community, his desires here may resonate with you. He's surrounded by six hundred men, but it's likely that none of them are on the same level with him here. They may not know God like he does, or they may be too impressed by the giant slayer to speak honestly with him. He probably feels very alone.

Today's final chapter, Psalm 142, has such depth of ache mingled with an abounding hope. David says, "I pour out my complaint before him; I tell my trouble before him." This is reminiscent of Hannah when she cried to the LORD in 1 Samuel 1:9–18. David feels utterly alone here, but not without faith that God will shift things for him soon.

TODAY'S GOD SHOT

God stores up David's tears, counting and recording all his tossings, being attentive to it all. David has lived in the palace, he's a war hero, he has worshipped at the tabernacle, he has a best friend who risked his life for him, yet here he is, living on a rock in the desert with six hundred men who don't really get him while he clings to a God he can't make sacrifices to. He can't keep the festal calendar in the city. He can't bring his tithe. He has nothing to offer God but prayer and praise and tears. *And God treasures every bit of it.* David knows that he comes to God empty-handed and that he's deeply in need of everything. He cries out to his only hope, who is also our only hope. Our God knows we have nothing to offer Him, but He delights in us still. You can take your needs and your nothing to Him—He's where the joy is!

1 SAMUEL 25–27

Saul has acknowledged that David is the next king, so the timing is right for Samuel to die, which is how our reading opens today. Meanwhile, David and his crew are protecting the flocks of a rich man named Nabal while he's out of town. They ask Nabal for provisions to keep the feast, but he refuses and even insults David, so they plan to attack his estate and take what he refused to give. David makes a vow to kill all the males in his house. It's interesting to see how different David's response to Nabal is from his response to Saul. One of Nabal's servants takes this information back to Nabal's wife, Abigail, telling her how honorable and helpful David's men have been to them.

She gets a lot of food and wine and takes it to David, without mentioning it to her husband. When she drops off the supplies, she humbles herself and accepts blame for everything that's gone wrong, even though it's not her fault. This defuses David's anger. She reasons with him, wishes him well, and indicates that she knows both David's past and future. Unlike Nabal, who insulted David, she references the way he killed Goliath with a slingshot and seems to know he'll be Israel's next king. She believes in and supports him, and it calms David down. He relents. This means he's breaking his vow to God, but we've learned by now that it's better to break a vow than to take a life. David realizes what a blessing she's been to him and that God sent her at just the right time, before he killed a bunch of innocent men in an act of revenge.

When Abigail tells Nabal about it, he physically responds with either a heart attack or a stroke or a coma, then God kills him. David goes back and marries her, and she continues to show him respect. She's leaving her wealthy estate behind to marry a man who moves around in the desert—at the moment, this isn't a lifestyle upgrade. Prior to all this, David's first marriage, to Michal, ended without his consent. Saul gave her to another man when he thought David betrayed him. We'll find out later that David was not okay with that.

David goes back to Ziph, and the locals tattle on him to Saul again. Despite the conversation they had outside the cave bathroom, Saul keeps hunting David. David and one of his men, Abishai, sneak into Saul's camp while he's sleeping. Just like the men in the cave, Abishai encourages David to kill Saul then and there—it would be quick and easy. But David refuses to do God's job for Him. Instead, he takes Saul's spear and water jar, and when he's a safe distance away, he calls out to them to make his point. He drives it home by saying, "If God sent you here, I receive this. But if you're here because of the words of men or the fear of man, then knock it off. Those men are cursed. They even said I should worship gods besides YHWH!"

Saul gets it and he blesses David—but this makes David wonder if there'll ever be a day when he doesn't have to run from Saul. Last time they talked, he thought he was in the clear, but it came unhinged again. Prolonged trials will always lead to despair and sin if we fail to trust God. And that's the path David heads down. He begins to think Saul will prevail, so he leaves Israel and goes back to King Achish in Philistia for asylum. He asks Achish for land to live in and turns his attention to raiding little towns on the edge of Philistia—like the Israelites should've done a long time ago. David is making strides to fulfill God's command, but instead of slaughtering the spoils, he brings them back to Achish and lies about their origin. He's pretending his raids are on Israel to earn Achish's trust. This is a holy war, but it's still not a good look for David.

TODAY'S GOD SHOT

God works beautifully through Abigail. He grants her wisdom to know how to de-escalate a situation that's about to get out of control. It takes real trust in God to enter into chaos and create peace. Scripture marks her as a woman of discernment, which is God-given. Proverbs 16:21 says, "The wise of heart is called discerning, and sweetness of speech increases persuasiveness." The wise in heart also know that joy isn't found in getting our own way—it's found in yielding to His way, because He's where the joy is!

PSALMS 17, 35, 54, 63

Since Samuel anointed David as king, life has only gotten tougher, so he turns his words godward. In Psalm 17, he claims his lips are free from deceit. We've seen his pattern of lying to Achish (even though that may be considered acceptable by wartime standards), but David isn't claiming to be morally perfect—he's saying he's innocent of the things he's been accused of by Saul and perhaps others. In this instance, Saul is the liar. David trusts that God will come to his rescue and acknowledges subtle ways God has already done that. He says, "With regard to the works of man, by the word of your lips I have avoided the ways of the violent." This has been true for him with Nabal and twice with Saul. Verse 10 in particular is reminiscent of his encounter with Nabal: "They close their hearts to pity; with their mouths they speak arrogantly." He affirms that worldly men often see benefits on this earth—both Saul and Nabal certainly did—but it's all they'll get. They have no eternal treasure. David knows that the presence of the LORD is the only place where true fulfillment exists.

In Psalm 35, David's prayers take a military turn. He uses battle imagery—some of it's literal, some of it's spiritual, and some of it may even be both. For instance, he asks the Father to send the Angel of the LORD (likely God the Son) to his rescue. Sometimes when the Angel of the LORD shows up, He's there to protect against enemies or as a force in battle. While it's true that God the Son is gentle and humble when He walks on earth, He's also a warrior.

David speaks promises of future praise, preaching the truth to himself. He knows God is attentive to the needy and weak, and David himself has demonstrated such godly characteristics toward his enemies when they were sick and mourning. But now they're falsely accusing him, so he asks God to rescue him. If you've ever been misunderstood or misrepresented, you can probably relate to a lot of his pleas. He asks God to vindicate him according to God's righteousness, not his own, and for

God's name's sake, not his own. He acts in humility while boldly praying for justice. This isn't a contradiction—this is trust in God's character.

Psalm 54 is about David's encounter with the Ziphites, who have twice exposed him to Saul. Will it be hard for him to serve them well when he's finally king over them? Will it be difficult not to hold a grudge? In verse 5, he says, "He will return the evil to my enemies; in your faithfulness put an end to them." It seems like he doesn't just want them to know the truth, but he wants them destroyed. And of course, some of this may be hyperbolic language—it's poetry, after all. So we have to hold it with a bit of an open hand.

Psalm 63 exudes confidence in God, even though it opens with longing. David is likely living in the wilderness when he writes this, and he says, "My soul thirsts for you; my flesh faints for you, as in a dry and weary land where there is no water." He recounts the days when he wasn't living in the desert, when he could worship God in the sanctuary. He recalls those days with fondness. Most of us have easy access to Christian communities and a church on every corner, but David has no idea how long it'll be before he's able to worship God in the ways the law requires of him. He longs for the day when he'll be able to participate in feasts and sacrificial offerings again instead of being a fugitive and an outcast.

TODAY'S GOD SHOT

David clings to God, because even though he's far from the tabernacle, God's presence is still with him. In the wilderness, when everything God promised him seems impossibly distant, David knows God is upholding him: "But the king shall rejoice in God; all who swear by him shall exult, for the mouths of liars will be stopped" (63:11). His faith is strengthened, and he knows these three things are true: (1) He'll be king, because God promised it, (2) God is trustworthy and praiseworthy and you can stake your life on that, and (3) in the end, that trustworthy, praiseworthy God will work justice. In David's desert wasteland, he opens his parched mouth to praise God. David knows He's where the joy is!

1 SAMUEL 28–31; PSALM 18

The Philistines want to attack the Israelites, and King Achish is relying on his buddy David to help him out. After all, David has been making raids on Israel for a while now, right? No? Uh-oh. What will David do? The narrative leaves us with a cliffhanger.

Not long ago, Saul had his second near-death experience with David. When you've stared death in the face, and your former mentor dies, and you're being tormented by a demon, and you're about to lose your job, and one of your powerful enemies is attacking you, that's a lot to deal with. This doesn't excuse Saul's actions, though. On the contrary, many of his trials are the consequences of his own actions. He tries to inquire of God, but that falls through, which highlights an interesting pattern we see in Scripture: When someone asks God for direction, but they aren't following His existing directions, He often won't tell them anything new. Saul experienced this earlier in 14:37. He's unrepentant, which is why God rejected him as king—it's all connected. So when he asks God what to do about the Philistines, God doesn't reply. Instead of repenting, Saul doubles down on his sin. He disguises himself and consults a medium, which God forbids. He's seeking answers from an enemy of YHWH, asking for help communicating with the dead, namely Samuel.

What happens isn't a normal occurrence for this medium, because when she calls Samuel he actually shows up, and she's shocked—she screams! So we can assume that whatever measure of power she normally operates in—whether fake or demonic—this rare occurrence is outside of her control. The narrator leaves us to assume that God has actually intervened here. What does Saul get for all his trouble? The same old prophecies but with two extra bits of bad news: He and his sons will die tomorrow, and the Philistines will defeat Israel.

Then we cut back to Achish, who is taking the Philistines to war with David in tow. The lords of the other Philistine cities don't trust him and tell Achish to send him back home. Through their mistrust of David, God saves him from potentially having divided loyalties, which could disqualify him from serving as Israel's king. He goes back to his home in Philistia and sees the Amalekites have attacked while the Philistines are away at war. His city has been burned, his family has been taken captive, and his people want to kill him. In the midst of this tragic loss, he knows where to turn for hope and strength: He inquires of God. God says to pursue the Amalekites and he'll win. Along the way, he meets an Egyptian who helps him. David had fled his homeland to escape his enemy, and he made a home in the midst of his other enemies, who were attacked by a third enemy, and then he gets help from another enemy. Wow.

He has four hundred men with him when he attacks, but two hundred others are too tired and stay behind. He raids the Amalekites and gets everything back, then shares the spoils with everyone, even the two hundred who were exhausted. Some of the four hundred aren't happy about this, but David shuts them down. He demonstrates God's generosity here, recognizing this is all a gift from God that he can freely share.

When Saul fights the Philistines, he loses, and he and three of his sons die. First Chronicles 10:13–14 says Saul died for his breach of faith, and it references his visit to the medium. And remember when God decapitated the Philistines' statue of their god Dagon? According to 1 Chronicles 10:10, it seems the Philistines took the head of Saul and affixed it to the headless body of Dagon. After the battle, the Israelites in the surrounding cities flee, and the Philistines take over their towns.

TODAY'S GOD SHOT

David wrote Psalm 18 on the day God saved him from all his enemies. He testifies to God's goodness through his trials. While he makes a lot of claims about his righteousness, he also says it and all his blessings are gifts from God. It's God who makes his way blameless, and God is the one who equips him, delivers him, and protects him. First Samuel 30:6 says, "David strengthened himself in the Lord his God." He doesn't strengthen himself in himself. He strengthens himself in the Lord his God! God is the source of all the good things we offer back to Him. And He's where the joy is!

PSALMS 121, 123–125, 128–130

These seven psalms are among the fifteen chapters known as the Songs of Ascent. To understand their purpose, we need a view of Israel's landscape. Jerusalem will eventually be Israel's capital, serving as the headquarters for the tabernacle and the temple. Jerusalem is at a high elevation, so no matter where you're coming from, you have to go *up* to Jerusalem—hence the ascent. Up to three times a year, all the tribes of Israel, who've been dispersed throughout the land, come together to celebrate the holy days. Scholars say they sing these fifteen songs as they make their pilgrimage. These are their road trip hymns—some even refer to travel or things travelers need to be mindful of. Psalm 121, for example, is a psalm of confidence in how YHWH is never tired or distracted, unlike the pagan gods, who require sleep and reportedly return to the underworld at night. Since the Israelites have to sleep along highways as they travel to Jerusalem, it's probably comforting to be reminded that YHWH is awake and watching over them. David also says God provides shade for them, which is especially nice if you happen to be traveling through the Judean desert.

Psalm 123 calls to God in the midst of distress and oppression, which the Israelites will continue to spend a lot of time dealing with. On their journey, they'll likely pass through areas where their enemies live, so they ask God for mercy. This flows right into Psalm 124, which says God's protection is the only way they've survived distress and oppression so far. Their trials have been abundant, but God is their help. It's good for them to have to sing this song three times a year, because we know how easy it is for them to forget God.

Psalm 125 affirms the blessings that will come to those who remember God and trust Him and says God will uproot the unrighteous. By the way, Mount Zion, which is referenced in this psalm, is the highest point in ancient Jerusalem, just outside the city gates. Because it's so noteworthy, it becomes a way of referring to Jerusalem; the two names are often used interchangeably.

In Psalm 128, we see references to God's covenant with the Israelites. He's told them if they keep the covenant, they'll live in the land and be fruitful and blessed, but if they break the covenant, they'll be oppressed and exiled. This song encourages them with the blessings of keeping the covenant.

Here's one important caveat for chapters like this: These texts present us with details about God's character and how He operates in general, but there's some stickiness in trying to apply them with the same one-to-one ratio today. For instance, not every obedient person is guaranteed to have children. These promises are based on God's covenant with the Israelites—a specific covenant with a specific people. It's important for us to honor context for a few reasons: (a) It helps us understand God's character rightly, (b) it saves us from the error of entitlement, and (c) in this specific instance, it also keeps us from judging others as obedient or disobedient based on their circumstances.

While Psalm 128 points out the blessings God brings to the home, Psalm 129 highlights all the ways God blessed Israel as a whole. And in Psalm 130, they recount the ultimate blessing: not just peace in the home or peace in the land, but peace with God Himself. He's the one who forgives their sins and redeems them!

TODAY'S GOD SHOT

"With you there is forgiveness, that you may be feared" (130:4). The fear of God consists primarily of delight and awe. If that weren't true, the two halves of this verse wouldn't fit together. It would have to say, "We know You're going to come down hard on us, that You may be feared" or "With You there is forgiveness, so we're drawn to You." Instead, we see that God's forgiveness of our sins inspires respect, awe, and delight—it draws us to Him! That's what the fear of God looks like. No matter how we've walked in iniquity and rebellion, we can come to Him for forgiveness, knowing that we have pardon and redemption because of Christ's full payment for our sins on the cross. The fear of the Lord enhances our lives in every way—He's where the joy is!

2 SAMUEL 1–4

Samuel appointed the new king before he died, but there's no precedent for this and no plan in place for how to move forward. Meanwhile, David has been living at his refugee home in Philistia, and he's just defeated the Amalekites. He was a three-day journey away from the battle Saul was fighting, but an excited messenger comes to tell David what he thinks will be good news: "Your enemy is dead and I killed him!" This guy obviously doesn't know David's character. Plus, his story is inconsistent with Scripture. First Samuel 31:4 says Saul fell on his own sword, but since David doesn't have access to 1 Samuel 31, he believes the messenger. Killing the king warrants the death penalty, so David orders it.

David asks God what to do next, and God sends him to Hebron in Judah. Judah is the largest tribe by far; they have their own army of sorts, and David is a Judahite. They make David king—but only over their tribe. Everything goes well until some of Saul's people want to stay in power. They anoint one of his surviving sons, Ish-bosheth, as king over the other eleven tribes. After about two years of having two kings in the promised land, the commanders of the two armies meet for a chat by the pool. Abner is the commander of Team Ish-bosheth, and Joab is the commander of Team David. They fight multiple battles, and eventually Abner calls a truce. It's a smart move, because Team Ish-bosheth lost nearly twenty times the men Team David did.

David's power grows, as does his family. He has six kids and six wives and concubines. Meanwhile, Abner also amasses power. But then something happens that shifts everything: Ish-bosheth accuses Abner of sleeping with one of Saul's concubines. Saul is long dead, so why is this a big deal to Ish-bosheth? Sleeping with a former king's wife or concubine is often a strategic display of power, a move to take over the throne. Ish-bosheth is essentially accusing Abner of attempting a coup against him.

For more information on today's reading, see thebiblerecap.com/links.

We never find out if it's true, but Abner is so offended by the accusation that he makes an oath to help David become king over all twelve tribes. God is working out His plan even through these accusations.

Abner tells David he wants to join his team, and David basically says, "Remember when your cousin Saul took my first wife, Michal, away from me without my consent? I may have several other wives now, but I want her back. Make it happen or the deal is off." Michal goes back to David, but she's still married to her second husband. When Abner gets the other tribes on board with David as king, he gives David the good news. But his timing is terrible because Joab, David's military commander, isn't there at the time. When Joab hears that Saul's former military commander is acting nice, he becomes suspicious and kills him. King Ish-bosheth is upset over Abner's death, even though they're recent enemies. Things begin to crumble for Ish-bosheth, and eventually he's killed by his military captains, who then brag to David that they've killed his enemy. David orders the death penalty, but even through their wicked actions, God's plan to position David as king moves another step forward.

Saul's surviving male family member is his grandson Mephibosheth, son of Jonathan. He's unlikely to make an attempt for the throne, because he's young and was crippled in an accident. At this point, it looks like we're poised for David to be the king over all twelve tribes of Israel!

TODAY'S GOD SHOT

People think they're pleasing David by killing his enemies, but he says, "I was gentle today, though anointed king" (3:39). The position of king makes people fear him as one who may be harsh and ruthless, but David says he's not that kind of king. God referred to David as "a man after his own heart" (1 Samuel 13:14), and his character here shows us glimpses of God's heart. In fact, God says something along these very lines about Himself: "I take no pleasure in the death of wicked people. I only want them to turn from their wicked ways so they can live" (Ezekiel 33:11 NLT). Though He's the King, He's gentle—the kind of King we can draw near to, instead of run from. And He's where the joy is!

PSALMS 6, 8–10, 14, 16, 19, 21

Psalmists often use poetic imagery and hyperbole to make a point about how they feel, and David is no exception. It's important to recognize when a psalmist's emotions are on display so we don't build theology on poetic imagery and hyperbole. This means we have to ask some questions of the text. Beyond its literary context (poetry), we have to look at its historical and scriptural contexts.

For instance, in Psalm 6, David seems to fear that his sin and eventual death will separate him from God. If that's what he's saying, this psalm contradicts the rest of the Bible's teachings on this topic—so what do we do with it? At this point in history, God hasn't revealed much to His people about the afterlife. He's been helping them build a society and get to know Him in *this* life, not talking about what happens in the next. We've read about Sheol, but that's mostly a reference to the grave, not the afterlife. And when Saul visited the medium, Samuel appeared to still exist after death, which contradicts what David's poetry implies here. All that to say: We have to be careful about building theology from the Psalms *unless* it can be backed up elsewhere in Scripture. The good news is, the really important stuff is backed up elsewhere repeatedly. For this example, the rest of Scripture makes it clear that Christ's death has covered our sins and that for God's kids, death is a uniter, not a divider.

In Psalm 8, David marvels at God's creation and the fact that man is given dominion over it. In Psalm 9, he praises God for turning back the efforts of his enemies. We've read a few psalms where David asked God to do that, and here he circles back to praise God for answering him with a yes. It's clear that David isn't just in this relationship for what he can get from God. He's in this for intimacy with God—he doesn't just come to Him selfishly with complaints and needs. He comes to Him with praise!

Psalm 10 implies God is distant and hiding Himself, because the wicked are prospering while oppressing the poor and mocking God. It's easy to conclude that God is inattentive when that kind of thing happens, isn't it? But David holds his feelings accountable to the truth: "But you do see, for you note mischief and vexation, that you may take it into your hands" (10:14). He returns to his accusations of God's distance, setting them right. This psalm expresses two conflicting ideas, but both feelings can sit in the human heart simultaneously—it's just helpful to know which feeling is true.

Psalm 14 shows up in Paul's letter to the Romans. David and Paul both say humans aren't good people; we have nothing to offer God. These verses may feel harsh, but if we read them in light of the gospel, they're praise inducing: "I'm a corrupt sinner who can't get my act together no matter how hard I try. The mantras and affirmations have failed me. But praise Christ, I've been made righteous through no effort of my own. It was His gift to me, as His child!" God seeks us out, pursues us, initiates—He takes the unrighteous and grants them the righteousness of Christ!

Psalm 16 feels more accessible after we've walked closely with David. We know why he's grateful for the saints in the land because we've met his enemies. We know what it means that God holds his lot and that his boundary lines are in good places, because we studied tribal allotments. Psalm 19 has a similar impact. In verse 7, David says, "The law of the LORD is perfect, reviving the soul; the testimony of the LORD is sure, making wise the simple." He wrote this about the Torah. Surely you've been surprisingly revived by passages in the Old Testament law books. Surely you've seen God making you wiser!

TODAY'S GOD SHOT

In Psalm 21, David says he has everything—all his heart's desires, a crown of fine gold, and a long life. But in verse 6, when he's talking to God and speaking in third person like kings sometimes do, he tells us where his true joy comes from: "You make him glad with the joy of your presence." We read something similar in Psalm 16:11: "In your presence there is fullness of joy." Despite all David's earthly blessings, he keeps pointing us back to God, reminding us that He's where the joy is!

1 CHRONICLES 1–2

We'll drop in on this book and 2 Chronicles over the next few months. These two books used to be one book but were divided because of scroll length. They were written to chronicle centuries of Israel's history, hence the name. Book 1 starts us back at the beginning—in fact, the first word in 1:1 is *Adam*. This refresher will help us to commit more of the story to memory as well as stir up new things in our hearts. Don't give up if this feels repetitive—reps are how you develop strength! It's also encouraging to realize you've heard something before, because that means it's sticking with you. Keep looking for God every day, even in spots that feel familiar or slow—He's in there!

Chronicles does spice things up a bit, though; it includes stories that aren't recorded elsewhere. Typically it adds positive stories and subtracts negative ones. That may sound deceptive, but Scripture doesn't let Chronicles off the hook—God has given us other books to help flesh out the story more fully. For instance, when we read a story in 2 Samuel one day and in 1 Chronicles the next, there will often be details that jump off the page in one account that weren't in the other account.

Today we traced the story of the family we've been following since Day 1. For most people, genealogies aren't fun to read. It seems like half the names sound like diseases, and the other half sound like medications—if that's hard for you, try having the Bible app or Bible.com read the passages to you aloud.

The early genealogies are really compressed; some aren't even complete sentences. Nimrod may have caught your eye in 1:10 because the verse says he was the first person on earth to be a mighty man. We first read about Nimrod in Genesis 10:8–12, which mentions that he was a mighty hunter before the LORD. There are two things worth noting here: (1) Some commentators think this was an entire people group of hunter-warriors—not just one person, and (2) the name Nimrod became

For more information on today's reading, see thebiblerecap.com/links.

a slang term for someone who was foolish. It was popularized by Bugs Bunny, who used the name to refer to Elmer Fudd, who was a hunter. Could the cartoonists at Looney Toons be better theologians than the Renaissance painters?

In 1:19, we see a note about Peleg: "In his days the earth was divided." What is this referring to? We first met Peleg briefly back in Genesis 10:25, which was right before the Tower of Babel incident, when God created multiple languages, separating the people. It's likely, but not certain, that this is the division the text is referring us back to. However, some scholars think this points to the continental drift theory and the way plate tectonics have impacted the globe.

The second chapter mostly hovers over the lineage of the tribe of Judah, because David comes from this tribe. The author wants to highlight his family line because they're Israelite royalty. As these genealogies continue in the following chapters, some of the other tribes barely even get mentioned. Naphtali only gets a sentence fragment!

According to 2:7, Achan is "the troubler of Israel." We met him in Joshua 7. After the Israelites made their first raid in the promised land and took the city of Jericho, he stole things devoted to God and hid them in his tent. How did that trouble the whole nation? In their next battle, against Ai, they lost thirty-six men, and God said it was because there was sin in the camp. Achan confessed and they stoned him. But dozens of men died because of his greed.

TODAY'S GOD SHOT

The tiny details of these three men's lives reveal more about God to us today. In this trio, we have someone who it seems is being praised—Nimrod the mighty hunter—someone identified more by the things around him than by anything he's done personally—Peleg the wallflower—and someone known for bringing trouble and death to God's people with his idolatry—Achan. God uses every story, from the great to the terrible to the person who never does anything historically significant. We're all written into His story of redemption. He sees us all, and genealogies remind us of that. They may be boring, but He's not. He's where the joy is!

PSALMS 43–45, 49, 84–85, 87

In Psalm 43, David is struggling and feels far from God but reminds his soul of the truth: "Why are you cast down, O my soul, and why are you in turmoil within me? Hope in God; for I shall again praise him, my salvation and my God" (43:5). He tells his heart and mind what to do. This is exactly what Moses told the Israelites to do in tough times: Remember who God is and what He has done. David is putting that counsel into practice hundreds of years later.

In Psalm 44, the writers, the sons of Korah, praise God for the things He's done for their ancestors, not just for them. They remember that God is the one who grants victory—not a man's strong arm or sword or bow—especially since Israel didn't even take any weapons to war sometimes! Again, the writers take Moses' words to heart, because this points back to his warning in Deuteronomy 8:17–18: "Beware lest you say in your heart, 'My power and the might of my hand have gotten me this wealth.' You shall remember the LORD your God, for it is he who gives you power to get wealth, that he may confirm his covenant that he swore to your fathers, as it is this day." Walking in humility leads to praising God.

But the sons of Korah are confused because God doesn't seem to be granting the kind of victory He did in the past. From their vantage point, it seems like God hasn't kept His end of the covenant, so they take that concern to God. Is some kind of sin prompting God's silence? Scripture doesn't say. But it's interesting that this is written to be a corporate song, because when people sing it, it may prompt some people toward individual reflection, which may, in turn, prompt repentance of any unconfessed sin among the people. By the way, the phrase *To the choirmaster* at the top is how we know this is a corporate song. Personal songs usually say something like *Of David* or *Of Asaph*.

Psalm 45 was written for the king's wedding—it wasn't written by David, but it's probably about David, or at least about one of his

---

For more information on today's reading, see thebiblerecap.com/links.

descendants. Even in the context of a wedding, the song still opens with praise of God. It's written for two specific people, but Psalm 49 is addressed to everyone—all peoples of the earth, rich and poor, low and high, wise and foolish. The psalmist has an important message for them all: You're going to die. It's a call to remember what matters in life, because that will drive out fear. In verse 5 he says, "Why should I fear in times of trouble?" and points out that God has ransomed his soul, so in the face of worldly oppression or even death, he can rejoice!

While Psalm 49 ends with its focus on death, Psalm 84 focuses on life—specifically the life of God's servant. The psalmist says he never feels more at home than in God's house. When he's away from it, he feels weak, but when he's there, he feels alive. He values nearness to God above everything else, and he's even willing to serve in humble positions just to draw near to God.

Psalm 85 is a corporate lament. It points to God's past faithfulness and asks Him to bless Israel again. One of the standout features of this psalm is how much it calls on the character of God and the name of God. God told Moses His name back in Exodus 34:6–7, and a lot of the words He used to describe Himself are sprinkled throughout this song: He forgives iniquity and sin, He shows steadfast love and faithfulness, He doesn't clear the guilty. It ends with beautiful imagery—Israel promises to let their faithfulness rise up from the ground and trusts that God's righteousness will look down from the sky, and those two things will meet each other in a holy kiss.

TODAY'S GOD SHOT

Psalm 87 doesn't just praise Zion or Jerusalem—it reveals something important about God. The person and cities it lists are all Gentiles: Rahab, which is likely a nickname for Egypt; Babylon, a wicked city; Philistia, their enemy; Tyre, another wicked city. This psalm celebrates that those people are all welcomed in Zion. It shows us Israel's unique relationship with God, but it also shows that He invites other nations to make their home among His people. It closes with a celebration of singing and dancing in honor of the God who provides for His people and who invites outsiders to be His people. Whether you're a Jew or a Gentile, all your springs are in Him too. Because He's where the joy is!

1 CHRONICLES 3–5

Today's genealogy picks up with David, whose kingship is the book's focus. In 4:9 the text goes from listing names to sharing a brief narrative about Jabez. He's an honorable man who seeks God, even though his name means "sorrow" or "pain"—which is all the more interesting given that he asks God to keep him from pain. Names often point toward character, so he could be asking God to protect him from himself, to make him a new man, to do something different than his name indicates. He knows part of avoiding pain and sorrow is avoiding sin and harm, so he asks God to keep him from those things too. He also asks God for an enlarged border, which is probably a literal prayer for more land, because as we've seen, that's a current focus. God answers his prayer with a yes.

Chapter 4 reveals that the tribe of Simeon is shrinking. Jacob hinted at this in his Genesis 49:7 prophecy: "Cursed be their anger, for it is fierce, and their wrath, for it is cruel! I will divide them in Jacob and scatter them in Israel." Moses also hinted at it when he blessed the tribes before his death and gave no blessing to Simeon. God has been dropping a trail of bread crumbs on this for a few thousand years. It has its roots in Genesis 34:25–29, when Simeon and Levi killed the men of Shechem to avenge their sister Dinah's rape. When Jacob prophesied, "I will divide them in Jacob and scatter them in Israel," it was for both Simeon and Levi. Levi has been scattered and divided as well. They don't have their own land; they live spread out among the other tribes. God fulfilled Jacob's prophecy for both tribes.

Chapter 5 recalls the sins of Reuben, another son of Jacob. He slept with Jacob's concubine and had his birthright taken away. Despite Reuben's wickedness, his descendants have been blessed. Reubenites are primarily herdsmen, and their flocks are multiplying. They live in the Transjordan with the tribes of Gad and East Manasseh. Those two and a half tribes seem to have a unique kind of unity—perhaps brought on by their isolation across the Jordan River. They have each other's backs, at least at this point. They seek God together and even go to war together and win. But alas, it's short-lived. Their beloved leaders eventually fall into idolatry and start worshipping pagan gods, so God raises up an enemy to cart them off, just like they'd done to their enemies.

TODAY'S GOD SHOT

We read two prayers today, and God's responses show us something about Him. The Transjordan tribes cry out to God during their war against the Hagrites, and "He granted their urgent plea because they trusted in him" (5:20). Is theirs a self-focused prayer or a God-focused prayer? Asking for help winning a war could be considered self-motivated, but maybe it's God-focused since this might be a holy war involving land occupied by the tribes (even though the Transjordan wasn't part of the original promised land). In 4:10, Jabez prayed, "Oh that you would bless me and enlarge my border, and that your hand might be with me, and that you would keep me from harm so that it might not bring me pain!" This prayer has elements of righteousness, but some elements pertain to personal desires. So is this a selfish prayer or a God-focused prayer? And does it matter?

God doesn't rebuke Jabez for asking for more land, and He doesn't tell the Transjordan tribes they should stick to the original promised land if they want to win battles. Many people struggle to pray for themselves, fearing it might be perceived as selfish. Jabez shows us that not only are both kinds of prayers acceptable to God, but they're both honorable to Him. These prayers come from a heart that knows God, trusts Him, and cries out to Him as the source of all good things—from victories to land to righteousness. God can be trusted to take all our prayers, sift them, and faithfully respond to us with what is best in each unique situation. When it comes to His kids, God leaves no prayer unanswered—there's no such thing as an unanswered prayer. He hears them, receives them, and always responds—with yes, no, or wait. He can be trusted with all our prayers, and He loves to hear from us! He's never busy and He's never bored—He's where the joy is!

PSALMS 73, 77–78

In the first half of Psalm 73, the psalmist Asaph bemoans the prosperity of the wicked; he sees them flourishing. Given what we know about human nature, this probably tells us something about what Asaph is going through as he writes this. There's a good chance he feels like he isn't prospering or flourishing. Perhaps he's comparing his life to the lives of the wicked and is frustrated that they're getting what he thinks he deserves. His perspective shifts when he goes to worship God—that's when he remembers what has eternal value, and earthly prosperity isn't on that list. Nearness to God is what truly feeds his soul. He has to take his eyes off others, and possibly off himself, before his heart can shift. Before his heart changed, his bitterness shaped his view of God: "When my soul was embittered, when I was pricked in heart, I was brutish and ignorant; I was like a beast toward you" (73:21–22).

Bitterness is often the result of deep wounding, and it carries the sting of unfulfilled hopes. Bitterness is an emotional problem that often rejects reasoning. The good news is that Asaph becomes a psalmist. He goes from being a person who accuses God to a person whose entire job is to praise God and serve Him. His heart's proximity to God determines his view of the world. Proximity gives us perspective—and the view is definitely better the closer you get to God.

The fact that Psalm 77 is a corporate lament reveals how much God wants His people to bring their honest feelings to Him—even publicly. Asaph wrote this song about being racked with anxiety and trouble; he can't even find respite in sleep. When God's people struggle, they shouldn't have to do it alone. The congregation of believers should be a safe place to bring our anxieties and our fears, knowing we'll be heard and loved and prayed for and that the truth isn't changed by our shifting emotions or uncertain circumstances. Asaph finally calms himself by speaking the past to his present. He reminds himself of God's past faithfulness. He points to the fact that God's character can be trusted, because those former times weren't easy either, but God came through.

In fact, verse 19 says, "Your way was through the sea"—*through* the sea, the way that seems impossible, the tough but miraculous way, the way that God gets the most glory, and the way that leaves us with an unforgettable story of His love and provision. All of this reminds Asaph that God is serious about His relationship with Israel.

Asaph gives us a parable in Psalm 78. It recounts Israel's history, including lots of the stories God has told them to teach their children. By writing this song, Asaph isn't just praising God for His faithfulness, he's also creating a teaching tool. Some scholars say that's what the word *maskil* (at the top of some psalms) means—a song to teach and enlighten us, to engage our minds.

In this psalm, the Ephraimites are front and center, but they're really serving as an example of the idolatry of all of Israel. Ephraim is the poster child for idolatry because of what happened in Judges 17 and 18 when Micah set up his own sanctuary, made his own ephod, hired his own priest, and had his own idols. That was the first major episode of an Israelite trying to counterfeit what God was doing in His tabernacle.

TODAY'S GOD SHOT

All three of today's psalms pertain to the direction of our eyes. If our eyes are on others or ourselves or our desires, inevitably we'll lose sight of God. In Psalm 73, Asaph's eyes are on himself and others. Some say comparison is the thief of joy, but here it seems that comparison is also the thief of faith. It prompts us to doubt God's goodness. In Psalm 77, Asaph's eyes are on himself and his struggle, but he repents—he turns his eyes—reminding himself of God's faithfulness. He preaches God's light to his darkness. In Psalm 78, the Israelites' eyes are on their idols, their current desires. Asaph encourages them to teach their hearts the history of who God has been to them. May God take our eyes off others, off our problems, off ourselves, and off our desires and fix them on Him, because Asaph knows and we know that He's where the joy is!

1 CHRONICLES 6

At this point, you may wonder if Chronicles is only genealogies. Don't worry—we've only got one more genealogy day coming up, and that day's reading also jumps into the narrative part of the book. But genealogies serve a few major purposes—not just for history but for us too. Today we encountered a portion that reveals one of the historical purposes, but it also is a bit of a spoiler on what will eventually happen with Israel. However, that spoiler probably comes as no surprise, so let's talk about it.

Verse 15 says, "Jehozadak went into exile when the LORD sent Judah and Jerusalem into exile by the hand of Nebuchadnezzar." God promised to send Israel into exile if they didn't keep the covenant, so this lets us know that Israel doesn't keep the covenant and God eventually raises up an enemy to carry them off into exile. They will eventually be leaving the promised land it took them so long to enter. But don't worry—when that happens, God isn't casting them off. He's already told us how this will go, and He says it's all part of His plan to bring them to repentance and to restore all things. Exile is less like punishment from an angry deity and more like discipline from a loving Father.

Israel will be in exile for a long time, but then they'll repent and God will bring them back into the promised land. When that happens, these genealogies will be a necessary part of restoring the tribes and families to their rightful allotments. It'll be vital to know who is from which tribe so they can go back to the right plot of land. Another thing they'll need to know is who is from the tribe of Judah and the line of David, because God has appointed that as the line of kings. They will also need to know who the Levites are—according to the clans of the Kohathites, the Merarites, and the Gershonites—because they need to set everything back up with the temple according to the specific job of each clan. By the way, you may have noticed that Gershon is called Gershom here, but don't worry—it's all the same.

All these lists serve the important role of verifying people's identities so they can reinstate things when they return to the land. It may seem boring to us, but it is vital for their obedience and thriving. To them, it isn't just a list—it's their life.

In verse 31 we see that David has set up some new positions in the service of the temple. Back in Numbers 4, God set up roles for the three clans of the Levites (Kohathites, Gershonites, and Merarites), but here David adds a fourth role from among those clans: musicians. Asaph was listed among these. We've been reading some of his psalms.

After the genealogies and the job assignments, the Levites are divided into their clans, and the cities of refuge are announced.

TODAY'S GOD SHOT

The fact that this chapter exists at all tells us something about God and His character. He intentionally put this here to help reestablish people in the land He gave them that they'll someday give up and that He'll eventually bring them back to. It not only shows us His forethought, but it shows us His passion for restoration and redemption. He's so patient and generous with them, even when they break His heart. But just like these genealogies, this kind of love isn't just historical—it impacts us today. This is how God interacts with each of His kids. He made us, we went astray, then He paid the ultimate price to buy us back—death on a cross. He planned it all before it even happened, just like with the Israelites! This chapter of genealogies is so much more than just names—it's a testament to His abundant kindness and His plan for restoration and redemption. He's where the joy is!

PSALMS 81, 88, 92–93

Psalm 81 is a corporate praise song, but it also has some elements of prophetic warning. We start out with a call to the musicians to play their instruments. Harps, tambourines, trumpets—God likes it all! At this time, a trumpet isn't made of brass; it's made of a ram's horn and is typically known as a shofar. The musicians are signaling the beginning of a feast in order to gather all the people together. They're essentially serving as an ancient dinner bell but with more spiritual significance. The people have come from all over Israel to the religious headquarters because God has commanded them to keep these feasts as a means of remembering and celebrating all He's done for them.

The lyrics of the song recount God's rescue from Egypt, His provision in the wilderness, and His command for them to be faithful to Him alone. It also recounts their rebellion, and it ends with God imploring His people to repent. The words *hear* and *listen* are repeated three times in this psalm. For all the noise God calls them to make with their instruments in the beginning, He's more concerned with them hearing Him and doing what He says.

Heman wrote Psalm 88, and he was apparently in a dark place at the time. He freely expresses his emotions to God, which demonstrates that God can handle our frustrations and questions without being threatened one bit. Heman opens by addressing YHWH as the "God of my salvation"—so he lets us know that he does have a relationship with God. He asks God to be attentive to his prayer. It sounds like he's either close to death or *feels* like he's dying emotionally—it's hard to say for sure. In verses 6–8 and again in verses 16–18, he names God as the source of his troubles; but he also makes it clear that God is the only solution to them. This psalm doesn't get tied up with a bow—he leaves it open-ended. These kinds of psalms show us that our prayers don't have to be perfect or polished—we can bring our hearts to the God who built our hearts, knowing He'll meet us in the mess. If you're afraid to pray, let

Heman's psalm set your heart at ease. There's very little chance you'll say something worse to God than he already has.

In my Bible, the subtitle for Psalm 92 is "A Song for the Sabbath." They have songs for the feasts, so it shouldn't surprise us that there's a song for the Sabbath as well. He starts out with a call to worship, reminding the listeners to bookend their days with worship. Then he contrasts the wicked and foolish with the righteous and wise. The wicked may seem to flourish in this life, but their blessings are temporary. And this kind of truth would likely serve as a timely reminder on the Sabbath—when God's people might be tempted to go back to work on the day He called them to rest just so they can keep up with the Canaanites.

Psalm 93 is a beautiful song of praise for God's reign over His creation. He's always been King of the earth, and the whole earth knows it! In the ancient Near East, the waters were viewed as a formidable enemy—they were chaotic, unknown, and terrifying. The psalmist reminds us that even the waters worship God and bow to His reign.

TODAY'S GOD SHOT

In Psalm 92, we see that the righteous are like palm trees planted in the house of God—they thrive and flourish, always bearing fruit. How do we become like those palm trees? What do we have to do to become the righteous ones? One of God's names is Jehovah Tsidkenu, which means "the LORD Our Righteousness." He's not just the one who makes us righteous, but He *is* our righteousness. Jesus says something similar in John 15:5: "Whoever abides in me and I in him, he it is that bears much fruit, for apart from me you can do nothing." Palm trees don't march into the house of God and plant themselves. And palm trees can't sustain themselves—they need water and sun to thrive and bear fruit. They have to stay connected to their supply of sustenance. Thank God, He does all that's required for us to be made righteous, to be planted in His house, to bear much fruit. He's where the fruit is, and He's where the joy is!

1 CHRONICLES 7–10

Today we wrap up the genealogies in this section, but we start with a double dose. In chapter 7 we see the genealogy of the tribe of Benjamin, then in chapter 8 we get a *second* genealogy of Benjamin that is almost entirely different. There are a few things going on here that contribute to this double genealogy. The chapter 8 genealogy focuses specifically on the line of Saul. Maybe you're wondering why they couldn't have just included that in the chapter 7 version instead of addressing it separately. We won't dive into this fully, but at a future point in the story, it seems that the tribe of Benjamin may have split. And since the author wrote this five hundred years after the time we're currently in, he might have been retroactively noting who went which way in that split. It's not vital information for us to retain, but it helps us understand why the genealogy is divided this way.

Remember how these genealogies serve to track who is a part of which tribe for when they return from exile? In chapter 9 we get a glimpse into that. It tells us who comes back and in what order and where they go to live. It focuses specifically on Jerusalem, because it's their religious capital. This chapter also shows just how many people are involved in running things at the temple after it's built. The temple work isn't just about making sacrifices—it involves mixing incense and counting utensils and leading worship and guarding gates and baking bread. So much goes into keeping things running smoothly, and all the people who work there are considered leaders, regardless of their specific task.

Chapter 10 gives us a quick review of Saul's death. In case there was any doubt, this affirms the earlier account of how Saul killed himself in battle. That's how it was recorded at the time, and that's how it's remembered five hundred years later. The Amalekite sojourner who came to David as a messenger in 2 Samuel 1:6–10 and claimed he had killed Saul was apparently lying to gain favor. He isn't even mentioned in this text.

The final two verses of today's reading summarize the sad story of the end of Saul's kingship. He was the leader of God's people, yet he wasn't seeking God. In fact, he was seeking counsel from people God had commanded him to kill, people who were enemies of God's kingdom. And in that way, Saul himself was a traitor and an idolater—and given how God portrays His relationship with His people as a marriage, Saul was also an adulterer. Even though Saul fell on his own sword, verse 14 says God put him to death. God is often referred to as "the God of the womb and the God of the tomb"—He's the giver and taker of life. That can be a hard concept to swallow, but it's what we see in Scripture, so we can't discount it just because it makes us feel uncomfortable or vulnerable. The fact that God claims credit for Saul's death might be a tough pill to swallow for a variety of reasons, but if we view it rightly, it can also be comforting because of what it shows us about God's heart.

TODAY'S GOD SHOT

God protects His people. God doesn't stand for a leader who is doing things his own way, disregarding the good of the people, betraying the God of the universe, and seeking selfish gain. God doesn't allow that person to continue leading this nation-state that He has put His own name on. God's protective nature helps us trust Him more. And even though we weren't part of that nation-state, He's protective of us too. Does harm happen to God's kids? Absolutely. But He preserves what is most important: our souls and our relationship with Him. He's vigilant when it comes to the things of eternal value. He has made us His forever, and He's the one who keeps us. He's where the joy is!

PSALMS 102–104

While Psalm 102 is a personal lament, the psalmist also applies his prayers and concerns to Israel at large. He's certain God will hear him and asks God to respond quickly. He feels utterly alone, and his body is breaking under the stress and sadness. We don't know the reason for his distress, and he doesn't seem to know either. In that way, this psalm is probably a comfort to anyone who can't seem to make sense of why things are happening the way they are. The psalmist attributes his pain to God's anger. Maybe he's wrong and God's not angry, and this is just an expression of emotion—but if he's right and God is angry with him, we can discern more about the why of his pain. The only thing that angers God is sin, so we can assume the psalmist's circumstances are the result of his sin and he's being disciplined into repentance.

He juxtaposes his temporary affliction with God's eternal reign. This transition to fixing his eyes on God seems to comfort him. By remembering God's relationship with His people, he reminds himself that God will rescue him somehow, someday. He knows YHWH will help Israel and that as a result other nations will be brought into Zion too!

While Psalm 102 looks ahead hopefully, Psalm 103 looks back, praising God for His goodness to His people through the years. Here, David praises God for things he didn't personally experience but that he benefits from. He truly grasps the metanarrative, the overarching story line of God and His people. He starts by commanding himself how to think, feel, and act, and he does it by remembering who God is and all the ways God has been good to him. He gives tribute to Exodus 34:6–7, where God tells Moses His name. It gives such a dense, rich display of God's character: He's merciful, gracious, slow to anger, and abounding in steadfast love, and He doesn't repay us according to what we deserve, and He's compassionate toward us like a father—all these ideas are copied and pasted from Exodus 34 into this psalm, which shows that David knows

Scripture well. He closes by pointing out that life is short and you'll be forgotten but God and His reign will continue forever.

Psalm 104 is another anonymous psalm of worship. It praises God as Creator, and a lot of creation themes are echoed here, so it's possible that this psalm is loosely based on Genesis 1–3. God didn't just create everything—He set systems in place for the survival of His creations as well as their deaths.

Verses 14 and 23 remind us that man was created to work hard. Work isn't a product of the fall—it preceded the fall. And in verse 15, we see that God didn't create just the basics for humanity—He gives us blessings above and beyond what we need: wine and facial oil are luxuries, not necessities. Along those same lines, God also made some creatures on earth solely for His enjoyment. Some of these are creatures we'll never encounter or appreciate. There are sea creatures that have lived on the ocean floor since creation that no one has ever seen, but God made them and delights in them. We don't know if Leviathan was a mythological sea monster or a real one or just an antique crocodile, but the psalmist portrays it like a puppy. He says God made it to play in the water!

He segues from showing God's sovereignty and might over all creation into asking God to use His power to wipe out the wicked. While this may sound harsh, we can probably view it less as some kind of personal vendetta and more as a desire for God's glory to be magnified.

TODAY'S GOD SHOT

Psalm 104:20 says, "You make darkness." Darkness seems to be the absence of something, not the presence of something. How can God create an absence? Maybe it's just poetic language to show that God created everything, but whether it's a great truth or just a great lyric, it gives glory to God. Scripture compares God to light, so it's easy to think of darkness as the absence of God, but Psalm 18:11 says He makes darkness His covering, and Psalm 97:2 says clouds and thick darkness surround Him. And even when we step out of the poetic parts of Scripture, 1 Kings 8:12 says, "The LORD has said that he would dwell in thick darkness." It seems nothing escapes Him. He's everywhere. And He's where the joy is!

2 SAMUEL 5; 1 CHRONICLES 11–12

When we read Chronicles, we'll often be reading stories for a second time, but with a different lens. Here's a refresher on where we are in David's story: He's been king of Judah for about seven years. The other tribes were following Saul's son Ish-bosheth until two of his military leaders murdered him. Right before that happened, his military commander stepped down from his role and set out to convince all the other tribes they should follow David instead.

David is finally anointed king over the other tribes, unifying the nation of Israel. He's thirty years old, which means he waited roughly fifteen years between being anointed as king over Israel and *being* king over Israel. He's been reigning in Hebron, but he's got his heart set on moving the religious capital to Jerusalem. There's only one problem: The Jebusites live there. The Israelites have failed in previous attempts to drive them out, in part because Jerusalem's landscape is like a topographical fortress with a natural moat—it's on a hill surrounded by valleys, surrounded by hills.

The Jebusites taunt David. They say Jerusalem is so fortified that they could appoint blind and lame people as their security guards and he still wouldn't manage to get in. Then, just like he did in the battle against Goliath, David opts for brains over brawn. He outwits them by going up through a water shaft instead of attacking the walls and gates. (By the way, David doesn't actually hate the blind and lame, despite what he says—this is likely a general reference to the Jebusites as a whole, because they said the blind and lame would be the ones to keep him out.) In summarizing the invasion, 1 Chronicles 11:5 says, "The inhabitants . . . said to David, 'You will not come in here.' Nevertheless, David took the stronghold of Zion, that is, the city of David." They forbid David from entering the city that's now named after him. David takes Jerusalem and makes it the new capital, so they move everything over from Hebron to Jerusalem. David builds his castle there, and if you visit Jerusalem, you can go there—it was discovered a few years ago!

Shortly after David is made king over all Israel, word gets back to the Philistines. Remember how David moved to Philistia when Saul was trying to kill him and pretended to be conquering Israelite cities but was actually conquering Philistine cities and lying about it? Well, now the Philistines finally realize that the guy they thought was on their side is actually the king of their enemies. When they come after him, he asks God what to do, and God promises and delivers victory. Scripture says the Lord of hosts was with him. *Lord* refers to YHWH and *hosts* refers to a group, which means it could either be an army or perhaps an army of angels—or maybe even both. In battle, David has a habit of inquiring of God and obeying Him, and he sees success in this area. But in his private life—like when it comes to women—he does not inquire of the Lord, and the outcomes reveal that he's off the rails. He has great victories, but Scripture makes it clear that he isn't perfect. He starts accumulating new wives and concubines right away, despite God's command against this in Deuteronomy 17:17.

In addition to accumulating women, he accumulates an army of mighty men, which includes three main warriors, a core group of thirty, and a few bonus guys who join in from time to time. They're often powerful and victorious, but they also make some foolish moves out of loyalty to David.

TODAY'S GOD SHOT

Second Samuel 5:10–12 makes it clear that David's greatness doesn't originate with David and doesn't terminate on David. It says he becomes greater because God is with him, just as He has been since David was anointed king. God exalts David's kingdom for the sake of His people, Israel. This is about something much bigger than just David. God is the source, supply, and goal of all of this. As Romans 11:36 says, "From him and through him and to him are all things." Both David's victories and his flaws point us to an eternal God who is working all things together according to His will, which is also for our joy. Because He's where the joy is!

PSALM 133

Even though it's short, there's a lot more to Psalm 133 than meets the eye. This is one of the Songs of Ascent, one of the songs the Israelites sing as they travel on foot—from wherever their tribal allotment happens to be—all the way to Jerusalem, three times a year. These are all hopeful, triumphant praise psalms, but they each have something different they're praising God for. So what are they singing about in this song?

Here's some background information on where this psalm likely came from. Remember back in Genesis 13:6 when Abram and Lot had to part ways because the land wouldn't support both of their families and flocks and possessions? This happened again in Genesis 36:7 with Jacob and Esau, who had just reconciled after years of fighting and being estranged from each other. But they had so many family members and such large flocks that the amount of land required to feed everyone was too great, so they had to separate. In both instances, the phrase used is the same phrase used for *dwell in unity*.

In 133:1 when David says, "How good and pleasant it is when brothers dwell in unity," it's not just a nod to a peaceful situation between the brothers. It's also a nod to God's provision: This isn't a desert land that can't feed many people like Abram and Lot and Jacob and Esau encountered—this land is flourishing and can provide for everyone! This verse also points to the good relationship between them and God. It demonstrates His faithfulness in giving them the land He promised.

This is not to diminish the fact that it does speak to peaceful unity between the people. That's huge on its own. Imagine the whole nation of Israel walking together to one city. All those millions of people from various tribes taking weeks-long journeys three times a year, sometimes with their kids and animals in tow—it sounds like a nightmare. They're all heading to Jerusalem, and they're going to have a feast to God and remember His provision and protection, but that kind of road trip is bound to incite some family fights. That's why this is probably a good song to sing in that situation!

Verse 2 also points them back to Israel's first priest, Aaron, on the day he was consecrated. God was pleased to set him apart and mark him as a servant, to demonstrate His presence with Aaron. And this psalm points out that living peacefully in the promised land is a lot like that—being set apart by God, being delighted in by God, being marked as God's servants, and experiencing God's nearness.

David's final comparison is to the dew falling on Mount Hermon, which is the highest mountain in Israel, and on Mount Zion, which is the highest point in Jerusalem. It's almost like the nation and its religious capital are being consecrated by God as well, but with dew instead of oil. That dew is also a means of keeping the land green and fruitful, which is another aspect of the blessing of God's provision.

TODAY'S GOD SHOT

In Deuteronomy 28:8, God said He would command His blessing on Israel in the promised land if they kept the covenant. We saw that again today in the final line of this psalm: "The LORD has commanded the blessing, life forevermore." The things David mentions in this psalm represent the best things of life on earth: unity, bounty, peace, blessing, provision. But God's blessings for His kids don't stop there. In fact, this closing verse seems to show that the thing God considers the real blessing is life forevermore. Eternal life with God where we live under the blessings of His presence—that is the real gift! A peaceful life of provision on earth is great, but it's such a flash in the pan. However, the future that awaits His kids when He restores all things and we live in that restored space *with Him*—that's where real life is found. He's where the joy is!

PSALMS 106–107

Today's psalms focus on the unity of the people of Israel—they point to corporate unfaithfulness to God, corporate repentance, and corporate forgiveness. And they both have aspects of lament and praise.

In Psalm 106, the psalmist recounts the sins of Israel's history and confesses a pattern of unfaithfulness to God. Despite their cycle of rebellion and unbelief, He hasn't given up on them, because He is a God of steadfast love. Verse 8 says something about God's motives that might seem to contradict that, however: "He saved them for his name's sake, that he might make known his mighty power." So which is it? Did He save them because of His steadfast love, or did He save them for His name's sake? This is one of those times when most theologians would simply say, "Yes." These two things aren't in conflict; they can reside in the same space.

Verse 23 says Moses "stood in the breach before him, to turn away his wrath from destroying them." Here, Moses is a Christ type, bridging the gap between man and God, absorbing His wrath on their behalf so that they aren't destroyed. This is the gospel, and Moses gave the Israelites a whisper of it long before Christ fulfilled it.

Then they enter the promised land, but the pattern they've established doesn't change, and they continue in idolatry, forgetting about their relationship with God. And God does what He promised to do: He raises up enemy nations to oppress them. But God hears them when they cry out to Him and saves them yet again. He keeps the covenant even when they break it.

Psalm 107 continues the theme of communal response. It lists four different kinds of people and their troubles, and all four stories share a common cycle: the problem, the cry for help, God's deliverance, and a call to praise.

The first person in trouble is the lost person who is wandering in the desert, hopeless, and hungry. We see no indication that they've caused their own trouble; it just seems like life is happening to them. But they cry to God for help, and He leads them out and satisfies their needs. The second person in trouble is the rebellious prisoner who is now being oppressed by other people. His suffering is definitely the result of his own actions—we see it in the text. Nevertheless, when he cries out to God, He delivers! Person three is the sinful fool who falls into sin because he doesn't seem to know better. He doesn't seek wisdom and becomes physically ill because of it. But when he cries out to God, He hears, heals, and restores.

Finally, there are the men in the ships. Scholars say some biblical writers had a negative view of international trade and seafaring businessmen, possibly because their trading suggests they believe God hasn't given them all they need in the promised land. Regardless, here's what we know: God sends a storm to wreck the ship, they cry out to God in deep sorrow, and He calms the storm.

All these people cry out to God, and He has mercy on them all, regardless of whether they arrived in their circumstances through oppression, evil, sorrow, or some combination of those. The psalmist tells all these people to thank the Lord for His unending love and for His work on their behalf.

TODAY'S GOD SHOT

Psalm 106:7 says, "Our fathers, when they were in Egypt, did not consider your wondrous works; they did not remember the abundance of your steadfast love, but rebelled by the sea, at the Red Sea." It's vital to remember God's works and His love for us—that is what will keep us abiding in Him and obeying Him. He doesn't say, "Remember the laws"—the psalm writer says, "Remember you're loved." Forgetting that God loves us leaves a space in our hearts where sin and rebellion sneak in. That's why reading His Word every day and looking for Him on these pages has a way of reshaping our hearts and lives. Will some of this reading feel repetitive? Yes. Will you see some of the same things about God from time to time? Sure. But do we still need to hear the gospel every day? Absolutely. Because we see how quickly the human heart wanders from the God we love when we don't actively remember Him. He loves you, despite you. And He's where the joy is!

1 CHRONICLES 13–16

As we drop into the books of Chronicles from time to time, events aren't always in the same order as in the books of Kings, so prepare to adjust accordingly. We open today with David making plans to move the ark of the covenant to Jerusalem, the newly seized, newly named capital. After the Philistines returned the ark to Israel, it was kept in the home of Abinadab. It stayed there as long as Saul was king, probably because Saul didn't understand how spiritually valuable it is. David does, though. He plans to bring the ark to Jerusalem and assembles the entire nation for this event. But there's one problem from the start: He has a lot of zeal but fails to yield to God's rules for how to treat the ark. It's only supposed to be moved by Levites, and it's supposed to be moved on poles, not a cart. The decision to move it on a cart may not be blatant disregard for God's commands, but it's carelessness at best. The Philistines sent it back to Israel on a cart, but they didn't have God's law. And we probably shouldn't take cues about obeying God from people who don't know or love Him.

During the parade the cows stumble, and Uzzah, who probably isn't a Levite, touches the ark. God strikes him dead. This is a hard scene to stomach, so let's look at a few important reminders. First, God told them in Numbers 4:15 that the penalty for touching the ark is death. Second, God is holy. We aren't. But He wants to be near us! He gave instructions on how to manage this kind of challenging relationship. We can't expect Him to make exceptions. It's already a big enough grace to us that He engages with us at all. Sometimes when people violate His rules, He might choose to be merciful, but we can't demand mercy from Him or say He's too harsh if He chooses to stand by His rules when we violate them.

David has a hard time with this too. He gets angry with God and may even be a little embarrassed, because it's his first big gathering as king

For more information on today's reading, see thebiblerecap.com/links.

of Israel and this is what happens. His heart is in the right place with wanting to bring the ark to Jerusalem, so it has to be especially defeating to leave such a tragic gap in the details of obeying God's commands. He's so discouraged that he decides to abandon the mission and leaves the ark at the home of a man named Obed-edom.

Chapter 14 reviews David's family and his defeat of the Philistines but also reveals that the king of Tyre approves of his reign. While it's not always important to have outside validation, it's probably helpful to know that other kings in the area support David as king. Verse 17 says God caused the nations around Israel to fear David; apparently God can create emotions, not just in His kids but even in His enemies. Even the hearts of people who aren't yielded to Him sit under the umbrella of His sovereign control.

By chapter 15, David has rallied from the discouragement of Uzzah's death and is ready to finish bringing the ark to Jerusalem. He's careful to make sure things are done right instead of just forging ahead on enthusiasm alone. He confesses his guilt in the first attempt and includes the Levites in that guilt. They didn't participate, but it seems they bear some of the guilt because of their passivity—their failure to step into the role God appointed for them. They bring the ark into the city, and everyone is thrilled except for Michal. We'll cover this more in the days ahead. They offer sacrifices, and David blesses and feeds them, appoints Levites, and sings a praise song that's a remix of other psalms.

TODAY'S GOD SHOT

"There is a way that seems right to a man, but its end is the way to death" (Proverbs 14:12). Both David and Uzzah do what is right in their own eyes—but without seeking God. Since God had already told them what to do, it doesn't even require seeking, just attention and obedience. God never requires something of us that He keeps us in the dark about. Many things are outlined for us in His Word, but for directions that aren't covered here, His Spirit serves as our Guide and Helper, showing us how to apply the principles of Scripture in each nuanced situation. We're never left to our own devices, because He knows His plan and He shares it. He's where the joy is!

PSALMS 1–2, 15, 22–24, 47, 68

Psalm 1 contrasts the wicked man with the righteous man—they think, act, and engage with the world differently. One thing the righteous man thinks about is God's Word—he *delights* in it. This delight causes him to flourish in every area that matters. No matter the circumstances around him, he'll be sustained and upheld by God's Word as his source of life.

In Psalm 2, the nations of the world have set themselves up against the new king, likely David. They want to overthrow Israel's power, but God looks at Israel's enemies—who are *His* enemies—and laughs. We should be careful not to imagine a maniacal laugh and Him rubbing his hands together and squinting down at them. He's not *cruel*; He's *just*.

Psalm 15 makes it sound impossible to get close to God, but David is specifically talking about the state of a man's heart when he enters the tabernacle or God's presence. God is holy and we aren't. His standards are higher than we could ever achieve. He shows so much mercy in drawing near to us and so much love in wanting to dwell with us!

The opening line of Psalm 22 is often taken out of context. It's important to view it rightly, because it informs our view of God. Jesus quoted the first line on the cross: "My God, my God, why have you forsaken me?" Some say this points to a separation between God the Son and God the Father, saying the Father can't look on sin. There's even a hymn that says, "The Father turned His face away."* But let's look at the historical context. David wrote Psalm 22, and parts of it are prophetic statements pointing to the Messiah. At this time, the books of the Bible hadn't been divided into chapters, so when they wanted to reference a certain psalm, they couldn't say, "Let's sing Psalm 5" or "Turn in your hymnal to page 23." Scholars say they referenced psalms by quoting the opening line. Given that information, here's what may have been happening: When

---

For more information on today's reading, see thebiblerecap.com/links.

*"How Deep the Father's Love for Us," by Stuart Townsend, Thankyou Music, 1995.

Jesus is on the cross, quoting the first line of this psalm, it's almost as if He's saying, "Remember that psalm about the coming Messiah? That prophecy David wrote? It's about Me. This is it. I'm it!"

Our faith is founded on who God is, and central to this is the doctrine of the Trinity: God the Father, God the Son, and God the Spirit. These three persons of the one true God have the same characteristics and personality but with different functions and roles. They're eternally distinct, but also eternally unified. It's theologically impossible for any person of the Trinity to be removed from the others even for a moment. And in fact, verse 24 says, "He has not hidden his face from him."

The idea that God can't look on sin comes from Habakkuk 1:13 taken out of context. God sees all sin—that's how He knows what to address. In the book of Job, God even has conversations with Satan. This is important to consider, because if we believe in a God who can't look at sin and who turns away *from Himself*, that can translate to the human heart as shame that drives us from God when we sin instead of encouraging us to run *to* Him. It's the same lie Adam and Eve believed as they hid from the God who came to clothe them.

Psalms 24, 47, and 68 celebrate the ark's return to Jerusalem. In Psalm 24, David personifies the gates of the city and tells them to look up and take notice, because the presence of God is approaching. Psalm 47 says God is king of the earth, not just Israel. Here, the defeat of their enemies isn't as great as having their enemies *join* them. The only way to be more than a conqueror is for your enemies to join your side! And Psalm 68 retraces the whole journey, starting with the desert. It shows God's victory over their enemies but ends by pointing to God as King over all kingdoms!

TODAY'S GOD SHOT

In Psalm 23, God keeps reiterating stillness and lack of motion. He says to lie down—not in front of Netflix, but by the still waters. It's interesting that He has to *make us* lie down. It's easy to despise stillness and waiting, but God invites us into the calm and the quiet. It's where He can get our attention long enough to restore our souls and comfort us. And isn't that part of the reason you're here in these pages? If so, we're in the right place, because He's where the joy is!

PSALMS 89, 96, 100–101, 105, 132

Psalm 89 has some confusing parts, so let's walk through them. First, verse 10 says God "crushed Rahab like a carcass." This isn't referring to Rahab the Canaanite. Here it most likely refers to Egypt or to a mythological beast who causes chaos. This verse is either showing God's victory over a world power or over chaos itself. The second confusing part is in verse 27 when David is called the "firstborn." As we've talked about previously, *Jesus* is the firstborn. So we have two firstborns—actually three, because Israel is called the firstborn. Israel is the firstborn of a people group, David is the firstborn of the kingly line God has established, and Jesus is the firstborn over all creation, meaning He's preeminent. There are lots of layered prophetic elements to this psalm, so it can refer to something in the present time of David while simultaneously referring to something else and something greater. Third, in verses 38–45, God is accused of forsaking Israel. But if we look back at verses 30–32, we see what's really happening: This is a time of discipline for sin, which God promised would happen when they rebel. Over time, God will show Himself faithful. And even the psalmist knows this in his heart, because he ends all these accusations with a call to bless the Lord forever.

Psalm 96 is similar to the song of thanks we read in 1 Chronicles 16 when they brought the ark to Jerusalem. Verse 5 says, "All the gods of the peoples are worthless idols," but the Hebrew has some humorous wordplay that basically translates to "these mighty beings are mighty useless!"

Psalm 100 celebrates God's kingship and goodness and reminds us that we belong to Him. Not only are we His creation—all things and people are His creation—but we're also His people and His sheep. He invited us into His courts, which is praiseworthy given that we're sinners and He's holy. It's worth celebrating! David spends a lot of time reminding himself to praise God, so when the music starts on Sunday and you're not feeling it, remind yourself of what He has invited you into. Remind your soul to celebrate.

In Psalm 101, David tells us what kind of king he wants to be. He's determined to be thoughtful and intentional about everything he does. He vows not to set worthless things before his eyes and to cut off wickedness from the land. The people who are allowed to speak into his life are the people who know and love God, and he'll be vigilant to protect his home and the city of Jerusalem. Perhaps his desire to be deliberate comes from how Uzzah died when David acted hastily.

Psalm 105 recounts the history of the Israelites from Abraham to the promised land. You may have noticed that the plagues are out of order and one is missing altogether. That's probably because this is a song of praise, so its purpose is to focus on the goodness of God's character, not the precise historical details.

Psalm 132 recalls God's promises to David and the people of Israel. However, it leaves out the promise that if the kings in David's line aren't faithful to God's covenant, Israel will suffer. It focuses mostly on the blessing. Some people believe this psalm was written when the Israelites were in exile, which means this focus on God's blessing would probably serve as hope for them to hold on to when times were tough.

TODAY'S GOD SHOT

Psalm 89:22–23 corresponds to a promise God made to David. It says, "The enemy shall not outwit him; the wicked shall not humble him. I will crush his foes before him and strike down those who hate him." When God settled David's future wins, He also settled the future losses of David's enemies. He doesn't just have things planned out for David and no one else or for Israel and no one else—His plans have to include *all* things. Otherwise, something outside those plans could go rogue and ruin them. If God weren't in control of all the details, prophecy would be virtually impossible. He'd just be guessing. The amount of detail this requires to plan for all of humanity, from creation onward, is mind-boggling. Our God is sovereign over details, and He's where the joy is!

2 SAMUEL 6–7; 1 CHRONICLES 17

Today we read more of the story in which David brings the ark into Jerusalem and Michal isn't pleased. After God strikes Uzzah dead, David becomes afraid of God. As we've learned, proper fear of the Lord is entirely different from being *afraid* of God. Proper fear of God—the kind that rightly understands His heart—consists of delight and awe, and it draws you to God. But the kind of fear David seems to be feeling is the kind that drives a person from God. David doesn't bring the ark to Jerusalem. He keeps it at the house of Obed-edom instead. But then, once David sees how God is blessing the people who are near to Him, his fears are dispelled, he remembers who God is, and he brings the ark to Jerusalem.

When he gets into the city, he encounters Michal and her displeasure. It's interesting that the text refers to her as Saul's daughter, not David's wife, even though she's both. This focus gives us a bit of insight into their relationship. She and David have a rocky past—her dad even gave her to another husband at one point, but later David demanded to have her back. And the rift between David and Saul may be affecting how she views David and even how she views the ark. The ark was never important to her dad when he was king, so maybe she wonders why David is making such a big deal about it.

When David comes dancing into the city, he's wearing a linen robe and a linen ephod, so he's actually quite covered and not naked at all, despite what she says. She seems to be displeased that he isn't covered with the royal robes. Maybe that goes against the royal protocol her dad kept, or maybe she thinks he's trying to look humble, or maybe she's still bitter about everything that happened in their marriage or even about his marrying other women. We have no idea. David tells her he isn't concerned about what people think, because this is just about him and the LORD—*that's* his motivation—and he'll humble himself in other ways that won't fit with the expectations for royalty. Then Scripture notes that Michal didn't have children. This *could be* because God thwarted her, but it could also suggest that the rift between her and David is never resolved to the point of intimacy.

Second Samuel 7 is one of the most important chapters in all of Scripture. It opens with David wanting to build a house for God. He talks to the prophet Nathan about it, who basically says, "Yes! Do whatever you want!" But it turns out Nathan spoke too soon and didn't seek God. People often say to follow your heart, but even the man after God's own heart doesn't get to follow his heart. And he doesn't always get everything he wants either. In fact, later that night, God corrects Nathan's advice, so he has to go back and tell David, "Oops. Don't follow your heart—follow your God. And by the way, God says the answer to your prayer is no."

This no is followed with good news, though, including what's known as the Davidic covenant, which has two parts: David's dynasty and Solomon's Temple. God lets him know, "I know you want to build Me a house, but I'm going to build *you* a house. Not an actual house, but a family. And one of your sons in this Davidic dynasty will build an actual house for Me." There are also parts of this prophecy that point to Christ and His eternal reign, which is why this chapter is so important.

David responds with, "Why are You so nice to me? I want everyone on earth to pay attention to how kind You are, so they can see what You're really like, because this promise You made me shows us a lot about who You are." David's humility and confidence combine beautifully here.

TODAY'S GOD SHOT

King David, the man after God's own heart, gets a no in response to his prayer. God doesn't respond to our prayers with a no because He's holding out on us. If God says no, it is His kindest possible answer. A yes would be a lesser kindness because it doesn't fit with His greater plan—to glorify Himself and to bless His people at the same time. His no is always for a greater yes. It probably won't always be an obvious upgrade like it is for David here, but if we trust His heart, we can believe it even when we can't see it: He's where the joy is!

PSALMS 25, 29, 33, 36, 39

Psalm 25:8 says, "Good and upright is the LORD, therefore he instructs sinners in the way." Jesus said a similar thing in Luke 5:31–32: "Those who are well have no need of a physician, but those who are sick. I have not come to call the righteous but sinners to repentance." His goodness and uprightness don't keep Him from sinners—they draw Him to them, to us! David is a sinner. In verse 11 he admits his guilt, which requires humility. He says, "For your name's sake, O LORD, pardon my guilt, for it is great." David links wisdom and humility throughout the chapter. Confessing sin shows wisdom. Notice he also appeals for pardon for God's sake, not for his own. Surely it's for his sake too, but this shows us that when God pardons sinners, it displays His character as one who is loving, forgiving, patient, and merciful. In the pardoning of sinners, the sinner is blessed and God's character is exalted. You'll notice this phrase "for your name's sake" attached to a lot of prayers in Scripture; it's an appeal to God to demonstrate who He is to the world.

Verse 14 says, "The friendship of the LORD is for those who fear him." Another translation (NASB) says, "The secret of the LORD is for those who fear Him." As we draw near to Him, His friendship and His secrets are heaped on us!

In Psalm 29, David portrays God as a thunderstorm moving across the land, leaving nothing untouched by His presence and power. Then amid His thunderous voice, lightning bolts, and flooding waters, God gives His people strength and peace. He is both *powerful* and *peaceful*.

Psalm 33 says praising God fits the righteous. It's not just good; it's right and fitting. When we fail to praise Him, we're acting *against* our created purpose. We also see that God's eye is on those who fear Him. For those who are afraid of Him, that probably sounds like a threat. But for those who rightly fear Him—who delight in Him and are in awe of Him—this is a comfort.

Psalm 36 opens with this: "Transgression speaks to the wicked deep in his heart." Then it describes the wicked. We've all been on this list at some point. Have you ever thought too highly of yourself? Ever thought you could get away with something? Ever lied? Ever planned to sin? Does that mean this psalm is calling all of us wicked? It seems to refer to the unrepentant person who follows a trajectory of sin and has given themselves over to it. Christ followers, however, are people who are for God but still sin. Even though we do wicked deeds, we're not defined by that—we're often called "the righteous" in Scripture, because Christ's righteousness has been transferred to us despite our sin.

In Psalm 39, David has sinned and admits his guilt. His sin has brought him pain, so he asks God to bring an end to his discipline—not because he doesn't deserve the discipline, but because God's rebuke is heavy and David feels like he's learned his lesson already. He's careful about how and when he talks about his struggles because he doesn't want to leave a bad impression about God on people who don't know God. So instead of complaining in public, he complains in private to God—which is totally fitting and right. He takes his complaints to the only One who can solve them. Remember how the Israelites grumbled about God in the desert and God rebuked and punished them and then Moses came along with the same complaints and it was no big deal? That's likely because when Moses had complaints, he took them to God, whereas the people just gossiped and complained to everyone around them. What we say matters, but whom we say it to also matters.

TODAY'S GOD SHOT

"Our heart is glad in him, because we trust in his holy name" (Psalm 33:21). If you've ever delighted in Him, that almost certainly means you trust Him. It's difficult—maybe even impossible—to delight in someone you don't trust, because you're always on your guard, trying to read their motives and self-protect. But if you've trusted God enough to let down your guard, there's a good chance you've delighted in Him. If you aren't there yet, stick around. He'll keep revealing His character to you and building up your trust in Him over time, and soon you'll be able to confidently say, "He's where the joy is!"

2 SAMUEL 8–9; 1 CHRONICLES 18

Today's reading recounts David's military victories. These battles aren't necessarily happening back to back; they're just grouped here together instead of spread out chronologically. This extensive list shows us how God is working to fulfill His covenant with David. Chronicles leaves out some personal stories about David that are included in 2 Samuel. The primary function of Chronicles is to show the trajectory of the covenant fulfillment, whereas 2 Samuel shows us more of David's personal growth and failure—it gives us more of an insider's look into his life. Chronicles is more of a news program, and 2 Samuel is more of a docuseries.

David wins often, but Scripture repeatedly points out that his victories are granted by God. Three times in our reading today it says, "The LORD gave victory." Victory is God's to give. David wins because of God's plan and favor, not because of David's strength or ability. God is the hero of the story. Given David's circumstances, it'd be easy to forget where the praise belongs. After all, he rose to power as the war hero, the guy who defeated the Philistines with one sling of a stone. So Scripture continues to remind us to give glory to God, not David. And David gives glory to God too. For instance, when other kings give him expensive gifts of gold and silver and bronze, he dedicates those gifts to the LORD.

In 1 Chronicles 18:7–8, when he comes back with spoils of war, he dedicates them to the LORD. Instead of filling his home office with signs of his victories, he offers them up for the good of all the people. That kind of humility and generosity makes for a great king. And guess what happens to those things years later? When his son Solomon eventually builds the temple for God, Solomon appoints those things to be made into holy vessels for use in the temple. Does this remind you of anything? This is reminiscent of when the Israelites fled Egypt and took the Egyptians' jewelry and clothes with them, then used those things to build the tabernacle. God continues to bless His people with things they can use for His glory and for the benefit of those around them!

As for the horses he captures in battle, David hamstrings them. Sometimes they do this so the enemy can't use their horses in battle anymore, but in this instance it might be because David is being careful to keep God's command from Deuteronomy 17:16, which says the king shouldn't acquire many horses. Scripture never tells us his motive, but those are two possibilities. And just to add more uncertainty, some scholars say this Hebrew word is better translated as "castrated" than "hamstrung," which would mean David turned all these war-horses into geldings.

David reigns with justice and equity, and he appoints a team of reputable leaders to run things for him, which shows his wisdom in delegation. He also displays a lot of integrity. For example, he remembers and keeps his promise to Jonathan from 1 Samuel 20:12–17. To keep your promise to a dead man really reveals your character, because the person isn't there to get angry if you don't follow through. But David's not just honoring Jonathan here—he's honoring God by keeping his word. In an effort to keep that promise, David actually *seeks out* someone from Jon's family to show kindness to them. He actively pursues the opportunity to bless others. When he finds out there's someone left alive in Jon's line, he responds immediately. Jon's son Mephibosheth is lame because of a terrible accident that happened when he was a child, so David has him brought to his home to live in his kingdom. He restores land to him and invites him to eat at his table for the rest of his life. All the work is done for Mephibosheth—all he needs is handed to him.

TODAY'S GOD SHOT

The way David treats Mephibosheth because of Jonathan is the way the Father treats us because of the Son. We're invited to live in His kingdom and eat at His table forever! And we could never get there on our own—we're too crippled by our sin. So He carries us. And all the work is done for us, because we can't do that either. *It is finished!* We get to live in His kingdom and eat at His table forever. Praise God for that, because He's where the joy is!

PSALMS 50, 53, 60, 75

Psalm 50 reveals that some Israelites view the sacrificial system as a trade-off for sinning—like a penalty you pay, a spiritual speeding ticket. God says that's never been what this is about. He doesn't want their bulls and goats and birds—He wants their hearts! This likely makes some of them wonder why He spends so much time telling them about the sacrifices. They are looking for a checklist and miss the very details that can reveal His heart to them. They view Him as greedy, as though He needs food to eat like all the pagan gods. Meanwhile their hearts are far from Him. They do wicked things, approve of others who are wicked, or just sit by idly when sin is committed. God rebukes them; He wants them to remember Him! One way to do that is to bring Him their gratitude and thanksgiving.

Psalm 53 is about the fool who dismisses God and does his own thing. When we live unaware of God's sovereignty and goodness, it becomes easy to think we're in control of our own future. And if we're the ones in charge, then lots of things can go wrong. And if lots of things can go wrong, then fear and striving are a natural response. Verse 5 says, "There they are, in great terror, when there is no terror." God says there's a way out for a person like this: The way of salvation and trusting God's goodness prompts rejoicing and gladness instead of fear and folly. It's counterintuitive, but surrender is the path to freedom. The only task the human will never be fatigued by is surrender.

In Psalm 60, David feels like God is angry and has rejected Israel. In verse 3 he uses a popular metaphor, comparing God's wrath to a cup of wine: "You have given us wine to drink that made us stagger," which basically translates to "This is some really intense wrath." God reminds him, "I love Israel. You're mine. I'm powerful and sovereign over your enemies—our enemies. I'll defeat them." David's still a little nervous but ultimately trusts God. In verse 5 he refers to Israel as God's *beloved*, despite their affliction. He knows who they are to God—he just doesn't see it at the moment. So he talks to God about it, God sets his heart straight, and he feels some emotional relief. This approach sounds far better than the downward spiral of despair and fear and anger we often fall into.

In Psalm 75, Asaph tells the wicked not to lift up their horns, but this isn't referring to a musical instrument. Horns represent strength, power, and victory, so for someone to lift up their horn would be an attempt (and probably an arrogant one) to demonstrate their power. Scripture refers to God as our horn, specifically the horn of our salvation. And sometimes in the prophetic books, we'll see images of beasts with multiple horns, which likely refers to a coalition with multiple powerful kings or kingdoms, each represented by a horn. All that to say: The horn itself is neither good nor bad—that's determined by who has the horn.

Verse 8 refers again to wine as God's wrath: "In the hand of the LORD there is a cup with foaming wine, well mixed, and he pours out from it, and all the wicked of the earth shall drain it down to the dregs." The wicked will fully know and experience God's wrath, because God executes judgment. This is a great reason to celebrate: The wicked will be cut off, the righteous will live, and God is just and can be trusted and praised!

TODAY'S GOD SHOT

"Mark this, then, you who forget God, lest I tear you apart, and there be none to deliver! The one who offers thanksgiving as his sacrifice glorifies me; to one who orders his way rightly I will show the salvation of God!" (Psalm 50:22–23). God wants to be remembered, and our remembering God is directly connected to our gratitude and thanksgiving. He wants to be the place where that thanksgiving is focused. Gratitude is an act of remembrance—we can't be grateful for something that hasn't happened yet or isn't currently happening. Gratitude connects us to God in our history, and it also compels us to obey Him in the future. Expressing gratitude knits our hearts to Him, which means we'll be much more likely to walk closely with Him. Because we know He's where the joy is!

2 SAMUEL 10; 1 CHRONICLES 19; PSALM 20

Today the Ammonite king dies. He's been friendly toward David, so David treats his son Hanun kindly. He's the likely heir to the throne, so it's a wise diplomatic move on David's part to keep peace with his neighbors. But Hanun's advisors are suspicious. They distrust his motives because they don't know him. They feel threatened, so they degrade his servants by shaving off half of their beards and cutting their clothes in half. Both of these things are emasculating. The beard is considered a mark of manhood, and the cutting of their garments in half symbolizes castration—something they do to prisoners of war to shame them. The men who came to serve Hanun are left half-naked and humiliated.

David isn't happy with the Ammonites, but he doesn't retaliate. The Ammonites go on the offense and hire more than thirty thousand mercenaries, including a bunch of Syrians who already hate Israel, to fight Israel on their behalf. David sends his army into battle led by Joab, whose trust in God is evident. In 10:12, he tells his brother Abishai, who is commanding another part of the army, "Be of good courage, and let us be courageous for our people, and for the cities of our God, and may the Lord do what seems good to him." This is what confidence and faith in God look like. He reminds his brother and himself that no matter what happens, God is in charge and He's trustworthy. And because of that, they can be courageous.

Israel's enemies flee before them but regret it and come back. When David hears, he goes out to fight against them and wins again. In the process, Israel kills a bunch of the Syrian mercenaries, and the surviving Syrians decide they're better off not helping the Ammonites anymore. Instead, the Syrians make peace with Israel and become their servants. Here the Israelites are "more than conquerors" yet again, turning their enemies into allies. As for the Ammonites, we leave their story hanging for now. This all started because David was trying to humbly send comforters to the new Ammonite king, Hanun, when his father died, but the Ammonite advisors mistrusted him. And in both battles, Israel was on the defense, not the offense.

You may have noticed a discrepancy in the number of chariots from today's two accounts. Second Samuel says there were seven hundred chariots, and 1 Chronicles says there were seven thousand. Your Bible may have a footnote about this, but if not, here's what's going on and why it's actually good that this discrepancy is left in: There are multiple ancient manuscripts, and when one says something different from the others, they'll often keep both bits of information in order to make sure that the truth is preserved somehow and that they don't accidentally delete the version that got it right. These kinds of things are rare, but it happens most often where numbers are involved. That kind of intentionality is worth the risk of confusion. But let's be honest: None of us are here for chariot numbers anyway. Our faith doesn't hinge on whether it was seven hundred or seven thousand, so don't lose sleep over the right number. We're here to see God, not chariots.

Psalm 20 is a corporate song of praise for God's promises to King David. Even though the promises of the Davidic covenant are specific to David, this psalm reveals God's heart for all His people. Verse 2 says, "May he send you help from the sanctuary." The word translated as "sanctuary" is most often translated as "holiness" elsewhere in Scripture: "May God send you help from His holiness." God's help originates from His holiness—He comes to us from His "set-apartness" to rescue us. He meets us in our need. He knows He's our only hope.

TODAY'S GOD SHOT

"May he grant you your heart's desire and fulfill all your plans" (Psalm 20:4). David knows that the only way God can answer this prayer with a yes is if those desires and plans align with God's desires and plans—otherwise, that would be less than the best, since God's plan is always best. This isn't a blanket request for God to reduce Himself to being a genie and doing whatever we want—it has the connotation of alignment, of being so in sync with God that we pray for what He has planned for. May He align our hearts with His, because He's where the joy is!

PSALMS 65–67, 69–70

Every line of Psalm 65 is rich. Verse 3 says, "When iniquities prevail against me, you atone for our transgressions." David's iniquities are stronger than his ability to rescue himself; they prevail against him. He knows he needs God's rescue and praises God for making atonement for his sins. God is also the Creator and Sustainer of all things. As they're harvesting the crops, David sees the abundance God has given them and praises His provision: "You crown the year with your bounty" (v. 11).

In Psalm 66, David praises God for triumphing over His enemies. He has a God-honoring view of the trials he's endured, and he's able to praise God even for hardships: "For you, O God, have tested us; you have tried us as silver is tried. You brought us into the net; you laid a crushing burden on our backs; you let men ride over our heads; we went through fire and through water; yet you have brought us out to a place of abundance" (vv. 10–12). He isn't holding a grudge against God because of what Israel has gone through; he's not saying, "I don't trust You anymore." Because of the parameters of the Davidic covenant, David knows Israel's struggles are the result of their rebellion, and even though he ascribes those hardships to God, he knows God did it in response to their sin. Despite their tough history, David has his heart set on praise: "Come and hear, all you who fear God, and I will tell what he has done for my soul" (v. 16). Wow.

Verse 18 gives us insight into God's attentiveness. Since God is everywhere and knows everything, then of course He hears all prayers—even prayers of those who don't know Him and who ask for things that don't glorify Him. He hears, but He's under no obligation to respond to people who don't know or love Him. Is it cruel for God not to heed their prayers? No. Those who cherish sin have no regard for what is best. Often, they only pray as a means to their selfish ends. So it's in *no one's* best interest for God to turn His ear to their prayers. This doesn't mean He never responds to them—just that He's under no obligation to. He always says yes when their prayers align with His will.

The author of Psalm 67 doesn't suffer from a scarcity mentality. This song features an Israelite asking God to save other nations, even their enemy nations. This psalmist knows how good and huge God is—big enough to be good to others without ignoring Israel. God has enough goodness to go around to people from all nations.

David wrote Psalms 69 and 70 as the representative of the people, so they can sing along with his lament. These laments are personal, but they're also public and even prophetic at times. Jesus echoed 69:4 in John 15:25: "They hated me without a cause," and He was given a sour drink when He was thirsty on the cross (69:21). "Zeal for your house has consumed me" (69:9) is a prophetic word about Jesus turning over tables in the temple in John 2:17. David is weary, surrounded by enemies who hate him without cause and lie about him. While he isn't altogether innocent, he's innocent of what he's been accused of. He doesn't want this to bring shame on Israel. He loves God and God's people, and he trusts God to rescue him. No one gets him except God—they're all cruel, adding to his pain. He prays for his enemies to be punished. This, of course, assumes they remain unrepentant. Nothing we've seen from David or God indicates an unwillingness to forgive those who repent. "May all who seek you rejoice and be glad in you!" (70:4). The punishment he asks God to deliver to his enemies is contingent on their position as God's enemies, not just *his* enemies—and those who repent are no longer God's enemies.

TODAY'S GOD SHOT

"Blessed is the one you choose and bring near" (Psalm 65:4). Do you realize how blessed you are? If you know God, it's because He chose you and He brought you near! We were far from Him—enemies by birth. But He bent down and adopted us into His family through no effort of our own. He brought us near and seated us at His table. We couldn't get there on our own. But He came and got us. And He put His Spirit inside us as a guarantee of the relationship we have with Him. It's the greatest blessing of our lives, because He's where the joy is!

2 SAMUEL 11–12; 1 CHRONICLES 20

Today is a dark day in David's story. Kings are typically involved in military exploits, but when it's time for war, David stays home, exposing a gap in his leadership: passivity. He shirks responsibility. While Israel is off to war, he sees Bathsheba bathing on a roof, which is where people bathe because rainwater collects there. She's keeping God's command, purifying herself. We have no reason to think she's trying to seduce David. She likely assumes the king is off to war like he's supposed to be, since that's where her husband, Uriah, is. As she's being obedient, armed guards show up at her door and bring her to David's palace. The common belief is that they had an affair, but Scripture never puts the blame on Bathsheba for what happens. God addresses the sin here, but it's always solely attributed to David. It seems likely that Bathsheba was raped while trying to be obedient to God's law. *Rape* is a strong word, but it doesn't always look like an act of violence. We can't tiptoe around Scripture just because it makes us uncomfortable or paints David in a negative light. Uriah is at war, and Bathsheba's pregnant, so it obviously can't be his baby. The punishment for adultery is death, so Uriah could have her killed. She's at the mercy of these two men. She can't appeal to the law, because the king is her offender.

David hatches a plan to bring her husband home so he'll have an excuse for the pregnancy. But he underestimates Uriah's commitment to Israel's wartime celibacy standard. Uriah refuses to see his wife, so David moves to plan B: Have Uriah murdered in battle. In a cruel move, David sends Uriah back to the battlefield holding the very letter that orders his death. Bathsheba is violated, pregnant, and widowed. She mourns her husband. "The thing that David had done displeased the LORD" (2 Samuel 11:27). Another translation says, "It was evil in the eyes of Yahweh" (LEB). There's no evidence of her complicity here. Only David is mentioned. She's forced to marry her offender, who murdered her husband, so she takes her place in his harem of women.

For more information on today's reading, see thebiblerecap.com/links.

God sends the prophet Nathan to tell David a parable *about David*, but he's so self-deceived that he doesn't catch on. He either thinks he hasn't sinned or that his sin won't be discovered. He pronounces judgment on himself by demanding a fourfold repayment. Nathan exposes David, and God has harsh words for him: He's entitled and ungrateful. This is tantamount to despising God's words, and it led him to do evil. David earned the death penalty twice over, but Nathan says God has put away his sin. What an incredible act of mercy!

While there's forgiveness, sin is not without consequence. The fourfold judgment David demanded is handed out to him: (1) There'll be division and death in his family, (2) his wives will be taken away from him in a humiliating way, (3) God will raise up evil against him from his own house, and (4) his child with Bathsheba will die. He fasts and prays over his son's sickness. God is the only one he can turn to. But God says no. The baby dies. God knows what it's like to have a son die, and David shares in that pain. In true repentance, he positions himself with humility. Even after his son's death and hearing such a harsh word from God, he trusts God's goodness and draws near to worship Him. Repentance is marked by worship. When David goes to comfort Bathsheba, they conceive again, and the child is Solomon. Israel defeats the Ammonites and the Philistines. These military victories are an act of mercy too. Given David's breaking of the covenant, Israel should've lost. But he goes back to war, bearing the responsibility that he previously shirked, and God grants victory.

TODAY'S GOD SHOT

In 2 Samuel 12:8, God lists all the things He's given David. He says, "If this were too little, I would add to you as much more!" David gets greedy, because he forgets how rich and generous God is. He forgets the Father's heart. God has already blessed him with more than enough and is still willing to give more. God is a good Father who wants to lavish gifts on His children! Jesus says, "Fear not, little flock, for it is your Father's good pleasure to give you the kingdom" (Luke 12:32). In a day filled with sadness, it's still true that He's where the joy is!

PSALMS 32, 51, 86, 122

As David praises God's forgiveness and mercy, we see his repentance. Psalm 32 thanks God for the ways He blesses His kids even when we sin. He doesn't bless our sin, but He blesses us when we sin by covering our sins and convicting us of our sins. If we try to cover our own sins, that usually means we're hiding them. But when God covers sin, He atones for it, pays for it—for all your sin and rebellion, past, present, and future. At the start of the psalm, David is the one doing the covering, but by the end, David uncovers his sin and God covers it. This is what God the Son did for us on the cross. God the Spirit plays a different role. He lives in believers and points out spots where our sin has trapped us so He can guide us out. John 16:8 calls this conviction, and it's different from condemnation. God's kids will never be condemned, because our sins have been covered by Jesus (Romans 8:1). Conviction, on the other hand, is when God the Spirit prompts us to grieve our sins and He changes our hearts and actions to align with His will.

When the Spirit's conviction comes, there's no true rest or happiness until we repent. David has been experiencing the heaviness of the Spirit's conviction, and it's exhausting, so he finally confesses. He says, "When I kept silent, my bones wasted away through my groaning all day long. For day and night your hand was heavy upon me; my strength was dried up as by the heat of summer. I acknowledged my sin to you, and I did not cover my iniquity; I said, 'I will confess my transgressions to the Lord,' and you forgave the iniquity of my sin" (vv. 3–5). He uses almost every possible word to describe his evil actions: sin, iniquity, transgression. It's so freeing for him that he encourages everyone to confess their sins to God.

In Psalm 51 he demonstrates confession. It's his psalm of repentance. In verse 4, he says he has only sinned against God. He knows he's sinned against Bathsheba, Uriah, and the whole nation of Israel, but his focus in this particular psalm is on restoring his broken intimacy with God. Nothing else can get set right until that is set right. He's been a sinner from birth—even from the womb—because he was born into the fall of man. From the first moment of his existence, sin dwelled in him. He's not passing the blame; it's more like he's saying, "This isn't the only time I've messed up. My whole life is full of things like this." He asks God to create a new heart in him, to change him. The word *create* means "to form out of nothing." When God gives us a new heart of flesh, it's not the same material as the heart of stone we were born with. We get new spiritual DNA. Then he asks God not to remove His Spirit. This was a legitimate prayer at the time, because God the Spirit moved around a lot. But now that God dwells *in* people, the expiration date on this prayer has passed. If you're a child of God, you never have to pray this or worry about this!

In Psalm 86, he asks God to teach him truth and change his heart. He knows he has a divided heart and asks God to fix it, to deal with his duplicity and unite his heart.

Psalm 122 is a Song of Ascent focused on God's relationship with all the people David rules over. David's sin had national consequences, so he prays for the city and its people, for peace and security, and he promises that he'll seek its good.

TODAY'S GOD SHOT

"I will instruct you and teach you in the way you should go; I will counsel you with my eye upon you. Be not like a horse or a mule, without understanding, which must be curbed with bit and bridle, or it will not stay near you" (Psalm 32:8–9). God wants us close! And He tells us what that looks like: (a) He offers guidance to His kids and doesn't leave us to figure things out on our own; He instructs us, teaches us, counsels us, and watches us; and (b) He tells us not to be foolish and stubborn in response to Him and to pay attention and yield to His leading, the conviction of His Spirit. The more we loosen our grip on the things we've been trying to control, the more we'll easily feel and follow His promptings, which keep us near Him. Hallelujah! That's where we want to be. He's where the joy is!

2 SAMUEL 13–15

Amnon, David's firstborn, falls in love with his half sister Tamar. His cousin gives him advice that isn't just bad—it's wicked: Amnon should pretend to be needy so he can prey on Tamar and rape her. Amnon sets the plan in motion, and Tamar tells him no and tries to reason with him, but he overpowers her. Lust is impatient, selfish, not open to reason—it's the *opposite* of what we read about love in 1 Corinthians 13. When Amnon's so-called love turns to hate, he kicks her out, adding to his wickedness. The law requires him to marry her or honor her with a bride price (Exodus 22:16–17), but he shirks responsibility.

Tamar's life is ruined. No one will marry her now—not in this culture. She's consigned to live childless and alone. As she mourns, she fills her brother Absalom in, and he begins to hate Amnon, so he hatches a plan to murder him. Absalom tricks him into coming on a road trip, gets him drunk, and has his servants murder him. He's now David's oldest living son. David gets a fake news report that Absalom killed all his sons, and he mourns. Even though he only killed one of his brothers, Absalom knows it won't go over well with his dad, so he flees to live with his maternal grandfather among the Transjordan tribes. David misses him and wants to make things right. He's already forgiven Absalom in his heart, but Absalom never repented and isn't looking to reconcile. He wants to take over. He's waiting for David to die. In fact, remember how he tried to convince David to go on the same road trip, but David declined? It's likely he was planning to murder David too, so he could slide onto the throne unhindered.

Meanwhile, David's nephew and military commander Joab hires an actress to tell David a fake story about having one son who killed the other so she can segue into telling him to bring Absalom back. David knows Joab put her up to it, so he calls Joab in and says, "Okay, bring Absalom home, but I won't see him." Absalom comes home, and they don't speak for two years. Absalom tries to summon Joab twice, but Joab doesn't reply, so Absalom burns his field to get his attention. It works. Absalom says he wants to talk to David even if David tries to kill him. But David doesn't kill him—he kisses him. It's a sign of reconciliation, but it's all a ruse on Absalom's part. He's acquiring a chariot and horses and other signs of wealth and power. He's making strides to take over the throne. He even undermines David's kingdom by intercepting people who want advice from David and taking their side in every argument. They fall for his deceptive charisma. Eventually he asks David for permission to "go pay a vow," but it's another ruse; he's staging a coup with two hundred men, including David's personal advisor Ahithophel.

When David hears, he escapes Jerusalem. As he flees, he leaves the ark behind because he hopes God will bring him back to Jerusalem. He asks a Levite priest and Ahithophel to keep him posted but then gets word that Ahithophel is a traitor and is on Team Absalom. Ahithophel is Bathsheba's grandfather, so it's possible he's seeking revenge for what David did years earlier. David prays that anyone Ahithophel counsels won't listen. God brings a yes to that prayer almost immediately. David's friend Hushai shows up and agrees to play the role of informant, and he makes it to Jerusalem just as Absalom arrives.

TODAY'S GOD SHOT

In this family feud God's timing is so kind. David has been betrayed by his mentor, who has now joined forces with his estranged son, and it looks like David might lose everything on top of that—his palace, his kingdom, even the city named after him. But God made David a promise, and even though David broke their covenant, God still shows mercy and honors His side of things. He's still working out His plan to bring the Messiah through David's line, despite David's sin. And like only God can, He works out the precise timing for David to get news of Ahithophel's betrayal and to run into Hushai, and then for Hushai to run into Absalom. It doesn't matter how many people the enemy ropes into his conspiracy against God's plan and God's people—nothing beats sovereignty. What a relief! He's still in control, and He's where the joy is!

PSALMS 3–4, 12–13, 28, 55

David wrote Psalm 3 when he fled Jerusalem during Absalom's coup. The people he once led are speaking ill of his soul, saying he's beyond saving. Not only is that hurtful to David, but it's an affront to God's character. God loves to save even the most wicked and vile—it displays His mercy and forgiveness! David has no idea how many people Absalom turned against him, but it's at least in the hundreds, if not thousands, especially given all those Absalom won over when he was flattering people at the city gates. Despite that, David knows who God is. He trusts God and asks Him to rescue him. These circumstances haven't dimmed the brightness of God's goodness to him.

Psalm 4 has similar themes except it's written for corporate worship, not personal worship. It expresses confidence in God and points out that the anger David feels for being mistreated has to be submitted to God too—that's part of what it looks like to put your trust in God. He knows that, ultimately, the nearness of God is where peace will be found, not in circumstances. He has more joy in knowing God than all his enemies have in their prosperity and abundance. God can't be taken away like wine, grain, and material blessings, so David doesn't lie awake at night anxious about losing everything. All that matters is secure, so he sleeps peacefully.

Psalm 12 addresses the utter lack of righteous people in the world. David is especially bothered by the lies people tell, their pride and arrogance, and the way they ignore the plight of the poor and needy. God distances Himself from liars and proud people, and since mistreatment of the poor and needy gets God's attention, David expects God to be moved to action when people are oppressed. He asks God to guard them from the wicked around them.

Psalm 13 is another example of how feelings don't always align with truth. David feels forgotten, but God hasn't forgotten him. He longs for God's nearness and counsel. He feels desperate, having to be his own counselor. He ends by reminding his soul that hope is coming—he knows

God is trustworthy, and he's going to praise Him for what He's already done while he waits to see what He'll do next. Psalm 28 reiterates a lot of these themes. When God seems distant, David feels like he's dying—going down to the pit. *The pit* likely refers to the grave or the realm of the dead, much like how *Sheol* is used, though some say it refers to prison, which often ends in death in these days. In addition to wanting God's nearness, David wants punishment for the wicked.

Psalm 55 is well suited to David's circumstances: He's been betrayed by his son and his mentor, he's fled his palace and his city, his son is attempting a coup, and he can't say for certain whether there's a bounty on his head. He wants to escape it all. He prays, "Destroy, O Lord, divide their tongues" (v. 9). This points back to the Tower of Babel, where God divided their language into many, causing confusion and division that thwarted their mission. David's enemies are people he once considered friends. Jesus certainly knows what that's like—He had Judas, so He can commiserate. David trusts God to humble his enemies and reminds himself in the meantime to trust God with the outcome.

TODAY'S GOD SHOT

"Be their shepherd and carry them forever" (Psalm 28:9). Jesus calls Himself the Good Shepherd (John 10:11), and Psalm 23 says, "The LORD is my Shepherd" (v. 1). It's fitting that we're compared to sheep. They do have lots of external enemies—like thieves and wolves—but their most dangerous enemy, the one who is always present, is themselves. And sheep can't be trusted; they're foolish animals with a short memory and can't see what's directly in front of them. The only way the sheep is safe from his outside enemies and himself is if the shepherd is carrying him. David knows this; he was a shepherd. Saying, "Be their shepherd and carry them forever" is like praying, "Protect them from their external enemies and protect them from themselves." As tough as it was for David to go to battle against a giant or to have King Saul trying to kill him, the worst things that have happened to him are things *he* initiated. "Be their shepherd and carry them forever." Our Good Shepherd—He's where the joy is!

2 SAMUEL 16–18

As David continues fleeing, he runs into Ziba, a servant of Mephibosheth. Ziba brings him gifts and says Mephibosheth is going to try to assume the throne David stole from his father, Jonathan. After all he's done for Mephibosheth, this is shocking. And God gave David the throne—he didn't take it! So David hands all of Mephibosheth's blessings over to Ziba. Then he encounters Shimei, who is cursing him and calling him a murderer—which is true, but not in regard to Saul. David's servant wants to kill him, but David's trust in God allows him to incur insult without fighting back; he humbly receives what comes to him as though it's from God's hand. Shimei is a Benjamite, a relative of Saul. The Benjamites never warmed up to having David as king, because he's a Judahite, and they think the royal line should continue through their tribe. Still, cursing the king is illegal and punishable by death, but David spares him.

Meanwhile in Jerusalem, Absalom runs into Hushai, David's double agent. Absalom is suspicious of him, but Hushai pretends to be on Team Absalom. When Absalom seeks counsel from Ahithophel, the advisor he stole from David, he advises him to sleep with David's concubines. Sleeping with a king's wife or concubine is a way of making a claim on the throne. Ahithophel's advice is highly regarded, so Absalom follows it. Without even knowing it, they bring about the fulfillment of one of the four consequences of David's sin: "I will take your wives before your eyes and give them to your neighbor, and he shall lie with your wives in the sight of this sun" (2 Samuel 12:11).

After this, Ahithophel unpacks his plan for killing David so Absalom can take the throne. Absalom asks Hushai for a second opinion. Hushai criticizes Ahithophel's advice and comes up with an elaborate plan that will allow David time to escape or retaliate. Hushai is sly in his delivery. He praises Absalom as he explains his plan while also giving him subtle reminders that his dad and his men are really good warriors, which likely plants hesitation in Absalom's mind. Absalom takes Hushai's advice instead of Ahithophel's, and Ahithophel sees the writing on the wall. God is not with his counsel and God is not with Absalom, because David is God's man for the throne. Ahithophel also knows this means he'll be killed for treason when David inevitably returns to Jerusalem, so he hangs himself.

Hushai secretly appoints messengers to fill David in, but some of Absalom's crew spot them. They hide in a well but eventually reach David and tell him to flee across the Jordan River. As David flees, three men bring food and provisions and beds for them from far away.

Following Hushai's advice, Absalom's army seeks David. David sends his army out but says not to harm Absalom if they find him. While Absalom is riding his mule through the forest, his head gets caught in a tree. Scholars think this refers to his thick hair getting caught in a branch. His mule rides off, so he's left hanging. A soldier reports this to Joab, and he's angry the soldier obeyed David's command and left Absalom alive. Joab finds Absalom and stabs him in the heart and declares an end to the battle. When messengers bring David the news and he hears that Absalom has died, he goes off to be alone, to weep and mourn.

TODAY'S GOD SHOT

God works through Ahithophel's advice. The first time he gives him counsel, Absalom takes it, which brings about the fulfillment of God's words in 12:11. The second time he gives counsel, Absalom doesn't take it, which is an answer to David's prayer in 15:31. Both responses line up perfectly with God's sovereign plan. "The LORD had ordained to defeat the good counsel of Ahithophel, so that the LORD might bring harm upon Absalom" (17:14). God is in the seemingly coincidental timing of David's encountering Hushai. He's in the curious timing of Hushai and Absalom reaching Jerusalem simultaneously. He's in the hesitation in Absalom's mind as he gets a second opinion. He's working in all things, seen and unseen, to bring about His good plan. He can be trusted with timing, He can be trusted with chance encounters, and He can be trusted even with the thoughts and plans of our enemies. He's in control, and He's where the joy is!

PSALMS 26, 40, 58, 61–62, 64

It seems like David is boasting about his righteousness in the beginning of Psalm 26, but then he says the source of his righteousness is God's steadfast love—*that's* what equips him. He's walking in God's faithfulness, not his own—a crucial distinction. Many of his friends betrayed him and joined forces with his estranged son, Absalom, so the references to hypocrites and men of falsehood are fitting. He wants to be markedly different as a man of integrity for the glory of God. He wants to be vindicated as he disassociates from the evildoers.

If we zoom out on the timeline of David's life, Psalm 40 fits it perfectly. He waits patiently before the Lord just like he waited fifteen years to be king. God drew him up out of the pit of destruction when Saul tried to kill him. He continued to praise God, and God continued to bless him. He proclaimed God's goodness for all to hear—in song, in conversation, among groups of people—he can't stop talking about God's goodness! But things take a rough turn in verse 12, just like they did in his life. His iniquity and sin—like with Bathsheba and Uriah—have overtaken him. He asks God to rescue him from the consequences of his sin; some of his enemies want to take his life—like Absalom and Ahithophel. When he claims to be poor and needy, he's pointing more to the state of his heart than to the size of his bank account. In the Sermon on the Mount, Jesus said, "Blessed are the poor in spirit" (Matthew 5:3), and this is what that spiritual poverty looks like. He knows he has nothing to offer God. He's humbled by his sin and his enemies, and God is his only hope.

His anger hits a boiling point in Psalm 58, but he never crosses into selfish revenge. He only wants justice. He never sets out to attain it for himself, even though as king, he could justify it. He knows God is a righteous judge and trusts Him to act. Things cool down in Psalm 61. God has been a refuge to him in the past, like when Saul sought his life, so David reminds himself of God's provision in the middle of his bleak circumstances. He wants to go back to Jerusalem, to the city God has set His name on, so that he can draw near to God.

In Psalm 62 those who betrayed him try to overthrow his position, but he knows God is his Rock, his stability. He's been surrounded by hypocrites and liars and has just found out the truth, and he'd rather keep silent than talk about it, because who knows who can be trusted? So he pours out his heart to God, because God can be trusted. Man's rank and position is ever changing, but God is solid ground. He's both powerful and loving, and He can be trusted to do what's right.

Psalm 64 recounts the steps of David's enemies. His words describe what happened when Absalom sought counsel from Ahithophel and Hushai: "They search out injustice" (v. 6). Absalom was trying to establish the best plan for carrying out evil. "But God shoots his arrows at them" (v. 7). Remember the three arrows Joab used to pierce through Absalom's heart? At the end of the song when David says, "Let the righteous one rejoice," it's almost as if he's preaching to himself. When we last saw him, he was mourning, but maybe soon he'll be able to rejoice amid tragedy. He rejoiced even when he lost his first son with Bathsheba, so it's possible. He knows how to take his sadness to God; he knows worship and lament aren't mutually exclusive.

TODAY'S GOD SHOT

"In sacrifice and offering you have not delighted, but you have given me an open ear. Burnt offering and sin offering you have not required. . . . 'I delight to do your will, O my God; your law is within my heart'" (Psalm 40:6–8). What does it reveal about God that these verses are in the Old Testament—the very place where all the sacrifices and offerings are listed out as commands? It reveals that the sacrificial system God set up was never fully sufficient, and it was never intended to be, because Jesus's death was always the plan. Goats and bulls have never been enough. God has always been after our hearts, not our sacrifices. He doesn't delight in people giving Him dead animals; instead, He delights in being the Giver—giving people ears that hear Him and hearts that know He's where the joy is!

2 SAMUEL 19–21

David mourns Absalom's death. Joab rebukes him for not being more grateful for the victory and for letting his enemy's death weigh him down. David responds to his rebuke, putting a stop to his grief and going home to Jerusalem to appear before the people, but it seems like he harbors resentment for Joab's harsh words. The people of Israel aren't sure what to do with David now. Should they still regard him as king? The responses are divided along tribal lines: David's tribe of Judah has one opinion, and the rest of Israel has another. Judah is hesitant about reinstating him. As he tries to convince their leaders to reinstate him, he unexpectedly replaces Joab, the commander of his army, with Amasa, who was the commander of Absalom's army twenty-four hours earlier. This could be motivated by David's bitterness over Joab's rebuke or by David's desire to get Judah back on his side. Regardless, Judah reinstates him. This probably feels like a slap in the face to Joab, even though he sticks by David.

Once David is king again, he pardons a bunch of his enemies. Shimei, the man who cursed at him, comes groveling before him, and David makes an oath not to kill him. Then Mephibosheth tells David an entirely different version of the story from what he heard from Ziba when he brought David the gifts in 16:1–4. Mephibosheth says he didn't try to take the kingdom away from David, and David seems to believe him. David has already given Ziba all of Mephibosheth's blessings, so he offers to split things up fifty-fifty in order to honor his commitment to both men, even though at least one of them is lying. He also makes a generous offer to Barzillai, one of the men who brought him food and provisions in exile. Barzillai rejects it and suggests David take another man—probably his son—back to Jerusalem with him.

Judah and the rest of Israel are still divided about David, but the tables have turned: Judah backs David and the other tribes oppose him. The Benjamites, Saul's tribe, think a Benjamite should be king. A Benjamite named Sheba calls for the men of Israel to leave David's army, and they do. David knows this is a problem, so he calls on his new military commander, Amasa, to gather their army and attack. Amasa procrastinates, so David calls in the second string, including Joab, the former commander. How awkward! When Amasa shows up, Joab pretends to greet him but stabs him instead. With Amasa dead, Joab resumes his role as commander and goes after Sheba. He besieges the city where Sheba is hiding. He's ready to destroy the whole city, but a peaceable, faithful woman reasons with him: "There's no reason for you to kill us all. Just tell us what you want." Joab says they're just there for Sheba, and she promises to toss his head over the wall, which she does, eliminating the most recent threat to David's throne. She's praised for her wisdom, and she saves an entire city!

When David asks God about a famine they're experiencing, God says it's because of Saul's sins. David has inherited not only the kingdom but the consequences of the previous king's decisions. Saul killed some Gibeonites after promising to spare them, so David asks them how he can make it right. They want to kill seven of Saul's descendants. David doesn't seem to consult God on the matter, and he decides it's better for seven people to die than for many more people to die from famine. God never endorses David's response, and in fact, the famine continues even after the men are killed and doesn't cease until they're buried, which some scholars view as a sign that God is displeased with David's actions.

TODAY'S GOD SHOT

God takes sin seriously. Israel is suffering because a dead king broke a promise. His sin happened a long time ago, but God cares about justice. He can be trusted to handle those things, which means we don't have to take matters into our own hands. We can pursue Him instead of vengeance. We can love both Him and our enemies. When we're wronged, God can be trusted to work on our behalf in the hearts of those who have wronged us. And when we've wronged others, He works in us on their behalf. He's working to restore all things, including not only our stories but our hearts! He's where the joy is!

PSALMS 5, 38, 41–42

In Psalm 5, David, the king, calls God *his* King. It's an act of humility and worship to recognize that even though he is the ruler of a nation, he's still subordinate to God. In verse 7, after pointing out that evil won't dwell in God's house, he recognizes that the only reason he gets to be in God's presence is not because he himself is good, but because God is good. He says, "I, through the abundance of your steadfast love, will enter your house." David knows his own wickedness; he hasn't forgotten. He doesn't think he's perfect—he just knows he's been forgiven for his sins because of his relationship with God. And again we see that his fear of God draws him near to God; it doesn't push him away.

In verse 10, when he asks God to punish his enemies, he doesn't ask God to do it in response to their evil against him but in response to their evil against God. He says, "Cast them out, for they have rebelled against you." David's love for justice is adjacent to his love for God.

We've probably all experienced a situation like David does in Psalm 38. He's enduring all kinds of pain and suffering simultaneously—physical, emotional, spiritual, relational—and he knows it's the result of his own sin and foolishness. He repents of his sin and accepts that these are his consequences, but he asks God to bring him relief—specifically, relief in the form of His nearness and salvation. When you've known the nearness of God like David has, feeling distant from Him is far more painful than any other kind of suffering. In the second-to-last verse, he says, "Do not forsake me, O Lord! O my God, be not far from me."

David opens Psalm 41 with an interesting line. He says those who consider the poor are the ones who are blessed, or happy. God is attentive to those who are attentive to the needy. Perhaps he points this out because he has been kind to the poor, and now he sees how God is being attentive to him, especially in his sickness. This is possibly the same physical suffering he mentions in Psalm 38. David's enemies think he's on the brink of death, but David is asking God to restore him. There's no entitlement in this request, though; he's humble, not demanding. In verse 10 he says, "Be gracious to me, and raise me up." He knows that physical healing would be God's grace—something he doesn't deserve. He closes by thanking God for upholding him up to this point, and he knows that the ultimate good is to be in God's presence.

In Psalm 42, the sons of Korah pick up on David's theme as they cry out for the nearness of God. It's written as a first-person psalm. He's desperate for God. He portrays himself as an animal who is dying of thirst. He remembers what it's like to feel near to God. He talks to his despairing soul and commands it to hope in God, and at the same time, he expresses his feelings that God has forgotten him—even though we know this is impossible. He trusts that there will be restoration, and he praises God in expectation of that time.

TODAY'S GOD SHOT

These psalms are so comforting when we're in situations like David's, when we feel distant from God. If you've ever felt parched in the desert, if you've ever felt the enemy's taunt, you probably know what it's like to wait for God's nearness and salvation to become evident. In those places, we can respond like David does, remembering the ways He has delivered us through trials in the past. Each of the psalms we read today ends with a request for God to act and an earnest belief that He will. David rehearses God's character and commands his soul to believe it. Sometimes it's in our darkest hours and when He feels the furthest from us that we finally realize He's where the joy is!

2 SAMUEL 22–23; PSALM 57

Today we approach the end of David's life, so we're beginning to look back at the many ways God has worked in his life through all the ups and downs. David's doing this too, in song form. His song in chapter 22 bears a lot of similarity to Psalm 18, so here's a reminder of what we talked about on that day:

David wrote Psalm 18 on the day God saved him from all his enemies. He testifies to God's goodness through his trials. While he makes a lot of claims about his righteousness, he also says it and all his blessings are gifts from God. It's God who makes his way blameless, and God is the one who equips him, delivers him, and protects him. First Samuel 30:6 says, "David strengthened himself in the LORD his God." He didn't strengthen himself in himself. He strengthened himself in the LORD his God! God is the source of all the good things we offer back to Him.

In chapter 23, David begins by identifying himself humbly—as the son of Jesse—then points out ways God exalted the lowly, raising him up and anointing him. God speaks to him and through him, and he serves as a prophet to Israel, not just a king. God is like sunlight and rain, bringing life and light to David as he rules by the fear of God—which is a stark contrast to Saul, who ruled by fear of man.

God made a covenant with David, and He continues to deal with David according to that covenant; it hasn't changed, and everything that has transpired in David's life has been a fixed part of God's precise, unshakeable plan. We close by recounting exploits and victories of his mighty men, including the incident when David happened to mention how he wanted some water from back home, which happened to be surrounded by the Philistines. David's men were so loyal to him that three of them risked their lives to go get him the water he casually referenced. But when they brought it back to him, he poured it out on the ground—not because he was ungrateful but because he wanted to show that their lives were more valuable than water or any of his fleeting desires. This may seem disrespectful to them, but this is a way of showing them loyalty in return. At the very end of the list, however, we see the man he was not loyal to: Uriah, Bathsheba's husband.

David wrote Psalm 57 when he hid from Saul in the cave. A lot of his life has involved crying out to God for help, and he's seen God deliver him in the most unlikely circumstances. By paying attention to God's consistent deliverance, he has grown to trust God over time, so when he encounters new trials or new lions or new enemies, his response is to praise God and expect God to deliver him. He may ask, "How long, O Lord?" from time to time, but he always seems to trust there's an answer. He knows that regardless of what happens, God is working in it all to fulfill His purpose. In verse 2, he says, "I cry out to God Most High, to God who fulfills his purpose for me." How comforting it is to be reminded that God is at work on our behalf and that His plans for us can't be thwarted, because He's God Most High!

TODAY'S GOD SHOT

Today showed us some unique things about God that we haven't seen elsewhere in our reading—at least not with the kind of poetry David uses here. In 2 Samuel 22:36 David says, "Your gentleness made me great." God's gentleness doesn't get a lot of press, but David says it directly corresponds to what has made him fruitful in life. David has been the recipient of God's gentleness—particularly in the way God showed him mercy despite his sins. And David has also displayed God's gentleness. He didn't lord his power or position over others. He spared Saul's life, he cared for Mephibosheth, he pardoned his enemies. This is what meekness looks like. Meekness isn't weakness; it's strength that has been disciplined by humility—and it manifests in David as gentleness. For God Himself to display gentleness is remarkable and noteworthy. God is gentle with us, and He's where the joy is!

PSALMS 95, 97–99

Psalm 95 opens with praise, reminding us that God isn't just supreme in the earthly realm, He's supreme in the spiritual realm too. He's worthy of worship—especially the worship of His people. Verse 6 says, "Oh come, let us worship and bow down; let us kneel before the LORD, our Maker!" It's not entirely evident in the English translation, but this short verse describes three different postures for worshipping God: *Bowing* and *down* are two separate acts, and *kneeling* is the third. These humble postures demonstrate honor and submission, which is how we should all relate to the One who made us. But then he goes on to describe another aspect of our relationship with God. It's not contradictory to the humble bowing toward our Maker—it's complementary. He portrays God as our Shepherd, the one who is attentive to us and feeds us and watches over us. He calls us "the sheep of his hand" (v. 7). It's a much more intimate, relational picture. Both things are true of our relationship with God. He's our Maker and He's our Shepherd. He doesn't just make us, then set us aside and move on to other things. He's with us all the time, watching over us.

The psalmist begs the listeners not to harden their hearts to such great truths, and he references the Israelites who did have hardened hearts. They didn't know God's ways, and they missed out on the beautiful complexity of this kind of relationship with Him, the kind that brings rest and restoration.

In Psalm 97, the psalmist reiterates God's supremacy over everything. He depicts God as a thunderstorm with lightning that strikes and consumes His enemies. He says God melts the mountains like wax, which is a direct affront to all the ancient pagan deities that were believed to live on those mountains. God shames them by bringing them low. Meanwhile, God's people rejoice.

Psalm 98 has a lot in common with Isaiah 52, which is a prophecy about the coming Messiah, so it's no surprise that this psalm repeatedly references God's salvation. When this song was written, the psalmist was

likely only referring to the military version of salvation—deliverance from enemies big and small. But there seems to be more going on here than the psalmist realized at the time. For instance, when he writes, "All the ends of the earth have seen the salvation of our God" in verse 3, he's likely just referring to how everyone saw the way God worked on Israel's behalf in military battles, or even His miraculous provision—like sending His manna in the wilderness. But in light of the Messianic promise to establish a relationship between God the Father and people from every nation, this verse takes on a whole new meaning: "All the ends of the earth have seen the salvation of our God." The psalmist probably had no idea how much more this verse would encompass, how God was layering truth upon truth throughout his song!

We ended with Psalm 99, another psalm praising God's kingship. Verse 1 positions God above the cherubim on the ark of the covenant, which is regarded as His earthly throne. Unlike many kings, He rules with equity and justice. This song reminds us of the great privilege we've experienced in having God come down to earth to establish a relationship with humankind. He's set up mediators, He speaks through them, He's given us His presence on earth, and He's given us His Word. We have everything we need to know Him better and respond to Him with worship. He even forgives us when we sin. We lack nothing!

TODAY'S GOD SHOT

Psalm 97:11 says, "Light is sown for the righteous, and joy for the upright in heart." You may wonder where God is in this sentence. His presence is never stated, but it's beautifully implied. Who do you think is doing the sowing? It's Him! He's sowing light and joy for the upright in heart! If you're in a dark season, the light and joy might not have bloomed yet, but God has planted them. Sometimes it takes a while for things that are planted to grow and bear fruit, but trust that they've been sown for you by His hand. May His light dawn on you so that you'll be able to confidently say, "He's where the joy is!"

2 SAMUEL 24;
1 CHRONICLES 21–22; PSALM 30

You may have noticed a discrepancy between the two accounts of David's census. Second Samuel says God incited David to take the census, and 1 Chronicles says Satan incited him. So which is it? Don't resist this tension—it's there for a reason. This may be the perfect scriptural example of how evil works *within* God's plan. Just like with Job, God's enemy wants to perpetrate evil against God's people, and God allows it. Because He allows it, it still falls under His sovereignty. And as with all things, He promises to use it for our good and His purposes.

Taking a census isn't bad; God even commands it at times—as we've read about at length. But here David does it of his own volition, not at God's command. Joab knows it's a bad idea and tries to dissuade David, but David forges ahead. Immediately, he feels conviction. Many scholars think the problem is that a census puts the focus on numbers instead of on God. Since nations put confidence in the size of their military, censuses are a routine part of planning for war. Israel has been under attack by the Philistines, and David may want to be confident in their numbers, but God wants his confidence to be in Him.

When David repents, God offers him a choice of consequences: famine, sword, or pestilence. David chooses three days of pestilence, and seventy thousand people die. The Angel of the LORD comes with His flaming sword to carry out justice but makes a turn for mercy when the Father commands it. He preserves Jerusalem. David offers himself up instead of the people, but God has him make an offering instead. Just like He did when He provided a sacrifice for Abraham to offer instead of Isaac, He provides David with an alternative. The only problem is they're supposed to offer burnt offerings at the site of the tabernacle, which is currently in Gibeon. The good news: God instructs him to offer the sacrifice at the threshing floor of Ornan the Jebusite. The bad

news: That's where the Angel of the Lord is positioned, which is kind of terrifying. Even Ornan's kids run and hide when they see the Angel.

David makes his sacrifice, then something significant happens. God sends fire to consume it on the threshing floor, signaling His approval of this site as the new location of His home. This is now the acceptable place where sacrifices will be made, right here on the threshing floor. But Ornan owns it and he's a Jebusite, one of the people who lived in Jerusalem before David conquered it. When the king wants your land, you give it to him. But David insists on paying for it, and he buys the land at Ornan's price. This is where the First Temple is built. Solomon is still young, but David gives him this charge. He tells Solomon how he wanted to build God a house and God said no, but comforted him with the promise that someday he'd have a son named Solomon who'd build the temple. He also tells Solomon the royal line of kings will descend through him.

TODAY'S GOD SHOT

God works for good, even through sin and evil. David's sin in ordering the census makes a way for him to have a reason to offer the sacrifice that establishes the site of the temple. Even though an evil spirit incites him, God is using the evil spirit's evil motives to bring about His plans for His people. And do you remember *when* in the timeline God told David he'd have a son named Solomon who'd build His house? It was before David ever met Bathsheba, Solomon's mom—before he sinned against her and murdered her husband. Before he ever committed those heinous sins, God had already told him how He planned to work through those sins for the good of all people, how He'd redeem it *all* on the other side. God is so generous and forgiving. And He's powerful! Sin never gets to win against God and His people—it always ultimately serves God's purposes somehow. That doesn't give us an excuse to sin, and it doesn't mean our sins and the sins of others don't cause horrific amounts of pain in the meantime. But it does mean we can sing the words of David from Psalm 30: "You have turned for me my mourning into dancing; you have loosed my sackcloth and clothed me with gladness. . . . O Lord my God, I will give thanks to you forever!" He's where the joy is!

PSALMS 108–110

When reading Psalm 108:7–9, it's helpful to know that the places David lists form a circle around Jerusalem. He's pointing out that God owns all the space around the city—tribal allotments, enemy territory, you name it—it's all His. Some of it He uses for reputable purposes, and some of it, like Moab, He uses as His washbasin. Edom is His footstool. He owns these places, but apparently they aren't His most prized possessions. And as for Israel, David feels like God has rejected them and isn't fighting on their behalf anymore. He cries to God for help, trusting He'll come to their rescue.

In Psalm 109, David laments to God and doesn't hold back. There are a few things to remember here. First, David isn't personally retaliating. He asks *God* to act; God can be trusted to do what's right even when our feelings are wrong. David is taking this to the One who'll resolve it righteously. Second, just because this prayer is in Scripture doesn't mean God agrees with it or answers it with a yes—it just shows us that God can handle the honest outpouring of our emotions, even the ones that don't honor Him or align with His plan. He's our safe space. Third, even though these offenses are primarily against David, they're against God too, because David is God's anointed over this unique nation-state. David treated Saul with respect when Saul was in this position, but here David suffers the betrayal and attack of many other Israelites—covenant people—who are acting against God and His covenant. With contempt in their hearts, they've rejected both David and God, so David asks God to act for His name's sake, not David's.

Many people compare David's situation here to Jesus's situation before His crucifixion. This isn't considered a prophetic psalm, but there are prophetic elements. For instance, Jesus is an innocent man who is accused and treated with contempt. And Jesus's apostles even reference verse 8 when they seek to replace Judas after his death. It says, "May another take his office!" Some scholars say it can't be prophetic, because they can't imagine Jesus saying most of the things David says here. But others point out that Scripture only records Jesus praying for the soldiers to be forgiven, not Pilate or Judas, who also participated in His death. Since it's hard to know how much of this might apply prophetically, it's probably wise just to read this as being David's emotional prayer.

Psalm 110, however, clearly points us to Jesus. It's a royal psalm with two halves: a prophecy and a divine oath. This psalm is quoted in at least six New Testament books, including three of the four gospels, where Jesus quotes it. Jesus says verse 1 is about Him: "The LORD says to my Lord: 'Sit at my right hand, until I make your enemies your footstool.'" YHWH has Jesus sit at His right hand, the position of honor, while YHWH gets to work making footstools out of enemies. And this ties in with what we read about Edom in Psalm 60:8: "Upon Edom I cast my shoe." God is at work even in His enemies' midst.

In Israel, the roles of king and priest are supposed to be separate, but in this unique situation, they've been fused—the king and priest are the same person. Verse 4 says YHWH has sworn, "You are a priest forever after the order of Melchizedek." Remember him? He was a priest and a king of a place called Salem. (By the way, Salem was also an ancient name for Jeru*salem*.) Here we see those roles fused again—the king who'll be from David's line and sit on David's throne will also be a priest. The book of Hebrews repeatedly refers to Jesus as our Great High Priest.

TODAY'S GOD SHOT

Psalm 108:12 says, "Vain is the salvation of man!" This is true on so many levels. We can't set our hopes on others, and we can't even set our hopes on ourselves. We can't save ourselves. The gospel isn't self-help. We can do nothing to accomplish our salvation, but He saves us, despite ourselves. Verse 13 reminds us that even though we do valiantly with God, He is the one at work: "With God we shall do valiantly; it is he who will tread down our foes." He does the doing as our Protector, our Savior, our Priest, and our King! He's where the joy is!

1 CHRONICLES 23–25

When we left off in David's story line, he was helping Solomon prepare to build the temple in Jerusalem, and today he continues equipping Solomon to be his successor. First, he makes him king. This only gets one sentence in today's reading, then we move on to the more important things: plans for God's house. Maybe it seems like more attention should be paid to this transition of kingship, and we'll cover that more over the next few days. But the reason the chronicler doesn't give it more time here is likely because it's truly secondary to the temple. While a relationship between a king and his people will always be temporary, a relationship between God and His people is forever. It's hard for us to grasp the importance of the temple today, since *we* are now the dwelling place of God, but it's difficult to overestimate how important the temple is to the Israelites. It's absolutely central to their relationship with God, just like the Spirit is for us today.

Since this is such a big deal, David offers his expert advice and connections to help Solomon prepare for the massive upgrade God's dwelling place is about to undergo from tabernacle (a tent) to temple (a building). David is thorough in all his details, which goes to show that not only is David a planner, but the temple is a big deal. It's similar to when God gave the original instructions for the tabernacle, except this is permanent. Even though the tabernacle has been stationary for a while, this news is probably most exciting for the Levites, who don't have to worry about moving it ever again. If you've ever been a part of a mobile church that eventually moved into a building, you can relate! Now all the Levites have to worry about is showbread and offerings and incense and daily worship and sacrifices and feasts and—okay, it's still a lot. So David sets up twenty-four divisions of priests to handle things. At first, he starts out with the minimum age requirement being thirty years old, but he later drops it to twenty years old. Either he needs more people than they have available at that age or he encounters twenty-year-olds who grasp the weight of these roles.

David organizes all the musicians. In the same way that the Levites have three divisions, the musicians have three divisions. They're divided under Asaph, Jeduthun, and Heman, each of whom wrote one or more of the Psalms. There are singers, psalmists, people who play stringed instruments, and percussionists. One of the unique things about the temple musicians is that they're only required to play music. They have no other tasks. The songwriters are considered musical prophets. According to 25:3, they prophesy in thanksgiving and praise to the LORD. There are 288 musicians in all, separated into twenty-four divisions like the priests, and the group includes a wide variety of ages. Some of them are teachers, and some are students—possibly people who are just learning to play their instruments.

TODAY'S GOD SHOT

In 23:25 David says, "The LORD, the God of Israel, has given rest to his people, and he dwells in Jerusalem forever." Think about the weight and beauty and relief this sentence holds for them. YHWH is the God of Israel. And He has taken them out of slavery. And He's given them rest instead. And they're His people. And He has come to live among them! And His home with them is not in the wilderness, where they have to move around all the time. It's in Jerusalem, the most glorious spot in all the promised land, the place where God has put His name! This sentence is one giant hallelujah: "The LORD, the God of Israel, has given rest to his people, and he dwells in Jerusalem forever." God is good, and He is with them, and He's where the joy is!

PSALMS 131, 138–139, 143–145

Psalm 131 is a Song of Ascent. It seems David may have written this song of confidence during a time of uncertainty. Maybe he's confused about all the things that are happening around him or why they're happening, but he resolves to trust God with the things he does know and leave the unknowns to God. One thing he knows is that God is sovereign over it all and can be trusted with the outcome.

In Psalm 138:1 David says, "Before the gods I sing your praise." The word for *gods* refers to spiritual beings of some sort. Some scholars believe it's better understood as *angels*, since David is in God's house when this happens and there are likely angels present. Others believe it's translated accurately as *gods* and that David is praising YHWH, the one true God, in front of all the false gods that exist in the world—pagan and demon gods, idols, created beings—because he wants them all to see his praise of YHWH. Acknowledging the existence of other gods isn't in conflict with monotheism. The idea behind monotheism is that we *worship* one God. He's the only true God.

This chapter gives rich descriptions of God's character. One thing that helps us understand His personality better is to search Scripture for what He loves, what He hates, and what motivates Him to do what He does. This chapter has all of that! Verse 2 shows us what He loves and what motivates Him: "You have exalted above all things your name and your word." Verse 6 shows us what He loves and what He hates, and James 4:6 reiterates this idea: "God opposes the proud, but gives grace to the humble." Verse 8 also shows us what motivates Him: "The Lord will fulfill his purpose for me; your steadfast love, O Lord, endures forever."

Psalm 139 is personal, intimate. David says he's fully known by God. That could feel threatening if you dwell in shame. But not David. He worships! He cherishes God's thoughts of him: "How precious to me are your thoughts, O God!" (v. 17). He even invites the One who knows him best to help him know himself better, to reveal his blind spots to him, to direct his steps. If David didn't trust God, he certainly wouldn't ask this of God. But he seems to understand that being known and loved is the best possible combination—one without the other falls short.

Psalm 143 is a penitent psalm. David is in dire straits and realizes that some of his problems may be the result of his own sin. David's humility and his proper understanding of God show up here—*before* he asks God to deliver him from his enemies, he asks God to deliver him from himself and his own sin.

In Psalm 144, David attributes his wartime victories to God, who has trained him to fight. He's humbled by the fact that such a huge, powerful God would pay attention to humanity at all. Then, knowing that he has God's attention, he asks Him to bless him again and promises to praise Him. He has high hopes for God's deliverance.

Psalm 145:3 says "his greatness is unsearchable." That doesn't mean we can't find it—we're finding it right now—it just means we'll never plumb the depths of it. There's always more greatness to find!

Verse 9 says God is good to all; that's what theologians call *common grace*. The fact that we all get to breathe His air and taste His food is His grace. It also says His mercy is over everything He has made. So even His enemies experience His mercy; He doesn't annihilate them the moment they rebel against Him. That's a kind of common mercy.

TODAY'S GOD SHOT

Psalm 145:17 says, "The Lord is righteous in all his ways and kind in all his works." Righteous and kind. It's in His *yes*, it's in His *no*, it's in His *wait*—every answer He gives to every prayer we pray is His kindest possible answer. If He says no to something we ask for, then His yes would be less kind. He is kind and His plans are good. Try reading Psalm 138:8 aloud and putting the emphasis on a different word each time. "The Lord will fulfill his purpose for me." He will, and He is doing it. And He's where the joy is!

1 CHRONICLES 26–29; PSALM 127

David continues making preparations for the First Temple. Even though it's God's house and David's doing the planning, it's commonly referred to as Solomon's Temple since he's the one who builds it. The gatekeepers have an incredibly important role; there are gates all around the city walls, serving as the city's first line of defense, so these men need to be agile and vigilant. Scripture regards east as the direction of holiness, so not only will the temple itself face east, but the gate of highest honor—and the one that requires the most guards—is the Eastern Gate, also called the King's Gate. This is the gate Jesus will return through when He comes back to earth at His second coming.

David sets up treasurers for the temple too. They aren't just in charge of money; they're in charge of any gifts dedicated to God and even the spoils of war. David has his own treasures too, as well as gardeners, farmers, vine keepers, and shepherds. Some of the Levites have the job of managing tribal relationships, which sounds a bit like being a diplomat or an ambassador. There are a lot of people involved in all of these rotating roles—24,000 per month, for a total of 288,000 people.

In case there was any doubt, 27:23–24 tells us why David wasn't supposed to take that census a few days ago. It was an act of unbelief in God's promise to make them a great nation. David felt like he needed to verify things and check in on God's progress.

In chapter 28, David gives his charge to all of Israel and to Solomon. He reminds them to seek and obey God and establishes that God has chosen Solomon for this project and to be king. He charges Solomon to yield his heart and mind to God in all things. David has suffered the consequences of setting his own course. He tells Solomon that God will be with him in all this work and won't leave him until he finishes building the temple. But that doesn't mean God's leaving Israel. When the temple is finished, He'll be dwelling above the mercy seat in the Most Holy Place.

David donates a lot of his personal wealth to build the temple, including over two hundred thousand pounds of gold and more than half a million pounds of silver. He models generosity toward God's house and leads the way in making donations and sacrifices before inviting the people to join in. They're excited to participate—they rejoice and give willingly, with their whole hearts. David blesses God, then asks God to continue to direct their hearts toward Him and to guide Solomon's heart. He passes off the throne to Solomon, then dies after ruling Israel for forty years. (But he'll still die one more time in our reading, so don't grieve just yet!)

We finished today with Psalm 127, a Song of Ascent likely written by Solomon. The first verse takes on so much more meaning in light of Solomon's calling to build the temple: "Unless the Lord builds the house, those who build it labor in vain." But this could also refer to Solomon's offspring and David's dynasty. God is establishing their family, just as He promised David, in order to bring about the Messiah. This psalm serves as a reminder that only what God initiates will be sustained and fulfilled. God is attentive to and involved in all areas of our lives—from something as minor as sleep to something as major as enemy warfare. We can strive all we want, but we'll gain nothing without Him working on our behalf!

TODAY'S GOD SHOT

God is the source of all things. In 29:12, David, says, "Both riches and honor come from you . . . and in your hand it is to make great and to give strength to all." Verse 14 says, "All things come from you, and of your own have we given you." Verse 16 says, "O Lord our God, all this abundance that we have provided for building you a house for your holy name comes from your hand and is all your own." This is true not just of money but of talents, time, and service. Everything we give back to Him originated with Him. God is the source of all good things, and He's what they all point to. He is the source, supply, and goal—and He's where the joy is!

PSALMS 111–118

Psalm 111:2 says, "Great are the works of the LORD, studied by all who delight in them." We're studying His works! Are you finding more ways to delight in Him? Delight also connects us to verse 10: "The fear of the LORD is the beginning of wisdom; all those who practice it have a good understanding." As we've seen, the fear of the Lord consists primarily of delight and awe. And viewing God rightly is where wisdom begins—those who practice delighting in Him have good understanding. Psalm 112 points to this too. Verse 1 says, "Blessed is the man who fears the LORD, who greatly delights in his commandments!" The word *blessed* can also be translated as *happy*. There's a happiness in the pursuit of God! Those who delight in God's laws will surely be living them out, right? This is how righteousness takes over a person's life—it starts in our heart and works its way out through our actions. We don't create our own righteousness. It happens when God changes our hearts.

Verse 4 says, "Light dawns in the darkness for the upright." God sends His light and brings the dawn at just the right time. For those who walk in the commands that they delight in, verses 7–10 serve as guideposts, reminding us that He keeps us steady in the meantime and that nothing can shake us when we're rooted in Christ. "He is not afraid of bad news; his heart is firm, trusting in the LORD. His heart is steady; he will not be afraid."

Psalm 113 rightly positions God as high above the earth, but that's less of a description of His physical location and more of a nod to His sovereignty over it; He's the ultimate authority. Though He's distinct and set apart, He bends down to connect with His people: "Who is like the LORD our God, who is seated on high, who looks far down on the heavens and the earth? He raises the poor from the dust and lifts the needy from the ash heap, to make them sit with princes, with the princes of his people" (vv. 5–8). From high above us, He turns His eyes toward us—He looks down. But He doesn't just look down, He *reaches* down, lifts us up, and seats us with royalty. This describes exactly what He's done by letting us share in the inheritance of King Jesus!

Psalm 114 looks back at the story of the Israelites with a summary so poetic it's easy to forget all the hardship they endured. It's entirely absent of the stories of dehydration and the quail tornado. The stories that got passed down—the ones that lodged in their collective memories—were the ones of God's provision.

In Psalm 115, Israel is being taunted by the nations around them. Unlike other nations' gods, YHWH doesn't have a statue or an idol to represent Him, so it appears as though Israel is worshipping nothing. Israel responds to the taunts, saying, "Our God is in the heavens; he does all that he pleases" (v. 3). If we know and trust God, this is one of the most comforting verses in Scripture. For Him to do whatever He pleases isn't a threat but a blessing, because what pleases Him is good for His kids!

Psalm 116 recounts a time when the psalmist desperately needed God's help. He praises God's deliverance of him against all odds. There's no way to repay God for what He has done, but out of the overflow of gratitude in his heart, he commits to praising and serving God forever.

Psalm 117 points us to the greatness, faithfulness, and steadfast love of God *and* to His affection for people from every nation, not just Israel.

TODAY'S GOD SHOT

Psalm 118 gives us a few prophecies about Jesus. Jesus calls Himself "the gate" and says, "If anyone enters by me, he will be saved" (John 10:9). When the psalmist talks about the gate of righteousness, he's definitely referring to the gates in Jerusalem, but there's a layer of prophecy here too. Verse 20 says, "This is the gate of the LORD; the righteous shall enter through it." Jesus is the way in. He's the gate to the Father. Verse 22 also prophesies of Jesus: "The stone that the builders rejected has become the cornerstone." He was rejected by the religious leaders of His day, but He's the very foundation of our faith. It's all built upon Him and His work. And He's the only solid foundation—everything else will crumble, but He's steady forever. And He's where the joy is!

1 KINGS 1–2; PSALMS 37, 71, 94

David is old and has bad circulation and heating pads don't exist yet, so they bring in a woman whose sole job is to keep him warm. Scripture is clear that nothing sketchy is happening, even though it's uncomfortable to read. Meanwhile, despite what we've already read in Chronicles, Solomon hasn't been anointed king in this book yet. All we know here is that David is close to death and one of his sons is supposed to succeed him. His oldest living son, Adonijah, wants the throne. Joab, David's advisor, and Abiathar, one of the high priests, are on board with it, but most of the leaders aren't, including Nathan the prophet and Zadok, the other high priest.

Adonijah rides his horses and chariots through town, which is like declaring himself king, then offers a public sacrifice but only invites those who don't oppose him. Nathan and Bathsheba both know God has chosen Solomon as king. David knows it too but he's old, so when Adonijah makes himself king it doesn't even catch David's attention. Nathan gets creative, subtly influencing David to obey. If David doesn't intervene, Adonijah will likely kill Bathsheba and Solomon to eliminate the threat they pose to him. David agrees to make things right. A group of leaders anoint Solomon as king, and when word gets back to Adonijah, he's terrified. He goes to grab the horns of the altar, a gesture indicating he's committed an accidental sin and is seeking asylum. He begs Solomon not to kill him, and Solomon says he'll live if he acts worthily.

On his deathbed, David has some final words for Solomon. He orders him to keep God's commands, but then he takes a hard left and commands Solomon to get revenge on his enemies. He says to kill Joab, who killed two of his commanders and his son Absalom, and to kill Shimei, the man who once cursed him but repented and became his servant. David swore to Shimei that he wouldn't kill him, and he may have found a legal loophole by having Solomon do it, but God isn't fooled. Just like

---

For more information on today's reading, see thebiblerecap.com/links.

with Uriah, David has someone else do his dirty work. He dies with murder on his heart.

After David dies, Adonijah wants Abishag to be his wife. He asks Bathsheba to make the request on his behalf, since Solomon listens to her. But since Abishag is in David's harem, this is seen as Adonijah attempting to overthrow Solomon. Solomon has him killed. Then Solomon continues fulfilling David's final wishes, killing Joab and Shimei. Technically, they both deserve the death penalty because one murdered and one cursed the king, so it seems this isn't considered wickedness on Solomon's part.

In Psalm 37, David says God grants the desires of those who delight in Him—and this is coming from a man who got a no in response to one of his major prayers! Some scholars say the meaning behind this verse has more to do with God giving us the desire itself, putting the right desires in us as we delight in Him. Others point out that if we delight in God, then He and His will are what our hearts desire.

The author of Psalm 71 is old and tired, but God has carried him throughout his life. He speaks of triumph over those who sought to harm him. This sounds a lot like David, doesn't it? Psalm 94 continues with this theme: "He will bring back on them their iniquity and wipe them out for their wickedness; the LORD our God will wipe them out" (v. 23).

TODAY'S GOD SHOT

David's deathbed speech leaves us with some tension. What do we make of his hate-filled words? Our aim isn't to figure out who David is—it's to figure out who God is. So what does this show us about God? What happens if one of God's kids dies with sin in their heart and doesn't repent? Does it ruin everything? What if it's revenge or even murder? Hebrews 11:1–12:2 answers our questions: David is listed in the "hall of faith" and counted among the forefathers of our faith. Our position in God's family isn't and has never been about our works or our perfection. Even in the Old Testament, it's about faith in the God who covers *all* our sins. Through David, God demonstrates His all-surpassing mercy and grace. What a gift to know that all the sins of all God's kids—past, present, future, intentional, confessed, and accidental—are covered by the blood of Christ! He's where the joy is!

PSALM 119

This is the longest chapter in the Bible as well as the center chapter of the Bible. It's written as a Hebrew acrostic poem, and each of the twenty-two sections starts with the subsequent letter of the Hebrew alphabet, and each of the eight verses within a section starts with that letter as well. For us, that would be like eight verses that start with *A*, then eight verses that start with *B*, and so forth. This was a labor of love. No one knows who wrote it, but many scholars think it was Ezra the priest and scribe. All we know is that this psalmist loves the Word of God. This kind of detailed, demanding songwriting isn't done in a halfhearted manner.

While the psalmist loves God's Word, he wants to love it even more. He's not a perfect man—he even ends the psalm by saying he's a lost sheep who has gone astray and asks God to come find him—but in all of this, he shows a deep understanding of God and His character. In fact, the psalm points out at least seven praiseworthy attributes of God and His character: righteousness, trustworthiness, truthfulness, faithfulness, unchangeableness, eternality, and light.

In verses 9–11, he shows us how possessing a heart-level knowledge of God and His Word keeps him walking in nearness and obedience to God. Unfortunately, we're helpless to change our own hearts. Fortunately, this chapter displays God as the active agent in wisdom giving and heart change! Verse 18 says, "Open my eyes"; verse 27 says, "Make me understand"; verse 32 says, "You enlarge my heart"; and verse 36 says, "Incline my heart." These are all great prayers to pray. *Turn my eyes, teach me, give me understanding, lead me, incline my heart.*

In verses 15–16, he coaches himself in the kind of behavior he wants to display. He says, "I will meditate on your precepts and fix my eyes on your ways. I will delight in your statutes; I will not forget your word." He wants to focus, treasure, and remember God. If this psalmist were to make a vision board, God's Word is what would be on it.

In verses 71–75, he even thanks God for the struggles God used to bring him near. He recognizes that God has an eternal purpose in mind: "It is good for me that I was afflicted, that I might learn your statutes . . . I know, O LORD, that your rules are righteous, and that in faithfulness you have afflicted me." But even this psalmist—a man whose hope is firmly planted in the LORD and who has knowledge of and love for God's Word—knows what it's like to feel pain and longing. In verse 82, he prays, "When will you comfort me?" Loving God doesn't preclude feeling pain and loss—it means we have a safe Person to be with us in our pain. We can ask God to draw near and comfort us. According to Psalm 34:18, He loves to do that!

TODAY'S GOD SHOT

Psalm 119:105 says, "Your word is a lamp to my feet and a light to my path." The word used for *lamp* in "a lamp to my feet" refers to a foot lamp, which is like a single candle. This kind of lamp only gives enough light for the next step. You can make the whole journey, step by step, with the candle—but you have to keep referring back to it, just like with the Word of God. The word for *light* in "a light to my path" is a different word. It's a floodlight. It's daybreak. It's the "God said let there be light" light. This is incredible! God's Word is both kinds of light—the whole earth flooded with the fires of a thousand suns kind of glorious absolute truth, *and* the individual, step-by-step kind of personal guidance we need in each moment. It's everything we need. Second Timothy 3:16–17 says, "All Scripture is breathed out by God and profitable for teaching, for reproof, for correction, and for training in righteousness, that the man of God may be complete, equipped for every good work." We have everything we need—the bright light, the personal light—all lighting up the same truths that we need for life and godliness and for every good work. God has generously given it all to us. His Word is where the joy is, because He's in it—and He's where the joy is!

1 KINGS 3–4

Solomon started out his reign by killing a few people—maybe righteously, maybe not—and by marrying a foreign woman, which is definitely not righteous. This marriage is for a political alliance, which suggests he doesn't trust God to act on Israel's behalf. He makes alliances that involve marrying the women God said not to marry. Being king doesn't mean he gets a pass on obedience. In fact, as the leader, he should be the one setting an example. Unfortunately, like his father, women are his weak spot—and that eventually causes his kingdom to crumble.

Solomon loves YHWH, but as we'll soon find out, he also likes to sacrifice to pagan gods. He has a divided heart. This isn't uncommon in his day—or even today. It's called *syncretism*—where people try to cover all their bases by synthesizing two religious beliefs. This works well with pretty much every god except YHWH, because they're all on the same team. Every false religion is opposed to the kingdom of light—even the false religion of morality that we see in cultural Christianity today. In Galatians 5:4, Paul says that those who believe in Jesus but rely on their own good works to add anything to their salvation are cut off from Christ: "You are severed from Christ, you who would be justified by the law." YHWH doesn't synthesize with anything else, not even our personal best efforts at living a good, clean life. And He certainly doesn't synthesize with pagan gods.

Solomon offers a thousand sacrifices—presumably to God, though it's hard to say for sure—then God shows up in a dream and says, "Ask Me for whatever you want, and it's yours." He knows what Solomon is going to ask for, and this is all part of His plan to use Solomon to lead His people and advance the Messiah's birth. Solomon knows this is a big deal and doesn't trust himself—he's smart enough to know that he's young and foolish. So he asks God for wisdom. (By the way, when he says he's a "little child," that's hyperbole—he's already a dad at this point.) God is pleased with Solomon's request and grants him wisdom and then some. He'll give him riches regardless, and He'll give him a long life if he walks in obedience.

Then the first test of his newly granted wisdom comes. Two women are fighting over a baby, and no one knows what to do. Solomon is discerning and a little sly and calls out the truth. All Israel sees he has divine wisdom. It's worth noting that these two women—who have a lower social status because of their jobs as prostitutes—are allowed to appear before the king. It shows us how Israel's ancient society valued women far more than most of us are inclined to think.

Solomon's dad fought many battles and acquired a lot of land, and Israel is enjoying the abundance. Not only is Solomon himself rich, but all the people are happy and provided for too. In fact, he and his crew eat more than 130 animals a day, and he has 40,000 horses. Did you notice a problem here? Remember Deuteronomy 17:16–17, where God forbid Israel's kings from amassing three things: wealth, women, and horses? In today's reading, we've seen a yellow flag on wealth, a red flag on women, and a red flag on horses. Israel is thriving, but Solomon's kingship is off to an unrighteous start.

TODAY'S GOD SHOT

Right before God shows up in a dream, Solomon makes sacrifices at a pagan altar. That night, God says, "Solomon, what is it you want? You know you'll only get that from Me, right? Come to Me. I've got everything you need." And let's be clear: Solomon doesn't clean up his act and walk in total obedience and perfection from this point on—it's not like this is a turning point for him where he looks to YHWH and never turns aside. He fails. But we're not here to learn about Solomon's heart—we're here to learn about God's heart. And what we see is that God showed up to Solomon's divided heart to say, "I'm what you're looking for." Like all of us, Solomon will forget this. And God will keep chasing him down. Solomon will have it all before it's all said and done—wisdom and wealth and women—but it will never get better than the nearness of God, even in the midst of our sins. He's where the joy is!

2 CHRONICLES 1; PSALM 72

Today we recount Solomon's encounter with God at Gibeon. God praises Solomon for not asking for the lives of his enemies. This feels like a reference to his dad, David, who asked for his enemies' lives on his deathbed. At the end of chapter 1 we're reminded that, despite his newly granted wisdom, Solomon starts hoarding wealth and horses.

The authorship of Psalm 72 is unclear. Is it by Solomon, like it says at the start? Or David, like it says at the end? Here's the case for each possibility: If it's by Solomon, then the line "Of Solomon" is telling us the author's name, and the last line, "The prayers of David, the son of Jesse, are ended," is prophesying David's death. If it's by David, then "Of Solomon" is telling us it's about Solomon—not by him—and the last line is giving us David's final sign-off before he dies. No one really knows, and nothing important hinges on it.

Here's what we do know about this psalm. It's about the blessing on the king—and probably Solomon specifically, regardless of who wrote it. God has big plans for this king. This is a prayer for a righteous king, but it's not praise *for* the king—it's asking God to grant all these good things *to* the king: a heart for righteousness, a hand for justice, an eye to see the poor and needy. Scripture attributes all these things to God and asks God to give them to the king. As we've seen, these positions of the heart and mind are granted by God.

The psalmist, who was a king himself at some point (regardless of whether David or Solomon wrote it) knows how much the king needs prayer. In verse 15, he asks for round-the-clock prayers for the king. Do you see how humble this viewpoint is? If he had exalted the king to God's status, then the king wouldn't need prayer. He would be elevated above the position of human neediness. But because the psalmist realizes all good things are given from God's hand, he knows the king needs God's help and asks the people to intercede on his behalf.

For more information on today's reading, see thebiblerecap.com/links.

He ends with a blessing for God Himself and says that God alone does wondrous things. There are so many things we need, and there's no one we can take those needs to except for God. So many people are afraid to ask God for things, afraid they're bothering Him. But God says to pray without ceasing. He wants us to keep talking to Him, to keep asking Him for things—in part because it helps us recognize that He's the source of all things and it helps us to acknowledge how desperately needy we are.

TODAY'S GOD SHOT

Even when people aren't asking God for anything, He's eager to display His heart of generosity. Solomon isn't even asking Him for anything, and God shows up and says, "Hey, Solomon, do you want anything?" Then, on top of that, God decides to triple the blessing—not just giving Solomon what he asks for, but also giving him things he doesn't ask for or deserve. God is marked by this kind of abundant generosity. He owns everything, and He loves to bless His kids. He seeks out opportunities to bless them. His heart is so kind! He's where the joy is!

SONG OF SOLOMON 1–8

This book is incredibly layered, and there's uncertainty about several aspects of it. For instance, we don't know if it was written by or about Solomon (or both) or if it was just written during his reign. If it's about him, it's about his relationship with his first wife, because it describes a monogamous relationship. He eventually had a harem of one thousand women—seven hundred wives and three hundred concubines—which doesn't go well for him, by the way. Scholars are divided over whether it's a story of human love, an allegory about God's love for His people, or both. Most scholars believe the ancient Jews regarded it as love poetry that belonged in Scripture's wisdom literature; in fact, young Hebrew boys were forbidden to read it because it was too risqué. For the sake of our conversation, we'll look at it like the ancient Jews likely did, but it's helpful to consider that it can also serve as an illustration.

If you hold to the romantic interpretation, you can see that it follows the ancient Jewish relationship from courtship to wedding to marriage. Much of the book is a conversation, and there are four primary speakers: the shepherdess, her entourage, the shepherd, and King Solomon. The shepherdess carries most of the conversation; in fact, she speaks more than any other woman in Scripture, followed closely by Esther. She begins by expressing her love for the shepherd. She also acknowledges that she's not conventionally attractive, but she knows she's beautiful nonetheless. She's dark-skinned in a culture that values light skin. Light skin means you aren't working class or poor; you get to spend your days inside, not in the fields under the hot sun. She lets this attractive, sought-after man know she's interested, and he reciprocates. Despite her appearance not meeting cultural standards, he finds her more attractive than the rest, and he lets her know repeatedly and at length.

For more information on today's reading, see thebiblerecap.com/links.

Three times, she speaks to the local women and begs them not to "stir up or awaken love until it pleases." This can be interpreted many different ways. Maybe it means, "Don't initiate things with a man; let him come to you," as though she regrets initiating things with the shepherd. Maybe it means, "Stay sexually pure until marriage." Or maybe it means, "Fix your mind on other things, and God will bring a relationship to you in His own timing." Maybe it means all of those things; they aren't mutually exclusive, and there's wisdom in all of them. But whatever it means, she's adamant about it. She also spends a good deal of time praising the shepherd to others. She thinks about him all the time and even has a dream that she can't find him and goes looking for him in the city streets at night. Later, she has another nightmare, it seems. As she's telling her friends, they ask her why this man is so spectacular. She goes on about him for so long that they want to meet him.

It's unclear exactly when the wedding happens, but there's probably a weeklong wedding feast happening during much of this time. When the day of the ceremony arrives, her brothers speak up, describing two types of women: a door—a woman who opens herself up for men without much discretion, and a wall—a woman who keeps herself closed off to men sexually. Her brothers want to be able to protect her. She reassures them that she's been a wall, which is consistent with the advice she's given to the local women. The shepherd confirms this when he says, "A garden locked is my sister, my bride."

TODAY'S GOD SHOT

God affirms His good design for marriage and sex. This book flies in the face of two juxtaposed ideas: (1) Sex is dirty and bad and God is disgusted by it, and (2) sex isn't a big deal. Despite the emotional and spiritual brokenness of the world's sexuality, our Creator had good things in mind when He invented relationships, marriage, and sex. He's not trying to steal joy from people by putting boundaries around those things. He invented them, and like any inventor, He wants us to know how to use what He made so that we don't break it or harm ourselves and others. He graciously tells us how these things He invented can function optimally for His glory and our joy. He's where the joy is!

PROVERBS 1–3

It's important to have proper expectations for this book; it's wisdom literature compiled by multiple authors over time, though Solomon is the primary author. Wisdom literature has to be handled differently than other categories of books in Scripture; it isn't God's laws or advice, and it isn't prophecies or promises. The proverbs are accumulated wisdom and general insights of people who observed the world closely and aimed to demonstrate the wisdom of God in every aspect of their lives. We have to be careful not to act like these wise sayings are promises we can cling to, because there are exceptions to these rules—and other wisdom books like Job and Ecclesiastes show us what those look like. For instance, Proverbs makes it sound like the wise and godly will avoid pain and suffering, but Job proves the exception. That's another reason it's important for us to read all of Scripture and not pluck things out of context that make us feel good, empowered, or entitled.

Three types of people are represented repeatedly in Proverbs: the wise, the foolish, and the simple. The wise person walks in righteousness and the fear of God, the fool leans on their own understanding and doesn't seek God or blatantly rebels against Him, and the simple is easily led astray or doesn't pay attention to the deeper realities of life. Be on the lookout for those three people. Adjusting your mind-set can be challenging—especially because Proverbs feels like a to-do list sometimes—but keep looking for God in this book. Many of the verses are stand-alone ideas, so we'll primarily cover the ones that are potentially confusing, problematic, or helpful.

The book opens with a dad giving instructions to his son, and it closes with a mom giving instructions to her son. The dad implores his son to seek and value wisdom, to be teachable. He personifies wisdom as a woman, but she's not all roses and sunshine. She has some firm words for the fool and the simpleton, and she says they'll be left to their own

For more information on today's reading, see thebiblerecap.com/links.

devices. Sometimes letting a person lie in the bed they've made is the best way to get them to buy a new mattress. This passage also points out that passivity is just as wicked and foolish as actively pursuing sin. Both the simple and the foolish die—whether as a result of action or inaction.

Chapter 2 lists desirable things that God provides and tells us to seek: wisdom, knowledge, understanding, and insight. They're like the muscles of your soul, empowered by God the Spirit. Chapter 3 calls us to trust God with the details of our lives and walk in His ways. When we walk in obedience to God and honor Him, we have more peace than when we do our own thing. It may even be a peace that doesn't make sense given your situation, but obedience adds peace where chaos seems natural. Wisdom can also protect us from being fearful in scary situations. These blessings aren't simply the result of knowledge or obedience—they're rooted in the nearness of God. And wisdom itself isn't what brings us peace, it's the nearness of the God of wisdom! And obedience doesn't amount to anything unless our hearts are engaged with the God we're obeying. In fact, obedience can feel a lot like striving if we're doing it to earn something instead of doing it in response to the God who loves us despite ourselves.

TODAY'S GOD SHOT

"Trust in the Lord with all your heart, and do not lean on your own understanding. In all your ways acknowledge him, and he will make straight your paths. Be not wise in your own eyes" (Proverbs 3:5–7). God wants us to talk to Him about everything. He wants to save us from the tyranny of self. Neither our hearts nor our minds should ultimately guide us. We don't want to trust in our hearts—we want to *entrust* our hearts to God. We don't want to lean on our own understanding—we want to fully lean on His. We don't want to do our own thing—we want to acknowledge Him in all our ways. We don't want to be wise in our own eyes—we want to affirm that we need His help. He makes our paths straight. He cares about every detail, and He's never too busy to speak into what we're going through. He's going through it with us, after all. And even here in the midst of it, He's where the joy is!

PROVERBS 4–6

The dad tells his son more general truths for living and walking in the fear of the LORD, engaging with God via delight and awe. Proverbs 4:7 says, "The beginning of wisdom is this: Get wisdom." To recognize that you need wisdom is wise, and when you pursue wisdom, you get even wiser. A relationship with God is very similar; sometimes the closer you get to Him the further you realize you are from Him. Being closer to the light of God illuminates the dark places in us, and we feel conviction about sins that never bothered us before and see positive changes in the negative attitudes we used to prize. He works a change in us that we can't make on our own power. He does the doing! Romans 11:36 addresses this circular, spiritual mystery: "From him and through him and to him are all things." He's the source, supply, and goal. He initiates, sustains, and fulfills. So here we are, midcycle, learning and growing because of His work in us.

In verses 14–15, the dad presses a specific concern. Six times he repeats the way to handle the path of the wicked: "Do not enter," "Do not walk," "Avoid it," "Do not go on it," "Turn away from it," "Pass on." Verse 23 is often applied to dating relationships: "Keep your heart with all vigilance, for from it flow the springs of life." There's wisdom in having good boundaries, but this is not a verse about disengaging from your emotions or trying not to get your hopes up that things might work out with your love interest. This verse is surrounded by verses about clinging to wisdom and about keeping your tongue from lies, your eyes from evil, and your feet from wicked paths. Guarding our hearts seems to be more about eradicating bitterness and malice from our hearts—not romantic feelings.

On the other hand, chapter 5 has a lot to say about relationships. The dad is emphatic about avoiding adultery and the adulteress. He describes her as a simpleton, someone who doesn't ponder her path. She doesn't weigh consequences and outcomes, because if she did, she'd never make the decision to commit adultery. The father is basically saying, "She's not thinking, so you'd better be thinking. And when you think, remember what I'm telling you right now: Don't do it. It's not worth it." He encourages his son to be faithful to his wife, praying a blessing over their marriage and their love life.

In chapter 6, the father tells the son not to cosign on someone else's loan. As a reminder, the Wisdom Literature isn't law. In fact, Scripture says that we should be generous to those in need, and God even forbids Israelites from charging interest to other Israelites they loan money to, so we know loans aren't against God's laws. This is just a dad passing down his experiential wisdom to his son. He also encourages him to develop a strong work ethic and to deal honestly with others.

Then Dad has more to say about adultery: If his son walks in wisdom, he'll naturally avoid the adulteress. But if he happens to find himself tempted, he should remember that you can't heap coals into your lap without being burned. Walking in wisdom and nearness with God ushers in peace, but walking outside of His ways ushers in destruction.

TODAY'S GOD SHOT

In 6:16–19, the author lists seven things that are an abomination to God and six things He hates: "Haughty eyes, a lying tongue, and hands that shed innocent blood, a heart that devises wicked plans, feet that make haste to run to evil, a false witness who breathes out lies, and one who sows discord among brothers." Much of that applies to us, which should prompt immense gratitude that Jesus paid our sin debt and that God's Spirit works in us. God's compassion, generosity, and forgiveness are evident here—He adopts sinners into His family even though He knows we do so many things He hates and that are an abomination to Him. Like all of us, God hates things that are an affront to what He loves. So what does He love? The opposites of these things are humility, honesty, innocence and justice, purity, righteousness, truth, and peacemaking and unity. Those things are so beautiful, and they're a great summary of what we've seen of Him in Scripture. May His Spirit empower us to be more like Him. He's where the joy is!

PROVERBS 7–9

Today we continue our progress through Proverbs, and we're still in the dad's advice to his son and his warning about adultery. He wants these words to be in his son's line of sight and on his hands and in his heart. All three of those areas—eyes, hands, and heart—are important aspects of walking in holiness and purity. If the son has this wisdom at the forefront of these places, he won't be drawn to the adulteress.

It's easy to hear the phrase *the adulteress* and think of someone who is intentionally seeking to seduce. While that's possible, it's not exclusively referring to that. It could be someone the son seeks out and pursues; in fact, 7:8 refers to the son walking to her house at night. She meets him on the way, but he seems to go of his own volition. As she lays the flattery on thick, the fool falls for it. The dad warns his son repeatedly that this is the path to death. It's not a subtle warning; he repeats it over and over, using different language, and even violent language, throughout the passage, just to make sure he gets the point across.

He describes the adulteress as a loud woman who sidles up to the son and seduces him in the street. Then he describes another woman who cries out in the street, but this woman is wisdom personified. She raises her voice to call out too. She tells the fools and simpletons to listen to her. She begins to describe herself: She lives with prudence, knowledge, and discretion, and she hates pride, arrogance, evil, and perverted speech. She talks about the benefits she offers to anyone in relationship with her: counsel, sound wisdom, insight, strength, leadership, justice, love, riches, honor, enduring wealth, and righteousness. She was a tool in the hand of God when He created the earth.

And as the fool pursued the adulteress by going down the path to her house, the woman Wisdom can be pursued in the same way. She says, "Blessed is the one who listens to me, watching daily at my gates, waiting beside my doors. For whoever finds me finds life and obtains favor from the Lord" (8:34–35). She doesn't tackle the son like the adulteress does or make a sneak attack. She asks to be pursued. And while the adulteress is the path to death, wisdom is the path to life. And to love God is to hate evil. These juxtapositions are obvious and intentional. The dad lays two options out for his son, and he's clearly indicating which path is right. Chapter 9 personifies both wisdom and folly, and they both cry out to the simpleminded person. Folly sounds a lot like the adulteress from chapter 7. Wisdom offers the son something lasting, and the adulteress takes something lasting from him.

The dad's advice concludes, and it's interesting to note what percentage of it is centered around encouraging the son to avoid sexual sin and pursue wisdom instead. Those pursuits are opposed to each other; you can't simultaneously pursue both. The results of those pursuits are juxtaposed too. The dad seems to know a lot about this—perhaps he's made this mistake in his own life and that's why he's so emphatic about it. Or maybe he pursued wisdom and realized how beneficial it was to him. Or maybe both, because Solomon is the one who wrote this. Solomon, the man who asked God for wisdom, had seven hundred wives and three hundred concubines. In his life, it seems like he learned both lessons: the value of wisdom and the foolishness of sexual sin. He tested the world out and came away with some advice based on his experiences. He hopes to spare his son from making the same mistakes he did.

TODAY'S GOD SHOT

Proverbs 8:30–31 describes wisdom, but some scholars say it also points to Christ. "I was beside him, like a master workman, and I was daily his delight, rejoicing before him always, rejoicing in his inhabited world and delighting in the children of man." The Hebrew words for *delight* and *rejoicing* carry the connotations of playing and frolicking. Just as wisdom delights in humankind and creation, God delights in wisdom. What's it like for God to *frolick*? He seems positively giddy at creation, smiling with affection and amusement. Can you imagine? That's how God feels about us and about wisdom, and that's how wisdom feel about us. God is happy! And He's where the joy is!

PROVERBS 10–12

Today Solomon gives wisdom for everyone, not just his son. The way we live impacts others, so he implores everyone to be intentional about seeking out truth and living by it. It may mean more work on the front end, but it'll bless us in the long run. Part of wisdom is being teachable. A wise person submits to leadership and authority: "The wise of heart will receive commandments, but a babbling fool will come to ruin" (10:8). The fool doesn't even listen to correction at all; he just keeps talking. Much of Proverbs pertains to our speech. While our words may not have the literal power of life and death—that power belongs to God alone—they certainly have a measured effect on our emotions and perspectives, whether they're the words we speak or the words we hear.

The words we speak have to be measured carefully. Solomon leans on this throughout chapter 10: "The mouth of the righteous is a fountain of life," and "On the lips of him who has understanding, wisdom is found," and "The mouth of a fool brings ruin near," and "Whoever utters slander is a fool. When words are many, transgression is not lacking, but whoever restrains his lips is prudent. The tongue of the righteous is choice silver. . . . The lips of the righteous feed many," and "The mouth of the righteous brings forth wisdom, but the perverse tongue will be cut off. The lips of the righteous know what is acceptable, but the mouth of the wicked, what is perverse." And that's just in one chapter!

Since this is wisdom literature, not promises or prophecies or law, it has to be weighed by its context and measured by the rest of Scripture, or we'll be led to believe something Scripture isn't actually saying. For example, 10:15 says, "A rich man's wealth is his strong city; the poverty of the poor is their ruin," but we've repeatedly seen that God renders wealth meaningless and lifts up the poor. Even 11:28 says, "Whoever trusts in his riches will fall." So what is Solomon trying to say? Is he contradicting himself? The message here seems to be more about work ethic than wealth. Laziness is frowned upon, and poverty shouldn't be romanticized because so many problems are adjacent to it. While hard work and poverty aren't always at odds, the proverbs speak general truths. There are always exceptions to the rule. Some people are "born on third," so even though they may work hard, they can more easily advance further than someone who was born in the dugout, for example.

Other proverbs require us to allow for nuance in how we interpret them, and they show us the attention to detail and balance that wisdom brings. For instance, 10:18 says, "The one who conceals hatred has lying lips, and whoever utters slander is a fool." This isn't contradictory either—it's telling us what to say and what not to say: We shouldn't lie about our feelings, but we shouldn't gossip about the person either.

Chapter 11 emphasizes the connections between humility and wisdom and between righteousness and wisdom. The humble person realizes that the wise thing to do is walk in God's ways, not their own. The righteous are not only blessed themselves, but also serve as a blessing to those around them: "One who waters will himself be watered." Chapter 12 dives back into our speech. The wise man might keep his mouth shut even if he has something great to say, but the fool blabbers on endlessly and it usually results in error, lies, and wounds.

TODAY'S GOD SHOT

According to 11:20 and 12:22, God hates a crooked heart and lying lips. The word *crooked* is most often translated as "perverse," which usually means behaving in a belligerent and unreasonable way, rebelling against God's standards. On the other hand, God loves those of blameless ways, who act faithfully. What if you see yourself in both categories? Haven't we all lied and rebelled? Aren't we all a bit like the Israelites who worship Him, then turn away, then come back, then turn away again? Does God love us or hate us? The good news is Christ's death covers not only our rebellious moments, but also the selfish motives behind our so-called good actions. Because He's covered our sins, He can delight in us as His righteous children! And in return, we can delight in Him. He's where the joy is!

PROVERBS 13–15

Solomon almost makes it sound like the wise person will live a charmed life with no problems. But think about the wisest person you know—have they suffered? They'd likely say suffering is what produced some of their wisdom, teaching them things they wouldn't know otherwise. Wisdom and suffering aren't mutually exclusive—and that's good news for all of us! If you're having a hard time, it doesn't mean you're foolish. It might just be a chance to grow in wisdom, which will always outlast the suffering.

"Whoever walks with the wise becomes wise, but the companion of fools will suffer harm" (13:20). You've likely heard the maxim "You're the average of the five people you spend the most time with." And Paul says it this way, "Do not be deceived: 'Bad company ruins good morals'" (1 Corinthians 15:33). The wise aren't just attentive to their words—they're attentive to their company as well. And certainly reading the Bible counts as walking with the wise!

Proverbs 14:6 gives us an interesting twist on seeking wisdom; it describes a person who appears to be seeking wisdom but is really a scoffer disguised as a seeker: "A scoffer seeks wisdom in vain, but knowledge is easy for a man of understanding." Scoffers prefer questions to answers; answers are a threat, because they require something of us—they require us to submit to the answers we find. If someone is truly seeking, they'll be delighted when you give them what they're after!

Proverbs 14:11 says, "The house of the wicked will be destroyed, but the tent of the upright will flourish." After all this talk that sounds like the wise live a charmed life, the wicked person has a house and the righteous person has only a tent. This proverb feels a little more aligned with the reality we see around us. In general, the wicked do seem to have more—or at least they start out that way. Proverbs 15:25 reiterates this idea: "The Lord tears down the house of the proud but maintains the widow's boundaries." The proud has a house, but all the widow has is land. But God blesses and protects what she has. Even when the upright have less than the wicked, what the upright have is blessed and will endure. Sometimes we have to have eternity in view to see it; we can't let our vision land on this life. The greater, eternal reality is that the upright will flourish and the house of the wicked will be destroyed. Not only does poverty not mean you're foolish, but God commands His people to be kind and attentive to the poor, which drives it home even further that the poor aren't foolish or wicked. According to 14:31, we honor our Maker when we're kind to the poor.

Proverbs 14:12 says, "There is a way that seems right to a man, but its end is the way to death." We've seen this played out over and over in what we've read so far. When man follows his own way and relies on his own understanding, things end poorly. And even if they don't, God isn't glorified or honored, and that's still a loss.

Chapter 15 revisits the theme of using wisdom in our speech. Verse 8 is reminiscent of Cain and Abel: "The sacrifice of the wicked is an abomination to the LORD, but the prayer of the upright is acceptable to him." Many people wonder why God rejected Cain's offering but not Abel's, and maybe this has something to do with it. After all, God knows hearts.

TODAY'S GOD SHOT

"The LORD is far from the wicked, but he hears the prayer of the righteous" (15:29). God is under no obligation to respond to the prayers of those who don't know Him, but if He's your Father, you can bet He's going to listen! He repeatedly tells us how much He wants to hear from His kids. He's near to those He has made righteous. Nearness is the blessing—it's even better than a yes. Ask Him to draw you nearer today. It probably won't happen in a dramatic way. It may just be a sense of peace when things are chaotic, or hope when things feel impossible, or strength to serve someone who annoys you. That may be what His nearness looks like today as His Spirit empowers you to look like Christ. Ask for His nearness, expect it, look for it—because He's where the joy is!

PROVERBS 16–18

Did you discover anything good today in our reading? Proverbs 16:20 says, "Whoever gives thought to the word will discover good." Ponder the Word. Dwell in it and let it dwell in you. Be intentional about it. Wisdom is never an accident. This chapter addresses not only our thoughts, but our words. It says, "The wise of heart is called discerning, and sweetness of speech increases persuasiveness" and "Gracious words are like a honeycomb, sweetness to the soul and health to the body." May we speak words like that—gracious, sweet, life-giving words! It's so easy to default to sarcasm or slander or skepticism, but He can transform our hearts in such a way that gracious words flow out of our mouths! Speech control and self-control go hand in hand: "Whoever is slow to anger is better than the mighty, and he who rules his spirit than he who takes a city" (16:32). It's more challenging to control ourselves than to win a war against others! More strength is demonstrated in acting peacefully than in acting out in anger. And we cannot do this on our own. Self-control is part of the fruit of the Spirit (Galatians 5:22–23)—it's evidence of God the Spirit at work in you. It's not you; it's Him!

Chapter 17 hits on a topic we haven't seen much of yet in Proverbs: forgiveness. Verse 9 says, "Whoever covers an offense seeks love, but he who repeats a matter separates close friends." This verse not only compels people to forgive but also compels the forgiven person to repent. If there's no repentance, forgiveness is disrupted, and in this instance, the relationship is ruined.

Chapter 18 hits on something we've talked about previously. Verses 10–11 say, "The name of the LORD is a strong tower; the righteous man runs into it and is safe. A rich man's wealth is his strong city, and like a high wall in his imagination." His wealth appears to provide him with safety and security, but it's an illusion. Almost every day, we see people stripped of everything they've spent their lives amassing: wealth, power, approval, fame—all gone in a second. There's nothing that can't be taken from us except for God and His family. It's humbling, and it helps us keep our focus on the right things. Proverbs 17:24 says, "The discerning sets his face toward wisdom, but the eyes of a fool are on the ends of the earth." The fool chases every possible unattainable goal, but the wise have the goal of wisdom, and they know it only comes from God.

Humility is another theme in today's reading, and it's frequently connected to wisdom. "Before destruction a man's heart is haughty, but humility comes before honor" (18:12). "Pride goes before destruction, and a haughty spirit before a fall" (16:18). This is where the saying "Pride goes before a fall" comes from. Humility doesn't make a lot of assumptions. Humility isn't entitled. Humility gives the benefit of the doubt. Humility shows up in our actions but starts in the heart—and that's where wisdom resides too. That's why 16:21 uses the phrase "wise *of heart*," because wisdom is related to heart capacity as much as mental capacity.

TODAY'S GOD SHOT

In Proverbs 16, Solomon spends a lot of time hovering over God's sovereignty as it pertains to various areas of life, such as what plans come to pass and what purposes things serve. Here are some of the places we see it: "The plans of the heart belong to man, but the answer of the tongue is from the LORD." "The LORD has made everything for its purpose, even the wicked for the day of trouble." "The heart of man plans his way, but the LORD establishes his steps." "The lot is cast into the lap, but its every decision is from the LORD." We've seen this theme painted in broad strokes and fine lines across the pages of Scripture over the past 159 days, but Solomon has such a poetic way of summarizing it. There are some days when discouragement threatens to take hold, or fear taunts us, or regret knocks on our door every hour—sometimes the only comfort is the reminder of God's sweet sovereignty, that He's working in everything to bring about the restoration of all the things we've broken, that He can't be defeated. He's working out His plan for good, and He's where the joy is!

PROVERBS 19–21

Chapter 19 offers wisdom on relationships, including our relationship with God. "Desire without knowledge is not good, and whoever makes haste with his feet misses his way" (19:2). If you were in a relationship with someone who said they loved you but didn't want to know anything about you, wouldn't you be skeptical of their so-called love? Many people have a relationship with God that is only driven by emotion, unsupported by any knowledge of who He is. Every day that you open your Bible and put your eyes on who God says He is, you're displaying the kind of wisdom this verse calls us to. Knowing Him takes time and effort, but seeking Him and His guidance is so much wiser than forging ahead on our own.

"When a man's folly brings his way to ruin, his heart rages against the Lord" (19:3). When our sins bring negative consequences, we often blame God instead of ourselves. And He's so patient with us—even while we're angry with Him, He keeps putting His true character in front of us, beckoning us to see the real Him. He forgives. "Good sense makes one slow to anger, and it is his glory to overlook an offense" (19:11). What Solomon is describing here is God; God describes Himself as "slow to anger" (Exodus 34:6). Because of Christ's death on the cross, our sins have been covered. There's great wisdom in being slow to anger and hard to offend. What things offend you? Are they related to your efforts to maintain your identity and sense of worth? God can be trusted to handle those things. And we can image Him to the world by laying down our so-called rights and reputations like Jesus did. According to 1 Corinthians 13, love isn't easily offended, it isn't irritable or resentful, and it keeps no record of wrongs. That chapter is describing God too. That means if you're His kid, He isn't mad at you. All your offenses have been paid for by Jesus!

Proverbs 20:15 says it's rare to live and walk in wisdom: "There is gold and abundance of costly stones, but the lips of knowledge are a

For more information on today's reading, see thebiblerecap.com/links.

precious jewel." Jewels are precious because they're rare. When you speak knowledge and wisdom to a foolish and simple world, you add value and beauty to a space that desperately needs it. That doesn't mean we should become arrogant and seize every opportunity to sound smart; after all, this book reminds us repeatedly about the links between wisdom, humility, and holding our tongues.

Solomon speaks wisdom to wives, women who hope to be wives, and any man in search of a wife. But these desirable traits for a wife are applicable to a husband as well. "It is better to live in a corner of the housetop than in a house shared with a quarrelsome wife" (21:9). "A wife's quarreling is a continual dripping of rain" (19:13). Being quarrelsome or antagonistic or nitpicky—those aren't desirable traits in any relationship, much less in the person you're binding yourself to for life. Verse 19 of chapter 21 adds another layer: "It is better to live in a desert land than with a quarrelsome and fretful woman." Fear is also an undesirable trait. When we're ruled by fear or live out of a scarcity mentality or a victim mentality, we miss out on the beauty and freedom of trusting God for provision and protection. We close our fists around our non-negotiables. It's exhausting to us and everyone around us. First Peter 3:6 paints a picture of what it's like not to fear things that are legitimately scary because we're eternally safe in the temporary storms.

TODAY'S GOD SHOT

In Proverbs 19:17, God identifies Himself with the poor: "Whoever is generous to the poor lends to the LORD, and he will repay him for his deed." In fact, Jesus says not to lend, but to give (see Matthew 5:42 and Luke 6:35). That doesn't preclude taking out or giving loans—it just highlights generosity as the right heart attitude. God also positions Himself as the one who reimburses the giver. And the good news is He usually pays in a different currency—the eternal kind, which is far superior. God not only identifies with the poor, but He's also generous to the rich. He's attentive to the poor and the rich, the needy and the content. No one is beyond His love and attention. He's attentive, He's generous, and He's where the joy is!

PROVERBS 22–24

Avoiding sin involves careful attention and thoughtful planning; it doesn't happen on accident. In Proverbs 22 Solomon says, "The prudent sees danger and hides himself" (v. 3), "Guard your soul," and "Apply your heart," and he encourages parents to "train up" their children with wisdom. "Thorns and snares are in the way of the crooked; whoever guards his soul will keep far from them" (v. 5). He says to steer clear of things that ensnare us. What things take your eyes and affections off God? What traps do you fall into? Proverbs 22:14 points out a common trap: "The mouth of forbidden women is a deep pit; he with whom the LORD is angry will fall into it." There's a deeper meaning to the phrase "he with whom the LORD is angry"—it's closer to meaning "he who is cursed of the LORD," which of course refers to the person who doesn't know God. It's important to remember that these wisdom nuggets aren't promises or prophecy; this doesn't mean God lures people into adultery. This is Solomon's way of imploring his readers to steer clear of things that are adultery adjacent, because they're a trap.

Then Solomon, one of the wealthiest men of all time, tells us something only a wealthy man could know from experience: Wealth is fleeting, unfulfilling, and not worth exhausting yourself over. In 23:4–5, he's basically saying, "Don't be foolish enough to chase these fleeting things. You'll be exhausted, and they'll be gone."

He frequently points to choosing friends wisely. "Make no friendship with a man given to anger, nor go with a wrathful man, lest you learn his ways and entangle yourself in a snare" (22:24–25). "Fear the LORD and the king, and do not join with those who do otherwise" (24:21). "Be not among drunkards or among gluttonous eaters of meat, for the drunkard and the glutton will come to poverty, and slumber will clothe them with rags" (23:20–21). The people we surround ourselves with have a measured influence on our lives. He also warns against drinking too much wine. Most scholars believe he wrote Ecclesiastes, which recounts feasts that last for multiple days with lots of food and wine, so he likely experienced these consequences or saw plenty of others suffer through them.

Then he gives us a crash course in what it means to learn, using a house as a metaphor: "By wisdom a house is built, and by understanding it is established; by knowledge the rooms are filled with all precious and pleasant riches" (24:3–4). What's the difference between wisdom, knowledge, and understanding? *Knowledge* is having the facts. *Understanding* is the ability to discern what the facts mean and how they fit together in the big picture. *Wisdom* is knowing how to apply your knowledge and understanding, translating it into the everyday life of a Christ follower.

TODAY'S GOD SHOT

God cares for those who are far from Him, including the fools and the simpletons: "Rescue those who are being taken away to death; hold back those who are stumbling to the slaughter. If you say, 'Behold, we did not know this,' does not he who weighs the heart perceive it? Does not he who keeps watch over your soul know it?" (24:11–12). God appoints the wise as watchers over those stumbling toward slaughter. Some scholars believe these verses are literal, referring to the unjustly oppressed. Some say they apply on a spiritual level as well. This idea is reiterated in 24:17–18: "Do not rejoice when your enemy falls, and let not your heart be glad when he stumbles, lest the LORD see it and be displeased, and turn away his anger from him." God wants our hearts to align with His heart. "As I live, declares the Lord God, I have no pleasure in the death of the wicked, but that the wicked turn from his way and live; turn back, turn back from your evil ways, for why will you die?" (Ezekiel 33:11). God wants the wicked to turn back, to repent and live, not to stumble into eternal death. What kind of person cares for His enemies like that? The same God who adopts them into His family, pays for their sins, and seats them at His table for an eternal feast. We all started out as His enemies, steeped in sin. But He gave us new hearts, opened our eyes, and helped us to see and believe that He's where the joy is!

1 KINGS 5–6; 2 CHRONICLES 2–3

Solomon is preparing to build the temple. He wants the best materials, so he negotiates with the king next door in Tyre of Lebanon, just north of Israel. King Hiram had a great relationship with Solomon's dad, David. Even though Hiram is a Gentile, he recognizes and blesses God and His work on Israel's behalf, so he and Solomon are off to a good start. Hiram's country has renowned cedar trees that can grow up to one hundred feet tall—that's a ten-story building—and their lumberjacks use secret logging techniques. As Solomon negotiates with them about using their cedar trees, he tries to send some of his guys to "help out" with the logging, but he's probably trying to get the scoop on their techniques. Hiram seems to assume Solomon is being sneaky, so he plays it cool: "Oh, that's so nice of you to offer! But we'll just bring it to you and save you the trip. Then you can just give us some food in exchange for it." But Solomon sends thirty thousand Canaanites from his work crew to Lebanon anyway, and he gets away with it somehow! He has 150,000 Israelites working on things too; that's nearly 200,000 people. This is a massive project.

Chapter 5 says they lay the foundation with dressed stones. These are stones that have been smoothed over into perfect cubes or boxes for a seamless fit. When you hear the word *stones*, don't imagine tiny rocks. The largest stone in the temple foundation today weighs 570 tons—that's over one million pounds. You can see and touch that stone if you take the tunnel tour underneath the Old City of Jerusalem. This kind of masonry is impressive, and for stones this size, it requires lots of workers.

Even though the temple's foundation is large, the temple itself is only ninety feet long, thirty feet wide, and forty-five feet high. That's pretty small by modern standards. In case you're not good at visualizing measurements, it's about half the footprint of a Chick-fil-A, but about twice the height. The temple construction takes seven years, and it's occurring approximately five hundred years after the Israelites came out of bondage in Egypt. This has been a long time coming. But finally it's here—God's glorious dwelling place, made of the finest materials on earth: gold and cypress and precious stones. They prepare the Most Holy Place for the arrival of the ark of the covenant by hanging a huge curtain to separate it from the Holy Place, blocking off the area where God's earthly throne will dwell. This curtain is important in the story line we'll continue to follow. The first-century historian Josephus Flavius may have described it as being four inches thick.*

Behind this curtain—or the veil, as it's commonly called—are two cherubim statues carved out of olive wood. Cherubim have four faces, and they have four wings covered in eyes. These statues are massive—they're about half the height of the temple, and their wings stretch from wall to wall. In Scripture, cherubim often serve as guards of holy places, like the garden of Eden and the Most Holy Place. The temple structure is magnificent, but God is quick to remind Solomon that impressive buildings aren't what guarantee His presence with them and His blessing over them. God says their covenant relationship is based on hearts that demonstrate their love for Him through obedience (6:12–13).

TODAY'S GOD SHOT

The temple is built on Ornan's threshing floor, which is on Mount Moriah. Do you remember what else happened on Mount Moriah? That's where Abraham offered Isaac before God stopped him and said He would provide the sacrifice (Genesis 22). Many scholars say the temple is built on that exact site, on the southern end of Mount Moriah. Something else happened on this mountain that we haven't read about yet. It's where God *did* provide the sacrifice. On the northern end of this mountain, the highest point is called Mount Calvary, or Golgotha, and it marks the site of Christ's death. From the start of the story to the fulfillment of the story, this mountaintop has been a focal point. He's not only been providing all along, but He's been foreshadowing His plan for ultimate provision all along too. He's writing a beautiful story with this mountaintop at the heart of the action. He's where the joy is!

*The Ryrie Study Bible: New American Standard, expanded edition (La Habra, CA: Moody Bible Institute, 1995), 133n.

1 KINGS 7; 2 CHRONICLES 4

Today we briefly interrupt the description of the temple details to zoom in on Solomon's house, dividing the temple description in half. This is probably an intentional move by the author to illustrate a sad point: Solomon has a divided heart. We saw a hint of this in yesterday's reading when Canaanite laborers worked in shifts, spending one month working on the temple followed by two months working on his house. Solomon's house is much larger, but houses that hold physical people have to be larger than ones that house God's Spirit and a few small pieces of furniture—so it's reasonable that it takes longer, but this interruption in the narrative is probably there to point toward what's happening in Solomon's heart, not just his house. He uses a lot of the same resources for his house, and he doesn't just build a house—he builds a whole palace complex. He has his own palace, his wife's palace, a throne hall, and the hall of pillars. While David had humble roots as a shepherd, Solomon's affinity for fine things will eventually become a problem for him.

As for the temple furniture, we've come a long way from the tabernacle. The temple is gorgeous! Solomon hires the most skilled craftsmen. For the bronze items, he uses an artist named Hiram, not to be confused with King Hiram of Tyre. Bronze worker Hiram doesn't just have skills—he has wisdom and understanding too. You may recall from our lengthy tabernacle descriptions that God empowered craftsman Bezalel along these same lines: "I have filled him with the Spirit of God, with ability and intelligence, with knowledge and all craftsmanship" (Exodus 31:3). When you have a task as important as this, it's vital to choose not only a person with talent, but one with wisdom and understanding. For a role related to the temple, character and integrity seem to be even more important than skill. While 1 Kings says Solomon made all the vessels (7:48), it's more likely that he commissioned the work. He also

For more information on today's reading, see thebiblerecap.com/links.

commissions the work that has to be done throughout the whole temple complex. That includes the bronze basin, which holds twelve thousand to eighteen thousand gallons—about as much as the average swimming pool—and which is suspended on the backs of twelve bronze oxen.

He also makes ten lampstands, or menorahs, even though God only asked for one. There are so many other details and extravagant decorations. In fact, in the 1980s, someone discovered what was believed to be one of the pomegranates mentioned in 2 Chronicles 4:13, and the Israel Museum, which is like the Smithsonian, bought it for over half a million dollars. It was the size of a thumb.

TODAY'S GOD SHOT

In 1 Kings 7:21, we read about the two exterior pillars of the temple, which faces east. It says, "He set up the pillar on the south and called its name Jachin, and he set up the pillar on the north and called its name Boaz." The name Jachin means "He will establish" and the name Boaz means "in strength." *He will establish in strength.* At the place where they enter the house of God, where they draw near to His presence, as they pass through the columns holding it up, they're reminded that God initiated all of this and that He's sustaining all of it. And what He initiates will not only be sustained, but it will be fulfilled, because He's doing it in strength. But don't get too attached to this beautiful new temple, because it eventually gets destroyed. But do you know what doesn't get destroyed? God's presence with His people. This temple was always meant to be a temporary house for Him. He doesn't dwell in buildings anymore. He dwells in His people. And did you know that He marks us with the very same promise? Philippians 1:6 says it this way, "He who began a good work in you will bring it to completion at the day of Jesus Christ." *He will establish in strength.* Established in strength. Established in Him. Kept secure until the day of Christ Jesus. He's where the joy is!

1 KINGS 8; 2 CHRONICLES 5

Yesterday Solomon finished building the temple, and now he needs to furnish it. Today he and the Levites move all the holy furniture, including the ark of the covenant, from the tabernacle to the temple. There's a good chance he's heard stories about the time his dad caused a man to die while moving the ark improperly, so he makes sure to transport it according to God's laws—on poles and carried by Levite priests. The priests deposit the ark in the Most Holy Place, then the cloud of God's presence swoops in and fills the place. As they're trying to leave the temple, they're falling over because they can't even stand in such a heavy concentration of God's presence. Even though God is everywhere, He can certainly dial up the saturation when He wants to.

In 1 Kings 8:12–13, Solomon offers a blessing, praising God for fulfilling His promise to David. He says, "The LORD has said that he would dwell in thick darkness. I have indeed built you an exalted house, a place for you to dwell in forever." While it's a nice thought that God would live in this particular house forever, that's never been God's plan. God never said that. Solomon is adding his own words to God's words here.

In 8:29, Solomon says, "That your eyes may be open night and day toward this house, the place of which you have said, 'My name shall be there.'" There are two things we need to address in this verse. First, he says God's name will be in the temple. Not God Himself? Just His name? This was likely Solomon's way of clarifying that God is not contained in this house. By saying His name is there—like God had said about Jerusalem at large—he's saying God's character and blessing and presence will be evident there, but that God isn't confined by those four walls. The second thing to notice is that Solomon himself clarifies this idea earlier in that verse: "That your eyes may be open night and day toward this house." He clarifies that even though God is inside it, He's also outside it. Just like He transcends time, God transcends location.

He asks God to be attentive to everything from the smallest matters of man-to-man sin to the largest matters of humanity-to-God sin and to act with justice and mercy, since God alone knows the hearts of all humankind. He anticipates a day when Israel will sin against God, and he knows that when they sin, they need both God's forgiveness and God's direction, so he asks God for both.

In 8:41–43, he prays a blessing for most of us. He asks God to spread His fame beyond Israel and transform the hearts of foreigners. He wants all the people of the earth to know God's name and fear Him. He knows that YHWH is the best, and he wants word to get out about it! Then he blesses the people, and in 8:57–58 he offers a beautiful benediction: "The LORD our God be with us, as he was with our fathers. May he not leave us or forsake us, that he may incline our hearts to him, to walk in all his ways and to keep his commandments, his statutes, and his rules, which he commanded our fathers." Solomon first reminds them of the blessing of God's nearness and also of the blessing of God's work in that nearness: "That he may incline our hearts to him, to walk in all his ways." God doesn't come near to condemn—He can do that from afar. He comes near to change hearts.

Solomon dedicates the house, and they offer so many sacrifices that they overflow the altar. Afterward, they have a weeklong feast, then the chapter ends by saying they "went to their homes joyful and glad of heart for all the goodness that the LORD had shown to David his servant and to Israel his people."

TODAY'S GOD SHOT

In this beautiful moment of promise fulfillment, we see foreshadowing of a promise that hadn't yet been fulfilled. In 1 Kings 8:27, Solomon says, "But will God indeed dwell on the earth?" *Solomon, you have no idea!* He's coming. And He's healing the blind, and He's feeding the hungry, and He's setting the captives free, and He's raising the dead. And if you think you know joy now, just wait, because it's about to go from zero to one hundred in the blink of an eye. He's where the joy is!

2 CHRONICLES 6–7; PSALM 136

Solomon remembers that when David told God he wanted to build the temple and God said no, He affirmed David by saying, "You did well that it was in your heart." God said David had a good desire, but the answer was no. Sometimes even good desires get a no, but it can be comforting to know that doesn't mean our desires are sinful. Good desires and God's no can coexist—David is proof. And we can rest assured that when God says no, it's His kindest possible answer.

Then we see more reminders that God isn't confined to the temple: "If they pray toward this place and acknowledge your name and turn from their sin . . . then hear in heaven and forgive" (6:26–27). The people will pray to God toward the temple, and God will hear *from heaven*. This reinforces the fact that YHWH is different from other gods. Those gods can only occupy one space, but YHWH occupies all space. He invented space! He's omnipresent—always present everywhere.

After Solomon's offerings, God sends fire to consume the food offered, and the people respond with praise. Somehow we've come to view lightning as evidence of God's anger, but the vast majority of His fire-throwing serves as a sign of acceptance, not rejection or condemnation. We also tend to have the wrong view of rain in Scripture. When Jesus says God sends rain on the just and the unjust (Matthew 5:45), it's easy to hear it as "Bad things happen to good people too." But these people live in a desert that only gets rain a few months out of the year, so rain is a needed blessing. Jesus is saying God extends His goodness and grace toward even the wicked, not just the righteous. This is common grace, meaning all the humans God created, not just His kids, get to have at least a base-level experience of His goodness, like breathing the air He engineered and feeling the sun He commands to shine and eating the food He invented.

After the weeklong party, God appears to Solomon in a night vision and tells him what's going to happen next. They have this big, beautiful new temple where God dwells, and there's been a majestic display of wealth and wonder and sacrificing and fire throwing, but it still won't make the Israelites love and follow God. They'll rebel, and He'll send them various forms of discipline: drought, locust, disease. If they repent and turn to Him, He'll keep the covenant despite their rebellion.

With passages like 7:14, we have to be careful about taking God's covenant with Israel and applying it to our own countries. Cherry-picking specific promises for ourselves that weren't made to us is dangerous. For instance, for most people it would be obvious that we can't take God's next promise to Solomon—that he'll always have a descendant on the throne—and apply that to ourselves. But what we can do with these promises is look for what they reveal to us about God's character. This verse shows us that He is the kind of God who stands ready to forgive and to bless. His covenant with Israel is contingent on their obedience, yet He's already telling them, "You're going to break this covenant. But when you return to Me, I'm going to forgive you. I've put My name on this family and this city, and I'm not going anywhere."

In Psalm 136, the other passage we read today, the psalmist is hung up, in the best way possible, on celebrating God's steadfast love that endures forever. He praises YHWH for His mighty works of creation and salvation, and even for a few acts of destruction.

TODAY'S GOD SHOT

Today Solomon said, "There is no one who does not sin" (2 Chronicles 6:36). This echoes other passages in Scripture: "There is none who does good, not even one" (Psalm 14:3) and "All have sinned and fall short of the glory of God" (Romans 3:23). Solomon delivers this sentence at the dedication of God's temple, and God comes to dwell there—the God whose presence is so powerful that even the priests among them can't stand up. The fact that every single human God created was and will be born into the fall, broken from the start and given to sin, shows us how remarkable it is that God comes down to live with us, to concentrate His perfect presence in the midst of our wickedness. He's here, and He's not going anywhere. He's where the joy is!

PSALMS 134, 146–150

Psalm 134 is the last of the Songs of Ascent. This prayer is still prayed as a blessing today. God's people have been saying these words for three thousand years: "May the LORD bless you from Zion, he who made heaven and earth!"

In Psalm 146, the psalmist reminds us not to put our trust in people. This isn't a call to be cynical and suspicious of everyone—it's more about not expecting people to rescue us or fulfill us. When we place on a human the kind of workload only God can carry, it crushes them and it disappoints us. Verse 5 says, "Blessed is he . . . whose hope is in the LORD his God." The person who puts their confidence in God—not in what He can do for you or how He can make all your dreams come true, but in God Himself—will be blessed. However, this isn't saying that if you hope in God, you'll get the material blessings you're tempted to try to claim. The word *blessed* here is often translated as "happy." So it boils down to this: When we trust God in all things, it brings a freedom that doesn't exist elsewhere. Because of His sovereignty over all things, we don't have to panic when we're delayed in traffic or when we don't get the job we think we're perfect for. Because we can trust Him, we can open our hand and loosen our grip. And because we know He's doing good things somehow, we can find joy in Him despite it all. *That's* the blessing.

Psalm 147 tells us God is attentive to the heartbroken and to a whole list of other things, even down to the blades of grass under your feet. But of all His creation, the thing He delights in most is humanity, specifically the humans who know and trust Him. Verse 11 says, "The LORD takes pleasure in those who fear him, in those who hope in his steadfast love." He loves to be delighted in and trusted. Don't we all? The two worst things you can say to someone are "I don't like you" and "I don't trust you." But to love God and to trust God invites His pleasure. If you struggle with either of those things, loving Him or trusting Him, ask Him for help! He can work changes in your heart that you aren't capable of.

Psalm 148 commands creation to praise God. Verse 14 says, "He has raised up a horn for his people." In Scripture, the horn represents strength and victory and salvation, and God has certainly raised that up for His people.

Psalm 149 opens with dancing and delight but takes a turn in the middle of verse 6. "Let the high praises of God be in their throats and two-edged swords in their hands, to execute vengeance on the nations and punishments on the peoples" (vv. 6–7). We go from praise to killing pretty quickly here. This is reminiscent of the time Ehud killed King Eglon with a two-edged sword (Judges 3). The mention of vengeance here can be easy to misunderstand. This likely refers to God's vengeance, not Israel's vengeance. Remember when God promised them the land and told them that He wasn't giving it to them because of their righteousness, but because of the unrighteousness of the Canaanites who lived there? And how He told Israel He'd use them as a tool to execute His justice? The end of this psalm seems to echo that idea.

We end the day with the very short Psalm 150, with all the instruments and everything that breathes praising God for who He is and what He does.

TODAY'S GOD SHOT

Psalm 146:7–9 says God is the one "who executes justice for the oppressed, who gives food to the hungry. The Lord sets the prisoners free; the Lord opens the eyes of the blind. The Lord lifts up those who are bowed down; the Lord loves the righteous. The Lord watches over the sojourners; he upholds the widow and the fatherless, but the way of the wicked he brings to ruin." That list of ten kinds of people covers many of the people Jesus had relationships with: the oppressed, the hungry, the imprisoned, the blind, the sorrowful, the righteous, the displaced, the widowed, the orphaned, and even the wicked. Where do you find yourself in that list? How has He shown His love to you in that place? If you want to be more godly, demonstrating these characteristics of Jesus is one way to do that. He's where the joy is!

1 KINGS 9; 2 CHRONICLES 8

Solomon spends twenty years building the temple and his house, and he also builds a separate house for his wife because, in his words, "My wife shall not live in the house of David king of Israel, for the places to which the ark of the LORD has come are holy" (2 Chronicles 8:11). When men in this day have multiple wives, they usually have a different house or tent for each wife, but the first or main wife often lives in the same house as the husband. But with Solomon, not even his main wife lives in the main house. The house he builds for her is in a location outside the city because she's a pagan, and he doesn't want her near the ark of the covenant. This whole arrangement sounds terrible, honestly.

Then Solomon builds twenty cities, possibly as a gift for King Hiram, but he apparently doesn't like them. And it's also possible that he gives them back to Solomon—these two chapters we read today aren't clear on that. In all his empire building, Solomon uses a lot of forced labor. God's law forbids the Israelites to enslave other Israelites, so Solomon works with the loophole and uses Canaanite laborers instead. They build things all throughout Israel and Lebanon to the north, where his friend King Hiram lives. He also builds a fleet of ships, which isn't one of his areas of expertise. Fortunately, King Hiram knows a lot of men who are skilled at seafaring, and they join forces to go do some international trade. Scholars are divided on whether international trade is acceptable or not. Does it imply that God hasn't provided for Israel and all their needs in the promised land? Does it mean they're joining forces with wicked nations? Is it driven by greed? Scripture isn't clear on any of those matters, so we hold it all with an open hand.

Despite all this building, Solomon still manages to keep the calendar of feasts and sacrifices. He tries to remain faithful to all the things that were clearly marked out in the law by Moses and David.

In 1 Kings 9:7–8, where God is discussing what will happen if Israel rebels, He says, "And the house that I have consecrated for my name I will cast out of my sight, and Israel will become a proverb and a byword among all peoples. And this house will become a heap of ruins. Everyone passing by it will be astonished and will hiss, and they will say, 'Why has the LORD done thus to this land and to this house?'" We already know that this temple will be destroyed eventually, and this all comes to pass. God knows, and we know, but Solomon probably didn't fully grasp what God meant in that moment. It's easy to think of God as harsh here, like He's saying, "If you don't do what I say, I'm taking my toys and going home!" But that's not what we see here for two reasons.

First, God has already laid out the plan of redemption and restoration. Solomon himself spoke about it on consecration day. A selfish god doesn't act like that. A selfish god is unyielding and vengeful. Second, God's compassion and priorities are evident even in these harsh words, because He always points back to the relationship He has with them: He rescued them. He brought them into this land. He came to dwell in this house with them. The whole conversation is peppered with reminders of their relationship. We see again and again that He's not just after their obedience, He's after their hearts.

TODAY'S GOD SHOT

God has rules and a right way for things to be done. We're broken and we need that. But He's also forgiving when we inevitably fall short, and we need that too. He even tells us in advance how He's going to operate in His relationship with us. What a gift that we never have to wonder where we stand with Him. If we have any problem with this passage, it should be with the wicked hearts of men, not with God's response to their wickedness. Wickedness deserves punishment. Yet God still has mercy. He's righteous, just, loving, and compassionate in all His ways. And He's where the joy is!

PROVERBS 25–26

Today we dig back into the wisdom of Solomon. Chapter 25 encourages us not to be presumptuous in relationships with others. We shouldn't elevate our level of importance with others; wisdom helps us stay humble. In the same way that wisdom doesn't esteem itself, wisdom also doesn't degrade others or their motives when it doesn't know the whole story, which requires humility and patience. Verses 9–10 encourage us in wise behavior when we have a problem with someone else. Talk about your problem with the person you have the problem with, not everyone else. That, too, requires humility and patience. Verse 15 says the humble, patient tongue wields great power: "With patience a ruler may be persuaded, and a soft tongue will break a bone." Patience and humility have a more powerful impact than arrogance and forcefulness.

Solomon also offers wisdom on self-control, tying that into humility as well. He urges self-control in everything from how much we eat to how often we visit our neighbor. The general theme in these proverbs is that too much of a good thing is a bad thing. Self-control also guides us in seemingly minor areas like what words we say to a grieving person or how we treat our enemies.

Verse 24 is similar to two other proverbs we've seen already: "It is better to live in a corner of the housetop than in a house shared with a quarrelsome wife." The other verses we've read on this topic said it's better to live in the desert and that this woman is like a constant dripping. Solomon has a lot of wives, so he probably has his fair share—or unfair share—of quarrelsome wives. He knows of which he speaks! And it bears repeating: This passage can be applied to either gender, but Solomon rightly assumes that most of his readers in that day are male. Regardless of your gender, it takes a lot of self-control not to be quarrelsome. The chapter ends with a call to self-control: "A man without self-control is like a city broken into and left without walls."

Proverbs 26 describes the foolish man as wasteful and worthless. On the surface, verses 4 and 5 seem to contradict each other: "Answer not a fool according to his folly, lest you be like him yourself. Answer a fool according to his folly, lest he be wise in his own eyes." This is a good place to reiterate that Proverbs isn't a book of biblical laws—it's a book of general principles for wise living. Some situations call for one type of wisdom, some for another type. These bits of wisdom complement each other. There are times when a fool needs to be corrected, and there are times when correcting a fool is a waste of your time and breath, because he won't receive it. We have to use discernment to know which wisdom applies. This is a good example of how knowledge and understanding work together with wisdom.

The foolish person, on the other hand, may speak words of wisdom, but they never grow or change accordingly. They don't retain lessons. They make the same mistakes repeatedly and aren't humble enough to care. Verse 12 says, "Do you see a man who is wise in his own eyes? There is more hope for a fool than for him." In other words, arrogance is worse than stupidity.

As the chapter wraps up, Solomon reminds us again of the power and importance of our words. Gossip, slander, and even flattery can be wicked: "A lying tongue hates its victims, and a flattering mouth works ruin."

TODAY'S GOD SHOT

Proverbs 25:2 says, "It is the glory of God to conceal things, but the glory of kings is to search things out." Sometimes God is more glorified in mystery than in revealing everything. And sometimes the only reason we seek answers is because we're proud or impatient or don't want to have to trust God. The leaders among men are supposed to have all the answers, but the ultimate Leader of all humankind is the only one who truly does, and sometimes, He just isn't telling. This is humbling to us but glorifying to God. Any time He conceals things from us, we can rest assured that it's ultimately in our best interest. He doesn't play hide-and-seek with anything we need to know to obey Him. He's not cruel. He's intentional with all the details and with His timing in revealing them. He's where the joy is!

PROVERBS 27–29

Proverbs 27 opens with a pair of reminders not to be presumptuous: "Do not boast about tomorrow, for you do not know what a day may bring. Let another praise you, and not your own mouth." Solomon advises us not to presume about tomorrow and not to presume about our importance in the world either.

Verse 6 digs into our relationships: "Faithful are the wounds of a friend." When someone loves you and they deliver a measured, intentional rebuke, the aim is to serve you well. It's like a loving parent disciplining their child. Verse 9 says, "The sweetness of a friend comes from his earnest counsel," and verse 17 says, "Iron sharpens iron." Whom have you invited to righteously wound you, to sharpen you or give you counsel? A good friend will do that, but an enemy won't hesitate to lie and manipulate in order to stay in good standing. "Profuse are the kisses of an enemy" (v. 6).

Verse 7 may seem like it's an encouragement not to overeat, but given its context, it likely means something more than that. "One who is full loathes honey, but to one who is hungry everything bitter is sweet." The next verse says, "Like a bird that strays from its nest is a man who strays from his home." Solomon may be covering two separate ideas here, but it's also possible they overlap like this: If a person engages fully in loving and being loved by their spouse, outside temptation won't have the same appeal, because "one who is full loathes honey." But if they find no satisfaction from investing in their marriage, then almost any kind of outside attention has the potential to be enticing. "To one who is hungry everything bitter is sweet." It's possible he's encouraging those who are married to invest in their marriage. In fact, much of this chapter is wisdom about investing in what you have, whether it's relationships or flocks or fruit.

Proverbs 28 says the mind-set of the righteous is and should be different from that of the wicked. For instance, do you find yourself inventing things to be afraid of? Verse 1 is a good reminder that we can trust God.

Ask Him to remind you that His Spirit within you equips you for everything He allows into your life. It is almost certainly more than you can handle—but it's never more than He can handle. Verse 5 steps into this space too, reminding us not to expect the wicked and foolish to understand what is right and just. People who don't know and love God won't act like they do. But because we love and trust Him, we *want* to walk in His ways. He gave us new eyes to see these things and a new heart to love them. Remembering this gives us more grace and compassion toward them and helps us not to feel so smart or self-righteous about our perspective. We didn't get here on our own. We didn't figure something out or get our act together—*He* made us new. It was His doing, not ours. That's humbling.

Verse 13 addresses the way the righteous should view their sins: "Whoever conceals his transgressions will not prosper, but he who confesses and forsakes them will obtain mercy." Verse 14 is a perfect continuation, reminding us of the importance of having a soft heart that responds to the Spirit's promptings when He makes us aware of our sins. The fear of the LORD goes hand in hand with a soft heart.

Chapter 29 shows us traits of the proud, foolish person. The proud aren't teachable. The fool lacks self-control and patience in an argument. But wisdom holds its tongue and thinks before it speaks.

TODAY'S GOD SHOT

"The fear of man lays a snare, but whoever trusts in the LORD is safe. Many seek the face of a ruler, but it is from the LORD that a man gets justice" (29:25–26). The approval of others is fleeting. If we seek it, we'll be forever imprisoned by needing to gain or maintain their affirmation. On the other hand, God's approval of us in Christ is immovable. It's the only thing about us that doesn't change, and it's the only thing about us that lasts. God's perspective is fixed, and His plan will be accomplished. He's not fickle. He knows the future, because He's already there. He knows all the ways we've yet to mess up and sin and rebel against Him, but He has set His heart on us forever. He never goes away, and He's where the joy is!

ECCLESIASTES 1–6

Ecclesiastes is wisdom literature written by "the Preacher," who likely either *is* Solomon or is meant to make the reader think of him. The main character has plenty of resources at his disposal, and he wants to find out how to live the most joyful life, so he performs an experiment and then tells us what he learns. He lets us know what's worth our time, energy, and money. He states his thesis up front: "Vanity of vanities! All is vanity." The word for *vanity* means "vapor or smoke," but it also carries the connotation of something that's hard to grasp. The word appears thirty-eight times in this book; it's part of the overarching theme.

First he leans into work. All hard work is eventually negated—buildings decay, technology becomes outdated, income is diminished by taxes. Even amassing knowledge doesn't enhance the preacher's life, and he basically says ignorance is bliss. He's worked hard, he's learned many things, yet he still feels empty—and maybe even worse off. So he decides to test his heart next, using things that seem to hold other kinds of value. Forget hard work and a legacy, let's go after joy and pleasure! He builds an estate, hires his favorite bands to play in his backyard, and even has lots of concubines. But it's all a vapor, a fleeting pleasure that fails to satisfy.

He gains wisdom through the process, but he's frustrated that even though he's wiser, he's still going to die. Wisdom can't keep him from meeting the same end as a fool. And any possessions he leaves behind will be handed off to someone else who may not appreciate them. It seems unfair, so then he decides to live in the moment and find contentment in working unto the Lord and trusting Him, not in trying to amass a fortune or a name for himself.

In chapter 3, he lists various seasons people encounter in life. There are fourteen pairs of seasons—"a time to be born, and a time to die," "a time to mourn, and a time to dance," for example. Two things in

---

For more information on today's reading, see thebiblerecap.com/links.

his list may be troubling, but they fit with the rest of Scripture. Let's look at them. First, "a time to kill" isn't suggesting murder. This is the nation-state of Israel, and God has established laws about when the death penalty should be enacted. So there is, in fact, a time to kill, but capital punishment in carrying out God's laws for their nation-state is different from revenge. Second, "a time to hate" isn't necessarily referring to humans. God Himself hates sin and calls us to hate it as well. Romans 12:9 says, "Abhor what is evil; hold fast to what is good." In Proverbs 6:16–19, Solomon listed out several things God hates. God's hatred doesn't mean He isn't loving—He hates things that threaten what He loves, as we all do. These two attributes of God aren't contradictory; they're complementary.

Ecclesiastes 3:11 captures the complexity of life and all its seasons. God is working in everything for a specific purpose—namely, redemption—and He's given us a desire to grasp it all but also the inability to do so. God leaves some things as mysteries even to the wise. It's a reminder that we aren't God, and it's also an incentive to trust Him with all the things we don't know. This is both comforting and humbling.

Chapter 4 says a lot of our work ethic is driven by our need for control and superiority, which is pointless and exhausting. We're motivated by competition, jealousy, and pride. But comparison is a terrible taskmaster—it never lets us rest. There's actually more joy and wisdom in working together. Greed wounds the greedy. If God has given you wealth, and you can live with an open hand, not focused on it, then that's where real blessing is found. Being occupied with God, not wealth, is the path to joy. We can't enjoy His gifts if we're focused on gaining more.

TODAY'S GOD SHOT

"I perceived that whatever God does endures forever; nothing can be added to it, nor anything taken from it" (3:14). We strive to gain things that are fleeting and exhaust ourselves over a vapor. But here we see that everything God sets in motion is immovable—it lasts. We can't add to it or take from it. It's fixed forever. How powerful He is, and how weak we are. He's where the joy is!

ECCLESIASTES 7–12

The preacher urges his readers to take life and death seriously and to let sadness do its job. Even though life is fleeting, there's weight to the human experience and value in the emotions that come with it. Waiting on God's timing requires humility. Trusting God means we live in contentment even as we wait.

In 7:16, he seems to frown on wisdom and righteousness: "Be not overly righteous, and do not make yourself too wise. Why should you destroy yourself?" The word translated as "righteous" most often refers to the judicial system, not personal morality. It's as if he's saying, "Don't be the person who always has to be right and have all the answers. That's arrogant and ultimately keeps you from being the kind of person you want to be."

At the end of chapter 7, he laments how challenging human relationships can be. Even with all his wisdom, he can't seem to comprehend women at all. And even among other men, he only understands one. Humans are complex creatures, and connecting is hard.

In chapter 8, he advises the king's counselor. He basically says, "You're dealing with a man who has almost no restraint on his power. You're going to need a lot of wisdom to know when to speak up and when to keep quiet. He's going to try to abuse his authority, and you're going to have to know exactly how to approach him to reign him in sometimes." But even in this, the preacher realizes that the impact this can have is fleeting. It's just another aspect of how we can spin our wheels trying to control things. We can't determine the outcome.

Chapter 9 reminds us we'll all die someday, so we should enjoy our days while we have them. In verse 10 he says, "Whatever your hand finds to do, do it with your might, for there is no work or thought or knowledge or wisdom in Sheol, to which you are going." You may have heard someone use the word *Sheol* as a reference to hell, but it points more to death or the grave. And at this point in time, God hasn't given His people much information about what happens after death, but they have a general view that the body goes to Sheol and the spirit goes to God. God will continue to reveal information to His people about this, but we're not there yet, so hang in there.

In chapters 10 and 11, the preacher gives us some Solomon-style proverbs: Even a *little* foolishness can lead to ruin (10:1), we should guard our thoughts as much as our words (10:20), and God is the giver of life, even in the womb (11:5). We can't understand God's ways, but they govern everything we do, so it's best and wisest to yield to Him and trust Him.

In the end, the preacher calls the reader to remember God, especially in youth, when we haven't yet gained the wisdom of years that often causes a person to reflect on the brevity of life. Then he gives a metaphor describing the failing body of an old man. "The strong men are bent" refers to his bones and joints decaying, and "the grinders cease because they are few" (12:3) refers to the way he has to stop eating because his teeth have fallen out. And verse 7 says, "The dust returns to the earth as it was, and the spirit returns to God who gave it." Then he gives the conclusion of his experiment: We'll see pain and joy in our lives, but our job is to enjoy and obey God regardless.

TODAY'S GOD SHOT

"Though a sinner does evil a hundred times and prolongs his life, yet I know that it will be well with those who fear God, because they fear before him" (8:12). There's no formula for a long and happy life. All we can do is delight in God, obey Him, and trust Him with the outcome. And that is what it looks like for things to go well regardless of what happens. Isn't that what you're really after anyway? A heart at peace? And haven't you seen time and again how getting the thing you want doesn't achieve that for you? And how striving after it produces the opposite of a heart at peace? The preacher has had palaces and parties and concerts and money in amounts we'll never be able to touch—and he says none of it brings the kind of peace and joy that comes from humbly walking with God. The preacher knows that He's where the joy is!

1 KINGS 10–11; 2 CHRONICLES 9

Word about Solomon's empire spreads quickly, and the queen of Sheba travels a long way to visit him, bringing many people and camels and gifts as well as a lot of questions. And Solomon answers them all. She's dumbfounded! She praises his wisdom, prosperity, and charisma—even the people who work for him seem to really like him. This pagan queen even praises God for establishing Solomon as king, pointing to God as the source of it all. This idea is reiterated in 10:24: "The whole earth sought the presence of Solomon to hear his wisdom, which God had put into his mind." There's no wisdom apart from God. He owns it all, and anyone who has it got it from Him. Solomon asked God for this wisdom, and we can too. "If any of you lacks wisdom, let him ask God, who gives generously to all without reproach, and it will be given him" (James 1:5). God promises to answer this prayer with a yes! Wisdom isn't only from God, but it points back to God. He's the source, supply, and goal of it all.

Despite his wisdom, Solomon isn't perfectly obedient to God's commands for Israel's kings. He amasses more gold and more horses, defying God's law. He also adds more women to his list. He marries and associates with women who turn his heart from God, accumulating seven hundred wives and three hundred concubines. But it all started with one—just one woman whose heart wasn't aligned with God. We lead our own hearts astray one act of disobedience at a time. Solomon's heart is ruled by lust, not by God, and it leads to the downfall of his kingdom. Things go just as God said they would: "You shall not intermarry with them, giving your daughters to their sons or taking their daughters for your sons, for they would turn away your sons from following me, to serve other gods" (Deuteronomy 7:3–4). God wasn't guessing—He knew.

Solomon also builds sites for worshipping idols, at least one of whom, Molech, is a god the pagans make child sacrifices to. Despite Solomon's sin, God is keeping His promise to David. He says that after Solomon dies, the majority of Israel will be torn away from his son. God effectively punishes Solomon's blatant disobedience while maintaining His promises to David and Israel. Talk about efficiency. God raises up an enemy to oppose Solomon—a man named Jeroboam, one of Solomon's servants. Jeroboam has been suspicious of Solomon for a while because the prophet Ahijah once tore his own brand-new clothes into twelve pieces, handed Jeroboam ten of those pieces, then explained: God will take ten of the tribes away from Solomon's line of descendants and give them to Jeroboam. From that point on, Jeroboam seems to eagerly await his rise to power. Solomon knows he's after the kingdom, so he tries to kill him, but Jeroboam flees to Egypt, where he stays until Solomon dies. Then Solomon's son Rehoboam takes over his throne. Since the names Jeroboam and Rehoboam are similar, we'll call them Jerry and Rey for short. Jerry is the outsider here. Rey is the son of Solomon. And here's a trick for easier recall: He's the son Rey, like the sun's rays.

TODAY'S GOD SHOT

The queen of Sheba blesses God in response to Solomon's prosperity and wisdom: "Blessed be the Lord your God, who has delighted in you and set you on his throne as king for the Lord your God!" (2 Chronicles 9:8). She doesn't say God set Solomon on Solomon's throne, but that God set Solomon on God's throne. This indicates that God owns positions of power, including the throne of Israel. He's in charge of who's in charge. These are His people, and He's establishing their rulers to work out His plan. This is easy to swallow when the people in power are guys like Solomon, but what about all those terrible judges? It's hard for us to see what God might be doing by positioning them in power. That's where we have to be openhanded and trust that He's working out something we can't see. For instance, He used those terrible judges to produce repentance in the hearts of His people. He has purposes we can't understand sometimes, but they're always righteous, good, and loving. And no matter who is on the throne, He's where the joy is!

PROVERBS 30–31

Chapter 30's author, Agur, says his wisdom in comparison to God's wisdom is zero. He uses lots of imagery that's reminiscent of when God spoke to Job, pointing out that God is much more powerful and wise than any of us, then ends with a question that could be prophetic: "Who has established all the ends of the earth? What is his name, and what is his son's name? Surely you know!" (v. 4). That sounds a lot like Jesus!

Verse 6 reminds us why our trip through Scripture is so important: "Do not add to his words, lest he rebuke you and you be found a liar." If we don't know what God says, how will we know if we're misquoting Him or adding to His words? Many ideas are presented as God's words, posted as mantras on Instagram images or wall art, claiming His promises—but they're far from God's truth, sometimes even the opposite of what He says. The more we read His truth, the more we'll be able to spot the lies.

Agur asks God to do two things: keep him honest and keep him from sin. He knows the human heart well enough to know that blessing and prosperity often lead to disregarding God and forgetting our need for Him, while poverty can lead to despair and sin. It's easy to view the latter as being a worse kind of sin—to become a thief or a criminal. The shinier option is to be so wealthy that you forget God, but that's still sin. Agur wants to be kept from both extremes. He calls the arrogant and self-righteous to account and encourages repentance for those who've puffed themselves up or who planned their sin. Planning sin is a sure sign of a calloused heart.

King Lemuel wrote chapter 31, but most scholars believe this is a pen name for Solomon. This chapter is wisdom his mom passed down to him, so it's possible that these are Bathsheba's words of wisdom from all she's endured. If these are Bathsheba's words, you can see how verse 3 fits Solomon's situation: "Do not give your strength to women, your ways to those who destroy kings." He lets his lust overpower him and destroy his kingdom. In verses 4–9, she encourages her son toward selflessness, basically saying, "You're in a position of power, so don't waste it. Don't open your mouth to fill it with wine, but open your mouth to work justice for the oppressed and the needy."

Then she gives the description most women are most familiar with. Interestingly, it was written for a man as his mother's advice on what kind of woman he should look for. The last section of Proverbs 31 often makes women feel inadequate because they can't really live up to this ideal, but be encouraged that this person is almost certainly imaginary. His mom is just putting together a prototype for him. As we imagine what this woman's life must look like, we may wonder if she's a robot. Does she ever sleep? When does she have time to shower? The good news is that this list of things might have spanned her entire life, not a twenty-four-hour period. She may not have been an entrepreneur while she was raising children. She may not have been feeding her family while feeding the poor. If you're a woman, hopefully it'll set you free to remember that this is wisdom literature, not law. The point of this chapter isn't to compare our lives to hers, but to take note of the wisdom in her heart and the things she values, which determine how she spends her time. She's a woman of substance. She's not entitled. She has a great work ethic. She's supportive. And most importantly, she trusts God: "Strength and dignity are her clothing, and she laughs at the time to come" (31:25). To live in fear of the LORD means we don't live in fear of tomorrow. And as verse 30 says, "A woman who fears the LORD is to be praised."

TODAY'S GOD SHOT

If a woman fears the LORD—delights in God, trusts God, stands in awe of God—she's ultimately relying on Him for everything that makes her the strong, dignified, praiseworthy woman we've seen described here. If we drill down, that means God is also and ultimately to be praised for who she is. This woman isn't the hero—she points to the Hero. She finds her strength in the Hero. She's granted her wisdom and dignity by the Hero. She's great, for sure, but she points to Someone far greater, and He's where the joy is!

1 KINGS 12–14

King Rey takes over his dad's throne, and King Jerry comes back from Egypt because a prophet told him *he'd* be king. He gathers people to approach King Rey about a problem they've been having: Solomon treated his workers like slaves, so they ask King Rey to lighten their load. Rey's counselors say the people are right, but he ignores their advice and listens to his friends, who aren't compassionate and have no leadership wisdom. They say to increase the workload, and Rey does. The text says God ordained that Rey would reject the people's request as a part of His plan to fulfill His prophecy to Jerry. And this is when the kingdom is divided.

The divided kingdom lasts for a while, so here are some helpful tips for understanding it all: Ten tribes become the northern kingdom known as Israel, or Northern Israel. During this time of division, the word *Israel* refers only to those ten tribes of the northern kingdom, not all twelve tribes. The other two tribes—Judah and Benjamin—become the southern kingdom collectively referred to as Judah, or Southern Judah.

Rey remains king but only over Southern Judah. Northern Israel makes Jerry their king. Rey isn't happy about the ten tribes breaking away from him, so he wants to fight them, but God says it'd be a fight against Him, so Rey shuts it down. Up north, Jerry worries his people might get nostalgic for the temple and decide to reunite with Southern Judah, and then Rey will kill him. Jerry thinks the best way to keep people from making that pilgrimage south to the temple is to set up his own worship site in Northern Israel. He sets up two altars, makes two golden calves, sets up his own temples, appoints his own non-Levite priests, establishes his own days for feasts and sacrifices, and generally does whatever he wants without any regard for God, simply because he's afraid of losing power. Fear will drive you to unholy ends.

For more information on today's reading, see thebiblerecap.com/links.

A man of God shows up to rebuke him, but Jerry isn't having it. Despite having his hand withered and healed by the man, Jerry doesn't repent. Word of all this reaches an old prophet who tracks down the man of God. He lies to him, "God said you're supposed to come to my house for dinner." Eventually the prophet tells the man of God he made a terrible mistake by listening to him instead of God and that the punishment is death. Wow. As it turns out, the prophet is right, and the man of God is killed by a lion that day. The moral of the story is to obey the voice of God, not the voice of man. Despite all that's happened, Jerry keeps rebelling.

When his son gets sick, he knows they need real help, not metal livestock. He sends his wife in disguise to see Ahijah—the prophet who told Jerry he'd be king. God gives Ahijah a heads-up that she's on her way, so he calls her out and then gives her terrible news: Their son will die. God's promise to Jerry was contingent upon obedience, and since Jerry doesn't follow YHWH, YHWH takes the kingdom from him. He and many others suffer the consequence of his sin. In Southern Judah, Rey still reigns, but things aren't going well there either. They're idolatrous too. The division between the two kingdoms persists.

TODAY'S GOD SHOT

God's compassion shows up in 14:13 when Jerry's son dies: "All Israel shall mourn for him and bury him, . . . because in him there is found something pleasing to the LORD, the God of Israel." When God takes someone in death, it's easy to think of it as a cruel and angry act. But here we see a different story: He takes the one who pleases Him. But just to clarify, God didn't "need another angel" like well-meaning people sometimes say, because (a) God doesn't need anything—He's self-sufficient, (b) people don't become angels when they die, (c) angels are an entirely different kind of being, and (d) angels are actually a lower order of created being—they aren't made in God's image like we are, so that would be a downgrade for us if we became angels when we died. God takes the boy because He delights in him. That's all. Just delight. He brings him home—to Himself. The boy escapes the wicked world his earthly father rules and goes to the peaceful home of his heavenly Father. That's a fantastic trade-off, because He's where the joy is!

2 CHRONICLES 10–12

During the divided kingdom, the ten tribes of Northern Israel reject the Levites as priests, so not only are the Levites fired from their jobs, but they're evicted from their homes too. They leave the tribal lands they've been appointed to serve and move to Southern Judah. They've served under the relatively good leadership of David and Solomon, and that legacy sticks with them for a while. They've set their hearts to seek God. For three years, they help keep Southern Judah on the straight and narrow, but it eventually falls apart. It's unclear whether the hearts of the Levites also turn away from God, or whether King Rey just stops caring and disregards God's laws and purposes for them.

King Rey has lots of wives and concubines, and as his family grows, he distributes his sons throughout the region. He provides for them and finds them wives. They serve as overseers in the region, making sure his power and influence take root in every part of Southern Judah. But as his power grows, his heart turns away from God. Weakness has a way of reminding us of our needs, whereas strength prompts us to lean into autonomy and forgetfulness. And as the king goes, so goes the kingdom. The people follow Rey's lead and turn away from God. Then the armies of Egypt come after Southern Judah. "Because they had been unfaithful to the Lord, Shishak king of Egypt came up against Jerusalem." There seems to be a direct correlation between Judah's unfaithfulness and Egypt's attack. Given how God has worked in the past when His people rebelled, it's possible He has raised up Egypt to oppress Southern Judah and prompt repentance.

Egypt takes a lot of land, but they don't capture Jerusalem. Shemaiah the prophet lets King Rey know that God is granting Egypt success in their efforts against Southern Judah. Finally, the people repent, but God doesn't immediately drive out Egypt. Instead, He says He's going to use the Egyptian armies to teach Judah something about Himself. Egypt invades Jerusalem and takes away some of their most valuable possessions from the temple and from the king's house, including their gold shields. King Rey replaces them with bronze shields, which is better armor anyway, considering how soft gold is. He has to keep his people armed at all times, which proves that the peace Solomon knew during his reign is gone. This feels more like David's reign, when there was continual war. But at least David was winning. Rey is losing, but just as his strength made him arrogant, his losses make him humble. And when he's humbled, God relents. Nevertheless, history records him as a wicked king.

Meanwhile, King Jerry in Northern Israel appoints his own priests from whatever tribes he wants to serve in the high places he builds and worship the idols he creates. He's like a cult leader, inventing his own religion pieced together with truth and heresy. He even has people sacrifice to goats, which Leviticus 17:7 refers to as demons. False religions worship demons—regardless of whether they take the shape of animals or mythical gods or even other humanlike deities, they're ultimately demonic. They're created beings who have either set themselves up against their Creator or who are being worshipped instead of the Creator.

TODAY'S GOD SHOT

When King Jerry takes the people away from King Rey, and Rey wants to attack him, God tells Rey, "You shall not go up or fight against your relatives. Return every man to his home, for this thing is from me" (11:4). God says to send the soldiers home, because he isn't allowed to retaliate. And Rey obeys. It's reminiscent of a much more significant event in John 18. When the soldiers show up to arrest Jesus before His crucifixion, Peter pulls out a sword to attack them, but Jesus says to put it away because this is all part of God's plan. The Son submits to the Father's will. God's plan isn't always easy. Sometimes He takes things from us or gives us tough assignments we'd rather avoid, but Christ has modeled for us—and even the evil King Rey has modeled for us—how to respond to God's plans. We gain things in surrendering to God that we'd never have otherwise. He can be trusted. He's where the joy is!

1 KINGS 15; 2 CHRONICLES 13–16

King Rey, the first king of Southern Judah, dies and is replaced by his son Abijam, also known as Abijah. Abijah doesn't follow God, just like his dad. Meanwhile, King Jerry is still king in Northern Israel. And these two obviously don't get along. King Jerry's people come out to attack King Abijah's people, and Abijah tells Jerry, "We know you're acting wickedly. We know all about your golden calves and your fake temple and your non-Levite priests. And if you attack us, it's bound to fail, because it's an attack against God!" Even though Abijah is also wicked, he's not wrong about this. In the battle, Abijah is outnumbered two-to-one, but he and his army kill more than half of Jerry's army and take some of his land too.

After Abijah dies, the next king of Judah is his son, Asa. Finally we have a God-fearing man on the throne in the south! Asa gets a serious pep talk from a man named Azariah, who acts as the mouthpiece of God the Spirit. After Azariah reminds him of his purpose as king and encourages him to be bold in making reforms, Asa does just that. He's not afraid to make things right in Judah, even if that means kicking family members out of their roles in the kingdom. He fires all the male cult prostitutes and tears down the idols. He makes rebellion against God punishable by death. He does leave some of the spots that are designated for idol worship intact, so he's not completely keeping others from worshipping idols. But as for his heart, he only worships YHWH. One thing you may begin to notice is that the kings in Southern Judah are always compared to whether or not they're like David. He set the standard for a good king.

Meanwhile in Northern Israel, Jerry dies and they get a new king named Nadab. He's an evil king who only has a two-year reign. He and his family are murdered by Baasha, who takes over the throne in Northern Israel. He's an evil king too, but God uses him to fulfill the words of the prophet Ahijah in 1 Kings 14:14–16, when he foretold that Jerry's family would be killed. After that massacre against his fellow

Northerners, Baasha devises a plan against Asa and Southern Judah, which involves setting up a blockade on one of their major highways.

Even though God has given Asa incredible military victories as the underdog, Asa decides to rely on his own plan for how to handle this. His decision seems logical and diplomatic and maybe even wise, especially since his army is likely outnumbered. But he doesn't seek God's counsel. He takes a bunch of valuable items out of storage and offers them to a neighboring king, asking him to attack Baasha and Israel instead. When Baasha realizes what's happening, he stops building the blockade. Then Asa takes all the supplies Baasha was using to build his blockade and uses them to build his own blockade against Baasha elsewhere.

A prophet named Hanani comes to Asa and says he may have gotten what he wants but God isn't pleased, and the consequence of not trusting God for victory is that he'll have many enemies who'll war against him. Asa doesn't receive correction well—he's furious. He imprisons Hanani and starts being cruel to others too. He's likely living in deep regret over his actions, but he can't see that he's only making things worse by letting his regret and anger rule him. He continues walking in autonomy, not seeking God, even when he comes down with the terrible disease that leads to his death. He seeks help from everyone but God. He rules Judah for a long time—long enough for five kings to come and go in the north. He started out wise but dies arrogant and angry. Then his son Jehoshaphat takes over the throne in the south.

TODAY'S GOD SHOT

God the Spirit speaks through Azariah and says, "If you seek him, he will be found by you" (2 Chronicles 15:2). You're seeking Him. You're at least 176 days into seeking Him. Have you been finding Him? What do you know about Him that you didn't know 177 days ago? You're probably finding Him in places you never thought possible—places like Leviticus and Numbers and genealogies. Keep seeking Him, because you probably know Him more today than you did yesterday, but not as much as you'll know Him tomorrow. He's where the joy is!

1 KINGS 16; 2 CHRONICLES 17

Baasha is king in Northern Israel when the prophet Jehu tells him his household will be wiped out. And they are—starting with Baasha himself. His son Elah reigns for two years before his servant Zimri murders him while he's drunk, then Zimri takes over the throne for a whopping seven days but still manages to accomplish something important: He fulfills Jehu's prophecy against the house of Baasha by wiping them out. During Zimri's short reign, word gets back to the Israelite army that he has killed their king. When they chase him down, he realizes the jig is up and sets his own house on fire—while he's inside. Meanwhile, Israel appoints Omri as their new king. Things are off to a rocky start for Omri. Not only is his palace a smoldering crime scene, but half the people of Northern Israel don't support him. There's a short-lived threat to his reign, but he prevails. Omri is a bad king too. He's a king in the north, and all their kings, without exception, are bad.

Ahab succeeds Omri. He's also in the north, so he's also terrible. You may not know much about him, but you've probably heard a few things about his wife, Jezebel. We'll get to her soon. First Kings 16:33 says, "Ahab did more to provoke the LORD, the God of Israel, to anger than all the kings of Israel who were before him." Yikes! That's a terrible epitaph. During his reign, one of his guys starts rebuilding Jericho, the first city the Israelites conquered when they entered the promised land. You may recall that Joshua pronounced a curse on anyone who rebuilt it: "Cursed before the LORD be the man who rises up and rebuilds this city, Jericho. 'At the cost of his firstborn shall he lay its foundation, and at the cost of his youngest son shall he set up its gates'" (Joshua 6:26). And that's exactly what happens to the man who rebuilds it. The text seems to indicate that his oldest and youngest sons die as a result of this endeavor.

Meanwhile in Southern Judah, Jehoshaphat takes over for his dad, Asa, after Asa dies from a foot disease. God is with Jehoshaphat, because his reign is similar to David's—he seeks God and keeps His laws.

Southern Judah as a whole is honoring God, while Northern Israel isn't. This continues to be a theme throughout the entirety of the divided kingdom; the only righteous kings are in Southern Judah.

Jehoshaphat tears down the high places and even sends officials and priests throughout Judah to teach people God's truths. Another astonishing feature of his reign is the way his enemies are turned into allies, including the Philistines—Goliath's people, the people who stole the ark of the covenant, the archenemies of the Israelites. Wow! Even his enemies are impacted by the way he rules with dignity and honor. Jehoshaphat is beloved and respected in Judah. Second Chronicles 17:6 says, "His heart was courageous in the ways of the LORD." That's a *great* epitaph! But he's not dead yet, so there's still time for him to make some less-than-wise decisions. Stay tuned.

TODAY'S GOD SHOT

"The fear of the LORD fell upon all the kingdoms of the lands that were around Judah, and they made no war against Jehoshaphat" (17:10). Is God turning the hearts of these enemy nations toward Himself? As it turns out, no. The Hebrew word for *fear* here is different from the word used to describe the good fear of the Lord. This word means "dread." The nations around Judah see that God's hand is with them, so they're afraid of them *and* of God, which makes them run. That's why Judah has peace—not because their enemies are falling in love with YHWH, unfortunately. But what this shows us about God is still an encouraging truth: He's sovereign over the hearts of our enemies. Whether He turns those hearts toward Himself or just away from harming His kids, it's the good and right thing, and it serves His purposes. Either way, His people are protected and His plan is accomplished. He's a bigger God than we realize, accomplishing far more than meets the eye, because He does a lot of His work at a heart level. He is sovereign over hearts, and He's where the joy is!

1 KINGS 17–19

The prophet Elijah tells Ahab, king of Northern Israel, that God is sending a drought. God feeds Elijah via birds, but then the creek dries up. He sends Elijah to a new spot and says a widow will feed him. But when he shows up she says, "You want food? My son and I are literally starving to death." He can't catch a break! But not to worry—God promises to multiply the food, and He does. When the widow's son gets sick, she blames Elijah. But it's for her benefit that he's there, because God works through him to heal her son. In Hebrew, the word translated as *life* refers to breath; the text says his *breath* left him. Of course, God can raise people from the dead—and maybe that is what happens here—but we just don't see it explicitly stated in the Hebrew like we do in other resurrection stories. Regardless, God uses Elijah to bring him back to *breath*, at the very least.

In year three of the drought, God tells Elijah it's time for rain, but Elijah has to confront Ahab first. Ahab blames the drought on Elijah, but Elijah says Ahab's sin and idolatry are the problem. He says, "Bring all your people and your 850 false prophets to meet me on the mountain, and we'll see whose god is superior." Elijah, Ahab, the people, and 450 prophets of Baal meet up on Mount Carmel (400 prophets are unaccounted for). Elijah calls the people to stop fence-sitting and trying to cover their bases by worshipping multiple gods. Unlike the pagan gods, YHWH requires exclusivity. This is a relationship, not a buffet. But they don't seem to care.

Elijah calls for two bulls, gives the false prophets first choice, and says, "Let's see whose god can burn this sacrifice." Baal's prophets cry out to him for hours, but nothing happens. Elijah taunts them. They cut themselves, thinking that will wake Baal up from his underworld nap, but he keeps snoozing. When it's Elijah's turn, he builds a trench around the altar and pours twelve jars of water over the altar, wood, and ground until it's all soaked and the trench is filled. If God doesn't come through, he just wasted a vital resource in a drought. But if YHWH can burn drenched wood, then He's really God and maybe the people will repent.

God sends fire from heaven, burning up not just the bull and the wood, but also the stones and dirt. The people confess that YHWH is Lord, and Elijah orders the 450 false prophets be killed. Elijah tells Ahab the drought is over. He keeps having his servant bring him the weather report, but the servant keeps coming back with bad news of sunny skies. Finally he says, "There's a baby cloud out there, but that's all." Elijah is thrilled. This is it!

Meanwhile, Ahab fills in his wife Jezebel on everything, including how Elijah killed the prophets of Baal. She's a devout Baal worshipper, so she's furious. She promises to kill Elijah, and he's terrified. He leaves Northern Israel to hide in Southern Judah. He goes into the wilderness, where he's afraid, depressed, and alone, and he begs God to kill him. But then the Angel of the Lord (maybe Jesus) shows up, wakes him, feeds him, and says to get moving. He moves to a cave, and God shows up to talk to him. He's despairing over Israel's rebellion. He feels as if he's the only one who cares about God and His Word. He probably doesn't know that Obadiah just saved one hundred prophets from Jezebel (18:4–13), but God doesn't correct him—He just gives him his next steps: Appoint two kings and a prophet. The prophet is Elisha. (Helpful tip: Think alphabetical order—Elijah with a *j* comes before Elisha with an *s*.) Elijah the old prophet begins to mentor Elisha the young prophet.

TODAY'S GOD SHOT

When God brings a tornado and an earthquake and a fire—massive displays of His power—the text says these demonstrations of power aren't the point. Elijah already knows God can do miracles on a massive scale. What Elijah needs to see is that God is in the whisper. He's seen that God can be big, so now God's showing him that He can be small too. He can be intimate. You have to be really close to someone to hear their whisper. Elijah is so close he has to cover his face. God's power is awe-inspiring, but sometimes what we really need is face-covering closeness. We want the whisper of His nearness. He's where the joy is!

1 KINGS 20–21

Ben-hadad, king of Syria, gathers an alliance of thirty-two other kings and chiefs and makes his demands on Northern Israel: He wants Ahab's wealth and the best of his women and offspring. Threatened by Ben-hadad's massive coalition, Ahab agrees. But the Syrian coalition takes things a step too far when they plan to raid Ahab's palace. Ben-hadad pushes harder, bragging on his military power, then Ahab says, "You might put your armor on tomorrow, but you won't be taking it off." This is ancient trash talk that basically amounts to a death threat. Ben-hadad is drunk and angry.

A prophet tells Ahab he'll win the war despite having an inferior army. Ahab follows the prophet's instructions, and Israel attacks the coalition and wins. The prophet warns Ahab that the Syrians will come back to mount another attack in the spring and says to get ready. The Syrians think the reason Israel won the last battle is because they had the home field advantage. But the prophet shows up again and tells Ahab, "Don't sweat this. God reigns everywhere, and God wins everywhere." Israel wins, and the twenty-seven thousand Syrians who don't die in the battle flee to a local city where the wall collapses and kills them. Meanwhile Ben-hadad is in hiding. He and his servants hatch a plan to beg Ahab for mercy in exchange for giving him back some land they took. Ahab agrees, which sounds good, but it defies what God commanded them to do in this situation. He was supposed to kill Ben-hadad, not negotiate.

God sends a prophet to call out Ahab's sin. Prophets often use a bit of theater to get their points across. This prophet forces another prophet to beat him up, then bandages himself and sits by the road where he knows Ahab will pass. He points out that by leaving Ben-hadad alive, Ahab has invited the death penalty for himself and for his people. Ahab isn't repentant. He resists and goes home angry and grumpy. He thinks what will make him happy again is more land. His neighbor Naboth has a nice plot of land he really wants, so he demands it. When Naboth says no—because it seems God would disapprove of it—Ahab is angry and grumpy again. His covetousness is intense.

Then we encounter his wife Jezebel, daughter of a pagan king. She's a murderer and a deceiver who sidles up to people of power and gives them everything they want in order to make herself feel important and get what she wants. She killed many prophets (1 Kings 18) and threatened the life of Elijah after he defeated her own prophets (1 Kings 19). Today we see her deceptive side too. She forges a letter, signs it with Ahab's seal, and uses his name to put together a gathering, presumably to honor God. She invites their neighbor Naboth, who shows up to honor God alongside everyone else, not knowing she's hired two men to sit beside him and falsely accuse him of cursing God and Ahab, which is punishable by death. So they stone him, right then and there. He never sees it coming.

Jezebel tells Ahab the "good news" about Naboth's land, so he takes it. But God holds Ahab responsible for his wife's sin, just like He held Adam responsible for Eve's sin. This may seem unfair, but leadership positions carry an added weight. God sends Elijah to condemn Ahab—he, Jezebel, and all their family will die. This devastates Ahab, and he demonstrates repentance. God shows mercy, delaying the complete punishment until the next generation.

TODAY'S GOD SHOT

Anytime God makes a promise, He keeps it. The only time He modifies it is for the sake of mercy or grace. We see that with Ahab. Scripture repeatedly says he was God's least favorite king in Israel: "There was none who sold himself to do what was evil in the sight of the LORD like Ahab, whom Jezebel his wife incited. He acted very abominably" (21:25–26). But in the very next paragraph, God relaxes His punishment on Ahab. God loves to show mercy to people, even the most wicked among us. He's eager to forgive—how can you not love a God like that? He's where the joy is!

1 KINGS 22; 2 CHRONICLES 18

We spent time in both Northern Israel and Southern Judah today, starting out in the north with wicked King Ahab. The kings of these two kingdoms make an alliance. They want to recapture Ramoth-gilead, a city that was taken from Judah by Syria. Before they put a strategy together, Jehoshaphat asks if they can seek God's counsel. Smart move! Ahab brings in 400 prophets, and they all say God will grant Israel success. But Jehoshaphat wants a second opinion. They just asked 400 prophets, who are all in agreement, so why does he need another opinion? One thing the original text hints at is that these prophets didn't inquire of YHWH. They're almost certainly the same 400 prophets of Asherah mentioned in 1 Kings 18:19. Remember how Ahab had 450 prophets of Baal and 400 prophets of Asherah when he met Elijah for the showdown on Mount Carmel? Only the 450 prophets of Baal showed up, and Elijah killed them; but we never heard anything from the 400 prophets of Asherah. These are almost certainly those prophets. Wicked King Ahab (of Israel) doesn't seem to fully grasp the concept of following YHWH, even though he repented under the consequence of death, and wise King Jehoshaphat (of Judah) seems to be discerning about that, so he wants a godly opinion.

Ahab says they could ask Micaiah the prophet, but Ahab doesn't like him because he never says what Ahab wants to hear. (Some commentators believe it was Micaiah who intentionally got himself beat up before he talked to Ahab.) Micaiah tells Ahab, "Go up . . . and triumph; the Lord will give it into the hand of the king" (1 Kings 22:12). Ahab doesn't believe him because this sounds too good to be true, especially coming from Micaiah, so he basically says, "Are you joking?" And that's when things get confusing. Micaiah had been mocking the king and his prophets, but this time he shoots straight: Evil spirits asked YHWH for permission to mislead Ahab by speaking lies through the 400 prophets. Evil spirits are subject to God's authority—they're on a leash and can only do what God allows and what ultimately fits into His sovereign plan. And God's plan, as He already said, is to remove King Ahab and his family. The means by which God planned to do that is through this war. And the false prophets prophesied falsely. Israel will meet with disaster, and Ahab will die in the battle. Ahab doesn't like this at all, of course, so he has Micaiah imprisoned.

When Ahab and Jehoshaphat partner up for war, Ahab tries to be tricky. He plans to wear a disguise, but tells Jehoshaphat to wear his royal robes, which will make him stand out as a target. Jehoshaphat agrees to this plan. Ahab's plan to disguise himself seems to work at first, because the Syrian archers go after Jehoshaphat in his royal robes, but they withdraw when they see it's not Ahab. Then, one of the archers randomly fires off one arrow that strikes and kills Ahab, and the events surrounding his death unfold in the ways Micaiah prophesied today and Elijah prophesied yesterday. His son Ahaziah takes the throne after him; he's Ahab all over again—Baal-worshipping and wicked in all the ways his dad was.

TODAY'S GOD SHOT

"A certain man drew his bow at random and struck the king of Israel between the scale armor and the breastplate" (2 Chronicles 18:33). God has laser focus on accomplishing His plan—nothing thwarts Him. Not Ahab's disguise, not the Syrian's mistaking Jehoshaphat for Ahab, and not even the call to stop firing, because the one man who fails to stop firing hits the very man God appointed to die in the very spot that would kill him. The man may have drawn his bow "at random," which can also be translated "in his innocence" or even "on accident," but that just goes to show that nothing is random where God is concerned. He's so intentional. He hears the cries of the righteous, He wipes out the wicked, and He can't be stopped. What a great comfort! He's where the joy is!

2 CHRONICLES 19–23

The prophet Jehu rebukes Jehoshaphat because of his alliance with wicked King Ahab, and Jehoshaphat seems to listen. He sets things in motion to honor God and point the people back to God. He appoints judges and commands them to judge righteously, as God does, saying God will help them. When a coalition comes to attack him, he has the people fast and seek God's will and God's help. He worships God in the temple and prays a beautiful, faith-filled prayer. Then a temple worship leader prophesies: "The battle is not yours but God's, . . . You will not need to fight in this battle. Stand firm. . . . Do not be afraid and do not be dismayed" (20:15, 17). Then the worshippers lead the army out to battle! You don't pull that kind of stunt unless you really trust God when He says you won't have to fight. As they worship, the enemy armies start to fight *each other*. By the time the people of Judah arrive on the scene, everyone is dead, and they spend three days gathering spoils of war from among the corpses. Just as God said, they didn't have to fight. The only time they lift a finger is to carry home treasure. When the surrounding nations hear about this, they're terrified of Judah—it's clear God is with them.

In his final days, Jehoshaphat makes another alliance with an evil king, just like he did with Ahab. He didn't learn his lesson. This alliance is with Ahaziah, the new king of Northern Israel. They build boats to go to Tarshish—probably for the purpose of foreign trade, because Tarshish is rich (2 Chronicles 9:21). But Jehoshaphat has joined himself to a king who doesn't know or worship YHWH, and as a consequence of his sin, God wrecks the ships.

After Jehoshaphat dies, his son Jehoram takes the throne. His first act is to kill his six brothers and any princes in the area who might be a threat to him. He also seems to have a role in ruining an important alliance with their nearest relatives, the Edomites (descendants of Esau). Edom had partnered with Judah, but they revolt under Jehoram's leadership, so he tries to kill a number of them (this will be important for tomorrow's reading). Not only does Jehoram not stop the evil practices in the land, but he initiates them. God prompts Elijah to send a letter saying his family will be killed and he'll die a slow, painful death from a mysterious illness. Then an army comes and kills his entire family except for one son, Jehoahaz, who also goes by the name Ahaziah (which is what we'll call him). Jehoram gets the mysterious disease, suffers for two years, and dies. No one is sad to see him go, and he doesn't even get a royal burial. His legacy is worthless.

His remaining son, Ahaziah, takes over the throne in Judah, and he's wicked as well. He too makes an alliance with Northern Israel. In a war against the Syrians, he gets wounded badly, then Jehu finds and kills him. The text says God appointed both this meeting and his death: "It was ordained by God that the downfall of Ahaziah should come about through his going to visit Joram" (22:7). After he dies, there's no one left in his family except his mom, Athaliah, who takes over the throne. She's the first queen of Judah, but most people don't consider her reign to be legitimate, because she's not from the line of David. She kills everyone who can threaten her reign—except Joash, a son raised in secret by the priest Jehoiada. The throne belongs to Joash, and Jehoiada works hard to make sure Joash gets it. He's the only legitimate heir, but he's seven, so Jehoiada handles a lot of the reforms. He reestablishes worship in the temple and destroys the altars and the priest of Baal. And the people of Judah rejoice!

TODAY'S GOD SHOT

In seeking God's help against the enemy armies, Jehoshaphat prays, "If disaster comes upon us, the sword, judgment, or pestilence, or famine, we will stand before this house and before you—for your name is in this house—and cry out to you in our affliction, and you will hear and save" (20:9). No matter what terrible things may happen to them, he knows they're in a relationship with a trustworthy God who will ultimately rescue them: "We do not know what to do, but our eyes are on you" (20:12). Plan A is to trust God. There is no plan B. He's where the joy is!

OBADIAH 1; PSALMS 82–83

No one knows when Obadiah was written; estimates range from 850 BC, which is approximately where we are in the story, to 400 BC. If it's happening around 850 BC, it likely connects to two events we just read about: Egypt's invasion of Jerusalem in 2 Chronicles 12 and Edom's revolt against King Jehoram of Judah in 2 Chronicles 21. Today, enemies come to take over Jerusalem, the capital of Southern Judah, and the prophet Obadiah rebukes the Edomites for it. Why? These are the descendants of Esau, the twin brother of Jacob-Israel (who is the father of the twelve tribes). Edom is Israel and Judah's closest relative, but family drama has plagued them since Esau sold his birthright to Jacob for stew. On top of that, Jacob tricked Esau out of the only thing he had left: his father's blessing. They made amends years later, but there's a lingering tension between these two people groups.

They also live next door to each other, which means the Edomites aren't just the closest relatives of the twelve tribes, but they're also the closest neighbors of Judah. When Jerusalem is invaded, Edom is expected to come to their aid. Instead, they not only *don't* help, but they add to the oppression the enemy nations inflict on Judah. God says Edom is too prideful to help Judah. He calls them out: "On the day that you stood aloof, on the day that strangers carried off his wealth and foreigners entered his gates and cast lots for Jerusalem, you were like one of them" (v. 11). Their passivity is just as bad as if they'd personally wielded the sword against Jerusalem. And some people believe they did wield the sword against Jerusalem, because God tells Edom not to do eight specific things to Judah: "Do not gloat over his disaster; . . . do not loot his wealth. . . . Do not hand over his survivors" (vv. 13–14). So it seems they're on the wrong track. Either way, Edom isn't the kind of neighbor or relative you want.

For more information on today's reading, see thebiblerecap.com/links.

Then Obadiah says something that has both immediate application and long-term implications: "The day of the LORD is near upon all the nations. As you have done, it shall be done to you; your deeds shall return on your own head" (v. 15). That phrase "the day of the LORD" encompasses both a general idea of a day when God will work out justice in a particular scenario as well as an ultimate, final day when God will do that. In the Old Testament, it typically refers to the more immediate scenario, and in the New Testament it typically refers to the final scenario—the day when Jesus will bring justice and free the world of corruption and evil through both judgment and restoration. In this short-term scenario, God says justice will unfold like this: The land and people of Edom will be devoured by the land and the people of Israel.

Psalm 82 was likely written much earlier, but it fits well here. It's about God's call to help the needy and oppressed, much like God called Edom to come to Judah's aid. However, there's evidence throughout this song that Asaph is talking to God's divine enemies here, not humans. In verses 6–7, either Asaph or God Himself seems to condemn them for the way they've acted wickedly: "You are gods, sons of the Most High, all of you; nevertheless, like men you shall die, and fall like any prince." What do we make of this psalm? If we zoom out, we see that God values justice and He values showing mercy and kindness to those in need, and He'll execute judgment even on the divine beings who fall short of that standard.

TODAY'S GOD SHOT

Psalm 83 is a cry for God to work justice on those who have opposed His people. "They lay crafty plans against your people; they consult together against your treasured ones. They say, 'Come, let us wipe them out as a nation; let the name of Israel be remembered no more!' . . . Against you they make a covenant" (vv. 3–5). God identifies so closely with His people that when they're mistreated, He takes it personally. God clearly isn't going to sit back and let Judah get bullied without doing something about it. His vengeance isn't like human revenge; it's perfect and it's just. He's so protective of His people that He works out justice not just in the human realm, but also in the supernatural realm. He's so powerful and protective, and He's where the joy is!

2 KINGS 1–4

King Ahaziah of Northern Israel falls through a roof and asks a false god if he'll recover. But God commissions Elijah to rebuke the king's people and let them know Ahaziah will die. The king repeatedly tries to threaten Elijah in return, but it only ends in more death. After Ahaziah dies, his younger brother Jehoram becomes Israel's new king (the current king of Judah is also named Jehoram, also called Joram).

Everybody knows Elijah is about to be taken away too, but Elisha seems devastated about it and asks Elijah for something only God can give: a double portion of the spirit Elijah has. He wants twice the God saturation. Elijah says, "It's not up to me, but we'll ask God and then see what He does." And what God does is wild! He sends a chariot of fire down from heaven to take Elijah away. People search in vain for his body, but he has vanished, taken by God. After this, Elisha's first three miracles signify his position as Elijah's replacement: (1) He parts the water, just like Elijah did earlier and like Moses and Joshua did in the past, (2) he speaks life to the waters of Jericho, and (3) he speaks death to the boys who mocked him. He may seem too harsh with the boys, but their rebellion against YHWH has put them under the death penalty anyway. They seem to be telling Elisha, God's prophet, that they want him dead—to "go up" like Elijah had gone up.

Then we jump back to Moab, who has rebelled against Israel (this may or may not refer to what we read yesterday). Israel and Judah team up to go to war with Moab, but they make a poor decision on what route to take. They end up in the desert with no water, and they finally decide to consult with Elisha. But Elisha says, "You want to talk to me? Don't you have pagan prophets back home? Ask them!" But they beg him, and since he has a weak spot for Jehoshaphat, one of the few good kings of Judah, he relents and agrees to talk to them. He says, "God will

For more information on today's reading, see thebiblerecap.com/links.

bring you water and you'll be refreshed, then you'll go defeat Moab. When you win, destroy everything on your way out of town." They follow his commands, and as they're winning, the king of Moab panics and makes an incredibly wicked plea to his god by offering his son as a burnt sacrifice in hopes it'll bring victory. Moab makes another strong push against Israel, but Israel had already effectively won the battle, so they head home.

Chapter 4 is full of miracles Elisha performs. They aren't all big things like national battles. They're things as seemingly small as helping a widow provide for her family. God provides enough to help her avoid selling her sons into slavery and enough for them to live on! And not only does God use Elisha to provide for the poor, but He also uses him to provide for the rich. Elisha meets a wealthy family who offers to help him with whatever he needs. He prophesies that the wife will have a son. And based on her reaction to the prophecy and the cultural norms at the time, a son is her greatest desire. But then the son dies. She seeks out Elisha's help, and here he performs his most dramatic miracle—raising the dead. The woman responds first with praise, before she even goes to pick up her son. Elisha's final miracle in this chapter is purifying some putrid stew and multiplying food during a famine. God uses him in such a wide array of situations!

TODAY'S GOD SHOT

Elisha prophesies to the kings about how they'll defeat Moab: "You shall not see wind or rain, but that streambed shall be filled with water" (3:17). God would provide in a way that's invisible to track. They won't be able to see any progress, just results. This kind of thing is always such a trust-building exercise—when we can't see how God is working but just have to believe that He is. God does some of His best work in the dark. Just because it's dark doesn't mean He doesn't have victory in store when the lights come on. Who knows what He's up to? Even earthly losses add up to eternal victories in God's economy, so our hearts can be at peace. Regardless of whether your next battle ends in a victory or a setback, He's where the joy is!

2 KINGS 5–8

Naaman is a Syrian military commander, one of Israel's enemies—but God grants him victories. In one raid on Israel, he captures a girl and brings her back to serve his family. She says she knows a guy who can heal his leprosy, so he goes through the red tape to enter an enemy nation for healing, but then he's disappointed because Elisha has weird advice: Take seven baths in a filthy river. Naaman is furious, but after his servants convince him to comply, he's healed. He offers Elisha a gift he rejects and also confesses that YHWH is God. He wants to take Israelite dirt back to Syria, because he believes the actual land of Israel belongs to YHWH and wants to use it to build an altar to YHWH. It's a good but misguided longing, and the answer appears to be no, likely because sacrifices are only supposed to be made in Jerusalem.

As Naaman heads home, Elisha's servant Gehazi runs after him. He lies about some needy people, so Naaman gives him clothes and approximately $35,000, which Gehazi hides. But God fills Elisha in, and he confronts Gehazi about it. When Gehazi lies, God gives him and his family leprosy. How ironic. One of God's enemies who doubts gets healed, and one of the Israelites who follows his own heart gets leprosy.

God gives attention not just to major things like disease but to tiny details like a borrowed axe. When a young prophet loses an axe-head in a river, Elisha miraculously recovers it. God works through Elisha in military exploits too. The Syrians keep trying to plot against Israel, but God reveals every plan to Elisha, and he tips off Israel's king. The Syrian king sends men to kill Elisha, but God tips him off again. His servant panics as the Syrian army approaches, so Elisha asks God to let his servant see what he can see: a literal army in the spiritual realm, surrounding and protecting them. Then he temporarily blinds the Syrians and leads them to the king. The king wants to kill them, but Elisha says to feed them dinner instead. Wow. They feed the people who are trying to kill them. Elisha wins peace with his enemies by treating them kindly. God does this with His enemies too.

A famine hits the land. It's so severe that people cannibalize their own families. The king holds Elisha responsible and orders his servant to behead him. But God warns Elisha and adds that the famine will end the next day. The servant doubts this, and Elisha says, "Yes, you'll see it fulfilled, but won't get to benefit from it." Meanwhile outside the city, four lepers want to eat one last meal before they die. They go to the Syrian military camp but find it abandoned. God drove the Syrians away in fear. The lepers alert the city's gatekeepers, and Israel plunders the camp. The Syrian spoils offset the Israelite famine, and the messenger who came to behead Elisha gets trampled in the gate. All of Elisha's prophecy is fulfilled.

Elisha warned the Shunammite woman about the famine, and now that it's over, she comes home and wants her house and land back. She shows up to appeal to the king at the very moment Gehazi is recounting what Elisha did for her. Because of this divine timing, the king gives her back all she left behind plus what she would've gained in the meantime! God's generosity is evident here.

King Ben-Hadad of Syria is sick and wants to know if he'll recover. He sends his servant Hazael to ask Elisha. Hazael takes the news and uses it to his own end: He murders Ben-Hadad to steal the throne.

TODAY'S GOD SHOT

In Naaman's story, God seeks out His enemy who doubts Him. He uses the theft of a little girl as a spoil of war, the permission of Naaman's own king, the doubt of Israel's king, and the encouragement of Naaman's servants. God isn't thwarted by Naaman's anger, and Naaman is humbled and repents. The God who has been granting Naaman favor all along grants him the greatest favor of all—an eternal relationship with Himself. God seeks out His enemies! He tracks them down to bless them. Despite their doubt and the doubt of those around them, He positions believers in their lives—even enemy servant girls—to point them toward Himself. Naaman doubts and resists, but God persists, and God always gets what He wants. Naaman finally finds out that He's where the joy is!

2 KINGS 9–11

Prophets are powerful people in ancient Israel. There's no voting because God runs their nation-state and speaks through the prophets. The prophets even anoint kings, especially when a line of heirs is interrupted. Elisha sends a prophet to anoint Jehu as Israel's next king and to assign him the weighty task of fulfilling God's prophecy to wipe out all of Ahab's descendants, including King Joram, Israel's current ruler.

Jehu sets out on his secret campaign and even convinces some of the king's watchmen to follow him. Either they have no idea what he's doing or they respect him enough to do what he says. King Joram of Israel and King Ahaziah of Judah both go out to meet Jehu and his crew, and they meet him in the most appropriate of spots: the land of Naboth. Naboth's vineyard is the whole reason this trouble started. Ahab wanted it, Jezebel killed for it, and God pronounced the death penalty on their whole family, which Jehu is here to enact. He kills both kings, then goes after Jezebel. She yells out the window and compares Jehu to Zimri, Israel's seven-day king, who killed King Elah. She's basically saying Jehu might get away with what he's trying to do, but his kingdom won't last long. When Jehu calls out, "Who's with me?" a few eunuchs give him a nod, then he tells them to throw her out the window. She dies in exactly the way Elijah prophesied she would.

Then Jehu goes after the remaining descendants of Ahab. He tells the people to appoint Ahab's best descendant as king, but the elders of the land resist. He replies, "So are you with *me* then?" He also adds a tricky line in his letter that can be interpreted two different ways: "If you are on my side, and if you are ready to obey me, take the heads of your master's sons and come to me at Jezreel tomorrow at this time" (10:6). This could mean bring your leaders with you when you come or behead your leaders and bring me the proof when you come. He doesn't clarify what he means, but it's a good test of their loyalty. They do the latter. Jehu absorbs any guilt for this act and reminds them that this has all been done according to the prophecy of Elijah, the word of God. Jehu continues this mission until it's complete. And it may seem extreme—because it is—but this is all part of God's covenant with these people. Jehu aims to destroy all the worshippers of Baal. And in order to do this, he uses some cunning techniques. He pretends to worship Baal and calls everyone to join him so he can weed out and spare any true servants of YHWH. He doesn't want to accidentally kill them while he's on his mission. After he kills the Baal worshippers, he destroys their pagan temple and turns it into an outhouse.

Despite all this, he leaves the two golden calves up in Dan and Bethel. God promises to bless Jehu even though he's not as thorough with the idol demolishing as he was with killing descendants of Ahab and worshippers of Baal. His heart eventually goes astray. The hardest enemies to defeat are the idols in our own hearts. During his twenty-eight-year reign, Israel begins to lose wars and land.

TODAY'S GOD SHOT

We didn't see God show up much in the text today, except in the spots the text says this is all happening to fulfill the word of the Lord. He's there in the cunning words and ways of Jehu; He's there in the appropriately located battle in Naboth's vineyard. He's there with the eunuchs in the tower alongside Jezebel. He's there working out His plan through all these acts. As terrible as they are, they're never less than righteous and just. When we zoom out on Him and His plans, we also see the wickedness and waywardness of a rebellious people, and we're reminded of how He has abundantly, generously provided for them in the past. But they go their own way. Even when He's not in the foreground, He's always in the background. And He's where the joy is!

2 KINGS 12–13; 2 CHRONICLES 24

Southern Judah's new king, Joash (also called Jehoash), is only seven years old. Fortunately, he has a wise advisor, the priest. And as long as the priest is alive, he seems to keep Joash in line. The priest does get two wives for Joash, but it's possible the second wife doesn't show up on the scene until after the first wife dies. For the most part, Joash follows God's commands—with the exception of tearing down the high places for idol worship—and even commands the restoration of the temple. It has fallen into disrepair, since the people have been so focused on worshipping idols; they've even used some of the temple instruments in their worship of Baal. But the priests of the temple don't follow Joash's orders for how to finance the restoration process. They either don't collect the taxes God required, or they collect them and embezzle them while they lounge around for twenty-three years. Joash finally puts his foot down and makes an offering box, and the people are actually happy to give to this cause. He uses their money to hire workers for the repairs since the priests can't be trusted. The workers are honest, and they do good work.

Joash's reign goes fairly well until the priest dies—then he goes off the rails. He starts seeking counsel from local princes who flatter him and eventually lead him into idolatry. The priest's son warns him about the consequences of this sin, and Joash's people stone him to death. Then God sends the judgment the priest's son prophesied in his last words; it comes in the form of the Syrian army. They're small, but they manage to defeat Judah's army and severely wound King Joash. While he's down for the count, his servants seize the opportunity to avenge the murder of the priest's son—their king has lost their trust, so they enact the death penalty on him. Then his son Amaziah takes the throne in Judah.

Meanwhile in Northern Israel, Jehu's son Jehoahaz is on the throne. He's wicked, but he does seem to recognize what God is doing in Israel. He notices they seem to be under God's judgment, so he seeks God's favor. But let's be honest—he's not really seeking God, he's seeking relief.

And God certainly knows the difference. The heart of Jehoahaz isn't repentant. Nevertheless, God demonstrates His mercy and sends someone to help them—possibly human help, possibly divine help; the text isn't clear on that. And even after all that, after God answers his prayer with a yes, Jehoahaz and the people still don't repent. When Jehoahaz dies, his son Joash, or Jehoash (a different one), takes the throne. To prevent confusion with Judah's King Joash, we'll call this king in Israel Jehoash.

Jehoash is a wicked king, as are all kings in Northern Israel. In his final days, when he's concerned that the Syrians might destroy them, he consults the prophet Elisha, who has him do some strange actions in preparation to face Syria in battle. As a prophet, Elisha often works through signs and theater, and in this scenario he uses arrow shooting and ground beating to convey his insight and wisdom from the LORD. Then Elisha dies. Later, as the locals are preparing to bury a dead man, they get distracted and accidentally throw the body into Elisha's open grave instead. When the body hits Elisha's bones, the man comes back to life. As our reading closes, Elisha's final prophecy about Jehoash and Israel's battle with Syria is fulfilled.

TODAY'S GOD SHOT

We only get two sentences about the accidental resurrection, but they serve to remind us that Elisha's powers of resurrection don't originate with him. They exist outside of him, granted to him by God, who—unlike Elisha—isn't lying dead in a tomb somewhere. He's living and active. His power isn't confined to our abilities. He's working even when we can't. And while it may wound our pride to recognize it, He doesn't need our help. He can accomplish His good and generous plans even without human intervention. God's goodness isn't contingent on our strengths or even on the strength of our faith. He's going to be good regardless. And He's where the joy is!

2 KINGS 14; 2 CHRONICLES 25

When King Joash, who became king at age seven, was killed by some of his servants in Southern Judah, his son Amaziah ascended the throne. One of Amaziah's first acts as king is to avenge his father's death by killing the men who killed him. It's a popular practice (although not one sanctioned by God) to kill the families of those who threaten a new king's reign, but Amaziah doesn't. He obeys God's commands and refuses to punish the children for the sins of their father. God commanded His people not to carry out justice generationally, even though He sometimes does. But He's the decider of what's just; He can be trusted with that kind of thing. He knows hearts, and we don't.

Amaziah is a good king, especially at first, but even his good actions aren't done with a fully yielded heart. This shows up in how he handles a few of God's commands. For instance, he leaves the high places of idol worship intact. Then, when he goes to war against their long-standing enemies, the Edomites, he spends the equivalent of $1.5 million to hire soldiers from Israel to join his army in Judah. When a man of God calls him on his lack of faith, he sends the soldiers home. They get angry and raid the cities of Judah in retaliation, killing three thousand. And he doesn't get the money back. We can look at this one of two ways: (1) We can say obedience is costly—and it is, or (2) we can say disobedience is costly—because it was his mistrust of God that got him into that spot to begin with. On top of that, he would've lost far more if he hadn't heeded the prophet's words.

Even without the help of the Israelite soldiers, Amaziah has a significant military victory over Edom. But this God-given victory leads him down a path of pride, because he forgets who granted him success. His first prideful (and foolish) move is to worship the gods of the people he defeated. That doesn't even make sense! When God sends a prophet to tell him how wicked and irrational this is, Amaziah is too proud to listen and threatens to kill the prophet. His second prideful move is to request a meeting with the king of Israel. It's possible this is actually an invitation to war, and that's how King Jehoash receives it. He sends Amaziah a snarky reply, laughing it off, but Amaziah's pride prompts him to pick a fight with Israel anyway. Israel wins, they raid Jerusalem, and they take Amaziah captive. He flees but is captured and killed, then his son Azariah becomes king.

Meanwhile in Northern Israel, Jeroboam II is king. We'll call him Jerry II. He's an evil king as far as God and His ways are concerned. Things get rough for Israel during his time, which is a fulfillment of Abijah's prophecy: "I will bring harm upon the house of Jeroboam and will cut off from Jeroboam every male, both bond and free in Israel, and will burn up the house of Jeroboam, as a man burns up dung until it is all gone" (1 Kings 14:10). God was only committed to wiping out Jeroboam's line, not all of Israel, so He uses Jerry II to accomplish some good things for the people of Israel. They've lost a lot of land in previous battles, but he gets it all back and restores Northern Israel to its original size. Even as an evil king, Jerry II still accomplishes what God ordained. This restoration was prophesied by Jonah (2 Kings 14:25), who was alive during King Jerry II's reign.

TODAY'S GOD SHOT

When the man of God rebukes Amaziah for hiring soldiers from outside of Judah, he says, "God has power to help or to cast down" (25:8). Both victory and loss are in God's hands; He can't give one without the other. His plan for Judah to win is also His plan for Edom to lose. And He turns the tables not long after that when Amaziah worships false gods and then picks a fight with Israel. Two people try to warn Amaziah, but "Amaziah would not listen, for it was of God, in order that he might give them into the hands of their enemies, because they had sought the gods of Edom" (25:20). God closes Amaziah's ears as punishment so that he might start and then lose the war. Many people prefer to think of God as neutral, not picking sides in anything, but Scripture paints a different picture. May we aim to be on His side. He is always victorious, and He's where the joy is!

JONAH 1–4

Around 750 BC, during King Jerry II's reign, Jonah lives and prophesies. Some regard this book as an allegory, but it's almost certainly not a parable. One marker of parables is that their characters are anonymous and fictional, but Jonah is mentioned by name here, in 2 Kings, and by Jesus in Matthew 12. And this story is far more complex than Scripture's other parables. Regardless of whether you view it as allegory or history, the things it reveals to us about God remain the same: He shows love and mercy to many of His enemies, choosing to adopt them into His family.

When God first commissions Jonah to rebuke the Ninevites for their wickedness, Jonah balks. He hates the Ninevites and doesn't want them to repent. He knows that if he rebukes them, they will. We're all naturally inclined toward people who are like us and who look, act, and dress like us—it's very natural, but that's the problem. Since God Himself isn't confined to a body and we're all made in His image, there's something in every single person that has a point of connection to Him. He spreads His love out to people from among every nation. And Jonah's arrogant attitude—whether it's racist, self-righteous, or both—isn't going to cut it for a person following YHWH. God doesn't let him off the hook.

Jonah tries to run, as though you can run from a God who is everywhere. He hops on a ship to Tarshish, which scholars say was in the opposite direction from Nineveh. When a storm hits, the sailors look for any god who can save them. Jonah confesses that he's the reason they're all about to die, and they're astonished at his rebellion. These pagan sailors have a higher regard for YHWH's commands than Jonah the prophet does. He says to throw him overboard, and they do—but not before they throw a bunch of cargo overboard first. We never sin in a vacuum; Jonah's sin impacts the people around him. But when he finally obeys, his obedience impacts them as well. The storm calms, and

For more information on today's reading, see thebiblerecap.com/links.

the sailors fear God—though we don't know if it's a fleeting response or actual heart change.

God demonstrates His sovereignty over animals by appointing a big fish to swallow Jonah. The text never says it's a whale, but that's a fair assumption. Jonah is there for three days and three nights, and Jesus quotes this incident in Matthew, paralleling His time in the grave with Jonah's time in the fish's belly.

Jonah prays a beautiful prayer of thanksgiving, despite being covered in digestive enzymes. He seems grateful to be alive and seems to trust that he's getting out of this fish one way or another. But repentance is entirely absent from his prayer. His heart hasn't changed, despite God's mercy toward him. After his prayer, the fish vomits him up on the shore, where God tells him again to call the Ninevites to repent. So Jonah, unrepentant, goes to Nineveh to tell *them* to repent. He shows up with his rebuke, and just like the sailors, the king of this notoriously wicked place shows more humility and obedience than the prophet sent to warn them. The whole country fasts in sackcloth and ashes, which are signs of repentance and mourning. God relents from bringing disaster. He's always eager to forgive. But Jonah isn't. God uses even reluctant and bitter people in His plan for redemption.

Jonah is full of pride, bitterness, and self-pity. He's so self-focused he can't rejoice that an entire nation has turned from their wicked ways. But even in his bitterness, God is kind to him, comforting him with shade. He begs God to kill him, but God won't. When God points out his irrational behavior, he gets moody and sassy. God reminds Jonah how merciful He is, but Jonah knows this already and hates it. He wants God's mercy for himself but not for anyone else.

TODAY'S GOD SHOT

"Those who pay regard to vain idols forsake their hope of steadfast love" (2:8). Have you seen this in your own life? Chasing fleeting joys to fill us up and satisfy us has a way of leaving us empty. But when we disengage from those things and engage with the one true God, we're always met with His steadfast love—it's been there all along. That's what steadfast love is. He's right there with you, patiently waiting for you to notice. He's where the joy is!

2 KINGS 15; 2 CHRONICLES 26

King Azariah of Judah also goes by the name Uzziah. He's just taken over after his father's death, and we don't hear much about him except that he's a pretty good king, high places notwithstanding. But then things take a turn. After his people have a series of military victories that make him rich and famous, Azariah grows prideful. He decides he wants to burn incense in the temple in Jerusalem, which is an act reserved only for priests.

When the text says, "He was unfaithful to the LORD his God" (2 Chronicles 26:16), it uses the same word that is often used for marital unfaithfulness. The priests are aghast, and eighty-one of them (including one who shares the name Azariah) rush in to rebuke him, but he's unrepentant. When he grows angry with the priests, God strikes him with leprosy. The text seems to indicate that he never actually lights the censer to burn the incense; apparently they stop him before he can. Even though he may not commit the physical act of sin, his heart is still set on it. So when God strikes him with leprosy, it seems like the motives of his heart are what are being judged here.

He has to leave the temple immediately to prevent defiling it, and after this, he lives in a separate house because of the cleanliness laws we read about in Leviticus 13:46. He likely either stops performing the roles of king when he becomes ill or he coreigns with his son Jotham until Jotham officially takes over for him. Jotham is considered to be a good king, mostly walking in God's ways, but as we've seen repeatedly, the high places in Judah remain untouched.

Meanwhile in the Northern Kingdom of Israel, we move quickly through five kings, most of whom kill the previous king. These short-lived kings and the way their reigns end reveal that Northern Israel is in rapid decline. This shouldn't surprise us, though, for two reasons. First, not only do we know that God's promise is connected to the other kingdom—the Southern Kingdom of Judah, the line of David—but we also got a heads-up from God that there is an end date for Northern

Israel. We read a reminder of this today in 15:12, but we first read it a few days ago in 2 Kings 10:30, when God said to Jehu: "Because you have done well in carrying out what is right in my eyes, and have done to the house of Ahab according to all that was in my heart, your sons of the fourth generation shall sit on the throne of Israel." As we see all these short-term, wicked kings cropping up, it's becoming evident that we've crossed that fourth-generation threshold, because Northern Israel is beginning to fall apart.

TODAY'S GOD SHOT

When God strikes Azariah with leprosy in the temple, it highlights God's holiness. He refuses to let the king defile His temple. He efficiently and thoroughly handles this situation, punishing Azariah's rebellion while effectively stopping him from lighting the incense and ensuring that he has to leave the premises and not return. He topples Azariah from the throne without killing him, which also demonstrates His mercy. So many of God's attributes are on display in this one story—not to mention the kind of wisdom it takes to come up with something that works on so many levels. He's righteous, efficient, thorough, merciful, and wise. He's where the joy is!

ISAIAH 1–4

Isaiah's prophetic ministry spans forty years. As we read his book, it's especially helpful to notice where the quotation marks occur to see whether he's quoting God, telling us about a vision, or prophesying. Much of it is laid out like poetry, rich with images and metaphors—which means the more you dig, the more layers of meaning you're likely to find.

In these sixty-six chapters, there are three general sections of prophecy. Isaiah is writing to Southern Judah, and in the first section (chapters 1–39), he primarily addresses what's been happening in Northern Israel and how God is dealing with their sins. As we saw yesterday, Northern Israel has just passed beyond the timeline of God's promised protection, and now they've been attacked, besieged, and destroyed by the invading Assyrian army. As of Isaiah's writing, the Northern Kingdom of Israel is finished, but we'll continue to read about them in the days to come. Here, Isaiah is using what has happened in Northern Israel to warn Southern Judah about what will happen to them in the future. He wants them to pay attention to what God's doing with their brothers, because if they don't repent, they're next. The middle section (chapters 40–55) includes prophecies of the coming Messiah, who will arrive roughly seven hundred years later. In the last section (chapters 56–66), Isaiah prophesies about the final judgment and restoration, when God establishes the new heavens and the new earth. Those are things we still await.

God's people have broken the covenant with Him, so He calls creation—heaven and earth, specifically—as His witness in what is presented as a legal trial between Him and His people. Isaiah depicts Assyria's attack on Israel as Israel's corporal punishment. They're beaten from head to toe—from the greatest to the least—and he implores them to repent. But in a situation that probably shocks them, God says repentance looks different than they think it does. He doesn't want their

For more information on today's reading, see thebiblerecap.com/links.

vain offerings; they disgust Him. Remember how long we spent reading about the offerings and altars and how important it all was? Why did God change His mind? He didn't—it was never about the animals. God doesn't need dead animals. It has always been about their hearts. When the offerings are just meaningless rituals, it's offensive to God. These sacrifices insult God's holiness and His love for His people. He's after their hearts, so He marks out what a changed heart would look like, which includes caring for the most vulnerable in their society. The leaders have become greedy, though, and greed and injustice go hand in hand.

In the promised land at large, Assyria has just destroyed Israel, which is next door to Judah. Judah grows fearful, making foreign alliances to protect themselves, as though God Himself were insufficient. This may look like Judah is making peace, but they aren't—they're rebelling against God so they can feel safe and flourish by their own means. Isaiah says Judah may be living in abundance and presumed safety, but they're prideful. He depicts them as vain women and says God is about to destroy all the vain things they find their pride in. Things take a turn for relief in his prophecy of "the branch of the LORD" (4:2), which refers to the Messiah. It's the same imagery Jesus uses when He says, "I am the true vine" (John 15:1).

TODAY'S GOD SHOT

Today we see lots of imagery from Israel's time in the wilderness. First we see the fire and the cloud, reminders of God's presence with them in the desert. But then our reading wraps up with a beautiful reminder that we're not in the wilderness anymore: There's a dwelling place, a place of protection and refuge—just like the tabernacle and the temple, where God came to dwell with them. The imagery is bound up together, demonstrating exponentially all the ways God is present with His people. Despite our fearful bargaining, idolatry, selfishness, and vanity, God still wants to unite Himself with us. The Father still sends the Son and the Spirit to make a home with His people, purify us, and dwell with us forever! He's where the joy is!

ISAIAH 5–8

Isaiah writes a love poem to God's people, comparing God to a vine keeper and the Israelites to wild grapes. But in the Hebrew, the term means "stinking things." That's not exactly what God wants to grow in His garden, so God removes the protective garden hedge and the grapes are trampled. He highlights six ways they stink and pronounces woe over them with a punishment corresponding to their particular brand of wickedness. Woe number one denounces the greedy who push the poor out of the land. God had established land allotment rules that they're disregarding, so their houses will become desolate. Woe number two addresses those whose lavish lives of excess and drunkenness lead them away from honoring Him. Instead of being filled, they'll be famished; instead of eating, they'll be swallowed by the grave. Woe number three is to those who mock God and doubt His judgment is coming. They seek out sin. Woe number four is to the prideful fool with no discernment or integrity who distorts the truth. Woe number five is for the arrogant, and woe number six doubles down on the drunkards mentioned earlier, adding that they rob people of justice. These people have despised God's Word, so He'll send judgment. Remember how God used Israel to drive out the wicked Canaanites from the promised land? Now He's using those nations to drive *Israel* out, because they've broken the covenant.

Chapter 6 is a stunning vision of God's throne room. Put yourself in Isaiah's shoes: God's people are sinning, and you don't even want Him to forgive them sometimes. It's a natural response, but if Isaiah is going to be God's mouthpiece, he has to not only have a proper view of God, but of himself in light of God. Yes, the Israelites have been acting wickedly, but Isaiah is a sinner in need of God's mercy too, and this vision is God's way of reminding him of that. He sees the outer fringes of God's glory, and he sees the six-winged seraphim covering their eyes as they cry, "Holy, holy, holy." A seraph puts a hot coal to his mouth, burning away the impurity. Confronted with God's holiness, Isaiah sees himself rightly. He's humbled—a necessary posture. Then God commissions him for the task at hand: Rebuke people who won't listen, which will heap more judgment on them. Isaiah is perplexed by this call, but God says despite all the judgment and destruction, He'll preserve a remnant of His people. He has set His heart on this family, this batch of stinking fruit, so He'll remove all the wickedness that has set itself up against Him.

When Southern Judah gets into military trouble, King Ahaz is likely tempted to make foreign alliances for protection, but Isaiah says to trust God for deliverance. God tells Ahaz to ask Him for a sign, but Ahaz refuses. This may seem like a humble response, but it's actually defiant, so God gives a sign anyway—and you may recognize it as the birth announcement for Jesus. But Ahaz doesn't know about Jesus; his focus is on enemy armies. How would he view this sign? It reads like a timeline: How long would it take a woman to carry and deliver a child, who would then be old enough to tell right from wrong? Before this hypothetical boy would reach that age, the two nations Ahaz fears will be desolate (7:16). Is the boy hypothetical or is he Jesus? He's both. For Ahaz, the boy is hypothetical. But for the grand scope of the timeline of all history, the boy is Jesus. This is the beautiful complexity of prophecy's layers: God can speak present truths and eternal truths simultaneously. They aren't in conflict; they work in tandem.

God tells Isaiah things are about to get bad. Judah is about to be destroyed. But in the midst of this impending doom, God says Isaiah shouldn't fear what everyone else fears.

TODAY'S GOD SHOT

At least two images of Jesus show up in the throne room vision. God's throne is in the temple, not in a palace, where thrones usually are. Kingship and priesthood overlap again, pointing us to Jesus. And in 6:6, when the seraph takes a burning coal from the altar and touches it to Isaiah's lips to purify him, it refers to the altar of sacrifice. What's on the altar of sacrifice that purifies us from our sin? Jesus! Thank God for the burning coal, for the death of Christ. He's where the joy is!

AMOS 1–5

Our timeline hasn't moved ahead for a few days; we're reading things from various people written in the same era, so much of what Amos says mirrors what we've read in Isaiah. Israel has been doing well financially, and they view it as a sign of God's blessing. They keep offering meaningless sacrifices to God, thinking it keeps them in good standing with Him. They anticipate the day when He'll rain down judgment on their enemies. However, He's about to turn everything they think on its head.

Amos gives eight separate statements from God. The first seven are against the nations surrounding Northern Israel. Of those seven, the first six speak specifically to nations that don't know YHWH as their God—despite not being in relationship with YHWH, they're still held to His baseline moral standard. But the seventh nation is Southern Judah, and they do know YHWH as their God. They've seen what He's capable of. They're in covenant with Him, so they may think they get a pass since He obviously likes them so much. On the contrary, He says they're held to an even higher standard because of that. They're accountable for what they know. And God makes it clear through these chapters that in order for Him to be a God of justice, no one can escape judgment—whether it's the base-level judgment or the higher-accountability judgment—because we're all guilty.

Specifically, the first six nations are guilty of cruelty, slave trade, treachery, harboring a grudge, murder, greed, and desecrating a corpse. When it comes to Judah, He gives a more general word: You've rejected Me. This has always been about the relationship between God and His people. His accusations against them may sound far more humane or tame, but they're also far more personal. For all seven nations, God promises fire as judgment. After addressing all the nations surrounding Israel, He addresses Israel directly, going into detail about their offenses:

For more information on today's reading, see thebiblerecap.com/links.

They sell people into debt slavery, they oppress the poor, they ignore the afflicted, they're sexually immoral and exploit people for their own pleasure, and they worship false gods and forget that YHWH is the one who rescued them when they were poor and afflicted and enslaved. They've broken the covenant, so God will bring oppression and destruction.

Not only are Israel's power and wealth *not* evidence of God's blessing, as they suspected, but they're actually evidence to the contrary. So God will destroy those things—their strength and riches won't be able to stand against Him. And while He'll judge the wickedness of the surrounding nations, He'll also judge their wickedness. Their sacrifices won't appease Him, because even those are done in a way that dishonors Him. Their so-called good deeds are tainted with pride and showy behavior, and their sacrifices break His laws. Lest we think He's being too harsh, He's already used less severe methods to prompt repentance—drought, famine, locusts, mildew, disease, death—but none of it has turned their hearts. He's been patient with them. He implores them to seek Him and live, to repent of oppressing the poor and seeking to build their own kingdoms, to hate the evil things that break His heart, and to love the things that align with His character. He says the day of the Lord is coming, which here refers to the day of His judgment.

TODAY'S GOD SHOT

"Does disaster come to a city, unless the Lord has done it?" (3:6). God takes ownership of disaster here. He's not always the active agent, but He's sovereign over all of it. This is a hard pill to swallow sometimes—it's okay to wrestle with this or feel the tension. And there are some important things to remember as we wrestle. First, while it may seem comforting to think of tragedy as coming only from the enemy, we don't actually want the enemy to have the upper hand, do we? Second, God's judgment for sin is always deserved and often even delayed, because He's patient. Third, we want a God who judges sin. He wouldn't be a good, trustworthy God if He ignored evil. Fourth, God's judgment on His people is ultimately for the purpose of restoration. This isn't the end. He's preserving a remnant. He's faithful to His people even when they rebel against Him. He's where the joy is!

AMOS 6–9

Amos calls out the leaders of the land who relax into lives of luxury, pay no mind to the needy and the poor, and fail to notice what's happened in their relationship with God. In chapter 7, God shows Amos three images that all foretell destruction. The first vision is of locusts devouring a field; the second is of a fire devouring everything. Twice Amos pleads with God to relent, and He does. But when the third vision appears, Amos realizes this is inevitable; it's a necessary part of God's process to turn His people's hearts back to Himself. The third is a construction image. Amos sees a plumb line—a tool used to make sure a wall is straight. If a wall isn't vertical, it'll eventually collapse. The meaning is that Northern Israel will collapse because they're so far off the standard and can't be set right.

None of this sits well with Amaziah the priest. He goes to King Jerry II, accuses Amos of conspiring against him, twists the prophecies to help his point, then tries to deport Amos. How heartbreaking for Amos. He's the one who begged God to relent! Obeying God doesn't mean everyone will understand your motives or honor your actions. Despite Amaziah's lies, Amos knows who God is, and he knows who he is to God—a humble servant sent to speak the truth. God has more words for Amaziah: He'll lose his land, his wife will become a prostitute, he and his kids will die, and Israel will still go into exile.

Amos has a fourth vision, this time of summer fruit. God is making a play on words; the Hebrew for *summer fruit* is a homonym for the word for *end*. The kingdom of Israel is coming to an end. Then God says He'll take His words away—there'll be a famine and a drought of His words. They've rejected and despised His words, so He'll stop speaking. This almost certainly refers to the four hundred years of silence that occur between the end of the Old Testament and the beginning of the New Testament. We're still three hundred years away from that, but it's coming.

The fifth vision is of the LORD standing beside the altar, commanding that the place be destroyed. What place? We're not sure, but it likely refers to the false places of worship—either places of idol worship or the shrine in Bethany where they're offering false sacrifices. This vision may feel harsh, but again, we have to zoom out and recall what they've done that led to this. God says He has fixed His eyes on His enemies "for evil and not for good" (9:4). This isn't easy to swallow, but it's not unjust either. And despite their sin, He's still preserving a remnant. They've earned destruction, but He promises mercy. Of all the people in this story, those who get mercy are the only ones who don't get what they deserve.

In the story of God's people, judgment isn't the end and destruction isn't the point. His goal in punishment is always restoration; these are steps on the path to that place. God hasn't cast off His people. They're suffering the consequences of their actions, but He still loves them. His discipline is part of His love, just like with any good parent. He promises to raise up, repair, rebuild, and restore. He has His heart set on restoration. He gives them a vision of what's to come so that they don't lose heart in the midst of the destruction. In a time when they're about to encounter what will feel like rejection, He reminds them of the great love He has for them.

TODAY'S GOD SHOT

When Amos describes the judgment of the day of the Lord (8:8–10), the imagery and events are strung together like this: The land trembles, the sun goes down at noon, the earth is darkened in broad daylight, and a feast turns to mourning, like the mourning of the death of an only son. Seven hundred years after Amos writes this, during the celebration of the Passover Feast, the land trembled and the sky went black in the middle of the day, when God the Son, the only Son, died. Everything God is about to put Israel through, He went through Himself. And He went through it for them, to bring them back to Himself. And He went through it for us too. Does sin require severe punishment? Yes. Does it seem unfair? Absolutely. And the most unfair thing of all is that we'll never receive that punishment ourselves, because Jesus took it for us. He's where the joy is!

2 CHRONICLES 27; ISAIAH 9–12

Northern Israel is falling, but Southern Judah is still plodding along. King Uzziah has just died, and his son Jotham, one of Judah's good kings, takes over the throne officially. He "became mighty, because he ordered his ways before the LORD his God" (27:6), and this corresponds directly to God's covenant promise with the kings of David's line, which says if they obey Him, they'll flourish, and if they don't, they won't. After Jotham dies, his son Ahaz takes over the throne, and he is not a great king. We'll read more about him in two days.

The early parts of Isaiah 9 include verses we recognize as Messianic prophecy, but what would the people in Isaiah's time think of these words? They live in a land that constantly sees war, they've experienced lots of oppression and exile, their nation-state exists in division and decay, and they currently live under the threat of Assyrian attack. So when Isaiah prophesies about the birth of a new king under whose reign light will dawn and oppression will cease, they think it's political; they expect a king who'll win every war. That sounds great, but in light of all it really means, it's incredibly shortsighted. There are a few hints in this passage that let us know it's more than what they expect. For instance, this king is referred to as "Mighty God" (v. 6).

In the meantime, God's wrath is coming for the wicked—and just because people are part of the kingdom of Israel doesn't mean they're part of the kingdom of God. He's shown us repeatedly that His family consists of people with new hearts, regardless of heritage. He's adopted foreigners into His family, and He's shown us that those born in Abraham's line don't get a free pass just because they share DNA. In one of the more shocking parts of this text, even those God usually has compassion on—orphans and widows—will be cut off too, because their hearts oppose Him. God will use Assyria as a tool in His hand to accomplish His plans. This could be confusing because it's often assumed that the side that wins the war has the most powerful god. But technically, this war is between two groups of people who both oppose God—the Assyrians and the godless among Israel. YHWH is still sovereign over the outcome, and He's still victorious. Assyria will win but won't get away clean either. It'll be punished for its wickedness too.

Whenever God describes the destruction, He tends to also remind them that He'll preserve a remnant. But at times, He says He'll make a complete end of them. So which is it? Of those who oppose Him, He will make a complete end. And those who *aren't* ended are the remnant. Since God knows the heart of each person, He can be trusted to be nuanced and specific in this process. He also promises to rescue them from the enemy He's sending to purify them. He has a plan in place.

Isaiah 11 also contains prophecies of Jesus's birth; He's a great ruler who will usher in peace. Again, they're expecting someone to topple foreign armies—not an eternal Savior who will pay their sin debt and set things right between them and God once and for all. That's not even slightly on their radar. Then we end with a prophecy of God gathering His people from among every nation, and they'll sing praises to Him for comforting and saving them.

TODAY'S GOD SHOT

In the latter half of Isaiah 9, the wrath of God is thick and heavy. It's hard to read. The wrath of God is real, and sin has to be punished. *Our* sin has to be punished. And the only person who doesn't deserve the Father's wrath stepped up to pay what we owe so that we don't ever have to face the Father's wrath. Jesus took all our punishment on the cross. That kind of act is love inducing. We get the love *and* the joy, because He's where the joy is!

MICAH 1–7

Our reading is hovering over the same time period, covering a variety of prophecies, plus narrative history portions where those prophecies are fulfilled. The prophet Micah speaks mainly to the general population. He tells them God is about to take action against their sins, and one of His first moves is to trample down the high places. Finally! He addresses the sins of Israel and its capital, Samaria, as well as Judah and its capital city, Jerusalem. And when God sends destruction, Micah tells them how to grieve and mourn: They should do it privately, possibly because if news of their grief reaches enemy nations, they'll rejoice.

Micah calls them out on the same things we've already talked about: stealing land from the poor and oppressing them. He says greed may start with just wanting more stuff, but it eventually becomes so all-encompassing that you begin to oppress others to get what you want. They oppress the poor to line their pockets, but God is a defender not only of the poor, but also of His own righteous standards.

Micah says the rulers, priests, and prophets are all wicked—they "detest justice and make crooked all that is straight" (3:9). These leaders in the land hate good and love evil. Amos addressed this same problem, instructing them to "hate evil, and love good, and establish justice in the gate" (5:15). The leaders and the people hear these oracles and think they'll avoid consequences because they're too powerful. They're arrogant and in denial, but Micah says they won't escape this destruction. Jerusalem will become a heap of ruins. He says, "You shall go out from the city and dwell in the open country; you shall go to Babylon" (4:10). This is so specific that it's helpful to know it all happens exactly like this roughly two hundred years later. Not only is Jerusalem destroyed, but the people are driven into exile in Babylon.

Micah offers several warnings but always follows with a reminder that destruction and exile aren't the end for them; a remnant will be preserved,

For more information on today's reading, see thebiblerecap.com/links.

and God will establish a kingdom of peace on the earth. He'll gather the ones He has wounded and driven out of the land, and He'll carry them back to the land. So even though they go into Babylonian captivity, they'll be back in this land again someday. And when they return, the King who will rule this new kingdom of peace will be born in Bethlehem Ephrathah (5:2). It's important for them to know their Savior will come from among them. They've been looking to other nations and the gods of other nations to rescue them for too long. But their Savior, the one true God, will dwell in their midst, even in this land of oppression. But again, they read this prophecy and imagine someone who can overpower Assyria and Babylon, not someone who can overpower death and the grave, like Jesus does seven hundred years later.

Micah also says the faithful remnant will be dispersed again to live among the nations. This happens roughly thirty years after Jesus dies, when the Romans destroy Jerusalem (its second destruction) and the Jews flee the city again. Except this time, when those Jewish and Gentile believers who make up the early church are dispersed among the nations, they take the gospel of the resurrected Jesus with them and spread it to the world. While this is still far off in the timeline, it's helpful to know that many of these prophecies have already been fulfilled in ways that history has recorded and verified. And while many of these prophecies sound tragic, God uses them to get the gospel to us today.

In chapter 6 Micah circles back around to remind the people that God is after their hearts and calls them to repent. He witnessed the destruction of Israel and knows the destruction of Jerusalem is coming. He knows a holy judge can't leave sin unpunished, and sin in Israel and Judah is rampant. But he keeps asking God for help and waiting expectantly for God's response.

TODAY'S GOD SHOT

Micah 5:4–5 shows us that God's greatness, not our own, is where our only peace and security are found: "They shall dwell secure, for now he shall be great to the ends of the earth. And he shall be their peace." When He increases and we decrease, that's where we find our greatest peace. He's where the joy is!

2 CHRONICLES 28; 2 KINGS 16–17

This narrative section of Scripture overlaps with the prophecies we're reading, and we see many of them being fulfilled. Some are fulfilled after this time period—like the birth of the Messiah, for instance—and some have yet to be fulfilled—like the Messiah coming back to reign in peace on the new earth. But in the meantime, in the final days of the kingdom of Judah, King Ahaz is wicked; he's building idols and initiating child sacrifices. Because of Judah's sins, God allows them to suffer defeat at the hands of both Syria and Israel. But when Israel tries to enslave them, some leaders and the prophet Oded rebuke them, so they release the captives.

Meanwhile, Judah is attacked again—this time by the Edomites. Ahaz is fearful, but instead of going to the King of the universe for help, he goes to the king of Assyria. He tries to bribe him into helping Judah, using money he stole from the temple, and even rearranges the temple to fit his demands. Talk about walking in the fear of man and not of God! The Assyrian king pretends he'll help but doesn't. So Ahaz sacrifices to more foreign gods, then destroys the temple's holy vessels and locks the temple. He commissions the priest Uriah to make a replica of a foreign altar for him, and the priest does. It's easy to see what Micah meant yesterday when he said all the leaders in the land—the kings, prophets, and priests—were wicked. King Ahaz sets up altars all over town, and "they were the ruin of him and of all Israel" (28:23).

Meanwhile Northern Israel is still heading toward their downfall under the leadership of wicked King Hoshea. During his reign, 2 Kings records the captivity of Israel. In this day it's common for a weaker or smaller country to act as a vassal to a larger country; it's called "paying tribute," and it basically amounts to paying a more powerful country not to destroy you or let anyone else destroy you. It's like bribing the bully. Assyria's king has been collecting regular payments from Israel's King Hoshea, but one year Hoshea skips out on that payment, and the Assyrian king finds out that Hoshea has been talking with the king of

Egypt, which he's not happy about. He besieges Samaria, Israel's capital city, for three years, until he finally captures it. He exiles the Israelites to Assyria, just as the prophets warned. The Israelites wouldn't turn from their idolatry, no matter how many warning flares were fired.

In Samaria, the vacant capital of the newly captured Israel, the Assyrian king wants to repopulate the city with other people he's captured. They all worship the false gods of their own countries, but YHWH is still working out His plan to sanctify the promised land, so He sends lions to kill the new inhabitants. Word gets back to the Assyrian king that things aren't going well, and he thinks sending Israelite priests back to teach them how to serve the God of that particular plot of land will get Him to dial back the problems.

But those priests aren't exactly walking in righteousness and honoring YHWH, so they probably aren't leading by example. While the people do learn reverence for YHWH, they try to fuse that with worship of their other gods. Syncretism is compatible with most religions, but not with YHWH.

TODAY'S GOD SHOT

In the long, sad narrative of Israel's demise, God displays immense patience with His people. "The LORD warned Israel and Judah by every prophet and every seer, saying, 'Turn from your evil ways and keep my commandments and my statutes, in accordance with all the Law that I commanded your fathers, and that I sent to you by my servants the prophets.' But they would not listen, but were stubborn, as their fathers had been, who did not believe in the LORD their God" (2 Kings 17:13–14). God not only established His covenant with them and showed them how to live in relationship with Himself, but He sent them multiple warnings over centuries when they continued to rebel against Him. Now He has brought captivity in order to reveal captivity—they're held captive to their idols, and only in exile will they realize it. This may feel like punishment for Israel, but it's an act of great mercy. He's patient, He's merciful, and He's where the joy is!

ISAIAH 13–17

While Isaiah is primarily concerned with warning God's people about their sins, today he prophesies against pagan nations, starting with Babylon, a ruling power of the ancient world. They'll eventually take Judah into captivity when Jerusalem falls in about one hundred years—and in today's reading, God pronounces judgment on them for the thing they haven't done yet. God's sovereignty is evident here—He refers to Babylon as "my consecrated ones." As far as they're concerned, they haven't consecrated themselves to YHWH. But *He* consecrated them—set them apart—for His own purposes. He will use their sinful ways to work out His long-term plans to bless His people—initially through discipline, then through restoration. Babylon will think they're doing their own thing, but they'll be fulfilling God's plan. Even though God uses their sin to accomplish His will (as He does with all sin), He still punishes it (as He does with all sin). They'll eventually be overtaken in return for what they do to His people. It's hard to wrap our minds around this kind of big-picture sovereignty; it can feel threatening to our ideas of self-sovereignty, and it's okay to wrestle with that.

While both Babylon and Judah will be destroyed, the end of Babylon's story is judgment and desolation, while the end of Judah's story is restoration and fulfillment. Then the people of Babylon—which probably represents all the ruling powers of the world—will eventually attach themselves to the people of the restored Israel and offer themselves up as servants. Isaiah says the king of Babylon will lose his power and position through arrogant attempts to exalt himself (14:12–15). Some scholars say Isaiah is also paralleling the king's situation to the story of a high-ranking angelic being. Most Bible versions call this being Day Star or Star of the Dawn, while others give the Latin translation, Lucifer. This creature wanted to be God instead of serve God, so he was cast from heaven. This may also overlap with Ezekiel 28:11–17, which seems to point to the same idea.

For more information on today's reading, see thebiblerecap.com/links.

The next oracle is for Assyria, who will destroy Northern Israel and mount an attack against Southern Judah. God will punish them, and the yoke they've placed on Israel will be broken, effectively freeing Israel. Next, Isaiah reminds the Philistines that God has only promised to preserve and protect *His* people, so even if they happen to see a reprieve from oppression, it won't last. God's heart is set on His people, and He'll be a refuge to them. Moab's oracle has a different tone from the other nations' oracles. God mourns over Moab's destruction. This is almost certainly because the Moabites are distant relatives of the Israelites. Regardless, they have to be judged for their sins like anyone else. Seeing God mourn over having to punish sin shows us that He's a real person with a real personality. He's multifaceted just like anyone else, though His characteristics never contradict each other. The Moabites will mourn their destruction—shaving their heads, putting on sackcloth—and they'll seek refuge in Judah.

Finally, the prophecy for Damascus says it'll be a heap of ruins. While it exists today, it is conquered at least three times over the next four hundred years and destroyed at least once. But God says there'll be a remnant here. Why does Damascus get a remnant when they're not part of His family? In this oracle, Ephraim (one of the twelve tribes) and Damascus are kind of blurred together. They're neighbors, and Ephraim has gotten so far off the path that they've effectively merged with this pagan nation. Despite that, God has mercy on them by preserving a remnant who will turn to worship Him again.

TODAY'S GOD SHOT

God mourns the destruction of Moab. His heart cries out for them. He even says, "I drench you with my tears" (16:9). It's incredible to see His tenderheartedness toward a pagan nation that has rejected Him. Most people don't expect to see compassion like this in the Old Testament, but His character has always been the same—God the Father, God the Son, and God the Spirit are not only consistent throughout eternity but within Themselves as well. Yesterday, today, and forever, He's where the joy is!

ISAIAH 18–22

Today we continue with more oracles to the pagan nations surrounding Judah. We open with a mystery nation located "beyond the rivers of Cush," which is likely modern Ethiopia. Isaiah warns them and the world that God is about to bring judgment, and eventually even the Gentile nations will bring tribute to YHWH and acknowledge His supremacy.

Next up is Egypt, the country who enslaved the Israelites for four hundred years and only let them go after God brought a string of plagues and death. They're a major world power, renowned for their knowledge, and prejudiced against Israel. God promises to confuse their wisdom, to oppress them the way they've oppressed others, and to turn them against each other. But still, YHWH has grace tucked up His sleeve: "In that day there will be five cities in the land of Egypt that speak the language of Canaan and swear allegiance to the LORD of hosts" (19:18). "And the LORD will make himself known to the Egyptians" (19:21). "In that day there will be a highway from Egypt to Assyria, and Assyria will come into Egypt, and Egypt into Assyria, and the Egyptians will worship with the Assyrians" (19:23). Assyria and Egypt, two of the most powerful enemies of God's people, will worship Him! He calls them, "Egypt, my people" and "Assyria, the work of my hands," right alongside "Israel, my inheritance" (19:25). This is a stunning revelation of God's heart for a multinational family. He continues to show us the beautiful diversity of His family.

The oracles are interrupted by Isaiah's prophetic sign pertaining to some present-day activity. He's dressed in sackcloth, the standard sign of mourning. Then the people of Ashdod, a Philistine city, are attacked by Assyria. Assyria is taking over the whole neighborhood, and Ashdod is just a few blocks over from Judah. Isaiah demonstrates this by going from a state of mourning in his sackcloth to a state of humiliation via nudity. The description sounds a lot like a prisoner of war who is being led away barefoot, naked, and ashamed. Apparently Isaiah does this for three years—either constantly or intermittently—to demonstrate this prophecy. He has a vision of two cities in Persia that will destroy Babylon, which they conquer two centuries later. Isaiah's grief over the destruction of such a wicked city shows us how tenderhearted he is; his compassion mirrors what we saw yesterday when God mourned over Moab.

Isaiah has a series of short oracles for other nations, all of which amount to destruction. They want to know how long it will last, and he says, "Dawn is breaking, but it will be followed by night." Yikes.

Today's final oracle is for Jerusalem. God's people are held to a higher standard, so what does Isaiah have to say to Judah here? He's crushed by what will happen to them. Jerusalem will be attacked and destroyed. They'll try to fortify the city and prepare it for an attack, but it won't save them from the attack, because God has planned it. When Judah realizes destruction is imminent, they don't repent. Instead, they spend their final moments in self-indulgence, revealing their hearts in the process.

Isaiah also has harsh words for the king's servant, who has made elaborate provisions for his own death, but God will thwart him, then replace him with a new chief of staff, Eliakim.

TODAY'S GOD SHOT

When God is talking to Egypt, His future people, He says, "I will confound their counsel" (19:3) and "The Lord has mingled within her a spirit of confusion, and they will make Egypt stagger in all its deeds" (19:14). The thought of God being sovereign over thoughts and words is humbling. But it can also be so encouraging. If God couldn't do that, how else could God the Spirit guide us into all truth, like Jesus promised in John 16:13, or remind us of what Jesus said, like He promised in John 14:26? While not every thought we think is Him speaking to us (Isaiah 55:8), He is willing and able to prompt His kids with His thoughts and His Word as we seek to live out His will in the world. He causes His Word to bear fruit in our lives! He's where the joy is!

ISAIAH 23–27

The last batch of judgment for foreign nations begins with Tyre and Sidon, Phoenician cities that specialize in international trade. Business is good, so they're wealthy, influential, popular, and prideful. Their line of work means they really need things to go well in the water, so they worship Yam, the god of the sea. So YHWH shows His power over their god. The ports they trade with mourn over their downfall and wonder who could've pulled off an upset like this over such great cities. As bad as things are, YHWH takes it easy on them. Tyre is destroyed but eventually restored. It seems like their hearts don't actually turn to God, but He still uses their business savvy to bless His people.

Chapter 24 describes judgment of the whole earth—from destruction to restoration. It's a dark passage, but it's not without hope. And for us as people who trust God's goodness and sovereignty, texts like this can be sobering without being frightening. YHWH can be trusted with this. He has a perfect track record.

No one is exempt from the coming day of cosmic judgment. Power and money can't protect anyone from it, because the whole earth has broken a covenant with God. But what covenant does the whole earth have with God? The covenant with His people is a totally different thing from this covenant with all people. The only covenant that encompasses all people is in Genesis 9:8–16, where God promised He wouldn't destroy the earth with a flood again, and that section immediately follows a section about how they are to honor life or God will require a reckoning. Because humankind has broken this law, they're under the curse of the covenant. This is heavy stuff, and it's real. This isn't just poetic imagery; this cosmic judgment will be like an undoing of creation, just like the flood was. This time the destruction seems to be more like an earthquake and a fire. When will all this happen? On the coming day of the Lord, whenever that is.

So where's the hope? First, we're sitting on the same earth that was destroyed in the flood. It's still here; God didn't give up on it. Second, this is how we get the new heaven and new earth Scripture talks about. Earth 3.0! The destruction scenes aren't the end. Even this weighty passage includes reminders about God's people singing praises to Him, and it continues with lots of other beautiful things that will happen as a result of all this: God puts death to death, there'll be no more tears, and He'll throw a big feast on the holy hill of Mount Zion! Everyone in Judah will sing a song of praise that says, "You keep him in perfect peace whose mind is stayed on you, because he trusts in you" (26:3). In getting to know God, your peace increases as a byproduct. And God will defeat all the chaotic forces of the enemy. In the great day of the LORD, this broken earth will be re-created new, the enemy of our souls will be defeated, and we'll live and feast on earth with God on the hills of Mount Zion in Jerusalem!

TODAY'S GOD SHOT

"O LORD, you will ordain peace for us, for you have indeed done for us all our works" (26:12). This theme is repeated in the New Testament a few times too. First, Jesus speaks it on the cross just before He dies, when He says, "It is finished" (John 19:30). He has done all our work for us. God the Son has fulfilled all God the Father's requirements to cover our sin debt. And as if that weren't enough, God the Spirit is equipping and enabling us to fulfill God's specific plans for us in our lives. "He who began a good work in you will bring it to completion at the day of Jesus Christ" (Philippians 1:6). He initiated it, He's sustaining it, and He will fulfill it. And "it is God who works in you, both to will and to work for his good pleasure" (Philippians 2:13). God is at work in you! He's creating both the desire in you *and* the actions through you that please Him. It's humbling that we don't get to take the credit for any good fruit our lives bear, but we get the joy of watching Him continue to work in and through us. Isaiah nailed it: "You have indeed done for us all our works." He does the doing, and He's where the joy is!

2 KINGS 18; 2 CHRONICLES 29–31; PSALM 48

While Judah's King Ahaz was terrible, his son Hezekiah is one of Judah's best kings—Scripture ranks him alongside King David. He makes aggressive religious reforms, restoring the temple and reinstating the sacrificial system. People bring so many animals to sacrifice that the priests have to call for backup. He also reinstates Passover, which they haven't celebrated in a long time. God told them to do that every year as a reminder of what He'd done, but when they stopped celebrating His goodness, their hearts disengaged from worshipping Him. Hezekiah also invites the people of Israel to celebrate Passover with His people—the Judahites—in Jerusalem. Though some of them mock and shame him, people from about half the tribes come. It's the first time since Solomon was king that both kingdoms celebrate together.

They're singing and praising God, and most importantly they're finally beginning to repent. These aren't empty sacrifices and vain words. Their hearts are in it. And we see who's behind it all: "The hand of God was also on Judah to give them one heart to do what the king and the princes commanded by the word of the LORD" (2 Chronicles 30:12). God is at work in them "to will and to work for his good pleasure" (Philippians 2:13). He's changing their hearts!

After Passover, Hezekiah tears down the high places and destroys the bronze serpent Moses used, because the people have started to worship it. In this demolition project, all the people participate, not just the leaders. As people from both kingdoms work together, the high places are torn down in both kingdoms! True worship prompts us to destroy our idols. It also prompts them to give generously to the LORD's work. The priests have more than what they need to live on.

Later, the Assyrians attack Judah, taking over cities and demanding money. King Hezekiah has a moment when he acts less than faithfully—which lets us know he's human—and he says, "Take whatever you need from us. What's mine is yours." So they take all the valuables from the temple. The Assyrian leaders want to know exactly what makes Judah so confident. Throughout the conversation, it's clear that Assyria's leaders misunderstand who YHWH is, so they're perplexed as to why Hezekiah trusts Him. Assyria thinks Judah must be trusting in Egypt now, because they mistakenly think the high places Judah just destroyed were used for worshipping YHWH. The people overhear this conversation, so the Assyrians address them directly, telling them not to trust YHWH, because it's all a sham. They even promise to give them wealth and prosperity if they follow Assyria instead. But the people don't respond.

Psalm 48:13–14 says, "Tell the next generation that this is God, our God forever and ever." As they reinstate all the long-forgotten practices, this is a timely reminder to teach God's ways to all the generations.

TODAY'S GOD SHOT

Hezekiah's people are ritually unclean, and Passover isn't going as God prescribed. If we hadn't read God's response already and didn't know how this went, what would you expect from God here? It's easy to expect judgment, but Hezekiah knows better. He knows God's heart for mercy, so in his letter of invitation, he promises the people: "The LORD your God is gracious and merciful and will not turn away his face from you, if you return to him" (2 Chronicles 30:9). Then he appeals to God on the basis of God's character, praying, "May the good LORD pardon everyone who sets his heart to seek God, the LORD, the God of his fathers, even though not according to the sanctuary's rules of cleanness" (vv. 18–19). Then verse 20 says, "The LORD heard Hezekiah and healed the people." Hezekiah knows God's character, and God knows the people's hearts. Remember how He despised all the ritually perfect sacrifices they made with unrepentant hearts? He's focused on the heart here too. He's always after the heart. These imperfect practices done with hearts of repentance are received with heavy doses of God's mercy. He's eager to forgive. "So there was great joy in Jerusalem" (v. 26). And do you know why? They were seeking God, finally. And He's where the joy is!

HOSEA 1–7

Hosea's message is likely intended for both kingdoms, Israel and Judah. During this time, the elite of Israel are flourishing financially, but their hearts have grown callous to God as they drift further from compassion, generosity, and a humble awareness of who is providing for them. God sends His prophet to intervene in an unusual way—by marrying a prostitute. God often calls prophets to personally feel and experience the weight of what's happening. Hosea's marriage points to God's relationship with Israel, and the adultery image is woven throughout the book to reveal God's character to His people.

Hosea's wife, Gomer, gives birth to three kids, but the text only clarifies that the first child is Hosea's; the others could be from one or more of her lovers. Even the names God tells Hosea to give them seem to distance him from them. And of course, this is about far more than just their family—those names symbolize God's distance from Israel at this point. His people give themselves up for mere things, as though He weren't providing for them, so He thwarts their idolatry. But He knows that the only thing that will bring lasting change is for them to love Him—not just to be forced to obey Him. He sets out to pursue them all over again, to show them how desirable a relationship with Him is. Likewise, when things fall apart in Hosea's relationship with Gomer, God says to go find her—she's apparently living with another man—pay off her debts, bring her home, and commit to her.

Northern Israel is often referred to collectively as Ephraim, which is probably a helpful way to distinguish Israel as a whole—all twelve tribes—from Israel the kingdom after the split. The second section of Hosea's prophecies details everything Israel has done wrong, forcing them to face it. It's important to remember that Israel is a theocracy and they're in a covenant with God, which they've broken, so they're living under the curse of that covenant. The consequences of their sins

For more information on today's reading, see thebiblerecap.com/links.

are reflected in their political and societal circumstances. God tells them, "My people are destroyed for lack of knowledge" (4:6). The leaders and elders were commanded to teach the people about YHWH, but they've been dropping the ball for so long that no one knows who God is anymore, much less has a relationship with Him. Instead, they've turned to idolatry, and idolatry has turned them into fools.

When he speaks directly to the priests and leaders, he continues to compare them to a prostitute and even says they don't know God at all. They take their animals to sacrifice to the God they don't know, not even realizing He isn't there. This is poetic imagery—of course, God is technically there, since He's everywhere, but the point of his prophecy is that God's blessing isn't present on their sacrifice and they're clueless about that. They appear to seek God, but they're only seeking relief, and God knows it. He watches their love evaporate and reminds them: I want your heart, not your bulls.

TODAY'S GOD SHOT

Gomer's kids' names seem cruel, but they actually tell the story of Jesus redeeming us. "Call his name Jezreel, for in just a little while I will punish the house of Jehu for the blood of Jezreel" (1:4). Here we see that sin exists and must be punished. "Call her name No Mercy, for I will no more have mercy on the house of Israel, to forgive them at all" (v. 6). Here we see that we were without mercy. "Call his name Not My People, for you are not my people, and I am not your God" (v. 9). In this name, we see that we were not His children. Together this reveals that our sins must be punished, we were without mercy, and we were not His children. But then He says, "In the place where it was said to them, 'You are not my people'"—in the very place of our brokenness and need—"it shall be said to them, 'Children of the living God' . . . Say to your brothers, 'You are my people,' and to your sisters, 'You have received mercy'" (1:10, 2:1). He redeems us right where we are—in the very place that means "you were not my people"—and makes us His people. Which means He's there with you right now. And He's where the joy is!

HOSEA 8–14

Hosea reminds God's people that there are consequences for their sins. Their hearts have wandered far from God, and it doesn't just show up in their religious practices. It shows when they choose leaders without consulting God about the decision. It shows when they look to other nations for help and pay tribute to pagans instead of trusting God for their needs. Our relationship with God isn't isolated to where we spend our Sunday mornings—nearness to God impacts every area of our lives, and so does turning away from Him. They try to solve the problem by becoming more religious, but they're just adding false gods and pagan altars into the mix instead of turning to YHWH.

He compares their actions to another tragic event we read about in Judges 19, when the leaders of Gibeah murdered the Levite's concubine. He says Israel as a whole has acted that way—a whole nation of people who do whatever they want, harm others in the process, and feel no remorse. As a result of the way they've abused God's blessings and forgotten Him, He'll reverse their freedom—they'll go back to Egypt and Assyria as captives and exiles. This will serve as discipline for them, training them to trust Him, because even after all this time, they still don't.

In chapter 11, God compares His relationship with Israel to that of a father and son: "Out of Egypt I called my son" (v. 1). While this refers to God's rescue of the Israelites from Egyptian slavery, it also foreshadows God calling Jesus and His parents out of Egypt, where they'll stay for two years when Jesus is a toddler (Matthew 2:15). God raises them up, teaches them how to walk, heals them, feeds them, comforts them, and eases their burdens, but they're bent on turning away from Him. His heart burns with anger, and He promises to punish them. But then His heart softens and He relents. His emotions are so complex!

In chapter 12, Hosea recounts the story of Israel's patriarch Jacob, and he urges them to live in the relationship God began with them back then. He lets them know they're not alone and reminds them that God is the one who started all this and that God can be trusted to continue it: "By the help of your God, return, hold fast to love and justice, and wait continually for your God" (v. 6). Their hope lies in the fact that God will help them do what He has called them to do. He'll equip them with what they need to repent and remain faithful. But Hosea knows they won't lean into His help. They'll keep doing things the way they've always done them. They'll pursue wealth and independence.

Hosea begs them to return to God, to break their foreign alliances and renounce their idolatry. He promises they'll be met with love. God initiated a relationship with them long ago, and they've consistently broken the covenant He made with them, yet here He is, pursuing them again to renew it. The story of Hosea and Gomer and the story of God and Israel serve to show us that God's love is bigger than our sin. God's words to Israel apply to all of us. We're all like this, more often than we aren't. And God's heart is to heal and save a people like us, meeting us in our sin with open arms.

TODAY'S GOD SHOT

In 11:7, God is furious and says He's going to cut Israel off: "My people are bent on turning away from me, and though they call out to the Most High, he shall not raise them up at all." But there's a tender shift when we hit verse 8, where His compassion and mercy swoop in: "How can I give you up, O Ephraim? How can I hand you over, O Israel? How can I make you like Admah? How can I treat you like Zeboiim? My heart recoils within me; my compassion grows warm and tender. I will not execute my burning anger; I will not again destroy Ephraim; for I am God and not a man, the Holy One in your midst, and I will not come in wrath" (vv. 8–9). Because of Christ, God's wrath has a landing place. He received it. We don't. We get the relationship and all its benefits: provision, hope, discipline, mercy, grace, and of course, joy. Because He's where the joy is!

ISAIAH 28–30

Today we read three of the six woes. The overarching theme is that we shouldn't rely on our own devices. In the first woe, Isaiah uses Israel's unfolding tragedy with Assyria as a warning for Judah. He says both kingdoms have spent too much time with wine and not enough time with God. The leaders respond by mocking Isaiah; in fact, 28:10 basically translates to "Blah blah blah." They've disrespected God's words, so everything He says will sound like "blah blah blah" to them now. One of the more challenging themes in Scripture is that God can open and close people's ears to the truth. He makes these mockers unable to understand His Word so that they may "go, and fall backward, and be broken, and snared, and taken" (28:13). This is a just response, but it's definitely tough to read and process.

In 28:16, we see a prophecy of Jesus: "Behold, I am the one who has laid as a foundation in Zion, a stone, a tested stone, a precious cornerstone, of a sure foundation: 'Whoever believes will not be in haste.'" Some of the people who hear this prophecy of "a sure foundation" mistakenly assume it means the temple in Jerusalem will never be destroyed, but it's about something much greater: God the Son. Then Isaiah makes another appeal for repentance. God has fought and won many victories on their behalf, but this time when He rises up it will be to fight against them. He compares God's people to wheat. The process of a harvest always involves threshing, but the point of threshing isn't to destroy the wheat—it's to make it usable. It exposes what's valuable in it.

The second woe is to Ariel, most likely a nickname for Jerusalem. God has an enemy set up a siege against the city, but then He shows up with His army of heaven, and the enemies flee. It happens so fast that the people think they must've dreamt it. While the leaders perform a bunch of religious activities, they don't actually love God. Often, this is the point when He brings discipline—but He doesn't. The next verse says, "Therefore, behold, I will again do wonderful things with this people, with wonder upon wonder" (29:14). *Because* their hearts are far from Him, He'll do wondrous things to reveal Himself to them.

The third woe is indirectly addressed to Judah. They want to make an alliance with Egypt to protect them from Assyria. They ignore God's counsel. They're running from God, striving, impatient, and afraid. Then God speaks to the remedy for each of those things: returning to Him, resting, quietness, and trusting. That's where they'll find their salvation and strength. But they aren't willing. Fear speaks with urgency; God whispers, "Trust." "Therefore the LORD waits to be gracious to you. . . . Blessed are all those who wait for him." It feels like Isaiah is saying, "You don't have to try so hard. You're striving, afraid things are going to go terribly if you don't step in with your solution. But slow down long enough to ask God what He has to say about this. He's ready to answer you if you'll just ask."

TODAY'S GOD SHOT

"Your Teacher will not hide himself anymore, but your eyes shall see your Teacher. And your ears shall hear a word behind you, saying, 'This is the way, walk in it,' when you turn to the right or when you turn to the left" (30:20–21). God just spent three chapters warning against walking in our own wisdom, so how cruel would He be if He didn't offer help or guidance, or if He told us He's too busy or that our needs are too frivolous? We'd be paralyzed! Thank God He promises to teach us and guide us. In fact, He's so serious about it that it's a title He has given Himself: Teacher, Guide. He invites us to seek Him for wisdom. This invitation isn't supposed to be paralyzing; it's supposed to free us up to talk to Him about things, to learn to hear and recognize His voice. The way we learn to recognize someone's voice is by talking to them more often. By being in His Word every day, you're starting to recognize the kinds of things He says, you're starting to develop a deeper awareness of His personality traits, and you're storing up His Word in your heart and mind. Based on what you know from His Word, listen for His voice today. He's where the joy is!

ISAIAH 31–34

Today we read the final three of six laments. We open with a reinforced woe to Judah. "Woe to those who go down to Egypt." God says they'll seek help from Egypt, but Egypt will be rendered helpless themselves. They may have horses and chariots, but God has weapons Judah can't even imagine. He can provide in ways that are supernatural. And He foretells a day when they'll finally turn to Him and destroy their idols. In that future day, a righteous king will reign. Any time we see this future righteous King reigning after the day of the LORD, it points to Jesus. Of course, the people in Isaiah's day don't know this—they naturally assume it will be an earthly king, except it will be a good one to contrast all the bad ones they've experienced. In that future day, fools and scoundrels won't be exalted anymore, but as for now, they still run rampant. The fool and the scoundrel are two distinct people. "The fool speaks folly, and his heart is busy with iniquity, to practice ungodliness, to utter error concerning the LORD, to leave the craving of the hungry unsatisfied, and to deprive the thirsty of drink" (32:6). And here's what he says about the scoundrel: "His devices are evil; he plans wicked schemes to ruin the poor with lying words, even when the plea of the needy is right" (32:7). One thing the fool and the scoundrel have in common, besides their hatred of God and His Word, is a disregard for the poor and needy.

In fact, a lot of people in Isaiah's day have this problem. Their wealth has made them complacent. He specifically calls the complacent women to repent. They're the focus of the fifth woe. They have a false sense of security, but in fact, things are about to get bad within the year. Then, as he always does, he reminds them of the message of hope beyond the desolation: God's Spirit will be poured out over the land, causing people's hearts to turn back to Him, and they'll begin to flourish again.

The sixth and final woe is for the destroyer and the traitor—which ultimately points to those who have wounded God's people in Judah. They'll serve God's purposes in bringing Judah to repentance, but then they'll be judged. Judah will be tempted to doubt God's trustworthiness as this unfolds. But Isaiah wants to remind them who YHWH is. While everything they know is being turned on its head and everything they've found their identity and hope in is being shaken, "He will be the stability of your times" (33:6). Nothing else is worth building your life on. He says, "The fear of the LORD is Zion's treasure" (33:6). In other words, the most valuable thing you have is your trust in God.

Then God promises to bring judgment on all the nations of the earth. Isaiah describes Edom as an abandoned wasteland full of tar and fire and terrible animals. It's a land God has cursed. Some scholars believe this passage alludes to hell as well.

TODAY'S GOD SHOT

In 32:15–16, Isaiah says God's Spirit will be poured out over the land, which will cause people's hearts to turn back to God and they'll begin to flourish again, because the active presence of God's Spirit brings justice and righteousness. In the next verse, he says, "The effect of righteousness will be peace, and the result of righteousness, quietness and trust forever." The thread we see running through these verses is that righteousness is what brings us quietness and trust and that God is the one who brings us righteousness. We don't have to manufacture our own righteousness. We couldn't if we had to. How freeing is that? Titus 3:5–6 says, "He saved us, not because of works done by us in righteousness, but according to his own mercy, by the washing of regeneration and renewal of the Holy Spirit, whom he poured out on us richly through Jesus Christ our Savior." Because of Christ's payment for our sins, the Holy Spirit is poured out on us, making us righteous—something we could never achieve on our own. And that is something that will set our hearts at peace and help us trust God forever. What a great relief! He's where the joy is!

ISAIAH 35–36

Yesterday we left off with Edom being turned into a sticky, smelly wasteland covered in weeds and birds. It represented a kind of undoing of creation, much like with the flood, when God destroyed the earth and then opened earth 2.0 for business. When God first made the earth, the words He used to describe it in Genesis 1:2 were "without form and void"—shapeless and empty, basically. The Hebrew words used here are *tohuw* and *bohuw*. And in yesterday's description of that wasteland, both of those words are used again. This seems to be an intentional move. Genesis 1 is the only other place where that combination exists, and the only other time the word *bohuw*—"void"—is used in all of Scripture is in Jeremiah 4:23, where he's describing this same situation. So we have the formless, void earth once again, after God's wrath has been poured out over all the nations, and today we read about how the ransomed captives are brought back to the land. So to understand this section well, we have to ask, "Does this refer to the time around 700 BC when this was written? Or is this a future prophecy of the final days?"

A popular opinion among scholars is that it's both—judgment on the earth then and judgment on the earth in the future. Prophecies can often speak to multiple layers, and it's possible that's what's happening here—a reference to the immediate scenario in 700 BC and a high-level reference to the future scenario. And when we read about the ransomed captives returning to the land, that could also point to both time frames: the already-fulfilled return of the Israelites to the promised land and the not-yet-fulfilled return of all God's adopted children to the newly restored earth 3.0.

Many of these prophecies have already been partially fulfilled. It speaks of the desert blooming, and it is. The Judean wilderness is currently a wealth of agriculture. Today, Israel exports tulips to Holland. Today, there are streams in the desert. *And* God brought back the

---

For more information on today's reading, see thebiblerecap.com/links.

ransomed Judean captives—that happened about seventy years after they were exiled to Babylon. He made a specific promise to a specific people, and He fulfilled that promise. God can be trusted to keep His word. Isaiah 35:4 says, "Say to those who have an anxious heart, 'Be strong; fear not!'" Why? Why shouldn't they fear? How can they be strong? He continues by saying, "Behold, your God will come with vengeance, with the recompense of God. He will come and save you." Does this mean they won't go into exile? No, they do. It just means exile is not the end of the story. He's coming to get them! The chapter ends with a promise we've seen before: no more tears, no more wickedness, no more threats to our peace—just everlasting joy.

Then in chapter 36 we revisit the time when the Assyrians confront the leaders who work for King Hezekiah, and they do it in front of the people of Judah. They use their best intimidation tactics to get the people to doubt God and follow them instead. They promise the people protection and provision, mocking God's ability to take care of His people. They also mock the people of Judah directly. They make a lot of false statements but also come up with a profound, true metaphor: "Behold, you are trusting in Egypt, that broken reed of a staff, which will pierce the hand of any man who leans on it" (v. 6). In other words, if they try to lean on Egypt for help, it'll end up stabbing them. And the Assyrians are right, here, in this one sentence. Even God Himself warned Judah against trusting Egypt. Idols may prop you up temporarily, but they'll wound you eventually. The rest of Assyria's speech is just a bunch of trash talk, intimidation tactics, and false promises. Fortunately, King Hezekiah was wise enough to tell his people not to respond.

TODAY'S GOD SHOT

The prophecies of chapter 35 point to the faithfulness of our promise-making, promise-keeping God. That desert is blooming today. Those waters are running today! He said it long before it happened. We have a promise-making, promise-keeping God. If God has brought about such great beauty in just this partial fulfillment, how much more beautiful will it be when He brings about the complete fulfillment of this prophecy in the future? And we'll get to see it with our own eyes. What an abundantly generous God—He's where the joy is!

ISAIAH 37–39; PSALM 76

Today Judah's King Hezekiah responds to Assyria's threats. His first response is to go to God. He trusts God to rebuke the Assyrians for their words. Meanwhile, he sends his staff to talk to Isaiah, who says God is in the process of dethroning the Assyrian king, just as Hezekiah hoped. He'll die by the sword.

When the messengers of Assyria send another threatening, mocking letter to Hezekiah, it's especially scary because now their army is surrounding Jerusalem and it seems they've already taken all the major cities of Judah. And once again, Hezekiah doesn't issue a response to them—he responds to *God*. He knows what God is capable of. He asks for God's deliverance not only because he wants it for himself but also because he believes it will show that YHWH is the one true God. While he's in the temple praying, Isaiah sends him a message with God's response to that prayer! God says He has already determined what will take place (37:26). He planned His actions long ago, and He will accomplish His plan. Assyria will have a few victories, but ultimately He'll thwart them. King Sennacherib and his army won't even enter Jerusalem again. Then the Angel of the Lord (likely Jesus) shows up and kills 185,000 Assyrians in one night. Then one day when King Sennacherib is at home worshipping an idol, his sons show up to kill him with a sword, just as God promised.

When King Hezekiah becomes sick, Isaiah says, "God says it's time for you to die." Hezekiah knows that often when prophets come with bad news, it's God's invitation to repent and avoid disaster. So he cries out to God, "I've been a good king and I've honored You, so would You delay my death?" Isaiah brings God's answer, "You've got another fifteen years. And in case you doubt that God can extend your years, He'll throw some shadows around in a very specific way to prove He's in control of time itself." And one interesting detail in this text is that God identifies Himself as the God of David. We're used to seeing Him refer to Himself as the God of Abraham, Isaac, and Jacob, so this nuance is significant. It seems to point to the fact that He's doing this in keeping with His covenant to David.

As God promised, shadows are thrown and years are lived. In that time, Hezekiah realizes his own selfishness: "Behold, it was for my welfare that I had great bitterness; but in love you have delivered my life from the pit of destruction" (38:17). He comes to terms with his own selfish entitlement. He was a great king, but he wasn't without sin. When he confesses, it leads him to praise God all the more for His goodness. But he also makes some bad moves. When he gets a friendly letter from a foreign king offering him a gift, he invites the king to visit. When the Babylonian king arrives, Hezekiah shows him all his treasures. Isaiah is aghast. He says this won't end well—the Babylonians will steal everything and kidnap some of Hezekiah's sons. Hezekiah affirms Isaiah's prophecy, but deep down he thinks, *None of that will happen. Everything will be fine.* He's become prideful. It's possible that what initially looked like naïvety when he was displaying all his riches to Babylon may have been arrogance. Regardless, his response to Isaiah reveals that his heart isn't in the same place as it was earlier in his reign. Despite—or perhaps because of—God's blessings, protection, and provision, Hezekiah's humility has faded.

Psalm 76 praises God for saving Judah from their enemies.

TODAY'S GOD SHOT

God declares His sovereignty over what happens with King Sennacherib: "Have you not heard that I determined it long ago? I planned from days of old what now I bring to pass" (37:26). This is terrifying if you're a pagan king who is an enemy of God, but for those of us who are His kids, this is so comforting. God has already set His very good plan in motion, and He's using it to bless us and glorify Himself. And we can't mess it up or derail it! He's working out His plan—we aren't living in a question or an uncertainty. We're living in His plan, right now. Your life isn't a decision you have to make; it's a secret you get to hear. And it's spoken from the heart of a sovereign, loving God. He's where the joy is!

ISAIAH 40–43

We've read Isaiah's prediction of Jerusalem's fall to Babylon, but he also prophesies to future generations of a hope beyond that, a future restoration postexile in Babylon. We enter that section of this book today. Israel's exile ends, they've been brought back in, and God is comforting them. Even though His creation passes away, His Word will stand. He is immovable. He's sovereign over all things, and in fact, if we were to give all His creation to Him as an offering, it would still fall short of praising Him as much as He deserves. But Israel struggles to trust and praise God. Both the rich and the poor build idols and fall into sin and entitlement. They act like God can't see their actions and their hearts and like He's being mean to them. Isaiah calls them to be servants of YHWH, but instead, just like they did in the wilderness, they complain and accuse God. They look to the gods of Babylon, just like the Israelites in the wilderness looked to the gods of Egypt. Once again, they're missing the point that YHWH has rescued them. That rescue does lead them through tough times, but Israel can't see the big picture. It involves using His enemies sometimes—like Cyrus, the leader of the Persian Empire. He isn't a God-fearing king, but he's God's servant because he serves God's purposes.

Isaiah tells Israel to trust God because He's doing things they can't possibly understand and He's capable of more than they can imagine. In 40:31 he says to wait for God because God will renew their strength as they wait for Him. The word *wait* is the Hebrew word *qavah*, which means "to bind together, to be joined, to meet, to expect, to be confident, trust, endure." If we read this verse with all those definitions included, it would say, "Those who are bound together with the Lord, joined with the Lord, who meet with the Lord, who confidently expect and trust and endure . . . will renew their strength." The image here is more than just an expression of time; it's an expression of *unity*. It's about

For more information on today's reading, see thebiblerecap.com/links.

relationship—knowing Him, trusting His character. When we live in that space, He strengthens us for whatever we're enduring.

God is with them—which is all they need for *qavah*-ing. He's in charge of things and three times He says not to fear. This is a big theme throughout Scripture. God promises to provide for and protect His people, which should set their hearts at ease. Those who don't believe Him are the ones who fall prey to worshipping idols, because as they perceive an absence of His protection and provision, they seek it elsewhere.

Chapter 42 gives us a prophecy of Christ. God refuses to give up on His people. He'll be compassionate and gentle toward wounded Israel: "A bruised reed he will not break" (v. 3). He continues to walk out His plan for restoration. It's clear that Israel can't adequately be God's servant, but God has provided a true servant to fulfill His mission, to restore Israel to Himself, and to serve as a light to the nations.

In chapter 43 God again says, "Fear not"—and not because things will be easy, but because they belong to Him. In fact, they'll go through trials, but He will prevail in those trials. He'll do miraculous things because He chose Israel to know and believe and understand who He is—the only Savior. He calls them to forget the things of the past, just as He has forgotten their sins. Despite their sin and their lack of offerings and sacrifices, He'll still make a way to blot out their sins for His own sake.

TODAY'S GOD SHOT

God calls Israel His "servant," Jacob His "chosen," and Abraham His "friend" (41:8). Israel sinned and rebelled, yet they're still serving His purposes. Jacob manipulated to get the blessing, he wrestled with God, yet he was God's chosen. Abraham had doubts and lied to preserve his own life, and he tried to fulfill God's promises instead of waiting on God's timing. Yet God still calls him "friend." There are no perfect people for God to use—we're all He's got, broken from the start. But He has written us into His story, and He blots out our sins for His own sake. Not just ours, but His own. What an incredible God and Father! He's where the joy is!

ISAIAH 44–48

While God has chosen Israel, there are some to whom He has given undiscerning hearts and closed eyes. This is His judgment on their idolatry. But part of His being sovereign means that even those whose hearts are far from Him are still used to serve His purposes. We see this with King Cyrus again today. We serve a God who makes even His enemies' plans bend to His will. He's the one who equips Cyrus even though Cyrus doesn't know Him. God is doing the heavy lifting here, breaking the doors of bronze and cutting the bars of iron, creating darkness and calamity, bringing rain and light and fruit. And ultimately, He uses all of this to set His people free from exile.

Babylon, Israel's captors, are idolaters. It should come as no surprise that the ones who took Israel into exile aren't followers of YHWH. He paints a picture of them lugging their idols around and being weighed down, which prevents any kind of forward motion and ultimately leads to bondage. For Babylon, this bondage happens when King Cyrus of Persia comes against them. In contrast to Babylon's carting their idols around, YHWH points out that He is the one who carries Israel—He's carried them from the womb and will carry them even when they're old. He has shown them who He is, and He can be trusted to keep being that Person in the future. His consistency is so comforting when we stop to recall it. But as for Babylon, Israel's captors, they're arrogant and entitled, and God promises to humble them. They'll seek help from an abundance of wicked sources—from idols to sorcerers to astrology—who will all fail to save them.

God speaks to Israel again in chapter 48. They're claiming God without actually knowing Him, so He says, "All that stuff you just went through—remember how I told you it was about to happen? I gave you a heads-up about it because it's one of the only ways to get your attention since you're so stubborn and forgetful. That way you'd have no excuse for thinking your idols were the ones who rescued you. It was Me all along. And now that you know My track record—that I do what I promise—I'm going to tell you some brand-new things I'm about to do. You've never heard anything like it." He's setting them up for the promise of the Messiah!

He'll do incredible things—defer His anger, restrain it, not cut them off—and He'll do them for His name's sake. What does that mean? When God restrains His anger toward the guilty, it displays His character; He's a God who seeks out opportunities for forgiveness. It isn't for Israel's sake that He withholds His anger. It's to show us and them and everyone what kind of God He is. He is a God who forgives sinners. And maybe that sounds selfish or showy to you, that God's priority is God's glory, and if so, then just think for a moment what things would be like if we were His first priority. How backward would it be for a holy, glorious God to worship fallen humanity? That kind of god isn't trustworthy. But to prioritize His glory—that's right and fitting. Not only that, but when the Father, Spirit, and Son are focused on displaying their glory and character throughout the universe, we reap the benefits. God withholds His anger from His kids, pays for our sins, and adopts us into His family. We are the recipients of the overflowing love of the Trinity!

TODAY'S GOD SHOT

In 45:19 God reminds Israel of the relationship He's had with them all along: "I did not speak in secret, in a land of darkness; I did not say to the offspring of Jacob, 'Seek me in vain.'" As we seek Him, God says none of it is in vain. Even on the days when you feel perplexed by what you're reading, none of it is in vain. God responds to your efforts to know Him—He's the one who initiated that desire in you to begin with. He doesn't thwart your desire to hear and know Him. He gave you that desire, He delights in that desire, and He's meeting you in that desire. And He's where the joy is!

2 KINGS 19; PSALMS 46, 80, 135

Today we revisited the story of Hezekiah's response to King Sennacherib's threats. He responds humbly when troubles come his way, he's blessed and stockpiles fortunes and gets to live an extra fifteen years, but his heart turns away from God. He becomes prideful, doubts God's words, and lives somewhat carelessly. God puts a spirit in Sennacherib that causes him to hear a lie. There are two noteworthy things in this section. First, God is in charge of evil spirits. They're on a leash. They have to do what He says and go where He commands. That's comforting! Second, God Himself didn't mislead Sennacherib. Scripture tells us repeatedly that God cannot lie. Hebrews 6:18 says He's incapable of it. It would be contrary to His character, because according to John 14:6, one of His names is The Truth.

But God certainly does use evil for His own purposes. When Romans 8:28 says that He works all things together for the good of those who love Him, evil is included in that list of all things. He uses the good, the bad, and the ugly. He works through the truth He speaks and the rumors others speak. He allows Sennacherib to be misled. If you think that's unjust, try to zoom out and remember how Sennacherib has openly mocked YHWH and how his leaders told the people of Judah that they shouldn't let YHWH trick them into trusting Him. God's response is merciful based on what Sennacherib actually deserves.

Isaiah also tells Hezekiah that they'll win this war easily, and he's right. Before Assyria can fire off an arrow toward Jerusalem, God's army—an army of One—shows up and wins! But it isn't really a balanced fight. The Assyrians are no match for the Angel of the Lord, who kills 185,000 of them in one night. Then King Sennacherib is assassinated just as God promised.

In light of what we just read, the reference to Jerusalem in Psalm 46:5 is encouraging: "God is in the midst of her; she shall not be moved. God will help her when morning dawns." This is certainly what plays out for Jerusalem over the course of the night when the Angel of the Lord shows up and wins the battle for them while they're sleeping. When morning dawns, they lay eyes on God's victory. Verse 10 says, "Be still, and know that I am God." One of the things we've seen repeated in Isaiah lately is the call to quietness, rest, and trust. This stillness fits in perfectly with those themes.

In Psalm 80, the corporate cry is for God to save and restore them. In this song, Israel knows its identity and echoes it back to the God who gave them that identity to begin with. Verse 8 says, "You brought a vine out of Egypt"—that vine is a reference to Israel the people, the ones He rescued from Egypt. Verses 8–9 continue, "You drove out the nations and planted it. You cleared the ground for it." This is a reference to Israel the place. God drove out the Canaanites and planted them there. Now they've been burned up, cut down, and plucked up, and they ask God to restore them and they promise to praise Him for it.

TODAY'S GOD SHOT

In Psalm 135, take note of all the action verbs that God is the subject of. Here's everything He does in this chapter: He chose Jacob and Israel, He does whatever He pleases, He makes the clouds rise, He makes lightning, He brings forth the wind, He struck down the Egyptians, He sent signs and wonders, He struck down many nations, He killed mighty kings, and He gave their land to Israel. He will vindicate His people. He will have compassion on His servants. He dwells in Jerusalem. As we look back at all the things God does here, we see His desire to bless His people, to restore and redeem the very ones who have repeatedly gone astray from Him. And He doesn't do it reluctantly. He does it willingly, joyfully. "He does whatever He pleases" (see v. 6). It pleases God to adopt sinners into His family and call them sons and daughters. It demonstrates His great heart for redemption. It pleases Him to vindicate His people and have compassion on His servants. It pleases Him! He's where the joy is!

ISAIAH 49–53

Coastlands is a catchall word for all the nations of the world, reaching to the far corners of the earth. God tells Israel, "I will make you as a light for the nations, that my salvation may reach to the end of the earth" (49:6). Though Israel is a despised nation, He's chosen them and will use them to bless all the nations that despise them. How will He do that? What exactly has He chosen them for? He's chosen them to be the lineage of the Messiah, and that Messiah will save people from every single nation. His love will reach to those who hate Him and His lineage, and then He will turn His enemies into family. In the meantime, though, Israel feels forgotten and ashamed. He reminds them that He cannot forget His people—they're engraved on the palms of His hands.

Chapter 50 brings us beautiful prophecies of Christ: He knows "how to sustain with a word him who is weary" (v. 4), and "I was not rebellious. I gave my back to those who strike, and my cheeks to those who pull out the beard; I hid not my face from disgrace and spitting" (vv. 5–6). Jesus spoke with compassion toward the outcasts, and He endured beatings at His crucifixion. This chapter also begins to draw a unique distinction for us. So far God has called a few people His servants, including the pagan king Cyrus and Israel as a whole, but these prophecies are pointing out that there's another servant, a superior servant, Christ the Messiah.

Chapter 51 says, "The earth will wear out like a garment" (v. 6)—and we're seeing that happen in real time—but His salvation will outlast even an undone earth.

Chapters 52 and 53 are a section often referred to as "The Suffering Servant," and they're filled with prophecies of Christ. In fact, for some Jewish people, chapter 53 is known as "the forbidden chapter," and they refuse to read it in the synagogues. It's been removed from some of their holy books. This section paints a clear picture of Jesus the Messiah. Isaiah 53:2 says He wasn't particularly attractive. One reason this

For more information on today's reading, see thebiblerecap.com/links.

is important is because it's human nature to follow people who have an attractive physical presence. But this goes to show that He was nothing special to look at, that people followed Him because of His message, not His muscles. The next verse calls Him a "man of sorrows and acquainted with grief." He was despised and rejected. If you've been any of those things, He knows your pain. Isaiah 53:5 says, "Upon him was the chastisement that brought us peace." Peace came to us through bloodshed. Isaiah 52:14 says He was beaten beyond human recognition when He was crucified. That's one reason people were so astonished when they saw Him three days later, because as far as they knew, bodies didn't rise from the dead, but they also didn't heal and regenerate that quickly. So when you see a crucifix with a tiny trickle of blood on the forehead, remember Isaiah 53 and know that's a gross misrepresentation of what He really endured when paying for our sins. He suffered to serve and save us.

TODAY'S GOD SHOT

The last part of chapter 53 shows us two of the three persons of the Trinity: It was the Father's will to crush the Son (see verse 10). What does that mean? This text displays a kind of hierarchy within the Trinity—they're all of equal value and Godhood, working in tandem for the same purpose and plan, but the Father is the authority, and the Son and Spirit walk out the Father's will, because they're united with it as well. The Trinity works in unity—the Son was on board with this plan. This was the plan to redeem our fallen world even before the world was created (Revelation 13:8). Jesus died willingly, submitting to the will of the Father (Luke 22:42). It's okay if this is challenging to process—everything about this is complex, including the emotions presented here. In fact, God is both anguished and satisfied (53:11). God has complex emotions; He's not a two-dimensional God. Christ did all this to make many be accounted righteous and to bear the sins of many. If you know Him, you're among the many. How ironic is it that our physically unattractive Savior is the most beautiful thing of all? He's where the joy is!

ISAIAH 54–58

God promises a blessing to the people of Israel: He'll enlarge His family through them, and it'll include people from all over the world. At present, these other nations are their enemies, so it may feel like a strange blessing to them. But He says this is nothing to fear and that this time of waiting is nothing to be ashamed of. He presents Israel as a bride and Himself as the husband—the one who redeems them. He compares their current situation to what Noah and his family went through in the flood. There was devastation and loss, but He protected all His people through the trial. He promises steadfast love, a covenant of peace, compassion—not anger or a rebuke. And not only will *He* not wipe them out, but no enemy will succeed in wiping them out. Their gates will be secure. And He promises to teach all their children. The fact that God the Spirit teaches us is such a gift!

Chapter 55 opens with His promise to feed His people for free. Is this actual food? No, it's better. It's the food of salvation, the feast of eternity. Then in 55:3, He says something paradigm shifting: He's had a covenant with Israel based on their behavior, and they kept giving Him every opportunity to withdraw from it, because they were not keeping up their end of the covenant. But God kept saying, "I'm not going anywhere. I'm here to bless you. Even though you've broken our covenant, I'm keeping it." And here, He says He's establishing an *everlasting* covenant with them. Lest you think it gives them a pass on loving God, He addresses that almost immediately. He calls them not only to a change of action but a change of thinking: "Let the wicked forsake his way, and the unrighteous man his thoughts; let him return to the LORD, that he may have compassion on him, and to our God, for he will abundantly pardon" (v. 7). It's always been and still is about the relationship, about the love, between God and His people.

He has good plans for His people, ideas that humans don't even have the capacity to come up with, and He'll fulfill all His plans. Everything He starts will accomplish what He intends it to. It'll take time, but He'll eventually restore all His creation, and that includes wiping out the briars and thorns that were a result of Adam's curse. This feels especially poignant given the fact that Jesus was mocked with a crown of thorns. And not only has God included the foreigner and the eunuch in His family, but He's also blessed them.

Isaiah has been prophesying about both immediate and future salvation. But the Israelites assume it will all be immediately and completely fulfilled, so Isaiah clarifies further. He says they're still called to put away their idols and worship God alone, because underneath their worship of false gods is a heart that doesn't yet believe YHWH can be trusted: "Whom did you dread and fear, so that you lied, and did not remember me, did not lay it to heart?" (57:11). Fear of man leads to forgetfulness of God. He says there's a wrong kind of "righteous" deed. The heart behind what they're doing matters. He'd rather they fast from selfishness than from food, from pride instead of wine, because all their fasting is still selfishly motivated. But proper fasting humbles us, blesses others, and honors God.

TODAY'S GOD SHOT

God doesn't run from sinners. He draws near to sinners to help them. He's the only one who *can* help them. He says, "I dwell in the high and holy place, and also with him who is of a contrite and lowly spirit." He's in the high and holy place, but He's with the lowly. And why? It's "to revive the spirit of the lowly, and to revive the heart of the contrite" (57:15). Wow. Isaiah 57:18 says it like this: "I have seen his ways, but I will heal him." God sees all our wickedness, and He draws near to help. When you sin, there's no need to run from Him and no way you could, even if you tried. He's with you, He loves you, and He's waiting for you with compassion and healing and joy. Because He's where the joy is!

ISAIAH 59–63

Today Isaiah records the people's confession. They know they can't fix what's broken in themselves, and it devastates them. But in 59:16 God shows up and does for each man what he can't do for himself. God Himself fulfills all that He requires. The end of chapter 59 can be kind of confusing in English, but in Hebrew, it's a bit clearer. It appears that God the Father is speaking to God the Son about God the Spirit and about the whole family of God: "'My Spirit that is upon you, and my words that I have put in your mouth, shall not depart out of your mouth, or out of the mouth of your offspring, or out of the mouth of your children's offspring,' says the LORD, 'from this time forth and forevermore.'" By the way, this isn't saying Jesus had literal offspring—this is a promise about everyone who comes into the family of God through His sacrifice, which is the only way to get into the family of God. Here, God promises that He'll continue what He has started. Israel's sin and rebellion haven't ruined His plan.

Chapter 60 is all about the future glory of Israel, when people from all nations will come to bless Zion and bless the Lord. While this points to a future fulfillment, there are aspects that could simultaneously point to the Messiah too. For instance, 60:1 says, "Your light has come," which is a reference to Jesus, and 60:3 says, "Nations shall come to your light, and kings to the brightness of your rising." That sounds a lot like the wise men who took a two-year trip from distant lands to see a toddler named Jesus and bring Him presents—all because they saw a star rising in the east.

The rest of the chapter paints Israel as a haven of peace and rest. As a part of His redemption plan, God has granted them beauty and majesty they don't possess on their own. He promises to improve on everything they'd hoped for—gold instead of bronze, silver instead of iron. And most of all, the presence of God Himself will be the light for the nation. He's done this before as the pillar of fire and cloud, but this time it'll be so bright that there'll be no need for the sun and moon. And

God says He'll do this in its perfect time. It won't happen a moment too soon or too late.

Chapter 61 is the messianic prophecy that Jesus read from in the synagogue of His childhood hometown of Nazareth (Luke 4:18–30). He says He's the fulfillment of this chapter—He's the one who will set the captives free and bind up the brokenhearted. The people marvel that their local guy could possibly be the Messiah. They're all for it until He starts telling them that this good news isn't just for them, but it's for the people they consider their enemies as well—the Syrians and the Sidonians. Suddenly they hate Him for it and try to kill Him on the spot by throwing Him off a cliff. People love to hear how God wants to bless them, but it's more challenging to hear that God might also want to bless people we hate or people who have hurt us.

TODAY'S GOD SHOT

Chapters 61–62 represent the year of the Lord's favor, but chapter 63 tells us about the day of the Lord's wrath. Reading them side by side here, we see how Isaiah's specific terminology points out that God's goodness far outweighs His wrath. Compare the day of His wrath to the *year* of His favor and redemption. That's 365 times more favor than wrath! This is reminiscent of Exodus 34:6–7, when God tells Moses His name by describing Himself. He says He keeps love for a thousand generations and only punishes to the third or fourth generation. From these two sections of Scripture, it looks like God is hinting that He's approximately three hundred times more loving toward His people. To be fair, these may all just be generalities. It might not fit on a scale quite like that. But God does communicate something to us here about who He is: Yes, sin has to be punished, but He's actually a benevolent God. He's also winsome and desirable. He's worth loving and worshipping. He's actually pretty awesome to be around—He's not a drag, and He's not looking to smite everyone who has a mean thought. He's already made a way to bridge that gap, so we can just enjoy being in His presence. After all . . . He's where the joy is!

ISAIAH 64–66

Context and culture are necessary for understanding 64:6. "We have all become like one who is unclean, and all our righteous deeds are like a polluted garment." This verse doesn't mean God turns up His nose at your Bible reading, volunteering, or tithing. He's pleased with your good works. After all, He's the one doing them through you, and He approves of His work. So what does it mean? A polluted garment refers to a woman's menstrual rag, and people who are unclean can't enter the temple without first being purified. The unclean person and the polluted garment are unacceptable in God's sight. Isaiah is comparing Israel's false worship to both of these. They sacrifice to God but also worship idols. They fast to be showy. They perform so-called righteous deeds with unrighteous motives. So it's true for them that their righteous deeds are like filthy rags—unacceptable to God.

Verse 7 says, "You have hidden your face from us." Does God hide His face when His kids sin? First, we have to remember that technically, God the Father doesn't have a face. He's not a physical, tangible being. He is spirit (John 4:24). So there's no face for Him to cover or hide. He doesn't have eyes, but He manages to see everything. When Scripture says He hides His face from Israel, it's clear that He still sees everything, because He talks about it and acts on it.

The feeling behind this statement is the more important thing to address. God being hidden from our eyes is more about the perceived distance we feel from Him when we sin, because we know in our hearts that this is a real relationship. We know He's a real person—and what do people do when we wound or offend them? They create distance until the situation is resolved. That's sort of what it's like with God too—except He's an infinitely loving being who has already paid for your sin and isn't holding a grudge. In any relationship, when we've sinned against someone, it's important that we demonstrate our repentance, turn from

For more information on today's reading, see thebiblerecap.com/links.

our sin. But it's also important that we don't misunderstand: We're not trying to earn God's trust. God's not trying to figure you out or see what you'll do next—He knows what's in you even more than you do. What we're doing is walking out a relationship in real time—learning, remembering, growing, strengthening the relationship. God's apparent distance serves as the catalyst for our repentance, driving us toward restoration and intimacy we don't feel in the moment. In fact, if God had removed His presence, we'd have no hope of repentance, because it's *His kindness* that produces repentance in us to begin with (Romans 2:4), so we know He's close, even when He feels distant.

Chapter 65 hovers over God's judgment and salvation—punishment for those who don't know Him and blessing for those who do. The kingdom of heaven isn't for people who are afraid of hell; it's for people who love God. In addition to a new earth, God will create a new heaven. Why? The current heaven has been tainted by sin too. Remember Lucifer's fall (14:12–14)? Jesus references the same incident (Luke 10:18), and John references it too (Revelation 12:7–12). Heaven isn't perfect, so it has to be re-created, just like earth. It's all part of God's plan to restore all of creation. The place where we'll be living after heaven and earth have both been re-created sounds a lot like earth. Jerusalem, in fact. Scholars are divided on whether this section refers to the eternal kingdom or a period of time known as the "millennial reign" or "thousand-year reign." Regardless of which view is right, the most important thing is that wherever we are, and whenever it is, we get to be with God forever.

TODAY'S GOD SHOT

Chapter 66 closes the book with a call to repentance and more reminders of God's judgment and salvation, yet He goes above and beyond in blessing the Gentiles. He'll send people throughout the world to reach them, and He'll even make some of them into priests and Levites! They won't be outsiders or sojourners—they'll be serving Him in the most exclusive roles. God is bent on loving His enemies. He's on a mission to bring people from every nation into His family. And He's where the joy is!

2 KINGS 20–21

We've been reading Isaiah's prophecies about Israel being taken captive by Babylon, but that hasn't happened yet. We're still a century away from when it actually happens, so we have a few final kings to meet. Today we read again about King Hezekiah's downfall. As a refresher, he starts out following God—reestablishing worship and feasts, tearing down high places, and generally not missing a step—but then he gets sick and God sends Isaiah to tell him it's time to die. He's devastated and begs God to let him live. God gives him a remedy for his ailments and another fifteen years to live. It seems like God said something would happen that didn't happen. Did God lie? Did He change His mind? Numbers 23:19 says, "God is not man, that he should lie, or a son of man, that he should change his mind." From what we can tell, it was His plan all along to let Hezekiah live another fifteen years and Isaiah's words of warning and Hezekiah's prayer worked in tandem to accomplish God's plan. God often sends prophets to give a call to repentance adjacent to a promise of consequence, like with Jonah and Nineveh, so this isn't unusual.

Hezekiah's prayer plays an interesting role in this process. Prayer is often the means God uses to achieve His appointed ends. Prayers are tools in God's hand to accomplish what He has planned for us. By talking to Him, by confessing our sins and sharing our fears and asking Him for what we want, we're playing a *vital* role in His will being made manifest. It's similar to the way God provides for you through your work. You're doing the actual work, but He enables you to do it, so He's doing the providing. In life and in prayer, we get to play an active role in God's will being worked out. Prayer isn't a means to get what we want *from* God, but to *get God*. And since He uses our prayers to accomplish His will, this encourages us all the more to pray, because He will use it!

Hezekiah lives another fifteen years, but he wastes God's yes. He's foolish, selfish, and prideful—he either disbelieves Isaiah's prophecy about his downfall or doesn't care since most of it pertains to what will happen after he dies. After he dies, his son Manasseh becomes king. He rebuilds the high places, after it took us centuries to get rid of them, and he consults mediums and fortune-tellers, sets up an idol of Asherah in the temple, and burns his son as a sacrifice. And his people follow suit. As goes the leader, so go the people. God promises them all that judgment is coming.

Then his son Amon becomes king. He's also horrible, and his servants kill him. Then the locals kill the servants who killed him and put his son Josiah on the throne.

TODAY'S GOD SHOT

God knows how the next fifteen years will go, but He's kind to Hezekiah despite it all. He hears the prayers of this selfish, arrogant man and answers them with a yes. Often our prayers are pleas to avoid pain, but the irony is that pain is often where we draw near to God. But when life is good and easy and we aren't desperately seeking God anymore, we begin to feel a sense of distance. We begin to grow complacent. And before we know it, we remember what intimacy with God is like, but we can't quite access it. So we start to do our own thing. We stop listening. That's what Hezekiah did when he had all kinds of treasures and blessings and suddenly felt like he didn't need to listen to God or His prophet anymore—the very God and prophet who told him yes in response to his prayer.

It's common to associate the enemy's attacks on us with negative things—flat tires and traffic jams and overdraft fees. We imagine him bringing all kinds of trials our way. But what if he knows human nature better than we do? What if his tactic is a more cunning one? What if, instead of trials, he brings abundance in a way that enables our hearts to get calloused and distracted, like Hezekiah's? What if the thing he wants to steal, kill, and destroy has less to do with our bank accounts and more to do with our peace and our intimacy with God? Satan certainly knows that's more valuable. King Hezekiah's rise and fall proves that nothing is worth putting our hope in besides God. He's where the joy is!

2 CHRONICLES 32–33

Today we see another perspective on the final days of King Hezekiah. In the chapters immediately before today's reading, there are several stories of Hezekiah's faithfulness. Then chapter 32 opens with an attack from an enemy nation, Assyria. At this point, Hezekiah is still a wise leader—his demise hasn't yet begun. He's living faithfully in Jerusalem, serving God and the people of Judah. Then Assyria and its king, Sennacherib, decide to attack Jerusalem. Hezekiah makes a plan to outsmart them. He cuts off the water supply to the city as a deterrent, builds up the wall around the city, fortifies their towers, stocks up on weapons, and organizes his army. Then he gives a pep talk to the army, encouraging them with reminders that God is on their side. He doesn't fixate on all the work he has done to defend the city or prepare them for battle—he centers his encouragement on the fact that God is with them. That is where their hope lies.

This is a big theme in Scripture. The message the world teaches us is more along the lines of "Believe in yourself. You've got this!" We don't see that in Scripture. In Scripture, the message is "Believe in your God. He's at work within you." True encouragement—the kind Hezekiah gives here—doesn't put the focus on our own abilities but on God's. It might make for a clunkier mantra or a less exciting social media post, but at least it doesn't miss the point.

After Hezekiah encourages the leaders who follow him, a few of the Assyrian leaders come to intimidate Judah. You probably remember this scene. While the Assyrian leaders are busy crying out to the people of Judah, Hezekiah is busy crying out to the Lord. Assyria thinks they're fighting a physical battle, but Hezekiah knows it's a spiritual one. And God sends His answer in the spiritual realm as well. He sends an angel—whom Isaiah 37:36 calls the Angel of the Lord—to fight the battle on behalf of Judah. And of course, nothing trumps the Angel of the Lord, because as we've talked about before, He's almost certainly a manifestation of God Himself.

Second Chronicles 32:23 says, "Many brought gifts to the LORD to Jerusalem and precious things to Hezekiah king of Judah, so that he was exalted in the sight of all nations from that time onward." This is likely connected to what happens next. People brought gifts to the LORD, but Hezekiah is the one who was exalted in the sight of all the other nations. And his pride seems to lead to his downfall, which we read about yesterday in 2 Kings 20:12–15. All that wealth he showed off—how much of it came from the gifts people brought to him? How much of what he was flaunting was treasure given to him as a result of God winning a battle that Hezekiah didn't even show up to fight? This kind of pride takes down kings and spiritual giants when they forget their Source.

Chapter 33 tells us about the reign of his son Manasseh after his death. He's an evil king. He reverses some of the best work of his father, undoing the good parts of his legacy. He burns his sons as an offering, seeks help from mediums and fortune-tellers, and sets up an idol in the temple.

TODAY'S GOD SHOT

In 33:10–11, God speaks to Manasseh and the people, but they don't listen at first. So God takes drastic measures to get his attention because His desire is to bless him. Eventually, Manasseh repents and turns to God. As it turns out, he lives the reverse story of his dad, Hezekiah. Hezekiah starts out strong but loses his way, and Manasseh starts out evil and repents. And the turning point in both of their stories has to do with the direction of their eyes. Hezekiah turns his eyes inward—we call this navel-gazing. He grows prideful and wanders from God. Manasseh turns his eyes upward and humbles himself, and God redeems his story. God is in the business of changing hearts and moving gazes. He's where the joy is!

NAHUM 1–3

Nahum's words are directed toward Nineveh, the capital of Assyria. We've read a lot about Assyria lately. Yesterday they planned an attack on Jerusalem but were thwarted by the Angel of the Lord. Before that, they attacked and destroyed Northern Israel and took its people into exile. And Nineveh is the city God sent Jonah to rebuke. At the time, they repented, but here we are a hundred years later, and they've fallen back into their wicked ways. Nahum only explicitly mentions Nineveh a few times. He mostly uses general terminology, which has an added benefit for this prophecy. It not only serves the immediate purpose of warning Assyria, but can also apply to future scenarios. Nahum's message is that God will always judge evil. There have been and will continue to be evil empires throughout time, and none of them will outlive God and His judgment.

Specifically, God is judging Assyria for the way they've treated His people. He starts out with a reminder of who He is, and it sounds a lot like Exodus 34:6–7, which has been a common refrain throughout the Old Testament. In the Exodus passage God describes Himself to Moses like this: "The Lord, the Lord, a God merciful and gracious, slow to anger, and abounding in steadfast love and faithfulness, keeping steadfast love for thousands, forgiving iniquity and transgression and sin, but who will by no means clear the guilty, visiting the iniquity of the fathers on the children and the children's children, to the third and the fourth generation."

Here, God is talking to one of His people and giving him a message to pass along to the rest of His people, and He starts with all these incredible qualities He possesses, but then He tacks on a reminder at the end that basically says, "But lest you think I'm a pushover, I still do punish sin." The order of a list can reveal what's being emphasized. For instance, according to the FDA, product labels have to list the ingredients in order

For more information on today's reading, see thebiblerecap.com/links.

of prominence—so the thing listed first is what the product contains the most of, and the thing listed last is what's least prominent. With that in mind, let's look at Nahum 1:2–3, where Nahum is talking to the enemies of God about who God is. "The LORD is a jealous and avenging God; the LORD is avenging and wrathful; the LORD takes vengeance on his adversaries and keeps wrath for his enemies. The LORD is slow to anger and great in power, and the LORD will by no means clear the guilty." Here, Nahum references the Exodus 34 passage but reverses the order. This is certainly intentional. How you view God and how God relates to you are entirely based on whether you know Him or not.

Throughout the book, Nahum offers reminders that God has His eyes not only on the wicked people He's going to punish, but also on the remnant of His people He plans to restore and bless. He encourages Israel with reminders that they'll be set free and will be able to celebrate their feasts again, which is something they couldn't do while Assyria was oppressing them. Their cities were destroyed and they were exiled, but that's never stopped God before. God undoes the undoing done by our enemies.

The Assyrian leaders fail to serve their people well—their princes and scribes flee, their royals are asleep at the wheel, and the people of the land have no one to lead them and they scatter. Meanwhile, the other nations around them—the ones who've been victims of their oppression—rejoice that they're being stopped in their tracks.

TODAY'S GOD SHOT

Nahum is a heavy book, but it shows that our God is a defender of His people. Our God addresses injustice. If you live in a country that has some form of systemic injustice or oppression, be encouraged to know that God will deal with it. It doesn't escape Him. It may take longer than you want, it may not be resolved in your lifetime, but our God isn't blind to it. It may seem like no one cares or speaks up about it loudly enough, but nothing is lost on our God. When leaders mislead, God can still be trusted. It's just another reminder of why we can't put our hope in nations or powers, because only God can rule in complete righteousness. He's our King forever, and He's where the joy is!

2 KINGS 22–23; 2 CHRONICLES 34–35

We're not too far off from the days prophesied by Isaiah when Southern Judah will be overthrown by the Babylonians. But as for now, we've got eight-year-old King Josiah on the throne. He's a good king. He has his servant Hilkiah make financial arrangements for God's house to be repaired. And at some point during the process of restoration, Hilkiah finds the book of the law, which is likely a reference to the scroll of Deuteronomy, somewhere in the temple. We don't know exactly where he found it, but given the state of the temple, it's probably shoved behind some idols somewhere and covered in dust. The Word of God was lost in the house of God. It's been a long time since anyone has read or reflected on the words of the law. Most people have probably forgotten what it says or maybe even that it exists at all. It seems like no one was looking for it or was distraught that it was missing. They were just doing their own thing—living their lives and fighting wars and making decisions, all without the guidance of God.

The book makes its way to Josiah, and it wrecks him. He realizes how far off track their hearts and lives are and how the kings before him have led the people astray for generations. As it turns out, what you don't know *can* hurt you. When we forget that truth exists, when it gets covered in the dust of our busyness, our hearts can't help but go astray. Josiah tells his leaders to seek God and see how they should proceed. His heart is so burdened by the whole thing that he gathers everyone to the temple, where he reads them the book of the covenant. Then he makes a covenant before God to obey Him with all his heart and soul, and the people join in.

He sets out like a man on a mission, removing and destroying idols in the temple, firing wicked priests and giving the death penalty to others, banishing the mediums and necromancers, and desecrating the places of idolatry and turning them into graveyards. He follows God with all

---

For more information on today's reading, see thebiblerecap.com/links.

his heart and soul and mind. He reestablishes the Passover feast, which has once again fallen by the wayside. The people of Judah follow God as long as Josiah is alive.

Josiah is the last good king Judah will have. After he dies, his son Jehoahaz replaces him on the throne. He's a wicked king and is eventually captured and taken back to Egypt by the same pharaoh who killed his dad. He dies there in captivity. The Egyptian pharaoh rules the roost now, so he appoints another one of Josiah's sons to be king instead. His given name is Eliakim, but Pharaoh Neco renames him Jehoiakim. He isn't a great king either, mainly because he's Neco's puppet, taxing the people to send money back to Egypt.

TODAY'S GOD SHOT

Josiah is the one good king we've read about so far whose heart never turned away from God. He remained faithful—unless you consider his final actions to be motivated by pride, which some do. His death came in a strange and unexpected way: While Pharaoh Neco was coming to join forces with Assyria and confront the Babylonians, Josiah wanted in on the action. The Pharaoh warned him to stay away, but Josiah disguised himself and went up to battle anyway, where Pharaoh Neco fatally wounded him.

Who would've expected that one of Judah's best kings would be taken out because he didn't listen to an Egyptian Pharaoh? According to 2 Chronicles 35:22, Pharaoh Neco was speaking the truth. God can work and speak truth through the mouths of those who oppose Him. He's not limited to working through His kids. He can use anyone and everyone to point to Himself and His truth, which should humble us and cause us to ask Him for more discernment. We can't dismiss something as a lie just because we don't like the person who said it. After all, God spoke to Balaam through his donkey, and today God spoke to Josiah through a pagan. Regardless of who or what He uses, He wants to speak to us. May He give us wisdom to discern what things line up with the truth of His Word. Seeking Him is the best place to start when we're seeking truth. He's where the truth is, and He's where the joy is!

ZEPHANIAH 1–3

Zephaniah is the great-great-grandson of Judah's King Hezekiah. He opens with a prophecy of destruction. He warns Judah about God's coming judgment in much the same way Isaiah did. Lots of scholars believe this book not only applies to Jerusalem's immediate future in the days of King Josiah, but also to the end times. He calls them out for the way they've mingled their worship of YHWH with the worship of false gods. Any time they feel like God isn't coming through for them, they don't seek Him or pray about things, but they seek help from idols instead. Zephaniah says God's judgment is coming; He'll punish not only those who are blatantly wicked and idolaters, but He'll punish the complacent too—those who are inattentive and inactive. Interestingly, their passivity seems to stem from a belief that *God* is passive, that He won't do anything about their actions, so they live lukewarm lives. But God does interact with humankind and says He'll judge that kind of complacency. For the few things they do put effort into—building houses and planting vineyards—they'll be laboring in vain. They won't get to live in the houses or drink the wine. It doesn't matter how high their walls are or how deep their pockets are; they won't be able to stand against God and His wrath.

Chapter 2 provides a potential solution, though, and that's repentance: "Seek the Lord, all you humble of the land, who do his just commands; seek righteousness, seek humility; perhaps you may be hidden on the day of the anger of the Lord" (v. 3). Zephaniah begins warning all the nations around Judah, because they don't follow YHWH either, and their sin will be judged too. In the midst of all this destruction and judgment, he offers a sweet reminder that there'll be a remnant of His people when it's all said and done.

The rebellious people of Jerusalem are proud, stubborn, faithless, and autonomous. They aren't teachable, yet God is still there and is

For more information on today's reading, see thebiblerecap.com/links.

still acting righteously. He gives them chance after chance to learn their lesson, but they refuse, so He promises judgment that will consume the whole earth.

Zephaniah wraps up the book with the same two promises we see in most prophetic books. First, God will save people from among all nations. In 3:9, He says He will "change the speech of the peoples to a pure speech." Remember the Tower of Babel, where God divided the tongues or languages of people? He's going to reunite those languages someday. And all those people from all those nations will serve God together in peace. Despite all the sins of His people, God says there will be no shame for them—they don't know this yet, but He's got a plan to pay for their sins once and for all. Second, God has preserved and will restore a remnant from among Israel as well. Israel has been through a lot, and He says, "The King of Israel, the LORD is in your midst; you shall never again fear evil" (3:15). God loves to banish the fears of His people, and He does it just by His presence with them. He rejoices over them with singing, and He quiets them with His love. He changes shame into praise and renown!

TODAY'S GOD SHOT

In 2:7–12, God promises the destruction of the enemy nations. He told the Israelites to do it when they moved into the promised land, but they didn't obey. So now He's saying He will do for them what they couldn't or wouldn't do for themselves—just like He always does. In the middle of that, Zephaniah references the remnant of Judah and says, "The LORD their God will be mindful of them and restore their fortunes." All they've done is sin and rebel, and God says someday they'll come back to build their houses in the lands that have been emptied of their enemies through this destruction. God is clearing out the wicked who have oppressed His people and mocked His name so He can make a peaceful home for His people. His patience and grace fill the pages of this story. He's where the joy is!

JEREMIAH 1–3

Jeremiah comes from a long line of priests, but God calls him to be a prophet. His time as a prophet spans forty years and five kings of Judah. In addition to prophecies, his scribe Baruch shares stories from Jeremiah's life—and it's not an easy one. He's known as the weeping prophet because he grieves over Judah's state. It's easy to imagine prophets as self-righteous people who go around telling everyone else what they're doing wrong, but more often, God puts them in tough circumstances so they can feel the pain of the people. It both keeps them humble and increases the potency of their message.

When God first calls Jeremiah, he refuses to prophesy, but God rebukes him and says, "I am with you" (1:8). He gives him three assignments: pluck up and break down, destroy and overthrow, and build and plant. There'll be destruction, but there'll also be restoration. God will send a conqueror (Babylon) from the north to destroy Jerusalem as judgment for turning their backs on Him. God tells Jeremiah not to be afraid, because while He does promise a battle, He also promises a victory.

Then God has Jeremiah walk through Jerusalem and tell the story of His relationship with Israel out loud: They used to love Him but gradually forgot all He's done for them. They're like thirsty people in the desert, and He's a spring of living water right behind them. But instead of turning to Him, they try to dig their own cisterns, which keep cracking and breaking. They try to find joy and fulfillment in things that aren't God, but those things always disappoint and exhaust us. God set them free, but they used their freedom to rebel against Him. They're like camels who wander in the desert. It's common for adult camels to change direction every few steps; they're aimless without guidance. Then he compares them to wild donkeys who follow every lust and desire; they can't be contained. Judah has worshipped the false gods of their pagan neighbors, and they've sought help from them instead of

For more information on today's reading, see thebiblerecap.com/links.

from God. And after all that, they still claim they haven't done anything wrong. They don't expect God to judge them for their actions, but He says it's coming.

God portrays Judah and Israel as His unfaithful bride. Judah had the chance to learn from Israel's mistakes but didn't—she just kept committing adultery. This image makes it seem like the husband would never want the wife back because of all she's done. But God is set apart here—He acknowledges Judah's adultery and His angry response to it, but He's not in the business of divorcing His bride. He's in the business of forgiving and staying. He pleads with them, "Return, faithless Israel. . . . I will not look on you in anger, for I am merciful" (3:12). He begs them to confess and repent. He wants to give them a home in Zion where they'll "no more say, 'The ark of the covenant of the LORD.' It shall not come to mind or be remembered or missed; it shall not be made again. At that time Jerusalem shall be called the throne of the LORD, and all nations shall gather to it, to the presence of the LORD in Jerusalem" (3:16–17).

What does this mean? The ark serves as the earthly throne where the especially dense presence of God came to dwell in the Most Holy Place. At some point—we don't know when or how or why—the ark went missing. Apparently, the people either currently are or will be distraught that it's missing, but Jeremiah says they'll get over it because they'll have something much better—the whole city of Jerusalem will serve as God's throne. His manifest presence won't be in a room most of us can never access. God insists on dwelling with His people, and nothing can stop Him!

TODAY'S GOD SHOT

According to 1:4–5, God not only created Jeremiah in the womb, but He also knew him and set him apart before he was created. God had already planned Jeremiah's future before he existed. Is Jeremiah special? Is this kind of thing specific to major prophets but not the rest of us? If we follow the thread of Scripture, we see this theme running through the whole book. Not a single one of us is an afterthought to God! He has a plan for each of us—to use us for His glory and our joy. And He's where the joy is!

JEREMIAH 4–6

Jeremiah pleads with Judah and Israel to repent. They've faked repentance before, but God makes it clear He's after their hearts. He compares this heart change to the way He marked them with circumcision: "Remove the foreskin of your hearts. . . . O Jerusalem, wash your heart from evil. . . . How long shall your wicked thoughts lodge within you? . . . Your ways and your deeds have brought this upon you. This is your doom, and it is bitter; it has reached your very heart" (4:4, 14, 18). God's problem with their sin goes far beyond their actions—it goes to their very hearts. So His consequences do too.

In 4:10, Jeremiah seems to accuse God of lying. It's a confusing time to be alive because up until this point, so-called prophets have been telling the Judahites that things will be fine; they've proclaimed "peace and safety," though things are actually speeding toward destruction. This is the first time Jeremiah is hearing the truth, and it's coming directly from God Himself. He's disoriented by it all but eventually realizes those prophets weren't speaking the words of God—they were just saying what people wanted to hear. As he warns the people, he gets some disturbing visions of the destruction Jerusalem will encounter. He can hardly sleep at night because it's so disheartening. Next, God has harsh words for His people: They're fools, and the only kind of wisdom they possess is the kind used for being crafty in sin.

Then Jeremiah has a vision of the undoing of creation, the reversing of all God's work in the Genesis 1 account. But God promises not to annihilate the earth. It'll still be there, just *emptied*. Jerusalem, portrayed as a desperate woman, tries in vain to save herself, but God says it won't be possible. In chapter 5, the struggle continues. The Jerusalemites are pros at offering up religious phrases and actions—taking oaths in God's name and such—but they don't keep their promises. Religious language can come from a corrupt heart.

Jeremiah thinks, *Maybe this is because they're poor and they can't afford to keep their oaths. Or maybe they just aren't educated enough to know better.* But then he finds that the same problem exists with the rich. They're *all* rebelling. God says nothing they have will be safe from His destruction—not their income, food, drink, family, or sense of security. Nothing is untouchable. Everything can be shaken or taken. But again, this is all the consequence of their sin. He says, "Your sins have kept good from you" (5:25). Sin is a thief—it steals good things from you. Not only does their sin keep good things from them, but it keeps good things from the poor too. The rich have gotten rich off their selfishness, and it turns into a total lack of concern for the poor. They lead and govern with injustice. But God will punish this too because a righteous judge has to punish sin.

Chapter 6 foretells the downfall: Jerusalem will be destroyed, the prophets will offer false comfort, and the people will refuse to repent and will have a complete lack of understanding that what they're doing is wrong. God pleads with them to remember the ancient paths of their forefathers—to turn back to the ways He has already marked out for them. But they refuse to listen.

TODAY'S GOD SHOT

God chose Jeremiah to beg His people to repent, knowing full well they wouldn't. Jeremiah endures sleepless nights and anguish and deep mourning to communicate this message to God's people—and he isn't the only one! We've read a few other prophets who are sent to the same people with the same message. What does it reveal about God's heart that He keeps sending this message, decade after decade, begging them to repent? We see His patience and His persistence. We also see His advance planning—He knew they wouldn't repent. He knew the day was coming when He'd exile them, and He also knew the day was coming when Jesus would claim victory over all the sins of His people: past, present, and future. Jeremiah and the prophets endured a lot, but not nearly as much as God the Father and God the Son endured in order to bring about the restoration of all things and to unite us with Him. He's where the joy is!

JEREMIAH 7–9

Today opens with Jeremiah prophesying to the people of Judah while standing outside the entrance of the temple, which is why chapter 7 is referred to as his temple sermon. The people have come to worship the God inside the temple, but outside the temple walls, they're sacrificing to idols and false gods, as though God isn't also outside the temple and can't see through walls. Apparently, the people treat the temple like a protective icon. Verse 4 shows them repeating a phrase like an incantation—it appears as though they're worshipping the temple itself, instead of the God in the temple. God rebukes them for it. They seem to think they've been protected from the Assyrian attack because they have the temple in the south, unlike the Israelites in the north. They've made an idol of the temple.

In addition to that, God says they're breaking nearly all the commandments—committing theft, murder, and adultery and lying and worshipping other gods. They're making His house into a house of robbers. You might recognize this verse because Jesus quotes it in Matthew 21:13 when the people of His day are doing a similar thing to oppress the poor and steal from people. God drills down to the heart of things. He calls them to change the way they treat others and Him. He promises to bless them if they do and cast them out if they don't.

What will they do? We get a hint based on what God says to Jeremiah after that. He tells him not to pray for the people. Prophets often intercede on behalf of the people, but here God says, "Don't waste your breath—it's too late. Talk to them about Me, but don't talk to Me about them." God's assignment to Jeremiah—to rebuke the people—is one that will fail to produce repentance, but that will still achieve God's plans. We've seen this before with other prophets. The people have trusted in their own minds, walked in their own counsel, and done what their stubborn hearts wanted instead of surrendering to God and His Word, and as a result, they moved backward in their walks with Him, not forward.

In chapter 8, God continues to speak out against their autonomy: "Everyone turns to his own course" (v. 6). Autonomy is idolatry—it's looking to ourselves for guidance instead of to God and His Word. But true wisdom and humility come from receiving the Word, and verse 9 points to this: "Behold, they have rejected the word of the LORD, so what wisdom is in them?" Even the scribes and wise men of that day will be exposed as fools and liars. They had access to His Word and disregarded it. The consequences of their sins are so harsh that some will prefer to die instead of live. And while God's methods may seem harsh, they're always righteous.

Jeremiah is heartbroken over all of this. When it comes to sin, we should be angry at our own and heartbroken over others'. How easy is it to look at the sins others commit and feel disgusted as though we aren't sinners too—and it's arrogant. So Jeremiah's response is fitting. He stays humble. He aches over Judah's actions. And God makes it clear that He's heartbroken too, because He continues to point out that He wants their hearts, not their begrudging obedience. Besides, the only kind of obedience that is complete and true is obedience that flows from a heart of love. But if all they are is circumcised in the flesh, they're no better than the pagan nations who don't even know Him. He wants transformation at a heart level.

TODAY'S GOD SHOT

We saw a lot of judgment in these three chapters. It's easy to skim over these lines and determine that God is harsh and unforgiving. But here's what He says about Himself in 9:24: "Let him who boasts boast in this, that he understands and knows me, that I am the LORD who practices steadfast love, justice, and righteousness in the earth. For in these things I delight." God leads with love. He delights in love, justice, and righteousness. He's always acting out of His motives—to display love, justice, and righteousness on the earth. God not only *does* what He loves, but He *is* what He loves. And there's nothing better to do or be. He's where the joy is!

JEREMIAH 10–13

Jeremiah exposes Judah's idols for what they really are: trees God made, cut down by a human God made, covered in gold God made. They can't hear or speak or move. Those blocks of wood alone can't do good *or* evil. They're completely impotent. Unless—and this is something the text doesn't quite dig into here—an evil spirit attaches itself to the object. This is what the people want to happen, although they aren't aware they're seeking evil spirits; they think they're just forces of power. In order to summon these forces, they do incantations, cut themselves, and perform magic and rituals. They want these forces to indwell the things they've just made. They worship idols in hopes of gaining safety, power, and happiness. Those are all good things, but when they take precedence in our hearts and thoughts, they take our eyes off YHWH. When our good desires become ultimate, when they become expectations and requirements, we're on the same path as Judah.

Jeremiah speaks on behalf of Jerusalem in 10:19–21, saying the leaders aren't seeking and following God. They're following their own hearts and impulses, and as a result, the people are scattered. Then Jeremiah prays as Jerusalem in verse 25, begging God to bring judgment on the pagan nations but not on Judah. Yesterday God commanded Jeremiah not to pray for Judah, so this seems to be his attempt to find a loophole—he's not praying for them, he's praying as them. In chapter 11, God says that's not okay either—Jeremiah isn't supposed to pray for them or as them.

Jeremiah talks to God about how he's suffering because of these prophecies. The people of his hometown don't like his words, and they've made a threat on his life. God says Jeremiah doesn't need to worry about those men or their threats, because He'll handle them. Jeremiah tells God he's really confused by His actions. He knows God is righteous and that they both want the wicked and the religious hypocrites to be punished, but God doesn't seem to be doing anything about it. In fact, the wicked seem to be thriving. God says, "It's worse than you think, and it's about to get even worse." God never promised Jeremiah an easy life. He just promised to be with him. And now Jeremiah is living in that reality: He's talking to the living God while all his family and friends betray him. God is with him, even if no one else is.

This hasn't been painless for God either—handing His people over to the consequences of their sins. Even as they're taken into exile, He keeps a watchful eye on them and He'll punish anyone who hurts them. He has a plan to bring them back into this land eventually. He also reminds us of His merciful promise to pardon any foreigners whose hearts turn to worship Him and include them in His family: "If they will diligently learn the ways of my people, to swear by my name, 'As the Lord lives,' even as they taught my people to swear by Baal, then they shall be built up in the midst of my people" (12:16).

Chapter 13 gives us a bit of prophecy theater: God has Jeremiah buy a linen loincloth, put it on, bury it, then dig it up. God says he'll treat Judah's pride this way, ruining it. The chapter closes with prophecies of death, destruction, and exile and reminders that God's plan prevails.

TODAY'S GOD SHOT

God is with us in every moment—not just in destinations and arrivals, but in steps. "I know, O Lord, that the way of man is not in himself, that it is not in man who walks to direct his steps" (10:23). And when God speaks about the covenant He made with His people, He says, "Listen to my voice and do all that I command you" (11:4). This is still the best advice: Listen to God. Do what He says. That very statement reveals that He is attentive, speaking, giving direction. He cares. He's not removed from you and your life—He's there to help you and guide you. You are not on your own! It's easy to feel lonely and confused and like we're on the verge of ruining our lives with one decision. But God says, "I'm here. Talk to Me. I know exactly what's next for you." While you're anxiously trying to decide which home to move to, He already knows where you'll keep your paper towels. He listens. He guides. He's with you. And He's where the joy is!

JEREMIAH 14–17

Judah is in a drought as part of their judgment. They cry to God for help, but they're not aiming for repentance, they're aiming for relief. While the prayer is beautiful, most scholars think it's actually Jeremiah praying on their behalf again, because we've seen no signs of repentance from them and God follows up by reminding Jeremiah *again* not to pray for them.

Regardless of who is praying, God's answer is no. His plan is to deliver them over to sword, famine, and pestilence. Jeremiah defends the people, perhaps thinking they've been misled by prophets who promised them no consequences. But even if they were misled, they're still guilty of idolatry, oppressing the poor, and slaughtering their kids. God makes it clear that those prophets are not *His* prophets. They're either making things up or saying things they've heard from demons, so God will devour them with the very things they say won't happen. God grieves over this.

Then either Jeremiah or Judah offers up another prayer on Judah's behalf. One reason to think it's Jeremiah praying is that, as a prophet, he's a mediator, so it's natural for him to continue pleading with God, hoping God will relent. On the other hand, one reason to think it's Judah praying is that they get one thing very wrong when the prayer says, "Do not break your covenant with us" (14:21). God isn't the one who breaks the covenant—they break it; but it would be just like Judah to blame God. To this prayer, God says, "Even if Moses and Samuel asked Me to spare these people the destruction, I'd still say no." Destruction is coming. And of the four possible outcomes—famine, sword, pestilence, exile—He has already determined the specific end for each person.

When it starts to feel like God's being harsh, it's wise to zoom out and remember exactly what has happened. In isolation, His response seems extreme. But in the overall story, He's given them everything, and they're not just worshipping idols—they're sacrificing their children to those idols! God does act severely, but He always acts justly. Jeremiah is struggling with this too. He thinks God is being too harsh, not just on the people but on him. He loves YHWH and His Word and he's willing to endure a lonely life to be used by God, but it's hard. Not only does everyone hate him for speaking the truth, but he knows these trials he's warning people about are coming for him too. It feels like too much to endure.

God responds with a bit of a rebuke but also a promise that He'll be with Jeremiah and strengthen him: "I will deliver you out of the hand of the wicked, and redeem you from the grasp of the ruthless" (15:21). That means they will have a grip on him at some point. God's people are never promised we'll be spared from trials, but we're always promised that we're not alone in them. But God is the only real companion Jeremiah will have. God forbids him to marry or have kids—not because He's cruel, but because He doesn't want any hypothetical family members to suffer. He also says no one should mourn over those who die in Judah. Their deaths are the result of their wickedness. But since they've paid no attention to God and His covenant, they won't know why He's doing this. They'll accuse Him of being unfair. But after all this, God will bring back a remnant. He'll send people to gather them and bring them home. They'll repent and fully know who God is. Finally!

Chapter 17 highlights two kinds of people. One is the man who trusts in man and doesn't rely on God—his soul will be parched. He's a fool because his heart can't be trusted. But the man who trusts in God—his soul flourishes even in a drought.

TODAY'S GOD SHOT

God calls His people to rest. What kind of God makes resting an act of worship? That's incredible! People tend to view God as an angry taskmaster, making demands on His people nonstop. While God does call us to work hard, He also knows our souls desperately need to reconnect with Him, which doesn't happen easily in chaos. Sabbath gives us space for intimacy with Him, time to slow down and fix our eyes on Him. What a gift it is that He wants to spend time with us, because He's where the joy is!

JEREMIAH 18–22

God sends Jeremiah to see a potter making jars. When one goes askew, he reshapes it into something new. Same lump of clay, different outcome. God says, "I'm the potter. The people are clay. I can do whatever I want with them. Because of Jerusalem's evil, My plan for them involves disaster. Call them to repent, but know that they won't. They'll do whatever they want, make their own plans, and follow their own hearts. They've forgotten Me." You can almost hear the heartache in God's voice when He says that last part. This image is potent. The potter is obviously engaged with the clay. This isn't a computerized assembly line—it's hands-on, creative work, much like how God formed man out of the dust of the earth, then breathed life into him (Genesis 2:7). God has always been involved with humanity in ways that are unlike His involvement with everything else He made. We're made with His hands, not His commands. We're made in His likeness, unlike His other creations. We are indeed the Potter's clay.

After this, the people plot against Jeremiah again, and he's finally had enough. He's been so compassionate toward them, pleading their case even when God told him to be quiet, but he's reached his breaking point. He's been resisting God's plan and doesn't get on board with it until the people oppose *him*. His heart has finally turned to desire the things God promised: famine, sword, and pestilence.

God has him perform some theater, telling him to buy a clay flask and smash it in front of the elders and priests, symbolizing how God will break this people in a way that they can't be mended. This is an important time to remember something about God's people: God has called Israel and Judah His people, but Scripture says repeatedly that God's people are made up of people from every nation—anyone whose heart turns to follow Him, including foreigners like Rahab and Ruth. And as far as natural-born Israelites, God says being born into the lineage of Abraham doesn't mean they're His kids, because His family is made up of people with new hearts, not just circumcised flesh. So technically, God's people, whom He calls Israel, includes some people who aren't biological Israelites and doesn't include some people who are. It all comes down to their hearts. His plan is to preserve those among Judah who do love Him—the remnant—and judge those who don't. And truly, only God knows hearts, so He can be trusted to make this kind of delineation.

After Jeremiah destroys the flask, a wicked priest beats him and puts him in stocks overnight. Jeremiah is obeying God and getting tortured for it. When the priest releases him, Jeremiah laments to God again: "O Lord, you have deceived me" (20:7). This is another example of why we can't take Scripture out of context. We know God didn't deceive Jeremiah. He's devastated by how things are going, but God has said all along that this won't be easy and people will reject his message. As much as Jeremiah hates his calling, he can't keep quiet. He wishes he'd never been born, but we know God had a plan for his life because we're reading his book.

King Zedekiah asks Jeremiah if they'll be spared when Babylon invades. Jeremiah says no and that the only way to survive is to surrender. Then God also says, "Stop oppressing the poor, orphans, and widows. Do justice and righteousness. That's your job. If you do, I'll let your kingdom survive. But if not, you're done."

TODAY'S GOD SHOT

"Do justice and righteousness, and deliver from the hand of the oppressor him who has been robbed. And do no wrong or violence to the resident alien, the fatherless, and the widow, nor shed innocent blood in this place" (22:3). Verses 15–16 echo these ideas and include a bold statement: "Did not your father eat and drink and do justice and righteousness? Then it was well with him. He judged the cause of the poor and needy: then it was well. Is not this to know me? declares the Lord." God says to know Him is to do what He says. Jesus reiterates this in John 14:15. Our deepest intimacy with God is found in obedience. Obeying God is where the joy is, because obeying God is where we connect with God on the deepest level. And He's where the joy is!

JEREMIAH 23–25

Jeremiah opens today with God rebuking Judah's leaders, and He seems to contradict Himself. Verse 2 says the leaders have scattered the people and driven them away, but in verse 3 God says, "I will gather the remnant of my flock out of all the countries where I have driven them." So who did the scattering and driving away—Judah's leaders or God? This is where scholars would answer, "Yes." The leaders are the active agent, but God uses their wicked actions in His good and righteous overarching plan. He'll bring His sheep back to the land, and He says, "They shall fear no more, nor be dismayed, neither shall any be missing." Fearlessness is a trait of God's sheep because He's proven Himself to be a good shepherd.

God promises to raise up a righteous king from the line of David—a prophecy of Christ. And when that new King reigns on earth, His people will have new things to praise Him for that will wildly surpass what they used to praise Him for. In the meantime, God is judging Judah. The sins of Judah and its capital, Jerusalem, are worse than the sins of Israel and its capital, Samaria, because Samaria and Israel prophesied by Baal, but the people of Jerusalem *pretended* to prophesy by YHWH and were lying, all the while worshipping false gods and oppressing the poor. The Judahites had access to the temple, the Levites, the scrolls—and they still disobeyed. They have a higher level of accountability and responsibility because of what they knew and had access to.

The false prophets speak good news from God-given dreams, but it's all made up. God says His Word is more powerful than a dream anyway, and if their dreams don't align with His Word, they're false. But they don't listen to His Word, so how can they speak it? How can they know if their dreams align? They're leading God's people astray and doubting Him, but He's watching their every move.

Jeremiah 23:33–40 is a play on words in Hebrew. The Hebrew word *massa* has two meanings, "message" and "burden." Here Jeremiah says, "If anyone asks you what the massa [message] of God is, tell them that *you* are the massa [burden]." It's a highbrow insult. God is so frustrated with their lies that He forbids the use of the word *massa*. He says, "I'll punish anyone who says they have the massa [message]. The only thing you're allowed to say is 'What has God already said about this?'" He tears it down to the studs: "If you really want to know what God is saying, pay attention to what God has already said." Or as one modern pastor says, "If you want to hear God speak, read your Bible out loud."

In this time, the words *Chaldean* and *Babylonian* are used interchangeably. Babylon's King Nebuchadnezzar—we'll call him King Nebby—takes Judah's prince and leaders captive. When Zedekiah becomes king, Jeremiah has a vision of two fig baskets in front of the temple—one very good and one very bad. The good figs are the remnant God will return to the land postexile. He'll give them a heart to know Him, and they'll be His people. The bad figs are Judah's wicked leaders; He'll send judgment on them: sword, famine, and pestilence.

Jeremiah tells them, "I've been begging you to repent for twenty-three years, but nothing has changed. I'm not the only one God sent to warn you, but you haven't listened to any of us. Because of this, God is about to drop the hammer. And the hammer's name is King Nebby. He's going to be your least favorite person for the next seventy years, because that's how long you'll be in captivity, if you survive. After seventy years pass, God will punish Babylon." God will pour out wrath across all the nations for their sins. His wrath is depicted like a cup of wine, which all His enemies will drink.

TODAY'S GOD SHOT

God promises to raise up a new king named "The LORD is our righteousness" (23:6). This is a *huge* promise. The Judahites certainly aren't righteous on their own. Neither are we. We need someone else to be righteousness for us. Jesus! He's the LORD—God the Son—and He grants us His righteousness. Even here in the Old Testament, Jesus is marked as God and King and Savior. We have no righteousness of our own, but our God-King-Savior came down and gave us His. He's where the joy is!

JEREMIAH 26–29

Jeremiah has three run-ins with local leadership. First, God sends him to prophesy to people entering the temple. This may be the same story from chapter 7 repeated. If so, we get a few more details in this version of events. He's arrested and accused of treason and false prophecy, offenses against political *and* religious groups. The penalty for a false prophet is death, and they want him dead. It's worth noting that their charge against him leaves out the part where God says He'll relent if they repent. Either his accusers didn't listen closely, or they tweaked his words in order to falsely accuse him. When confronted with their accusations, he clarifies the rebuke they've misquoted but does it with humble confidence, submitted to their authority. He trusts God regardless of the outcome. After hearing his side of the story, they acquit him. They still want to kill him, but Ahikam the son of Shaphan spares his life.

Jeremiah's scribe, Baruch, who wrote this book, doesn't always order the stories chronologically, so as far as we can tell, the rest of today's reading happens after Babylon invades Judah. Jeremiah meets with the kings of five other nations, and God has him do some prophecy theater, telling him to wear a yoke—the piece of wood that goes behind an animal's neck so it can pull a plow. This image displays how God will make the nations submit to Babylon and King Nebby. Some of the nations are plotting a revolt, having been emboldened by the false prophets, but God says it won't happen. God is using Nebby to serve His purposes. He's not a follower of YHWH, but he's still a servant of YHWH. Jeremiah says Judah has to submit to Babylon too, and Babylon will take all the temple furniture, but God will bring it back to Jerusalem when He's ready.

Jeremiah's third confrontation is with the prophet Hananiah, who claims to be a prophet of YHWH. In front of everyone, Hananiah contradicts some of Jeremiah's prophecies: "That yoke we're supposed to wear? God has broken it. Babylon's not in charge of us anymore! Within

For more information on today's reading, see thebiblerecap.com/links.

two years, God will bring back the temple furniture, exiles, and captives." Jeremiah says, "That sounds great! Since we know all prophecies from God come true, let's wait two years and see what happens." This may be humble hopefulness on Jeremiah's part, but it could also be a subtle rebuke. He knows time will expose false prophecies. Then Hananiah walks over to Jeremiah and breaks the yoke he's wearing. Later, God gives Jeremiah a twofold message for Hananiah. First, that metaphorical yoke of wood on the necks of the nations has been replaced with a yoke of iron. Hananiah's lies led to greater oppression for the people. Second, Hananiah's consequence for being a false prophet is that God will enact the death penalty on him.

Chapter 29 recounts Jeremiah's words to the exiles in Babylon: "You'll be in exile for seventy years, so in the meantime make the most of where God has put you. Build houses, plant gardens, and raise families. Try to improve the lives of the people around you. Try to bless the very city that has taken you captive. It won't just be good for them, it'll be good for you too. And don't listen to any of the prophets around you—they're liars. You're not coming home early. God has a plan, and it's a good one, but it's going to take seventy years. Then He'll bring you back here and restore everything."

But anyone who doesn't listen to God's warnings and doesn't go into exile will be punished with sword, famine, and pestilence. The exiles are the remnant, the ones He's preserving. Then God directly addresses and punishes a false prophet named Shemaiah who shamed and contradicted Jeremiah.

TODAY'S GOD SHOT

Every time Jeremiah receives a false accusation, God protects him. From death threats to yoke breakers to Shemaiah the shamer, God keeps proving Himself. All Jeremiah has to do is stand firm on God's word. He doesn't need a clever argument, and he doesn't have to miraculously fuse the broken yoke back together. He just has to trust God in the place where God put him, which is what he tells the exiles to do too. That's so much easier to do when we know the God who knows—that's what God calls Himself in 29:23: "I am the one who knows." He's with you. He knows. And He's where the joy is!

JEREMIAH 30–31

Today is filled with reminders of God's plan for Israel and Judah. Here are all the things He says He'll do for them in chapter 30: "I will restore the fortunes of My people, I will bring them back to the land, I will break his yoke from off your neck, I will burst your bonds, I will raise up a King, I will save you, I am with you, I will make a full end of all the opposing nations, I will discipline you in just measure, I will not leave you unpunished, I have dealt you the blow of an enemy, I have done these things to you, I will make your predators into prey, I will restore health to you, I will heal your wounds, I will restore Jacob's fortunes, I will have compassion, I will multiply them, I will make them honored, I will punish their oppressors, I will make them draw near, I will be your God."

On the surface, some of this may sound cruel. But this process is necessary in order for the scales to fall from their eyes and their hearts to be softened. God is wounding them, but all His wounds are ways to heal. He can be trusted. Trials are formative—they build character, teach us what's important, and hopefully shape us into people who are more humble, less entitled, more compassionate, less impatient, and ultimately more like God. At this point, they're bound to Babylon, but He'll break their yokes eventually. And when they're set free, they'll turn to serve Him instead. True freedom isn't doing whatever they want—that's what got them in this place to begin with—true freedom is serving God instead of our oppressors or ourselves.

God promises to restore people from among all the tribes of Israel and Judah, not just people from the kingdom of Judah. Sometimes He states this outright; other times He hints at it when He refers to them as *Jacob*, the collective term for all the tribes. All along this journey, He's protecting them. Even as He drives them out of their land, they not only survive the sword but they "found grace in the wilderness" (31:2). He gave them rest, appeared to them, and reminded them of His everlasting love and promise of restoration. When the time comes for them to return, He really wants them to do it. If they refuse and stay in the place of their exile, that will reveal that they don't believe His promise of restoration. So He reiterates this promise over and over, in case they're tempted to doubt Him. He promises the everlasting covenant through which He'll write the law on their hearts. Since their hearts have been the problem all along, His plan involves getting to the root and addressing the real issue. Then they'll *know* Him. This all points to Christ's death on the cross and the indwelling of the Holy Spirit. That's when heart change happens—when God gives us a new heart and His Spirit comes to live in us forever. Without new hearts, we're stuck trying to modify our behavior and be "good people," which leaves us exhausted, disappointed, arrogant, and fearful. But the work of His Spirit in us is a different thing altogether. He brings us peace!

Chapter 31 seems to give prophecies in chronological order: God will be with them in exile, He'll bring them back to the land and restore their fortunes, the new covenant will come to fruition (with the coming of Jesus and the indwelling of the Holy Spirit), and Jerusalem will never be uprooted again. The reason most scholars think this is still a future prophecy is because, at this point, Jerusalem *is* uprooted again. Jesus even prophesies about that uprooting, which happens in AD 70. The last few verses seem to point to a future Jerusalem, a final Jerusalem (Revelation 3:12; 21:2). It sounds like a place where the new heaven and the new earth are finally joined together to create the new Jerusalem as heaven *on* earth.

TODAY'S GOD SHOT

"They shall be radiant over the goodness of the LORD" (31:12). This doesn't just say, "They'll be radiant." The point isn't that they'll look beautiful or be happy. The point has to do with *why* they are radiant. It's because of God's goodness. He's the source of their radiance! "My people shall be satisfied with my goodness, declares the LORD" (31:14). His goodness apart from any other gift is all-satisfying. Just Him. May we always be radiant and be satisfied because we have Him and He's where the joy is!

JEREMIAH 32–34

Jeremiah is in prison when we open today's reading. Judah's King Zedekiah didn't like his prophecies, so he's punishing him. God tells Jeremiah that his cousin will try to sell him some land, and when his cousin shows up with a deed, Jeremiah follows through. The fact that Jeremiah has money while in prison indicates that he's pretty wealthy. This is noteworthy because he's been coming down pretty hard on the rich in his prophecies. So is he a hypocrite? No. His problem with the rich isn't with what's in their bank accounts; it's with what's in their hearts. They're oppressing people in order to get and stay rich.

Jeremiah buys the field and stores the proof, since it'll be seventy years before he needs it. He really believes God will bring them back to the land. So this isn't a financial investment; it's an act of faith. But even Jeremiah is still human, because immediately after this he says, "God, I know nothing is too hard for You. You've done everything You've promised. But I'm struggling with this field purchase. The Babylonians are already in the land I just paid for." He takes his questions and doubts to God. God knows them anyway; He can be trusted to speak truth to our fears and our questions. God patiently reminds Jeremiah that the presence of the Babylonians is all part of His process, as if He hasn't said it a thousand times already. And as if Jeremiah hasn't said it himself! But we all need to keep circling back to the truth. One of the big problems with Israel and Judah is that they don't do that. We need to remember the gospel of Jesus regularly—to speak it to others and have them speak it to us. So after Jeremiah tells God who God is, God tells Jeremiah who God is. He's the God who will gather His people back to this land and restore their fortunes. He's not just sovereign over wars and lands, He's sovereign over hearts. He says, "I will put the fear of me in their hearts" (32:40). The good fear, the mix of awe and delight, the kind of thing

For more information on today's reading, see thebiblerecap.com/links.

that draws us *to* Him—He grants that! Not only that, but He rejoices in doing good to His people.

God reminds Jeremiah that someday Jerusalem will have a righteous King and priests—things they haven't had in a long time. We already know Jesus is the King this passage refers to, but if you're a part of a faith tradition that doesn't have priests, that part may feel odd. Here's something that may make it less strange: According to 1 Peter 2:5–9, *you* are a priest if you're a child of God. This doctrine is called the priesthood of believers.

In chapter 34, we flash back to the conversation Jeremiah had with Zedekiah that landed him in prison. For context, we need to recall the rules God established about slavery: Israelites can only be indentured servants to pay off debt, and only for seven years, then they have to be set free. Apparently that seven-year clause was being ignored, which isn't surprising given all the injustice. One day, when Babylon has the area under siege, Zedekiah frees all the slaves. We don't know his motives behind this act—maybe he does it because he needs more free men to serve as warriors, or maybe he does it to try to appease God. Regardless, the slave owners set their slaves free but enslave them again as soon as the siege lifts. God isn't okay with that. It makes a mockery of His character. He's the God who set them free. And since they don't truly grasp that, He promises judgment.

TODAY'S GOD SHOT

"I will fulfill the promise I made to the house of Israel and the house of Judah. . . . I will cause a righteous Branch to spring up for David, and he shall execute justice and righteousness in the land. . . . And this is the name by which it will be called: 'The Lord is our righteousness'" (33:14–16). We may be tempted to think of righteousness and good deeds as things we bring to God as a peace offering—"Look at all the good stuff I did" or "I promise, I'll do better next time. Please don't be mad at me." But the problem is, we have no righteousness to give Him. None. As it turns out, righteousness isn't something we present to God, it's something *He* presents to *us*. He is our righteousness, granted to us for free. And He's where the joy is!

JEREMIAH 35–37

Much of the rest of the book of Jeremiah will take us back and forth in the timeline, but it's all purposeful. For instance, yesterday ended with Judah's unfaithfulness. Today we open with the strict obedience of the Rechabites. Scholars think God intended to highlight the contrast between the two, so He had Baruch put the stories side by side. The Rechabites are nomads, and even though they're not genetically a part of the Israelites, they've lived alongside them for a long time and some seem to be followers of YHWH.

God has Jeremiah invite them to the temple and offer them wine, but they refuse because one of their ancestors commanded their family to avoid alcohol. They've honored his command for over two hundred years. Their heritage of obedience puts Israel's to shame. God highlights this to both groups, telling the Israelites they'll be punished for rebelling and telling the Rechabites He'll preserve a remnant from among them too because of their faithful obedience. Some "insiders" are cut off, and some "outsiders" are welcomed in—this is a theme in God's kingdom.

God has Jeremiah write down everything He's said—twenty-two years' worth of details. He wants the people to hear it all, but it seems Jeremiah has been banned from going to the temple, probably because of the sermon he preached in chapter 7, so he sends Baruch on the mission. Word gets out about what's happening, and the officials send for Baruch and his scroll, because they want to hear it for themselves. When he reads it to them, they're aghast. They seem to believe the prophecies and warnings. They want to tell the king but fear he won't respond positively; they tell Baruch and Jeremiah to go into hiding, because this likely won't go over well. And they're right.

When the king hears the scroll's words, he cuts it into pieces and burns it. A popular belief of the time is that words have power to make things happen. So the king isn't just being unrepentant, he's also trying to play God by destroying the words in hopes that will prevent the disaster. Some of his officials try unsuccessfully to get him to pay attention. He sends people to find Jeremiah and Baruch, but God hides them. Then God has Jeremiah start writing all over again. This time he expands the scroll by adding a few new things—including the story we just read. Then He promises to bring judgment on the king, including that he won't have a son to succeed him. God fulfills that promise by having Babylon's king appoint Zedekiah as Judah's new king.

Around this time, Babylon has besieged Jerusalem, but then Egypt's army shows up on the scene, so the Babylonians back off a bit. This seems like a good thing in the king's eyes. He sends some guys to ask Jeremiah to pray, but Jeremiah sends bad news: This is only a temporary reprieve, and Babylon will kick things back into high gear again soon. While all this is happening, Jeremiah decides to take a road trip, but a soldier assumes he's trying to join the Babylonians in their fight against Jerusalem. Jeremiah tries to explain, but no one believes him. They beat him and throw him into prison over motives they've misunderstood. Still, he persists in following and submitting to God. The king secretly sends for Jeremiah occasionally, seeking wisdom and insight. Jeremiah always delivers the truth humbly. In fact, his posture brings him favor with the king, who moves him to a better prison and feeds him even during a local famine.

TODAY'S GOD SHOT

God vigilantly preserves His Word. He wants people to hear what He has to say. He wants to be known. Nothing can thwart His efforts to communicate with humankind. Not only has He been repeating the same words to the people over and over, but He also has Jeremiah write the scroll again after it's destroyed. "Heaven and earth will pass away, but my words will not pass away" (Mark 13:31). The building you live in will someday be rubble. The car you drive will eventually stop running. But the words you spent time reading today, the God you're investing in knowing, He and His Word are forever. You're investing in something eternal! You're building something that will last. And He's not just eternal—He's where the joy is!

JEREMIAH 38–40; PSALMS 74, 79

Jeremiah is still preaching repentance to Judah, and his warning still lands on people as though it's a pro-Babylon message. The local officials think his prophecies are bad for morale and want him killed. It seems to be the only way to silence him. King Zedekiah, who has an amicable relationship with Jeremiah, realizes he can't stop them from taking action, and he's probably afraid of what they might do to him if he tries to oppose them. The officials throw Jeremiah into a cistern, a place for underground water storage, but Jerusalem has been under siege and is near the end of their water supply, so this cistern is empty. Cisterns can be 120 feet deep, but most average 20 feet—that's a two-story building. The opening at the top is usually two feet wide, and the walls are often coated with plaster. These details make it clear that this situation is designed to kill Jeremiah. This isn't prison. There's no way he can climb up smooth plaster walls for two stories to escape. In fact, he sinks into the muddy bottom of the cistern. This is a desperate situation, but back in 1:19, God promised him, "They will fight against you, but they shall not prevail against you, for I am with you, declares the Lord, to deliver you."

This time God delivers Jeremiah by bringing his situation to the attention of an Ethiopian eunuch who lives in the king's house. The Ethiopian asks for permission to rescue him, and Zedekiah approves. After his rescue, the king summons him, and they both bring their fears to the table. Jeremiah fears more punishment, and the king fears everything Jeremiah has ever told him. Despite his fears and all he's been through, Jeremiah's directions to the king remain unchanged. "Surrender to Babylon," he says. But the king is afraid of being punished by his people if he does that. He tells Jeremiah how to respond when people ask about their conversation later, feeding him lines from a prior conversation they had. Jeremiah responds accordingly. It's a bit of a technical loophole since they did have that conversation at one point. It's definitely misleading, but God doesn't seem to punish him for it, perhaps because a human life is at stake.

After one and a half years of being under siege, Jerusalem falls to Babylon in 586 BC. It all happens just like God promised, including Zedekiah's capture and punishment. The Babylonians cart the rest of the people into exile, except a few of the poor who pose no threat. Then King Nebby of Babylon tells his people to get Jeremiah. As far as Nebby is concerned, Jeremiah seems to be on his side, because he kept telling Zedekiah to surrender to him. So he says to take good care of Jeremiah and do whatever he says. God gives Jeremiah a word for the Ethiopian who saved his life: God will spare him because he demonstrated faith in God. Once again, the outsider is welcomed into God's family.

In chapter 40, it seems Jeremiah is accidentally taken captive with the exiles. The captain gives him two options: go to Babylon with him or stay in Judah and live with Governor Gedaliah, the guy Nebby appointed to run things. Jeremiah stays in Judah with Gedaliah. When word gets out that Gedaliah's governing Judah, many people who fled to the country come back because life isn't so bad there by now. Meanwhile, military leaders warn Gedaliah that one of his supporters is plotting his death, but Gedaliah dismisses it as a lie.

Psalms 74 and 79 are perfectly suited to what's happening in Judah. In Psalm 79, the psalmist holds the people of Jacob responsible for breaking the covenant. This is the consequence they were promised. But the psalmist begs for mercy and relief, appealing to God on the basis of His name and His power.

TODAY'S GOD SHOT

"Deliver us, and atone for our sins, for your name's sake!" (Psalm 79:9). This plea is answered with a yes when Christ dies for the sins of God's people—past, present, and future. His death covers the sins of Asaph the psalmist and the remnant among Judah. For God's glory, He adopted sinners into His family, showing Himself merciful and gracious and generous. He's our Deliverer, and He's where the joy is!

2 KINGS 24–25; 2 CHRONICLES 36

Today we read about the last five kings of Judah; they're often lumped together because they're the final turning point for Judah. After Josiah dies, his son Jehoahaz takes the throne. He's barely a blip on the radar because he only reigns for three months before the Egyptian Pharaoh Neco, who killed his dad, captures him and carts him off to Egypt, where he dies in captivity. Now we're down to three remaining kings.

At the time, Egypt is dominating Judah. Pharaoh Neco appoints their new king and even changes his name from Eliakim to Jehoiakim. Then Neco demands that Judah act as a vassal nation to Egypt—the arrangement where a weaker nation pays money, or tribute, to a stronger nation for protection, but they're often just being protected from the nation they're paying. But then Babylon shows up on the scene and dominates both Judah and Egypt, and Egypt goes home with its tail between its legs. Then Judah becomes a vassal of Babylon, but at some point they rebel and Babylon turns up the heat. They take Jehoiakim captive, along with many of the holy vessels from the temple. And now we're down to two more kings.

Next on deck is Jehoia*kim*'s son, Jehoia*chin*. After Kim dies, Chin is only on the throne for three months before Babylon comes to besiege Jerusalem. He decides to surrender to Babylon, so they make him a prisoner and also take the opportunity to destroy a bunch of his stuff as well as some of the temple vessels. Remember in 2 Kings 20:16–17 when King Hezekiah showed off all the riches to Babylon and Isaiah told him someday they'd carry it all away? This is it—exactly what Isaiah prophesied.

While Chin is in prison, the king of Babylon appoints a new king for Judah, who is our one remaining king. He appoints Mattaniah, but when other nations appoint a new king, they tend to change their name. They call him Zedekiah. He's Judah's final king. Jeremiah prophesies a lot of hard things during his reign. Zed wants a different outcome, but

Jeremiah says, "This is God's word to you, and it's not going to change." But Zed doesn't listen. Not only does Babylon destroy Jerusalem like Jeremiah prophesied, but Zed dies a prolonged, painful death. Babylon also kills many of the other leaders of Judah and steals more temple treasures. Only a few people remain in the land at this point. And since Babylon has defeated Judah, they don't have any reason to set up a new king, so they just appoint a governor to watch over things. Yesterday we met the guy they appointed, Gedaliah, but some of his trusted inner circle murder him.

Jerusalem falls and is destroyed, but we end with a reminder that God already has His sights set on restoration. The final verses of 2 Chronicles point us to King Cyrus of Persia. He doesn't know God, yet God appoints him to head up the rebuilding of the temple.

TODAY'S GOD SHOT

In 2 Kings 25:27–30, we follow up with King Chin, who surrendered to Babylon as soon as things got tough. He's been imprisoned there under the reign of King Nebby. But today Nebby dies and a new king takes the throne in Babylon. His name is Evil-merodach, and he shows us a beautiful picture of who God is: "Evil-merodach king of Babylon, in the year that he began to reign, graciously freed Jehoiachin king of Judah from prison. And he spoke kindly to him and gave him a seat above the seats of the kings who were with him in Babylon. So Jehoiachin put off his prison garments. And every day of his life he dined regularly at the king's table, and for his allowance, a regular allowance was given him by the king, according to his daily needs, as long as he lived." This is exactly what God does for His kids! He graciously frees us. He speaks kindly to us. He seats us at His table. He provides for us daily according to our needs as long as we live. This is the gospel of Jesus! Jehoiachin is an enemy king to Babylon, but he gets to experience freedom and provision and protection. Just like us. God took your prison garments, your orange jumpsuit, and clothed you in robes of righteousness and seated you at His table. You are a prisoner set free, dining with the King! He's where the joy is!

HABAKKUK 1–3

Habakkuk is a prophet to Southern Judah prior to the Babylonian exile, around the same time as Zephaniah and Jeremiah. Prophets are mediators between God and His people. We usually think of them as talking to the people on behalf of God, but Habakkuk mostly works from the other end of the spectrum: He talks to God on behalf of the people. He's focused on justice, and he brings his complaints about injustice to God. God is concerned about justice too, so they're on the same page. But just because they care about the same thing doesn't mean they have the same ideas about how that should be accomplished. Habakkuk mistakenly thinks God isn't listening to his prayers since God isn't doing what he asks. He says, "God, are You seeing what I'm seeing? If so, why aren't You doing anything about it?" He forgets that God's no is also an answer. God can hear him. God is listening. God just denies his request, because His process involves using a wicked nation to accomplish a righteous plan.

In this conversation, we encounter a verse that's often taken out of context: "Look among the nations, and see: wonder and be astounded. For I am doing a work in your days that you would not believe if told" (1:5). Some misread this verse as though it's painting a beautiful picture: "You wouldn't believe the wonderful works God is doing!" But in context we see that the thing God is doing that they won't believe is the raising up of the Babylonians to destroy them. And God is right—they don't believe Him.

Habakkuk responds to God by saying, "I know You're sovereign over this and You've chosen to use the Babylonians to bring correction to Your people, but they're wicked! They're way worse than Judah. This isn't fair." He's in the middle of the process and can't see what God sees, so God gives him some perspective via a vision. God says to write it down, because it'll be a while before it's fulfilled and people need to remember

---

For more information on today's reading, see thebiblerecap.com/links.

God's truth in the meantime. He wants to bolster their faith in Him as things get dark. He wants them to draw near to Him. "The righteous shall live by his faith" (2:4)—remembering God and His promises will keep their souls afloat during Judah's destruction, when a wicked nation prevails over them.

Then God pronounces five categories of woe on Babylon, warning them against putting their hope in wealth, security, power, pleasure, and control. Those who look to wealth as their ultimate hope will steal and cheat to get it. Those who look to security as their ultimate hope will oppress others to protect themselves. Those who look to power as their ultimate hope will enslave people, kill people, and work themselves to death. Those who look to pleasure as their ultimate hope will engage in drunkenness and debauchery but will end up with shame instead. Those who look to control as their ultimate hope will try to grasp it anywhere they can, even through idols and false gods. Pursuing each of those things as ultimate leads to unique kinds of sin. God calls them to turn from their false hopes, remember that He exists, and honor Him. He sees their wickedness clearly, and He'll deal with it accordingly.

Habakkuk asks God to show Himself mighty. He knows what God is capable of—he's seen God's works in the past and wants to see those kinds of mighty works again in the present. But he resolves to wait for God's timing. He commits to trust God and not object to God's process.

TODAY'S GOD SHOT

"Though the fig tree should not blossom, nor fruit be on the vines, the produce of the olive fail and the fields yield no food, the flock be cut off from the fold and there be no herd in the stalls, yet I will rejoice in the LORD; I will take joy in the God of my salvation. God, the Lord, is my strength; he makes my feet like the deer's; he makes me tread on my high places" (3:17–19). This is what faith looks like. Faith says, "Nothing is going the way I want it to. Everything is falling apart. But I won't put my hope in wealth or security or power or pleasure or control, because I know they'll fail me. I can be strengthened and fulfilled regardless. Because fruitful vines and filled stalls aren't where the joy is. *He's* where the joy is!"

JEREMIAH 41–45

Judah's governor, Gedaliah, is murdered by a member of the royal family named Ishmael. He and his crew kill many others in the process, including Judeans and Babylonian soldiers. He takes everyone else captive, forcing them to move east with him, across the Jordan River. On the way, they run into Johanan, the man who gave Gedaliah the heads-up about Ishmael's assassination plot. They fight and Johanan wins. The captives are set free, but Ishmael escapes.

They're living in a land that has erupted in chaos. They're terrified and with good reason. Their country has been dismantled, their new, enemy-appointed leader has been assassinated, they've been kidnapped, and they have no idea what their enemies will do next. They want to flee to Egypt in hopes of finding protection, so they seek counsel from Jeremiah and promise to do whatever God says. He spends ten days in prayer, then says, "Don't go to Egypt. The reason you want to go is that you're afraid of what will happen here. But if you let fear drive, it'll lead you to the very thing you're afraid of. On the other hand, if you trust God and stay, He'll protect you and provide for you here." They should trust him; his prophecy record is spot-on. But he knows they won't listen. He tells them, "God says to stay here. Don't go to Egypt. But you're going to disobey."

He's right; they don't believe him. In fact, they accuse him of conspiring against them and being a false prophet. They kidnap Jeremiah and take him with them to Egypt, forcing him to disobey God's command. God has him remind them that they disobeyed and aren't safe there. They've run to the very spot where their most feared enemy will attack. Babylon will come to Egypt and overthrow them. Jeremiah even marks the spot where Babylon's King Nebby will set up his throne. God has been persistent and patient in warning them, He's given them counsel on how to avoid disaster, but they never listen. As a consequence, those who fled to Egypt will see destruction; only a few will escape disaster.

When Jeremiah tells them this, they reply, "We're not interested in your words. We've been thinking about it and realized all our troubles started when we stopped making offerings to the queen of heaven. Everything was great until then. So we're starting that up again." They're referring to the time during good King Josiah's reign when he stopped the pagan sacrifices and tore down the high places. After his death, things in Judah began to decline under the leadership of the last four evil kings, and they think it's because they stopped idol worship. Then Jeremiah says the scariest thing he's ever said: "Go ahead. Worship your idols. God is done with you."

TODAY'S GOD SHOT

Exodus 34:6–7, the passage we've seen over and over, says God is slow to anger—but it doesn't say He never gets angry. It says He's merciful—not giving people what they deserve. That's been true here. He's gracious, giving them blessings they don't deserve. He has continued speaking to people who lie to Him and disobey and disregard Him. But Exodus 34 also says He won't leave the guilty unpunished. He knows when the timing is right for that punishment to be doled out, and He says the time is now. He's not rebuking them anymore. Paul talks about this in Romans 1:18–32. Sometimes God gives people over to their sins—He no longer begs them to repent but lets them continue sinning without any feelings of guilt. On the surface, it looks like mercy, but at its core, it's God's passive wrath. Mercy would be calling them to repent. But wrath lets them continue in sin unchecked.

God's kids never have to fear His wrath. He promises His Spirit will convict His kids of their sins. We can never exhaust His persistent love. God even reminds Baruch of that personally, drawing a distinction between how He deals with His kids and those who don't know Him. When you're convicted about your sin, the enemy of your soul wants you to feel ashamed about it, but God says it's a mark of adoption—evidence of His love, proof you're His child—because that's His Spirit at work in you! Thank God the Spirit is with us to draw us out of sin and back to the Father's heart. He's where the joy is!

JEREMIAH 46–48

In many of the books of prophecy, we read about prophecies not only for Israel and Judah, but also for the enemy nations. The book of Jeremiah is no exception. Jeremiah spends the next few chapters directly addressing the surrounding nations. In chapter 46, he holds Egypt accountable. He's already told us what's coming for them, but today God tells *them* what's coming for them. Though they're in a position of power, they'll be brought low. Their towns will be destroyed, their soldiers will attempt (and fail) to flee, and as their nation is crumbling, their pharaoh will be rendered powerless; he's all bark and no bite. Then God tells the Egyptians, "Pack your bags—you're going into exile. A nation will invade you from the north, and they'll demolish all the things you expect to save you. Your forest may be impenetrable, but they'll chop it down. Nothing can withstand My command."

Then God circles back to talk to the Israelites who disobeyed Him and fled to Egypt. He's much more gentle with them than He was last time He spoke about this. He reminds them not to be afraid. By now you know why they can be fearless. Because He's with them! Throughout Scripture, the most common reason given for God's kids not to be afraid is that His presence is with them no matter what. If we can remember who God is and how much He loves us, then the awareness of His nearness is the antidote to fear. He tells them a few ways He'll handle things with them in the midst of dealing with Egypt, where they're currently hiding out. He'll offer protection and deliverance, but He'll also bring discipline and punishment.

Next is an oracle to the Philistines, another long-standing enemy of the Israelites. When they're invaded from the north, they'll cut themselves, either as an act of mourning or as a prayer to their gods. Cutting themselves is a common part of their pagan worship rituals. If their gods don't do what they ask, they sometimes assume their gods are asleep, so they wake up the gods by spilling blood on the ground. Since they're cutting themselves, YHWH says He'll bring a sword too, but it won't be to wake up their gods. It will be to destroy them.

Then God addresses Moab. The Moabites have had it pretty easy—they're wealthy, they haven't experienced trials or exile, and life has generally been smooth sailing. Since character is often formed through suffering, Moab doesn't have much to speak of. They've become entitled and arrogant. They've put their hope in their strength and wealth. But God has all the strength. And God has all the wealth. He can take it from them in a second, and He says He will, because they've exalted themselves against Him. As a result of their arrogance, He'll make them drunk on the cup of His wrath. But still, He shows mercy and grace. Moab is a pagan nation, but God says, "I will restore the fortunes of Moab in the latter days, declares the LORD." Moab is an enemy of Israel, but they also have some familial ties with Israel. Ruth was a Moabite, so David and Jesus both have ties to the Moabites. It's almost certain that God offers them this unique benefit because of their connection to His people Israel.

TODAY'S GOD SHOT

In book after book, God sends prophets to talk to His enemies, not just His people. Why does He spend so much time addressing others who aren't in His family? One of the purposes behind this is to display that God is sovereign over all nations and all people. In this day, nations attach themselves to specific gods and believe they're only accountable to the gods they attach themselves to and vice versa. By talking to His enemies, YHWH shows He's a different kind of God than all the rest. He's sovereign over His people Israel, and He's sovereign over everyone everywhere, and everyone is accountable to Him, whether they worship Him or not. He's unique in this way, set apart from other gods. Our God is the universal God, sovereign over all those lesser gods—false gods, pagan gods, demon gods. They all answer to Him, and they'll all bow to Him. Not only is He the God of gods, but He's also your Father. Your Father is the sovereign God of all creation, and He loves you! He's where the joy is!

JEREMIAH 49–50

Chapter 49 holds a lot of destruction. We start out with Ammon. God will drive the Ammonites out of their land, but like we saw with Moab yesterday, He will also bring restoration afterward. We never find out why—it appears that God is just being merciful and generous toward His enemies! Next is God's judgment against Edom, the descendants of Esau. God promises judgment and destruction for them too, but He adds an interesting caveat: He'll be the one who takes care of their orphans and widows.

Verse 12 says, "If those who did not deserve to drink the cup must drink it, will you go unpunished?" This verse has two possible layers of prophecy. First, at the time, this meant there were people who suffered through the effects of God's judgment who had been faithful to Him. The remnant of Israel still had to be driven out of their land as a result of the sins of those who were destroyed. Sin has consequences that reach far beyond the sinner. No one sins in a vacuum. So God is basically saying, "Look, if the remnant of My people have had to endure exile and destruction because of sin and rebellion, then you're definitely not getting off the hook, because you're not even My people." Second, this may point to Christ. He had to drink the cup He didn't deserve to drink. Three times He asked the Father if there was any other way, and three times the Father said no. Jesus drank the cup of the Father's wrath toward the sins of His people. He paid for those sins. But those who don't know God must pay for their own sins; He says His cup is filled to the brim for them.

Next up is Damascus, a city in modern-day Syria. He promises to burn it with fire. It's worth noting that the phrases God associates with His enemies and their circumstances are the opposite of what He associates with His kids. God's people will not be afraid, because He's with them. But about His enemies, He says things like, "They melt in fear, they are troubled like the sea that cannot be quiet. . . . Panic seized her; anguish and sorrows have taken hold of her" (49:23–24). While

God's people experience His presence to bless, His enemies experience His presence to judge.

Kedar and Hazor, cities in Northern Arabia, have managed to avoid a lot of the drama other nations experience. Things are so low-key for them that they don't even have city gates. They're vulnerable but probably don't even realize it. King Nebby will come in and take advantage of that for his gain and for their destruction.

Then judgment comes for Elam, another enemy nation He promises to restore for no obvious reason. In Matthew 5:45, Jesus said that the rain falls on the just and on the unjust. In modern language, this sounds like it's saying bad things happen to everyone. But in ancient language, rain was a blessing. So Jesus was actually saying God sends out some of His blessings to all humankind—like common grace. And here, nations like Elam and Ammon get caught up in the current of His kindness.

After God uses Babylon to cause Israel and Judah to repent, He judges Babylon and lays it to waste. He says it'll be the last of the nations, which sounds like it'll be the final survivor, but this actually means it'll be the least prominent in position, the bottom tier. God's destruction of Babylon will end the captivity of His people who are there. Then the remnant from Israel and Judah will return to Zion with hearts that love God and that remember and rejoice in the everlasting covenant He made with them!

TODAY'S GOD SHOT

"In those days and in that time, declares the LORD, iniquity shall be sought in Israel, and there shall be none, and sin in Judah, and none shall be found, for I will pardon those whom I leave as a remnant" (50:20). This says a lot more about God than it does about people. God isn't saying His people will be sinless—He's saying their sins will be pardoned. The very act of pardoning suggests there's been sin. God's people do sin. But when God looks at His kids, He doesn't point to our sin—He points to our righteousness, which is Christ's righteousness. Christ's death on the cross made atonement for our sins, and because He paid the penalty, we receive the pardon. He's where the joy is!

JEREMIAH 51–52

Today we pick up where we left off yesterday with the destruction of Babylon. As we're reading, it's important to remember that some of the exiles of Judah are there when this invasion and destruction are taking place. Given their track record for remembering God's words and His promises, there's a strong chance they may have forgotten His promise to rescue them and bring them back to Israel. It's possible that all they recall is that they were driven out of Judah into exile, and now they're being attacked again in the land of their exile. So one of the first things He says to them is, "Israel and Judah have not been forsaken by their God" (51:5). He reminds them that He's with them. They're not alone—He's active in this process and will bring them back and restore their fortunes. He'll plead their cause and take vengeance on their behalf, destroying Babylon.

When the destruction comes, all they need to do is pack up and go back to Jerusalem. This is reminiscent of their exodus from Egypt. God will punish Babylon for what they did to Israel, and they'll be so thoroughly destroyed that nothing useful will come from them. They're like a nuclear waste site—not even a stone will be removed to use elsewhere. In order to make this happen, God will prompt the king of Persia to destroy Babylon. It's as good as done. While the Babylonians will be ashamed of their worthless idols, God's people don't have to be ashamed, and they don't have to be afraid. The situation is frightening, but God says He can be trusted. His people don't have to fear frightening things. Jeremiah writes all this down and tells one of King Zedekiah's military officials. By the way, when he does this, it's still seven years prior to the start of the Babylonian captivity, which is decades before Babylon is defeated by Persia.

Chapter 52 gives us an overview of the story, particularly the fulfillment of some of the early prophecies. Jerusalem is overthrown; the

---

For more information on today's reading, see thebiblerecap.com/links.

temple is plundered, burned, and destroyed; kings and leaders are killed; people are exiled—and in fact, there are three rounds of deportation to Babylon. Yet there are stories of redemption, freedom, and hope in the midst of it all. And redemption isn't just for those who do everything perfectly—it even includes people like wicked King Chin in his orange jumpsuit. By the way, when Jeremiah prophesied that Judah should surrender to Babylon, King Chin was the only one who obeyed. He surrendered just three months into his reign. He was a wicked king by most accounts, but he did what God commanded, and God took care of him. God provides for and protects people we'd never expect to receive His blessing.

TODAY'S GOD SHOT

After God talks about the Babylonians' idols, Jeremiah 51:19 says, "Not like these is he who is the portion of Jacob, for he is the one who formed all things, and Israel is the tribe of his inheritance; the LORD of hosts is his name." The God who made everything gives His people Himself. He owns everything and says, "I'm the best gift. I'm better than all the things I've made. I'll give you plenty of those things, but none of them will be as good of a gift as Me." And He's right. Ask anyone who has everything, and they'll tell you it doesn't satisfy. On the other hand, some of the most content people you'll ever meet are those who have very little apart from Jesus. They understand His value in a way that's hard for the rest of us to grasp. When God gives us the gift of Himself, it's evidence that He gives the very best gifts, because there's nothing better than Him. That's good news for us, because He's where the joy is!

LAMENTATIONS 1–2

No one knows who wrote Lamentations, but many scholars suggest it was Jeremiah. It's a book of poetry lamenting Jerusalem's destruction and the Babylonian exile. Not only is this the worst thing that has ever happened to the people of Israel by far, but Jeremiah spent years warning the people about it while also suffering the consequences of their unwillingness to listen.

Chapter 1 focuses on the destruction of the city of Jerusalem (also called Zion). The once-thriving capital of Judah has been emptied, her enemies rule over her former inhabitants, and she's lost everything. All along, God has told them to remember. And when they finally do, they don't remember Him, but they remember the things they used to have and the peace they used to experience. They forget what God did in their past, and they forget what He's promised for their future. Any time we choose sin, we fail to consider the future. Sin occurs when we live so much in the present that we forget about the eternal kingdom. Sin is shortsighted. The Israelites are nostalgic for a time when they were disobedient to God. They long for the days when things were easier for them, but if you recall, those were days when they were sacrificing their children and worshipping idols. This isn't righteous mourning. There's a way to grieve and mourn to the glory of God, but this isn't it.

The author describes all the ways God has directed this destruction: He afflicted them, inflicted sorrow, sent fire, thwarted their efforts, weakened them, and handed them over to their enemies. They're not wrong in attributing this to God, but His actions are the discipline for theirs. He said all along that He'd do these things if they didn't repent. Finally, Judah owns their role in this: "The LORD is in the right, for I have rebelled against his word" (1:18). Not only does this verse remind us that God is just, but it also makes the truths of 1:12–16 bearable. And in verse 20, it sounds like Jerusalem truly repents: "My heart is wrung within me,

For more information on today's reading, see thebiblerecap.com/links.

because I have been very rebellious." They mourn and grieve their actions, not just their consequences. Meanwhile, their enemies gloat over what's happened to them.

In chapter 2, we get a second poem about the fall and destruction of Jerusalem. Their relationship with God has been affected by this disaster: "The Lord has become like an enemy" (2:5). He's not an enemy, but it certainly feels like He is to them. But they know His actions are justified—He enacted a necessary discipline for their sins. The consequences of this discipline reach further than just the destruction of their home. In addition, God Himself seems to go radio silent. The prophets have no visions or words from God. The elders sit on the ground in silence. The silence of God is devastating, and it exacerbates the pain of trials. They know this is all part of God's plan, though. Verse 17 says, "The Lord has done what he purposed; he has carried out his word, which he commanded long ago." Maybe they're finally remembering that this is what He's been warning them about. This isn't a knee-jerk reaction to their sin; God hasn't lost His temper. In Judah's worst tragedy, we're reminded that God is patient and methodical. We aren't walking on eggshells around Him—He isn't volatile and unpredictable.

TODAY'S GOD SHOT

What does it reveal to us about God that He gave this book to us? He's a God who can handle our feelings and frustrations and emotions and who values them and invites us to engage with Him on that level. "Pour out your heart like water before the presence of the Lord" (2:19). The author pours it out unguarded before the Lord, knowing God receives our emotions, even when they're the result of our sins. He wants us to talk with Him about what we're feeling. We've seen all along how He's after our hearts. He doesn't just want a one-dimensional, glossy love—He engages with the good, the bad, and the ugly in our hearts. How can He work with us on those levels if we keep the ugly emotions back from Him? Who will speak truth to our struggles if we keep them in the dark? Throw some light on them! Talk to Him about them. He'll meet you there in them. He's where the joy is!

LAMENTATIONS 3–5

God is faithful in the midst of all the evil that seems so prevalent. The author doesn't hold back from attributing their trials to God, but as we know, the trials are God's response to the people's sins. Despite attributing their situation to God, the author says, "The steadfast love of the LORD never ceases; his mercies never come to an end; they are new every morning; great is your faithfulness. 'The LORD is my portion,' says my soul, 'therefore I will hope in him'" (3:22–24).

During Judah's struggle, the author preaches the gospel to himself, reminding himself of the truth when it seems most untrue and inaccessible: "The LORD is good to those who wait for him, to the soul who seeks him. It is good that one should wait quietly for the salvation of the LORD. It is good for a man that he bear the yoke in his youth" (3:25–27). Remember the yoke? The author's point is that challenges are beneficial—character and knowledge of God are formed in those times. These trials can be especially helpful when they come in our youth, because we'll have the rest of our lives to live in the benefits.

When the author says, "Why should a living man complain, a man, about the punishment of his sins?" (3:39), he points out that any punishment we receive for our sins is justified. This kind of humility is a step toward repentance, which is exactly what happens next. He calls them to examine their ways, confess, and repent. God draws near when they repent, and the first thing He says to them is "Do not fear!" (3:57). He's always telling His kids not to be afraid—He's near! The author also knows God has promised to take vengeance on their enemies. His enemies don't get the final word. His people can find hope in the fact that sin and evil don't get to win.

In chapter 4, we read a poem about the two-year siege of Jerusalem and its subsequent destruction. The author looks back longingly at the way they used to live in luxury and ease and how the wealthy, who were raised wearing expensive purple garments, now live in ash heaps. But not everyone lived in luxury and ease—the rich were oppressing the poor, sacrificing their children, and enslaving people illegally. So even though the author reminisces about how things used to be wonderful, they weren't so wonderful for everyone. He says Jerusalem has it worse than Sodom. Sodom was destroyed immediately, but Jerusalem's struggle lasted for years. Why is God acting more harshly toward His kids? Most scholars say immediate destruction was fitting for Sodom, since they were His enemies. But with His kids, His aim is to discipline and restore, so He keeps the long term in mind. He's trying to train them toward obedience and trust, and that doesn't happen overnight.

Meanwhile in Jerusalem, there's a famine so bad people resort to cannibalism, their king has been captured, and they have no leaders—which often means chaos. Their neighbor Edom gloats over their plight, so the author reminds them that the day is coming when God will punish them for rejoicing over Jerusalem's demise.

Chapter 5 closes with a communal prayer for God's mercy and restoration. The discipline God brought yielded the repentance He intended. The people say, "Woe to us, for we have sinned! For this our heart has become sick." And they praise God in their trying circumstances: "But you, O Lord, reign forever; your throne endures to all generations."

TODAY'S GOD SHOT

Lamentations 3:32–33 points out the complexity of God's desires: "Though he cause grief, he will have compassion according to the abundance of his steadfast love; for he does not afflict from his heart or grieve the children of men." Just like us, He can have desires that are in contrast with each other. But unlike us, none of His desires are sinful and He always does what's right and best. He causes grief, but it's not His preference. But even more than He doesn't want to cause grief, He wants to produce obedience in the children He loves. And He does that through discipline, which does cause grief sometimes, but He disciplines in conjunction with His compassion and steadfast love. In the layers of His will, He always lands on what serves His utmost glory and the greater joy of His kids. He's after His glory. He's after our joy. And He's where the joy is!

EZEKIEL 1–4

Ezekiel is from the line of priests, but he's exiled to Babylon and prophesying roughly seven years before Jerusalem falls. He goes the extra mile to give details, and when he has a hard time giving concrete descriptions of his visions, he says things like, "They had the appearance of" or "the likeness of" to let us know it's his closest approximation. Despite all his details and metaphors, he doesn't get lost in the weeds. He continually reminds the reader of the main point: God wants to be known. One of the most common phrases in the book is "then they will know that I am the LORD."

His first vision involves creatures that look kind of human but have four wings and four faces—they have a face on the back of their head as well as one on each side of their head, allowing them to see in all directions. Later, he calls them cherubim (10:3–22). His descriptions match what we see about cherubim in Psalm 18:10 and Revelation 4:6–8, but it's possible that the Revelation creatures are seraphim—a different kind of creature that has six wings. Each cherub is attached to a gyroscope-like base covered in eyes, so they can move and see in any direction. Cherubim are associated with the presence of God and places God has called sacred. In this instance, it's the former, because God shows up, enthroned. Ezekiel sees rainbows, fire, light, metals, and jewels. God tells him to stand, then the Spirit enters him and lifts him to his feet in obedience to the Father's commands. A few noteworthy things: (a) The Spirit lifts him three more times in today's reading, (b) the Spirit also does some implied teleportation, where he's moved to a different place, and (c) it's rare for the Spirit to enter people in the Old Testament, but it happens here.

God appoints him to speak to Israel because they're rebellious, and God patiently and lovingly pursues the rebel. Israel may not obey, but at least they won't doubt—they'll know for sure that Ezekiel is a true

For more information on today's reading, see thebiblerecap.com/links.

prophet. Unfortunately, you can know the truth and still not be changed by it. Then God has Ezekiel eat a scroll—a bit of prophecy theater. God tells him to speak to the exiles from Judah, not to the Babylonians holding them captive—which is a bummer because the Babylonians would've listened, but the exiles won't. Their hearts are hard.

Ezekiel sits with the exiles for a week, then God lays out His instructions in a format called case law, which gives different outcomes for different scenarios (e.g., "Here's what happens if you warn a wicked person and they don't repent," "Here's what happens if you warn a righteous person who stumbles and they don't repent," and "Here's what happens if you don't warn someone at all."). The consequences for all the sins are the same, regardless of whether the person has lived a wicked life or a righteous life and stumbled. All sin gets the death penalty. And since Ezekiel's failure to warn people would be equated with murder, he'll get the death penalty if he doesn't warn them. After God commands him to speak, He shuts him up in his house, binds him, and makes him mute so that he can't give the message. God has him set up a model of Jerusalem's siege and lie on his left side, facing it for 390 days. Then he's supposed to move the siege model to the other side and lie on his right side for forty days. He's allowed twenty-one ounces of water each day and eight ounces of food, cooked over human dung. But he reminds God, as if God has forgotten, that he's a priest, so that's not allowed; God approves the use of animal dung instead. This is a humbling, desperate situation in which Ezekiel is called to experience physically what the exiles are experiencing spiritually. They're bound, starving, and parched. This is a picture of Christ, who also intentionally experienced human trials and bore our burdens.

TODAY'S GOD SHOT

God says He made Ezekiel stubborn and insensitive to fulfill His purposes. Ezekiel's God-given personality was designed to keep him from fearing or faltering in delivering God's message to an equally stubborn and insensitive people (3:8–9). God is intentional about how He makes each of us. And it isn't just intentional, it's *kind*. His plans are good, His heart is kind, and He's where the joy is!

EZEKIEL 5–8

At this point in the timeline, the destruction of Jerusalem is still a few years off. There's been one round of deportation and exile, but there are still two rounds left to go. Today God has Ezekiel shave his head, weigh the hair, divide it into thirds, then follow specific instructions for each third. This pertains to God's people back in Jerusalem, symbolizing the three ways He'll respond to their rebellion: sword, pestilence, and famine. These are the punishments He listed as consequences back in Leviticus (20:14; 21:9; 26:25; 26:30; 26:33) before Judah committed these sins. God isn't making these punishments up on the spot.

Another thing God does in response to their sin is turn their sins back onto them. For instance, they oppressed the poor to get rich, so now all the money they've amassed will be worthless. They sacrificed their children, and now there'll be cannibalism in families. And He'll scatter their bones in front of the idols they worshipped and trusted to bring them full, easy lives. In other words, God makes the punishment fit the crime.

As for the remnant, there'll be punishment for some of them too, but He addresses the others in 6:8–10: "I will leave some of you alive. . . . Then those of you who escape will remember me among the nations where they are carried captive. . . . And they shall know that I am the LORD." The phrase "they shall know that I am the LORD" appears eight times in today's reading. God wants to be known, and He's turning the hearts of the remnant back to Himself. In the end, everyone will know who He is, but not everyone will submit to Him and love Him. Those who do are the ones adopted into His family.

It's important to note that the remnant hasn't been set apart because they've earned it. They aren't innocent. "They will be loathsome in their own sight for the evils that they have committed, for all their abominations" (6:9). "If any survivors escape, they will be on the mountains, like doves of the valleys, all of them moaning, each one over his iniquity"

(7:16). So if they don't earn it, if they're sinning just like everyone else in Jerusalem, how do they get to be the remnant? This is important: It's granted to them solely by God's grace and sovereign choice, not by their actions. He preserves some people to magnify His name, display His mercy, and continue working out His plan to restore humanity. He wants to be known. His justice is one thing He wants us to know about Him, and the sword, famine, and pestilence display that aspect of His character. And mercy is another thing He wants us to know about Him, and the remnant displays that aspect of His character.

God says He'll remove His presence from the temple and leave it empty to be defiled. Those who remain in Jerusalem will finally seek wisdom, but it'll be too late. No one will be able to offer them guidance or help. Then, as Ezekiel sits with the exiles, he has another vision. It's of a manlike being made of what appears to be fire, light, and metal. Then the Spirit takes him in a vision to Jerusalem. He sees terrible things going on outside the temple, then he goes through the wall to see what's happening inside, and things are even worse. Jerusalem's leaders are worshipping graven images. Since God's presence isn't in the temple anymore, they think He can't see them and won't punish them. When Ezekiel goes back outside, he sees women worshipping the god of fertile soil and men worshipping the sun.

TODAY'S GOD SHOT

In 6:9, God says their idolatry has broken His heart. While we see His fury and lack of pity, they come on the heels of centuries of compassion and mercy toward sinners. And 7:13 says, "Because of his iniquity, none can maintain his life." Paul says something similar in Romans 6:23: "For the wages of sin is death," but then he goes on to say, "but the free gift of God is eternal life in Jesus Christ our Lord." Your sin broke God's heart. You deserved His wrath. Because of your iniquity you can't maintain your life. But He maintained it *for you*. For free! God the Son came to die in your place. He's where the joy is!

EZEKIEL 9–12

Yesterday we left off in Ezekiel's vision of Jerusalem's evil. Today the vision continues with God calling for death. He summons executioners—almost certainly angels—to the temple. The text calls them men, but angels always appear as men. Of the seven men, six are there to slaughter, but one is dressed in linen and has a writing kit. His job is to mark those who are grieved over the evil; God will spare them. The word *mark* is *tav*—the last letter of the Hebrew alphabet, and it looks like either a cross or an X. This scene is reminiscent of the Passover, where those whose doorways were marked with blood—also in the shape of the cross—were spared. It also parallels Revelation 9:4, where the righteous will be marked with God's seal on their foreheads.

God says to stack the dead bodies inside the temple. This is against God's cleanliness laws, but it's in line with His plan to leave the temple. Ezekiel is distraught because he knows how wicked the people are; he seems nervous that God will kill *everyone*—that there won't be anyone marked for saving and Israel will be wiped out forever. God says they've sinned against Him long enough, the days of mercy have passed, and it's time for judgment, starting with the leaders. Not to worry, though—the man in linen does his job completely, saving everyone God commands him to save. While there's nothing in the text indicating he is a theophany or Christophany, he's a Christ figure at the very least.

Ezekiel has another vision of cherubim—heavenly creatures that often guard holy places. Here, they carry the throne that God's presence will dwell on when He leaves the temple. His cherubim chariot waits outside the temple as God has the man in linen send holy fire as judgment on the city. Then He leaves the temple on the cherubim chariot and heads east. God has left the temple, but He *hasn't* left His people—those worshipping idols aren't His people; they aren't among the remnant.

For more information on today's reading, see thebiblerecap.com/links.

In the vision, God's Spirit moves Ezekiel to another part of the city, where he prophesies to twenty-five men, including leaders. They've been acting like they'll die in the city—cooked like meat in a pot—possibly because of the fires the man in linen caused with his coal throwing. But God says He'll kill them outside Jerusalem and things will be worse than they fear. It all happens by the book in 2 Kings 25:4. (We read about it on Day 231, but Ezekiel's prophecy here was written before it happened.) While Ezekiel is delivering this prophecy, one of the men falls over dead.

Then God sets the record straight on something: The temple isn't their sanctuary; *He* is their sanctuary. And God the Sanctuary goes anywhere He wants. He isn't confined to one spot.

At this time, people believe your god changes when you cross a border, so they think YHWH is confined to Israel and when they leave, they won't be able to worship Him and He won't have any power. This is wildly inconsistent with what He's shown them through the years—He even rescued them from Egypt through a series of signs and miracles. But their default mind-set is cultural, not spiritual, so they forget.

God promises His people new hearts. Then Ezekiel performs a sign-act in front of the exiles. A sign-act is a theatrical way of communicating a prophecy that relies on images instead of, or in addition to, words. When they're unmoved, he adds some emotion to show them the kind of fear and trembling the future exiles will endure. They seem calloused by years of false prophecies and even as-yet-unfulfilled true prophecies, so God lets them know this will happen soon.

TODAY'S GOD SHOT

In 10:19, the glory of the Lord is leaving the temple with the cherubim. God and the cherubim "stood at the entrance of the east gate of the house of the LORD." The word *stood* implies that God lingers at the threshold before leaving through the Eastern Gate. It's almost like a final look back as He's feeling the grief over what's been lost, the pain over the way His people have broken His heart, the loss of the land He promised them and the blessings He gave them. But all is not lost. Because then the presence of God heads east toward Babylon. God *follows His people* into the land of their exile, pursuing them still. Even in exile, He's our sanctuary. Even in exile, He's where the joy is!

EZEKIEL 13–15

Ezekiel prophesies against other prophets—false prophets, specifically. They prophesy things they've dreamed up in their own minds or "just have a feeling about" in their spirits. They see false and lying visions, and it's unclear whether they're lying about what they see or the enemy is faking these visions. The prophets also believe they have the power to speak things into existence as long as they attach God's name to it, because then His hands will be tied and He'll be forced to comply with what they've said. But God says He isn't the one informing them and He won't bend to their will. Not only are His hands not tied, but His hands will be used against them. He compares their prophecies to a wall they've built and painted white—it looks fresh and clean, but He'll crush it and it'll fall on them. Their false prophecies will ultimately be turned back on them.

Then God turns His attention to the magicians or sorcerers, those who sew magic bands on people's wrists to protect against evil. How deceptive is the enemy! He uses the fear of evil to entice people *into* evil. The sorcerers promise protection to people who'll die and promise death to people who are among the remnant. God says their efforts will be thwarted, because they're not all-powerful. He is. They aren't the Creator who can speak things into existence—He is.

In chapter 14, some elders come to Ezekiel, and God knows what's happening in their hearts so He tips him off that they've taken idols into their hearts. God asks Ezekiel, "They're here to ask you for guidance. But based on the status of their hearts, should I give you any guidance to give to them?" Surprisingly, the answer is yes. God still welcomes these idolaters to seek His guidance—He wants them to come to Him, not their idols. He'll even respond to them directly. And here's what He'll say: "I'm not going to answer any of your questions as long as you worship idols. I'm not going to tell you what to do in whatever scenario you're coming to Me about. I'll only deal with the problem of your idols until that changes." Whatever our sins may be, we can go to Him. He loves us, and He wants us to walk in freedom from whatever is obstructing our path. Then He says, "If you do ask a prophet for guidance and he gives you a so-called word from God, you'll both be guilty of sinning against Me, because I've already told you it's not going to happen."

God says He'll send judgment on the land via famine, sword, pestilence, and wild animals. In fact, things are so bad that even if Noah, Daniel, and Job were a part of this judgment, they'd be the only survivors and would barely get out alive. Not even their kids would survive. These men are probably given as illustrations for two reasons: (1) Scripture emphasizes their God-given righteousness, and (2) God preserved them through astonishing circumstances. God says there'll be some survivors when He destroys Jerusalem too—people who apparently fall into the same two categories as these three men. In the end, these survivors will be an encouragement to Ezekiel, serving as evidence of God's goodness and justice.

Then God asks Ezekiel another rhetorical question. He compares the people of Jerusalem to a vine and points out that they're useless. He'll punish them with fire for their wickedness.

TODAY'S GOD SHOT

God promises punishment for the false prophets and sorcerers because "you have disheartened the righteous falsely, although I have not grieved him, and you have encouraged the wicked, that he should not turn from his evil way to save his life" (13:22). This verse mentions two things that are unsuitable: peace for the wicked and lack of peace for the righteous. God wants His people to be at peace and walk in truth. And He wants the wicked to hear the truth too! Because He cares so deeply about those things, He'll punish those who discourage and dishearten His people. He doesn't just care about our eternal destination, He cares about the peace we carry with us day by day as children who know and love the truth of who their Father is. Truly, He's where the joy is!

EZEKIEL 16–17

God uses an extended metaphor in telling Ezekiel about His relationship with Israel. While the overall point of the metaphor is clear, scholars warn against getting into the weeds, because every comparison breaks down at some level. Here's what we see: Israel is an abandoned orphan, unloved and left to die. But then someone, the King of the universe, rescues her and nurses her to health. He includes nineteen verbs when describing what He did for her: "I passed by you, I saw you, . . . I said to you, 'Live!', I made you flourish, . . . I spread the corner of My garment over you, I covered your nakedness, I made My vow to you, I entered into a covenant with you, . . . I bathed you with water, I washed off your blood, I anointed you with oil, I clothed you with embroidered cloth, I shod you with fine leather, I wrapped you in fine linen, I covered you with silk, I adorned you with ornaments, I put bracelets on your wrists and a chain on your neck, I put a ring on your nose and earrings in your ears and a beautiful crown on your head. . . . I bestowed splendor on you."

Eventually she loves the King's gifts more than the King Himself. She's beautiful, so she trusts in her beauty to get her whatever she wants. She uses all the King's gifts to lure in other lovers, making idols out of them. Eventually she forgets that she was once a helpless child and sacrifices her own children. Her idolatry grows unsatisfying, but instead of turning away from it, she dives deeper. Idolatry always demands more, making us needier, more frantic and insecure. She goes from being a prostitute who receives gifts from her lovers to one who is so desperate for love and security that she gives *them* gifts to keep them around.

God's judgment for her sins, which are worse than Sodom's and Gomorrah's, will bring them to a screeching halt. Only one manifestation of Sodom's sin is described, but as always, God goes to the heart of the issue: "This was the guilt of your sister Sodom: she and her daughters had pride, excess of food, and prosperous ease, but did not aid the poor and needy. They were haughty and did an abomination before me. So

I removed them" (16:49–50). God addresses their sexual sin elsewhere (Genesis 19:4–9; Jude 1:7) and doesn't ignore it here either, but He digs deeper than their abominable actions and points to their pride and arrogance. Their sinful attitudes manifested in other areas: God gave them much, but they lived in luxury without caring for the poor and needy. And Jerusalem, He says, is even worse. His punishment for her sins will look a lot like death, but He will restore her fortunes.

Chapter 17 gives us a nature parable. A big eagle—Babylon's King Nebby—plucks up a shoot and drops it down elsewhere, and it grows into a tall vine. The shoot is King Chin, the one who surrendered to Nebby, was captured, then was provided for all the days of his life. Nebby does more gardening, planting King Zedekiah in Judah to handle things. But unlike the first vine, Zedekiah reaches out to a different eagle, Egypt, who happens to fly overhead. Zedekiah wants to be plucked up and transplanted, but instead he withers and dies, because Egypt isn't God's appointed people. God promised all this long ago. He sent Jeremiah to warn Judah's kings to surrender to Babylon, but only King Chin followed the plan. Everyone else looked for an escape route and got what God promised: judgment and exile. God will plant a sprig in Israel, and it'll grow up into a cedar that will bear fruit and make shade and be a home for all kinds of birds. This points to the Messiah and His coming kingdom.

TODAY'S GOD SHOT

Israel has despised God and broken the covenant. And do you know what His response is? He leans in. He broadens and deepens His relationship with His people by expanding the covenant. They broke the conditional covenant, so He makes an eternal one. They've forgotten the covenant, but He'll remember it. They've broken it, and He'll atone for their sins. He will cover the cost Himself! Do you see Him tipping them off to the plan for Jesus's arrival on the scene? This has been His plan all along to restore His people to Himself. God's excessive love is shocking, stupefying, and praise inducing. He's where the joy is!

EZEKIEL 18–20

Today God addresses a common saying that has misinformed Israel's theology. The saying conveys the idea that a child is punished for a parent's sins. While children are certainly impacted by their parents' sins and may even inherit some sinful traits, they aren't punished for them. Despite the corporate impact and effects of sin, God judges people individually. So how will they be judged? And who will be among the remnant He's preserving? God says righteousness demonstrates His character to the world—that's what life in the kingdom of God looks like. And for those who don't live according to His ways, that's what death looks like. He gives an illustration of a righteous father with a wicked son *and* a wicked father with a righteous son to show how everyone will be judged individually. Righteousness doesn't transfer genetically, and wickedness doesn't either.

But the point of this passage isn't that we're saved by doing good works or being "good people"—that's contrary to the rest of Scripture. The point is that our righteous works are *evidence* of our faith in God, and faith like that is individual, not inherited. God reminds them it's never too late to turn to Him and have the debt of their sins paid for. He doesn't want to kill the wicked; it's a much better scenario if they repent. Unfortunately, for those who don't repent, His righteousness requires justice. Israel's response to this great news is to object to everything God said. They think it's not fair for God to pardon the wicked if they repent, which is ironic, because that's Israel's only hope at this point! They object to the mercy He's extending to them.

Ezekiel laments, portraying Judah as both a lioness and a vine. The lioness raises one cub who gets captured and taken to Egypt. This likely refers to Jehoahaz. Then she raises another cub—probably Zedekiah, the final king—but things don't go any better for him; he's taken to Babylon. This is a major defeat for the tribe associated with such esteemed lion imagery. In the vine metaphor, Judah is like a vine that has grown so tall and strong that it gets turned into a scepter, then eventually burned. Again, Ezekiel laments over Judah's demise.

The leaders of Israel have questions for God. In chapter 14, He said if they came to Him before repenting of idolatry, He'd only speak to them about their idols. They haven't repented yet, so He says, "No, I won't answer you. But while you're listening, let's walk through the story of our relationship." He recounts how He's provided for them as they have rebelled and disobeyed. It happened in Egypt, in the wilderness, in the promised land, and now in Babylon. No matter their circumstances—enslaved, challenged, blessed, or oppressed—they reject God and their hearts go after idols. God speaks the truth to each new generation, but they all do the same thing. So, no, He won't let them ask their questions, but He still reminds them He'll restore things in the end. We can hardly go three chapters without Him bringing up restoration!

In 20:25–26, it sounds like God is saying He misled them and ordered them to do a bunch of terrible things. This statement could be sarcastic, or it could be His expressing the Israelites' viewpoint of His laws—or even some combination of the two. But there is a deeper point to it as well, one that is echoed in Romans 7:7–25, which goes on at length about the purpose and the effect of the law. On their own, God's laws don't bring life. They reveal how helpless we are and how righteous God is. We can't keep the law even if we try. The law doesn't lead to life—it points to death. And it *is* devastating.

TODAY'S GOD SHOT

"You shall know that I am the LORD, when I deal with you for My name's sake, not according to your evil ways, nor according to your corrupt deeds, O house of Israel" (Ezekiel 20:44). The law is necessary, but keeping the law isn't the gospel. *Gospel* means "good news," and the thought of having to keep the law is certainly not good news. What's good news is that God the Son kept it perfectly and paid the debt for those God adopted into His family. Praise Him! He saves us for *His* name's sake. He's where the joy is!

EZEKIEL 21–22

God's words to Ezekiel today come down pretty strong. He doesn't sugarcoat these two chapters. God draws a sword against the land of Israel, and it's especially unsettling because He says He'll cut off the righteous and wicked. The righteous too? Why? We don't find out until the end of today's reading. Next, God tells Ezekiel to mourn and grieve over what's happening and to spread the word about it to everyone who asks, which likely involves public mourning. After this, it sounds like he's supposed to demonstrate some of God's actions using an actual sword in front of the people. And after the sword, he demonstrates a highway with a fork in the road. The road is coming out of Babylon; one path leads to the capital city of Ammon, where the Ammonites live, and the other leads to Jerusalem. God says King Nebby is using divination, seeking the direction of evil spirits, to determine which path he should take first (that is, who's getting destroyed first).

Jerusalem is chosen. And in 21:27, God says this "ruin, ruin, ruin" will happen when King Zedekiah comes—although he isn't mentioned by name. God has promised to judge him, and He won't withhold it. We read about his downfall in Jeremiah 52:1–30, and it was a "ruin, ruin, ruin" indeed. But the Ammonites aren't off the hook. They've been getting false promises and prophecies just like Judah has, but they're next on the chopping block.

Then God circles back to Jerusalem, calling them the "bloody city" because they've killed so many people. God's penalty for murder is death, and He's held back their judgment long enough—it's time for Him to act. During the time He's given them to repent, their sin has increased. The list of their sins is lengthy: They've murdered, worshipped idols, shown contempt for their parents, extorted foreigners who live in their land, disregarded the needs of the most vulnerable in their society, disregarded the Sabbath, lied, and committed sexual impurities of all kinds. Basically, no commandment is left unbroken. But they probably don't even remember the commandments, because the priests aren't teaching anyone anything and the prophets are lying and using witchcraft! In fact, things have gotten so bad in Israel that the nations around them shake their heads in disgust and roll their eyes. Even the pagan nations have grown to hate Israel because of the magnitude of Israel's wickedness. God compares Israel to dross, the impure byproduct that comes from refining silver, so He'll burn them up. They've profaned themselves. He's the one destroying them, but it's in response to their own actions.

Remember how the sword will devour the righteous too? It seems unfair, right? Before we get to what happens, think back to Genesis 18, when Abraham tried to talk God out of destroying Sodom if He could find just ten righteous men. There weren't ten so God destroyed them, but He still mercifully spared Lot and his daughters. The end of chapter 22 is a similar scenario; God gives Israel an even better chance at being spared—this time all He needs is *one* righteous man, and that'll be enough to keep Him from destroying Jerusalem. But there aren't any righteous men. Not even one. So we finally find out that God isn't being unfair after all, because there aren't any righteous people in the path of destruction.

TODAY'S GOD SHOT

God's wrath toward sin is marked out so clearly here. Most of us probably hate some sins but are fond of others or have a love-hate relationship with them—we enjoy them in the moment but feel guilty later. But God doesn't know this kind of ambivalence toward sin. He hates it, full stop. He hates it because He loves His glory and He loves His kids. And sin mars both of those things. But despite God's hatred for our sins, which He most certainly sees, He can also see beyond that to the righteousness Christ has granted us. While sin can affect the intimacy of our relationship with God, it doesn't affect the *status* of our relationship with God. We're still His kids. He still loves us. His wrath toward the sins of His kids was absorbed by His only begotten Son. He's where the joy is!

EZEKIEL 23–24

The prophets often use metaphor and hyperbole; their prophecies aren't always literal. Because of their style and intended purpose, we don't look at them with a microscope—we zoom out to see the big picture. For instance, yesterday God compared the people of Jerusalem to dross and said He'll burn them up. That doesn't necessarily mean they'll die by fire. The prophets humble us because they refuse to let us be controlling about details; the metaphors and imagery loosen our grip. Today's metaphors are dark and graphic, but in every heavy paragraph, there's still something to learn about God.

Chapter 23 compares two women to two cities: Samaria (Northern Israel's capital) and Jerusalem (Southern Judah's capital). God often compares His relationship with His people to marriage; when His people wander off to other gods, He compares it to adultery. This picture of intimate betrayal shows what's happening on a spiritual level. So while there definitely was sexual sin happening in these cities, that's only a fraction of the broader problem. The people have turned their eyes away from YHWH, who has always provided for them and protected them. They've looked to other nations to save them, paid them tribute for protection, become enamored with their gods, and worshipped their gods instead of YHWH. Verse 7 shows the trajectory of their sin: It started with lust and ended with idol worship. Sin always wants more from us. It's never satisfied.

God begs them to repent, but even when their sin and idolatry isn't satisfying anymore, they still don't turn back to Him—they double down on idolatry. And even though Jerusalem witnesses Samaria's demise, she doesn't learn anything from it. The whole process becomes a chore to the two cities. They're abused and unloved by their lovers. They're "worn out by adultery." But God says it's too late for them to repent and calls Ezekiel to judge them. They'll drink the cup of His wrath and bear the penalty for their sins.

In Ezekiel's day, news took weeks or months to travel from one nation to another. So it's a big deal that Ezekiel, who is nearly nine hundred miles away from Jerusalem while he's exiled in Babylon, gets a personal notice from God about the siege in Jerusalem. He compares Israel to the choicest cuts of meat. But as they're being prepared, it becomes clear that they're spoiled. Not only does the meat itself have to be discarded, but it's even ruined the cauldron. As the meat is being removed, it's dripping with blood, and Israel leaves it out for everyone to see and encounter. In other words, Israel is ignoring God's laws and they aren't even embarrassed or ashamed about it. They feel no remorse. Their hearts are hard.

Ezekiel's heart isn't hard, but God's about to put him through the wringer nonetheless. Once again, he gets an assignment to feel the pain of the situation Israel will go through. His wife is going to die, and he's only allowed to mourn in private. The ancient Jews had very detailed, prolonged ways to mourn the dead, but God says to disregard the traditions. This catches the attention of the exiles, which opens up the conversation in which Ezekiel lets them know about the tragedy in Jerusalem. He says to respond in the same way, because ultimately, they don't have a right to grieve since this is the result of their sins. This is what they'd been moving toward all along as they disregarded God's warnings.

God tells Ezekiel that when Jerusalem finally falls, a fugitive will confirm it, then Ezekiel won't be mute anymore. If he's still mute, how has he been prophesying? Put a pin in this, because we'll come back to it.

TODAY'S GOD SHOT

God, in His great love and provision, gave Judah a prophet who understood her pain. Ezekiel lost his wife right before the people of Judah lost everything. He knew there was a greater purpose in this loss. What he probably didn't know is that his purpose extended far beyond commiserating with Israel and giving them a proper understanding of the situation. He was also imaging Christ, the one who bears our burdens, to people 2,500 years in the future. God the Son, who knows exactly how hard it is to be human, aches on our behalf. He mourns and grieves with us, and still, He's where the joy is!

EZEKIEL 25–27

God's enemies are pagan nations who have been acting wickedly. Ezekiel prophesies first against the Ammonites. God's main problem with them is that they find pleasure in Judah's struggles. They loved watching the temple be defiled, the land be destroyed, and the people of Judah be killed and exiled. They literally celebrated death and destruction. God will send people from the east to destroy the Ammonites. We already know from prior prophecies in 21:21–29 that this refers to the Babylonians; this is where they take the second fork in the road after having destroyed Jerusalem.

Next up are Moab and Seir, but probably just Moab. There might be a note in your Bible that the word *Seir* doesn't appear in a lot of the ancient texts, so we'll just deal with Moab here. The Moabites are distant relatives of the Israelites, but apparently their sin is that they don't acknowledge Israel's uniqueness based on their relationship with YHWH. They regard them as indistinct from pagans.

Then God moves on to Edom—they acted with vengeance and cruelty toward Judah. God will use Israel to punish Edom in response. Israel will be the tool God uses to demonstrate His anger and wrath. Philistia had the same sin as Edom, but God doesn't specify who their attackers will be. He just promises that justice will be served.

In chapter 26, God brings a harsh word to Tyre, a major shipping port located north of Israel. The main part of the city of Tyre is an island. They're wealthy, and because of their trade business, they have relationships with all the powerful nations of the day. The kings of Israel had an amicable relationship with the king of Tyre for a long time; in fact, he supplied the cedar for David's palace and for Solomon's Temple. But things went wrong with Tyre over the years. And when Jerusalem falls, Tyre thinks Judah's demise will result in their advancement. They don't care what's been lost—they only care that they'll benefit from it. God will send the Babylonians to attack Tyre and destroy it.

Things went somewhat differently than Ezekiel prophesied. The Babylonians did lay siege to Tyre for thirteen years, but it didn't completely fall until later, when it was attacked by the Greeks.

There are a handful of ways scholars respond to this: Some don't address it at all because they say it's a nonissue. And some say Ezekiel was primarily using hyperbolic and metaphorical language, so there's flexibility here because it isn't intended to be read with literal detail. As an example of hyperbolic language, Ezekiel says Babylon will build a siege mound against Tyre, knowing full well that it's an island. You can't build a siege mound against an island, so this seems to be intentionally exaggerated language. Others say there's no timeline given on when this prophecy would be fulfilled, so the Greek attack suffices. In 29:18, Ezekiel himself acknowledges the failure of Babylon's attempted siege. Prophecies are almost always fulfilled in ways that don't seem obvious at first. Metaphors and imagery set us up to understand it one way, but in hindsight, we often see it differently.

The final chapter of today's reading is a lament for Tyre, demonstrating at length how wealthy the city is. They're massively influential on an international scale—and that's not always a good thing. They traded clothes and silver and honey and wheat, but they also traded ivory and human beings. And this lament calls the people of Tyre arrogant.

TODAY'S GOD SHOT

God is so protective. Throughout these prophecies, it's evident that He's against the people who are against His people. Even after all Israel has done to betray Him and break His heart, He's still committed to working justice for their enemies. His protective nature and His promise of justice is good news for us, because it means we don't have to take things into our own hands. We can trust Him to mete out justice more precisely than we ever could and in His perfect timing. You can lay down your weapons, even if they're just words. You can lay down your bitterness, because it says you don't trust Him. And you can lay down your will, knowing His is better anyway. He is your defender, and He's where the joy is!

EZEKIEL 28–30

Today we repeatedly see how God opposes the pride of the nations, even if their pride corresponds to gifts and skills He's given them. For instance, He affirms that Tyre is beautiful and its leaders are wise, but they've corrupted those good gifts through the pride in their beauty, wisdom, and wealth. Likewise, Egypt is proud of its power and position. People who take credit for their own strengths or who fixate on them too much steal the credit that belongs to the Giver of those gifts.

We open with prophecies directed at the leadership of Tyre. A person in a significant position is claiming to be a god, and this is the tipping point for YHWH. The very things Tyre and its leader put confidence in will be attacked and destroyed. Beginning in verse 12, God addresses the king of Tyre—who might be the same person He addressed in verses 1–10—with poetic words that may have multiple layers. Some scholars believe the language used to describe the king isn't intended to be read as fact—that it's referring to the king, but with hyperbolic language, saying things like "You were the signet of perfection" and "You were in Eden, the garden of God" and "You were on the holy mountain of God." Other scholars believe Ezekiel isn't just addressing the king of Tyre, but he's also comparing him to a cherub appointed to guard the garden of Eden in Genesis 3:24. They believe that in addition to telling us what's going on with the king of Tyre, it informs us about something that happened with that cherub. Among those scholars, some say this dual prophecy points also to the serpent in the garden of Eden, who might also overlap with Lucifer or Satan. They say this creature could be the appointed cherub, and that he possibly even possessed the king of Tyre and lived out the same story line all over again, trying to exalt himself to the position of God.

Sidon, another neighboring city to the north, lands on the hit list too—they've treated Israel with contempt. Then chapter 29 brings us

For more information on today's reading, see thebiblerecap.com/links.

to Egypt, where God compares their pharaoh to a water dragon. This might be a reference to Leviathan (Job 41:1; Psalm 104:26; Isaiah 27:1). Pharaoh begins to act like he's the one who made the Nile, as if he's YHWH. God will fish Pharaoh out, and all the other fish—which probably symbolize the people of Egypt—will get caught on his scales on the way out, then they'll be thrown into the desert. God will punish Egypt because of how they appeared to help Israel but just ended up torturing them instead. After Egypt's long punishment, God promises again to restore them (see Isaiah 19:25). God is consistent with His prophecies, even though they come from a variety of prophets and over the course of many centuries.

Ezekiel circles back to what happened with Tyre after yesterday's prophecies. Babylon besieged Tyre for thirteen years but didn't get any spoils. God says, "Don't worry—even though you didn't get payment from Tyre like you expected, you're still going to get paid. It's just going to come from Egypt. You're doing My work, and I'm going to provide for you." Chapter 30 laments Egypt; God will destroy it and all the countries that support it. He'll break Pharaoh's arms but strengthen Nebby's arms. God is the one who gives and takes away strength.

TODAY'S GOD SHOT

God hates human pride—not because He's envious of what we've got (after all, He gave it to us!), but because it's built on a lie. We are not gods. He is. While we may be powerful, we aren't powerful on our own; our strength is from Him. While we may be wise, we aren't wise on our own; He is the source of all wisdom. While we may be beautiful, we aren't beautiful on our own; He invented DNA. He's the rightful object of praise for all our beauty, wisdom, position, might, height, you name it. God should be the target of our praise and gratitude. Giving praise to Him helps eradicate the pride He hates so much, *and* it focuses our eyes on our Father! And He's where the joy is!

EZEKIEL 31–33

Today God opens by talking to Pharaoh Hophra and the Egyptians, but He spends most of the chapter talking about Assyria. He compares Assyria to the tallest, most significant cedar tree that ever existed. Assyria was the most powerful nation in the world for approximately three hundred years, until it got chopped down by Babylon. God is the one who supplied it with water for its growth and abundance, but then He commands it to be chopped down. Ezekiel tells this story about Assyria for two reasons: to illustrate that no nation is indestructible and to let Egypt know they'll see the same end.

After Ezekiel prophesies about a nation's destruction, he often follows with a lament. Since chapter 31 prophesies against Pharaoh, chapter 32 is a lament for him. Pharaoh thinks of himself as a lion, a mighty predator among all the nations, but God says he's not very self-aware. He's more like a water dragon, which is the same imagery God used for him in 29:1–12. God reiterates His promise to catch Pharaoh and the Egyptians in His net and hurl them onto land, where they'll be eaten by wild animals. But as we've talked about before, much of prophecy involves metaphorical language, so this isn't necessarily the precise way they'll die.

When Egypt is overthrown, the other nations will be terrified, because if Egypt can be toppled, everyone is vulnerable. Pharaoh is comforted to know that other great nations have been toppled too, but God adds insult to injury by telling him he'll share the pit with all those uncircumcised nations. Egypt practiced circumcision and hated the nations that didn't, so this idea would disgust them.

Chapter 33 compares Ezekiel to the guy who blows the trumpet to let people know about an attack on the city. Ezekiel is only responsible for his obedience to God; he isn't responsible for how others respond to God or to him. He knows his lane, and his lane is not something as

For more information on today's reading, see thebiblerecap.com/links.

big as changing hearts or even as small as modifying behaviors—that's the Spirit's lane. His lane is trumpeting. He's been blowing the horn for thirty-three chapters, and Israel still hasn't listened.

Finally the people say, "Wow. We've really messed up here. What should we do?" He reminds them that no matter how wicked they've been, it's never too late to repent. True repentance is a sign of a new heart. And no matter how righteous they've been—even though we know they haven't been righteous, despite what they think—their actions won't save them. People who think of themselves as good people still sin. God is clear here that their actions aren't saving them. He isn't putting good deeds and bad deeds on a scale and weighing them—that idea is nowhere in Scripture. It is, however, a core belief of something known as Moralistic Therapeutic Deism, which is centered around the idea that God just wants us to do good and be happy. It's a self-focused antigospel.

When Jerusalem falls to Babylon, a fugitive comes to Ezekiel to let him know, just like God promised. And also like God promised, Ezekiel is no longer mute. Most scholars believe his muteness was related to anything that was not prophecy—he'd been able to call people to repentance but unable to talk about the weather or lunch or to openly mourn the death of his wife. For years, his words only existed to warn others about God's judgment.

TODAY'S GOD SHOT

"I have no pleasure in the death of the wicked" (18:23; 33:11). We've talked about how important it is to look for God and His character in Scripture—the things He loves, the things He hates, the things that motivate His actions. And we've talked about how the things He hates are things that run contrary to what He loves. So if God does not delight in the death of the wicked, then He does delight in their salvation. God's delight, God's *joy*, is expressed in saving the wicked. When sinners repent and turn to Him, we see His delight at work. We see His joy and affection in the spotlight. God loves to save sinners and sanctify them. His delight is the best thing that has ever happened to us. He's where the joy is!

EZEKIEL 34–36

God calls wicked kings to account, comparing them to shepherds who haven't looked over their flocks. They've been selfish, using the sheep's wool and meat without taking care of the sheep. They've made life unnecessarily hard for the sheep. God provided Israel with more than enough for its kings to care for their people well, but they didn't. Since the shepherds acted harshly and abdicated their responsibilities, the sheep scattered and some were devoured by wild animals. God will hold the shepherds responsible for how they've treated the sheep, but He won't just punish the shepherds—He'll rescue the sheep. He'll seek them out, separating the sheep that are His, and He'll care for them and bring them back into the land. He'll do all the things their shepherds neglected to do. Kings will always fail us, but God has given us a Good Shepherd, a King from the line of David, who is our Shepherd forever—He never abdicates His role. Because of that, God's sheep "shall dwell securely and none shall make them afraid." Again we're reminded that God is actively engaged in driving out our fears.

Then Ezekiel prophesies against Edom again. He uses the word *because* often in this oracle; God wants them to know *why* He's responding to them this way. Edom is guilty of many sins; God doesn't punish them out of cruelty or because He likes to see them suffer. He always has a reason and He doesn't want to hide it, because then they'd miss out on understanding who He is and what He's about.

The first part of chapter 36 addresses the actual land of Israel. Other nations, like Edom, think they're going to come in and possess it. But God says, "No, this land isn't yours to take. It's Mine. And I'm bringing My people back to live in My land and thrive there." As we know, God isn't doing this because of Israel's goodness—they've been terrible—but because He wants His reputation and His character to be widely known. Sometimes it's hard for us to hear this. We like to think of ourselves as

For more information on today's reading, see thebiblerecap.com/links.

the center of God's universe. But how ill fitting would it be if things were human-centric instead of God-centric? God loves us, that's absolutely clear, but before us and through us and with us, God's goal is the glory of God. Loving us is one of the many ways that's displayed throughout creation, but He is the point. Humans aren't weighty enough to be the point.

Then God uses eighteen verbs to tell us how He'll initiate, sustain, and fulfill His plan for restoration: "I will take you, I will gather you, I will bring you, I will cleanse you, I will give you a new heart and a new spirit, I will put them in you, I will remove your heart of stone, I will give you a heart of flesh, I will put my Spirit within you, I will cause you to walk in My statutes and obey My rules, I gave the land to your fathers, you shall be My people, I will be your God, I will deliver you from all your uncleannesses, I will summon your food, I will make it abundant, I will keep you from famine, I will make fruit increase."

There are three noteworthy things in this section. First, these verbs are all future tense except in "I gave the land to your fathers." He's letting them know nothing has changed; that's still their home even though they don't live there anymore. Second, God is the author of heart change and obedience. *He* will remove the heart of stone, and *He* will give the heart of flesh. In biblical times, the perspective on the heart is that it isn't just where your emotions come from, but where your will and your thoughts come from too. So God is saying He'll give them a new will and new desires. How will He do this? He'll put His Spirit in His kids, and He'll cause them to walk in His ways and obey His rules. Third, in 36:37, God essentially says, "Ask Me for these things, because it's a guaranteed yes." God wants to be asked even for things He has promised, because it's about the relationship, not just about the outcome.

TODAY'S GOD SHOT

"[I] will do more good to you than ever before" (36:11). This is what God is saying to the people who are currently rebelling against Him. Who is like that? Only YHWH. Only the God who has always been good would look at a bunch of sinners and promise to be even better. He's where the joy is!

EZEKIEL 37–39

Ezekiel has a vision of a valley filled with dry bones. As far as the eye can see, there's nothing but femurs and fibulas. Through Ezekiel, God commands the bones to live. God is the one who issues the command, and God is the one who breathes life into the army. And of course, God could've done it without Ezekiel, but He loves him and He's using him, so Ezekiel gets the joy of being part of God's process. The vision represents the twelve tribes—people from both Judah and Israel. God will give them new life and bring them back to their land. There are three noteworthy things about this vision. First, it connects us back to God's original creation of humankind in the garden of Eden in Genesis 2:7, where God breathed life into Adam. Second, the word *breath* is from the Hebrew word *ruwach*, which is more often translated as *spirit*. Third, God doesn't command the bodies to breathe; He commands the breath to enter the bodies. They can't breathe without breath. The breath has to come first.

Then God has Ezekiel perform a sign-act: Take a stick and write "Judah and company" on it to represent Southern Judah, then write "Joseph and Ephraim and company" on another stick to represent Northern Israel. Then tie the sticks together to represent the restoration of all that has been broken relationally in the 350 years since the kingdom divided. God has preserved a remnant from both kingdoms, and He'll bring them all back to their land and set one Shepherd over them—a King from the line of David. The remnant of all Israel will be restored, reunited, and repentant, because God Himself will be among them, He'll sanctify them, and He'll live out His eternal covenant of peace with them!

In chapter 38 we meet a king named Gog who rules a nation named Magog. No one knows who he is or where this is; even the details Ezekiel gives make things more uncertain. For instance, his army is composed of people from far and wide, which doesn't help us narrow down his location. Lots of scholars think Ezekiel invents this king as an amalgam of all the powerful nations that have opposed God's people throughout history. Ezekiel even uses a lot of the same imagery he used earlier with Tyre and Egypt. So Gog seems to be an archetype that represents God's enemies. Since God twice says this will happen "in the latter days," most scholars think this is a yet-to-be-fulfilled prophecy about the end times.

Peculiar things will happen in the future that involve both Gog and the restored remnant. They'll be dwelling securely, then Gog will show up to attack them. But why is God bringing this enemy against His people? In verse 16, God says, "In the latter days I will bring you against my land, that the nations may know me, when through you, O Gog, I vindicate my holiness before their eyes." He'll do it to remind all the nations around Israel not to mess with Him or His people. When He demonstrates His dominance over a powerful enemy, the less-powerful enemies won't risk attacking God's people. So when Gog shows up on the scene, God will send an earthquake, fire, hail, pestilence, and mass confusion, causing the people of Gog's army to accidentally kill each other. "Then they will know that I am the Lord."

TODAY'S GOD SHOT

God isn't just going to show up at the site of Gog's army and attack them; He'll also throw fire on Magog, their homeland. Israel will take all the weapons Gog was going to use against them and recycle them into fuel. Then Israel will get the spoils of a war they didn't even have to fight. God takes the enemy's efforts to destroy His people and turns them to bless His people instead! God isn't working everything out so that it's perfectly fair—nothing about this is fair. This is absolutely undeserved generosity and unmerited favor. Nothing God's people have done has earned them anything but eternal separation from Him. But He doesn't just say, "I forgive you. Now leave Me alone." He says, "Here's a new heart to love Me with. And here's My Spirit to empower your obedience. And here's an eternal kingdom you're going to inherit." No one is like Him! He's where the joy is!

EZEKIEL 40–42

Ezekiel 40–48 is one of the most challenging sections in all of Scripture. Scholars are at odds on how to view this text, so here's what we need to know for now: God gives Ezekiel this vision in 573 BC, at a time when His people are in exile in a foreign land. For God to go on for nine chapters about the temple here is like Him showing up and saying, "I know you've lost everything. I know the First Temple was destroyed—the one Solomon built about 350 years ago. I know we're all living here in the land of our enemies, but I want you to remember that I've got a detailed plan for restoration. You're not forgotten, and I'm with you!"

The day Ezekiel has this vision isn't just any day. It's the beginning of the preparation for Passover, which commemorates the Israelites' exodus from Egyptian slavery. Passover also corresponds to our modern-day celebration of Easter, because Jesus had gone to Jerusalem to celebrate Passover when He was crucified. As part of Ezekiel's Passover vision, God gives him a tour guide we'll call Bronze Man. Certain aspects of this man resemble the fiery man from 8:2 and the man in linen from 9:2. Bronze Man brings two tools for measuring—a reed and a cord, which serve kind of like a ruler and a tape measure.

Bronze Man and Ezekiel measure everything from the gates to the outer and inner courts to the priests' chambers, then they head into the inner temple area. Bronze Man leads Ezekiel up to the Most Holy Place, but Ezekiel doesn't go inside. Next, he describes the walls of the nave and the vestibule, which feature carved cherubim—the created beings who serve as guardians of the holy places. Even though Scripture says they have four faces, they only have two visible faces here since wall surfaces are two-dimensional.

In chapter 42, Ezekiel sees into the temple's chambers. The measurements described in this vision are massive, especially compared to

---

For more information on today's reading, see thebiblerecap.com/links.

Solomon's Temple (which was the First Temple). In fact, the temple courts are almost one square mile, which is bigger than the surface of the whole Temple Mount! This gives us reason to consider that perhaps this vision is a metaphor using hyperbolic descriptions as opposed to a literal blueprint. We'll continue to read more about this in the days ahead.

TODAY'S GOD SHOT

Today's tour ends where it began, back at the Eastern Gate. The Eastern Gate is also known as the Golden Gate and the King's Gate, and it's the gate Jesus will come through when He returns. Ezekiel describes an outer wall along the perimeter of the massive temple complex. It's a large wall, as far as circumference is concerned, but it's not a tall wall. According to 40:5, it's only about ten-and-a-half-feet high, which means it's not for defense. Ezekiel 42:20 says its purpose is to be a line of demarcation between the holy and the common.

One of the accusations people make toward Christianity is that it's exclusive. But the gospel of Christ isn't *exclusive*; it's just *specific*. It says, "Here is the truth. All who believe the truth are invited in." The Truth, the Way in, and the Life everlasting is Jesus. He's the only way to the Father. Jesus said, "No one comes to the Father except through me" (John 14:6). The walls aren't to keep people out; they're to show who has come in! The Way is open, and He's where the joy is!

EZEKIEL 43–45

Today in Ezekiel's vision of a new temple design, we see it filled with people, their jobs, and even YHWH Himself! God returns to the temple the same way He left—through the Eastern Gate. Ezekiel falls on his face in worship, then the Spirit lifts him up again and takes him from the outer court to the inner court, where he hears God speaking to him from inside the temple. In the layout of the temple complex, the outer courts are large, the inner courts are smaller, the Holy Place is smaller still, and the Most Holy Place—where God's manifest presence dwells—is the smallest of all. While God's room is the smallest, He's actually everywhere. He certainly isn't confined to this nine-hundred-square-foot space; He's in dimensions that we haven't even accessed yet! There's also some meaningful symbolism in this layout, corresponding to the separation of the holy and the common.

When God speaks to Ezekiel, He has him do two main things: (1) write down all the dimensions of this temple and tell the people about it, because it'll humble them, and (2) write down all the laws God gives and command the people to obey Him. God never actually tells Ezekiel to build the temple. He just says, "Here are some dimensions—that should put people in their place. And here are some laws; tell them to do them." It sounds like the description itself is what will produce the proper response in people. Put a pin in this—we'll come back to it tomorrow.

In chapter 44, they seal off the Eastern Gate since it's the one God's cherubim chariot came through. Then, another interesting thing is set in motion in today's chapters. Just like Moses met with God on Mount Sinai, then told the people God's laws, Ezekiel meets with God on the Temple Mount and sets out God's new laws for the people. With Moses, God set out specific rules, and the people proved over time that they couldn't keep them. So you might think God would relax the law at this point, but He doesn't. The requirements are even higher from here on out. Have God's standards of holiness changed? No. Complete perfection in deed and thought has always been required. He's always been after us at a heart level. But when YHWH first entered into a relationship with His people, He gave them the amount of information they could handle at the time. And as He continues building this relationship with them over the centuries, He brings progressive revelation of who He is and what He requires. Even though God is raising the law bar, His standards have always been the same. Regardless of how strict or loose His laws are, people won't be able to keep them. The law will always point to our need for a Savior.

God says the priests aren't allowed to marry divorced women or widows, unless they're the widow of another priest. This may sound harsh, but there's a practical reason behind it. Women who have been married are likely to have children, which would add confusion to the question of who could serve in the priestly roles as the generations progressed. This debate about priestly roles is a big deal during the Second Temple period, when the families return from exile. In chapter 45, Ezekiel makes land requirements that include even the prince, who is also supposed to concern himself with peace, justice, and care for the poor.

TODAY'S GOD SHOT

God's utter holiness—or set-apartness—is so evident in this passage. Since He keeps pursuing His rebellious people in their sin, it's easy to forget what a big deal His holiness is. The way He holds back the fullness of His presence seems to be for our protection, not His. In Exodus 33:20, He told Moses that no one can see His fullness and live. And today in 44:19, the priests have to change clothes before they go to the outer courts where the people are, because they might transmit holiness. As we've already seen with Uzzah and the ark (2 Samuel 6:1–8), God's manifest presence can be lethal when it comes in contact with evil or common things. But He gets as close to us as we can handle. May we draw near, knowing every step closer fuels our love and delight in Him. He's where the joy is!

EZEKIEL 46–48

During the descriptions of feasts and festivals, God instructs them to exit through a different gate from the one they enter through. Hebrew culture is rich with symbolism, and there's a deeper meaning here beyond functionality. It points to each person leaving different than they came—it represents the change that takes place in us when we come before God to worship Him. Then God forbids the political leader from acquiring any more land. Pre-exile the leaders were greedy, oppressing the poor to acquire more land for themselves. Here, God raises the bar in a way that stops their greedy desires from becoming greedy actions.

Then Ezekiel sees a vision of water flowing from the temple, through what is currently desert, and into the Dead Sea, where the water is too salty for anything to live. In the vision, the desert is blooming because of the water, and the water even purifies the Dead Sea basin so that it's no longer dead! In addition to being symbolic, this may also be literal. In 2011, scientists started finding freshwater springs at the bottom of the Dead Sea, along with new bacterial life forms. While this isn't a precise fulfillment of the Scripture (since the vision's river flows from the temple), some say it could be the early phases being put into motion.

In chapter 48, God makes other adjustments to things He commanded through Moses. Yesterday He raised the bar on laws, and today He raises the bar on generosity. In Numbers 18:20–24, He said the Levites would have no land inheritance because He was their inheritance, but in 48:10–14, He portions off land for all the tribes, including the Levites. In the restored land, the priests and Levites have land too. They don't get to possess it as an inheritance (44:28), but they get to live there nonetheless.

This temple blueprint is magnificent. However, it's never been built. When the Jews built the Second Temple, it didn't meet these specifications;

For more information on today's reading, see thebiblerecap.com/links.

it was much smaller. What happened? Did they disobey God's vision? Or did God lie? Or was Ezekiel a false prophet? There are three primary views, each rooted in a different belief about the end times. View A: The description is literal, and God will build this temple at some point in the future. He wouldn't describe things in such great detail if He only intended this to be a metaphor.

View B: This vision is intentionally symbolic; the exact reason it's described in such great detail is to reveal that. Jews see imagery when they read words, and they give special meaning to numbers; every letter of the Hebrew alphabet has an assigned numerical value. So when they read these specific dimensions, they believed they were intended to convey the superior magnitude and beauty of God's dwelling place with humankind, not to be a literal blueprint. This view also fits with what we talked about yesterday when God didn't explicitly tell them to build this temple from the vision. If the ancient Jews had somehow misunderstood and these instructions were intended to be taken literally, then God would've rebuked them for not following His blueprint when they built the Second Temple. And there are two other reasons for view B's popularity. First, it takes into account the fact that God calls *us* His dwelling place in 2 Corinthians 6:16, which means there isn't a need for another structure. Second, this vision gives details in 40:39 and elsewhere about the sin and guilt sacrifices, but we definitely won't need sacrifices, because Hebrews 10:1–18 tells us Jesus was the final sacrifice.

View C: The text has some prophecies that are literal and others that are symbolic, while some may be both. It's not vital to reach a conclusion here. Prophetic texts are hard to find clarity in sometimes—so we don't scream where Scripture whispers, and we don't whisper where Scripture screams.

TODAY'S GOD SHOT

"The name of the city from that time on shall be The Lord Is There." So whenever this comes to complete fruition, God says He's not going anywhere. No more trekking through the wilderness, no more captivity or exile. And He promises to stay there forever. So of course, that's where I want to be, because He's there, and He's where the joy is!

JOEL 1–3

The book of Joel contains a lot of mystery. Joel doesn't name any of Israel's sins and barely mentions which enemy nations he's referring to. He opens with a locust plague swarming the land, and it isn't just a nuisance—it's a total agricultural devastation. They've destroyed the vines and fig trees, both of which are things locusts only attack if they've already eaten everything else in the land. On top of lacking food for themselves, the people also lack grain and wine and oil for daily offerings at the temple. Joel tells the priests to lament and call for a fast, likely as an act of repentance.

A day of judgment is coming, the day of the Lord we've read about many times. Joel points to a future military invasion by an army sent by God Himself. However, prophets' warnings often serve as God's escape hatch. The people can avoid disaster if they repent and obey. So there seems to be a hope that He'll relent. God wants them to truly repent—not just so the bugs will go away or the army won't come, but because their hearts are turned toward Him and they want to walk in His ways. He wants them to draw near to Him out of delight and not as a form of escapism. There's a difference, and God knows it. He knows there's more available for them, so He says: "Don't just come to Me because you're in trouble. Come to Me, but bring your broken heart, not the clothes you've torn in some kind of surface-level repentance." In this passage, Joel quotes the verses we've seen so often in our reading: Exodus 34:6–7, where God tells Moses who He is. Joel reminds the people who God has always been and says, "We don't know what He'll do, but we know who He is. So repent!"

Then God responds: "The Lord became jealous for his land and had pity on his people" (2:18). What does it mean that God became jealous for His land? To be jealous *for* something is different from being jealous or envious *of* something. God has an appropriate possessiveness

For more information on today's reading, see thebiblerecap.com/links.

that wants what's best in the situation. So He promises to send them things they lack for the daily offerings—grain and wine and oil. He'll get rid of the invading army from the north. And the fig tree and vine will bloom again.

God even tells the land and the animals not to be afraid. He also promises to send the early and late rain, bookending the harvest season. And in a sweet turn of events, God will restore the damage the locusts did, the locusts He sent among them. He'll restore all that was lost through His necessary punishment of their sins. In this section we seem to have another dual prophecy, where there's a partial fulfillment in the centuries to come and a complete fulfillment in the end times. He says, "It shall come to pass afterward, that I will pour out my Spirit on all flesh." Several hundred years later, a week after Jesus ascended to heaven, God's Spirit came to dwell in His people. And He says all who call on the name of the LORD will be saved and that all those who are saved are those whom God has called. And that's still happening today!

But there are also things yet to be fulfilled. For instance, He promises cosmic phenomena, but it's hard to know if that's figurative or literal. Will the sun actually be blotted out? Or does that just mean that all the false gods and ruling powers apart from YHWH will be defeated? God will bring His people—and all people, it seems—back to the land for what sounds like war but could be His judgment for the nations. From then on, only He and His kids will live in Zion.

TODAY'S GOD SHOT

In just three chapters, Joel references seven other prophets and the book of Exodus. Joel knows Scripture! While it helps him grasp Israel's current situation, it also helps him keep perspective for the future. God wants us to read His Word because He wants to be known but also because He cares about how hopeful we are. Paul says these things were written that "we might have hope" (Romans 15:4). The more we know God and His Word, the more hopeful we'll be—not full of hope in our desired outcome, but hope in *Him*. From fixing his eyes on Scripture, Joel has learned both God's track record and God's promises for the future. He knows where hope is found; he knows He's where the joy is!

DANIEL 1–3

The first half of the book of Daniel is known as hope literature, and the second half is filled with apocalyptic prophecies. When Daniel is a teenager, the Babylonians raid his hometown of Jerusalem, destroying the temple and taking captives, including Daniel and three of his friends. King Nebby wants the most impressive captives to be trained in Babylon's best schools and fed like kings. This isn't a generous move on Nebby's part—it's how captors make their captives loyal to them. Then after the captives are sufficiently indoctrinated, they send them back to their homelands so they can win other people over to their side.

Daniel struggles with this because the king, who isn't Jewish, doesn't eat according to the dietary laws God commanded. Daniel negotiates with his overseers, promising that he and his friends won't lose weight if they eat kosher. Their diet proves beneficial, so their overseers agree to let them be vegan. God gives Daniel's overseers compassion, He gives Daniel and his three friends skill and wisdom, and He also gives Daniel a gift for interpreting dreams and visions.

Their overseer takes away their names that point to YHWH and assigns them new names that seem to point to the Babylonian gods instead. Daniel's friends become Shadrach, Meshach, and Abednego, and Daniel becomes Belteshazzar. King Nebby loves him. When he has a nightmare, he calls a staff meeting and says, "I don't just want the interpretation—I want you to tell me the dream itself. Anyone who can't will die." But no one can help, so Nebby orders all the wise men—the whole priestly class, including Daniel and his friends—to be dismembered, even though some of them weren't even there! Then Daniel offers to help. He and his friends beg God for mercy, knowing only God can do what's required. God answers his prayer with a yes. When he goes to Nebby, he's the picture of humble confidence. He says, "Humans can't do what you've asked, but God can and has."

For more information on today's reading, see thebiblerecap.com/links.

The dream is of a large statue made of different substances, each one representing a different kingdom. Nebby and Babylon are the gold head, some other kingdoms are the body, decreasing in value but increasing in strength from head to foot. The feet are a mix of clay and iron, representing a divided kingdom. When the two-feet kingdom is the ruling power, the statue is smashed by a rock, which almost certainly represents Jesus, then God establishes His eternal kingdom on earth. The king is in awe. He bows to Daniel and gives him presents and a promotion. Daniel's friends get promotions too, and the wise men are spared. Nebby pays tribute to YHWH as the one true God.

But then he sets up a ninety-foot gold statue. He was the gold head in the dream, so whether the statue is of Nebby himself or of a Babylonian god, the connection is clear: He's made an idol of his own identity. He's so prideful that he misses the dream's message: Kingdoms are temporary, and God is sovereign over them all. He orders everyone, including foreign dignitaries, to worship his statue, but Daniel's friends resist, even at the threat of death. When Nebby finds out, he's furious but gives them another chance. They still resist, saying, "We know you'll try to kill us, but we think we'll survive, because we know what God can do. But regardless of what He chooses to do, we'll worship only Him." They don't demand a specific outcome from God; they just trust Him. Nebby turns up the heat so hot that the workers are burned alive.

The trio should also die in the fire, but they're alive and unbound! And someone is with them. Some believe it's an angel. Others believe it's a Christophany. Nebby orders them out, and they don't even smell like smoke. The only thing the fire did to them was set them free from the things that bound them. Nebby not only repents but commands everyone else to repent and worship YHWH too.

TODAY'S GOD SHOT

In Daniel's prayer of praise, after God gives him the dream and the interpretation, he lists things God is sovereign over: wisdom, strength, timing, authorities, knowledge, understanding, giftings, revelation, and sight. And in just three chapters, we've seen God display His sovereignty in all those areas. As Daniel said, "Blessed be the name of God forever and ever." He's where the joy is!

DANIEL 4–6

King Nebby writes a letter to his people praising YHWH. It shows an unexpectedly humble side of him—he's actually praising God for thwarting his plans! He has another perplexing dream, but no one can interpret it until Daniel shows up. In his dream, a tree grows big and strong and its impact, which is mostly positive, reaches the whole earth. A messenger of YHWH commands that the tree be chopped down and stripped of its branches and fruit but that its stump, which represents a man, should be left to soak in the ground for seven years.

Daniel says, "This isn't great. You and Babylon are the tree. Your reign will be chopped down, and you will live in the fields among the beasts for seven years. But if you repent and show mercy to the oppressed, God might delay this." A year later, Nebby is walking on his roof writing a praise song to himself, and God makes the dream a reality. After seven years of eating grass, Nebby is humbled and his reign is reinstated. He sings another praise song, but this time it's for YHWH.

In chapter 5, we meet Belshazzar—probably Nebby's grandson. He's throwing a pagan worship ceremony and wants to serve the wine in the stolen temple vessels. But then God shows up and shocks everyone. Belshazzar almost passes out because he sees the hand and the writing. He calls in his wicked interpreters, but they can't make sense of it. It's possible they understand the words but not the meaning, or it could be written in a foreign language, like Hebrew.

A woman (probably Belshazzar's mom) tells him how Daniel helped Nebby, so they call him in. Belshazzar promises Daniel he'll be third in the kingdom if he can interpret the writing. Daniel doesn't seem to like Belshazzar. Not only does he reject his gifts, but he leaves off the traditional "O King, live forever" in his greeting. Daniel rebukes Belshazzar for using the holy vessels, worshipping pagan gods, and dishonoring YHWH. He boils the writing down to this: "God has deemed you an unworthy leader, and He's going to remove you and divide the kingdom between the Medes and the Persians." Belshazzar gives Daniel the gifts, then dies later that night, and the kingdom is given to Darius the Mede. The new Persian king, Darius, leaves Daniel in his new role, so he's now in charge of many other politicians in Babylon. When Darius wants to give him a promotion, the other politicians are jealous. They try to find fault in Daniel but come up empty-handed. The only way they can trap him is to make it illegal to pray to anyone except King Darius for thirty days. They propose the law, and Darius hastily agrees.

When Daniel finds out, he doesn't change his behavior. He doesn't try to change the law or run and hide in fear. He just goes about his faithful business as usual, praying three times a day. The men catch him praying and alert Darius. He's devastated because he really likes Daniel. He tries to get the law overturned, but when he fails, he lets Daniel know he's rooting for him and fasting for him. They throw Daniel into the pit with the lions and seal it with a big stone. By the way, Daniel is at least eighty-two years old when this happens. He survives the pit because God sends His angel to shut the lions' mouths. Then Darius orders his conspirators to be executed by lions instead, and he writes a decree praising YHWH.

TODAY'S GOD SHOT

God granted Daniel faithfulness and integrity that turned the hearts of kings and nations not just once, but twice. But even with all his great victories and qualities, he's still not the hero of the story. Daniel doesn't understand the visions on his own. Daniel doesn't close the lions' mouths. Daniel doesn't fulfill the prophecy against wicked King Belshazzar. YHWH is the active agent. YHWH is the hero of every story. And He's where the joy is!

DANIEL 7–9

Today we transition out of the hope literature portion of this book and into the apocalyptic prophecies. Daniel opens today with a flashback to an earlier vision, but even he can't figure things out; he needs help from an angel. His dream is about beasts, which represent empires or kingdoms, and horns, which represent kings. The worst horn will rise up and try to destroy God's people. He'll try to abolish their laws and will punish them for an amount of time that most commentators believe amounts to three and a half years. That period of time shows up a lot in Scripture's apocalyptic books. Numbers are significant in Judaism. Seven symbolizes completion and perfection, and some say three and a half carries the idea of incompletion or possibly even failure. This time period could be literal or could symbolize the horn's failure. Regardless of whether it's literal or figurative, the result is the same; the horn doesn't win. Because God—the Ancient of Days—is on the scene, ready to issue judgment. He's on His fiery chariot throne, and His servants—who are probably angels—are with Him. The horn mouths off to God, so God annihilates him. Then someone called the Son of Man begins to reign, and His rule will never end. The Son of Man is Jesus; He claims this title in Mark 14:61–62, among other places. In fact, it's His favorite way of referring to Himself.

Some scholars believe these four beasts represent the same four empires Nebby dreamed about in his statue dream, so it's possible God could be communicating the same information but with different imagery. Scholars are divided on which four empires are represented here, but most believe the strongest beast represents either ancient Greece or ancient Rome. Some believe these prophecies were fulfilled a few hundred years later, in Jesus's time, and others believe they apply to the future.

Chapter 8 gives us more animals and horns in a vision that is so historically precise it could make a believer out of a skeptic. It's perplexing

---

For more information on today's reading, see thebiblerecap.com/links.

to Daniel, but the angel Gabriel explains everything. It refers to Greece, specifically when Alexander the Great is ruling the empire. A ruler after him, who is almost certainly Antiochus IV, will punish God's people and succeed at bringing destruction to many of the things they cherish. History tells us that he slaughters thousands of Jews, sacrifices a pig on the altar in the temple, and sets up offerings to Zeus there. God says He'll personally destroy him. Daniel is so disturbed that he has to call in sick for a few days.

When Daniel reads Jeremiah, he realizes that the seventy years prophesied for their captivity are almost over. He seems grieved! He puts on sackcloth, smears himself with ashes, fasts, prays, and begs God for mercy. He acknowledges Israel's wickedness and God's just response to the broken covenant. He asks God to bring their judgment to an end and restore them, not because they're righteous, but because God is merciful. While Daniel is midsentence, the angel Gabriel shows up again. Some translations say Gabriel came "in swift flight," but the original Hebrew says he came to Daniel in the midst of Daniel's extreme weariness, as though Daniel were the one swiftly slipping away. Regardless, we shouldn't take it to mean that angels fly—they seem to travel at the speed of thought. Gabriel gives timelines for exile and restoration. There'll be setbacks—namely, Jerusalem will be destroyed again and there'll be wars and more devastation and desolation—but there's a decreed end to the tragedies.

TODAY'S GOD SHOT

Little phrases in these visions show us how all of this is part of God's plan, how His enemies are on a leash, and how the clock is ticking on their part of the story. Dominion is both "given" to and "taken away" from the four beasts (7:6; 7:12). There's an "appointed time" for things, and there'll be a "limit" on transgression (8:19; 8:23). And there's a "decreed end" (9:27). God is sovereign over His enemies, over His timeline, over His plan. Still, with all the nation-sized things on His to-do list, He sends a messenger to remind His prophet, "You are greatly loved." He's in the rise and fall of kingdoms, and He's in the tiny whispers to His servants. And He's where the joy is!

DANIEL 10–12

Daniel mourns and seeks God for three weeks, then sees a vision of a metal-looking man dressed in linen and gold. Many scholars think this is Gabriel again. The angel gives a glimpse into the spiritual realm, saying he's been fighting with the prince of Persia. Remember how each nation has their own set of gods to worship? Those gods are often connected to demonic powers. So the angel probably wasn't fighting a literal human prince; he was probably fighting the demonic power in charge of Persia. Some scholars believe those demonic powers indwell the leaders of those countries, so it could be a both/and situation, where he was fighting the demon indwelling the prince.

This fight lasted three weeks, and it turns out he wasn't just fighting one demon but many demons over Persia. When the archangel Michael came in as backup, they won. Daniel is stupefied, so the angel touches him, strengthens him, and encourages him: "O man greatly loved, fear not, peace be with you; be strong and of good courage" (10:19). The angel fills Daniel in, then leaves to fight another spiritual battle. This time, some Greek demons will be added to the mix. Fortunately, Michael will be there to help. By the way, Michael is the angel assigned to protect Daniel and all God's people.

The angel says Persia will flourish until a powerful Greek ruler—probably Alexander the Great—takes over. His reign will end when his kingdom is divided into fourths. Earthly power, even when aided and abetted by demons, is temporary. Control is an illusion. All kingdoms crumble except one. There'll be wars between unnamed kingdoms, but they're easily recognizable to modern historians looking back on these prophecies. These kings and kingdoms use murder, manipulation, and marriage alliances to maintain positions of power. One king will stand "in the glorious land, with destruction in his hand"; this almost certainly refers to the terror Antiochus IV will bring to Jerusalem.

But didn't God promise to bring the remnant back to the land after seventy years and establish an eternal kingdom and that there would be peace forever? So why is He saying there'll be more wars? What about the peace He promised? The trajectory of God's redemption has always been a process. His people still haven't repented. They still don't have new hearts. He still hasn't put His Spirit in them. And the eternal Messiah-King hasn't established His reign on earth yet. God's seventy-year timeline was for the return to Jerusalem, but the promises of peace have always been pointing us to Christ and His eternal kingdom. In the meantime, though, there'll be transgression and war, but on the upside, there is more time for people to repent. Some of the wise will be persecuted, but persecution isn't the end for them. Glory is. However, the wicked king "shall come to his end, with none to help him." Israel will endure a terrible war—the worst they've ever seen—but all of God's people have been accounted for by name and will survive it.

Then, for the first time in the Hebrew Bible, Scripture explicitly addresses the afterlife. Up until this point, we've mostly just heard death referred to as "the grave," with only a few hints about life after death. Here, the angel says those who sleep in the dust (that is, the dead) will wake to face one of two realities: everlasting life, or shame and everlasting contempt. God tells Daniel He's already appointed a specific place for him in the afterlife. Then two other angels appear, and one wants to know when these things will take place. The main angel replies with a phrase that typically indicates three and a half years.

TODAY'S GOD SHOT

Sometimes we want to know exactly what to expect because it lets us off the hook of having to trust God. We treat details about the future like a security blanket. But the only knowledge that brings security is knowledge of who God is. There are many things in this book that God only told Daniel. Other things He doesn't share even when Daniel asks (12:8). Even some angels aren't informed about certain things. As we read these prophecies, we can rest knowing that we don't have to master the book of Daniel and map out what may or may not happen in the future, because YHWH is already there, and He's where the joy is!

EZRA 1–3

This historical narrative covers almost a century, and we don't meet Ezra until several chapters in. The book opens with King Cyrus of Persia, who has just defeated Babylon. He's a pagan, but God stirs up his spirit to rebuild the temple in Jerusalem, so he sends fifty thousand exiles home with the best provisions and the 5,400 stolen temple vessels. The historical record of the families that return traces them back to the families that left Jerusalem in the exile. For those who can't be traced, the author says, "These people are going back to Israel from Babylon, but we're not sure they came from Israel originally. To be on the safe side, they aren't allowed to be priests."

After they've been back in Israel for seven months and have settled into their towns and homes, they gather in Jerusalem. They've started to grow fearful because they're encountering the people who moved into their land while they were in exile, so they put down roots that connect them back to God. They rebuild the altar in Jerusalem and make burnt offerings and freewill offerings.

We see the word *freewill* three times in today's reading. It roughly translates to "voluntary." Each time we see it in Scripture, it's followed by the word *offering*, so the phrase *freewill offering* pertains to a voluntary offering—something the people are giving God above and beyond the baseline of what He has required of them. In modern times, we've mostly ditched the words *freewill* and *voluntary* and just call it an offering—but church language varies in each denomination and culture. All that to say, when people use the phrase *tithes and offerings*, both words are money related, but they usually pertain to two different aspects of giving. *Tithe* literally means "tenth," and offerings are often considered to be any portion above and beyond that. This can be a controversial topic. Some scholars say we aren't required to tithe anymore, so everything we give God would fall in the offering category. And others say tithing is still

For more information on today's reading, see thebiblerecap.com/links.

something God asks of His people as a demonstration of their faith in His provision and as a means of sustaining the people who serve His kingdom and His church with their lives.

The newly returned exiles are giving to God generously, and they're also using some of the grant money Cyrus gave them to buy supplies in preparation for building the temple. And after about two years, under the leadership of Zerubbabel and Jeshua, they start appointing priests. They also start laying a foundation, and lots of people are very excited about this. They have a worship service, like the kind that David and Solomon led the people of Israel in generations ago.

But in the midst of all the guitars and drums and fog machines, some of the older people, who have been around long enough to remember the First Temple, are sitting in the back row wailing. Some commentators say they're mourning over the fact that this temple falls short of the First Temple. Others say they're just remembering all they've been through and that their eyes are so fixed on the past that they can't actively celebrate what God is doing in the present.

TODAY'S GOD SHOT

"For he is good, for his steadfast love endures forever [toward Israel]" (Psalm 136:1). We're standing in the middle of a promise fulfilled today. The Israelites are back in the land after being driven into exile. Finally! Offerings are being made on the altar, the priests are being reestablished, the foundation is being built up, and regardless of what this temple was or will be, we're seeing the fulfillment of God's promises to His people. He's been working even in the hearts of His enemies to bless His people. He's bringing them back to the land. He's restoring, He's remaking, and He's where the joy is!

EZRA 4–6; PSALM 137

Yesterday the returned exiles started rebuilding the temple. Today that comes to a screeching halt. A few of their local enemies try to stop the plan by offering false help, but Zerubbabel and Jeshua send them packing because Cyrus said the Israelites who returned from exile should rebuild it. The enemies' next plan is to bribe officials and lie; it works for a while—the construction project is put on hold for roughly fifteen years. When the new king, Ahasuerus, begins his reign, they write him a letter to make sure he knows why they've asked for the construction project to be stopped. When his successor, Artaxerxes, takes over, they write another letter, calling the Jews rebels. Artaxerxes investigates and sees their point, so he decides to shut things down. Israel's enemies get the king's mandate and rush over to Jerusalem and force them to stop building again.

In chapter 5, the prophets Haggai and Zechariah encourage the Jews amid their enemies' attacks. As a result, Zerubbabel and Jeshua, the current leaders of the returned exiles, rally the troops to start rebuilding. Meanwhile the governor and his crew swing by to inspect the site, then they send a letter to Persia's new king, Darius, saying, "The Jews in Jerusalem are rebuilding the temple. Apparently, their ancestors built it a long time ago, but then they angered God so He drove them into exile. Now they're saying Cyrus sent them back home and said they could rebuild their temple and even gave them a bunch of vessels for it. Could you double-check the records to see if that's true? Because we're really not sure how to proceed."

Darius looks through all the archives and finally finds the information in one of the storage rooms in the king's summer home in the mountains. It reveals that not only had Cyrus given them the permit to rebuild the temple, but he also gave permission to build it *six times larger* than before, and then he'd followed that by saying, "Let the cost be paid from the royal treasury." Darius writes the governor back and says, "Back off. Let them rebuild. The only time you need to bother them is to write them a check, because you're footing the bill for it. Give them whatever supplies they need and whatever they need for sacrifices and offerings every day. Do whatever they need so that they can continue to seek God and pray for me and my family. P.S. No one can change this command, or he'll get the death penalty and I'll turn his house into a landfill. And may God overthrow anyone who tries to overthrow the Jews or destroy their temple." Wow!

The governor does as commanded, and the Jews prosper. Haggai and Zechariah continue to prophesy, and the construction crew keeps working until they finish the temple and dedicate it to God. Then they celebrate Passover seventy years after their exile, just like God promised. And what's more, this Passover isn't just for the Jews. It's for anyone who worships YHWH, Gentiles included. They're welcomed into the family of the Israelites.

Psalm 137 references Jerusalem's destruction and recounts the time when they were exiles in Babylon and remembering life in Jerusalem. While it felt like torture to think about their homeland, it was also torture to think of forgetting their homeland. They ask God to punish their enemies and bring justice. It ends with a shocking expression of anger and grief, reminding us again that God can handle our worst emotions.

TODAY'S GOD SHOT

If the enemy hadn't tried to stop the Jews from rebuilding, the Jews would've rebuilt, but they would've had to pay their own bills. Instead, God works it out so that the enemy's efforts to thwart His plans result in a better outcome for His people! God's enemies deceive, frustrate, and accuse. They wield fear as a weapon, and if they can't stop you outright, they'll try to discourage you into quitting. *But God.* He says, "I'll take their lies and their scheming and their manipulation, and I'll use them as tools to expose the truth, bless My people, and advance My kingdom." No one can pull off that kind of redemption story like YHWH. He's where the joy is!

HAGGAI 1–2

We first met the minor prophet Haggai yesterday in Ezra. He and Zechariah were encouraging the returned exiles of Judah as they worked to rebuild the temple. Today we find out what he said. After the exiles return from Babylon, their first high priest is Jeshua (also called Joshua). Haggai has a conversation with Jeshua and Zerubbabel, the local ruler over Judah, confronting them both about the people's misplaced priorities. Haggai says, "No matter what you do to your own homes and lifestyles, it'll never be enough. You'll always want more. But do you know what would be a wise use of your time and a righteous use of your energy? Rebuilding God's house. And until you focus on what matters, God is going to withhold everything you're trying to gain." Jeshua and Zerubbabel know Haggai's words are true. But it's not all correction—Haggai offers consolation too: God is with them. Then God stirs up the spirits of all the people to obey Him. In a few weeks, they're building again.

When they've been rebuilding for about a month, God tells Haggai to identify all the people who saw the First Temple with their own eyes before Babylon destroyed it. Then he says, "This new temple we're building doesn't look like much, does it? It's a shadow of the first one, right? But don't worry—this is just the beginning." Then God says, "Work, for I am with you, declares the LORD of hosts. . . . My Spirit remains in your midst. Fear not." He reminds them to keep their heads down and keep working because He's with them. He's in the process of building something they can't see yet. He owns all the silver and gold and all the treasures of all the nations, and someday all of that will be evidenced in the place where He chooses to dwell. He doesn't say when, but He's going to make His dwelling place magnificent.

Months later, while they're still rebuilding, God gives Haggai a question for Jeshua the high priest: "If a piece of holy food touches a piece

For more information on today's reading, see thebiblerecap.com/links.

of common food, does it make the common food holy?" No. But why? If the priests' garments can transmit holiness, why can't meat used for a sacrifice do the same? The unique thing about the priests' garments is that they've been in the presence of the glory of YHWH, whereas the food Haggai describes is just holy in the sense that it's been set apart to be used for a sacrifice. The glory of YHWH's holiness far outweighs something that's just been designated for sacrifice.

Then Haggai has another question: "Can uncleanness be transmitted?" This time the answer is yes. Even though modern Western culture is very different from ancient Jewish culture, this makes sense to us. If our clean hand touches a dirty faucet, the faucet doesn't become clean, but our hand does become dirty. Then Haggai gets to the point he's been driving toward. God says, "Since that's how things work, we have a problem with the people building the temple. Their hearts aren't clean, so their hands aren't clean, so they're building a defiled temple from the ground up. Maybe you've noticed that I keep thwarting their efforts to finish it. Maybe you've seen how it's all 'two steps forward and one step back.' That's Me. I'm doing that. I don't want you to get to the end of this project and have it be an unclean building that I can't dwell in and you can't worship in. I want their hearts, not their hard work! We've got a heart problem, not a construction problem. But the good news is I'm here to change that." Then God says He's got big things in store for Zerubbabel, who is a direct descendant of King David.

TODAY'S GOD SHOT

"The latter glory of this house shall be greater than the former" (2:9). After all Israel has done to break God's heart through the years, they deserve a downgrade, at best. It's not like they've learned their lesson. Even today they selfishly focus on their own houses instead of His, being greedy and foolish again, building with unclean hands and hearts. But He still promises them that He'll dwell among them again and that it'll be even better than before. Wow. No matter what is destroyed, God can rebuild. And when God rebuilds something, He improves on it. He's where the joy is!

ZECHARIAH 1–4

Zechariah is one of two prophets to the returned exiles, and he's also a priest. Through him, God wants the current generation to know how much their ancestors' sins impacted things, and He begs them not to walk the same path. Those people are gone, and even the prophets He sent to warn them are gone, but He's still here with the same message, because the truth doesn't die. Their ancestors eventually repented while in exile and acknowledged their sins deserved punishment.

Then we launch into vision one of nine in this book, and the first eight likely happen back to back on the same night. Vision one is of a bunch of horses sent to patrol the earth. They report that everything is at rest. The problem is the nations should not be at rest. They've mistreated God's people, and He's not going to let it slide. While He has returned to Jerusalem with mercy, that mercy is for His people and not for those who oppose Him. He'll comfort Zion and choose Jerusalem, not His enemies. For those who oppose Him, His anger has increased. During all of this, there's a man in the trees—the Angel of the Lord—so it's quite possible that the preincarnate Jesus is the one acting as a mediator between God the Father and His patrolling horses.

Vision two is of horns and skilled workers, like stonemasons and blacksmiths. The four horns represent nations and empires—specifically those that have scattered God's people (possibly Assyria, Babylon, Greece, and Rome). The blacksmiths smash them as punishment.

In vision three, a man measures Jerusalem. Two angels tell Zechariah to let the man know that God will fill Jerusalem and that He'll be their protection all around them. He tells the exiles to return home to Jerusalem, because He'll personally deal with anyone who messes with them—they're the apple of His eye. Then He reiterates that foreigners will be joined with Israel as His people: "Many nations shall join themselves to the Lord in that day, and shall be my people."

For more information on today's reading, see thebiblerecap.com/links.

The high priest Jeshua is a key figure in vision four. He's standing in front of the Angel of the LORD (likely Jesus), and Satan is there too, accusing Jeshua. The word *satan* means "accuser," so it makes sense that the accuser is accusing. Despite the fact that Jeshua is wearing filthy garments, the LORD rebukes Satan for his accusations against Jeshua, then refers to Jeshua as a stick that was snatched from the fire. God gives him clean clothes and a clean turban to wear, then says, "If you obey My ways, you'll be part of the redemption story I'm writing." God's references to His servant *the branch* are almost certainly pointing to Christ, who is called *the branch* elsewhere in Scripture. And when God mentions the day when iniquity is removed (3:9), that's a reference to Christ's triumph over sin. God is letting Jeshua know that he's set up to be a part of ushering in the kingdom; God calls him to be faithful.

Vision five is of a golden lampstand (that is, a menorah) with seven lamps that each have seven wicks, for a total of forty-nine lights, plus a bowl at the top. Beside it are two olive trees, and their oil fuels the lamp. In Scripture, oil often represents God the Spirit. The trees represent the anointed ones—"sons of fresh oil" in Hebrew. Most scholars say these are Jeshua and Zerubbabel, who have been newly appointed and anointed to serve God's purposes with the returned exiles. And as the vision implies, they won't be doing it by their own strength or power, but by God's Spirit—the oil flowing through them!

TODAY'S GOD SHOT

When Satan accuses Jeshua before God, God makes a command to strip him of his filthy garments and put clean clothes on him. Then God says, "I will clothe you with pure vestments." It's incredible that we get clothed in robes of righteousness instead of our sin-soaked clothes, but it's even more astonishing that God doesn't tell *Jeshua* to take off his dirty clothes or to put on the clean clothes. God Himself takes responsibility for it. This is God's doing, not Jeshua's. Righteousness is something done to us and for us, not by us. We can't clean ourselves up, but He can, and by His grace, He does. He's where the righteousness is, and He's where the joy is!

ZECHARIAH 5–9

We ended yesterday halfway through Zechariah's strange night of multiple visions. Today we pick up with vision six, which features a flying scroll roughly the size of a billboard. It flies over the city, bringing judgment to everyone who disobeys God's laws. The two laws mentioned in the vision represent the two types of sin: sin against our neighbor and sin against God, which ultimately represent all God's laws. The angel calls this scroll a curse—some say this means the scroll only held the curses for breaking the covenant, not the benefits of keeping it. Others say this reminds us that the law's purpose is to reveal that we all deserve death. Only in Christ do we find life and freedom from the curse of the law (Galatians 3:13).

Vision seven is of a woman who represents wickedness. The angel seals her up in a basket before she's carried away by stork-like women to Babylon, where they'll build a house for her and the basket. Some believe the woman represents the pagan goddess Asherah, and others say she's just a symbol. This vision seems to suggest that Babylon is the new representation for evil; after all, it's where evil's home is being built. The book of Revelation spends a lot of time addressing Babylon's wickedness.

We get more horses in vision eight. Horses symbolize power and strength, and as these four chariots go to the four corners of the earth, it demonstrates that YHWH's power extends over the whole earth—even in the directions associated with His enemies. God has Zechariah get gold and silver from the exiles, fashion a crown out of it, and set it on the head of Jeshua the high priest. Then Zechariah has a bonus vision filled with a mixture of priestly and royal imagery. They're putting a crown on the head of a priest, who traditionally wears a turban. Then there's a priest sitting on a throne in the temple, and there's also a crown. All this blending together is foreshadowing Jesus, the Messianic King. And Jeshua the high priest is the branch that is the forerunner of *the* Branch.

In chapter 7, some men ask Zechariah for advice. They've been in the habit of fasting for two months each year and want to know if they should continue. Scholars speculate on their motivation for asking—either they want praise for fasting regularly or they want a pass on religious practices since things in Jerusalem aren't quite up to their standards. God compares them to their ancestors: "When you fasted, you weren't fasting with Me in mind. When you ate, you weren't eating with Me in mind. Everything you do is self-serving. I don't want your religious actions without heart change. And it'll be evident when your hearts have changed because you'll care about the things I care about—justice, kindness, and mercy. Your ancestors never quite got there. Instead of becoming more like Me, their hearts grew harder, so I scattered them."

Not all the promises God has made to their people have been fulfilled yet, and not all the things their ancestors lost have been restored yet. God knows it has traumatized them, and He speaks truth to their lost hopes and their deep aches. He describes children playing in the streets—a prophecy that has been fulfilled, at least in part, today. He says someday foreigners will long to travel to Jerusalem—that has been fulfilled too! And He keeps telling them that it's coming and that they play a vital role in His plan for restoration.

TODAY'S GOD SHOT

Jesus shows up repeatedly in today's reading. "Behold your king is coming to you; righteous and having salvation is he, humble and mounted on a donkey, on a colt, the foal of a donkey" (9:9). We recognize the donkey part, because Jesus rode through Jerusalem on a donkey in Matthew 21, but even without the donkey, He's unmistakable. He speaks peace to the nations in verse 10. He rules to the end of the earth. Through the blood of His covenant, in verse 11, He sets prisoners free. He restores double to prisoners of hope in verse 12. He saves His people, and they shine like jewels in His crown in verse 16. And verse 17 says, "How great is his goodness, and how great his beauty!" When we gaze at Him, we can't deny it—everything about Him is what our souls know is missing. He's where the joy is!

ZECHARIAH 10–14

God promises to punish Judah's wicked leaders. Because of their passivity, the people sought guidance from wicked sources—diviners and false gods. Then, when God's sheep are under His care, they'll grow strong and have victory over the enemy. He'll bring them back from the nations where they've been scattered and multiply them in the promised land again. God has Zechariah shepherd the flock destined for destruction. Some say this is a prophetic parable intended to help him better understand God's perspective. Others say it's a sign-act, where he becomes the literal shepherd of the group of animals known as the flock doomed to slaughter. This title likely refers to the animals kept near the temple for sacrificial offerings. Since not everyone owns animals, some people have to buy animals to sacrifice. But the animal owners and shepherds are wicked people who only care about the money, not the animals. This parallels the relationship between Judah's leaders and God's people.

Zechariah initially takes pity on the sheep, firing wicked shepherds. He guides them with two staffs, which he names Favor and Union—or Kindness and Unity—representing not only his relationship to the sheep individually but also the relationship the sheep have as a flock. But he loses patience with them because they hate him. He snaps his staff in half and quits his job. He gets a payout of thirty pieces of silver, but God says to give it to the person who makes the clay pots for the temple.

Chapter 12 prophesies a day yet to come when the nations will attack Jerusalem, but God will fight on Judah's behalf and destroy those who come against them using panic as His weapon. Judah will recognize YHWH as the reason for their victory. He'll pour out on His people His spirit of grace and mercy, which changes people. Verse 10 says they will "look on me, on him whom they have pierced, they shall mourn for him, as one mourns for an only child, and weep bitterly over him, as one weeps over a firstborn." John 19:37 points to this verse as a prophecy of Jesus—they pierced Him and will mourn over Him, the firstborn Son.

Chapter 13 gives us more prophecies of Jesus. He is the fountain who washes His people clean from their sins and uncleanness. Someday, He'll cut off all the idols and false prophets in the land. You don't need prophets anymore when all the prophecies have been fulfilled. The false prophets will go into hiding, but they won't be able to keep up the ruse, because their backs will be covered in the scars they got from the cutting practices associated with worshipping false gods. Verse 7 is quoted in Mark 14:27 when Jesus dies. "Strike the shepherd, and the sheep will be scattered." And that's what happened when Jesus died—the sheep were scattered. But in God's great plan, that's exactly how the gospel spread to all the nations. There will be trials and sanctification, but what appears to be only tragic is used for God's glory and the good of all His people.

Chapter 14 recounts the future prophecies of the coming day of the LORD again, some of which sounds like chemical warfare. On that day, God, presumably God the Son, will stand on the Mount of Olives, which will be split, probably by an earthquake, causing a river to flow out of Jerusalem. God will reign on the earth and over everything in it!

TODAY'S GOD SHOT

Zechariah becomes the shepherd of the flock destined for slaughter. This prophecy points us to Jesus repeatedly. Thirty pieces of silver is the price Judas Iscariot is paid for betraying Jesus to the authorities (Matthew 26:14–16). Zechariah gives his to the temple potters, and when Judas regrets betraying Jesus, he throws the silver into the temple, and it's used to buy his burial plot in a potter's field (Matthew 27:3–10). And of course, Jesus is the "lamb destined for slaughter"; this was the Father's plan before the world was even formed (Revelation 13:8). Zechariah 11 is dark, but it points us to Jesus the Good Shepherd, who was first rejected by His sheep, then took the place of those sheep in the slaughter. He's the shepherd *and* the sacrifice—because when it comes to His kids, God provides all He requires. He's where the joy is!

ESTHER 1–5

Esther is the only book in Scripture that doesn't mention God's name, but we see Him in the shadows of every scene, working things out in keeping with His plan and promises. Ahasuerus is king of Persia. He's not a follower of YHWH; he's just a pagan king in a pagan empire. He throws a massive six-month party, presumably for himself. As the grand finale, he wants his beautiful Queen Vashti to come out and take a lap in her crown—and possibly nothing else. She refuses to come, which is an affront to his ego and his throne. He calls a staff meeting to find out what kind of punishment he's allowed to give her. His advisors are personally offended by her actions because now their wives will feel like they can do whatever they want too! They write a law banishing and replacing her.

They throw a mandatory beauty pageant to find her replacement. They gather all the beautiful young virgins from the 127 provinces in King A's territory, essentially kidnapping them and forcing them into the king's harem. Some scholars suggest this could be voluntary, but given how King A and his advisors seem to view females, it's unlikely. This is more along the lines of human trafficking of girls in the age range of twelve to fourteen. His staff spends about a year preparing each girl and then dresses them up so he can decide which one he wants that night. For King A, choosing a new queen is an audition process in which each girl spends a night with him and is sent away in the morning. Essentially, the king spends years systematically deflowering all the girls he's kidnapped to decide which one he likes best. After their night with the king, they're added to his growing list of concubines while he moves on to the next, devastating an entire generation of females in Persia.

Among those is a girl named Esther. She's been raised by her cousin Mordecai. He's protective of her and has a good position, despite being a Jew in Persia. He has her keep her nationality a secret. Four years after

For more information on today's reading, see thebiblerecap.com/links.

Vashti is dismissed, the king finally chooses Esther for the night. That's almost 1,500 days—and possibly 1,500 girls—later. Esther exercises wisdom and humility, and God grants her favor with the king, who makes her his new queen. When Mordecai overhears a plot to attack King A, he passes the word to Esther, who tells her new husband. The conspirators get hanged, and normally Mordecai would be honored, but he's forgotten. This divine oversight sets the table for what's next.

King A establishes a new second-in-command, Haman the Agagite, a descendant of one of Israel's oldest enemies, the Amalekites. Mordecai refuses to bow to him, so now Haman wants to kill all the Jews. He tells King A these outsiders are disobeying the law and must be stopped. He even offers to pay for the execution himself! King A says yes, and they send letters to all the provinces on the day before Passover, saying the Jews in Persia will be slaughtered in eleven months. Mordecai tells Esther her life is on the line too, and this may be the very reason she's in this position. She seems emboldened by his rebuke and says, "Let's fast for three days, then perhaps the king will see me. If I die trying, it's a risk worth taking."

When the king invites her in, she returns the favor by inviting him and Haman to dinner. He offers her anything she wants, and she asks for another feast tomorrow night. Haman is overjoyed until Mordecai refuses to bow to him. His wife tries to console him by saying he should build a giant gallows for Mordecai, and he has it constructed overnight.

TODAY'S GOD SHOT

In 4:14 Mordecai says, "If you keep silent at this time, relief and deliverance will rise for the Jews from another place. . . . And who knows whether you have not come to the kingdom for such a time as this?" Mordecai knows God has promised to preserve His people, and he trusts that God will be faithful to His Word. He lets Esther know that she may be the very tool God uses to accomplish His plans and fulfill His promises. Despite being in mourning, despite being under a death threat, Mordecai leans into what he knows to be true about YHWH. He's our only hope, and He's where the joy is!

ESTHER 6–10

Haman's crew is working on the gallows, which are more like a big spike to impale a person on. Meanwhile, King A can't fall asleep, which is God's providence at work. To combat his insomnia, he asks one of his staff to read him a bedtime story about everything that has happened since he took office. That's when he realizes he never thanked that nice man who saved his life. That divine oversight from four years ago led up to this very moment! Just as it dawns on the king, Haman walks in to ask for permission to kill Mordecai. But before he can get the question out, King A says, "Suppose I want to honor someone? What's the best way to do that?" Haman pulls out his list of bullet points—all the ways he wants to be honored and is expecting the king to honor him, of course. When he finishes, King A says, "Great! Go do all those things for Mordecai!" Haman is humiliated, leading a parade through the center of town on behalf of Mordecai.

Haman heads back for another banquet with the king and queen. Once again, the king offers the queen whatever she wants, and that's when she fills him in on what Haman has done to her and her people. The king is furious, so he goes outside to cool off. Meanwhile, Haman begs Esther to save his life. The wine is mentioned a lot in this passage, so perhaps Haman is tipsy when he falls on the couch where Esther is seated. And since God is sovereign even over the stumbling of a drunk fool, it happens just as the king walks back inside. He thinks it's an assault of some sort, and his bodyguards grab Haman and take him away to kill him. The death Haman planned for Mordecai is doled out to him instead.

Esther tells King A that Mordecai is her cousin and guardian, then sets him over Haman's inheritance. The king moves him into Haman's position. But the clock is still ticking toward the pronounced edict against the Jews in Persia's provinces. Esther begs the king to reverse the edict,

For more information on today's reading, see thebiblerecap.com/links.

but royal edicts are irreversible. The king gives Esther and Mordecai permission to write whatever they please, and they come up with a brilliant plan: Since they can't stop people from attacking the Jews, they'll give the Jews permission to fight back and plunder the goods of anyone who attacks them. They hope this new edict will deter people from attacking the Jews at all, but for those who still do attack, the Jews will at least have legal grounds to fight back.

This is a great relief to the Jews. In fact, lots of the locals either convert to Judaism or claim to be Jews just to be associated with the people who have the upper hand. If it's the latter, nobody is endorsing their lies—it just shows us how this impacts the political climate.

When the day comes, the Jews are attacked, so they fight back and kill seventy-five thousand attackers. But they don't take the plunder. This could sound like a foolish move, but it seems more like a move of honor. Here's why: Remember how Haman is a descendant of the Amalekites, the long-standing enemies of the Israelites? When they fought against each other in 1 Samuel 15, God commanded the Israelites not to take any of the spoils from their victory, but Saul did, and God punished him for it. It's possible they're trying to set right what Saul had gotten wrong in the war of their fathers six hundred years ago by aiming to honor God's commands instead of taking advantage of what's available to them. They kill Haman's sons, then celebrate their victory. They also make this an annual celebration known as Purim.

TODAY'S GOD SHOT

God is hands-on despite His apparent absence. He's at work flipping the plans of the wicked to fall back on them. He's at work flipping things for the righteous too—to bless them! He's at work fulfilling His promises despite an irreversible edict from the king. Esther isn't the hero here, and Mordecai isn't the hero—YHWH is obviously orchestrating every detail of this story to be the Rescuer of His people. Time will reveal how God is rescuing you in your current situation. He may appear to be absent, but He is always at work, fulfilling His promises for our good and His glory. He can be trusted. He's where the joy is!

EZRA 7–10

Today's events occur roughly sixty years after the first six chapters. Ezra lives in Babylon until Persia conquers it, then Persia's King Artaxerxes sends him and some other Jews back to Jerusalem, offering massive blessings and provisions and promising to take care of anything Ezra needs. He has Ezra appoint magistrates and judges to teach and enact YHWH's laws. And the temple will get a pass on paying taxes. This is an exciting assignment for Ezra; he's a Torah scholar who was born into exile, and now he'll be teaching the Scriptures in Jerusalem! He's probably twenty-two years old, and this is a lot of authority for such a young man, but he knows where the assignment has come from and he knows where his strength lies. He praises God for putting these plans in the king's heart and says, "I took courage, for the hand of the LORD my God was on me" (7:28). The awareness of God's nearness imparts courage!

They set out on their months-long journey, and as he's counting his men, he realizes they forgot the Levites, who are necessary for running the temple. They send for some temple servants and are provided for "by the good hand of our God on us." Then fear begins to creep in. This trip takes them through potentially hostile territory. The king offered to send bodyguards, but he said, "No thanks, God will take care of us." He stated it as fact but had never actually asked God for it. So he fasts and asks God for help, which is exactly where his hope lies. He divides the holy vessels among the priests, and although they encounter some thieves, "the hand of our God was on us, and He delivered us from the hand of the enemy and from ambushes on the way." They arrive in Jerusalem safely and all the holy vessels are accounted for, so they make offerings to YHWH.

In chapter 9 they learn how bad things are in Jerusalem, even though the exiles have only been back for a few decades. The main issue is that the returned exiles started marrying locals who don't know or love YHWH, which was also a problem in the past. Marrying foreigners isn't an issue if they're followers of YHWH—it's just that so few of the foreigners are. God forbade marrying people of other religions because it would lead them to worship false gods, and it did. To make matters worse, the leaders and priests are the ones leading the way in this.

Ezra is devastated. He pulls out his hair and beard, tears his clothes, mourns, and goes to the only place he knows to go: YHWH. He confesses their sins and recounts God's great love to them through all their rebellion, acknowledging that God hasn't punished them according to what they deserve. He's shown mercy in response to their sins, and He's shown grace by giving them favor in the eyes of foreign kings. Ezra seems terrified that God will say, "Enough! I've given you a second chance and you've blown it!" and kill them all. This is a wake-up call. They confess their sins and create a covenant with God to divorce any pagans they've married. And here's where we hit a problem: They make a covenant with God to do something God never told them to do. He said not to marry pagans, but He never said to divorce pagans. They assume it's what He wants, but as we've seen, they don't know God's Word or His ways.

So what does God think of their oath? Some scholars say the word used here for *marry* is different from the usual word, that this is more along the lines of cohabitating. So it's possible that they're living together but not married, which means Ezra isn't commanding a divorce so much as a breakup. Other scholars say Ezra mourns but doesn't ask God for direction; he just rolls with the suggestion of the people. The book ends with him calling everyone to gather and repent as they promised.

TODAY'S GOD SHOT

Despite how messed up the whole last scene is—sin on sin on sin—Shecaniah has beautiful words as he confesses his sins: "Even now there is hope for Israel in spite of this." Their hope isn't that they're finally going to get things right. Their hope is that God has entered into a covenant with them, God has preserved them despite their sin, God offers forgiveness, and God extends hope. Hope is a person—and He's where the joy is!

NEHEMIAH 1–5

Nehemiah is an Israelite official who works as the king's personal assistant, giving him an inside track for getting the king's support. When we open today, he's got a family member in town from Jerusalem who says things aren't going well there. The exiles have been back for almost a century but still haven't rebuilt the walls. He's distraught, and he mourns, fasts, and prays. He also quotes God back to God, regarding the promises in Deuteronomy 30:1–4. God has lived up to what He said He'd do, but the people haven't done what God asked, so Nehemiah wants to do something about it.

When he asks for the king's approval, the king gives him everything he wants: time off work, a travel visa, and building supplies. He also sends military officers with him for the journey. Nehemiah acknowledges God's role in every level of this plan moving forward. God put the idea in his heart (2:12), and God granted him favor with the king when working out the plan (2:8). What God initiates, He will sustain and He will fulfill. That's not to say it won't come with opposition—Nehemiah encounters that right away. Sanballat and Tobiah are governors of the areas surrounding Judah, and they're not pleased that anyone who works for Persia would help the people of Judah. Even though the king sent Nehemiah on this journey, they think it was a bad military decision.

When Nehemiah gets to Jerusalem, he stays quiet about his plans, sneaking out at night to inspect the city's roads and walls before showing up as the new governor and presenting his plan to the locals. His pep talk is a hit, and all the people are on board. But when word gets back to Sanballat, Tobiah, and another governor, they falsely accuse him of rebelling against Persia. He isn't deterred. He says they'll keep working on what God started, trusting God will finish it. He reminds the neighboring governors that Jerusalem doesn't belong to them—it belongs to God and His people.

For more information on today's reading, see thebiblerecap.com/links.

Chapter 3 lists the projects and workers and even calls out a few nobles who think they're too good to help. In chapter 4, Sanballat and Tobiah make more threats, and Nehemiah asks God to turn their words back on them. The people continue building, no matter what their enemies say or do. Then, since the enemy can't discourage them, they attack them. Nehemiah asks God for help and sets up a guard for protection. But as word gets out to Jerusalem that their enemies want to kill them to stop their progress, their morale drops. They're in an especially vulnerable situation because they're rebuilding the very wall that would normally serve as a military defense, and they're barely halfway done, so the enemy has ample opportunity to invade. After the enemy sees God working on their behalf, they back off. But the Jews aren't letting their guard down. They take off their construction vests and put on armor, and they pick up weapons and work with one hand on offense and one hand on defense.

All this is happening during a famine. And because of the supply shortage, some locals have started enslaving other Jews. Nehemiah is furious. He commands the leaders to give back the land they've taken and stop charging interest, because those things go against God's laws and heart. They promise to do what he says. Nehemiah does his part to solve the problem too. Even though governors have the right to take an income from the people, he doesn't, because he knows they're already hard-pressed, plus he has the financial support of King Artaxerxes. For twelve years, the king pays Nehemiah's bills, and the money also blesses the locals.

TODAY'S GOD SHOT

God works in a variety of ways, sometimes in the miraculous, sometimes in the mundane. Sometimes Israel didn't even have to lift a finger to win a battle—God just did it all on His own! But sometimes, like today, He works *through* His people—they're praying, working, and ready to defend His city. It's key to stay tuned in to God like Nehemiah does, always asking Him for direction. He has a plan; we just have to ask what role we play in it. Sometimes He calls us to be active, sometimes He calls us to wait for Him to work, but He always has a plan. His plan is good, and He's where the joy is!

NEHEMIAH 6–7

Yesterday we left off with Nehemiah and his crew working on the wall—each with a sword in one hand and a shovel in the other. Today as they're about to wrap up the finishing touches on the wall, two of his bullies, Sanballat and Geshem, send him a threatening letter. It's veiled as a party invitation, but Nehemiah knows better. So he says, "Sorry, guys, I can't make it. I've got a big project due at work." They write back three more times, then Sanballat's servant shows up with *another* invitation that includes more false accusations. They say he wants to be king and he's making prophets lie about everything. He calls their bluff, because he knows it's part of their plan to intimidate him. As they're trying to weaken his resolve, he prays, "Now, O God, strengthen my hands."

God answers that prayer with a yes. We'll see it in the discernment God continues to give Nehemiah. He seeks guidance from a local prophet named Shemaiah, but he realizes something is off when Shemaiah suggests he go hide in the temple. He knows he's not allowed in the temple, because he's not a priest. God reveals to Nehemiah that his enemies had hired the prophet to lie to him—Shemaiah was in on the conspiracy. If Nehemiah had responded to his fears and not to his God, he would've committed an egregious sin. He stands firm, and the wall is finished in just fifty-two days. What had been lying in ruins for nearly a century was completed in under two months of God-appointed work. The surrounding nations fear Judah because they realize this task was impossible apart from God; God is definitely working on behalf of these returned exiles they don't like. Despite the wall being finished and God being glorified, Nehemiah's personal life is rough. He continues to suffer taunts, lies, betrayal, manipulation, and public humiliation.

In chapter 7, he sets everything in order for the grand opening. He hires his brother and the castle governor to run things in Jerusalem, because he knows this job will require a man who is faithful and God-fearing. Even though Jerusalem is big, not many people live inside the city walls yet, so he gives the gatekeepers orders about when to open and close the gates; they should be closed most of the day. This probably helps them avoid potential attacks.

Then God has Nehemiah record all the heads of families who have returned from exile and the number of people in their households as well as the Levites, priests, temple servants, and descendants of Solomon's servants. As for the people who claim to be Israelites but don't have their paper work, they're allowed to live among the Israelites but can't be priests—unless or until a priest can seek God on the matter and get a definitive yes. Altogether, there are fifty thousand people and eight thousand animals. They donated from their own wealth to the work of restoring the city and the temple. All told, they gave nearly eight hundred pounds of gold and over six hundred pounds of silver.

TODAY'S GOD SHOT

God grants Nehemiah incredible discernment and strength in the midst of the conspiracy of powerful people around him. They're threatening his livelihood and even his life, they're trying to get the people under his authority to doubt him and rebel against him, and they're relentless in their campaign against him, even though he keeps taking the high road. Since Nehemiah repeatedly seeks God for strength, direction, and discernment, it's clear that he knows where those things originate: with God, not with him. Since he got his start as an assistant, he's used to taking orders and following authority, which helps him stay humble. And when he gets promoted, he doesn't grow arrogant and show it off or pull out any false humility. True humility is confident humility—the confidence comes from looking to God as our source, and the humility comes from seeing ourselves in light of who God is. Confident humility is when you're not building yourself up or beating yourself up. Nehemiah walks in confident humility not because he's awesome, but because he knows the source of his strength lies in the God who calls him and equips him. Nehemiah knows He's where the joy is!

NEHEMIAH 8–10

The exiles are back, the temple is rebuilt, and the walls are restored. But God isn't concerned only with the details of where they live and worship, He's concerned with their hearts. Ezra and Nehemiah team up to address this. All the men, women, and children old enough to understand gather together to listen as Ezra reads the Word, probably the five books of Moses, aloud. When there's a confusing spot, the Levites help them understand. It's necessary for people to not just hear the Word but to understand the Word—because we can't and won't respond properly to something we misunderstand. They're grieved over what they hear, but the priests say it's worth rejoicing over. Today is to be celebrated, because it's a day God set apart to remind them about their relationship with Him. So they end the day with a feast.

On day two, the heads of the households come back for more reading. That's when they cover Leviticus 23:33–43 and realize there's a feast they've forgotten—one God commanded a long time ago but that they haven't celebrated in almost one thousand years. The Feast of Booths is a seven-day fall festival commemorating God's provision for the Israelites for forty years while they lived in the wilderness. On each day of the feast, Ezra reads more of the law to them while the Levites help them understand it. On the eighth day, after they'd finished celebrating, they have a sacred gathering.

Later that month, they gather again for the reading of the Word, fasting, worship, and repentance. Ezra offers a prayer recounting all God has done for His people, which is an abridged version of everything we've read since Day 1: He alone is God. He made heaven and earth and everything, He preserves everything He made, He chose Abraham and brought him out and gave him a new name, He paid attention to Abraham's heart, and He made a covenant with him and kept His promise because He's righteous. He saw the affliction of His people in Egypt and heard their cries and performed signs and wonders to protect them, because He knew they were being oppressed. He made a name for Himself. He divided the sea. He cast their pursuers down. He led them by cloud and by fire. He came down the mountain to speak with them. He gave them rules and laws. He made His ways known to them. He gave them food. He brought them water. He told them to go to the promised land. He swore to give it to them.

He performed wonders. He's ready to forgive. He's gracious and merciful, slow to anger, abounding in steadfast love. He doesn't forsake His people, even when they sin and rebel. He doesn't depart from them. He gave His Spirit to instruct them. He didn't withhold food or water. He made sure they lacked nothing. He gave them kingdoms and people. He multiplied their children. He brought them into the promised land. He subdued their enemies and gave them victory. When they rebelled, He gave them into the hands of their enemies. He heard their cries. He sent people to rescue them. They rebelled again, and He abandoned them until they cried out to Him. He heard their cries and delivered them. He warned them to repent. He bore with them. He warned them through His Spirit and His prophets. He gave them over to other nations, but He didn't make an end of them or forsake them.

Then Ezra says, "You keep Your Word. We've seen Your steadfast love. You've dealt with us righteously and faithfully, no matter how wicked we've been. Please take notice of our present hardships and trials." This prayer isn't demanding or entitled. It's a humble prayer of repentance and hope, honoring God and His character while appealing for mercy. The leaders promise to do all God commands.

TODAY'S GOD SHOT

God makes Himself known to people who have long forgotten or ignored who He is. They've never really known what His Word said, and they've abandoned one of His feasts for nearly a thousand years, and still, He says, "I'm not giving up on you." God is committed to being known by His people and being in relationship with them. He's so patient and persistent! And their hearts respond with an ache and a shout of joy. After all this time, they're finally seeing Him. And hopefully they're realizing He's where the joy is!

NEHEMIAH 11–13; PSALM 126

The leaders live in Jerusalem, but they need others to live there too, probably to keep a strong military presence. Via lottery, 10 percent of the people are chosen to move to the city, while others go voluntarily. Then Nehemiah holds a grand opening ceremony to dedicate the wall. They sing and praise God, then march along the Broad Wall, which you can still see in Jerusalem today, and around to the temple. They offer sacrifices and shouts of praise so loud that neighboring towns hear them! They appoint people to new jobs—storehouse manager, gatekeeper, singer, musician—and the people are thrilled because it signals that things are moving forward with their new life in the old city. They read from the Torah to keep learning what God says and realize they're accidentally disobeying some of His commands. But as soon as they discover their sin, they set out to obey.

Meanwhile, Tobiah is back. He's the neighboring governor who tried to stop Nehemiah from rebuilding the wall. While Nehemiah was out of town, Tobiah plotted with an insider to build a room for him in the temple courts. Nehemiah is furious, and with good cause. He throws Tobiah's furniture into the street, then purifies the space and puts everything back in order. He also learns that the Levites and singers haven't been paid or fed and have been fending for themselves. This is not what the people promised they'd do when they made a covenant to give generously to the temple and its workers. He calls them to account, and they bring what they've been withholding. They're also working on the Sabbath again, and every Sabbath is basically a flea market where foreigners bring things to sell to the locals. First, Nehemiah warns the locals that they're inviting disaster because they're breaking the covenant, then he starts locking the city gates every Sabbath so outsiders can't come in and sell things. He threatens to physically harm them if they return. He'd

For more information on today's reading, see thebiblerecap.com/links.

rather fight the vendors than have God bring punishment on Jerusalem for breaking the covenant.

They also start marrying people who don't love YHWH again. They have kids with pagans and don't teach them about YHWH. This is the biggest problem of all because it has indefinite consequences. Nehemiah can't just lock a gate to solve this—this will impact generations. God's people are rebelling against the covenant, so Nehemiah takes matters into his own hands, literally. He pulls out their hair, curses at them, beats them up, and makes them promise to stop. He reminds them how this has gone poorly in the past, even for some of their most noteworthy ancestors, like Solomon. He knows how this story ends, and he'd rather get into a few fistfights hoping to stop it than to see the demise of Israel as a nation. Scripture doesn't defend or rebuke his violence. He seems to have a clear conscience about it, though, because he keeps asking God to remember that he did these things, that he cared about justice and obedience, and he asks God to remember what they've done too.

Psalm 126 praises God for bringing restoration. Their mouths are filled with shouts of joy—like we saw today when their praise could be heard from far away. But even the psalm acknowledges there are things yet to be restored. In all of today's reading, we see that restoration hasn't transformed them; they're still the same people—they've just moved a few times. No matter where they go, they take their same stone hearts with them. They need the new hearts of flesh God promised them.

TODAY'S GOD SHOT

"They offered great sacrifices that day and rejoiced, for God had made them rejoice with great joy" (12:43). God made them rejoice with great joy. How did He do that? Did He force them to rejoice with great joy? Did He threaten them with punishment if they weren't filled with joy? You can't force someone to have joy. You may be able to force someone to act joyful, but you can't force them to *be* joyful. When it says God made them rejoice with great joy, it's a testament to His work on them at a heart level—He produces a joy in them that they wouldn't have otherwise. Yes, they've still got miles to go, and they still fail and break His laws, but their hearts know deep down that He's where the joy is!

MALACHI 1–4

God tells Israel how much He loves them, but they don't believe Him. He contrasts them to Edom and says, "If you don't believe Me, just look at how I've blessed My kids versus how I've treated the Edomites, who aren't in My family." He even says, "I have loved Jacob, but Esau I have hated." This raises a lot of questions: Does this really mean God hated Esau? Or does it mean He loves him less by comparison? Or is it referring to the two people groups but not the people themselves? Or is this showing that God isn't bound by the cultural norms to show preference to the firstborn? The only way to start finding answers is to look at the greater context of Scripture. God's emotions are complex; few things have only one layer with Him. We've seen that God does hate some things—primarily things that are in opposition to the things He loves. And we've seen that God's family is made up of those who've been adopted into it, regardless of genetics or even the fact that He made us all. If this passage is hard for you, don't give up; ask God to keep revealing Himself to you as you dig in.

The priests have rejected God even after all He's done for them. They mock Him and His laws, so He'll send a curse on them if they don't repent—but He doesn't want to. He made a covenant of life and peace with Levi, the head of their tribe, and Levi demonstrated godly leadership. But these priests are neglecting that and causing people to stumble. In 2:10, Malachi inserts himself into the conversation between God and the people of Judah, saying, "We are God's people, so why aren't we acting like it? Why are we oppressing our brothers and sisters and disobeying our Father's rules? May God cut off anyone who loves their own ways more than God's ways." He also addresses God's intentions for marriage: God hates adultery, divorce, and marriage to those who don't love Him. He encourages them twice to "guard yourselves in your spirit, and do not be faithless."

For more information on today's reading, see thebiblerecap.com/links.

Judah makes two contradictory accusations against God that are both wrong. The first is, "Evil isn't a big deal to God," and the other is, "God never brings justice! When will He punish the evil done to us?" Judah wants to have their cake and eat it too; they want their sins to be okay by God, but not the sins done to them.

Chapter 3 prophesies of a messenger who'll prepare the way for a messenger who *is* the way. The second messenger is Jesus. He'll refine His people like silver and gold, purifying them, then God will draw near for judgment. The first messenger, who prepares the way for Jesus, is John the Baptist (Mark 1:2). Most scholars say the reference to Elijah in 4:5 also refers to John the Baptist and that Elijah is as an archetype of John the Baptist, but others believe it refers to the literal return of Elijah.

God begs His people to return, but they want to know what it'll cost them. God says anything it costs will be repaid in ways they can't even imagine. He offers a practical example with tithing, saying, "If you think I'm here to rob you and not bless you, lean into this and see what happens!" Some of them respond by saying, "No thanks. We don't see any benefit in serving You. The wicked have better lives." But others, those who fear the LORD, are remembered by God, and He calls them "Mine" and sets them apart.

TODAY'S GOD SHOT

Chapter 4 paints a picture of the great day of the LORD, the day of God's judgment over sin. On that day, those who don't know Him will be brought to justice for their evil. He uses the imagery of an oven by which they're set ablaze. But those who fear His name will be granted healing and joy when the sun of righteousness rises. There are two fires in this section: the oven and the sun. One brings death and one brings life. Through these fires, God shows that He's a God of both justice and mercy; those two things aren't opposed to each other—they work in tandem. God demonstrates the great complexity of His character here. God's kids don't deserve any of the mercy He's granted us. We all deserve the oven. But in His great mercy, He has provided the healing that comes from the sun of righteousness instead. And He's where the joy is!

Four Hundred Years of Silence

The end of the Old Testament marks the beginning of a period known as the four hundred years of silence. During that time, God doesn't send prophets, and we have no written records of His engagement with humankind. But we know He's there, working out His plan in and through His people, and that a lot is happening historically and politically. This is important because it tells us the kind of political climate Jesus was born into.

At this point in our reading, the Jews are home in Israel after being driven out by the Babylonian Empire, but now they're under the control of the Persian Empire—the ones who defeated Babylon. A few hundred years from now, *another* empire, Rome, rises up and takes control of Israel in 63 BC. If you care to remember the order of empires, it's alphabetical: *BPR*. Babylon, Persia, Rome. If you don't, here's all you need to remember for when we launch into the Gospels and the New Testament: The Jews are tired and they're ready for rescue. They've been driven from their land, had their cities destroyed, lived as exiles and as slaves, and had to rebuild their cities, and they are now living back in their homeland under the oppression of one of the cruelest empires in the history of humankind. They remember God's promise to send them a new King who will conquer all their enemies, but they have no idea yet what that means or how or when that promise will be fulfilled.

When our New Testament reading opens, it's roughly 7 BC. Contrary to our current calendar, Jesus is probably born around 6 BC, not in year 0, because our calendar is off by a few years. We know Jesus has to be born before King Herod dies (we'll read about that in a few days), which happens in 4 BC. So we open in Israel in 7 BC, approximately a year before Jesus is born, and the Jewish people are both ready for their new king *and* they're understandably skeptical of anyone with power.

In the Gospels, we'll be reading some of the stories multiple times. Three of the four gospels overlap often: Matthew, Mark, and Luke. They're called the Synoptic Gospels, meaning they cover a lot of the same territory. John is the non-Synoptic gospel; John takes a different approach to storytelling, writing like a movie director more than a biographer. Each of the gospels has its own style and gives us a unique lens through which to see Jesus, so there's something new to learn or look for, even when we're reading the same story for the second or third time.

After the Gospels, we'll read the story of the early church—its leaders and strengths and weaknesses. We'll read about how it all began, then we'll see churches planted outside the Jewish population in various Gentile countries as the message of God's redemption spreads to people of every nation, just as He's been promising all along! There will be trials and struggles, but the light of the gospel can't be stopped by darkness and doubt. It will continue advancing. It has advanced to you today, and it will advance even beyond you, because joy is contagious and He's where the joy is!

LUKE 1; JOHN 1

The four gospels are narrative accounts of the life of Jesus, and they're primarily eyewitness accounts, with the exception of the book of Luke. Luke saw some of the events but is more of an investigative reporter collecting eyewitness accounts. Each gospel writer has a unique lens on who Jesus is. Luke's primary lens is "Jesus as man," and John's primary lens is "Jesus as God." Jesus was 100 percent human and 100 percent divine, so it's fitting to start with those two books.

Luke writes to a Greek man named Theophilus. He opens with the story of Zechariah and Elizabeth, who are righteous but infertile. Zechariah is assigned to burn incense in the Holy Place of the temple, which usually happens once in a priest's life; he's greeted by the angel Gabriel, who says he'll have a son named John. God has a special assignment for John, which includes strict rules for his life according to the Nazirite vow (Numbers 6:1–21). He'll eventually be called John the Baptist (we'll call him JTB). He'll be filled with the Spirit of God, even when he's in the womb! At this time, God the Spirit doesn't dwell in people yet, so this is a big deal. In fact, Gabriel says JTB's life will be like Elijah's, which recalls what we read in Malachi 4:5–6. Essentially, his life will be a flashing arrow pointing toward the Messiah.

A few months later, Gabriel delivers a message to another unsuspecting person—Mary. She'll be pregnant soon, and her son's name will be Jesus. He'll be a king like his ancestor David, except His kingdom will be eternal. She's a virgin, but Gabriel says the baby's Father isn't human—He's divine and has access to dimensions we don't. Gabriel tells her Elizabeth is pregnant too, so she goes to visit. When the women see each other, JTB jumps for joy in the womb; he's already using his God-given gift of prophecy. Then Elizabeth prophesies about Mary being pregnant with the Lord. The first human to prophesy aloud about Jesus being the Messiah is an elderly woman. Mary rejoices and breaks into song.

For more information on today's reading, see thebiblerecap.com/links.

John's gospel was likely written by an apostle, but we can't be absolutely certain it is John because the writer doesn't use his own name. Instead, he calls himself "the disciple Jesus loved," perhaps in an effort to remain anonymous at a time when Christians were being martyred. John opens by taking us back to the beginning of time and putting Jesus at the start of it all. John 1 echoes Genesis 1, where God the Son (Jesus) does the manual labor of creation. God the Son wasn't created. He has always existed as God the Son; He took on the name Jesus when He was born on earth. Even though Jesus made the world, the world doesn't recognize Him. But John gives us hope: Among fallen humanity, there are some whom God has adopted into His family, and He calls those people the children of God.

One day, JTB is in the desert baptizing people, which is similar to the ritual purification baths from Leviticus 14:8, except John is doing it in the wilderness rivers with dirty water. The Pharisees, the Jewish religious leaders at the time, send people to interrogate JTB, and he says, "Remember how our prophets foretold the coming Messiah? He's here. It's not me, but I'm here to point to Him." The next day, Jesus shows up and JTB says, "This is Him!" Jesus and JTB live far apart, so they may not have met before, but even if they have, JTB first sees Jesus *as the Messiah* when the Holy Spirit affirms His divinity. Later, two of JTB's disciples follow Jesus and begin inviting others. Jesus heads back to Galilee, and when He arrives, He recruits more disciples by demonstrating His ability to read minds, know hearts, and see things others can't.

TODAY'S GOD SHOT

The songs of Mary and Zechariah demonstrate that they know what matters. Mary rejoices even though she gets something she didn't ask for, because it's far greater than her wants or desires. On the other hand, Zechariah just got a yes to a long-prayed prayer, but he skips past praising God for the birth of his son and goes straight to praising God for the upcoming birth of Jesus. He knows what's most important—it's not the yes to his own desires, it's the yes to all humanity's long-awaited redemption. The birth of Christ is the yes that surpasses all our prayers and the peace that surpasses all our fears! He's where the joy is!

MATTHEW 1; LUKE 2

Matthew's unique lens on Jesus is "Jesus as King," and this book is likely written by the apostle who was a tax collector before Jesus called him. He opens with the lineage of Jesus, and there are three things worth noting. First, it includes women, which is unheard of in ancient Jewish genealogies. Jesus sent His disciples a message of women's inclusion and value. Second, His inclusion extends beyond gender: This genealogy mentions Gentiles and people with scandalous histories. The message God sends in this genealogy is one of redemption. Third, Matthew says there are "fourteen generations," but those numbers likely aren't precise—not because he's lying but because in Jewish culture, numbers often represent ideas, so "fourteen generations" may be a way to say "doubly perfect" since the number seven represents perfection and completion.

Jesus is the culmination of this perfect and complete setup for the redemption of humankind. God works out His plan through the fear and resistance of Joseph, Mary's fiancé; an angel confirms Mary's version of events and tells him not to be afraid. Mary remains a virgin until after she has Jesus, and Matthew confirms twice that she and Joseph consummate their marriage (1:18, 25) and their other seven or more children are conceived naturally. Mary has no divinity or perfection; she's a regular human, which is one thing that makes this story so remarkable.

Luke 2 tells us of Christ's birth, which unfolds far differently than it does in most imagery we've seen. Everyone has to go to their ancestral hometown for the census, so Mary and Joseph likely travel in a large group of extended family, not alone. They probably aim to stay with distant family in Bethlehem, but because everyone is in town for the census, the guest room is full. The word translated as *inn* isn't a hotel; it's likely a basement cave. Most homes in this day are built on caves, which serve as basements and animal pens. The feeding troughs are often

For more information on today's reading, see thebiblerecap.com/links.

hollowed-out stone, because wood isn't abundant in Israel. Jesus is likely born between June and September, which is census season and the right time of year for sheep and shepherds to be in the fields at night. The shepherds are likely Levitical shepherds who raise sheep used in temple sacrifices. When a sacrificial lamb is born, they wrap it in swaddling cloth to keep it from getting bruised or injured, because only a perfect lamb can be a sacrifice. So when an angel tells them the Savior is wrapped in swaddling cloths, this points to Him as the perfect, sacrificial lamb. The shepherds go to see this Savior of the world, this peace on earth, and when they tell Jesus's family that angels alerted them, the family is shocked.

When Jesus's parents dedicate Him at the temple, they bring the offering of the poor (Leviticus 12:8). God came to the lowly, to the humble—His is an upside-down kingdom. We see this again at the temple with the widow Anna and the elderly prophet Simeon, who knows the "consolation of Israel" means far more than just the Jews coming out from under Roman oppression. He also knows the Messiah will be a light to the Gentiles.

The family goes home to Nazareth, then when Jesus is twelve, they go to Jerusalem with extended family for Passover. On the trip home, they realize that Jesus isn't with other family members, so they go back. On day three, they find Him on the steps of the temple, talking with the elders, who are amazed at His wisdom. He knows He's God the Son but humbly submits to His parents.

TODAY'S GOD SHOT

At some point during the four hundred years of silence, God the Spirit speaks to Simeon and makes him a promise—it's recorded in Scripture. Those four hundred years are dark times for God's people, but here we have evidence that God hasn't forsaken them. His Spirit is still at work; He's still drawing near to His people, directing them, producing obedience and hope in them despite the darkest of circumstances and the oppression of the enemy. Nothing can keep God from drawing near to His people. He does it through His Word and through His Spirit. And these are the things Simeon relies on and clings to when all seems lost. Simeon longs for Him and awaits Him, because even in the dark times, Simeon knows He's where the joy is!

MATTHEW 2

Yesterday we read Luke's account of the birth of Jesus, and today we get more information from Matthew's account. Jesus is born in a village called Bethlehem, in a kingdom called Judea. At the time He's born, all of Judea is under Roman rule and occupation. Imagine that a large and powerful country takes over the country where you live, stations soldiers in every major city, is involved with every level of your government, and makes you pay taxes to support that occupying army. That's what's happening here. Rome is in charge, and they appoint Herod the Great over Judea.

Herod's a great builder, making port cities and aqueducts and even renovating the Second Temple complex so that it's much bigger and more magnificent. He's even the president of the Olympics! But in his later years, he becomes jealous and paranoid. He's driven by fear, which prompts him to try to control everything around him. One day, some foreign wise men show up at Herod's palace and say, "We're here to see the new King. We saw a sign in the sky that let us know He's been born, and we want to worship Him." Herod says, "Now that you mention it, I'm just as curious as you are! When you find Him, let me know where He is, because I want to worship Him too." But it turns out they don't need directions, because God sends the star to guide them again and it leads them to Jesus.

Let's look at a few details more closely. First, what is a wise man? Are they kings, like in the Christmas carol? Do they wear crowns? We don't have any evidence of that. Most scholars say they're astrologers who work for a king, kind of like the guys in Daniel who were on King Nebby's dream team. Second, are there three of them? Probably not. There are three gifts, but there are probably several wise men, and their names are never given in Scripture. Third, where is the east? We don't know. Scholars have a wide variety of guesses, ranging anywhere from

For more information on today's reading, see thebiblerecap.com/links.

five hundred to two thousand miles away. Fourth, what's the astronomical phenomenon they saw? They call it a star. It's not a comet, because it appears, disappears, reappears and moves, then rests in one spot.

Their journey probably takes several months, which means neither the wise men nor the star are at the cave on the night of Jesus's birth. Verse 11 calls Him a child and says they come to His house to see Him. They worship Him and give Him gifts, and Mary stands off to the side with her chin on the floor. Then God warns them in a dream not to go back to Herod, so they take another route. When they don't come back, Herod makes an order to kill all the boys age two and under in the whole region, because apparently, they'd said the new King would be about two years old. But God warns Joseph in a dream, so they move to Egypt, outside Herod's jurisdiction. Not long after this, in 4 BC, Herod dies, and God gives Joseph a dream saying that they can return, but when they learn Herod's son has replaced him, Joseph decides they should start over in a new town.

TODAY'S GOD SHOT

God goes to great lengths in order to provide for and protect His people according to His plan. He sends dreams and angels and angels in dreams, and not just to Joseph and his family, but to the wise men too. We're already seeing how Jesus is the King of people from among every nation—these wise men come from a foreign country to worship Him. These non-Jews follow a star and travel for months to give expensive gifts to a toddler, because they believe God's Word. Jesus is already drawing people from among every nation, and He's still in diapers! Then God protects the wise men on their way home, and God protects Joseph's family when Herod turns to murder. Does God's protective nature mean bad things won't ever happen to His kids? No—in fact, He spared the life of His Son at age two, but thirty-one years later, things go quite differently. God's protective nature means that whatever comes our way, He can be trusted. He's attentive. He's at work on our behalf in all things. And He's where the joy is!

MATTHEW 3; MARK 1; LUKE 3

John the Baptist (JTB) lives in the desert eating locusts and honey. Scholars say *locust* may refer to the fruit of the carob tree that grows in the wilderness. Its fruit grows in a bean pod called a locust, and it tastes like cacao, so it's possible JTB was eating dessert!

His message opens with a call to repent—to turn and go the other direction—but it's more of an inward turning, and it implies a level of remorse. He commands them to repent and be baptized, but then he rebukes some people for coming to be baptized. Why? Those he rebukes, the Pharisees and Sadducees, are the ruling class of Jews. They're *very* religious. But they're also prideful, greedy, dishonest, and cruel to the poor. This is the same problem God has been addressing for centuries with Israel's corrupt leaders. JTB calls them a snake pit *to their faces* and says that just because they're Jews by birth doesn't mean they're true Israelites, true children of Abraham. Lineage doesn't equal heritage. He doesn't want them to be baptized, because their lives prove they haven't repented. And until they do, baptism will be a meaningless act.

Then Jesus asks John to baptize Him. JTB knows Jesus doesn't need to repent, and it even seems like he wants to refuse Him, but he concedes. In this moment, all three persons of the Trinity show up in one place, just like at creation. God the Son is in the water, God the Spirit descends on Him like a dove, and God the Father's voice booms through the atmosphere, approving of Jesus and identifying Him. Jesus and JTB seem to be the only ones who see and hear what happens in the spiritual realm.

There are lots of different viewpoints on baptism—immersion or sprinkling, believers or babies. Those views may sound worlds apart, but they have one major and vital thing in common: They don't believe baptism is something man does to achieve salvation or righteousness by his own works. God does the doing. This is important. Scripture repeatedly

---

For more information on today's reading, see thebiblerecap.com/links.

says we're saved by grace alone, through faith alone, in Christ alone, not by our works. We are saved entirely and eternally by His works.

After His baptism, God the Spirit leads Jesus into the wilderness. He's there for forty days, fasting and being tempted by Satan. Then He launches His ministry when He's around thirty years old. Just as things are kicking off, JTB is arrested because he rebukes the new king for having an affair with his sister-in-law. When Jesus begins preaching, His message mirrors JTB's. His first command is "Repent and believe the good news." His ministry is geographically centered around a freshwater lake called the Sea of Galilee, which is surrounded by mountains. It's thirteen miles long and eight miles wide. There, Jesus runs into Simon Peter and Andrew, disciples of JTB. Now that JTB's in prison, they're back working for their dad's fishing business. Jesus invites them to follow Him instead. They come and invite two others: James and John. Within a few days, they see Jesus preach with more authority than Torah scholars, be recognized by a demon, silence the demon, heal the man with the demon, and heal Peter's mother-in-law! They're awestruck by His obvious power and must be so grateful He handpicked them.

By the way, Mark's unique lens on Jesus is "Jesus as servant." The four lenses present ideas that seem juxtaposed—king and servant, man and God—but they work together to show us a fuller picture of Jesus.

TODAY'S GOD SHOT

Luke's genealogy is broader than Matthew's and goes further back. Matthew is a Jew, and his lineage traces the Jewish line to Abraham. Luke, on the other hand, is probably a Gentile; he traces the line of Jesus all the way back to the beginning to show Jesus is connected to all of human history, even pre-Abraham, before God invented the Israelites. By giving us two genealogies from different vantage points, Scripture gives us a fuller view of Christ. We all have strengths and blind spots. God, in His wisdom and generosity, knows we need each other, so He gives us each other. He has adopted kids into His family with different histories, experiences, races, languages, gifts, weaknesses, and baptism practices. He continues to open our eyes, to correct us and broaden our understanding, so we can know Him better and see more clearly that He's where the joy is!

MATTHEW 4; LUKE 4–5

After His baptism, the Spirit leads Jesus into the desert to be tempted. The Spirit doesn't tempt Jesus, but He leads Him to where the enemy tempts Him. Satan's whole aim is to derail God's plan for redemption. He wants to get Jesus to give up now instead of going to the cross. Satan is more afraid of the cross than Jesus is, because he knows it means his eternal defeat. The enemy's weapon of choice is Scripture—*twisted* Scripture. He pulls verses out of context, shifting their meaning, making promises he has no power to fulfill. The enemy knows Scripture and knows how to use it to his advantage. But Jesus fights with Scripture too, speaking truth to the false accusations.

After His forty-day fast, He learns JTB has been arrested and goes back to the Galilee region, where He grew up. He preaches His first public sermon in Nazareth, reading from Isaiah 61:1–2 about how God has sent Him to proclaim good news to the poor and liberty to the captives. Then He says, "I *am* it. I'm the fulfillment of this prophecy." The locals are thrilled about this at first, but things take a turn when He starts recounting stories of God's love for outsiders—like when God sent Elijah to feed a foreign widow while the Israelites were starving in a famine. Or 2 Kings 5, when the Syrian leper was the only one who was cleansed. Suddenly they don't like the idea of proclaiming good news, freedom, and favor, because they want it to apply only to them, not to people of other nations, not their enemies. One minute they're praising Him, and the next they're trying to throw Him off a cliff, but He *passes through their midst* (maybe by teleportation, like during His temptation).

Then He moves to Capernaum, one of the most culturally and ethnically diverse areas of Israel. Luke recounts the story of when He calls some of His first disciples. They're fishing by the lake of Gennesaret (the Sea of Galilee) and are failing miserably at their job until Jesus says to throw the nets out in the deep. They catch so many fish that the nets

For more information on today's reading, see thebiblerecap.com/links.

are breaking and the boats are sinking. They immediately know there's something special about Him. Contrary to what Renaissance paintings portray, the disciples are young, probably thirteen to fifteen years old. They're still young enough to follow a rabbi, which usually happens at age twelve, but it appears they've been rejected by other rabbis, so they've started working in their family businesses. Now they're following thirty-year-old Jesus, who keeps referring to them as little children.

He also calls Matthew the tax collector. In the text, he's named Levi, but evidence points to this being the same person as Matthew the gospel writer. Tax collectors like Matthew are especially hated in Jesus's day. This is not only because they overcharge people, but primarily because their job is to collect money from the Jews to fund the Roman army—the occupying army that has moved into their country and is oppressing them, making their lives miserable, and even killing their family members.

Jesus heals Peter's mother-in-law while she is lying down at home, which leads scholars to believe Jesus lives in that house too, because those outside the household can't enter a woman's chambers. Jesus also teaches with authority and heals a demonized man and a leper.

TODAY'S GOD SHOT

Jesus sought out the people who were rejected by rabbis and hated by locals. He's seeking out the unwanted and the unloved, He's pointing to Old Testament stories of healing and provision for the foreigners, and He's saying He has come to bring freedom for prisoners and liberty for the oppressed and sight for the blind and good news for the poor. This is encouraging if you're the oppressed or imprisoned, but it's not good news for jailers and oppressors. When you set prisoners free, the jailers grow even more furious, entitled, and self-righteous. When Jesus points this out to the people of Nazareth, they try to kill Him. He knew they would reject Him—He prophesies it in Luke 4. He knew it from the beginning, yet still He came to be rejected by the people He loved, to feel their pain so He could lead them out of bondage and into joy—to lead them to Himself. Because He's where the joy is!

JOHN 2–4

At His mother's request, Jesus performs His first public miracle: turning water into wine. It's clear she knows what He's capable of, so she asks Him for help. His response seems harsh in English, but *woman* is a common way to address a female in His day, and His words are more along the lines of "You and I don't need to get involved with this." He's measured and intentional about when, where, and in front of whom He displays His power. His primary concern is keeping the Father's timeline for revealing His identity as the Messiah. Mary persists, though, and Jesus saves the day.

John has less concern for chronology, so he jumps to the last week of Jesus's life, when He's in Jerusalem for Passover. It's a standard practice to sell animals outside the temple—it provides a service to travelers who are either too poor to own animals or who don't want to bring animals to Jerusalem. The problem isn't necessarily that people are selling animals; it seems to be that (a) they're selling them *inside* the temple complex, instead of outside, disrupting what's supposed to be peaceful, and (b) they're price gouging the tourists, being greedy in the very place that most represents God's generosity. So Jesus sits down and *makes* a whip, then drives them out of the temple. He loves the place where God in His holiness comes to dwell with humankind, so He hates what's happening to it. And in the very next paragraph, He compares His body to that place—they're both ways God came to dwell with humankind. And these people have no respect for either. All of this happens a few days before Jesus goes to the cross. Today, Jesus uses a whip, and in a few days, *they'll* use a whip. Both whips reveal that they don't get it; they've missed the Truth.

A Pharisee named Nicodemus visits Jesus at night. He's watched Jesus for a while, and something in his heart is starting to shift. Jesus says that shift is God the Spirit blowing like wind across his life, moving Nicodemus and waking him to life. The Spirit is the one who gives

---

For more information on today's reading, see thebiblerecap.com/links.

new birth and new life. We're born dead, and only through believing in Him do we gain life in the kingdom. Those who don't believe in Him are condemned already. John reiterates this in his own words: "Whoever believes in the Son has eternal life; whoever does not obey the Son shall not see life, but the wrath of God remains on him." Part of the good news for those who do believe in Christ is that, because of Christ, we will never see God's wrath. Never. Christ absorbed all the Father's wrath for our sins—past, present, and future—on the cross.

When the Pharisees learn that Jesus's ministry has surpassed JTB's, Jesus leaves town. On His way back to Galilee, He passes through an area Jews avoid: Samaria. Centuries prior, Jews in Samaria married Gentiles, disobeying God's law to only marry His followers. This evolved into prejudice against the new biracial Samaritans. The Jews avoid Samaria, but Jesus walks straight through it and even stops for lunch. He stops to rest at a well, talks to a Samaritan woman, and tells her everything about herself. A Jewish rabbi is talking with a Samaritan woman alone! But even more shocking is His offer of grace, mercy, and love that she's never experienced. He knows all the worst things about her, all her shame, and He offers her life. She comes from a long line of rejection. She has wounds and betrayals that probably feel like identity markers. But she hasn't lost hope. She is waiting for the Messiah. And He looks her in the face and says, "You don't have to wait anymore. Your hope is fulfilled right now." She becomes an unlikely missionary, seeking out those in town who've rejected her. And Jesus stays for two more days preaching the good news to the outcasts of Samaria.

TODAY'S GOD SHOT

The Jews revere Moses, whose first public miracle was turning water into blood. Blood symbolizes death. And here we have Jesus's first miracle: turning water into wine, which symbolizes life. Moses was the lawgiver, and these Jews don't know it yet, but Jesus is the life giver and the law fulfiller. This is God announcing, "Ladies and gentlemen, the greater Moses has arrived. The fulfillment has arrived. The LIFE has arrived." And He's where the joy is!

MATTHEW 8; MARK 2

A leper defies the cleanliness laws by kneeling at Jesus's feet and asks for healing, which shows that Jesus is known for His kindness and humility. Jesus heals him but says to keep it quiet. He did this in Luke 5:12–14 too, but the woman in John 4 was allowed to tell everyone about Him. Why does He respond differently in these situations? He tells people to spread the news when He's in Gentile regions or dealing with non-Jews. But with the Jews, He says to keep quiet. There's a danger in having them know He's the Messiah, because they'll want to crown Him as King, they'll expect Him to overthrow the Roman oppressors, and Rome will want to kill Him. In order to preserve the specific timing God has planned for His revealing and His death, Jesus is measured in His approach. Every healing exposes Him and brings Him one step closer to death.

In Jesus's current hometown, Capernaum, a Roman military official has a sick servant and asks Jesus for help. The locals don't want Jesus to help the enemy, their oppressor, but Jesus defies the status quo. He says, "This guy has more faith in the Jewish Messiah than the Jews do. My Father's kingdom includes foreigners. And those in Israel who think they're in the kingdom *just because* they're born into the lineage of Abraham will be cast out." Then, with a word, He performs His first long-distance healing.

Jesus says following Him will cost comfort and control and our own plans and timing. It challenges preferences and priorities. When Jesus tells His followers they're going to the other side of Galilee, it challenges the norm. It's the Gentile side, the unclean side they've spent most of their lives avoiding. They hit a storm along the way, and with a word, Jesus turns it from "a great storm" to "a great calm." His disciples are in awe. They're probably relieved to hit the shore on the other side, until they meet up with a bunch of demons. Jesus has been demonstrating

For more information on today's reading, see thebiblerecap.com/links.

complete power over various domains: beverages, human bodies and diseases, weather, and now spiritual forces of darkness. Demons recognize Him and are afraid of Him. They know what awaits them in the future, and they ask, "Have you come here to torment us before the time?" (8:29). He casts them out, they go into the pigs, the pigs run into the sea, and the locals are furious—those pigs were costly! They forget that two men are no longer demonized. They don't understand the upside-down kingdom.

In Mark 2, Jesus is at home in Capernaum, likely living at Peter's house. When people find out He's there, they gather around to hear Him preach. A paralytic man wants in, but he can't get there on his own. Four friends carry him over, but the place is too full, so they remove part of the roof! Jesus is moved by the man's situation and says his sins have been forgiven. Some people aren't pleased about this—who does Jesus think He is? So Jesus shows them by healing the man's legs, not just his future.

When Jesus calls Matthew the tax collector to follow Him, the Pharisees are outraged that He'd keep company with a tax collector. They also give Him grief because His disciples are eating too much and at the wrong times. The Pharisees' traditions and rules extend beyond God's commands, so Jesus continually pushes on them.

TODAY'S GOD SHOT

Some people say that if your faith is strong enough, God will heal you. But the centurion's servant did nothing to get the healing Jesus gave him. It was a gift. He never sought it out, and he never saw it coming. Jesus just said, "I can heal him, so I'm going to." What an incredibly generous God. He reaches out to bless people who can offer Him nothing—not even their faith. He shows mercy to those who are so bound up by the oppression of the enemy that they can't even ask for help! He shows mercy to the paralytic man, who can't even seek Him on his own. Jesus seems to have a great affection for those who are desperate. "Those who are well have no need of a physician, but those who are sick. I came not to call the righteous, but sinners" (Mark 2:17). Our only hope of finding the deep healing and joy of knowing Jesus is to realize we were born sick sinners. Thank God He found us, because He's where the joy is!

JOHN 5

The invalids of Jerusalem gather at the pool of Bethesda. There's a belief that these waters have healing powers and that the first to jump in when the waters move will be healed. Some believed an angel stirred the waters, but there's evidence that the swirling is likely from a natural spring, which sometimes do have the effect of helping aches and pains. Regardless, it's a place of hope for invalids. When Jesus shows up there, He asks a man who has been there for thirty-eight years if he wants to be healed, and the man responds by telling Jesus why healing seems impossible for him. But Jesus meets him in his hopelessness and gives him the thing he can't even hope for. The man picks up his mat and walks off.

The first place he goes with his new legs is the temple. He hasn't been allowed to go there in almost forty years because he's considered unclean. But the minute he's healed, he goes to worship God. Unfortunately, he gets in an argument with the Pharisees because he brought his mat with him. It's the Sabbath and this is against the law. God established Sabbath rules early in His relationship with Israel, but they were terrible at obeying Him. So the Pharisees, who are *very* strict, decide to create more laws in order to force people to obey. They beef up God's laws by writing their own amendments. For instance, God said you can't work on the Sabbath. So they said, "Brick masonry is work. It combines water and dirt. So to be on the safe side, we'll make that illegal. Therefore, it's illegal to spit on the dirt on the Sabbath. You can spit on a rock, but you can't spit on the dirt." They call this "building a fence around the law"—a fence to protect it. But they start treating their fence like it's God's law.

These Pharisees tell the man that he's not allowed to be healed on the Sabbath, and that the Man who healed him broke the law. Jesus finds the man in the temple and encourages him: "You're better! Isn't this amazing? Look, you've had a hard life already, and sin has consequences I want you to avoid so that no more harm will come to you. Let today mark a turning point for you."

When the Pharisees find out that Jesus was the one who healed the man, they want Him dead. So Jesus pushes back. He doesn't do it to be defiant; He does it because *they* are being defiant—defying God's commands not to add to His words. They're giving man-made traditions equal standing with God's laws. They repeatedly accuse Jesus of breaking the law, but He's only breaking man-made traditions and rules. He goes on to tell them that He's working through His Father's power. He says He can give life to the dead when He speaks to them—this is spiritually *and* physically true. The Father has given the role of judgment to Him, but all His judgments are the ones the Father has handed down. In verse 30, He says, "I seek not my own will but the will of him who sent me." God the Son submits to the plan of God the Father. What remarkable humility He demonstrates in His time on earth!

Jesus tells the Pharisees they don't know God's Word at all, because the Old Testament Scriptures point to Him, and they don't even see Him there. If they actually understood Moses, and hadn't just memorized the law, they'd know who Christ is. But knowing Scripture without knowing Christ is pointless. The Pharisees have built their hope on the law, but all those laws were given to show how impossible they are to keep, to humble humankind into seeing our great need for Him, the law fulfiller and the life giver. The law—checked boxes and moral uprightness—will never have the power to save.

TODAY'S GOD SHOT

Jesus is so much more valuable than everything, and the healed man knows it. The first place he goes is to the temple. He knows the value of drawing near to God. God found him and his entire world changed—but not because he got his legs fixed. If he'd gotten his legs fixed and didn't *get God*, we'd feel sorry for him, because he was right there, face-to-face with the King. If he'd missed it and just skipped off with his mat, our hearts would shatter at this story. But thank God, Jesus spoke to that dead man's heart and called him to life. And now that man knows for sure that He's where the joy is!

MATTHEW 12; MARK 3; LUKE 6

When the Pharisees accuse the disciples of breaking the Sabbath, Jesus creates a teaching opportunity. He says the temple is important, but there's something more important than the dwelling place of God: *God Himself.* Then He says sacrifice is important, but there's something more important than sacrifice: *mercy*. The point He seems to be making is that the law is important but there's something greater than the law: *the God who made it*. God made the Sabbath law to serve people, so even the people's needs are greater than the Sabbath law. The law reveals our brokenness and what righteousness looks like—and that's important—but it never terminates on itself; it points to Him. When the Pharisees misinterpret and misapply God's law, they twist it into a version that no longer points to His heart.

When Jesus gives examples of people disobeying the law yet being guiltless, He isn't endorsing anarchy; the standard for holiness is still intact. Nothing has changed. So what does He mean? Like with the Egyptian midwives who lied to save babies, or King Hezekiah's unclean Passover celebration, the law points toward doing good, but mercy points toward the greater good. He presses on their legalism when He heals a man at the synagogue on a Sabbath. The Pharisees likely planted this man to trap Jesus. He points out their hypocrisy—they'd rescue a sheep on the Sabbath, but humans are more important than animals. Sabbath is about bringing rest and well-being, and healing is consistent with that.

The Pharisees conspire against Him, so He leaves. He can't be distracted from His current assignment to let the Gentiles know He's the Messiah and that He's for them too. The Gentiles don't know to expect a Messiah like the Jews do, because they haven't read the Hebrew Scriptures that speak of a Messiah for all nations. Jesus engages with the Jews first but needs to keep His identity secret while also spreading the word to the Gentiles. He needs to keep it a secret because the Jewish leaders will try to kill Him. He knows this is the plan, but it can't happen until "His hour has come." So when He heals people in Jewish regions, He begs them to keep it quiet. Every time He heals someone, He takes a step closer to His own death, trading His safety and well-being for theirs.

He handpicks twelve disciples to follow Him closely, but His family thinks He's lost His mind. Maybe they disbelieve He's the Messiah or think He needs to stop inciting the Pharisees—we don't know. The people with Him say, "Your family is outside looking for you," and He says, "You are My family. My family is everyone who does the will of God." This sounds harsh, but we'll see an encounter with His brothers soon that gives more context to this. Also, this is probably less of a downgrade for His blood relatives and more of an upgrade for all believers. He emphasizes the connection of the kingdom over the connection of genetics.

When He heals a man who is blind and mute because of a demon, the locals wonder if He might be the Messiah, so the Pharisees start a rumor that He can only do that because He's possessed by a demon too. Jesus essentially says, "If I were possessed by a demon, why would I drive out My own team?" He mentions blasphemy of the Holy Spirit, which seems to refer to the Pharisees' repeatedly and insistently attributing His work to Satan. They're rejecting the truth that Jesus is God. Other scholars say blasphemy of the Holy Spirit is the rejection of Jesus as God, which is true of anyone who isn't in God's family. Regardless of which it is, it seems a true believer can't commit this sin—accidentally or intentionally.

TODAY'S GOD SHOT

Jesus is the fulfillment of Isaiah's prophecies, one of which says, "A bruised reed he will not break" (42:3). Jesus is falsely accused by religious leaders, His name is on a wanted poster, and His closest friends and family turn against Him. He knows what it's like to be spiritually abused and suffer the relational consequences, so He's compassionate toward others who are mistreated. The man with the withered hand may be just a pawn to the Pharisees, but Jesus enters in with gentleness, mercy, and healing. We can draw near, because He's where the joy is!

MATTHEW 5–7

In His Sermon on the Mount, Jesus describes the upside-down kingdom of God. He opens with eight blessings, and many scholars believe they're cumulative—the first blessing is the foundation of the rest of the sermon. It all starts with poverty of spirit, recognizing that we're spiritually poor. We have nothing to offer God, no reason for Him to choose us or love us. That's square one. This stands in stark contrast to the attitudes of the Pharisees, who think they're nailing it. Can you see why that's an affront to God? Life in the kingdom begins with recognizing your desperate need for God. Here's how these blessings might accumulate in a person's life:

When we realize our spiritual poverty, we mourn it, which produces meekness in us as we engage the world. Meekness gives way to a desire for God to increase our righteousness. It becomes easier to show mercy to others, because we know what it's like to struggle. God continues to purify us as we engage with Him. We become people who don't run from conflict, but who enter into the chaos and create peace. Peace*makers*, not peace*keepers*. The life of a humble, hungry, meek, merciful, and pure peacemaker won't be easy—Jesus knows that personally—but despite trials, it'll be the most joyful life we can imagine, especially because it doesn't end when the end comes. The best reward is still ahead!

It's easy to turn this sermon into a checklist, but we desperately need it not to be. The requirements are impossible. However, Jesus doesn't say, "You won't be able to earn your own righteousness, so we're going to lower the bar. Do whatever you want, because God is a God of love." Instead, He points out that God isn't just after right actions; He's after a right heart, which means the standard is even higher. He says, "You therefore must be perfect, as your heavenly Father is perfect." That's what God requires. That's devastating. We can't do it. So what now? Our only hope is to be declared righteous because of what Jesus did,

For more information on today's reading, see thebiblerecap.com/links.

not what we do. It's such a relief that He has completed and fulfilled the requirements of the law through His perfect life and perfect death.

Jesus says we, as people who know our brokenness, shouldn't try to show off our good deeds to impress others—giving and fasting and praying—because then we're not living from square one. The problem with trying to be spiritually rich is that it's all Monopoly money anyway. Jesus says to fix our eyes and time and efforts on something that will last. If we value the eternal things above all else, our concerns about the temporary things will be displaced. It's normal for people who don't know God as their Father to be concerned about provision, but to God's kids, Jesus says, "Remember how much the Father loves you! He values you above everything else He's created. If you're focused on fleeting things, you'll be filled with fear. And fear usurps your allegiance to God's kingdom because it never stops demanding your attention. Instead, remember who your Father is. He's providing for you."

Jesus says we should be careful not to act like God, the Judge of all humankind. God's judgment happens at a heart level and we don't have eyes to see that, so it's best to direct our discernment toward an action being right or wrong instead of a person being good or bad. We inspect the fruit, because we can't see the root. When we venture into that territory, it becomes far too easy to lose sight of square one: our own spiritual poverty.

TODAY'S GOD SHOT

"Let your light shine before others, so that they may see your good works and give glory to your Father who is in heaven" (5:16). The point of our good works is to glorify God, not us. But why would God want glory for something He didn't do, something *we* did? Because He *is* the one doing it. His Spirit is producing good works in us: "It is God who works in you, both to will and to work for his good pleasure" (Philippians 2:13). "From him and through him and to him are all things" (Romans 11:36). He deserves the glory, because He does the doing! But He doesn't leave us empty-handed. He gets the glory, and we get the joy. Because He's where the joy is!

MATTHEW 9; LUKE 7

Matthew recounts the time when Jesus called him to be a disciple. It mirrors Levi's calling, which is why many scholars believe it's the same man who perhaps has two names. The Pharisees harass Jesus for eating with sinners, like tax collectors, and His response shuts them down. He acknowledges Matthew's sinfulness and says, "Sinners don't scare Me. They're the whole reason I'm here."

We read a series of healing stories that reveal a lot about the cultural mind-set. A synagogue ruler, Jairus, has a twelve-year-old daughter who is dying. He asks Jesus for help, and Jesus agrees but gets sidetracked. Technically it's only a sidetrack if you're Jairus. For Jesus, it's part of the plan. And for the woman He runs into along the way, it's an answer to prayer. She's been sick for as long as Jairus's daughter has been alive. She's ceremonially unclean, so she's a social outcast and can't go to the temple. If you're Jairus, these things seem less important than death. It probably feels like Jesus doesn't care and He's ruining everything. As Jesus walks past the woman, she grabs His prayer tassel—"the fringe of His garment" like in Deuteronomy 22:12. And in her interaction with Jesus, she finds healing from the thing that has ailed her, alienated her, and impoverished her for twelve years. Finally! Meanwhile, a twelve-year-old is breathing her final breaths.

When Jesus arrives at Jairus's house, mourners are wailing. Their wails turn to laughter when Jesus says the girl is just sleeping. He isn't denying her condition, just the permanence of it. Her body doesn't have the final word. He does. He made her body, and He raises it. Mark's gospel tells this story too, and his version seems to say she's at the point of death, not dead. Most scholars say she was alive when Jairus left her to find Jesus but dead by the time He arrived. Whether it's with her or with the widow's son, today is the first time in His public ministry that He raises someone from the dead.

For more information on today's reading, see thebiblerecap.com/links.

Next, He heals two blind men and says to keep quiet, but they tell everyone. Then He takes a road trip and passes a funeral procession as He's entering the city. The only son of a widow has died; now there's no one to provide for her, which is likely a death sentence for her too. She doesn't ask Him for anything; she may not even know who He is, but He enters in with compassion and raises her son from the dead.

Simon the Pharisee invites Jesus to dinner, and a "woman of the city who was a sinner" crashes the party. She's likely a prostitute. Not only is Jesus drawn to sinners, but sinners are drawn to Jesus. Simon is repulsed by her presence in his home and can't believe Jesus is letting her touch Him. But she weeps as she anoints His feet with oil that probably costs more than she makes in a year. Jesus speaks to Simon's thoughts. He acknowledges that she's a sinner and says the greater our awareness of our need for Him, the greater our joy and gratitude will be in knowing Him. If we pride ourselves on being morally upright, we'll miss out on that joy and gratitude. The more we can find ourselves at square one, spiritual poverty, the more we'll be able to grasp all the blessings of knowing Him.

TODAY'S GOD SHOT

A few times in today's reading, Jesus says things like, "Your faith has healed you." In order to see what He's communicating, not just what He's saying, we have to look at the whole story He's telling us. If their faith healed them, Jesus wouldn't need to show up or act, because their action of belief would be sufficient. But it wasn't. Jesus is necessary. He has to make it happen. He even heals people who don't have faith, like the lame man, the dead man, and the dead girl. He heals people who don't ask for it, people who don't ask for it but do have faith, and people who do ask for it but don't have faith. There's no formula. This isn't a combination lock; it's a relationship with a compassionate God. Faith, no matter how strong, can't heal on its own. But the object of our faith can—and it's not what we're believing for, it's whom we're believing in. Faith in our faith is foolish. But faith in our God, who is powerful and loves us, is worship. He's where the joy is!

MATTHEW 11

After Jesus appoints the twelve apostles, they preach in their hometowns. While they're going from town to town, John the Baptist (JTB) seems to be having an internal struggle. He's seen the Spirit descend on Jesus like a dove, and he's heard the voice of the Father affirm Jesus as His Son, but then Jesus went away into the wilderness and JTB got thrown into prison. Their paths barely crossed, and now JTB keeps hearing that Jesus is doing miracles for everyone. Surely if Jesus is the Messiah, He'll miraculously get him out of prison, right? This seems less like doubt and more like despair. We don't know what JTB is thinking. All we know is that he sends messengers to ask Jesus to confirm or deny that He is the Messiah.

Jesus sends word back, telling the messengers to let JTB know they've seen Him do the things Isaiah said the Messiah would do when He comes. He quotes prophecies JTB probably knows by heart, but He leaves off a part of the prophecy that almost certainly catches JTB's attention: the part where the prisoners get set free. It must've been difficult to be on the receiving end of this message: "Yes. I'm the Messiah Isaiah prophesied about and the one you pointed toward. It has all been fulfilled, but you will die in prison." Jesus ends by saying, "Blessed is the one who is not offended by Me." And while this certainly had wider implications, it has personal implications for JTB—it's almost an acknowledgment from Jesus that He's delivering hard news.

As they go on their way, Jesus praises JTB to His disciples. He says JTB is the fulfillment of Malachi's (3:1; 4:5) prophecy about the coming of Elijah. This doesn't mean JTB is a reincarnation of Elijah; it indicates that Elijah was the archetype and JTB has followed suit. Jesus calls him the greatest man who has ever lived, but then says everyone in the kingdom is greater than JTB. Does that mean JTB isn't in the kingdom? Jesus seems to be pointing to a future kingdom, one that has

---

For more information on today's reading, see thebiblerecap.com/links.

already been inaugurated but hasn't been fulfilled. Sometimes He talks about the kingdom in the present tense, and sometimes He talks about it in the future tense. It's not uncommon to read the words of Jesus and think, "So is it now or is it coming?" Scholars say the answer is yes; they call this the "already but not yet." The tension is intentional and hopeful. We live in this tension when we think about how God has declared us righteous and views us as righteous even though we're still sinners and He still sees our sin. Kingdom realities may not be fulfilled until the future, but Christ calls us to be presently mindful of them. That's how we live out kingdom values instead of earthly values.

Jesus's generation doesn't have a taste for the kingdom. Nothing satisfies them. They'll always find something to condemn, because they don't want to submit to the deity of Christ. He lists cities that have seen Him do miracles but refuse to believe He's the Messiah. He does 90 percent of His miracles in His hometown of Capernaum; they see the most but believe the least. Only soft hearts can submit to the evidence. Hard hearts resist it. Jesus thanks His Father for the soft hearts of those who accept Him. Those who consider themselves wise miss it, but those who are humble and needy receive it. He thanks the Father for pouring out grace for them to hear the truth; He'll reveal Himself and the Father to whomever He chooses. He sends out an invitation to the weary and burdened. And it seems this message is especially for those who are wearied by an attempt to live up to the law—either God's law or the rules the Pharisees added to it. The yoke of the law and the yoke of the Pharisees are crushing. But His yoke is easy and His burden is light.

TODAY'S GOD SHOT

It's interesting to imagine where Jesus might put the emphasis when He says, "Come to me, all who labor and are heavy laden, and I will give you rest" (v. 28). The context makes it seem like He puts the emphasis on Himself: "Come to *me* . . . I will give you rest." As we learn His character, it's more evident every day—He's where the rest is, and He's where the joy is!

LUKE 11

Even the apostles asked Jesus to teach them how to pray. Just like any kind of conversation you have with a person, prayer is a skill you can learn. There are a few things worth noting in the prayer Jesus teaches His followers. First, Jesus says to pray to the Father, not to Him. If we aren't careful, we end up putting the three persons of the Trinity in a blender and mixing them all up together, as though they're the same. While they are one and are unified in their will and purpose, they're also distinct in their roles. In Scripture, the normative prayer model is to pray to the Father, through the Son, by the Spirit. The Father is the supreme authority, Jesus is the mediator between us and the Father, and the Spirit empowers our prayers through the Son to the Father. That's not to say we can't or shouldn't pray to the Son or the Spirit—it enriches our relationship and deepens our understanding of God when we think intentionally about each person of the Trinity and talk to them according to their roles. The more we get to know Him, the more natural this becomes.

It's astonishing that we can boldly approach the Father. For some people this can be challenging; it may feel easier to pray to the Son or the Spirit. He knows our aches; He extends grace to us in this. He's also capable of redeeming the word *Father* for those who struggle with it.

Jesus demonstrates yielding in this prayer. He prioritizes the Father and His kingdom, giving everything else its proper landing spot. Our praise, repentance, and asking fall under the heading of submission to God and His kingdom. While prayer is submitting to God, it's primarily *talking* with God.

In the next section, the Pharisees accuse Jesus of being demon possessed, then a woman in the crowd cries out, blessing His mother. "But he said, 'Blessed rather are those who hear the word of God and keep it.'" It's worth noting that Jesus doesn't show Mary any special reverence.

For more information on today's reading, see thebiblerecap.com/links.

He's not demoting or disrespecting Mary; He's just rightly positioning her alongside everyone else. She's a sinner in need of a Savior, just like all of us. This is similar to what we read in Mark 3:31–35, where Jesus elevates those in the family of God, showing that kingdom relationships have greater significance than genetic relationships.

The crowds ask Him for a sign to prove He's the Messiah, and He rebukes them. When Jesus performs miracles, it's to help people in need, not to prove Himself. His miracles weren't enough for the people of Capernaum or the other cities He pronounced woe to. Signs don't soften hearts. Jesus says the only sign they'll get will be the one of His death and resurrection—the "sign of Jonah." In Matthew's account, Jesus said He'll spend three days and nights in the grave just like Jonah spent three days and nights in the fish (12:38–41).

Much like in Luke 7:36–50, Jesus has dinner with a Pharisee and doesn't hesitate to rebuke him in his own home. The host is shocked that Jesus doesn't wash up before dinner. It's not a law; it's just a tradition of the Pharisees. Jesus says, "You're concerned with being clean on the outside, but you're dead inside." A lawyer pushes back, "That's harsh!" Jesus says, "What's harsh is that you make burdens unnecessarily hard for some people and refuse to offer any help at all." His strongest words are for the self-righteous. He pushes back to His own detriment.

TODAY'S GOD SHOT

Jesus wants His followers to know how much the Father loves to communicate with His kids, even about little things. He uses examples like eggs, fish, and bread. He says to be persistent in prayer. The Father can be trusted to hear our prayers, sift through them, and answer with whatever is best. Everyone who asks receives! That means there's no such thing as an unanswered prayer—He answers all of them, with yes, no, or wait. We tend to forget that no and wait are answers too. God doesn't always give us what we ask for, because sometimes He has better ideas, but He always hears and responds to us. That's what a good father does. And He's where the joy is!

MATTHEW 13; LUKE 8

Parables are one of Jesus's favorite teaching tools. A parable is a short story that often has one main point and names no specific people or places. In His first parable today, He compares the gospel to a seed that is spread all around and falls on four different types of soil, showing four ways the gospel can be received. Three of the soils don't receive the gospel well, but the one soil that does produces a hundredfold increase! Soil number one is the path, where birds devour the seed. This person hears the gospel but doesn't really understand it, then the enemy snatches it away. Soil number two is rocky and shallow. This person responds quickly and joyfully to the gospel, but when tough times come, the plant can't take the heat. Trials reveal our hearts—are we only after God's blessings, or are we truly after God Himself? Soil number three is thorny soil, where the seed takes root but thorns choke it and crowd it out. Jesus compares the thorns to the cares of the world and the deceitfulness of riches. Here, *abundance* is what overtakes the seed, just like trials did in soil number two. Finally, there's soil number four, the good soil—the one who hears the gospel, understands it, and bears fruit.

When Jesus first tells this parable, He doesn't give the explanation. He's talking to a big group of people from various towns when His disciples pull Him aside and say, "No one knows what You're talking about." He says, "Yes, I'm doing that on purpose. You guys will get it, but the people with hard hearts won't. Be grateful for the blessing of your soft hearts and open ears, because you're seeing something very few people have experienced." Then He explains the parable to His disciples, but not the whole crowd.

Jesus goes back to Capernaum and teaches in the synagogue. We've read about this scene before, but there are two things worth noting in Matthew's account. First, He has at least seven brothers and sisters: James, Joseph, Simon, Judas, and "all" His sisters, which means there are at least three. Second, they call His dad Joseph a carpenter, but this is actually a misunderstanding from the original translation. The word used here in Greek is *tekton*, which means a builder or a craftsman. When England first translated the Bible to English, they assumed this meant *carpenter* because builders and craftsmen in England used wood. But builders and craftsmen in Israel work primarily with stone since it's far more abundant there than wood. So Jesus is probably more of a stonemason than a carpenter, which fits well with the stories He tells and the analogies He uses. Scripture calls Him "the Rock" and "the stone that the builders rejected" who became the cornerstone. As a *tekton*, He's been shaping things out of rock since the first day of creation, starting with the earth itself!

In addition to the twelve apostles, there are a few women who likely travel with them too—Mary Magdalene, Joanna, Susanna, and many more. This is remarkable, especially in His day. It's clear that He values the contributions of women in the kingdom. These women seem to be caretakers because they "provided for them out of their means" (8:3). Some of these women probably have great wealth and status—like Joanna, who is married to King Herod's household manager—and others have poor social standing—like Mary Magdalene, who had seven demons before Jesus cast them out.

TODAY'S GOD SHOT

There is great diversity among Jesus's closest followers. He travels with poor fishermen, wealthy tax collectors, family members of the king's entourage, and a formerly demonized woman. He keeps a wide range of company. Jesus isn't just for all nations of people, but all types of people—rich, poor, polished, and unkempt. He proves that the thorny pleasure of wealth and status can't choke out every seed and that the scorching trials of the demonic can't wither all seedlings. And the simple fishermen who may appear to be rocky soil might even be rocks themselves—like Peter, whose name means Pebble; and they can still, against all odds, bear fruit. One of the beautiful things about a sovereign God is that He can take the most unlikely soil and turn it into a garden. He's where the joy is!

MARK 4–5

Today we open with Mark's account of the parable of the four soils, which he immediately follows with a question about the purpose of a lamp. You don't hide lamps—you display them. These two illustrations back to back suggest that Jesus wants the light and the seed to go everywhere. Some people may hide their eyes from the light, but it shines in the darkness nonetheless. The seed must fall even on the three bad soils, not just the one good soil. Everyone who has eyes to see and everyone who has soil to receive *will see* and *will receive*, and they'll respond accordingly. In several other parables, He explains the kingdom of heaven—not describing the experience but describing its unstoppable power despite its small beginnings. It's a seed that grows into ripe grain, but no one knows how it happens. Like a mustard seed, which is practically impossible to kill, it slowly takes over everything.

That night they take a boat to the Gentile side of the Sea of Galilee. We've read this story before, but this account tells what happens on the water. A storm hits, and the boat starts to fill with water. Meanwhile, Jesus is asleep. They wake Him and accuse Him of not caring about what's happening to them, even though He's in the storm too. He rebukes the storm—which carries the idea of a sharp response—but He *encourages* His disciples. He has compassion on them in the midst of their fears, despite their false accusations that He doesn't care about them. He reminds them to lean into their faith in Him when scary things happen and remember what they've learned about Him.

The word *rebuke* is used nearly thirty times in the New Testament, but in the original language, it appears to never be directed toward the disciples. Jesus rebukes the storm, those who reject Him as Savior, an illness, and most often, demons. It's possible that He's rebuking a disciple when He says to Peter, "Get behind me, Satan" (Mark 8:33), which many scholars believe is actually addressed to Satan, not Peter. Rebuking someone isn't wrong. In fact, Jesus later gives His followers instructions on how and when to rebuke each other. In today's text, He leans into compassion.

He chooses not to rebuke them because of their fear, but to rebuke the cause of their fear instead. If you battle with your own fears and even feel shame over your inability to quiet them, remember that He doesn't shame you. He's in the storm with you. And He cares.

While it's comforting to know that Jesus cares and is sovereign over storms, it's also interesting to note that the whole reason they get into the storm to begin with is because they're obeying God. When things go sideways in our life and our boat starts to fill with water, it's common to wonder what we've done wrong. We want to find the offensive action so we can avoid it in the future. But this trial was the result of obedience, not sin or error. Often, these situations serve to teach us something valuable and necessary that we wouldn't know otherwise.

TODAY'S GOD SHOT

Our relationship with God is the most important thing in our lives, and it impacts every other area of our lives. Everything we learn about and experience of Him builds on our eternal relationship. In the storm, the disciples learn something about Him they wouldn't know otherwise: He's sovereign over whatever comes their way. This is just one of many times when He demonstrates His power to them. They need to see this repeatedly because they'll all face much bigger storms in their lives—from watching their leader die on a cross to facing their own horrible deaths. He's so generous to let them see more of who He is, to strengthen their faith. He's slowly but surely growing their hearts of faith from tiny mustard seeds into something that takes over and can't be killed. His kingdom goes on forever, and He's where the joy is!

MATTHEW 10

Jesus chose twelve of His many disciples to be in His inner circle, and Scripture begins referring to them as apostles. *Disciple* means "learner," and *apostle* refers to "a messenger who is sent out." Jesus sends the twelve out but first gives them authority over things He knows they'll encounter: demons, disease, and affliction. He instructs them as they set out. First, He gives directions: Go *only* to Jews, not Gentiles or even Samaritans (Samaritans are half-Gentile, half-Jew). God's plan has always involved getting the message to the Jews first, then to the Gentiles. Jesus does roughly 90 percent of His miracles in the Jewish town of Capernaum. But He has a specific timeline and a specific mission to fulfill before His death, and the more He speaks among the Jews, the more their leaders recognize Him as a threat and try to eliminate Him. His followers, however, can heal and help people without being in the same danger. Second, He gives them a message and mission: Proclaim the kingdom of God, heal the sick, and raise the dead. Third, He gives them limits: Pack light and choose lodging wisely. They're learning to trust Him for all their provision—food, bills, and beds. He'll be providing for them through other people, which is both faith building and humbling; in order to rely on Him, they have to rely on others. He says to stay only in places that welcome His message, and He promises to deal with those who don't handle them with care.

What they're doing will result in persecution. People will falsely accuse them, and they'll be mistreated, questioned, and brought to trial. And He says, "Don't try to plan ahead for this. You won't be able to. But don't worry either—when the time comes, you'll know exactly what to say. God the Spirit will equip you with words." God is calling them and equipping them. And what God initiates, He will sustain and He will fulfill. So those who endure to the end are the ones He has called and equipped—endurance serves as evidence of His relationship with them.

For more information on today's reading, see thebiblerecap.com/links.

Otherwise they'd bail when persecution comes. Like with the four soils, persecution serves as a sifting tool, separating true believers from those whose faith is shallow and false.

Their families may turn against them and people may hate them, but nothing their enemies can do to them is eternal. Then He talks about swords and rewards; these sections point to what we ultimately value. It's not wrong to love our families—God loves them too. But Jesus says commitment to God should always take precedence. That'll be especially important when their families turn against them. If they're driven by fear of man, people pleasing, or peacekeeping, their allegiance will be divided. But if they're driven by fear of God and peacemaking, they can move forward without being distracted by or hindered by conflict. God so identifies with His people that He says those who reject His people are rejecting Him, and those who accept His people are accepting Him. In trials and oppression, those who dare to open their homes to the apostles are welcoming the kingdom of God and the God of the kingdom. The apostles spread the message we heard from both JTB and Jesus: Repent. They heal and cast out demons and spread the good news about Jesus.

TODAY'S GOD SHOT

Jesus pays attention to details big and small. Not only is He watching over the biggest detail of all—their eternal souls—and keeping them for eternity, but He's also tuned into medium-sized details like providing them with clothes and food and lodging. He even watches over the tiny details—giving them the very words they speak. Sometimes it's easy to think of God as only being concerned with the majors. God seems to care about everything, though, because He's the only one who sees how it all fits together in His sovereign plan. Our minds are finite. But His mind is infinite, and it's never preoccupied. Romans 8:28 tells us He's at work in every detail. He listens to all our prayers of various levels of importance, and He always answers in one way or another. He shows us repeatedly that He's in the details. And He's where the joy is!

MATTHEW 14; MARK 6; LUKE 9

John the Baptist (JTB) has been in prison since the early days of Jesus's ministry. Herod Antipas arrested JTB after he rebuked Herod for marrying his brother's wife, Herodias. She wants JTB dead, but Herod is torn. On Herod's birthday, Herodias's daughter does a dance for him at his party. In ancient Greco-Roman culture, these dances are seductive, so it's highly inappropriate that his stepdaughter is his "entertainment." He loves it and offers her anything she wants. Herodias is likely using her daughter as a pawn in order to achieve this very outcome—she says to ask for JTB's head. So the sins of the king and the selfish plotting of his mistress lead to JTB's beheading in prison. He dies an unjust death, the one Jesus hinted at not long ago when JTB sent Him a message asking if He was really the Messiah.

After Herod kills JTB, he begins to hear about the miraculous things Jesus is doing, and he's confused, because he sees a lot of similarities between these two guys. He's left wondering if Jesus is the ghost or the resurrection of JTB because of how their ministries run along the same trajectory. Some people even suggest that Jesus is the resurrected Elijah because of the types of miracles He's performing.

When Jesus gets word of JTB's death, He and the disciples go off in a boat alone. He likely wants to grieve and talk to the Father about everything that's happening. But the locals see them on the water and run to meet Him when He docks. Scripture records the five thousand men, but there are also women and children to account for. They're probably there for a variety of reasons. Some probably just want healing. Others have likely heard about what happened to JTB, and their first thought is to go to Jesus—maybe to offer Him their condolences or maybe they want to know the plan for moving forward now that one of the leaders of this new kingdom has been executed. For them, this must be kind of like a presidential assassination—Rome just killed one of their Jewish leaders.

For more information on today's reading, see thebiblerecap.com/links.

Jesus just got news of the unjust death of the man who was His forerunner, whose entire life was dedicated to preparing the way for Him and pointing people toward Him. And in the not-too-distant future, the same government will play a role in His own death. And now fifteen thousand people want something from Him. Despite all that, He leans in. He doesn't send the crowd home, as the disciples suggest. Instead, He tells the disciples to do something impossible: feed them. As they begin to take steps of obedience, they see that *He* is the one doing the feeding. He does the miraculous.

Jesus gives thanks to the Father for the food, breaks it, and gives it out. There are twelve baskets of food leftover—one for each of the apostles. These leftovers serve as evidence of His power as well as serving a practical purpose: to feed them on their journey. This whole story shows that Jesus isn't just concerned with spiritual provision, but practical provision too. Then He wants more time to pray, so He sends the disciples away. At three in the morning, a storm hits. Jesus can see them from the spot where He's praying, so while the wind is giving them a beating, He strolls past their boat, walking on the water. Until they realize it's Him, they're terrified. Peter says, "If it's really You, invite me out there." But the moment Peter pays more attention to the frightening things around him than to the God who is sovereign over those things, his fears overtake him. Jesus rescues him, and immediately the wind stops. When they land in Gennesaret, they're swamped by people in need of healing, and Jesus heals them.

TODAY'S GOD SHOT

For the disciples, the storm is bad enough. The storm plus being sleep deprived and emotionally exhausted from serving people and mourning the death of JTB is worse. They're tired, they're sad, and now their lives are in danger. Just when they think things can't get worse, they see a ghost coming toward them! But what they perceive as tragic or terrifying is actually God moving in their lives to show them He's with them, to show them He's powerful, and for a moment, to bring them some joy. Even in our storms in the middle of the night, He's where the joy is!

JOHN 6

Yesterday Jesus fed fifteen thousand people. Today when they wake up, they think He's still with them. They saw the boat go out and He wasn't on it, but now they can't find Him anywhere. Eventually some boats swing by the dock, and they convince the fishermen to take them on a manhunt for Jesus. When they track Him down, they say, "How'd You get here?" And He says, "You're only following Me because I fed you." Instead of being blown away by the Man who can do miracles, they just want the miracles. He's not interested in giving the temporary at the expense of the eternal, so He points out that He has a lot more to offer them than they're aware of: "Don't labor for the temporary things—work for the food that lasts."

They latch on to the word *work* and totally miss His point. But in missing the point, they ask a crucial question: "What must we do to be doing the works of God?" This is one of the most important questions of all time—what does God require? And Jesus answers, plain and simple, "This is the work of God, that you believe in him whom he has sent" (v. 29). The one thing God requires is belief in the gospel of Jesus. That's it. End of list. But this isn't just a belief that He exists or even a belief that He is God. As we've seen, even the demons believe that, and it doesn't make them Christians. The word *believe* means "to commit your trust, to place confidence in"—it's heart-level belief, not just acknowledgment or cognizant assent. This isn't knowing the truth—it's *surrendering* to the Truth. The crowd misses the point and says, "If we're supposed to believe in You, we need some signs—like the kind Moses did. He gave miracle bread from heaven." That's exactly what Jesus did for them last night, but they've forgotten. And as for Moses, he wasn't the origin of that bread—God the Father was. Jesus says, "There's an eternal bread available: Me. *I'm* the way for your souls never to hunger again."

For more information on today's reading, see thebiblerecap.com/links.

Then He segues into some deep theological points that are also over their heads. In verse 38, He indicates that there's an authority structure within the Trinity: "I have come down from heaven, not to do my own will but the will of him who sent me." God the Father has a plan, and God the Son submits to the will of God the Father. That authority structure also translates to humanity—we are dependent on the Father's plan. Jesus says, "All that the Father gives me will come to me. . . . No one can come to me unless the Father who sent me draws him. . . . Everyone who has heard and learned from the Father comes to me." Our salvation starts with the Father. Other Scriptures we'll encounter reveal that the Father uses the Spirit as a means of drawing us, just like the Son is the means of redeeming us, but it all starts with the Father's plan, and He's working it out through all the persons of the Trinity.

All that Jesus is saying—especially the part where He tells them to eat His body and drink His blood—is hard for the Jews to stomach. And it's definitely against Jewish laws. They think He's speaking in literal terms, not spiritual terms, but Jesus is almost always pointing to things on a deeper level; He uses tangible imagery to make His points, and that's what confuses them. So He just meets them in that moment and says, "You're right. It is hard. And the only ones among you who get it will be the ones God reveals it to."

TODAY'S GOD SHOT

This sermon is a seat emptier for Jesus. He loses a lot of people here because they can't handle the truth. And it seems to make Him sad. Jesus has twelve apostles, and two of them are going to walk away from their relationship with Him during the toughest moment of His life—Simon Peter and Judas Iscariot. Jesus knows it, but still He keeps them close, submitting to the Father's plan. This is how it has to go. He's going to share life with people who will wound and betray Him. It's probably always in the back of His mind. And in this moment, He asks them, "Are you going to leave Me too? Just like the others?" Then Peter says one of the best things he ever says: "Where else would we go? Only You have the words of eternal life." Yes and amen. Peter knows He's where the joy is!

MATTHEW 15; MARK 7

Today we open with Jesus dealing with the complaints of the Pharisees again. They're upset that His disciples don't wash their hands before meals. If this sounds familiar, it should. Jesus dealt with this Himself when He went to dinner at a Pharisee's house. But this time the scribes and Pharisees have traveled eighty miles from Jerusalem to Galilee to address this situation. Jesus says they aren't breaking God's law, just man's traditions. According to God's law, only the priests have to wash their hands before meals. Jesus points out their hypocrisy—they break the actual law in order to keep their man-made traditions. He quotes Isaiah in reference to people who do and say all the right things but don't actually love God. They love their religious acts and being "right," but they don't know anything about righteousness, because that only comes through a relationship with God.

Later when He's talking to just His disciples, He says, "Wash your hands or don't—it doesn't matter. What does matter is what comes out of your mouth; it testifies to what's in your heart. That's where evil thoughts, murder, adultery, sexual immorality, theft, false witness, and slander originate." What Jesus says here about food has some other far-reaching implications. In Mark 7:19, Jesus declares all the forbidden foods clean. Then He gives a brief commentary on the Pharisees: They aren't God's kids, and they're blind.

Then they head to a Gentile region. As soon as they arrive, a Gentile woman begs Him to help her demonized daughter. She calls Him Lord, but that's just a way of showing honor. However, when she calls Him Son of David, it indicates that she knows something. She's onto Him. On the surface, it seems like He's being cruel to her. But based on how she approaches Him right away and seems to know who He is, and the fact that He's hiding from everyone else in town, it seems she may be the whole reason He came to this area. The disciples try to send her away, but Jesus engages in a conversation with her. He says He's not there for her—He's there for the people of Israel. And yes, that's His first mission, but this seems more like He's testing her faith, because of how it all ends. It's similar to the time He walked on water *past* the boat at first or the time He was reluctant to turn water into wine. Being the sovereign God of the universe—the heart reader and mind reader we've seen Him to be, the one who knows the future already—He knows exactly what He's going to do here. And even though He calls her a dog, the tone of the original language is affectionate, not derogatory. He praises her for her faith, and He heals her daughter. Then they turn around and go home, having just made a seventy-mile road trip that was probably only for one Gentile woman who happened to know, somehow, that Jesus is the Messiah.

Back in Galilee, He heals a deaf man and tells him to keep quiet, but of course, he doesn't. Then when He's on a mountainside in what's considered a Gentile region, the locals bring sick people to Him and He does a three-day healing marathon. While they're all there, He has His disciples feed them. Just like the last time. Jesus always has enough of everything we need. There's no need to despair. Ever. This time there are seven baskets of leftovers, which represents completion and perfection in Jewish culture.

TODAY'S GOD SHOT

"Great crowds came to him, bringing with them the lame, the blind, the crippled, the mute, and many others, and they put them at his feet, and he healed them" (15:30). In Revelation 4:10–11, Jesus is on His throne in the eternal kingdom, where the elders will "cast their crowns before the throne, saying, 'Worthy are you, our Lord and God, to receive glory and honor and power.'" What a vast difference in the things placed at His feet. On earth, it's the crippled, and in the kingdom, it's crowns. And Jesus welcomes all of it. He doesn't just take the crowns and the glory. He stays for three days to heal everyone who needs His help. What a compassionate Savior. He's where the joy is!

MATTHEW 16; MARK 8

After rebuking the Pharisees and Sadducees, Jesus turns the experience into a teaching tool. He often uses things around them in His metaphors, but sometimes it confuses the disciples because they take Him literally. He compares the teachings of the Pharisees and Sadducees to leaven—even getting a little bit mixed in with what you believe will impact everything. The teachings of both groups focus on morality. When morality is the goal, we focus on our actions instead of on the saving action of Christ. Morality hijacks the gospel while wearing a Sunday suit. And that mentality infects everything.

When His disciples misunderstand, He fills them in, but not the Pharisees and Sadducees, on the truth. He has warned His disciples, "Do not throw your pearls before pigs, lest they trample them underfoot and turn to attack you" (Matthew 7:6), and He demonstrates this here. Not even a good and true argument can change a hard heart.

Jesus can heal immediately and with a word, so why does He heal a blind man using spit? Possibly because spit is considered disgusting, so when He heals using a contaminant, it shows His power all the more. This healing is a two-step process. Why? It happens immediately after the disciples demonstrate their own partial vision. They're starting to see and understand who Jesus is, but they don't see fully yet. So it seems like He's letting them know He'll bear with them until they see clearly.

Then they go to Caesarea Philippi—the site of pagan worship rituals, including bestiality and child sacrifice. Pagans believe the mouth of a cave there is the gate to the underworld; they call it the Gates of Hell. They throw babies into it as an offering to the gods. Jesus brings His disciples here to make a point. He starts by asking a question: "Do people think I'm the Son of Man?" That title comes from Daniel 7:13 and refers to the Messiah. Then He gets personal and asks who *they* think He is. He's

---

For more information on today's reading, see thebiblerecap.com/links.

asking for them, not for Himself. He's a mind reader and doesn't need validation from teenagers.

Peter says He's the Christ, and Jesus says God blessed him with that information because there's no way he would've figured it out on his own. Then He continues: "And I tell you, you are Peter, and on this rock I will build my church, and the gates of hell shall not prevail against it" (16:18). The name *Peter* is *petras*, which means "a fragment of loose rock, a pebble." The word for *rock* is *petra*, which means "a mass of earth that is rock, a mountain." The sentence basically says, "You are a pebble, and on this mountain I will build My church." Peter isn't the foundation of everything; he can't be. But His statement of Christ's divinity is. We see it in Matthew 21:42, Ephesians 2:20, Acts 4:11, and 1 Corinthians 3:11. Jesus is the cornerstone, the foundation. In stone masonry, that's the most important piece. If it's removed, the whole thing collapses. But Jesus says His church will outlast everything because it's built on His divinity.

Peter's role in the early church is important; Jesus gives him a significant amount of authority, but we see immediately and repeatedly that he isn't infallible. When Jesus says He'll die soon, Peter rebukes Him. Then Jesus says, "Get behind me, Satan." Jesus has to go to the cross. He knows what He will endure (John 18:4). Satan knows the prophecies about the Messiah too, and he wants to stop it from happening because Jesus's victory seals Satan's defeat. But Revelation 13:8 says the cross has been the plan since before the world was created.

TODAY'S GOD SHOT

Jesus knows He's going to the cross soon. He's prepping the apostles for His death and the aftermath. He knows they'll be tempted to think this was all for nothing. He doesn't want them to shrink back when they face oppression. He takes this trip to the worst place imaginable and says none of this wickedness will stop His kingdom—it's not a threat to His church, which will outlast everything. He's also giving them a charge to storm the gates of hell. Gates are defensive—no one attacks with their gates. So this isn't just a promise that the enemy won't defeat them, but it's a call to go on the offense because we win! Nothing you encounter today can stop His kingdom. You can be bold in your faith because He's our King, and He's where the joy is!

MATTHEW 17; MARK 9

In Mark 9, Jesus says, "There are some standing here who will not taste death until they see the kingdom of God after it has come with power." Most scholars say this points to one of the following: (a) the transfiguration, which happens about a week later, (b) the resurrection, which is about six months away, or (c) the Holy Spirit showing up at the Feast of Pentecost, which is still about eight months away. All three events are times when God's power and His kingdom are displayed in unique ways. At the resurrection, God demonstrates His power over death and the grave. At Pentecost, the Holy Spirit comes to indwell believers. And the transfiguration is what we encounter next in today's reading.

About a week after He tells them He's going to suffer and die, He takes Peter, James, and John up on a mountain and lets them see behind the curtain of the spiritual dimension. They see things human eyes can't see. Jesus physically transforms or reveals some aspect of His deity that is normally hidden. His face shines like the sun, and His clothes turn white. Then two Old Testament leaders, Moses and Elijah, show up to talk with Him. How'd they get there? This is definitely a one-off. As the lawgiver, Moses represents the law, and Elijah represents the prophets, since he was one of the most prominent prophets. Whenever Jesus summarizes the Old Testament Scriptures, He refers to them collectively as "the Law and the Prophets." So these two men represent the whole thing—all of the words that testified to Jesus all along.

Peter doesn't want this to end. He throws out ideas about how they can stay there but gets interrupted by God the Father. And just like He did at Jesus's baptism, the Father affirms the person and work of the Son. The disciples are facedown; Jesus tells them not to fear and to get up. Then suddenly, Moses and Elijah are gone. Jesus says to keep this a secret until after He dies. Again, He's telling them He's going to suffer and die, and later, He tells them He'll be killed then raised from the dead,

---

For more information on today's reading, see thebiblerecap.com/links.

but they don't grasp any of this. Luke's account of this story indicates that God keeps them from understanding—quite likely because they can't handle it.

Finally, Matthew, the former tax collector, includes a story we don't get in any other gospel, and it's about tax season. The tax collectors approach Peter and ask if Jesus plans to pay His taxes. This is a temple tax required by God's law in Exodus 30, and Jesus hasn't paid it yet. They don't ask Peter about his taxes, because he's probably not of age yet. It's only required of men aged twenty and up. Jesus tells Peter that He personally shouldn't have to pay a tax to fund His Father's house, but His language also indicates that all sons of God, all the people who are adopted into God's family, should be exempt from this tax. Still, He lays down His rights and privileges and says, "I'll pay it anyway. I don't want to offend anyone by opting out. It would set a bad example." He has no problem breaking the Pharisees' traditions, but He always honors God's laws. He pays His bill in a miraculous way. He has Peter catch a fish and says it'll have a coin in its mouth for the exact amount to cover both of their taxes. He's paying Peter's tax too, even though Peter likely doesn't owe tax legally. He's paying more than what's required.

TODAY'S GOD SHOT

The father of the demonized boy confesses his doubt to Jesus—his fifty-fifty faith: "I believe. Help my unbelief." Both components are there, belief and unbelief, and he asks Jesus for help believing. God can grant faith! The disciples seem to have a faith problem too. One account says the demon can only be driven out by prayer, and the other says the demon wasn't driven out because the disciples didn't have faith. This seems to add up to show that they had faith in themselves but not in God, and their self-reliance meant they didn't even ask God for help; they tried to access the power of God without connecting to the person of God. God *wants* us to ask Him for help. He wants us to acknowledge our reliance on Him and rightly view Him as the source of all things. He's the source, and He's where the joy is!

MATTHEW 18

The disciples ask Jesus which one of them is the greatest. Jesus says humility is connected to greatness, and if they aren't humble, they won't be in the kingdom at all, much less be the greatest there. In stark contrast to the cultural mind-set, God values humility. Jesus also uses kids in His illustrations, which is unique because kids are viewed more like property. By using them as illustrations, He's showing the value of children as humans and image bearers. He says we should take notice of things that tempt us to sin and avoid them at all costs. He uses some pretty intense hyperbole for these illustrations—cutting off your hand, plucking out your eye—because sin is a big deal, and those who love God take their own sin seriously. Then He tells us how to respond to people when we've been sinned against.

Step one: Try to resolve it one-on-one with the person. By the way, there's no step zero—there's no space allotted for us to talk to others about that person and how they've sinned against us. If step one doesn't resolve things, then step two is our first opportunity to involve others in a conversation with the person. This isn't an ambush; they should know it's coming based on the conversation you had with them in step one. If step two doesn't resolve things, take it to the church for resolution—and again, the person should know this is coming. If step three doesn't resolve things, then the church exercises their discretion and wisdom. Jesus promises to be with them in their effort to reach unity on how to handle the situation. He says two or three should be able to agree on how to handle things and promises to give them guidance toward that end. When Jesus says to treat the person like a Gentile or a tax collector, it's helpful to recall that we've seen Him ministering to both kinds of people, associating with them, eating with them, seeking them out. So while this does seem like a call to remove them from the church, it doesn't seem to endorse wholesale excommunication. This is a call to love them well and share the gospel with them and to prevent them from being divisive in the church until they repent or the problem is resolved.

Then He goes straight into a message about forgiveness. Peter wants to know how many times he has to forgive someone who keeps sinning against him. Jesus tells a parable about a man who has great debt. He's repentant and wants to make things right with his master, and his master forgives his debt ($4–6 billion in today's money). Then the man runs into a man who owes him about $1,000. This man is repentant and wants to make things right—he isn't flippant or rebellious. But the man who had the huge debt forgiven won't forgive this small debt. In this parable, we're the one who owes $6 billion. Our sin debt is so massive we could never pay it. God is the generous master who forgave us. The fact that this parable revolves around this one man in the middle seems to show that forgiveness is our response to God, not the person who sinned against us. We respond to our forgiveness by forgiving those who are repentant. We extend what's been given to us. If we don't do that, then we probably don't really understand what we've received or how much we were in debt.

Jesus adds a little weight to this at the end of the parable by saying forgiveness has to be from the heart. In Scripture, the heart is the seat of the thoughts, emotions, and will—it's like a combination of your mind and your heart. So this could be referring to feeling forgiveness, but more likely, it's referring to making a decisive effort to continually choose forgiveness even when you don't feel it.

TODAY'S GOD SHOT

"If a man has a hundred sheep, and one of them has gone astray, does he not leave the ninety-nine on the mountains and go in search of the one that went astray?" (18:12). God pays individual attention to His kids. He notices what's happening, and He acts. He moves toward us when we run away. He comes to carry us back. And He rejoices over us! He's not far off, and He's not inattentive. He's actively working on our behalf, even when we're running away from Him. He finds us and brings us back so that we can see He's where the joy is!

JOHN 7–8

There are three feasts each year for which Jews travel to Jerusalem. Before one feast, Jesus's brothers say He should publicly demonstrate His power there, but their words are almost certainly mocking, because they don't believe in Him. Jesus says they're part of the world, not the kingdom. Those who don't submit to Christ belong to the world, and the world doesn't hate its own. He addresses this again in John 15:18–25, which helps us understand this better. He tells them He's not going to the feast—and the Greek phrase here often includes the word *yet*, meaning He's not going right now, but He goes later.

When He arrives, He teaches in the temple, a role typically reserved for educated rabbis. They're perplexed that He knows things. He says, "I know these things because I speak with God's authority—which is why it's completely irrational that you're trying to kill Me." They accuse Him of having a demon. He lets the insult slide and tries to reason with them: "You circumcise babies on the eighth day, even if that day happens to be the Sabbath, and everyone's fine with it. Why the double standard? Why can't I heal someone if you're cutting someone?" Some people watching wonder if He's the Messiah but dismiss the thought when they get confused by an inaccurate rabbinical theory (Micah 5:2 says the Messiah will be born in Bethlehem). As He's being attacked, He leans into the Father's authority, submitting to His role as the Son. They try to capture Him, but again He escapes because "His hour had not yet come." They send people to arrest Him, and He says, "Not yet. You'll get Me soon, but even when you do, it won't be for long. And when I leave, you can't go where I'm heading." None of His words makes sense to them at the time, but He's setting them up to understand retrospectively. Nicodemus, the Pharisee who met with Him at night to ask Him questions, tries and fails to reason with them.

When Jesus returns to the temple, the Pharisees bring a woman caught in adultery. They ask Him if they should stone her like the law commands. He says, "Sure. Let's stone her. The person who should lead the way is whoever is sinless." He is the only one qualified to stone her, but instead, He uses His power to bless, not to curse, then tells her to leave her life of sin.

Back in the temple, He says He's the Light of the World. The Pharisees say, "You're making big claims about Yourself. Can anyone else back up what You're saying?" And He says, "My Father testifies about Me. That should suffice." They say, "Where's this Dad You speak of?" And Jesus says, "Oh, you don't know Him." They think He's talking about a human, but He's saying, "You have no relationship with the God of the universe. He's a stranger to you. The only way you can know Him is if you know Me, and you clearly don't know Me. And you can't hear God's words, because you don't belong to Him." He says they'll die in their sins and that their father is the devil. God isn't the Father of all the people He created; He's only the Father of those He adopts into His family, those who come to know Him through Jesus.

He says He'll be lifted up soon—a reference to the cross—and then they'll understand. They may not submit to it, but they won't be able to deny it. He incites their attempts at murder when He says He's been around longer than Abraham, that He's both preexistent and divine. He's using the language of YHWH in Exodus 3:14, identifying Himself as the great I Am, the self-existent one. He is I Am.

TODAY'S GOD SHOT

Jesus says He's the Light of the World, the very thing by which we can see. Most scholars say Genesis 3:15 is the first prophecy about Jesus in Scripture; it talks about His victory over the enemy. But perhaps the first prophecy is actually in Genesis 1:3, where God the Father looks out over the dark, chaotic world, knowing all the brokenness that will take place after He finishes creating it, and says, "Let there be light." Maybe that's more than just a creation command. Maybe it's a promise, as if He's saying, "Things are about to get very dark, but Light is coming. Hold on—Light is coming." If that's a prophecy, Jesus is certainly the fulfillment of it. And He's where the joy is!

JOHN 9–10

In this culture, people associate sickness or physical disability with sin. While it's true that occasionally there may be a link—like with the demonic—many of the healing cases we've seen haven't had mentions of sin at all. There's no direct, consistent cause-and-effect relationship. When Jesus's disciples display the cultural mind-set instead of biblical truth, He sets them straight. They ask who's to blame for a man's blindness, and He says, "He's blind because this will be used to glorify God." Their mind-set had evolved as an attempt to avoid blaming God for suffering, but Jesus seems to put the onus on God. This can be especially hard if we still struggle to trust that God is doing what's good and best. Fortunately, God is still at work in this man's story to heal and redeem.

It's the Sabbath when God chooses to do this work, of course. Remember how the Pharisees build a fence around the law? Remember how they made it illegal to spit on the dirt on the Sabbath? So of course, Jesus steps over their fence and heals the man by spitting on the dirt, making mud, and putting it on the man's eyes. He's showing that He can break two of their rules by making mud and healing on the Sabbath while still honoring the heart of the law. The Pharisees ask who healed the man, but he's never seen Jesus, so he can't pick Him out of a lineup. He only knows His name. The Pharisees round up his parents to verify the story, but they're nervous about the investigation because they don't want to be expelled from the synagogue community. The Pharisees interrogate the man again, and he gets salty with them: "You're so curious about Jesus. Sounds like you want to follow Him too!" He uses their words to reason them into a corner, so they throw him out. Jesus finds him again and says, "I'm the Messiah. I'm here to help blind people like you get their sight and people who have sight to lose theirs." He's talking about spiritual eyes. Those who think they can see—who aren't aware of their own spiritual poverty—He's going to blind them. He condemns the religious and saves the lost. He's always pointing back to square one: spiritual poverty.

Jesus calls Himself the Good Shepherd. In Ezekiel 34:23, God promised to raise up a good shepherd for His people, Someone unlike their wicked leaders. Other leaders may be sneaky and violent, but He's got a personal relationship with the sheep, His followers. They know His voice, and He's protective of them. Then He calls Himself the door of the sheep. So is He the shepherd or the door? Their sheep pens are made of stacked rocks with one section left open as an entrance and exit. After the shepherd rounds up the sheep and puts them in the pen for the night, he lies down and sleeps in that spot. That way the sheep can't get out, and thieves and robbers can't get in. The Shepherd *is* the door. During the day, the sheep go out to feed in green pastures. At night, they come in and are safe. They have enemies—humans who want to steal them, animals who want to devour them—but Jesus says He owns the sheep; He's personally invested. He isn't a hired hand who clocks out and takes his paycheck. Then He gives a nod to the Gentiles when He says, "I have other sheep that are not of this fold." He closes this metaphor with a reference to His willing death; no one takes His life from Him. This is the Father's plan.

The Pharisees want Him to shoot straight—is He the Messiah or not? When He answers, the cause-and-effect relationship He mentions is noteworthy. He doesn't say, "You aren't My sheep because you don't believe," He says, "You don't believe because you aren't My sheep."

TODAY'S GOD SHOT

"I give them eternal life, and they will never perish, and no one will snatch them out of my hand. My Father, who has given them to me, is greater than all, and no one is able to snatch them out of the Father's hand. I and the Father are one" (10:28–30). For God's kids, the single most comforting thing is that nothing can snatch us from His hand. Nothing is stronger than Him—not even us. He says no one can do it, and we're someone. He promises us eternal life *and* eternal security in His hand. What He initiates, He will sustain and He will fulfill. He can and does and He keeps doing. He's where the joy is!

LUKE 10

In Matthew 10, Jesus sent out His twelve apostles. Today He sends out seventy-two people. It's likely the same scenario, and Matthew focused on telling the personal story he and the other eleven apostles experienced, whereas Luke, who isn't an apostle, prefers to zoom out on the whole group. Their job is to bring the kingdom near, to let the towns know that Jesus the Messiah is coming to visit. As ambassadors for Christ and agents of His healing power, they bring the benefits and truth of the kingdom near to those far from the kingdom. When they return, they're overjoyed. They feel so powerful! They can do things they've seen Jesus doing. Jesus responds by saying He saw Satan fall like lightning from heaven, then He moves on without explanation. Scripture may fill in the blanks elsewhere. Some scholars say this refers to Isaiah 14:12 or Ezekiel 28:11–19, which record a fall from heaven, power, or both in the past, and others say it refers to a future fall, like in Revelation 20:1–10, which records Satan's final defeat.

When we collect the passages about Satan throughout Scripture we see that he's one of God's created angels who rebelled in heaven, along with one-third of the other angels. They were all evicted, but since they weren't destroyed, they've mounted a doomed attack against the kingdom of God and will ultimately be put to shame. So when Jesus casually mentions this here in the context of their personal encounters with the demonic, it seems like He's trying to say, "Of course you have power over demons. You're on the winning team. But the main point isn't what you can do here on earth—that's all temporary. The point is that your eternal future with Me is secure." In fact, Jesus gets so excited about these eternal things that He may have even done a little dance. Verse 21 says, "He rejoiced in the Holy Spirit" as He thanked God. The word *rejoice* carries the idea that He "jumped for joy," and apparently it was often accompanied by a song and dance!

As He continues talking, a lawyer, who is probably a Pharisee, asks Him how to get this eternal life He keeps mentioning. He wants to test

Jesus and justify himself by his good deeds. Since Jesus is talking to a lawyer, He meets the man where he is by going straight to the law: "Based on the law, what do you think the answer is?" The man says, "Love God with everything I have and love my neighbor as myself. But who is my neighbor?" It seems like an attempt to avoid loving others. Jesus answers with a story about a man who is attacked when he takes a dangerous journey through an area known for thieves and robbers. A priest walks past and won't touch him. A Levite walks past and ignores him. Their jobs are to be mediators between God and man, but they won't extend God's help to the man in need. Then Jesus throws a shocking twist into the story: A Samaritan stops to help. Samaritans and Jews have mutual disdain for each other. Jesus paints a Samaritan as the good guy in this story and tells the Pharisee to take notes. The word *neighbor* refers to everyone you encounter, even if they're your enemy.

Later, two of Jesus's friends have Him over for lunch. Mary is talking to Jesus while Martha is trying to handle the details. She's frustrated that Mary is relaxing while she's stressed. She even asks Jesus, "Do You not see the problem here?" Jesus leans into compassion. He acknowledges her emotions, then says, "Don't let this work ruin your day. What matters is that the time you spend with Me can't be taken away from you."

TODAY'S GOD SHOT

The Samaritan has many things in common with Jesus. They both have a mixed lineage. They're both rejected and despised yet compassionate toward the hurting. They both pour out wine and oil—for Jesus these symbolize His blood and God the Spirit. They both pay the price for healing and rest. And they both promise to return. What the Good Samaritan does here is good and beautiful and true, but it's a temporary thing pointing to an eternal reality. Jesus is showing us what *He* has done. This parable serves as a reminder that we are the ones in the ditch. It turns out the Good Samaritan isn't even the hero of his own parable—Jesus is! And He's where the joy is!

LUKE 12–13

Jesus is preaching about trusting God's provision and gets heckled by a man who asks Him to settle a financial dispute. Jesus says, "That's not why I'm here, but since you brought it up, don't put your hope in money." Then He launches into a parable about a fool who builds new barns to hold his wealth. He preaches a false gospel to himself, finding comfort in his possessions. But he'll die that night, and his wealth will be divided. He stored up the wrong things. Death can come at any moment, and we have no idea when Jesus will return, so He says to be prepared. Preparation can only mean one thing. *Do we know Him or not?* Relationship is the only preparation possible or necessary. Daniel 12:1–3 and Malachi 4 tell us the two possible outcomes based on knowing God and not knowing God. When Peter asks, "Is that doomsday prep stuff for everyone to hear? Or just for us?" Jesus answers with a parable about a servant who is supposed to feed the master's other servants. Later, He'll tell Peter to feed His sheep. Connecting these details seems to answer Peter's question. Jesus does tell the disciples more, but He'll also require more of them.

Pontius Pilate is the governor in Judea, and he recently killed some Jews. The people tell Jesus about this, and He says, "This isn't punishment for their sins; that's not how things work." He gives a parallel account of mass death and says, "Your level of suffering doesn't tell us anything about your heart. You can't look at trials and tragedies and assume they're punishment from God." But He ends with a warning: Judgment *is* coming, and the only way to survive it is to turn to God.

Then he tells a parable: A man plants a tree and has a gardener tend to it, but it's fruitless for three years. The owner is frustrated, but the gardener who cares for it every day says, "Be patient with it." He's invested in this tree and doesn't want to cut it down. He keeps fertilizing it and caring for it as they wait to see what happens. This is a metaphor

For more information on today's reading, see thebiblerecap.com/links.

for Israel at the time—Israel is the fig tree, Jesus is the vinedresser, and the Father owns the vineyard. It's been three years since Jesus began His ministry, but Israel shows no signs of repenting. God is willing to chop down a fruitless tree, but He's also patient with a tree that hasn't yet produced fruit. Fruit takes time, so He tends to us, waters us, and fertilizes us.

Someone asks Him how many people will be saved. Saved from Rome? Saved from their sins? Jesus doesn't let the man get away with generalities. He makes it personal, saying, "Here's what *you* need to do," then tells a parable imploring the man to respond to God's invitation. Some people spent time with and near God, but then God said, "I don't know you." He says we may be surprised to know who is, and who isn't, in God's kingdom, because it's not about your race, nationality, or deeds—it's about who you know.

Herod wants to kill Jesus, so He sends Herod a message: "I've got work to do, but I'm heading your way. I have to die in Jerusalem, after all. I want to shower Jerusalem with love, but its people reject Me. I'll be there soon, though, and the people will greet Me by saying, 'Blessed is He who comes in the name of the Lord!'" He is prophesying Palm Sunday.

TODAY'S GOD SHOT

Warnings about judgment are important—they're a call to repentance for those who don't know Jesus and a call to evangelize for those who do. But they're never supposed to leave us more terrified of judgment than in love with Jesus. Peter and Paul encourage believers to check their hearts to make sure they're in the faith (2 Corinthians 13:5; 2 Peter 1:10–11), but they both imply that we can reach a conclusion. We can *know* that we've been adopted into God's family. God doesn't want us to carry that fear. Jesus even tells His disciples they don't need to be anxious because their Father is attentive and delights in them: "Fear not, little flock, for it is your Father's good pleasure to give you the kingdom" (12:32). God delights to give good gifts to His kids. And there's no greater gift than Himself. He's where the joy is!

LUKE 14–15

Jesus goes to dinner at a Pharisee's house, where He meets a man with dropsy, a swelling condition. And, of course, it's the Sabbath. A Pharisee likely wouldn't allow this man in his home, since they associated sickness with sin, so this is likely a trap. Jesus asks if it's legal to heal on the Sabbath. He regularly asks questions He knows the answers to. They don't respond, so He heals the guy and sends him home. Then Jesus says, "Humble yourself or you'll be humbled. When you have dinners like this, invite the poor and sick—the people you regard as sinners. You won't get repaid for it on earth, but in the long run, that's the path to blessing." Someone else jumps in to smooth over the awkwardness, saying, "Everyone will be blessed who eats and drinks in the kingdom of God!" But Jesus then tells a parable about the kingdom, showing how the discarded and poor know they need God's provision but the wealthy and important have other priorities that take up their time: possessions, work, and relationships. The poor and homeless don't have those distractions. Often, the things that creep in and push God out are things we primarily count as blessings.

Following Jesus will mean self-denial, putting an end to our self-determination. He's not calling people to hate others; He's saying that by comparison, everything else comes in a distant second. He wants the people who are caught up in the emotions of His miracles to really consider if they're interested in a life of following Him. He warns them this life won't be easy.

Then He tells three parables about recovering lost things: a sheep, a coin, and a son. (We covered the lost sheep in Matthew 18.) The lost coin was only worth about a day's wages, but Jesus paints a picture of complete joy when the woman finds it. God rejoices at finding the lost, even when they may not seem valuable to anyone else. The inhabitants of heaven celebrate when a sinner repents! Then He tells the parable of the prodigal son. Many people think *prodigal* means "rebellious" or "wandering off." But it really means "wasteful." So this is the parable of the wasteful son. A man has two sons, and the younger son wants his inheritance now; he wants to do his own thing and doesn't seem to have a great relationship with his dad. He gets his third of the inheritance, because the oldest son typically gets a double portion, and sets out to burn through it all. Then, the best thing that could've happened happens: a famine. He comes to the end of his money and has to get a job. He's hungry and has to feed pigs for a living. This detail adds shock value for the Pharisees, because pigs are unclean. His circumstances wake him up and soften his heart. His entitlement has been starved out of him. He becomes repentant and wants to go home to work as a servant. But when his dad sees him in the distance, he runs to him. He doesn't punish him for running off. He doesn't shame him. He celebrates! When the older son skips the party, his dad begs him to come but he refuses. His dad doesn't rebuke him for being self-centered; he says, "All I have is yours. It always has been!"

We resonate with the story of the father welcoming a sinner and celebrating that what was dead is alive. But given Jesus's audience—Jewish followers who are "tax collectors and sinners," plus Pharisees—it seems He may have a different angle. He seems to be portraying the tax collectors and sinners as the younger son and the Pharisees as the older son. If we look at it that way, who is the real prodigal son, the truly wasteful one? The older son is the one who really misses out, just as the Pharisees are missing out on the Father's heart because they're too busy hating the sinners.

TODAY'S GOD SHOT

Jesus shows God celebrating our nearness to Him (15:23–24, 32). He celebrates! It's easy to feel the weight of our sin and forget that He calls us clean. One of the great things about serving a God who is outside of time is that He sees our future as a present reality. He sees us as holy, because Jesus has already taken our debt and traded it for His righteousness. The fact that God would celebrate us feels a little odd, but He calls it fitting. He is so merciful and gracious. And He's where the joy is!

LUKE 16–17

Jesus tells His disciples a parable while the Pharisees listen in. A rich man's household manager has slacked on collecting money people owe his boss. He gets fired, but his pride motivates him to hustle to reclaim his job; he manages to collect most of the debt. Being fair to the boss isn't his goal, but it works out in his favor. Jesus doesn't seem to be on board with his methods; it's just an illustration to show how pagans are wiser in worldly matters than the disciples are in eternal matters. He wants them to wise up. He inserts some confusing irony but seems to be saying, "This guy is so concerned about being welcomed into people's homes that he's willing to lie. If you attempt that with My eternal dwelling place, you'll fail. No amount of wealth or shrewdness can get you there." He implores them to value true and eternal things, saying, "You can be a slave to your bank account or a slave to God, but you can't be both."

His next story is often referred to as a parable, but if it is, it's the only one in which a person is named. A rich man dies, as does a beggar named Lazarus, who has a skin disease. Lazarus is carried away and dropped down beside Abraham; his proximity to Abraham is emphasized because the Pharisee listeners would assume Abraham is in the best possible eternal destination (i.e., heaven). It would disgust the Pharisees that a sinner is in the kingdom and that Abraham has to be near him. As the rich man is being tormented in Hades, he begs Abraham for water, but Abraham says, "Impossible. There's no path from here to there." Their eternal destinations are fixed. The text doesn't reference purgatory or any second-chance option. He begs Abraham to send messengers to warn his family, but Abraham says, "If the Hebrew Scriptures don't convince them to repent, they wouldn't be convinced even if someone rose from the dead!" Foreshadowing!

In the parable of the unworthy servant, Jesus encourages His disciples to be humble and remember they're servants of the one true God. As He continues toward Jerusalem, heading toward His death, He runs into a group of lepers. All ten lepers beg Him for healing, and He sends them to see the priest, in accordance with the law. And they're healed on the way! But the only leper who returns to thank Him is the foreigner, the Samaritan.

The Pharisees want to know when God's kingdom will be established. The Hebrew Scriptures promise a Messiah, an eternal kingdom, peace on earth, and the elimination of their enemies, so they expect God to set up a political or military leader to make this happen. But Jesus says it won't be like that. Then He makes a statement that's frequently taken out of context, misquoted, and misapplied: "The kingdom of God is in the midst of you." Some versions say "within you," and others say "among you." The Greek word can mean both things, but they communicate different ideas. Jesus is saying, "I *am* the kingdom of God. I'm right here in front of you—among you, in the midst of you." But He's definitely not saying, "The kingdom of God is within you," because (a) He's talking to Pharisees, whom He has previously called whitewashed tombs and children of Satan, and (b) even if He were talking to His disciples, the Holy Spirit hasn't come to dwell in people yet.

TODAY'S GOD SHOT

Jesus is specific with how He speaks to different audiences. He meets them where they are—the Pharisees in their unbelief and the disciples in their confusion and bewilderment. But to their dismay, He doesn't always give straight answers. He says things to prepare them that don't make sense to them yet: "You'll want the kingdom to come soon. People will try to convince you it's about to happen, but they're liars. No one knows when it's happening." Some say today's final verses—about one person being taken and the other left—refer to God taking the righteous into heaven while pagans are left behind. Others believe it refers to God killing off the wicked—taking them in death—and leaving the faithful alive to be united with Him in the new heaven and new earth. Either way, Jesus speaks to His disciples with a comfort and a promise: He's coming back, and we'll be united with Him. And He's where the joy is!

JOHN 11

Today we visit with Mary, Martha, and Lazarus. You may recognize the sisters—we met them in Luke 10:38–42—but this Lazarus is different from the one we read about yesterday. Lazarus gets sick and the sisters send for Jesus, but He continues with what He's doing and says, "This illness won't lead to death. It'll be used to glorify God." He doesn't go to their house right away but stays two more days before heading there. His delay has to be excruciating for the sisters and confusing for His disciples. The disciples don't want to go to Bethany, where the family lives, because it's right outside Jerusalem's walls and the people there are always trying to kill Jesus. But Jesus knows it's still not time for Him to die, so they head to Bethany.

When they arrive, Lazarus is four days dead. Mary stays inside, mourning, but Martha, ever the doer herself, runs out to meet Jesus and asks Him to do something, though she doesn't know exactly what. Then, one of the most ironic moments in Jesus's ministry happens. Often, when He's talking about things on a spiritual and eternal level, people think He's talking about physical things, but this time He's talking about a physical thing, and He still gets misunderstood. Martha thinks He's speaking spiritually. Jesus says, "I'm going to raise Lazarus from the dead." And she says, "Yes, in the resurrection to eternal life." But instead of spilling the beans, He reasons with her about what He's capable of and saves the surprise for later. Martha's faith in Jesus isn't specific to His ability to raise Lazarus—that hasn't even occurred to her—her faith is rooted in the fact that Jesus is good and strong and loving. She isn't entitled or demanding. She doesn't claim anything other than the goodness of God. That's where she drops her anchor.

Then Jesus goes to talk with Mary, the more emotionally-driven sister. She says the same thing Martha said, but Jesus responds to her in a totally different way. He weeps. His responses to people are so personal, specific, attentive—He meets people where they are. We see His humanity here as well. He's moved by their pain and enters into their grief. Even knowing He's about to raise Lazarus from the dead, He doesn't brush off the weight of what has happened. But there are scoffers who say, "If You really cared, You would've stopped this from happening!" They don't understand His ways or His timing, and they mistrust His heart. He says to roll the stone away, then He thanks the Father aloud and calls Lazarus out of the tomb. Some who see this believe and worship Jesus. Others can't get back to Jerusalem fast enough, because they want to report this to the Pharisees. They're worked into a frenzy because if Jesus keeps doing these things, everyone will follow Him, and then Rome will think the Jews are out of control and will oppress and deport them. Caiaphas the high priest speaks up and becomes an unwitting prophet; he's speaking God's truth but doesn't know it. He wants Jesus to die, so he says, "It's better that one man die for the people than for all the people to die." At that point, the religious leaders start plotting Jesus's death. Jesus knows this, so He keeps a low profile, but He isn't living in fear of His future. He's actively working things out to correspond to the Father's appointed timing for His death.

TODAY'S GOD SHOT

Jesus loves this family, so why doesn't He go when they call Him? He's waiting for Lazarus to die. You can't raise a person who isn't dead. He intentionally designs a situation where things get far worse in order for His power to be made known all the more. He's always pointing to the Father and His glory, just like He did in His prayer of thanks. And this miracle sets in motion the plan to crucify Him. He knew this would be costly. Perhaps that's even part of what moved Him to tears—the tomb and the stone and the graveclothes aren't too far off for Him, and He knows it. He's about to put death to death and this is a preview. From His intentional timing that somehow always seems too late, to His sweet, personal interaction with the sisters, to His power over death and the grave—He's where the joy is!

LUKE 18

Jesus encourages His disciples to pray about what's really on their hearts, to not give up asking. He tells a parable of a wicked judge who finally caves to the persistent nagging of a widow. He isn't drawing a direct parallel—He's portraying God as *better than* the example. This judge doesn't fear God or man, so if he relents and hears the widow's cry, how much more would a loving Father hear and respond to the cries of His kids? Scripture encourages us to pray for things big, medium, and small—God doesn't discriminate when it comes to conversation with His kids. Jesus knows His disciples need to be reminded that God is attentive, because it's the awareness of God's attention and love that will invite their own faithfulness. If they feel forgotten by God, they won't walk closely with Him, which is why Jesus ends this parable with a question about His return: "Nevertheless, when the Son of Man comes, will he find faith on earth?" (v. 8). As usual, He asks this question for *them* to think about; He knows the answer.

Then He tells a parable about a Pharisee and a tax collector, and He's telling it to people who have completely missed square one: spiritual poverty. So we can expect that to be the point He's going to make here. While praying in the temple, the Pharisee thanks God for all his good works—and he has certainly found the right person to thank, because God is the source of all his good works. The problem is that his words carry a tone of arrogance. Meanwhile, the tax collector, who has no good works to speak of, is wailing, acknowledging his sin, and begging God for mercy. Jesus says the tax collector is the one God justifies, not the Pharisee. The gospel is an inversion of religion.

The rich ruler has wealth and power, and he's been obedient as far as the law is concerned—at least on the surface. He asks Jesus how to have eternal life. Jesus has been talking about it a lot, so he wants to know how to get it. Jesus leans into the question, forcing the man to search his own heart and see what's really in there. He pushes him one step at a time. He starts by telling him to keep the law, and the man says, "Done!"

Clearly that's not true—we all fail to keep the Ten Commandments, not to mention the other six hundred–plus laws. But the ruler is confident, so Jesus says, "You've kept the law? Great! Then you need to come be one of My followers. Go sell everything you own and come with Me." This invitation reveals the man's heart. Jesus makes him an offer that He makes to no one else in the Gospels but the twelve disciples: "Come follow Me." This ruler could've been the thirteenth apostle, but Jesus knows all along what's in his heart. The problem is that the ruler doesn't know what's in his own heart, until he has to choose between following Jesus and sticking with wealth and power. To be clear, the command and invitation Jesus gives him *isn't* the path to eternal life. Nothing else we've read says, "Sell everything you own. That's how to know God." Jesus is just meeting the ruler where he is to reveal his own heart to him. He exposes his priorities. The ruler may think he wants to follow God, but he really prefers his own path, so he goes away sad.

Jesus tells His disciples for the third time that He'll die soon, giving more details than usual. He even includes the fact that people will spit on Him. They still don't understand; God is hiding it from them even as He's telling them. They keep moving toward Jerusalem, undeterred. On the way there, they pass Jericho, where Jesus heals a blind beggar.

TODAY'S GOD SHOT

"Truly, I say to you, there is no one who has left house or wife or brothers or parents or children, for the sake of the kingdom of God, who will not receive many times more in this time, and in the age to come eternal life" (18:29–30). Abundant, eternal life in the kingdom won't look the same as a life focused on the here and now—nor should it. Jesus promises there will be some necessary losses along the way. But He also promises that what we gain for following Christ will always trump what we lose. Even His taking is giving. He's always in the business of giving: life, hope, peace, healing, freedom, justice . . . and joy! Because He's where the joy is!

MATTHEW 19; MARK 10

No area of our lives is untouched by God; there's no space He's restricted from or inactive in or that He doesn't have plans for. Sovereignty knows no bounds. So when Jesus gives a sermon on divorce, He can be trusted. If you haven't lived up to His words, it just means you're human. We all fall short of His teachings, but He paid for our sins and took our shame. "There is therefore now no condemnation for those who are in Christ Jesus" (Romans 8:1).

The Pharisees ask Him, "Is it lawful to divorce one's wife for any reason?" This could mean, "Are there any circumstances under which divorce is acceptable?" or "Can we divorce our wives for any reason we want?" Typically, they add to God's laws with their own traditions, but they also ignore His laws when it serves their own purposes—like with honoring their parents. Where they add to God's law with their traditions, Jesus breaks those traditions. Where they subtract from God's law, Jesus dials it back in. With divorce laws, they tend to loosen the reins, so He dials in, pointing out that God's standard is higher than the law—it goes to the heart. Moses allowed men to divorce their wives, but only because their hearts were hard. The goal isn't hardness of heart; the goal is a soft heart. According to Jesus, divorce wouldn't be an issue if hearts were soft. His disciples say, "That's pretty strict stuff. Sounds like we're better off staying single!" He says, "You're right. It's a tough teaching. If it's too difficult for you, you should stay single—God promises to help you." Both marriage and singleness are tough paths, but we don't walk either path alone.

Teachings on divorce and on remarriage vary in different faith traditions—some say it's one unified issue, while others say they're separate issues. In Jesus's day, a woman is often unable to support herself without a husband to provide for her, so being divorced almost forces her to be remarried in order to survive, so He addresses this too. In Mark 10:11–12, He touches briefly on remarriage, and Paul talks about it in 1 Corinthians 7:10–11: "To the married, I give this charge (not I, but the

Lord): the wife should not separate from her husband (but if she does, she should remain unmarried or else be reconciled to her husband), and the husband should not divorce his wife." In verses 12–15, Paul basically says, "To the rest I say—I, not the Lord—if the unbelieving partner separates, let it be so. In such cases the brother or sister is not enslaved." Some say "not being enslaved" means they're free to remarry, while others say he's indicating that they aren't bound to stay married. It's helpful that Paul distinguishes between his opinion and God's law, but these teachings aren't easy either way.

Jesus keeps talking about the eternal kingdom, and James and John want to sit on either side of Him there. But Jesus is seated at the right hand of the Father, so that seat is taken. He says, "You can't do what that requires." They say, "Sure we can!" Then in His veiled way, He says, "You're kind of right. You'll die and be persecuted like Me, but I'm not in charge of those details and the answer is still no." Even two men in His inner circle get a no to something they ask Him for.

TODAY'S GOD SHOT

"Whoever would be great among you must be your servant, and whoever would be first among you must be slave of all. For even the Son of Man came not to be served but to serve, and to give his life as a ransom for many" (10:43–45). In dying for the people, Jesus is taking Himself away from their physical presence but leaving them something eternal. By saying no to the requests of James and John, He's giving them something better—they just don't understand at the time. When they enter the kingdom and see Jesus seated at the right hand of the Father, there's no chance they'll protest it. They'll realize in retrospect that no was the best response to their request. God is always doing what is eternally best, and He's too efficient to have something that's best for one person but bad for another. In the grand scheme of things, whatever is best for John is best for James and even best for you. He's always serving us and giving the best gifts. He's where the joy is!

MATTHEW 20–21

Jesus compares the kingdom to a vineyard and its workers. The owner brings in workers at various times but pays them all the same amount. The ones who worked longer get upset, but he says, "Stop comparing yourselves to those who worked less. Take what I'm giving you." This parable shows the tremendous amounts of grace God pours out—grace is when you get what you don't deserve. It also shows that entitlement has no place in the hearts of God's kids. Since everything God gives us is undeserved, it's *all* blessing and generosity. Comparing ourselves to others is evidence that we've lost sight of our spiritual poverty and God's immense generosity. There will be unexpected people in the kingdom—people who spend their lives in sin and turn to Him in their final moments. They may not accomplish much on earth for the sake of His kingdom, but they receive the same rescue.

Jesus continues heading to Jerusalem to celebrate the Passover and be crucified. His actions and parables intensify during His final days. When He curses a fig tree because it's fruitless, it withers immediately. Jesus knows it's not fig season—that's still months away. So why is He so angry? Remember the parable of the fruitless fig tree in Luke 13:6–9? Israel is this fig tree. Prophets have been making this comparison for hundreds of years, painting Israel as a fruitless fig tree (Jeremiah 8:13; Micah 7:1). Jesus desperately wants Israel to bear fruit, but it hasn't. The withering is a sign of judgment because of fruitlessness. Jesus knows His days on earth are almost over. He knows how this all unfolds. It probably breaks His heart to see that Israel hasn't produced fruit. When He curses the fig tree, it's hard to imagine it isn't devastating to Him, even though none of it comes as a surprise.

He goes to the temple to teach—putting Himself in front of the very people who will arrest Him soon. The chief priests and elders question His authority, and He turns the tables on them. He gives them a riddle about JTB's ministry, asking where it came from. The answer to that question is also the answer to their question. John's ministry and Jesus's authority both come from heaven. The chief priests and the elders can't accept and receive these truths, but they can't refute them either.

The final two parables today represent condemnation for those Jews who have rejected Jesus as Messiah. First is the parable of the two sons. One takes his time in being obedient, while the other pretends to be obedient right away but is actually disobedient. Jesus says tax collectors, sinners, and prostitutes may seem to take the long way around, but if they eventually repent, that's better than faking obedience. Verbal assent to the truth isn't enough—it has to come from a yielded heart.

The parable of the wicked tenants is a picture of Christ's death. The tenants of the vineyard don't want to give the master what's rightfully His, so they kill everyone who comes to get it—the prophets, JTB, and now Jesus—so they can have the inheritance instead. Herod and Satan have already tried to kill Jesus to benefit themselves, and soon Judas Iscariot will do the same. But here, Jesus is talking to the chief priests and Pharisees, who also play a role. He says they are not producing the fruit of the kingdom. They're producing lots of fruit, but it's human fruit, not kingdom fruit. Kingdom fruit is Spirit grown, and it has a few defining characteristics: love, joy, peace, patience, kindness, goodness, faithfulness, gentleness, and self-control. Those are its attributes.

TODAY'S GOD SHOT

Jesus often speaks life and healing, so it's interesting to encounter a place where He speaks death. To have the power of life is to have the power of death too—He holds them simultaneously. He even has the power to speak death over those who will kill Him. He could wither their bodies with a word or a thought. But He doesn't. He walks in meekness, humbly submitting to the Father's plan. He does it to magnify God's greatness throughout the universe, to fulfill the story of redemption, and to bring all God's adopted children into His kingdom forever. What a rescue and what a Rescuer! He's where the joy is!

LUKE 19

In Luke's account, Jesus hasn't yet entered Jerusalem. He's on His way there, along with the rest of the crowd. While He's passing through Jericho, Zaccheus the tax collector is curious about Him and wants to see Him. He doesn't need anything tangible from Jesus—he's not sick, he's not demonized, and all seems to be well in his world. In fact, he's one of the most wealthy, powerful men in town. It's easy to realize our need for God when we have a tangible need, but for a wealthy businessman to be curious about Jesus is a different thing altogether. He's so intrigued that he climbs a tree to see Him. What prompts a person like Zaccheus to have curiosity like that?

Jesus looks up at him, calls him by name, then invites Himself to dinner. The locals are shocked that He wants to eat with a sinner. Jesus reminds them that sinners are His priority—He came to seek and save the lost, not those who think they're found. After being found by Jesus, Zaccheus sets out to do everything in his power to make right what he's done wrong. It's clear he has a heart of repentance. Zaccheus has some things in common with the rich ruler in Luke 18:18–30—they're both wealthy and powerful. But the rich ruler thought he was acing life and morality, whereas Zaccheus is fully aware of his own spiritual poverty. The rich ruler saw how much he had to lose by following Jesus, but Zaccheus sees how much he has to gain!

Jesus continues on, and as they approach Bethany on the outskirts of Jerusalem, He sends two disciples to get a colt. His instructions are precise and vague at the same time and almost certainly require divine arrangement. Why does Jesus need a colt? He's walked all this way, so why now, at the end of His long journey, does He ask for a ride? There are many Old Testament prophecies about the Messiah, and Jesus is fulfilling them all, bit by bit. This particular prophecy comes from Zechariah 9:9: "Rejoice greatly, O daughter of Zion! Shout aloud, O daughter of Jerusalem! Behold, your king is coming to you; righteous and having salvation is he, humble and mounted on a donkey, on a colt, the foal of a donkey." And this is exactly how He enters Jerusalem. When He arrives, the people fulfill a prophecy too, one He spoke over them in Luke 13:31–35. As He promised, they're saying, "Blessed is He who comes in the name of the Lord" as they walk down the Mount of Olives into Jerusalem. Other accounts say they're shouting, "Hosanna," which means, "Save us!" Most likely, it's a cry to save them from Roman oppression, not a cry to save them from their sins.

We don't know the exact path they took down the Mount of Olives, but for three thousand years much of that hillside has been covered with thousands of tombs. They're still there today—mostly above-ground burial plots with limestone markers. As the disciples are shouting their praises, the Pharisees don't like the uproar, so they tell Jesus to rebuke His people. He says that if they go silent, the very stones will cry out. While it's possible Jesus is referring to actual rocks, it's more likely that He's referring to the thousands of gravestones they're passing on the hillside. He's basically saying, "If you try to stop the living from praising Me, the eternal souls of the dead will do it instead. My praise will echo through the universe regardless."

They don't get it, though, and it's heartbreaking for Him. In the verses immediately following that, He weeps over Jerusalem. He loves Jerusalem and its people, but they don't have eyes to see Him for who He really is. He prophesies the destruction of the city that will happen in approximately forty years.

TODAY'S GOD SHOT

"The Son of Man came to seek and to save the lost." It may not be immediately evident, especially since you weren't alive back then, but you are in that story. Do you know what you're doing in it? Nothing. You're just lost. That's all. But Jesus is doing a *lot* in that story. He comes, He seeks, He saves. He is the active agent in your salvation. And thank God, because we never would've found our way out. We might not have known we were lost if He hadn't shown up. We desperately need His rescue, because He's where the joy is!

MARK 11; JOHN 12

Jesus and His apostles go to the outskirts of Jerusalem to spend the night. The next morning as they're heading back into the city, they pass the fig tree Jesus cursed. Peter says, "Whoa! It's withered down to the root!" And while this is actually a bad sign as far as Israel is concerned, Jesus takes the opportunity to redeem the image. He turns it into an object lesson for Peter, pointing out aspects of faith, prayer, and forgiveness that He expounds on more elsewhere in Scripture. Since Scripture interprets Scripture, we have to be careful not to isolate these passages from everything else Jesus says about these things, or we'll end up with an incomplete doctrine and a skewed theology. These verses aren't giving us the power to make things happen if we believe strongly enough. They aren't putting the onus on you to create enough faith in yourself. And the verses on forgiveness can make it sound like some kind of work we do to earn our way into a relationship with God, but that's not what the greater teaching of Scripture says. Hold these things with an open hand for now, and we'll continue to dig into them more as we keep reading.

Mary, Martha, and Lazarus invite Jesus and His apostles to dinner. As usual, Martha is doing the work, Lazarus is talking with Jesus and the guys, and Mary is cherishing every second with Jesus. She pulls out expensive perfumed oil, about a pint-sized jar of it, and pours it on His feet. Washing feet is the work of a servant—that's not what she's doing, but it's close. She takes her humility further by using the thing viewed as a woman's physical crown of beauty to wipe His feet. This is rich with symbolism—she's placing her head at His feet, almost like the crowns cast at His feet that we've talked about before. It's a dramatic, poetic demonstration of humility. Matthew and Mark say she also anoints His head (and the jar is large enough to provide for both).

Judas is watching this, and he appeals to them with an argument for generosity and charity, but underneath his whitewashed argument is a spirit of greed, manipulation, and criticism. John tells us that Judas is a thief, so it seems his motivation has more to do with wanting to steal money. He's not concerned for Jesus or for the poor; he's looking out for himself. Judas is their treasurer, the one who keeps the money and pays for things they need along the way. Jesus tells Judas to leave her alone and says, "She'll need the rest of that oil for My burial."

Word gets out that Jesus is in town, so people start to gather. They also want to see His friend Lazarus, who was raised from the dead. The leaders aren't happy about it and want to put Lazarus to death. A few Gentile followers of YHWH recognize that Jesus is the Messiah, and they want to meet Him. But Jesus says, "I'm busy right now. It's time for Me to die. But don't worry—this will bear much fruit. And pretty soon you'll be following in My footsteps."

His heart is troubled. He wants to be rescued from what He's about to endure, but He knows this is the Father's plan. If there's any other way for God's kids to be reconciled to Him, then Jesus doesn't have to die. If any path to God is sufficient, or if we can earn our way into that relationship by being good, then Jesus's death is unnecessary. He can be spared the pain of death, because it's pointless. But there is no other way. We can't fix ourselves. Brokenness can't repair itself to a state of perfection. We *must* have the perfect sacrifice to pay our sin debt. And only Jesus can be the perfect sacrifice, because only He is perfect. Only He is the fully God, fully man Savior Messiah King. The audible voice of the Father booms through the atmosphere, affirming Jesus.

TODAY'S GOD SHOT

Jesus can bring the dead to life, boss the weather around, and make food materialize, yet He humbly submits to the Father. Jesus is God the Son—not just a powerful prophet or a good teacher of morality. He repeatedly claims to be God Himself, and the Father affirms it. Jesus is God and still obeys God, demonstrating humble submission to a greater degree than is even possible for us. He's where the joy is!

MATTHEW 22; MARK 12

The parable of the wedding feast is similar to the parable of the tenants. Both include a master and his son, sending multiple rounds of servants to get a response from people who refuse and even kill them, bringing justice for those who refuse the master, and showing generosity to others. In the wedding feast parable, the master orders his servants to invite both the bad and the good, which would shock the Pharisees and offend the pride of the self-righteous. Everyone who is invited in gets a wedding garment, but those who don't belong, who have no wedding garment, will be cast out. This sounds like the robe of righteousness God gives His kids. Whether the robes are figurative or literal doesn't matter—the point is that they mark us as God's righteous children.

As the Pharisees and other leaders grow more desperate to accuse Him, they try to trap Him with a question about taxes. Jesus paid His temple tax, which was ordained by God (Matthew 17:24–27). Will He respond differently if the tax is imposed by the oppressive ruling government? The Jews hate giving money to Rome—it funds the army that oppresses them and kills their families. But Jesus says it's lawful to pay taxes and to submit to the authorities God has placed over you, even if they're wicked and you're in the process of opposing them. It's possible to humbly honor God by keeping the law while rebelling against wicked authorities.

Next, the Sadducees try to trap Him by creating a hypothetical scenario built around resurrection. They don't believe in resurrection or the afterlife, but they present this question as if they did, thinking it'll prove that resurrection is a ridiculous idea. The question: A woman has married many brothers (levirate marriage) and they've all died, so whom will she be married to in the kingdom? Jesus answers, "You don't know Scripture or the power of God. In the kingdom, people will be like angels, who don't get married. And as far as resurrection is concerned, remember

For more information on today's reading, see thebiblerecap.com/links.

how YHWH said He's the God of Abraham, Isaac, and Jacob? Those guys were dead by the time He said that to Moses. And since He's not the God of the dead, then they must be alive—just not in this dimension. So your attempt at a trick question reveals your ignorance of Scripture."

There are two other important things to note here: (1) The church is the bride of Christ, so technically, we're all married in the kingdom, and (2) the angels don't marry or procreate with each other, possibly because they're apparently all male.

As they're talking, a Pharisee scribe is impressed with Jesus, so he asks which commandment is the most important. Jesus encapsulates all 613 Old Testament laws into just two—the vertical, man-to-God law and the horizontal, man-to-man law. Jesus isn't eliminating any laws; He's just summarizing them. The scribe is impressed, and Jesus says, "You are not far from the Kingdom of God." Literally. Because the King of the kingdom is speaking to him.

They ask how the Messiah can be a descendant of David but also somehow predate David. God the Son has always existed, even though Jesus is only in His thirties. In His reply, He also affirms that when Psalm 110 was written by David, the Holy Spirit was engaged in that process. The Spirit authored Scripture through human hands!

Jesus says to beware of those who do things to be seen and admired. Long robes and long prayers aren't wrong, but arrogance is. Jesus knows the Pharisees' hearts when they do these things. He contrasts them with a woman who doesn't have anything to show off but who gives generously from her heart.

TODAY'S GOD SHOT

Jesus is drawn to the poor and the sinners. The world ignores those who have nothing to offer it, but God says, "People who have nothing to offer are My sweet spot." In this relationship, He's the only one who has anything to offer anyway. He already owns all we give back to Him. Money, faith, good deeds—those are all things He gives us that we return to Him. It all starts and ends with Him, and our hearts get to feel the blessing of being caught up in the cycle. How incredibly generous of Him to invite us into that! He's where the joy is!

MATTHEW 23; LUKE 20–21

Jesus covers a lot of ground with the Pharisees that may seem familiar. It's possible that Matthew has collected all His sayings to the Pharisees and put them in one convenient filing cabinet labeled chapter 23. His words are full of woe—seven woes, to be exact. Woe to (1) those who don't enter the kingdom and who, by their lies, prevent others from entering too; (2) those who make converts to false religions, taking them from one lie to another; (3) the blind guides who value the symbol over the source and the creation over the Creator; (4) those who neglect the weightier things, who tithe religiously while oppressing others; (5) those who try to look righteous though they're greedy and selfish; (6) those who work hard to seem perfect on the outside when they're full of sin and death; and (7) those who repeat the sins of their fathers, killing the prophets.

Jesus tells the crowds to follow the commands of the scribes and Pharisees but not their actions. He doesn't wholesale condemn their practices—they're teaching the Hebrew Scriptures, after all. The primary problem is that their hearts are off, and because of that, they're adding to God's laws to prove themselves. So Jesus doesn't throw the baby out with the bathwater. He knows that obedience to the truth is a good thing, even if the truth is preached by hypocrites. They "make their phylacteries broad and their fringes long" (23:5). Phylacteries are small leather boxes that hold Scripture, and they are worn on the forehead or arm as a way to literally obey Deuteronomy 11:18: "Lay up these words of mine in your heart and in your soul, and you shall bind them as a sign on your hand, and they shall be as frontlets between your eyes." The fringe refers to the four tasseled ends of a prayer shawl, which God ordained in Numbers 15:37–41 as a reminder that they belong to YHWH. Jesus isn't condemning wearing a prayer shawl. He wears one; the sick woman touches the fringe of His prayer shawl in Matthew 9:20. He's condemning using these things to show off.

For more information on today's reading, see thebiblerecap.com/links.

Jesus says not to consider anyone your father or teacher—but why? The Pharisees aspire to these titles in order to establish power. By giving His disciples this instruction, He directs them away from feeding the Pharisees' pride or becoming like them. He also says the Pharisees kill the prophets, just like their ancestors who killed Abel and Zechariah. Abel was the first person murdered in the Old Testament and Zechariah was likely the last, so Jesus encapsulates all the Old Testament martyrs here, knowing He's next.

Luke 20:36 says God's kids will become "equal to angels" when they die. It doesn't mean we'll *become* angels; the original word means "like." They're a different kind of created being, and unlike humans, they aren't made in God's image. But like them, we won't be able to die after the resurrection. We'll be immortal.

In 21:10–19, Jesus warns His disciples about wars and persecution that Judea and Jerusalem will encounter soon. Much of this is directed toward these specific people. Some will be put to death, but "not a hair on your head will perish." This is only possible if He's pointing to eternal life. Endurance in the faith is what marks the believer, but perseverance is His doing, not ours. We display and demonstrate the preserving He does. He promises to finish what He started in us.

Jesus says to live intentionally. Don't get caught up in too much of anything, least of all alcohol, or it'll weigh your hearts down. And don't let your attentions and affections fall on fleeting things—the cares of this life—because the things that matter are eternal.

TODAY'S GOD SHOT

"When you hear of wars and tumults, do not be terrified, for these things must first take place, but the end will not be at once" (Luke 21:9). Jesus says not to be terrified of these things. He knows it sounds frightening, but He also knows how it ends, so He's the only person who can say this with any kind of authority. He doesn't say things won't be scary or hard; He just promises that we don't go through those things alone and that on the other side of it, we'll live with Him eternally. Whatever darkness comes our way is no threat to His light. He's where the joy is!

MARK 13

It's always helpful to look at Scripture's context and ask, "Who is this message for?" and "What parts are information, and what parts are instruction?" Is Jesus telling us something God is going to do, something the disciples are supposed to do, or something we are supposed to do? If He's telling us what God is going to do, it's information. If He's telling us what the disciples are supposed to do, it's information (for us). But if He's telling us something we're supposed to do, it's instruction.

Jesus has been teaching in the temple, and as they're leaving, one of His disciples says, "Isn't this place the best?" Jesus rains all over his parade by saying, "Enjoy this while you can, because it's about to be rubble." The temple is a huge complex built of massive stones—the largest of which weighs 570 tons. That's more than one million pounds! But Jesus says the temple will be destroyed. Less than forty years after He prophesies this, Rome fulfills that prophecy. After the Jews mount an ongoing revolt, Rome will retaliate by razing the temple, just like Jesus said. Earlier, we read a prophecy in which Jesus compared His body to the temple. He said, "Destroy this temple, and in three days I will raise it up" (John 2:19). That prophecy refers to His body, and John clarifies that point in the verses that follow. So it's a different situation, but it's easy to confuse these two prophecies since they both refer to temple destruction of one kind or another.

After they leave the temple, they go to the Mount of Olives, where His inner circle asks Him questions about when this will happen and what signs to expect. He spends more time on the part of their question about the signs but never gives them a straight answer about the time—that's important to note. In fact, He says that when terrible things happen, they'll assume it's the end, but it's not; these are just the beginning of the birth pains. He gives some instructions that seem to be for these specific people at this specific time. Then He mentions something called the abomination of desolation. Most scholars believe this is a person, not a thing—but who or what is it? And when will that happen? Scholars are divided; some say it refers to Rome taking over Jerusalem forty years later when the temple is destroyed and the Jews have to flee Jerusalem and persecution. Others think it pertains to something still yet to come in the final days before God unites heaven and earth.

If you believe this already happened, this text doesn't alarm you. But if you believe this is yet to come, and you find that frightening, here are a few things in this text that are intended to bring you peace: Jesus says not to fear the end. "Do not be alarmed. . . . Do not be anxious." Bad things will happen, but you have a kingdom assignment in the midst of it all. Your priority is to talk about the good news of Jesus. Jesus also says to stay awake and stay focused on the main thing—don't be lulled to sleep by the comforts and ways of the world. Matthew 24:14 says, "This gospel of the kingdom will be proclaimed throughout the whole world as a testimony to all nations, *and then* the end will come." What this boils down to is talking about whom you love. Our relationship with God is personal, but it's never supposed to be private. Jesus says the gospel must go everywhere, and we're the ones who have it to share!

TODAY'S GOD SHOT

In the conversation Jesus is having with His disciples, He promises that God's elect—those people God has chosen to be in His family—will endure hard times, but He'll protect them from eternal harm. He says it's impossible to lead the elect away from the faith; nothing can snatch you out of His hand. But He gets painfully honest about it when He says, "If anything could lead the elect astray, it would be this thing I'm describing. But it's not possible." He encourages them: "You'll see opposition and even death, but this thing I'm building—you're a part of it, and it's going to outlast all this. So before, during, and after the trials, take heart!" We're part of an unstoppable kingdom, He's our King, and He's where the joy is!

MATTHEW 24

In the final week of His life, Jesus tells His inner circle that the temple will be destroyed, Jerusalem will fall to Rome, and they'll endure trials and struggles. He seems to list things chronologically in conjunction with His return to earth after His death, resurrection, and ascension to heaven. He pulls back the curtain a bit on what will happen after that, but we still don't see it clearly. There are a few major perspectives on how things unfold, but in general, this is one place in Scripture where it's wise to hold things with an open hand. We don't want to scream where Scripture whispers. When He returns, there'll be some strange astronomical phenomenon—or maybe this is metaphor. Will the actual stars fall? Or is this one of the times when He speaks of things in spiritual terms, not physical terms? Perhaps this refers to kings and kingdoms? Or to spiritual forces of evil—like Satan, who many believe is the Day Star in Isaiah 14:12? After that, Jesus will send His angels to gather His elect from the four corners of the earth and the four corners of heaven, and we'll be united with Him through eternal life, a merging of heaven and earth.

Luke's account of this in chapter 21 says people will faint with fear when this happens. But God's kids don't need to fear. The so-called end times are the beginning times for believers! In Luke 21:28, Jesus says, "When these things begin to take place, straighten up and raise your heads, because your redemption is drawing near." It's tempting to read His words about the future and focus on the hard parts. Some people are so consumed by the hard parts that they try to determine when it will happen, but Jesus says that's an impossible task. Many people have made fools of themselves through the centuries by trying to name dates of His return, saying certain world leaders are the ones prophesied in Scripture to do specific things—then those dates pass and those people die and here we still are. It's a foolish focus. Here's what Jesus says to think about instead: "Straighten up and raise your heads for your redemption is drawing near!" By the way, the phrase "straighten up" isn't a call to get your act together—it's His way of saying we don't have to cower in fear. This is one of the clearest things He says in the whole passage.

Then He says something that isn't clear: "This generation will not pass away until all these things take place." Was He lying? Those guys have definitely passed away. Here are two things worth noting. First, Jesus definitely isn't referring to these guys specifically, because He tells a few of them how they'll die and that it'll happen before His return. Second, Jesus says He doesn't know when He'll return—only the Father knows. So He can't be telling them it'll be within their lifetime. Most scholars believe "this generation" refers either to humanity itself or to the line of descendants of God's family, but it's inconsequential which it is, because God's family will last as long as humanity lasts, so both options have the same end point. He's encouraging His followers with reminders that His kingdom will keep advancing into the future. What they're building is eternal. The gospel isn't going to die out or be killed off. It's going to keep reaching the peoples and the nations, then He'll return.

TODAY'S GOD SHOT

Along with "don't be afraid" Jesus also calls His followers to "stay awake." Amid all the partial information He gives, this is one of His clear commands. He never says, "Try to figure out when I'm coming back." He never says, "See if you can piece this all together like a big puzzle." Instead, He says, "Stay awake. Don't be lulled to sleep by the world. And when things get crazy, don't be afraid. Share the gospel no matter what." When we know Him, it becomes easier to trust Him. And when we trust Him, we can have the kind of peace only He can bring, even amid uncertainty. We can walk out the values of His upside-down kingdom when we aren't trying to grab all we can get or make sure our earthly future is secure. We can trust that He's granted us an eternal inheritance. Knowing Jesus helps us live with open hands, no matter what happens. Because He's where the joy is!

MATTHEW 25

As Jesus gets closer to His death, He coaches His followers on waiting well, because they and the rest of the church will be waiting for His return for quite some time. We still are, in fact. Jesus knows we're more likely to treat His return like something we're not excited about. We don't have any concept of what we're entering into, so it's more common to be scared, since it's unknown. But waiting well is important.

The parable of the ten virgins is a call to steward our *time* wisely while we wait. The virgins have money to buy oil for their lamps—they just don't think about the future. They live in the moment, forgetting there's something they need to prepare for. Jesus has been saying, "Stay awake! Don't be lulled to sleep by the world and its priorities." But the virgins zone out and forget to prepare. In Scripture, oil often represents the Holy Spirit. This parable is essentially saying that the only way to be prepared for the return of Christ our bridegroom (the Light of the World) is to have the Holy Spirit (the oil). At this point, the Holy Spirit hasn't come to dwell inside believers—that'll happen after Jesus dies, resurrects, and ascends to heaven. But since Jesus won't be here, He's preparing them now to understand that better when it happens.

The parable of the talents is a call to steward our *gifts* wisely while we wait. A master gives his servants talents to use while he's away. *Talent* is a financial term; it's roughly fifteen to twenty years' wages. He gives them each a specific number of talents based on their abilities. So the talents aren't the abilities themselves—they're funds given based on how the servants are already gifted. Servants One and Two invest the money well, but Servant Three has a different approach. He doesn't trust the master's heart and actions, and mistrust always leads to fear and hiding, which is exactly what Servant Three does with the money; he buries it. Not only does he miss out on the master's joy, but when the master gives his talent to Servant One, he loses the very thing he was trying to protect. He accuses the master of being a hard and unfair man, but the text reveals the opposite: The master invites his servants into his *joy*. When you're trying to serve a God you don't know or trust, you'll always miss the mark.

Ultimately, we're responsible for how we use the time and money and gifts God has entrusted us with. The more we have, the more we're responsible for. The more we trust our Father's heart, the more we'll use what He's given us in ways that please Him and bless us.

In explaining the final judgment, Jesus says the flocks will be brought before God and He'll separate the sheep from the goats—the sheep are in God's family, and the goats aren't. The goats go to the eternal fire prepared for the forces of darkness, including Satan and his angels. While God created all angels (spiritual messengers and assistants), not all serve Him. Just like humankind fell, some angels fell as well—at least a third of them. Of that third, the highest-ranking angel is named Lucifer. We generally refer to him as Satan, but that's more of a title than a name. It means "accuser." So the lead accuser and his fallen angels will be punished in eternal fire. Despite what we see in movies, Satan doesn't rule over hell; he's being punished there, just like the goats. As for the sheep, we go into the kingdom of eternal life with God.

TODAY'S GOD SHOT

"Come, you who are blessed by my Father, inherit the kingdom prepared for you from the foundation of the world" (25:34). He's been preparing this for us for so long. Like the master who invites his servants into his joy, Jesus invites the servants of God into His joy. Our Father is eager to share His blessings with His kids. What a beautiful day that will be! We're invited into His joy, and He's where the joy is!

MATTHEW 26; MARK 14

Jesus tells His disciples He only has a few days to live. The authorities are plotting, waiting for the right moment. Judas sees an opportunity to make some cash from it by turning Jesus in; they arrange to pay him thirty pieces of silver—about four months' wages.

There are a few noteworthy things here. First, God's will always comes to pass. Second, there are passive and active agents involved in accomplishing that. Third, Judas, the active agent, has woe pronounced on him. Verse 24 says it would be better *for him* if he hadn't been born, but his birth is a necessary part of God's redemption plan. Fourth, it's easy to feel sorry for Judas, but he gets what he deserves—what we all deserve, in fact. But Jesus does *not* get what He deserves.

At dinner, Jesus says there's a betrayer at the table. They're mortified, asking if it could be them. They all call Him Lord except for Judas, who calls Him Master. Jesus affirms that it's him. Judas isn't shocked by this; he's already got the silver in hand.

Then He reminds them of something He said earlier (John 6:54–58) about eating His flesh and drinking His blood. He feeds them the Lord's Supper (i.e., Communion or Eucharist), giving them a physical action that connects them to a spiritual reality. Like with baptism, there are various perspectives on how, when, and why this should be practiced. The Lord's Supper may not taste like much, but it's the best feast we'll eat on this side of eternity. It's the most privileged meal in the universe. It helps our forgetful hearts remember that His body was broken and His blood was poured out for many. We need that reminder, or we'll become like the people we read about yesterday who didn't wait well and who were sidetracked, foolish, and fearful. So we partake and we remember.

After dinner, they go to the Mount of Olives. The Passover dinner is a big deal, but there's no mention of them eating anything here besides bread. We never see them eat the Passover lamb, which is a command.

For more information on today's reading, see thebiblerecap.com/links.

Why isn't it mentioned? Here's a theory: Exodus 12:1–28 gives us a picture of what happens at Passover (or the Feast of Unleavened Bread). It's a weeklong celebration, but some scholars say that it lasted eight days in Jesus's time, with the extra day serving as a chance to finish off any existing leaven in their homes before the event starts. So while they're eating a Passover meal, it may just be the first day of the feast, on which they eat the leavened bread. The Greek reflects this too; *azymos* is the word for unleavened, and *artos* is leavened bread. Jesus and His disciples are eating *artos*. So if this isn't *the* Passover Feast, that explains why they haven't eaten lamb—and the reason that's important is because *Jesus* is the Passover Lamb.

In the four days prior to Passover, each family selects their own lamb to sacrifice. They bring it into their home, live with it, feed it, and inspect it for flaws—because it has to be perfect—then on the day of Preparation, they sacrifice it and eat it after sundown. They paint its blood on the doorways of their homes—on the top, left, and right sides of the door—to commemorate what their ancestors did in Egypt when God "passed over" their homes and saved their lives. Palm Sunday is the only day Jesus lets people publicly affirm and approve of Him as the Messiah King. Then He lives in Jerusalem, is interrogated and inspected, and is put through trials and questioning, and He's still found to be without blemish. The perfect, spotless, sacrificial Lamb of our Passover. And on the day of Preparation, He's sacrificed. He is the Passover Lamb.

TODAY'S GOD SHOT

Jesus fed Judas Communion—something reserved only for true followers of Christ. Why? While we don't know Jesus's motives, this reveals something important to us: The act of taking the Lord's Supper isn't magical. It doesn't hold any power to save us. Similar to when the gospel fell on deaf ears and hard soil, Jesus feeds a hard heart. This is a foretaste—as He tells them to eat His flesh and drink His blood in the elements, they are, in a way, eating the sacrificial Lamb. And by His blood our sins are covered. And by His death our lives are spared. And by His provision, we can know one thing for sure and forever: He's where the joy is!

LUKE 22; JOHN 13

John's account of the Last Supper includes a detail no other gospels mention—Jesus's washing of the disciples' feet. It's the job of a servant or slave to wash guests' filthy, sandal-wearing feet. Peter knows how humbling this is, so he tries to refuse it, but Jesus does it anyway.

John says Satan put it into Judas's heart to betray Jesus and that Satan entered into him. Still, Jesus trusts the Father's plan; He doesn't try to overpower Judas while He has the chance. Evil must play out its role, but what the enemy means for evil, God uses for the good of His people. So Jesus serves even the one He knows will betray Him. Then He gives a new command: He says to love each other like He has loved them. He's always been saying this, so how is this new? He's raising the stakes, making it about a willingness to lay down your life for your brothers and sisters in the faith. The timing is ironic, because in Matthew's account, Jesus says they'll all turn their backs on Him and that Peter will deny Him. Satan demanded (the Greek implies more of a tortured begging) to test Peter. Jesus knows the testing will help equip Peter for all God has in store for him, so Jesus comforts Peter: "Satan is after you. But I've prayed for your faith to be strengthened." Trials produce things in us that we wouldn't be able to access otherwise, and since God has big things in store for Peter in the early church, his character has to be developed to that level.

Jesus reminds them that He has always provided them with everything they need, then gives them new instructions: Get a sword. Are they finally going to overthrow Rome? No, that's never been the plan. There are three primary perspectives on what Jesus means: (1) He's speaking of a spiritual readiness, so when the disciples produce actual swords, He's dismissive of their weapons; (2) He's giving them the opportunity to physically defend themselves against attackers, even if they can't go on the offense; or (3) He knows they'll need legal cause to arrest Him, so He's arranging for the disciples to have "proof" that they're insurrectionists.

For more information on today's reading, see thebiblerecap.com/links.

When they go to the garden of Gethsemane to pray, Jesus asks the Father for what He wants and acknowledges that the Father has the power to do it but yields to the Father's will. Jesus is fully God and fully man. It's not His divinity that wants to avoid the cross—it's His humanity. The will of His divinity is perfectly aligned with the will of the Father, but His humanity overcomes temptation by submitting to the Father's will. His humanity submits to His divinity, just like our humanity must submit to His divinity.

He's so troubled and sorrowful that He sweats blood (hematidrosis). Meanwhile, the disciples keep falling asleep. He invites them into His pain, even knowing they're moments away from turning their backs on Him. He sees the authorities walking through the valley with their torches. It comes as no surprise. Peter pulls out a sword and cuts off a soldier's ear, but Jesus stops him and heals the man.

In John's account, the soldiers are looking for Jesus of Nazareth, and when He says, "I am He," they fall to the ground. This wasn't voluntary; they aren't there to worship Him. This seems like an involuntary response to the revelation of His deity. Someday every knee will bow at the name of Jesus (Philippians 2:10–11), and this foreshadows that day. They take Jesus to the high priest's house, and Peter follows. As he waits in the courtyard, people associate him with Jesus, and he denies it three times. Then the rooster crows. When Jesus catches his eye, Peter leaves to weep. Those holding Jesus in custody blindfold, beat, and mock Him. He undergoes six trials in eight hours—three religious trials before the Jews and three civil trials before the Romans—and most of them are performed illegally.

TODAY'S GOD SHOT

Gethsemane means "olive press." It's where olives are crushed to produce their most valuable resource: oil. In Scripture, oil often represents God the Spirit. An oil press is where the crushing of Jesus begins, and it's through this process that we receive the thing He says is most valuable to us: the Holy Spirit, the very presence of God dwelling in His kids forever. He never leaves us, and He's where the joy is!

JOHN 14–17

Jesus is going away and they won't be able to follow Him immediately, but they'll follow Him eventually and eternally. Yesterday He told us where He's heading: "From now on the Son of Man shall be seated at the right hand of the power of God" (Luke 22:69). He'll prepare a room for them in His Father's house, which, in Jewish culture, implies they're family now. He says He's the way, the truth, and the life—no one can bridge the gap between humankind and God the Father except for Jesus, who is fully God and fully man. When people claim He's just a good prophet or a good teacher of morality, they must not know He said this. Because if these things *aren't* true, He's either crazy or lying—which means He's not a good moral teacher.

He says they'll do greater works than Him. The word for *greater* means "more," so this could say, "You'll continue to do powerful and miraculous works of God after I'm gone." And He'll give them anything they ask in His name in the context of walking out His power and will. For a request to be made "in His name" means it's in accordance with His character and will. He's generously built a safety valve into this promise—He'll say yes to anything that corresponds to His will and glorifies His name, and thankfully, He'll say no to anything that doesn't. This means we don't have to figure out what's best before we pray—we can just ask and trust Him to do what's best!

He promises His Spirit to all who believe in Him. This will happen for the disciples in about fifty days. God the Spirit has always existed. In the Old Testament, He empowered people for specific tasks and then moved on, but Jesus's death ushers in the next part of God's plan: the Spirit dwelling in them. He'll bless them in various ways. He's the reminder, helping us recall what Jesus has said and done. He's a spotlight that shines on Jesus. While He's often associated with mysterious things like signs, wonders, and tongues, those are just a handful of ways He

---

For more information on today's reading, see thebiblerecap.com/links.

points to Jesus. Wherever Jesus is being preached, the Holy Spirit is active, even if He isn't mentioned. He guides us into truth, convicts us of sin, and affirms that we belong to the Father. He is exclusively present with followers of Christ. The world doesn't have Him. He works among them, but His relationship to the world is a different one.

Jesus spends a lot of chapter 15 on an image: He's the vine and we're the branches, and God is glorified when we bear fruit. He compels the disciples to be engaged with what He's doing because bearing fruit will lead to their joy! He knows they'll need this reminder, because hard times are coming. He promises them trials and persecution, but one of their greatest encouragements is that He's the one who chose them and appointed them. Knowing all their strengths and weaknesses, all their fears and failures, He still chose them. He prays for them to be upheld when the world persecutes them, and since God is the one who initiated this in them and He is their source, their hope is secure.

Chapter 17 is the High Priestly Prayer, where He prays for all believers, including you. He prays for the spiritual offspring of His apostles, for unity among us, and for the Father to be glorified. The glory of God is our shared purpose!

TODAY'S GOD SHOT

Jesus keeps reiterating the joy and peace He has for us: "Let not your hearts be troubled. Believe in God; believe also in me" (14:1). "Peace I leave with you; my peace I give to you. Not as the world gives do I give to you. Let not your hearts be troubled, neither let them be afraid" (14:27). "These things I have spoken to you, that my joy may be in you, and that your joy may be full" (15:11). "I have said these things to you, that in me you may have peace. In the world you will have tribulation. But take heart; I have overcome the world" (16:33). "You have sorrow now, but I will see you again, and your hearts will rejoice, and no one will take your joy from you. In that day you will ask nothing of me" (16:22–23). The fullness of joy that comes from His presence will leave us wantless. How complete will our joy be if we can't think of a single thing to ask for? We have fullness of joy, forevermore, because He's where the joy is!

MATTHEW 27; MARK 15

Jesus has been declared guilty in three religious trials. The next step is to present Him to the Roman governor, Pontius Pilate, because only Rome can hand down the death penalty. He's taken from His religious trials to a civil trial. To Pilate, the people accuse Him of claiming to be a king, since that poses a threat to Roman authorities. In Luke's account they say He forbade them from paying taxes to Caesar, but we know that's a lie (Luke 20:20–26). Pilate asks Him about being a king, and in John's account, Jesus explains that His kingdom is not of this world because otherwise His followers would be fighting. He's not there to fight but to speak truth. Then Pilate responds with a question that has always been a popular response to the gospel, "What is truth?"

In Luke's account, Pilate seems to be trying to avoid making a judgment, so he sends Jesus to King Herod, a higher authority. The king and his soldiers wound and shame Jesus, putting a purple robe and a crown of thorns on Him, mocking His royalty—then send him back to Pilate, likely because the crimes were committed in Jerusalem. So Pilate is required to make a judgment call. But before Jesus had been brought to him the first time, Pilate's wife had a nightmare about Him. It was so upsetting that she told Pilate to leave Jesus alone.

Pilate declares Jesus innocent but offers the people an option: "I can release Jesus or Barabbas. Who should it be?" Barabbas is a convicted felon who committed multiple crimes, including robbery, insurrection, and murder. The people choose to set Barabbas free. Remember the Day of Atonement (Leviticus 16:6–10), when one goat is sacrificed as a sin offering and the other is set free into the wilderness? This is a picture of that, and it's also a picture of us. We are Barabbas—set free because Christ is the sin offering. The people demand that Jesus be crucified. Pilate tries to dodge responsibility by handing Him over to the people, but no matter how dismissive he is or how many times he washes his hands, passivity doesn't equal innocence. As the people respond, they accidentally speak a truth that is everyone's only hope: "His blood be on us and on our children!" (Matthew 27:25). They don't realize it, but that is the only hope for any of us—that the blood of His sacrifice would cover our sins.

God is the one who sets rulers in their places of power (John 19:11). He is sovereign over every trial Jesus encounters and every ruler who hands down a verdict and even the verdict that results in Christ's death. The cross has always been the plan (Revelation 13:8). But with God's great attention to detail, why are there only six trials instead of seven? If God loves numbers and symbolism as much as He seems to, why did this stop one short of perfection and completion? Scripture doesn't tell us, but perhaps after the three religious trials declaring Him guilty and the three civil trials declaring Him innocent, the seventh and final verdict is the one handed out by God the Father, affirming and approving of the finished work of Christ on the cross—His beloved Son, in whom He is well pleased. The perfect, complete verdict is handed down by the one righteous Judge.

While all the trials are taking place, Judas realizes the magnitude of what he's done in handing over an innocent man. He feels like he can't live with the weight of that guilt, so he throws the money back into the temple. The priests use it to buy a field that serves as a cemetery. Judas dies by suicide. Matthew says Judas changed his mind, but a changed mind is different from a changed heart. Worldly sorrow is different from repentance and godly sorrow. Worldly sorrow has no hope. And that's where Judas found himself.

TODAY'S GOD SHOT

Jesus displays such humility as He submits to the Father's plans, receiving false accusations and mocking and the rejection of the people He loves so much—the people He wept over not long ago. And we have done this to Him just as much as Judas, just as much as Pilate, just as much as the crowds. And still, He covers us with the blood of His sacrifice, bringing us the peace and hope that He promised before this all started. And still and always, He's where the joy is!

LUKE 23; JOHN 18–19

Jesus has been tried, mocked, beaten, and crowned with thorns, and then on His way to the cross, Pilate has Him flogged. The Jewish rule says a person can only be flogged thirty-nine times, but Pilate is a Roman governor and those rules don't apply to Rome, so we don't know how many times He's beaten. Isaiah 52:14 says He's beaten beyond human recognition, which means He has more than a few cuts and a trickle of blood like we see in many renderings that seem to be a mockery compared to what He actually endures. This beating is a total undoing of His body.

He's so weak that Simon has to carry His crossbeam—the part that goes behind the arms. This is likely all he's carrying, because wood is scarce in Israel, so the Romans often reused a fixed upright, which was likely a bare tree trunk at the side of a highway. They crucify people on main roads going into the city to serve as a warning to incoming visitors not to defy Rome. Jesus is likely crucified at street level—eye to eye with people walking past. In fact, He's close enough to talk with onlookers at a time when He hardly has breath in his lungs from the torture. This happens at Golgotha ("The Place of the Skull," *Calvary* in Latin). Some say that name describes any place of death, while others say it refers to a hill that resembles a skull. On the road to Damascus, a northbound highway out of Jerusalem, there's a hill just outside the city gates that looks like a skull face, and some believe this could be the spot; it's adjacent to the Garden Tomb site. Others say He was crucified on the Mount of Olives, east of Jerusalem, and still others say it was on the west side of the city, marked by the Church of the Holy Sepulchre. The Garden Tomb and the Church of the Holy Sepulchre are both on Mount Moriah—the hill where Abraham offered Isaac as a sacrifice, foreshadowing this event two thousand years later when God provided the true sacrifice, His Son.

For more information on today's reading, see thebiblerecap.com/links.

The soldiers cast lots over His clothes, fulfilling prophecy. He not only asks the Father to forgive His crucifers, but He spends His final moments inviting sinners into the kingdom. Two criminals are crucified beside Him—one mocks Him, but one hails Him as King and asks Him to remember him when He comes into His kingdom. And Jesus says, "That's today. I'll see you there." This man spent his life in sin but turns to Christ at the last possible moment, and Jesus says, "You are welcome in My kingdom. You get a seat at the table too."

Rome performed crucifixions for roughly a thousand years, and they probably changed up the methods over time—sometimes tying limbs and sometimes nailing them. We don't know the exact process they used on Jesus, but Luke 24:39 says there are nails in His hands and feet. As He hangs on the cross, He quotes the first line of Psalm 22, "My God, my God, why have you forsaken me?" referencing a Psalm about the Messiah and identifying Himself as such (see Day 125).

He commits His Spirit into the Father's hands and cries out, "It is finished," letting us know we can add nothing to His saving work. When they come to make sure He's dead, they pierce His side and blood and water pour out, which often indicates a heart attack.

The sun is setting, and the new day is about to start—one when the Jews can't work—so they get Him off the cross quickly. A wealthy man named Joseph asks for His body and moves Him to his own tomb nearby, then Joseph, Nicodemus, and a few women wrap and anoint Him and then roll the stone over the tomb's entrance. These tombs are often cave-like, and a big rock is used to seal the mouth of the cave.

TODAY'S GOD SHOT

God does miraculous things in each gospel account that barely get a sentence. In Matthew 27:52–53, there's a great earthquake and people who are dead and buried suddenly rise and walk through the city. He brings the dead to life! In John, Pilate accidentally prophesies, writing that Jesus *is* the King of the Jews. And Matthew, Mark, and Luke all say the sky goes dark at noon, and in the temple, the curtain is torn from top to bottom, from heaven to earth—indicating that it's an act of God, opening up His presence to His people in a way they haven't had access to before. Hallelujah and praise God! He's where the joy is!

MATTHEW 28; MARK 16

Today we'll focus on the events immediately surrounding the resurrection, so fair warning that there will be a few spoilers about tomorrow's reading. Roughly three days have passed since Jesus was crucified, and it's now the predawn hours of Sunday morning. Another earthquake happens concurrent with the appearance of an angel, and it seems they may work in tandem to roll away the stone. Angels always appear as human males, which is why Mark's gospel refers to the angel as a young man. They're most often dressed in white, and while they don't have wings or halos, they're often described as radiant or "like lightning." Angels can be terrifying; when the guards see him, they become catatonic.

Mary Magdalene, another Mary, Joanna, and Salome come to visit the tomb. (Some gospels record two angels, and some gospels record only Mary Magdalene, but as we've seen, the authors tell the part of the story that shines a light on the point they're trying to make.) When the women arrive, the angel tells them not to be afraid. You may have a note in your Bible that the oldest manuscripts of Mark's gospel end at the rising of Christ in verse 8. A lot of what is said in verses 9–20 can be found elsewhere in Scripture, so we'll address those parts when we get to them. But for the questionable parts that appear only here, we'll let Scripture whisper.

The angel tells the women that Jesus has been raised from the dead, invites them to see the empty tomb, and tells them to spread the word, even though it seems they still don't quite understand. The timeline of the four gospel accounts isn't clear, but a rough outline seems to be that the women show up and see the angel and the empty tomb, they leave and tell the disciples, Peter and John run back to check things out, and then Mary goes back and some other women join her later. Meanwhile, the guards have gone to tell the authorities what they saw. The elders bribe them to say that His body was stolen by His disciples. Peter and John see the linen graveclothes are folded up and set aside. This is noteworthy

For more information on today's reading, see thebiblerecap.com/links.

because thieves don't fold laundry, so it's one of their first clues that Jesus has risen from the dead.

Meanwhile, Mary is outside sobbing, probably dealing with a mixture of emotions. She looks in the tomb and sees two angels sitting where Jesus's body had been—one at the head, one at the foot. This parallels the description of the mercy seat, the cover for the ark of the covenant, where God's presence dwelled in the temple. The mercy seat has two cherubim, one on each end. In Exodus 25:22 God told the Israelites, "I will meet with you there above the mercy seat, between the two cherubim that are over the ark of the Testimony." And there, between those two angels, God's presence had been made manifest not only in the death of His Son but in the raising of His Son.

When Mary turns around, she's in the darkness of the tomb. It's probably still dark outside, or maybe the sun is starting to breach the horizon, and she sees a Man outside the tomb. She assumes He's the gardener. In this day, most men only have one tunic and they wear it every day, making them easy to recognize. But Jesus doesn't have His tunic anymore—the soldiers cast lots for it. Here He stands in His new clothes, backlit by the rising sun, and Mary has tears in her eyes and no way of knowing that the man she thinks is a gardener is actually the risen Christ standing in front of her.

But He speaks her name and suddenly she knows. She falls at His feet and worships Him. He's not an apparition or a ghost—she's touching His real, risen body. If someone were making this story up, they would've chosen a more reliable witness than a woman, because in this culture women aren't even allowed to testify in court. But Jesus has always gone to the rejected, the outcasts, those considered "less than." It's such a Jesus move to have His first resurrected revealing be to a formerly demonized woman.

TODAY'S GOD SHOT

Jesus tells Mary to let His brothers, the disciples, know He's alive. The last time we saw them all together, He told them they'd all fall away on account of Him. And they did, and it was in the moment of His deepest need. But despite their betrayals, He still calls them His brothers, and He still can't wait to see them. What great love and forgiveness He has for the sinners in His family! He's where the joy is!

LUKE 24; JOHN 20–21

Jesus's followers are buzzing about the recent events. Two of them are making the seven-mile trip from Jerusalem to Emmaus on Sunday—resurrection day—and they run into Jesus, but God keeps them from recognizing Him. Maybe His resurrection body is different somehow, or maybe it's because His old tunic and turban, which cover most of a man's body, have been replaced with new clothes and the body that was utterly destroyed a few days ago has miraculously healed.

He asks what they're talking about. They say, "What is *anyone* talking about?" and explain the resurrection. Jesus says all of this was necessary. He unpacks the story for them from the beginning. As they get closer to Emmaus, they convince Him to stay for dinner, and when He blesses the food, their eyes are opened to recognize Him. He loves surprising people—first Mary, now these guys. As soon as they recognize Him, He vanishes! They go back to Jerusalem to tell the disciples about this, and as they're talking, Jesus appears in the room despite the locked doors. They think He's a ghost, so He shows His wounds and even eats fish. He explains that the whole Old Testament is about Him. They couldn't see it then, but it's clear now. Thomas isn't there, so when word gets back to him, he says, "Show me and I'll believe it." We've called him Doubting Thomas, but Jesus never called him that. All the disciples doubted until they saw Jesus with their own eyes. Jesus never shames Thomas for questioning things; instead, He meets Thomas in his doubts and questions. Then He blesses us all: "Blessed are those who have not seen and yet have believed."

Yesterday, the angel said Jesus would go before the disciples to Galilee, and the time has come for that to happen. God may have given these instructions to keep them safe from the authorities in Jerusalem who were surely trying to get to the bottom of things. One night, they're fishing in the Sea of Galilee and don't have a single catch. As the sun rises, Someone calls from the shore, "Children, do you have any fish?" They say no, and Jesus says, "Throw the net on the other side of the boat."

They do, and their nets are nearly bursting with fish. This is like what He did on the day He recruited them (Luke 5:1–11). It feels a bit like He's making an inside joke with His friends, pointing back to the start of their relationship. When they pull up the net and it's breaking, they realize who the Man is. Peter jumps in the water and swims to shore to meet Him.

They catch 153 fish. Scholars say that's how many species of fish are in the Sea of Galilee, indicating they catch one of each type. When Jesus filled their nets in Luke 5, He said He'd make them fishers of men from now on; these 153 serve as a reminder that they'll be catching people from every nation, that the gospel net will pull in fish of every kind.

Jesus cooks them breakfast over a charcoal fire, like the one Peter was at when he denied Him. They have a beautiful moment of restoration. Jesus asks Peter if he loves Him three times to meet with Peter's three denials. Peter's responses indicate he may feel shame or insecurity, but Jesus gives him a weighty assignment: "I'm putting you in charge of things now. Steward this well." He reminds Peter, just like He reminds all His followers at the end of every gospel, that His gospel must go to all nations. When He tells Peter how he'll die—he'll be crucified too—Peter starts comparing his assignment to John's. Jesus reminds Peter to stay in his lane: sheep feeding and Christ following. A few weeks later, forty days after His resurrection, Jesus ascends to heaven from the Mount of Olives.

TODAY'S GOD SHOT

The men on the road to Emmaus say, "Did not our hearts burn within us while he talked to us on the road, while he opened to us the Scriptures?" (Luke 24:32). Talking to God, opening Scripture—that's prayer and Bible study! That's what we're doing here. Those two things set their hearts aflame *because God is in them*. God is the one who makes His Word come alive! God is the one who makes our relationship with Him so rich and beautiful. It's *nothing* without Him—it's a sad, dry, seven-mile walk through the desert. But with Him, our hearts burn within us. May you feel it and know it and live it—He's where the joy is!

ACTS 1–3

Luke the gospel writer wrote Acts to record what happens after the life of Christ as the gospel spreads to all nations. Jesus stays on earth for forty days after the resurrection, and He tells the apostles to stay in Jerusalem until the Holy Spirit comes to them. The next phase of God's plan is about to be rolled out. Just like when God the Son came to live alongside His people, now God the Spirit will come to dwell *in* His people. It'll be a new kind of baptism. The disciples say, "Now that You've been raised from the dead, You'll overthrow Rome, right?" Jesus says, "You're asking the wrong questions. There's no political takeover. The only thing you need to be concerned about is when the Spirit will come to dwell in you. He'll equip you to take the gospel from this place to the whole world."

Forty days after His resurrection, Jesus ascends to heaven from the Mount of Olives. Then the disciples go to the upper room, which has become their headquarters. The apostles and female disciples meet regularly to pray, along with Jesus's mom and siblings, who've had a change of heart. Eleven apostles remain, so they replace Judas with Matthias, a disciple who has walked with them all along.

A week later, there's a holiday called Pentecost. All the disciples gather, probably at the temple, the house of God. A strong wind blows through the interior, and "divided tongues as of fire" (2:3) appear over their heads. Fire represents the presence and power of God. What does "divided tongues" mean? This takes us back to the Tower of Babel, where the people sinned against God and He divided their languages—the same word used for tongues. These divided languages, or tongues, appeared over their heads like fire.

They're filled with the Holy Spirit, who empowers their words to be understood in languages they aren't even speaking. Verse 5 tells us why this is important. Devout Jews from different nations are in Jerusalem for Pentecost and hear Galilean disciples speak their native languages.

For more information on today's reading, see thebiblerecap.com/links.

So the disciples are speaking Aramaic, but they're being heard in Latin and other languages. The foreign believers are blown away, but some locals don't understand what's happening since they understand the native language regardless and don't see the miracle, but Peter says this is the fulfillment of Joel's prophecy!

Just as God divided the languages at Babel, He undoes that undoing, bringing unity by the power of His Spirit. *This* is how the gospel begins to spread to all nations—by the miraculous power of the God who invented languages and knows them all. In this instance, *speaking in tongues* means "speaking in human languages." It isn't filled with chaos and confusion—on the contrary, it brings clarity, understanding, and unity. There are some other scenarios we'll look at in the future, but here there is no translator—just the gospel for all to hear and understand, though some don't believe what they see.

Peter addresses them and preaches the gospel, saying God's plan for redemption involves the crucifixion and resurrection of Jesus; he preaches repentance, just like JTB and Jesus did, and three thousand people repent and are baptized! On that site, there are 125 mikvahs—ritual purification baths the Jews used regularly. People continue to be saved by God every day as the apostles keep applying what they learned from Jesus. Believers eat meals and pray together, sharing their lives sacrificially with each other daily.

In chapter 3, Peter and John heal a lame man who was only asking for money, and of course, they credit Jesus with the healing. The healing serves as a launchpad for Peter's next sermon, during which he quotes lots of Scripture. He knows you can't feed sheep with something you don't have!

TODAY'S GOD SHOT

Rarely does God do something exactly like we think He will. Even with His repeated promise to send the Holy Spirit, we probably never would've imagined an indoor tornado, fire holograms, and a language convention. His ways are higher than ours, but He's kind enough to share occasional bits of His big plans with our tiny brains, and He doesn't grow impatient with us when we misunderstand. He has the best ideas and the kindest heart, and He's where the joy is!

ACTS 4–6

Peter and John heal a crippled man, then take that opportunity to preach the gospel. But it brings more pushback. The actions of Jesus heightened local tensions and the oppression of His followers. Peter and others are thrown in jail for preaching, but they keep preaching and five thousand people repent and follow Jesus. The leaders ask Peter and John where they got their power and authority. Peter says, "Jesus. The guy you killed. By the way, there's no other name by which people are saved." The leaders are perplexed—they've got two uneducated men who speak with wisdom and authority, plus a healed lame man, all three of whom say that Jesus, who has mysteriously disappeared, is responsible for it all. So they let them go but tell them to stop the Jesus talk. Peter says, "Nope." When they meet with the other disciples, they even pray to be *more* bold. They only want relief from persecution in order to preach the gospel more, not for the sake of comfort and ease, and God says yes to the prayer.

As their trials heighten, Barnabas sells some land so the apostles can provide for needy church members. Ananias and Sapphira want to look as generous as Barnabas, so they sell land and give part of the money to the church but act like they gave it all. The Spirit gives Peter discernment about it; he says if they hadn't sold the field or even if they'd kept the money, there'd be no problem. They're free to do what they want with their stuff, but they're not free to lie to God. In faking generosity, their hearts are revealed. Peter prophetically questions Ananias about this, and he dies. Sapphira repeats the lie and dies too. This section is bracketed by the activity of the Spirit—Peter isn't commanding their death; he's *communicating* it. Death and judgment are what we all, as sinners, deserve, so this isn't unfair.

Outsiders are intrigued by everything they see happening with the Christ followers, but they also seem fearful. They want in on the healings and the community, but they probably fear the judgment of Ananias and Sapphira. People keep dipping their toes in, though, testing things out.

There's even a local rumor that Peter's shadow heals people, but the text never confirms or denies it.

The authorities grow jealous of their power, fearlessness, and community. They arrest them again, but God sends an angel to unlock the doors, so they go back to the temple to talk about Jesus again. Meanwhile, the authorities ask to see them, but the jailers can't find them until somebody tips them off. The apostles don't back down from their message—one that makes the religious leaders look bad to locals. But a Pharisee named Gamaliel says, "We've seen this before with two other guys. Remember? It'll blow over. And if it doesn't, we may want to pay attention, because maybe it's true." The leaders beat the apostles and send them home, and they rejoice that they're allowed to suffer for the gospel.

As the church crosses more cultural divides, they learn hard lessons about working for unity. The Hellenist widows aren't being cared for, so the apostles find a solution that allows them to continue to focus on preaching. They delegate the care of the widows to seven wise, godly men. One of them is Stephen, who, like Jesus and the apostles, can do signs and wonders. It's going great until he encounters Jews from a synagogue that doesn't believe in Jesus. They twist his words in a trial before the council, but as the council looks at him, he has the radiance angels have when they appear on earth, the radiance that comes from being in the presence of God.

TODAY'S GOD SHOT

"There is salvation in no one else, for there is no other name under heaven given among men by which we must be saved" (4:12). Peter isn't placing emphasis on the name Jesus here. In Jewish culture, your name is a shorthand way of summarizing you as a person, your character, your will. Saving power isn't in the word *Jesus*; it's in the person of Jesus. He's showing how specific the gospel is. People often say Christianity is too exclusive—but the gospel isn't exclusive; it's just specific. He's our only hope for salvation. He's where the rescue is, and He's where the joy is!

ACTS 7–8

Stephen has been falsely accused by unbelieving Jews and is on trial before the Sanhedrin—a ruling council, like the Supreme Court. In his defense statement, he doesn't say a single thing about himself for fifty-three verses. Instead he gives a synopsis of the gospel story line: God pursues His people, who keep rejecting Him. They kill prophets He sends to speak truth to them. They've killed the Righteous One the prophets spoke of. As he recounts the horrible ways God's people have acted in the past, the Sanhedrin likely recognize their forefathers' evil actions but don't realize he's building to a crescendo where the greatest burden of wickedness is the one they're legally responsible for—rejecting God's pursuit by killing His Son.

They're furious, but Stephen is at peace. God pulls back the curtain of eternity and gives him a glimpse into heaven. He sees Jesus standing at the right hand of the Father. Elsewhere Scripture says He's seated at the right hand of the Father, so why is He standing? Scholars say Jesus may be rising up to be his advocate and testify before the great Judge on his behalf or to greet and welcome Stephen into the afterlife. Or both. His work is finished, but Jesus hasn't tuned out. He's paying attention. He's involved and engaged. He's praying for us (Romans 8:34), and He's cheering us on.

Stephen tells the Sanhedrin what he sees, but they scream and attack him. Once outside the city gates, they can enact the death penalty. When the Sanhedrin get outside what's now known as Stephen's Gate, they take off their cloaks to stone him and lay them at the feet of Saul. He may be a member of the Sanhedrin, but if not, he's still a powerful leader among the Jews. It's almost certain that he heard Stephen preach the message of Christ moments earlier, and now he stands by, approving as Stephen becomes the first martyr of the church. Saul has one foot in each enemy camp: He's a Pharisee who rejects Jesus, and he's a Roman citizen. His dual citizenship

For more information on today's reading, see thebiblerecap.com/links.

puts him in a uniquely privileged position. Saul is his Hebrew name, but the Romans primarily speak Latin, so they call him Paul.

Stephen's death escalates the persecution of Christians. Saul starts going door to door in Jerusalem, dragging Christians from their homes and throwing them into prison, so all the Christians in Jerusalem flee, except for the apostles. When Philip flees, he goes to Samaria. Jesus commanded that the gospel be brought to Samaria, even though the Jews and Samaritans hate each other. Philip preaches and performs signs, and people begin to believe. When the apostles hear that Samaritans are repenting, they send Peter and John to make sure everything is going smoothly. Peter and John realize the Samaritans have been baptized by water, but they haven't heard of or received the Holy Spirit. Some say this is because the apostles would need to see this happen, so they could confirm that the Spirit is actively working in Samaritans, otherwise they might be tempted to dismiss it.

The apostles' power and the message catch the attention of Simon the magician, who seems to work through demonic intervention. He notices the difference between his magic and God's miracles, but he seems to want power more than he wants to surrender, and Peter rebukes him. Trying to access the power of God and not the person of God is selfish idolatry.

An angel sends Philip to the desert, where he meets an Ethiopian official who is confused by the words of Isaiah. He's reading what some Jews call the "forbidden chapter." Starting there, Philip unpacks the gospel, and the official finally understands. He goes from confusion to joy! He asks to be baptized, and as they're climbing out of the water, Philip departs (possibly by Holy Spirit teleportation) and appears at the coast.

TODAY'S GOD SHOT

What the enemy means for evil, God uses for good. When the Sanhedrin murdered Stephen, they were trying to stop the spread of the gospel, but the exact opposite occurs. The believers in Jerusalem disperse and take the gospel with them. They're fleeing persecution in Jerusalem, but they don't run and hide, they go and tell! "Those who were scattered went about preaching the word" (8:4). Their fear of persecution doesn't stop them. They know God will fulfill His assignment through them. He's where the joy is!

ACTS 9–10

Today Saul hunts down anyone who belongs to "the Way," which is how they refer to the church. He gets permission from the high priest to track down Christ followers and extradite them to Jerusalem for punishment. But God has a different plan.

As he heads north out of the city toward Damascus, a holy lightning bolt (or something like that) knocks him to the ground. He and his men hear a voice from heaven that asks, "Saul, Saul, why are you persecuting Me?" Jesus is in heaven, at the right hand of the Father, so how can Saul be persecuting Him? Jesus has united Himself with the church. As the church is persecuted, Jesus feels it; He enters into the pain of His people. He identifies himself to Saul and sends him to Damascus. The experience leaves Saul blind. He fasts for three days, then God gives a vision to a local believer named Ananias and tells him where to find Saul. Ananias says, "Lord, I have heard from many about this man, how much evil he has done to your saints at Jerusalem" (9:13). Aren't saints dead people? How is Saul harming dead people? He isn't. Scripture repeatedly identifies all believers as saints—dead or alive. This shows up all across Scripture, even in the Old Testament; it's a doctrine called the sainthood of the believer.

God explains the plan to Ananias: "I've given Saul a vision; he's expecting you. Go pray for him to receive his sight." Why does God do this instead of just heal Saul Himself? God wants His people to be engaged in His process; we get the joy of being part of His plan of redemption. Ananias prays and Saul regains his sight, is filled with the Spirit, is baptized, and starts declaring Jesus as Lord. His preaching causes such an uproar in the local synagogue that some of the local religious leaders plot to kill him! He goes back to Jerusalem, but the disciples there are skeptical of him too—except Barnabas. He vouches for Saul, who begins preaching locally but then gets threats from others who aren't

For more information on today's reading, see thebiblerecap.com/links.

buying it. The apostles send him to his hometown, Tarsus, until things simmer down.

The church is facing a rise of persecution and death threats, and yet it experiences increasing peace, comfort, and fear of the Lord. They're remembering what Jesus said. They're living out His peace and primary focus. Why don't they forget things like their forefathers did? Why are things so different now? This is the work of God the Spirit as He indwells believers. He is the Reminder! Not only do they live in peace, but they live in power. Peter heals people and even raises a woman from the dead.

One day he has a strange vision of a sheet with animals on it, and a voice says to kill and eat them. He's confused, so God repeats it twice. God is declaring all foods edible. Jesus did this in Mark 7:19, and God repeats it here. This scene may be confusing because it seems like He's saying some Old Testament laws no longer apply. So how do we know which ones to disregard? God gave three types of laws: civil, ceremonial, and moral (see Day 50). Peter is in the awkward transition phase where the ceremonial laws have just been fulfilled by Jesus, so he resists what God tells him because it goes against what has always been in place. But it's important for him to get it, because there's a greater purpose behind what's happening. A Roman centurion named Cornelius has a vision directing him to send servants to Peter. They arrive right after his vision. He goes to meet Cornelius, who has a packed house waiting for Peter. Peter says Jews frown on associating with foreigners, but God has been correcting his thinking. He now sees that there's racial *diversity*, not division, in God's family. He preaches the gospel, and they all believe. The Spirit verifies their conversion, and they're baptized.

TODAY'S GOD SHOT

God is sovereign over the salvation of His people. Saul's story is evidence that when God wants someone, they're His. If you've prayed for friends or family who've rejected the gospel, take heart: God has the final word. Saul wasn't pursuing God; he was actively rebelling against Him. But still, he was captured by the God of the universe and caught up in the greatest redemption story the human heart has ever known. He's where the joy is!

ACTS 11–12

When Peter gets back to Jerusalem, trouble is brewing. Everyone has heard what happened with the Gentiles in Caesarea. Jews aren't supposed to associate with foreigners. God corrected Peter's thinking on that, but the Christ followers back in Jerusalem weren't privy to his vision. A group some of the believers refer to as the circumcision party confronts Peter about it, saying foreigners who commit to following a Jewish Messiah should have to convert to Judaism and be circumcised. Being set apart has been a major part of their culture. Anytime foreigners have followed YHWH, they've assimilated into Judaism. Now that the Messiah has come and said the gospel would go everywhere, they know many foreigners will be converting, and they want to preserve their culture.

Peter tells them how God approved of everything he did via the Spirit. He even points to a teaching of Jesus that foretold this. Jesus was always dropping little time capsules of truth along the way—things that didn't make sense in the moment but that He knew they'd need in the future. Peter says, "If God approves of them, who am I to deny them?" Not only does the circumcision party agree that Peter is right, but they praise God for welcoming outsiders. This is an important turning point for the early church—it's where we start to see that, more than anything else, the Holy Spirit is the marker of God's people, not circumcision. He's the unifier of His people across all racial and cultural divides.

In these early days of the church, things can feel clunky. There are adjustments to make, but God patiently walks them through the transitions. As they try to follow Jesus's command to spread the gospel, they need to get God's seal of approval on any new decisions to verify they're making the right ones. That's why they need to see the activity of the Spirit, the obvious evidence that God is the one at the helm of anything new.

Some believers who fled Jerusalem are preaching the gospel, but only to the Jews. Others preach to Greek-speaking Jews known as the

---

For more information on today's reading, see thebiblerecap.com/links.

Hellenists, who start a church in their city, Antioch, which is in modern-day Turkey. Barnabas goes to make sure everything is running smoothly, then brings Saul with him and they stay for a year, teaching and building them up. The Antioch church is thriving and even sending money back to Jerusalem to care for the Christians there during a famine.

Then we meet a new King Herod. Herod the Great was king when Jesus was born. Herod Antipas was king when He was crucified. And now Herod Agrippa is on the throne. He's a major persecutor of Christians, and he murders James, an apostle in Jesus's inner circle. The local Jews are thrilled about this, and Herod wants to make them love him even more, so he arrests Peter during Passover.

The church prays fervently for him. He's locked up with two chains, between two soldiers, being watched by two guards. During the night, an angel wakes him by punching him in the side. When he gets up, his chains fall off, and they walk straight out as the iron door opens in front of them. He goes to the house of Mary (John Mark's mom), where the disciples have the doors locked. Once inside, he whispers everything that happened—the fear of persecution is real—and tells them to fill the other disciples in. The next day, the guards know they're in trouble with Peter gone. Herod orders them killed, then goes to meet with rulers from Tyre and Sidon. He's upset with them, so they flatter and praise him as a god. Immediately an angel of the Lord strikes him dead because he received glory that belongs to God alone. After his death, the church continues to thrive and grow, and Saul and Barnabas head back to Antioch from Jerusalem, but this time John Mark goes with them.

TODAY'S GOD SHOT

"To the Gentiles also God has granted repentance that leads to life" (11:18). The Greek word for *granted* means "given." God has *given* repentance to the Gentiles. It's easy to think of repentance as something we offer to God, but this verse says it's something He gives to us. He's the one who initiates our repentance. What an incredible gift—to be given eyes to see, ears to hear, and a heart to know the truth and surrender to it! He's where the joy is!

ACTS 13–14

The Antioch church is led by a bunch of rebels and former enemies. Together, they're worshipping God and fasting when they get direction from the Holy Spirit. He says to appoint Barnabas and Saul as missionaries, so the two men leave on their first missionary journey! Stop number one is Cyprus. John Mark joins Saul, and as they're preaching their way across the island, the governor hears about it and summons them. He's hanging out with a false prophet and magician who relies on the power of the enemy. The governor is starting to come around to the gospel, but the magician tries to dissuade him, so Saul calls him a son of the devil and speaks temporary blindness over him. The governor is convinced. This is the first time Scripture uses Saul's other name, Paul. It is the primary name he uses henceforth, because this is where the spread of the gospel to the Gentiles increases, so it makes sense for him to use the Gentile version of his name. He's adapting to the cultures he encounters, making sacrifices to get any stumbling blocks out of the way.

For stop number two, the Spirit sends Paul and Barnabas to a different Antioch—but John Mark goes back to Jerusalem. They listen to the teaching in the synagogue, then the leaders ask them for encouragement. Paul's version of encouragement focuses on what Jesus has done for them: "Through this man forgiveness of sins is proclaimed to you, and by him everyone who believes is freed from everything from which you could not be freed by the law of Moses" (13:38–39). In a room full of law-abiding Jews and devout foreigners, Paul says the law isn't where their hope lies—Christ is. They beg them to come back next week, and when he does, nearly the whole city shows up, but it doesn't go as well. The Jews who aren't Christ followers turn their noses up at the Gentiles. Paul says it had to happen this way. The Jews had to be presented with the gospel and reject it so that it could go to the Gentiles. God has a detailed process and intentional timing for everything. Everyone God

For more information on today's reading, see thebiblerecap.com/links.

has appointed for eternal life believes (13:48), and God has appointed so many that a revival starts in the area, primarily among Gentiles.

Stop number three is Iconium. Many Jews and Greeks believe the gospel there, but once again, they have trouble from those who don't. They actively work against Paul and Barnabas. So what do Paul and Barnabas do? They stay longer. But when they find out the people are about to stone them, they leave. Stop number four is Lystra. When Paul heals a lame man, people start worshipping him and Barnabas. They both lose their minds over it and try to shut it down, but the people want to offer sacrifices to them! Meanwhile, the Jews from stops two and three have followed Paul and Barnabas to stop four. They rally the locals in Lystra, stone Paul, and drag his body out of the city because they think they've killed him. These people wanted to offer him sacrifices moments earlier. After the stoning, the disciples gather around him, he gets up, and he goes back into the city. The next day they head to stop number five, Derbe, and preach the gospel, then decide to go back to the three towns that wanted to kill them. They don't go back for revenge or even to change their enemies' minds; they go back to strengthen and encourage the believers there. They appoint elders in their local churches, pray, fast, and commit the elders to God. They make a few more stops, then head back to the first Antioch to report on everything that has happened, how God opened the hearts of Gentiles to believe!

TODAY'S GOD SHOT

"In past generations he allowed all the nations to walk in their own ways. Yet he did not leave himself without witness, for he did good by giving you rains from heaven and fruitful seasons, satisfying your hearts with food and gladness" (14:16–17). The Greek word for *allowed* is often translated "suffered"—God suffered all the nations to walk in their own ways. And even though their complete rejection of God wounds Him, He makes Himself known to them nonetheless through His blessings—rain and fruit and food and gladness. What a generous God, using His kindness and grace as a means of making Himself known even among His enemies. He's where the joy is!

JAMES 1–5

This book was written by the half brother of Jesus, who used to mock Him. It shows what an incredible change of heart James went through, because it opens with the author calling himself "a servant of God and of the Lord Jesus Christ." The author is actually named *Jacob*. The name was mistranslated in the King James Version, and somehow it stuck. Jacob writes to the church outside of Israel. It's *vital* to remember that this is for believers. Out of context, this book sounds like a list of things we do to earn God's approval instead of things that serve as markers of knowing Him.

The church is encountering trials, but Jacob says steadfastness is developed in those trials, and steadfastness is part of being whole. Wholeness, or completion, is the idea behind the word *perfect* that often appears in this book. Only God can bring that kind of wholeness. Not long after this, Jacob dies as a martyr; so he not only knows what he's talking about, but he also lives it. He says to ask God for wisdom—it's a prayer we'll always get a yes to! True wisdom is the knowledge of God, and it's one of the tools He uses to reshape and restore our fractured lives into wholeness—it's how we persevere through trials, resist temptation, handle riches and blessings, and walk in humility and faith.

Jacob repeatedly talks about the challenge of taming the tongue. He knows this well, since he once used his tongue to mock Jesus. But he's had a change of heart and knows that heart change shows up in the ways we talk. It's easy to lie to ourselves about our motives (1:22 and 26), but our actions reveal what's in our hearts. And if our hearts really trust and believe Jesus, then we'll obey His teachings. None of us are where we want to be, but God adopted us in the midst of our sin and is committed to sanctifying us!

What does Jacob mean when he says, "You see that a person is justified by works and not by faith alone" (2:24)? *Justified* means "to prove

For more information on today's reading, see thebiblerecap.com/links.

or demonstrate." This verse is essentially saying, "A person's works demonstrate or prove what's happening in their heart." This is about what other people see, not what God sees. Because as we've seen repeatedly, God sees the heart. Humans are the ones who have to have it demonstrated to them. This is especially important to the church as they live under oppression and experience new conversions. Lots of people are claiming to believe but aren't showing evidence of having a new heart, so Jacob addresses this directly. When the Holy Spirit isn't falling in major and obvious ways, their only evidence that someone is a true believer is when they prove it by their actions, which justifies them to others.

Jacob says wisdom is pure, peaceable, gentle, open to reason, full of mercy, full of good fruits, impartial, and sincere. Chapters 3 and 4 are connected with the idea of being a peacemaker—someone who enters into the chaos and brings the peace of Christ. The world and the church are full of fights and division, and chapter 4 says we bring peace to those situations by being content and humble, by prioritizing the things of God in our lives. Chapter 5 gives us more examples of living out wholeness in the wisdom of God—and it connects us again to prioritizing the things of God in our lives. If we do, we'll handle our wealth in a way that honors God, our suffering in a way that honors God, and even our sins in a way that honors God.

TODAY'S GOD SHOT

No one leaves this book feeling like they're nailing it. It points out our blind spots and weak spots. But remember, it's good for us to be at square one. Not so we can feel like a failure, but so we can take our eyes off ourselves and put them back on Him—where grace and mercy abound. And that's how Jacob ends this book. He says, "You're a sinner. Don't try to hide it. Throw some light on it and ask for help! Tell other people where you struggle—they are strugglers and sinners too. Together, you can ask God to help you, because He will. You're not alone in this!" He even points to Elijah—a human just like us—as an example of what's possible when sinners seek God. So let's draw near! He's where the joy is!

ACTS 15–16

Men from Jerusalem come to Antioch and teach circumcision, inciting the old chaos again. Paul and Barnabas go to Jerusalem in hopes of putting a stop to it for good. Pharisees are behind this, even though they're also Christ followers. As they debate, Peter says, "Remember how God used a Jew like me to preach to the Gentiles? Those uncircumcised people received the Holy Spirit. God makes no distinction between us. By saying He requires them to be circumcised, you're heaping a burden on them that none of us could bear anyway, and you're testing God. He's made Himself clear. All who are saved are saved through His grace alone, not by keeping the law."

Then Jacob (James) says, "Simeon reported the same thing as Peter. But this isn't a new idea—Amos prophesied about this eight hundred years ago. God calls these Gentiles by His name. Their relationship with Him is intact. So let's only be concerned with things that disrupt the harmony of our relationships. Our code of conduct should be about creating unity in the family of Christ. Let's figure out what those things are." They hold a meeting called the Jerusalem Council to decide what to require of Gentiles. This list isn't a way to obtain righteousness—it's a way to make sure things go smoothly as the church fills with people from different cultures. They list the divisive deal breakers: eating things sacrificed to idols, eating blood, eating things that've been strangled, and sexual immorality. Gentile cultures are engaged in these things and even use them in their worship, so it's important to stop doing them. The only parts of their culture new converts have to lay down are things that conflict with Christ and the unity of His body. And the only culture they have to pick up is the culture of Christ and His kingdom—not that of Judaism. The Spirit doesn't homogenize; He unifies. When the church reads this letter from the Jerusalem Council, they're thrilled!

Paul and Barnabas plan to visit the churches from their first trip, and Barnabas wants to bring John Mark, but something happened when John Mark left their first trip early (Acts 13:13), so Paul doesn't trust him and refuses to travel with him. Still, God uses this division to create more missionary trips.

In Lystra, Paul and Silas meet Timothy, who is half-Jewish, half-Greek. Paul invites him to join them and has him circumcised. He knows Timothy will be preaching to Jews who reject uncircumcised people, so he's proactively addressing anything they might use to discredit Timothy's message. All their steps are carefully directed by the Holy Spirit and visions. In Philippi, they meet Lydia, and God "opened her heart to pay attention to what was said by Paul" (16:14). God makes her interested in and receptive to their message, and there's a domino effect in her family—they're baptized that day.

A demonized girl, who is enslaved for the demon's powers, disrupts their message by claiming they serve the Most High God. To a community that doesn't know YHWH, this likely sounds like they worship Zeus. Paul commands the demon to come out, then her masters arrest them and accuse them of disturbing the peace. They're beaten and thrown into prison. But they never waste a jail sentence. When an earthquake opens the doors, the prisoners are so captivated by their message that they stay put. The jailer panics, thinking they're gone, but Paul comforts him. When he asks how to be saved, they say, "Believe in the Lord Jesus." This echoes what Jesus said in John 6:28–29. On one hand this seems freeing—no long list of laws! But on the other hand, belief seems even harder. Have you ever tried to make yourself believe something? Fortunately, God opens hearts to believe, like He did for Lydia. The jailer's family believes and are baptized, then Paul and Silas go back to prison. They sacrifice their freedom for the jailer's life; he'd be killed if they disappeared. Then the magistrate frees them and even apologizes!

TODAY'S GOD SHOT

God cleanses our hearts by faith (15:9). He uses faith like a silversmith uses a furnace—it's like a purging fire that purifies our hearts and refines them. The presence of a godward faith in your heart drives out whatever needs to go. Praise God! He's the active agent in that, and He's where the joy is!

GALATIANS 1–3

This is the first of Paul's letters (called epistles in Greek) to churches, and it's to a church he planted on his first missionary journey. They're Gentiles, but some Jewish believers have been trying to force their culture on them, circumcision specifically. Paul has already addressed this topic with the early church, and they attempted to resolve it at the Jerusalem Council, but some Jews aren't complying. They're known as Judaizers—people who combine God's grace with human effort. Paul is furious with them and seems to be furious with the Galatians for believing them.

Distortion of the gospel is a false gospel, and Paul pronounces God's judgment on anyone who preaches it. He tells his own story to give credibility to his argument. He was a zealous Jew, eager to live out the traditions of the fathers to the point of violently persecuting those who disagreed. But God chose him before he was born, and at the right time, God graciously called him and revealed Christ, and Paul spent three years being taught the Scriptures—by the Spirit and the Word—before he met with the apostles in Jerusalem. Then God directed his steps to preach the gospel to the Gentiles. He mentions Titus, an uncircumcised Greek with no Jewish ties. If the Jews in Jerusalem didn't insist on circumcising Titus, then Jerusalem obviously wasn't requiring it. But some people thought Paul's message needed less freedom, more laws.

Regardless, the apostles sent Paul to the Gentiles and Peter to the Jews. They asked Paul not to forget the poor—likely referring to the persecuted Jews in Jerusalem—even though his ministry was to the Gentiles. Paul was all about inclusion. In fact, there was a time when Paul had to call Peter out. Peter had been eating with both Jews and Gentiles, but when James sent people to visit them, Peter started eating with only Jews because of his fear of man, and others followed his lead. Paul had to publicly correct him so they'd be corrected too.

For more information on today's reading, see thebiblerecap.com/links.

Paul says, "I'm a Jew, and even I know that actions don't save. Only faith in Christ saves. If I attempted to earn my own righteousness, I'd be rejecting His death on the cross. Why would He need to die if I could do this on my own? If I can earn my own righteousness, He died for nothing!"

In chapter 3, he says, "You have the Spirit. How did that happen? Did you do some action that summoned Him? Or did He come to you through the faith God granted you? Now that you've got the Spirit, why are you trying to do something to gain God's approval? The Spirit is God's seal of approval!"

Then he summarizes an important idea in a succinct way, twice. "It is those of faith who are the sons of Abraham" (3:7). And, "If you are Christ's, then you are Abraham's offspring, heirs according to promise" (3:29). He's writing this letter to Gentiles. Even though God has a unique, irreplaceable relationship with ethnic Israel, Gentiles are still counted among the descendants of Abraham. That relationship isn't contingent on ethnicity or circumcision; it's contingent on faith in Christ and available to anyone of any ethnicity, Jew or Gentile. Four hundred thirty years before God gave the law to Moses, He promised Abraham that all the nations of the earth would be blessed through him. Salvation has always been about faith in YHWH and has always been available for anyone who has that.

Paul has approached his argument from every angle, trying to dismantle any potential counterarguments before they arise. He points to his own story, Abraham's story, the guidance of Scripture and the Spirit, and the decisions of the apostles, all to drive home one point: Salvation is the gift of God, by grace alone, through faith alone, in Christ alone.

TODAY'S GOD SHOT

If the only way to enter the kingdom were through circumcision, and only men were circumcised, how could women enter the kingdom? These new female Gentile converts may have wondered the same thing, feeling hopeless or overlooked. Paul leans into that question: "There is neither Jew nor Greek, there is neither slave nor free, there is no male and female, for you are all one in Christ Jesus" (3:28). What an incredible relief! Because of Christ, the door is open to everyone. And because of the Spirit, we're united across our differences. He's where the joy is!

GALATIANS 4–6

Paul opens with great news today: As sons of God, we are fellow heirs with Christ, and as coheirs, we inherit everything! But what's more, we inherit the Spirit of the Son (that is, the Holy Spirit). The presence of the Spirit in us is what enables us to call God our Father; those without the Spirit don't have God as their Father. Since we have that status as a child of God indwelled by God, it's ridiculous to go back to being a slave—and that's what happens when we try to rely on the law; it enslaves. He implores them not to turn back to their old ways. These are Gentiles whose past doesn't include the law, but they were enslaved by other things. Specifically, they worshipped and sought guidance from things that aren't God, like the sun, moon, stars, and planets in their culture of astrology.

Their observance of days, months, seasons, and years (4:10) may refer to astrology; he calls those "the weak and worthless elementary principles of the world," which is translated as "elemental spirits" elsewhere in Scripture, possibly indicating demonic involvement. Others say he's referring to keeping Jewish holidays and festivals, which aren't part of their culture since they're Gentiles. He's not saying it's wrong to celebrate events—even as Gentiles—he's saying God doesn't require it of them. If Paul had forbidden it, he'd just be flipping the law on them; to require and to forbid are just different types of laws. Paul shows this later, saying, "In Christ Jesus neither circumcision nor uncircumcision counts for anything, but only faith working through love" (5:6).

When Paul first preached to them it was because of a bodily ailment, which likely had to do with his eyes based on this information: He says they would've gouged their eyes out and given them to him (4:15). He writes to them with large letters—which likely means large handwriting because this letter is fairly short compared to his others (6:11). He says, "I bear on my body the marks of Jesus" (6:17). Maybe he's talking about scars from his beatings, but maybe it's his eyes, a constant reminder for as long as he lives that he encountered Jesus, was temporarily blinded, and had his whole life changed. This eye problem could also be his "thorn in the flesh" in 2 Corinthians 12:1–10.

He uses intense language to say that if they rely on works at all, they've missed the gospel and they've missed Christ: "You are severed from Christ, you who would be justified by the law" (5:4). He isn't saying they'll lose their salvation—he's saying they clearly don't grasp the gospel. At the end of that verse, he says, "You have fallen away from grace." *Grace* means "unmerited favor"—it's when we get what we don't deserve. The phrase "fall from grace" is often misused as a way of saying someone has fallen into sin. But Paul shows us that falling from grace is more like falling into self-righteousness (which, to be fair, is also sin), making an effort to earn what has been freely given.

He says our freedom doesn't terminate on us. It's not a pass to live for ourselves and sin all we want. Freedom is an opportunity to magnify God's character and model His love to the world around us. We only get this freedom to begin with because the Spirit lives in us, and there's only one thing He wants to do: Magnify God—which is what the Spirit does in us, producing His fruit in us. And Paul shows us what this Spirit fruit looks like on display: If another Christian is ensnared in sin patterns and can't get free, lean in with gentleness to help. Don't become arrogant that you're helping, because that could be you next week. Share with those who teach, and don't tire of doing good—especially to other believers. He reminds them what it looks like to be a family.

TODAY'S GOD SHOT

When God planted us like trees in His garden, the Spirit started working in us, producing Spirit fruit in us. This word *fruit* in 5:22 is singular—it's one fruit with nine characteristics. When these things begin to show up in us, that's His signature. Do you see love, joy, peace, patience, kindness, goodness, faithfulness, gentleness, and self-control on the increase in your life? If so, thank Him for it! That's His doing. He gets the glory, and you get the joy, because He's where the joy is!

ACTS 17

Paul and Silas head for Thessalonica, where they're staying with Jason. Paul spends three days going to the synagogue to reason with people about the Scriptures, showing how Jesus is the Messiah the prophets wrote about. He isn't just sharing his personal testimony—even though he has a great story. Instead, he shares Scripture's testimony of Christ. Personal stories are moving, but Paul knows that subjective experiences can be easily dismissed by anyone who has a different experience. So he takes an objective and logic-based approach, sharing facts, not feelings. He lets Scripture speak for itself.

As usual, the audience is split. Some believe and some don't. The Jews who don't believe him form a mob, start a riot, and go to Jason's house to find Paul and Silas. When they can't find them, they drag Jason and a few others out of the house and take them to the authorities. They say the church is rebelling against the establishment—Caesar in particular this time. Jason posts bail for everyone, and the authorities let them go home. This money probably has a bit of a promise attached to it as well—in the way bail serves as a promise that you'll return for your court date, Jason's money probably serves as a promise that Paul and Silas will leave town.

They leave in the middle of the night and head to Berea. First stop: the synagogue. Paul testifies about Jesus, and they don't just take his word as fact—they crack open their scrolls every day and check his words against Scripture. They walk in wisdom and humility; they're open to receive—but not just anything. They'll only receive the truth. Because of that, many of them believe in Jesus. When word gets back to Thessalonica, they march over to Berea to try to shut Paul's preaching down. Paul packs up to leave, but Silas and Timothy stay behind.

When Paul gets to Athens, he sends word that he needs Silas and Timothy. Luke may be with him—we don't know for sure. Athens is full of idolatry; the people there worship so many different things, in part because they're open to different ideas and philosophies. They're inundated with religious options, and the people love hearing new ideas. In fact, many of the prominent people Paul encounters are professional seekers. They're always following the current trends, which change frequently. They love to seek, but they don't like to find; they prefer to keep seeking. This is new territory for Paul. He's used to talking to Jews and Gentiles who have some understanding of the Hebrew Scriptures, but the Athenians aren't on that page at all. Still, they're intrigued by his message—not because they're moved by their own sinfulness and God's great mercy, but because it's a new idea they haven't heard yet.

Paul is educated and knows how to lean into that when it's helpful, so he uses intellectual language they understand, much like how Jesus used agricultural analogies when talking to farmers and fishermen. Paul quotes philosophers and poets they're acquainted with. He points out that they know something is missing—amid all their religious paraphernalia, they have an altar dedicated to an unknown god. He says, "I know the God you're missing. But you didn't make Him like you made these idols and their altars. In fact, He made you. And when He did, He was intentional about every detail, including the time and location of your birth—it all serves to point you back to Him. Turn to Him. Someday He'll judge the earth through the One He raised from the dead." Some of them mock the idea of the resurrection, but others believe, including Dionysius and Damaris.

TODAY'S GOD SHOT

"In him we live and move and have our being" (17:28). Here, Paul clips a quote from a Greek poet and pastes it into his conversation about God, because it speaks to the truth of who God is. Ultimately, all truth is God's truth. Anything that is true points back to Him, the author of truth—the way, the truth, and the life. And that's kind of what this verse says: "In Him, we live," He's the life; "and move," He's the way; "and have our being," He's the very truth at the core of who we are. And He's where the joy is!

1 THESSALONIANS 1–5; 2 THESSALONIANS 1–3

Paul wrote two letters to the church at Thessalonica. He tells them a few ways their lives demonstrate that God has chosen them to be a part of His family: (a) They received the gospel wholeheartedly and the Holy Spirit came to them; (b) they started spreading the word to other people, taking what they learned from Paul and making Macedonian mentees; and (c) they've turned from their idolatry to worship the one true God. Overall, they received, lived out, and shared the gospel.

He recounts the story of how they met. In the face of opposition, he came to Thessalonica to share the gospel with them—not to be popular, powerful, or rich. The apostles had a right to demand that the church take care of them but didn't make use of that right. They worked overtime to share the gospel and their lives. As they all lived out the gospel, persecution came. Struggles shouldn't come as a surprise to Christ followers.

Paul sent Timothy to check on them, and he came back with an encouraging update, making Paul all the more excited to visit, so he prays that God will open that door. So far, Satan has hindered him. Some scholars say this refers to what happened the last time he was there; perhaps he is forbidden to return. He loves them and calls them his "crown of boasting" before God. Some scholars say these are the crowns we'll lay at His feet—those we've led to Him and built up in Him. Even their ancestors who believed in the Promise—though they never heard of Jesus—were saved by Him through faith in God's promise (4:14). People in the Old Testament were saved by faith, not by works, just like those of us who live after Christ died.

He says to keep living lives of honor and purity, even with things that are culturally dishonored, like sex, because that's God's will. It's one of the few places where God's will is stated loud and clear: "This is the

For more information on today's reading, see thebiblerecap.com/links.

will of God, your sanctification: that you abstain from sexual immorality; that each one of you know how to control his own body in holiness and honor, not in the passion of lust like the Gentiles who do not know God" (4:3–5). God's will is that we be sanctified (made clean). And God Himself is the one who sanctifies us (5:23). Another clear declaration of His will says, "Rejoice always, pray without ceasing, give thanks in all circumstances; for this is the will of God in Christ Jesus for you" (5:16–18).

After Paul's first letter, things grow worse. They're under more persecution, and false teachers are spreading lies and claiming their false messages are from Paul—probably by forging a letter. They're scared and confused, so Paul writes his second letter to help set the record straight.

He says God will give them relief and can be trusted to judge their persecutors, who will suffer eternal destruction (1:9). He addresses the false teachers' lie. They say Jesus has already returned and they've been forgotten and abandoned by Him, but Paul says we'd know if it had happened. There'll be a major rebellion against God, led by the "man of lawlessness," who'll try to take control of the temple of God. This phrase has a lot of flexibility; it doesn't necessarily refer to the temple in Jerusalem (which was destroyed in 70 AD, after this letter was written). It could be a pagan temple or a position of church leadership. Regardless, Paul says they don't need to lose sleep over it, because Jesus will stop it by the breath of His mouth and God will protect His kids from Satan and his lies. And as for those who want nothing to do with God, He's finally and eternally giving them what they want. They refused the truth, and God gave them over to believe the lie.

TODAY'S GOD SHOT

Paul consistently gives God the credit for the good works of His people. He asks God to grow their love, to establish their hearts in holiness, to make them worthy of His calling and fulfill every resolve for good, every work of faith. He thanks God—not them—for their growth in faith and love and for choosing and sanctifying them. He credits God as the initiator of faith and love. Look at all the *doing* He's doing! God does all He requires. He's where the joy is!

ACTS 18–19

Today we jump back into Paul's second missionary journey. In Corinth, he meets Aquila and Priscilla (we'll call them A&P), a married couple who just moved from Italy because the Jews were forced out of Rome. They're tentmakers by trade, as is Paul. Paul shakes out his tunic at the Corinthian Jews. Jesus told the apostles to shake the dust off their feet in the towns that rejected them (Matthew 10:14), and Nehemiah shook out his tunic for a similar reason (Nehemiah 5:13). Paul shared the gospel with them and they rejected it, so while he's in Corinth, he decides to talk to the Gentiles instead. This is location specific—he isn't dismissing the Jews at large; in fact, by the end of the chapter, Jews have turned to Christ. In a vision, God encourages Paul to keep at it: He'll protect him and his work will bear fruit, because God has plans to save a lot of people there. As Paul stays for a year and a half, preaching the gospel, the local Jews eventually bring an accusation against him, but the governor dismisses it and lets Paul go. God protects him just like He promised.

After leaving Corinth, Paul gets a haircut, likely because he kept the Nazirite vow while in a city known for its worldliness. It sets him apart as someone who is serious about the things of God. Then he drops off A&P in Ephesus, where they meet Apollos, a compelling, precise teacher, despite the fact that he doesn't even have the Holy Spirit. They explain things, filling out his theology a bit more, and he becomes a huge asset to the early church. Apollos heads to Corinth, and Paul goes back to Ephesus, where he meets others who aren't aware of the Spirit. They were baptized by JTB before Jesus started His public ministry and probably moved out of the area at that point. When they hear about Jesus and the Spirit, they're on board. They're filled with the Spirit and start prophesying and speaking in tongues; it's hard to say how tongues were used here specifically because the text doesn't give us many details.

Paul's sermons are persuasive, but he eventually gets pushback from those who've been hearing the gospel repeatedly but not yielding to it.

Seeing their resistance, he goes to teach in a different building, one that's more of a cultural space where nonreligious people gather, Tyrannus Hall. He teaches there daily for two years. Ephesus is a major city for business and travel, so people passing through hear his teaching and take it home with them, and the Word spreads through Asia.

God does uniquely miraculous things through his ministry. People are even healed by Paul's handkerchiefs. These things are so unique that even Scripture notes how odd it is. But the power hungry want in on the action. Local exorcists start mimicking what they've seen Paul do, treating Jesus's name like an incantation. But there isn't power in the *word* Jesus; there's power in the *person* of Jesus. When demons prove more powerful than magicians and Jesus proves more powerful than demons, people start repenting and renouncing idolatry. In fact, a silversmith gets nervous that his livelihood is in jeopardy because he makes statues of false gods for a living. What's more, their culture is built around the goddess Artemis, an idol. He whips the local silversmith union into a frenzy, and they begin to riot.

The town clerk knows if they don't calm down, Rome will intervene, so he says, "We all know Artemis is in charge. We have her statue and her holy meteorite. So you can all relax."

TODAY'S GOD SHOT

God is sovereign over timing and every detail. If Paul hadn't been a tentmaker, and if A&P hadn't been forced out of Rome, they never would've met and bonded, and they wouldn't have gone with him to Ephesus, where they eventually met Apollos. The early church is built up through Apollos! If the Jews in the synagogue at Ephesus hadn't grown stubborn, Paul wouldn't have moved to a new location where people from all over the world would hear about Jesus. That's how the gospel spreads to Asia. From jobs to timing to rejection, God has His hands in everything, which is how He "works all things together for the good of those that love Him" (Romans 8:28). He's always at work on our behalf, and He's where the joy is!

1 CORINTHIANS 1–4

Paul lived in Corinth for eighteen months, and he checks in on the church there from time to time, sending letters like this one in response to what he hears. Before he wrote 1 Corinthians, he wrote a letter that we've never found. He follows up with this letter to address upsetting problems he's heard about, as well as some questions they have.

He opens with encouragement that Jesus will sustain them to the end and make them guiltless. God is the one who called them into His family, and He'll be the one to keep them there. What God initiates, He will sustain and He will fulfill. Paul has some rebukes to deliver and knows that when you're about to be confronted with your sin, it's nice to be reminded that none of it changes the way God views you or revokes your status as His beloved child. The first problem he addresses is their leader worship. They're divided over their favorite church leaders. But their leaders didn't die for them. All Paul does is plant seeds—he has no power to make them grow. God is the one who gives growth! Paul won't even baptize people. He's not diminishing the importance of baptism; he's pointing out that it's secondary to preaching the gospel.

The gospel makes no sense to those who don't believe it—it's foolishness. The Jews were seeking signs, and the Greeks (like those we met in Athens) were seeking wisdom, but all Paul had for them was the gospel of Christ. For the Jews, Paul threw a wrench in things, and to the Greeks he just seemed crazy. It's so easy to dismiss the gospel, but for those who believe it, it's the power that enables everything they do. Somehow, the unpolished, lower-class Corinthians actually got it. God intentionally chose them because they understand what it means to be at square one—spiritual poverty. They're not under the illusion that they have anything to offer God, unlike the self-righteous Pharisees or the educated Greeks. Because of that, they gained the righteousness and wisdom of Christ. So they don't need to boast in whatever teacher

For more information on today's reading, see thebiblerecap.com/links.

they follow, including him. They should boast in the finished work of Christ!

Paul wants to help those who have been given the wisdom of God to grow in it by communicating with the Spirit, who imparts wisdom. One of the primary ways to communicate with the Spirit is through reading Scripture, because He wrote it. As God, the Spirit knows the mind of God. And as our Teacher, He helps us understand God's thoughts. Paul refers to this kind of connection and access as "having the mind of Christ." Paul wants to teach them deeper things, but their actions prove they aren't ready for it. First, they have to learn to live out what they do know. To try to teach them more now would be cruel, overwhelming, and unfruitful. He trusts that God will keep growing them, because He finishes what He starts.

Paul talks about what judgment is and who judges whom, and it can be confusing if we forget the context. He's talking about what it means to be a Christian leader. Leaders are servants to the people, but they're primarily accountable to God. He's not seeking their approval or trying to feel good about himself; he's seeking God's approval. It's a hard path—he doesn't make a lot of money, he doesn't sleep much, and people speak poorly of him—but he does it because he loves them and they love God. He doesn't want to have to rebuke them when he visits—he wants to come in gentleness and love, but he'll do whatever is best for them, whatever they need at the time.

TODAY'S GOD SHOT

Paul describes three things that are given to us in Christ: "righteousness and sanctification and redemption" (1:30). They point to different time frames in our life. Past: We've been declared righteous. Present: Sanctification is the ongoing process through which we're made clean. Future: Jesus said our redemption is drawing near (Luke 21:28); we eagerly await the redemption of our bodies (Romans 8:23). Your past, present, and future are all handled by Jesus. There's no frame in the story of your life where He isn't active. He's at work in all of it to bring you into the fullness of relationship with Himself. He's got your past, present, and future. He's in all of it, and He's where the joy is!

1 CORINTHIANS 5–8

The Corinthians engage in debauchery, using God's grace as an excuse. Freedom in Christ isn't freedom to sin—it means we're no longer enslaved to sin; we have the Spirit to help us obey God! Grace is an agent of change—it's God's favor on us to help us walk according to His ways. Anything that lets us continue in sin unchecked and carefree isn't grace—it's passive wrath. Paul says to *flee* sexual immorality. Sexual sin dishonors people by dissociating their body from their soul, using them for our own pleasure. He addresses this in chapter 6 with even heavier words. He says if you're a believer, you have the Spirit of God living inside of you, and forcing God into situations He doesn't want to be in is a form of abuse.

He tells the church how to respond to those in the church who actively rebel against God's call for sexual integrity—not those who struggle to obey, but those who refuse. There's a big difference. Rebellion and repentance move in opposing directions; when it comes to sin, there's no such thing as standing still. They're supposed to judge those in the church. He doesn't mean the church takes the place of God as final judge, determining the destination of that person's soul. He's saying to act as fruit inspectors and spade callers. If a Christ follower is in blatant rebellion against God, address it; if they continue to rebel, "deliver them over to Satan for the destruction of the flesh." Why? "So that his spirit may be saved in the day of the Lord." This is intended to bring repentance by letting them hit rock bottom. Restoration is always the goal. However, the response is different for people outside the church who don't profess to love God. Why would they live their lives according to the laws of a God they don't love or believe in?

Next, Paul doesn't forbid lawsuits against other believers; he just says there's a better way to handle disputes: Find someone in the church wise enough to make peace amid the chaos. If you can't find that person, maybe it's better to accept being wronged instead of to fight for what's yours. He also lists types of people who won't inherit the kingdom; we've all been on this list at least once. Paul says that's who we *were*—people whose identities were rooted in sin; but now we aren't just sinners, we're saints who sin. We're God's children, who bear His name and His Spirit. He changes our identity!

When Paul speaks about marriage, singleness, widowhood, and divorce, he distinguishes between his opinion and God's instruction. He believes his opinions are endorsed by the Holy Spirit, but he's humble enough to be openhanded. Both marriage and singleness are gifts given by God, and the one who gives the gift is the one who chooses what to give. In marriage, you don't own your own body; this unity reflects what happens in our relationship with Christ. For those married to unbelievers, Paul says stick it out so that the unbelieving spouse and children can be set apart to live in a space where God is honored and regarded. He says, "We don't know how it'll turn out, but give it a shot!" In Paul's opinion, marriage is good but singleness is better. We find freedom in accepting the positions God has given us. If at some point He gives us something different, we'll accept that too. We don't hold tightly to anything. It frees us up to focus on eternal things.

Finally, new believers who still worship idols are eating food they've sacrificed in worship to those idols. Experienced believers eat the same food but with a different aim and perspective. That means the new believers might misunderstand their motives and see it as an endorsement of idolatry. Paul tells the seasoned believers, "You're right, but being right has made you arrogant. You may not be sinning by eating the food, but you're sinning by not loving your brother while eating the food."

TODAY'S GOD SHOT

"There is one God, the Father, from whom are all things and for whom we exist, and one Lord, Jesus Christ, through whom are all things and through whom we exist" (8:6). All things are from Him, through Him, and for Him. He starts it all and sustains and completes it all, and it all points back to Him. He's the source, supply, and goal. And He's where the joy is!

1 CORINTHIANS 9–11

Some Corinthians discredit Paul or refuse to view him as an apostle since he doesn't receive money from them. But he says, "A paycheck isn't what makes me an apostle. I'm an apostle because God appointed me." He has every right to receive support from them but has chosen to deny that right so they can't second-guess his motives—but it backfires on him. Essentially, he says, "You didn't hire me, so you can't fire me. I'm going to preach the gospel regardless." Paul is restricting his freedoms for their sake.

God's people have always struggled with idolatry, despite His presence, protection, and provision. Idolatry often leads them into sexual sin. In Numbers 25:1–9, God brought divine judgment on the people who rebelled against Him in that way. Paul urges them to turn from sexual sin and from grumbling and testing God. Whether our sins are subtle or drastic, they represent self-idolatry; they attempt to dethrone God and position us in His place. We're all capable of these sins, so we have to stay humble and on guard against them. If someone thinks they're above these sins, they're demonstrating the same kind of arrogance that is the very heart of these sins—an elevated view of self. Temptation will come to everyone, but when it shows up, so does the God-given power to resist it.

Then Paul addresses food offered to idols again, expounding more here since he's talking about idolatry. The Corinthians go to pagan temples, hang around after the sacrifices, and eat the food. It's a potential snare for them, an easy first step into idolatry, because false religions aren't just made-up ideas; pagan gods are demons. But what if they're eating food sacrificed to idols in someone's home and not at a pagan temple? Paul says, "If no one mentions where it came from, eat up! But if they tell you and you still eat it, they're going to think you're okay with idolatry, so you should refuse to eat it." In the temple scenario the problem is idolatry, and in the house scenario the problem is the other person's mind-set. The problem is never the food itself. These are specific scenarios in Corinth, but they potentially have broader application.

Paul addresses some touchy topics in chapter 11, but they were less touchy then because of the culture. He compares marriage to our relationship with God and with the church. It's helpful to remember that Paul continually lays down his freedoms and doesn't argue for his own rights so that he can let his humility lay the groundwork for him to share the gospel. Remembering the character of Paul and God will help us view this rightly. He unpacks the authority structure in marriage, which is a lot like the authority structure of the Trinity. Anything without a head is dead. *Glory* means "to give the right opinion of something," and Paul says this is what's happening with men as the head. Women are made in the image of God, giving them equal value to men, but value and roles are different things. He isn't discrediting or diminishing women—men and women are mutually dependent. In their Roman culture, pagan men who pray in pagan temples cover their heads, so he says to be set apart. Married women typically wear veils to cover their heads—similar to wearing a wedding ring—but some married women are taking off their veils, which is problematic here because of their abundant sexual sin.

The churches often meet in the homes of the rich, but the poor have to work long days, and then by the time they arrive, all the food is gone. Jesus said to eat the bread and drink the cup in remembrance of Him, but it seems they're eating and drinking but have forgotten Him and His command to love others. They should examine themselves before taking Communion—do they really understand that it's about the unity of His body who partakes in His body?

TODAY'S GOD SHOT

God won't let us be tempted beyond what He'll empower us to resist (10:12–13). In other words, when Satan gives you temptation, God will give you the strength to say no, so lean into His strength. This isn't about having the strength in ourselves; it's about trusting Him to provide us with what we need to obey Him. He is our escape hatch in every temptation! And He's where the joy is!

1 CORINTHIANS 12–14

Paul addresses problems the Corinthian church experiences in their meetings, beginning with a lack of information about the Spirit's gifts. A common misunderstanding about spiritual gifts is that they're like a personality assessment. But since these gifts are given by the Spirit, they only show up when we get the Spirit. Our natural gifts can benefit the church too, but they differ from our supernatural gifts. A good way to know your spiritual gifts is to ask others how the church is being built up by your presence. We can also ask God to give us gifts we don't have, which means our gifts can change over time, but they're given by God and the giver is the one who chooses what to give.

Some believe the gifts that are signs of the Spirit's indwelling were only used in the first century to give validity to God's work in the early church. This is called cessationism. Others believe these gifts are alive and well today, though there are nuanced beliefs about how certain gifts should be used. This is called continuationism. This gifts list isn't exhaustive; others are listed in Romans 12:6–8, Ephesians 4:11–16, and 1 Peter 4:10–11. However, Paul does seem to give a ranking, referring to the "higher gifts." The Corinthians were fixated primarily on tongues. Paul mentions it last in his apparent hierarchy. He encourages them to use their gifts with love as the motivation. Otherwise, all their good deeds are multiplied by zero or are *harmful* to the body. He describes love and says it'll outlast everything—even faith and hope. When our faith is made manifest, faith won't need to exist—it'll be proven. And when our hopes are fulfilled, we won't have to hope for those things anymore—they'll be realities. We'll be faithless and hopeless. But love will remain.

Some say Paul also references a "prayer language," since it seems to be directed toward God, not others, and it seems to be unintelligible, whereas the languages in Acts 2 were clearly understood. He wants them all to speak in tongues, but not as much as he wants them to prophesy,

For more information on today's reading, see thebiblerecap.com/links.

because prophecy holds greater value for the church. He also gives instructions on interpreters, whom some believe to be bilingual people who can verify the message and others believe to be people God has revealed the message to. Paul speaks in tongues more than anyone—which may or may not just mean he knows more languages than others—but says that prophecy is his preference. Moses said something similar in Numbers 11:29.

There's debate over the final verses of this chapter. Some say this passage means women shouldn't be allowed to speak in tongues or prophesy in church, but in 1 Corinthians 11:5 and 11:13, he said women *can* prophesy and pray in the church, so this can't be forbidden. Some say his words apply to all churches, and others say he's addressing specific problems at Corinth, possibly related to their Greco-Roman culture. It's possible that the women were only allowed *outside* the meeting area and were calling to their husbands inside to see what was being said. If that's what was happening, you can see how it'd be disruptive. So Paul wants them to hold their questions for later; it might be like asking people not to talk on the phone during church. The Corinthian women also don't treat their husbands with honor and respect—something God calls both parties to do—so Paul addresses it. When we take in everything he says about women in the church, his words seem to be more about creating peace and unity than about prohibiting women from talking. Elsewhere in Scripture, he affirms the gifts of women in serving the church. Priscilla is one of the founders of this particular church, and Paul affirms her as his co-laborer (Romans 16:3).

TODAY'S GOD SHOT

God loves diversity and works in and through us to display more angles, textures, and colors of His glory. And because He's efficient, it not only glorifies Him, but it benefits us too. Through God's work in us, we actually enhance each other's lives. He isn't building a one-dimensional kingdom where we all look and act the same. He gives His diverse body unique gifts to offer back to Him and connects them all in an orderly fashion like only He can do. He's where the joy is!

1 CORINTHIANS 15–16

Some Corinthians don't believe in the resurrection of anyone, much like the Sadducees. Paul confronts them with evidence that Jesus rose, including five hundred eyewitnesses, many of whom are still alive at the time. It's almost like Paul is saying, "If you don't believe me, go ask them!" Christ's resurrection is the most important thing about our faith. If Jesus didn't have victory over death, we'd be hopeless. But since He did, that hope permeates every area of our lives. And time will reveal whether we truly believe and have that hope. If God has given us new hearts, then He's given us His Spirit, and His Spirit reminds us of the truth and seals us for the day of redemption. So if we truly belong to God, He'll finish what He started in us. But those who only *affirm* the truth without it taking root believe in vain—like the rocky soil and the thorny soil (Mark 4:1–20).

If Jesus wasn't raised from the dead, we're still in bondage to sin and there's no afterlife and no hope. But Christ's resurrection brings a hope Paul compares to firstfruits. This is a nod to the Feast of Firstfruits (Leviticus 23:10), which praises God for the first harvest of the season because it represents a greater harvest ahead; they trust there's more coming. In the same way, Jesus's resurrection foreshadows the resurrection of all God's kids into eternal life. Adam brought death, but Jesus ("the second Adam" or "the last Adam") brings life. He'll put all His enemies under His feet, He'll destroy death itself, and He'll reign forever.

Paul's reference to being baptized on behalf of the dead can be misleading if we don't treat this according to the rules of Scripture interpretation: (a) This is descriptive, not prescriptive, and Paul never endorses it; (b) since this isn't referenced anywhere else in Scripture, we don't scream where Scripture whispers; and (c) it's unclear what's happening, and we don't build a doctrine or a practice around something unclear. Some say they're washing dead bodies as a kind of baptism; others say the living are serving as baptism stand-ins for the dead. Either way, Paul makes his point: "If you don't believe in the resurrection, why are you doing that?"

The Corinthians who don't believe in the afterlife are wandering off into sin. One of the wicked side effects of disbelieving the resurrection is that people feel like their actions don't matter. Paul says, "Don't deceive yourselves. This life isn't all there is." To help them out, Paul describes their resurrection bodies but without painting a full picture: They're powerful, glorified, imperishable, distinct. Our resurrection bodies are more glorious than our earthly bodies, because the image of God isn't tainted by our sin nature.

Paul asked the churches to collect money to support the oppressed believers in Jerusalem. Since Paul has them collect this money on the first day of each week, some scholars say this indicates that the church now meets on Sundays to commemorate resurrection day, instead of the traditional Jewish meeting day (the Sabbath, Saturday).

Paul will visit when he finishes his time in Ephesus, but he wants to stay for a while since there are lots of enemies of the gospel there. In the meantime he's sending Timothy, who has two strikes against him. First, he's Paul's mentee, and the tension between Paul and Corinth means they may resist him. Second, he's young. But Paul says to offer him honor and help. Paul wants Apollos to visit too, but he resists, likely because of the tension.

TODAY'S GOD SHOT

Paul has a right view of himself and of God. He doesn't deserve to serve God as an apostle, but this scenario reveals God's great mercy. He doesn't punish Paul for his wicked past; instead He gives him a vital role in building the church. Paul's unworthiness doesn't call the shots; God's calling calls the shots. Paul jumps at the chance to serve the kingdom and sees God working through him: "I worked harder than any of them, though it was not I, but the grace of God that is with me" (15:10). He knows his good works were done by grace-driven effort, not Paul-driven effort. God is the source, supply, and goal. And He's where the joy is!

2 CORINTHIANS 1–4

In Paul's last letter to Corinth, he promised to visit, asked them to collect money for the needy believers in Jerusalem, and confronted many of their sin patterns and errant beliefs. After that letter, some people repented of things he addressed, while others rebelled all the more. For some who rebelled, God used his subsequent visit to turn their hearts back to Him. Paul writes this letter in response to the situation.

Paul and his traveling companions endured many trials in Asia, and they despaired of life itself. But God carried them through, and Paul hopes God will continue to do so. He asks them to pray for him and says that it helps. Prayer isn't pointless; it engages with God and it encourages believers. Even though he wasn't able to visit them when he planned, it wasn't because he didn't want to. He knew his last letter caused tension, and he likely wanted to leave time for the Spirit to work in their hearts instead of coming to them in the midst of hurt feelings and grief. He wanted even the sinners to feel loved and comforted so Satan couldn't use it as an opportunity for division. He wants beauty and unity, even though Christ can be divisive. He says Christians are God's perfume spritzer—we're the bottle, Christ is the perfume. Some people don't like the fragrance of Christ; they'll cover their noses and leave the room. But others will want to get it for themselves!

Other speakers have started coming to the church, and they're rich and flashy and they come with letters of recommendation. The not-so-wealthy Corinthians are impressed. Some church members question Paul's legitimacy as an apostle. He loves the locals and doesn't want them to be led astray by false teachers, so he has to disprove their claims of his inadequacy and defend himself. He says, "You are my letter of recommendation! I planted this church." But even then, he's quick to point out that all his worth and his only sufficiency come from God. Through God's power, Paul brings the ministry of life—which is far

For more information on today's reading, see thebiblerecap.com/links.

more glorious than the law, the ministry of death. The law can't solve sin, it can only name it. The ministry of death was glorious and necessary in its own right, but the ministry of life and grace far outshines it. But Paul knows some won't connect with it, no matter how powerful and bold his words are, because their hearts are covered with a veil only God can remove. Some people—possibly other itinerant speakers—don't understand what Paul is doing and don't believe the gospel. Paul says their eyes are veiled to the truth. Satan has blinded them to the glory of Christ; Satan is referred to as the "god of this world" here, but that doesn't mean he's in charge of the world. We've seen multiple times that he's absolutely subject to God's authority. This likely points to the fact that the world follows his ways. He does have some level of power here, but only as it applies to accomplishing God's ultimate will.

Those who carry Christ carry a light in them that God shined into their hearts. And that light lives in fragile vessels—human bodies—but you can't kill light. Many things can hurt the vessel, but the light will remain unscathed. In fact, every chip and crack is just another way for the light to spread. Paul and his traveling companions are being physically tortured, but the light is spilling out all around them—to prisoners, jail guards, governors, Jews, and Gentiles. He can't help but speak what he believes; and if it ends up being the death of them, it'll be for the life of others. His body is being destroyed in persecution, but his spirit is being renewed as he looks past the afflictions to the eternal.

TODAY'S GOD SHOT

"For God, who said, 'Let light shine out of darkness,' has shone in our hearts to give the light of the knowledge of the glory of God in the face of Jesus Christ" (4:6). God shone in our dark hearts, our hearts of stone, and He gave us new hearts of flesh. He drenched them with His light, which Paul calls "the knowledge of the glory of God in the face of Jesus Christ." *The knowledge of the glory of God* means "to know and see God rightly," to see Him in the face of Jesus. Are you growing in the knowledge of the glory of God as you behold Him? He's where the joy is!

2 CORINTHIANS 5–9

Yesterday Paul compared our bodies to jars of clay, and today he continues his third letter to the Corinthians by comparing them to tents. These tents need an eternal mansion around them—our resurrection bodies—because our tents suffer from the elements and from attackers. God says that'll happen someday. In fact, inside these tents lives the mansion maker: the Spirit. And He's preparing us for the mansion!

In the midst of all Paul's trials, it's not death he's wishing for—it's eternal life. He'll either be alive here or alive with Christ, because for anyone with the Spirit, there's no such thing as death. There are a few views on this particular timeline in a person's life, but the prominent view is this: Paul and all believers who die before Christ's return (which may also include us someday) will live in an "unclothed" state (5:4)—their spirits are disembodied and they're with God, but they haven't yet been given resurrection bodies, because that won't happen until Jesus returns to earth. For now, Paul is "away from the body and at home with the Lord." His body is no longer a tent, but he won't have his mansion body until after Christ returns. In the meantime, his spirit is with God in heaven. We'll all appear before the Judge, who in this instance is Jesus Himself. The Father has handed judgment over to Him. Many scholars say this particular judgment is about the rewards that God will give believers based on their lives. There's no greater reward than Jesus Himself, so anything else we receive will pale in comparison. Paul's words should give us pause, but they should always point us back to Jesus, not ourselves. If we're too busy being fearful, we'll lose sight of our calling to be ministers of reconciliation. God reconciled us to Himself through Christ—He ended the hostility between us—and it's our job to point others toward that reconciliation.

He urges them to receive his message with open hearts. When our hearts love the right things, we won't fall prey to loving the wrong things.

For more information on today's reading, see thebiblerecap.com/links.

If we love Christ most of all, it'll be easier to follow his instructions: "Do not be unequally yoked with unbelievers." Paul gives this as a warning for those who aren't yet married and compares it to joining yourself with the enemy. These words are probably hard for many of his readers to hear, especially in their worldly culture. But God has used Paul's rebukes to produce grief and repentance in them. Godly grief—like the kind Peter had—leads to repentance and life, whereas worldly grief, like Judas had, leads to death.

Paul asked all the churches to collect money every Sunday as a relief fund for Christians in Jerusalem. The Macedonian church was abundantly generous, but the Corinthians have either forgotten or ignored this. Paul urges them to be generous. God was generous toward them—Jesus became poor so that they might gain spiritual wealth. And now, by comparison, they have physical wealth too, which he encourages them to share with other believers who are in need. He isn't forcing them to give but says those who give will be blessed in return—and possibly even in ways that are better and longer lasting than money. God will provide everything they need, whether financial or spiritual! In fact, God is interested in giving to people who give: "You will be enriched in every way to be generous in every way, which through us will produce thanksgiving to God." We're blessed in order to bless so that God might be praised. We're conduits of His provision and praise!

TODAY'S GOD SHOT

In their extreme trials, there's one thing they won't stop talking about: their persistent joy! They were "sorrowful, yet always rejoicing" (6:10). Paul says, "In all our affliction, I am overflowing with joy" (7:4). And "In a severe test of affliction, their abundance of joy and their extreme poverty have overflowed in a wealth of generosity on their part" (8:2). Trials have a way of revealing what matters—not only *to* us but *through* us. The world and its trials may crack our jars of clay, but that's how the light gets out. In all our trials, we have the light and we have the joy, because He's where the joy is!

2 CORINTHIANS 10–13

Paul plans to visit Corinth again and wants them to deal with their sin first so he won't have to have any hard conversations. In light of all the lies that have been circulating about him, he says he won't fight back with actual weapons, but he'll wage spiritual war via prayer, faith, truth, and obedience. Through the power of the Spirit, he'll bring the truth to light, punish disobedience, and tear down the enemy's lies about him and his ministry. He hopes they'll all be changed by it and that their faith will grow as a result—because when a person's faith grows, the spread of the gospel grows. As believers grow in depth, the gospel grows in width.

Then, while talking to the most wicked and debauchery-filled church in Scripture, Paul says he wants to present them as "a pure virgin to Christ." The gospel of Christ takes sinners and makes them clean. In the meantime, though, there are many people trying to entice them with distortions and perversions of the gospel. Paul is upset about it and says, "I'm not as impressive as the popular speakers, but I'm preaching a better message. That may sound prideful, but it has nothing to do with me; it's because I preach the truth! These so-called super apostles are servants of Satan!"

Paul has gone to great lengths to prove his intentions with the Corinthians—in fact, he's being fully financially supported by other churches so he can minister to them for free. By contrast, the super apostles are taking advantage of them—taking their money and spiritually abusing them while lying to them. Meanwhile, the list of what Paul has endured is astonishing. He's living fully committed to the gospel of Christ, and his life looks like a tragedy. The super apostles use this against him, basically saying, "You don't want to be like that guy, do you?" But Paul continues to embrace everything God has called him to, which includes beatings, imprisonments, near-death experiences, lashings, being stoned, shipwrecks, dangers, being robbed, toil, hardships, sleeplessness, hunger, thirst, freezing, exposure, and torture. But the thing that caps off his list is his persistent love and ache for the people he ministers to.

Then he tells a personal story of a vision from fourteen years ago—which was ten years after his conversion experience on the road to Damascus. He doesn't know if this vision or revelation happened in the spiritual realm or if it was physical. In the vision, he went to heaven. He calls it "the third heaven," which reflects the cultural language and viewpoint of the time: the first heaven is where birds fly, the second heaven is where the stars are, and the third heaven is where God dwells. "He heard things that cannot be told, which man may not utter." Some say this means he's forbidden to speak what he hears, but others say there are no words to describe it. With this incredible gift comes a lifelong trial—he calls it a "thorn in his flesh" and a "messenger from Satan" (see Day 329). God allows this in order to keep him humble. He's trading physical comfort for a greater knowledge of God. Three times he begs God to take it away, but God answers his prayer with a no. He won't take the thorn away, but He'll pour out grace to sustain him through this lifelong trial. Paul's weakness is a great canvas to display God's strength.

Paul reminds them of his upcoming visit and that he doesn't want to have to rebuke anyone. He wants to see a transformation in them. He says, "Examine yourselves, to see whether you are in the faith. Test yourselves. Or do you not realize this about yourselves, that Jesus Christ is in you?—unless indeed you fail to meet the test!" (13:5). A test implies a result. Paul implies we can *know* if we have a relationship with God. It's the most important question we can ask ourselves.

TODAY'S GOD SHOT

"I will boast all the more gladly of my weaknesses, so that the power of Christ may rest upon me" (12:9). The phrase "so that" is doing a lot of work here. Paul will boast in his weakness *in order for* him to access the power of Christ. Merely speaking of Christ's sufficiency has the effect of strengthening us to endure trials! Praising Him strengthens us. Blessed be the name of the Lord. He's where the joy is!

ROMANS 1–3

A few years ago, Rome's governor banished the Jews from Italy. They're allowed to return, but now the church looks dramatically different—the Gentiles have diluted their Jewish culture, causing a lot of division and frustration. Paul has seen this problem everywhere, so he writes to address it with this new group of people, and as always, the gospel is his solution. He addresses his letter to all in Rome who are loved by God and called to be saints—every Christ follower from every culture and ethnicity—and says Christ gives them all the gifts of grace, obedience, faith, and apostleship.

Paul preaches the gospel to anyone who'll listen and trusts it'll save all who believe it. Everyone needs to hear it because everyone is born into a fallen world. Some have even resigned themselves to the fallenness. God has made the truth obvious—that there's a Creator in charge of all of this—but they ignore the truth and live life on their own terms, suppressing the truth. They know God but don't honor or thank Him. Their lack of humility and gratitude adds to the hardness of their hearts, catapulting them further down the trajectory of disbelief and disobedience. Instead of worshipping the Creator, they worship the things He made—humans and animals—as they distort worship, sexuality, and creation. God responds with inaction. He doesn't grant them repentance; they feel no guilt over their actions—in fact, they celebrate them. This is God's passive wrath. It lets people continue in sin unchecked.

While believers in Christ will never experience any version of God's wrath—passive or active—it's important to remember that we've all been on or currently are on the list from 1:29–30. We deserve death and separation from God, but He grants us grace instead. Remembering that keeps us humble. We can't grow prideful, as if we did anything to earn grace; that's legalism and moralism. Paul says, "When you look down on others, you act like you don't do these things too, but you do!

For more information on today's reading, see thebiblerecap.com/links.

So don't abuse God's kindness in not giving you over to your sins. His grace isn't a free pass for sinning; it's a change agent. If you miss that, you prove that you don't have a new heart after all, in which case the same judgment is coming for you." This message is probably directed primarily toward his Jewish readers who may be relying on the law and the old covenant to keep them in good standing with God. It's probably easy for them to look at the Gentiles with disdain. So Paul says, "Whether you're a Jew or a Gentile, you'll see God's righteous judgment in response to your heart."

When Paul talks about obeying the law, he's likely referring to all 613 Old Testament laws, which Jesus summed up as vertical laws and horizontal laws: Love God and love people. Paul says the Gentiles, who don't even have these 613 laws, are proving by their actions that they love and honor God—and that kind of love only comes from a transformed heart. He assumes his Jewish listeners might be wondering, *What's the point of having the law if you don't* have *to have the law to know and love God?* Paul says, "The law revealed God to us and made us carriers of the promise and the covenant. It revealed our need for God's great rescue. It shows us so much about God and ourselves!" Then he imagines his Jewish readers asking, "Is there any advantage to being an ethnic Jew instead of a Gentile?" He says, "No, there isn't. Being Jewish doesn't protect you from God's righteous judgment. We're all under the curse of sin and need God's rescue, and Jesus is the only Savior for all ethnicities. His great gift of faith and salvation is adjacent to a changed heart that makes us *want* to obey and honor God and His law."

TODAY'S GOD SHOT

"All have sinned and fall short of the glory of God, and are justified by his grace as a gift, through the redemption that is in Christ Jesus" (3:23–24). *All* of these things are gifts—the grace, the faith, the justification, the redemption. He gives the best gifts! Everything we need and everything we didn't know we needed. He gives it all. And He's where the joy is!

ROMANS 4–7

The church in Rome is diverse, but Paul's letter primarily addresses issues pertaining to the Christians who are ethnic Jews. He opens by continuing his point from yesterday: "Abraham was the first Jew, and even he was declared righteous because of his faith in YHWH, not because he kept the law. In fact, the law didn't even exist for 430 more years! So how did he get his saving faith? By being circumcised? No, his faith preceded his circumcision. If he had to do something to receive the faith, then it wasn't a free gift—it was something he had to earn. So if he received righteousness and faith as an uncircumcised man, then the same thing can happen for the Gentiles." He wants them to embrace the Gentiles as Abraham's offspring, as God's family. Though Jesus hadn't been born yet and Abraham didn't know the particulars—Jesus's incarnation, crucifixion, and resurrection—he responded to what he knew of YHWH. And according to YHWH, who exists outside of time, even though Jesus hadn't been born when Abraham died, Jesus had already died on the cross before the world was made. It was always the plan.

Being justified (declared righteous) in Christ ends the hostility between us and God. Our sin is the problem, but when our sins are covered—past, present, and future—we have good standing with the Father. And because of that, we can rejoice even in our sufferings. Suffering produces endurance, which we'll need because suffering always lasts longer than we want it to. If we never had to suffer, we'd be insufferable. But as we suffer, God develops character in us, which leads to hope—and not just hope in anything, but hope in the glory of God. God is being glorified and made known in our suffering. God can be trusted with our suffering, just as He can be trusted with our sin.

Jesus came to set right what was destroyed by God's enemies and set in motion by Adam, who consigned all to death. Jesus, the second Adam, came to bring life. It doesn't seem like one man could accomplish that—but it isn't a one-to-one trade. An imperfect man could die to pay for his own sins, but what about a perfect God-Man? How many sinful humans can be covered by the blood of a perfect God? As many as accept it. "By the one man's obedience the many will be made righteous." Many! You're one of the many. And because His blood covers you, you can't sin your way out of it. "Where sin increased, grace abounded all the more" (5:20). In other words, if your sin is a valley and His grace is a mountain, you could push the mountain into the valley and it'd still be a mountain. But His grace is no reason to continue in sin. We may struggle, but we're no longer enslaved to that struggle. By the Spirit's power in us, we're continually killing off the old self. It may be easy to fall back into our old patterns, but sin isn't worth it: "What fruit were you getting at that time from the things of which you are now ashamed?" The fruit of sin brings shame. The fruit of righteousness, on the other hand, is sanctification and eternal life.

All of this could make it seem like Paul hates the law, but he says it's helpful—it taught him what sin is. We need to know we're sinners in need of a Savior. But as sinners, we want to push back on boundaries and laws. So while the law helps us, it also provokes our pride. That's one reason the law can never be an end unto itself—it invites more problems than it could ever solve.

Paul lives in the struggle between the old self and the new self, between the flesh and the Spirit. In those circumstances he looks past his surface desires to see what his heart, not his flesh, really wants. What is his true desire, the one that will last? The other desire will be fruitless and produce shame. He digs down to find what's in his inner being—the part of him that delights in God.

TODAY'S GOD SHOT

Jesus our Lord was "delivered up for our trespasses and raised for our justification" (4:25). Not only does Christ's death—not our works— save us, but our sins aren't counted against us! We got grace and mercy. We got forgiveness and adoption. We got our sins erased and our lives restored! Not just the absence of punishment but the presence of blessing. What a Savior! He's where the joy is!

ROMANS 8–10

Those who have received Christ's deliverance will never be condemned! The new Spirit we've received wars against our old flesh, so we must set our mind on the things of the Spirit, choosing wisely what we think about because our thoughts become our actions. The Spirit empowers us to do this, but the lost are helpless to fight sin with anything besides more sin. They fight gluttony with vanity or fear with control, but sin still wins. That isn't victory and it isn't freedom. But God's kids have His Spirit as the sign of our adoption into His family. And not only are we God's children, but we're also coheirs with Jesus!

In the meantime, we live in a broken world that longs for redemption. The Spirit helps and prays for us as we wait, always praying for things that align with the Father's will, which means His requests will always be granted. The verses that follow tell us how we became believers and how we came to inherit such great kindness from God: He foreknew us, predestined us to be His kids, called us, justified us, and glorified us. And because God has done all that work in our lives, nothing and no one can stand against it. Jesus is praying for us too. In Him, we're more than conquerors against distress, persecution, and danger. How do you do *more* than conquer? By turning your enemies into your servants, making what tried to kill you serve you—which is exactly what God says He does for His kids (8:28).

Paul wishes everyone knew this kind of freedom and love. He aches for the Jews who don't believe in Jesus. They have everything that points them to Jesus—covenants, patriarchs, laws—but they can't see or believe it. Being an ethnic Jew isn't the same thing as being a child of Abraham. This is probably a hard concept for his Jewish readers to grasp, so he compares it to two other stories they're familiar with: (1) Abraham had Ishmael first, but God's promise landed on his second son, Isaac; and (2) Esau was born first, so he should've had the inheritance, but through

For more information on today's reading, see thebiblerecap.com/links.

a series of events it was handed over to Jacob, the second born. God's promise hasn't failed—it's just distributed differently than people expect. Like with salvation, none of this is based on anything they've done—God declared this plan before they were born.

He knows this will be hard for his readers, so he says, "God isn't being mean or unfair. He's incapable of injustice. While we may question God's actions, the reality is we're the pottery and He's the potter. He can do whatever He wants with us. He made us. None of us deserve anything from Him except punishment, death, and separation. The fact that He chooses to adopt any of us into His family is astonishing. That displays His great mercy and kindness. And for those who aren't adopted into His family, His wrath and power are displayed. God seems to delight in doing the unexpected, calling people into His family who were outcasts, calling them 'beloved.'"

Some Gentiles who don't even have the law have been adopted into God's family, while Jews who've spent their lives trying to live up to it perfectly have not been. They obey the law to attain self-righteousness, which never works. Nevertheless, Paul reminds them of God's promise through the prophet Isaiah: He'll preserve a remnant from among Israel who'll love and follow Jesus, not the law. Paul longs for them to know God, not just His laws. They're zealous—just like Paul was in his terrorist days—but their zeal isn't based on knowing God. Zeal without knowledge is dangerous. He wants them to realize that salvation is surrendering and fully relying on what Christ has done, and it's available to anyone of any ethnicity. Because of this, Paul implores them to spread the knowledge of God.

TODAY'S GOD SHOT

Paul says we must share the gospel, because the people God is going to adopt into His family have to hear the news. We must go, share, and tell. And Paul models this well, going from country to country, enduring persecution, and writing letters—to those who love him and those who disagree with him—to spread the knowledge of God and the hope of the gospel. And God can give people the ears to hear it, so we must be the mouths to speak it. Spread the word that He's where the joy is!

ROMANS 11–13

Paul has focused on spreading the gospel to the Gentiles, so he addresses a question that may exist about ethnic Israel: Has God written them off? No! The elect among ethnic Israel have been preserved as a remnant, just like God did in Elijah's day. Those who know God will be preserved, but that divide falls along faith lines, not ethnic lines. God has never rejected His elect in the past, and that remains true in the present. They've been chosen by grace, but some received it and some didn't. And because God wants His kingdom to be full and diverse, their rejection is an opportunity to spread the gospel to the Gentiles. But even that is an opportunity to entice ethnic Israel back to God.

In John 15:1–11, Jesus said He's the vine and we're the branches, and Paul continues this metaphor. The original branches are ethnic Israel; those who rejected Christ and proved to be dead branches, like Judas, were trimmed off. In the vacancy, God the gardener grafted in wild branches, Gentiles, making the vine lush and full. But Paul says, "Don't get boastful about this. You didn't graft yourself in or earn this. You're only here because of the Gardener's kindness." God's severity is displayed with those who are cut off, and His kindness is displayed with those who are grafted in. This metaphor may sound like it's possible to lose our salvation, but that's not the case. Consider Judas. He had the appearance of being a follower of Jesus, but his heart wasn't in it. God sees hearts and knows who really believes, and He makes His judgments based on that reality, cutting off the imposters. Theologians use two phrases to help distinguish and clarify this: *the church visible* and *the church invisible*. Judas was part of the church visible—what could be seen by human eyes. But he was cut off from the vine, since he didn't truly believe. Perseverance in the faith is what reveals our hearts over time. So it's never too late for anyone who has been cut off to be grafted back in!

For more information on today's reading, see \thebiblerecap.com/links.

God's plan is for many Jews to resist Him until all of the Gentiles have been reached, and then the hardening of the Jews will be brought to an end and He'll show them more mercy. He offers no details about how or when this will happen but says Jews will continue to be saved. There are a few perspectives on what it means that "all Israel" will be saved (11:26). Some say this refers to all believers, both Jew and Gentile, some say it means all Jewish people, for all time, but most say it refers to a vast number of Jews at some point in the future, when God brings the partial hardening to an end. Because we trust Him, we can offer ourselves and our lives to Him, resist getting caught up in the current of any culture, and seek His glory—and that's how we discern His will! And as a part of God's diverse family, we are both God-dependent and interdependent.

God is sovereign over authorities. Even through evil authorities who defy His ways, He's working out His plan, bending their evil back on their own heads, while preserving His people. No matter who's in charge, God can be trusted. Authorities are working out God's goodness toward His kids in the long run. As people who trust God, we should be subject to authorities even if we don't like or respect them (Titus 3:1; 1 Peter 2:13). God makes no commands about how to feel about their position—only how to *act* toward their position. In a body as diverse as this church in Rome—Jews, Gentiles, Pharisees, and former pagans—there's sure to be many opinions about local authorities, so Paul reminds them of the higher law: "Love your neighbor as yourself," which echoes the words of Christ (John 13:34). The time for complacency has ended; it's time to put to death the deeds of darkness and walk in the light!

TODAY'S GOD SHOT

"Oh, the depth of the riches and wisdom and knowledge of God! How unsearchable are his judgments and how inscrutable his ways!" (11:33). A god who can fully fit inside our tiny brains is no god at all. But our God is unsearchable. Yet in His generosity, He makes Himself knowable. We can always know Him better yet never quite plumb the depths of Him. What a glorious mystery! He's where the joy is!

ROMANS 14–16

Paul reminds us that there's room for different opinions and preferences in the body of Christ. Quarreling can provoke feelings of superiority and inferiority; it incites our flesh and promotes pride, bringing more division than unity. We should each follow the Spirit's guidance in our own convictions while also trusting Him to guide others—they're at a different part of the journey, and God is sovereign over their steps too. He's the one who upholds us and sustains our obedience. When it comes to the nonessentials of life—even the religious ones—Paul says it's better to agree to disagree than to argue for your point. The time we should be concerned with another believer's actions is when our actions are tripping them up. If we have to lay down rights and preferences for them, that's okay—love is a good reason to pivot. Peace doesn't naturally occur; we have to actively pursue it by disengaging from the flesh and engaging with the Spirit. In addition to peace, we should aim for mutual upbuilding.

When Paul says, "The faith that you have, keep between yourself and God" (14:22), it's not a call to be private about your faith. The word *keep* means "hold firmly"; this is a call to hold firmly to faith in God, to live our convictions, letting our faith show up in everything. Our faith must be personal, but never private.

The Old Testament exists to instruct us, encourage us, and give us hope: "Whatever was written in former days was written for our instruction, that through endurance and through the encouragement of the Scriptures we might have hope." The Hebrew Scriptures, Genesis to Malachi, are stacked with instruction, encouragement, and hope. Paul reiterates God's interest in our hopefulness in 15:13: "May the God of hope fill you with all joy and peace in believing, so that by the power of the Holy Spirit you may abound in hope." The Spirit brings us hope too—which makes sense, because He wrote the Scriptures!

For more information on today's reading, see thebiblerecap.com/links.

The Old Testament also contains God's promise to save the Gentiles. He has always wanted a diverse family, so Paul encourages them again to live in harmony with each other. Harmony means people are singing different notes—not the same note. A symphony is beautiful because people are playing different instruments and different parts, but in a way that works together to reveal the beauty of the song. Our harmony must be not only with each other, but also with Jesus, and our song points to the glory of God.

Paul also wants them to peaceably instruct each other. This is "mutual upbuilding," and it happens when we all aim to grow in wisdom and surround ourselves with wise people. We can learn not only from what God is teaching us, but from what He's teaching other people as well. Paul begins to close out his letter to the Roman church by letting them know he loves them and that he's heading to Jerusalem to deliver the financial support he's been collecting from the churches. But he hopes to visit later, on his way to Spain.

Paul's letter is probably being delivered to the church by Phoebe; he says to welcome her as a servant of the church and give her whatever she needs. The word used for *servant* is *diakonos*, also translated as *deacon*; so Phoebe was likely a deacon in one of the churches near Athens. He lists other men and women he wants them to greet, including Aquila and Priscilla, whom he says risked their lives for him, probably during the riots in Ephesus.

In closing, he warns them about people who do not serve and help the church, people who "deceive the hearts of the naïve." This short line points out that what we know informs our hearts. Knowledge helps protect us from deception.

TODAY'S GOD SHOT

"The God of peace will soon crush Satan under your feet" (16:20). In order to bring peace to any situation, you can't ignore chaos; you have to address it. God addresses the chaos of Satan and evil by crushing it. And we're participants in the battle God has won. *God* crushes Satan under *our* feet. He does the crushing, and He's the one who strengthens us (16:25) for it—making us strong, moving our feet, and crushing our enemy. He's where the joy is!

ACTS 20–23

Paul continues preaching through Europe and Asia, heading toward Jerusalem to deliver the financial support. While he's preaching in Troas, a man named Eutychus falls asleep and plummets three stories to his death. Paul raises him from the dead and goes on preaching until sunrise, before setting out again. The Spirit keeps reminding Paul that imprisonment and affliction await him. But God is the one who gave him this ministry, so Paul receives it even though it comes with persecution and trials. He expects to die soon. At their stop in Tyre, Paul gets a strange message from the people. Acts 20:22 says the Spirit is leading Paul to Jerusalem, but 21:4 says, "Through the Spirit they were telling Paul not to go on to Jerusalem." Is the Spirit contradicting Himself? Scholars say it's likely that the Holy Spirit has revealed to others what He revealed to Paul—that things won't go well for him in Jerusalem. However, the people receive this as a warning, not a fact, so they try to deter him from going. Paul, on the other hand, probably sees it as confirmation of what God has already revealed.

They stop in Caesarea, where Philip and his four unmarried prophetess daughters live. They're visited by the prophet Agabus, who does a sign-act showing Paul how he'll be bound and delivered to the Gentiles in Jerusalem. They beg Paul not to go, but this only serves as more confirmation. He knows he can't outrun God's plan; he heads to Jerusalem. Shortly after they arrive, Jacob (James) gives them good news—there are lots of Jews who believe there—and bad news—rumors about Paul are marring his reputation. Since the Jerusalem Council established that Gentiles don't have to convert to Judaism or obey Jewish laws, people are saying Paul told the Jews to disregard those laws too. Jacob has an idea to help Paul set things straight: There are four men who are under a vow (likely the Nazirite vow), and if Paul joins them in that vow, it'll show he's not opposed to Jews keeping Jewish traditions.

For more information on today's reading, see thebiblerecap.com/links.

Paul has always been willing to lay down his rights to advance the gospel, so he does it again here. But then some Jews spread rumors that he brought a Gentile into the temple, defiling it—an act punishable by death. They riot and beat him. A local leader arrests him because he has him confused with someone else, but when he realizes Paul is an educated Roman citizen, he lets him speak to the people. Paul speaks in Hebrew, recounting his story. They're listening until he says God told him to share the gospel with the Gentiles—then they demand he be killed. The leader wants to flog him, but they can't because he's a Roman citizen, so they interrogate him instead. While he's speaking, he accidentally disrespects the high priests and apologizes, practicing what he preached in his letters.

He realizes the crowd is part Pharisee, part Sadducee—groups that disagree about the resurrection of the dead. Paul crafts his response in a way that takes the focus off their problem with him and puts it on their problem with each other. The Pharisees take his side, and Paul is imprisoned for another night. God tells him, "You won't die here. You've got to tell Rome about Me first." Meanwhile, a team of people go on a hunger strike until someone kills Paul. His nephew tips him off and informs the tribune, who orders nearly half of Jerusalem's army to take Paul to Governor Felix in Caesarea.

TODAY'S GOD SHOT

God lined everything up from before Paul was born—just like He said—to work it all together so that the gospel is advanced. In order for Paul to be arrested and survive, he has to have dual citizenship, speak Hebrew and Greek, be a knowledgeable Pharisee, and even be mistaken for an Egyptian. He may be in prison, but his ministry hasn't been thwarted. He's not done preaching the gospel. And God has always been in every detail. He has infinite power, has an infinite attention span, and can handle every kind of complexity and nuance imaginable. God isn't just in the grand scheme of things; He's also in the tiny scheme of things. And in all the schemes of all the things, He's where the joy is!

ACTS 24–26

Today we pick up five days after Paul is delivered to Governor Felix in Caesarea. Authorities from Jerusalem have come to talk to Felix about Paul. Their lawyer and spokesman begins by flattering Felix before accusing Paul of starting riots and defiling the temple—neither of which he's done. Paul defends himself with the truth. He goes to great lengths to live with integrity and honor YHWH, including doing everything written in the Law and the Prophets (i.e., the Old Testament). Felix is familiar with Christianity, or "the Way," as Paul calls it, possibly because he lives in Caesarea among prominent evangelists like Philip. He wants to hear more from Paul, so he tells the Jerusalem authorities he'll make a decision later and sends them home. He tells the soldiers to keep Paul in prison but to be nice to him. In this day, prisons aren't required to care for you; you have to rely on family and friends for that, and sometimes prison guards prevent them from doing it.

Felix keeps calling Paul to talk to him about the Way, but it's never enough for him. He also hopes Paul will bribe him to get out of prison, but Paul maintains his integrity, sharing the gospel and obeying the rules. After two years Felix leaves office unexpectedly. History tells us he was kicked out of office because he couldn't keep peace between Jews and Gentiles. In order to make things less awkward with the Jews, he leaves Paul in prison. Festus takes over after Felix, and Paul's situation is one of the first things addressed when he takes office. While he's in Jerusalem, the authorities say, "Bring Paul to us so we can deal with this." They've hatched another plan to kill him. But Felix tells them to come to Caesarea instead. When they come and make their case against Paul, he maintains that he hasn't broken any laws—Jewish *or* Roman. Festus wants to keep peace with the Jews too and doesn't want to be evicted from office like Felix, so he offers to take Paul back to Jerusalem for trial. As a Roman citizen, Paul opts to appeal to Caesar instead. He wants to be elevated to a higher court, one that should in theory weigh more in his favor. Festus agrees.

A few days later, King Herod Agrippa II comes to town. While Governor Festus and King Agrippa are talking, Festus tells him the whole tale and Agrippa asks to hear Paul's side of the story. When they bring Paul before Agrippa and other prominent leaders, Festus introduces him by saying, "Everyone wants him to die, but I don't think he's done anything wrong. What should I do?" This feels reminiscent of Jesus's trials. Paul opens by asking the king to be patient with him as he tells his story about his days as a persecutor, followed by his conversion. Festus interrupts and says Paul is losing his mind. Paul has just given a beautiful explanation of the gospel, but Festus doesn't get it. As Paul wrote in 1 Corinthians 1:18, "The word of the cross is folly to those who are perishing."

Paul says, "I'm not crazy. And the king knows it too. You believe all of this don't you, King Agrippa?" Agrippa probably feels like he's on the spot, so he says, "I'm not ready to convert just yet, Paul. Give me some time." And Paul says, "As long as it takes. I want everyone here to know the God I know and love the God I love—my only hope is that it doesn't land you in prison too." They wrap things up, and the leaders privately agree that Paul is innocent and that if he hadn't appealed to Caesar, King Agrippa would've set him free.

TODAY'S GOD SHOT

"To this day I have had the help that comes from God" (26:22). Even in what seems like terrible timing, God is at work directing Paul's steps according to His plan. He's been through trial after trial, false accusations, character assassination, torture interrogations, beatings, shipwrecks, and imprisonment—and even in all of that, he sees God's help every step of the way. Paul has his eyes set on eternity and his heart set on God's glory, and help looks very different with that mind-set than if he were seeking his own good. He refuses to trade the temporary for the eternal. Even though the road is hard and lonely and frustrating, God equips him with all he needs. God is our helper, and He's where the joy is!

ACTS 27–28

Paul defended himself in front of King Agrippa and Governor Felix yesterday, and today we launch into the aftermath of that trial, where he's transported to Rome to appeal to Caesar. He's taken by sea, and the authorities allow his friends to travel with him, including the narrator, Luke. This is a ship with sails and anchors, not a little fishing boat; there are nearly three hundred people on board. The trip is taking longer than usual because they hit rough autumn winds and have to reroute. At this time of year, most shipping expeditions are halted because of bad weather. Paul has a bad feeling about it and says, "If we continue, we'll probably end up losing supplies and shipmates." We don't have any evidence that this is a message from God; Paul could be speaking from experience. Either way, they don't listen to him. A storm comes, and they start throwing cargo overboard, which probably includes exports like wheat. Next they throw tools and maybe even parts of the ship overboard. They feel hopeless and haven't eaten in days. Paul says, "I wish you had taken my words to heart. But hopefully now that you've seen me give good advice, you'll listen to me, especially because I have a message from an angel. He says we'll lose the boat, but we'll all live. So be encouraged!"

After two weeks, they're approaching land. They start making preparations to go to shore by dropping anchors from a dinghy, but Paul says to stay in the big boat instead. They listen to him and cut the dinghy free. The next day they shipwreck at the island of Malta. The soldiers plan to kill the prisoners before they're able to escape, but God has promised that no one will die, and He thwarts their plan via the compassion of Paul's guard, Julius. And just like God promised, they all survive. The Maltans are hospitable, making sure everyone is taken care of. As Paul is building a fire, a snake latches on to his hand. The locals are steeped in Greek mythology and see this as a sign that he's evil—a murderer, in fact.

For more information on today's reading, see thebiblerecap.com/links.

They're not wrong. They say the Greek goddess Justice is making sure he doesn't get away unpunished. Meanwhile, Paul demonstrates YHWH's supremacy by shaking off the snake. Since he shows no symptoms, they decide he's a god. He's invited to stay at the home of the chief official, and while he's there he heals the man's dad. This starts a domino effect with other sick people on the island, and Paul keeps healing them all.

After about three months, when the worst of winter has passed, they set sail for Rome, where they're greeted by friends. Paul gets to stay in his own cell—just him and his soldier. Because of his high status as a prisoner, he seems to be granted more freedoms than other prisoners. He calls a meeting of the local Jewish leaders in Rome and explains his situation. They say, "We haven't heard anything negative about you, but we have heard bad things about followers of Jesus." They plan for him to hold a seminar to fill them in on everything, and many people show up at his prison cell to hear the truth. He talks from morning until night. Some believe him and some don't—because it doesn't depend on how well we make our argument or present the facts; the Spirit has to open hearts to hear the truth. Paul points that out to them and says, "This is just like what Isaiah prophesied."

After attempting to share the message with Jews and being met mostly with rejection, he moves on to share the message with Gentiles. Even though he's primarily been called to minister to Gentiles, he always starts with the Jews.

TODAY'S GOD SHOT

God provided for Paul by appointing Julius to be his centurion—the one who would eventually come to listen to him and even spare his life. After seeing God speak to and through Paul and after watching Paul humbly encourage his enemies on the ship, survive a snakebite, and heal people for three months in Malta, he likely couldn't deny the truth. Perhaps God assigned Julius to be Paul's centurion not just for Paul's sake, but for Julius's sake too. God reaches across enemy lines to show mercy and save those who oppose Him. That's where He found all of us. He's where the joy is!

COLOSSIANS 1–4; PHILEMON 1

Paul wrote today's two letters while in prison (probably in Rome). The first letter is to a church at Colossae; he doesn't know them, but he's friends with one of their church leaders, who filled him in on some problems they're having. He wants them to know and love God with their minds, and he also wants their knowledge and love of God to bear fruit in their lives, empowered by His Spirit. He says, "I am filling up what is lacking in Christ's afflictions for the sake of his body, that is, the church" (Colossians 1:24). Since there's nothing lacking in what Jesus did on the cross (John 19:30), most scholars think Paul is saying his sufferings are a necessary part of fulfilling his role of spreading the gospel of Christ. The more they dig into knowing Christ, the less they'll be led astray by two primary deceptions: (1) local philosophies and idol worship, and (2) Jewish laws and traditions, which don't apply to them as Gentiles. Paul says, "You don't need to be circumcised. Your hearts were circumcised in Christ. You were dead and God made you alive and forgave your sins. That's all the evidence you need!" He warns against participating in spiritual and religious practices that aren't connected to Jesus, especially because some of those things have demonic connections.

When they died to those things, they were raised to a new life in Christ. He says to disconnect from earthly things: sexual immorality, impurity, passion, evil desire, covetousness, idolatry, anger, wrath, malice, slander, obscene talk, and lies. Instead, he reminds them that they're God's kids and calls them to engage with the things of God: compassion, kindness, humility, meekness, patience, forbearance, forgiveness, love, peace, thankfulness, and the words of Christ. This will impact the way they live in their homes. In this culture, the man is king of his domain, and everyone else is treated as lesser. But he tells husbands to be loving and gentle, and he reminds fathers not to discourage their children. He tells servants to act with honor and tells masters to treat them with

For more information on today's reading, see thebiblerecap.com/links.

honor. Bondservice was designed as a mutually beneficial arrangement where someone could pay off debt and have their needs met, but some masters abused the arrangement. Paul wants to make sure that those who are followers of Christ treat everyone with dignity and honor regardless of position.

Paul writes his letter to Philemon on behalf of Onesimus, who is like a son to him. Onesimus had been a bondservant or slave to Philemon until he stole from Philemon and escaped. But Onesimus has since converted to Christianity and become an assistant to Paul. While Paul would love to keep Onesimus around, he knows the better thing to do is to send him back to Philemon and aim for restoration between them, begging him to welcome Onesimus back not as a slave, but as an equal—a brother in Christ. He offers to pay any remaining debt Onesimus has—just like Christ did with our debts.

TODAY'S GOD SHOT

Colossians 1:15–20 is a beautiful description of Christ: "He is the image of the invisible God." If we want to see what the Father is like, we look to Christ; He reveals God—"the firstborn of all creation." The word *firstborn* is a declaration of His authority over all creation, *not* an indication that He was created; He has always existed. "For by him all things were created, in heaven and on earth, visible and invisible, whether thrones or dominions or rulers or authorities—all things were created through him and for him." He made everything and everything serves His purposes. "And he is before all things, and in him all things hold together." Not only did He make everything, but He sustains it all. "He is the head of the body, the church. He is the beginning, the firstborn from the dead, that in everything he might be preeminent." Jesus rules over everything, even death. There isn't an atom in all of creation over which He doesn't reign. "For in him all the fullness of God was pleased to dwell." He is God. Fully. "And through him to reconcile to himself all things, whether on earth or in heaven, making peace by the blood of his cross." Jesus brings the fullness of His deity to the cross, and its impact echoes through all of His creation, bringing restoration to all things! He's where the joy is!

EPHESIANS 1–6

Scholars say Paul may have written this as a mass letter to lots of churches in the area, which could be why it doesn't address any specific problems but instead offers general encouragement and vision casting. Paul reminds them that they were chosen by God before He made the world and that reconciliation has always been His plan, even before things fell apart. God gave His kids an inheritance with Christ, and the Spirit sealed the deal. Paul gives an overview of the past, present, and future of every believer. We were dead in our sins, slaves to our flesh, doing whatever it wanted. By nature, we were children of wrath, just like everyone else. We weren't especially good or moral, but then God intervened and made us alive in Christ, raising us from the dead. And that's not the end of His kindness to us; it's just the beginning. He'll keep being kind to us forever!

A few of the gifts He gives us are grace, salvation, and faith: "By grace you have been saved through faith. And this is not your own doing; it is the gift of God, not a result of works, so that no one may boast" (2:8–9). And now we're living out the good works God prepared beforehand for us to do. God isn't a haphazard creator; He's intentional and thoughtful. He put purpose and love into His design, and our good works are part of what He planned for us. For Gentiles, the reminder is even more intense. Paul essentially says, "Not only were you far from God because of your sins, but you didn't even have proximity to His covenant promises. God's people weren't allowed to go near you. He showed great mercy to come and get you." The Jews have heard this reminder for millennia too. And when God drew both people groups near, He did two simultaneous acts of reconciliation: He reconciled His kids to Himself and His kids to each other, "killing the hostility."

God's inclusion of the Gentiles was a shock to both Jews and Gentiles, even though God mentioned it all throughout the Old Testament.

For more information on today's reading, see thebiblerecap.com/links.

Paul knows it's a mystery that God chose anyone, including him. He urges them to be humble and use their gifts to serve the church. Serving will help mature them in the faith. He calls them to live differently and gives examples of ways God's Spirit transforms us. Words are a major area where we see that occur as we echo kindness, tenderheartedness, forgiveness, and thanksgiving. He even makes an interesting connection between offering thanksgiving and avoiding sexual sin. Gratitude helps us rightly view God, and when we rightly view God, we love God more, and when we love God more, our hearts are drawn away from sin—it doesn't hold the power over us that it once did!

He explains the high calling of both parties in marriage. The wife has the role of trusting the husband and letting him care for her, which is challenging. But most people agree the husband has the harder role: He's called to love his wife like Christ loves the church. Christ died for the church and worked to help her flourish, to build her up, to bless her. He was patient with her. He lost sleep over her and prayed for her, even when she treated Him poorly. This is a weighty call, but the Spirit equips us with what we need. Paul gives similar instructions to children and bondservants about trusting those in authority over them, then he tells parents and masters, "Be someone who is easy to trust."

TODAY'S GOD SHOT

We have real, unseen enemies. God has equipped us against them, but He leaves a gap in our armor in a vital spot: Our backs are completely exposed. In ancient battles, archers stood back-to-back so they could see each others' blind spots and protect each others' weak spots. God never intended for us to walk alone or fight alone. We need each other. In the armor, every item is defensive except for one thing: the Word of God. It's our only weapon against the enemy. It's a fitting weapon because the word *satan* means "accuser." He fights with lies, and we fight with the truth. By being in God's Word today, you are strengthened for another day of fighting the lies of the flesh and the enemy. For every battle, He gives us each other and He gives us Himself. And during and after every battle, may we remember that He's where the joy is!

PHILIPPIANS 1–4

Paul writes an encouraging letter to the church in Philippi, which likely includes Lydia and her family, his former jailer and his family, and the demonized girl he healed. He planted this church and watched it grow, and he's confident that God will finish what He started in them. "He who began a good work in you will bring it to completion at the day of Jesus Christ" (1:6). "Work out your own salvation with fear and trembling, for it is God who works in you, both to will and to work for his good pleasure" (2:12–13). God is the one doing good works through them and even creating the desire in them to do those things. His charge to "work out your own salvation" isn't a call to figure out how to save yourself; if we could do that, we wouldn't need a Savior. The context helps clarify: Our lives should demonstrate the gratitude and awe we feel toward God for saving us. This is a nod to the process of sanctification—where God works in us to conform us to the image of His Son.

Paul is in prison as he writes. The Philippians know how he responds to prison, because when they imprisoned him, he shared the gospel with his captive audience. He knows his trials have purpose. He doesn't know what will happen, but he's hopeful and surrendered. He says, "I'd rather step over death into the other realm and be with Jesus right now. But on the other hand, it's probably better for you if I stick around a little longer, so that's probably what He has in store." He encourages them to be strong in the face of persecution too and not be frightened by it, because suffering has been granted to us. We should live in harmony in the midst of suffering. This is important, because suffering can bring out the worst in us. So Paul reminds them to count others as more significant—not equal, but *better*—and to look to their interests, like Jesus did.

He warns them about people who insist on circumcision, because they're adding to the gospel. He says, "As a Jew, I'm circumcised—but

---

For more information on today's reading, see thebiblerecap.com/links.

it has no impact on my relationship with God. In fact, my whole list of credentials means absolutely nothing compared to knowing Jesus. Everything I worked so hard for and everything that was given to me in my privilege—it's garbage." The word Paul uses for *rubbish* would be a curse word in modern language; that's how he views what the world values compared to the all-surpassing value of knowing Jesus.

There's a rift between two women who have been co-laborers with him in ministry, and he wants to help restore the relationship. He tells them to rejoice and to be reasonable, prayerful, and peaceful. These things are all tied together in one stream of thought. Rejoicing sets the tone—it arcs our hearts toward God and His goodness. When that's our focus, we can respond reasonably. Another translation uses the word *gentleness* here. When we're aware of the nearness of the Lord, we don't strive after things, because we can trust Him to work on our behalf. The peace that comes from trusting Him and remembering His nearness will act like a bodyguard at the door of our hearts and minds. And truly, only one thing matters. Paul says, "Whether I'm rich or poor, or regardless of what challenges or blessings I face—with Christ, I can endure all things." He thanks them for helping provide for him in prison. They've repeatedly been generous to Paul in ways other churches haven't, so he reminds them, "Just as you've provided for me, God is providing for you."

TODAY'S GOD SHOT

"Whatever is true, whatever is honorable, whatever is just, whatever is pure, whatever is lovely, whatever is commendable, if there is any excellence, if there is anything worthy of praise, think about these things" (4:8). Most of our fears don't make it through these filters; they get stopped at the first one—*is this true?* But the gospel of Christ passes every filter: true, honorable, just, pure, lovely, commendable, excellent, praiseworthy. It is all of those things and more. What we fix our minds on shows up in our hearts and our actions, bearing fruit in things like rejoicing, gentleness, prayer, and peace. God is all those beautiful things, and by fixing our eyes and minds on who He is, our thoughts are filled with beauty. He's where the joy is!

1 TIMOTHY 1–6

Today and tomorrow, Paul is writing letters to the new leaders of relatively young churches. It's helpful to notice what information he shares with both leaders and what is specific to just one leader. That helps us discern which instructions and counsel are universal to all churches.

Timothy is a leader at the church in Ephesus, which Paul planted. The Ephesians are so steeped in their culture of pagan worship that Timothy has a battle on his hands when it comes to good doctrine and orderly practice. They're proud and unteachable—and to make matters worse, they want to be teachers and leaders! But there's hope for these sinners yet. After all, God saved Paul. His story is a canvas on which God's mercy and patience shine. And that's his hope for the two men he hands over to Satan here, much like in 1 Corinthians 5:5; Paul always aims for restoration and repentance.

He wants them to be dignified and respectable—to help them avoid persecution and to be winsome to outsiders, drawing people *to* the faith, instead of repelling them. Their men are prideful and inclined to fight, and their women are flashy, arrogant, and loud—so he says to reel it in. His statements to their women are complex, but it's worth noting that *silence* means "quietness"; it's more of a posture than a volume; it carries a tone of humility. This is positioned as the opposite of exercising authority over men. The Greek for *have authority* is only used in this one spot, so we have nothing to compare it to. The perspectives on what Scripture teaches here are wide and varied: (a) Women can serve in all roles, (b) women can serve in most roles as long as they serve under a male authority, (c) it's okay for women to teach about God as long as it's outside the church, (d) they can teach in the church but not on Sundays, and so forth. Even among Spirit-filled people, it's challenging to reach total agreement on what Scripture means here *and* whether it applies universally or not. The primary interpretation of 2:15 is that Christ

For more information on today's reading, see thebiblerecap.com/links.

was born to a woman and that's how salvation came to the world. But scholars agree that Paul isn't saying women are granted eternal life by having babies. That would be contradictory to everything else he says about how salvation is granted to us.

The list of qualifications for elders points to character more than skill set. The only skill is "able to teach." Then he addresses deacons, which is a gender-neutral term that means "servant." Paul seems to establish this as a role in the church under the leadership of the elders. The requirements are high, but not as high as for elders.

The Ephesians are used to worshipping multiple gods, so it feels normal to tack something else onto their worship of Jesus. They're prone to believing false teaching—whether it's blatantly wicked or the law repackaged. Some false teachers are commanding them to avoid a whole list of things, but Paul says if they can legitimately praise God for something, they're free to enjoy it. But this is not a call to live with abandon; we should intentionally train ourselves for godliness.

When Paul says God is the Savior of all people (4:10), this doesn't mean everyone is saved. If it does, why is Paul risking his life to share the gospel? Most scholars believe this verse is saying, "God will save people from among every people group, and more specifically, the people He'll save are the ones who believe in Him."

Paul continues to help Timothy walk in humility while creating order in the church, setting up boundaries and processes. He says money is a blessing that should be used to honor God, who wants us to delight in the things He gives us. Money isn't the problem; *the love of money* is. Paul doesn't condemn their wealth or command them to get rid of it. Instead, he says, "Hold it loosely and view it rightly. It's not sturdy enough to set your hopes on."

TODAY'S GOD SHOT

"Godliness with contentment is great gain, for we brought nothing into the world, and we cannot take anything out of the world" (6:6–7). Being godly and content is the best setup imaginable. That also serves to remind us that our obedience to God isn't a claim ticket for our desires. Is godliness enough for your contentment? Is knowing Christ sufficient for your joy? Scripture says it's true, so may our hearts echo it: He's where the joy is!

TITUS 1–3

Paul writes this letter to his friend and coworker who has been assigned to ministry on the Greek island of Crete. The people there have a challenging culture that goes against the grain of Christ's teachings, and all of this is reinforced by local leaders in a battle for power. Paul reminds Titus that he positioned him over the church in Crete to get things running smoothly. But when you're dropped down at a relatively new church with a bunch of bad leaders and false teachers, it's not an easy task. Titus has a lot of the same problems Timothy faced yesterday, so there's some overlap in Paul's advice. It's interesting to note what advice shows up in both books, because it helps us understand which things are situational and which are universal.

He gives Titus guidelines for choosing elders—the people who'll govern the church, its leaders, and its decisions. It's vital that they reflect Christ not just in their doctrine, but in their lives as well, because people will look to them for guidance and truth. They also have to be willing to correct those in the church who teach bad doctrine. That's a big problem at the church in Crete. There are lots of false teachers, especially among the Jews of the "circumcision party," as Paul calls them in 1:10. And some of the local Cretans are foolish and vulgar and engage in debauchery; their lives prove they don't actually love God. So Paul tells Titus to rebuke the church members who act like that, because if and when a person actually *receives* a rebuke, their faith increases and their doctrine is refined.

Paul demonstrates what godliness and good doctrine look like in a pagan culture. He gives broad counsel to different groups of people in the church, primarily addressing areas where they may struggle. Though he sections off people by age and gender, he's not making a division so much as a distinction. His counsel is general in nature, because the greater purpose is to point them toward what it looks like to honor God in the

---

For more information on today's reading, see thebiblerecap.com/links.

most basic institution, the family. He wants their lives to be set apart in the eyes of outsiders. He tells them to adorn the doctrine of God, to present their faith as beautiful to the world, because God poured out grace on them, and grace changes everything. Grace is a change agent. God's grace brought them salvation, trained them to renounce sin and worldly passion, and trained them to be upright and godly, even in a wicked culture. God's grace reminds them to wait for the hope of Christ's return, because Christ is in the process of purifying them for Himself.

Paul takes his message outside the home and into the immediate culture and the larger realm of politics and leaders. This is another area where the church needs to stand out by demonstrating humble submission. Our humility has its greatest opportunity to show up when we disagree with someone. And in those circumstances, we should aim to speak evil of no one, avoid quarreling, be gentle, and show perfect courtesy toward all people. We do that by remembering that "we ourselves were once foolish, disobedient, led astray, slaves to various passions and pleasures, passing our days in malice and envy, hated by others and hating one another" (3:3). Paul enriches our humility by reminding us that we weren't the ones who got ourselves to where we are today—it was entirely the goodness and loving-kindness of God our Savior. If we believe that, we must be careful to live what we believe. We must aim for humility and peace and rebuke those who don't.

TODAY'S GOD SHOT

God promised us eternal life "before the ages began, and at the proper time manifested in his word" (1:2–3). The gospel of our salvation has been on the lips of our eternal God since before the ages began. Nothing has thrown His plan off or set it back. And at the right time, He set it all in motion. He created the world, carried us through the fall, and sent His Son to earth to live as a divine human who would die for the sins of fallen humanity so that we could be rescued and resurrected into a perfection and a position we never would've had on our own. We're not just His creation, but His children, His heirs. Praise God! He's where the joy is!

1 PETER 1–5

Gentile believers are Peter's primary audience for this letter. Rome is still in control, and Nero, a renowned persecutor of Christians, is likely the emperor. The Roman Empire is so wicked that Peter nicknames it Babylon, which was an evil empire from the Old Testament. Rome is Babylon 2.0, and the church is under severe persecution in a culture that's openly rebelling against God and His kingdom. Peter writes to encourage them, reminding them that God has chosen them. They likely feel forgotten or betrayed by God, but Peter says, "God caused you to be born again. And He's keeping you forever. These trials aren't His rejection of you—they're purifying you. It feels like you're growing weaker, but these trials are actually strengthening your faith. The prophets endured this, and it was purposeful."

Because of their identity as God's kids, Peter reminds them to be attentive to the things of God, to live fully for what's ahead—not for what's currently happening—and to be holy, which means "set apart." He wants them to mature in the faith, because they have a high calling: They are a holy priesthood. But how is that possible? These aren't Levites—they aren't even Jews. These are Gentiles! Peter is pointing to a doctrine called the priesthood of the believer, establishing that every believer is a priest and every believer can approach God directly because Christ is the only mediator we need.

He wants their honorable conduct to catch people's attention, but he isn't just angling for good morals; he's urging them to trust God when the world comes unhinged and to be kind to their persecutors. He says, "In your suffering, remember God—it'll help you display His worth to those around you and strengthen your soul." Then he broadens the view of submitting to authority, applying it to other areas, like Paul did in his letters. Peter encourages women about their appearance: "There's nothing wrong with nice clothes and hair, but I hope you know that's

---

For more information on today's reading, see thebiblerecap.com/links.

not the point. The thing God wants people to notice about you is your beautiful *soul*. Let people see what it looks like to trust God in trials. A woman whose heart is at rest shows God as glorious!" When Peter praises a gentle and quiet spirit, he's pointing to a heart posture, not a word count. Then he tells husbands to be gentle with their wives and describes women as the weaker vessel. Some take offense at this, but it was almost certainly a relief to his readers. It's not a derogatory term; the phrase refers to porcelain. He's telling the husbands to be tender and careful, not aggressive, selfish, or haphazard. He ascribes value to women and tells husbands God will hold them accountable for how they treat their wives. This is revolutionary in a day when women are treated as property.

When Peter says in 3:21, "Baptism, which corresponds to this, now saves you," he goes on to clarify what he means by *baptism*: "Not as a removal of dirt from the body but as an appeal to God for a good conscience, through the resurrection of Jesus Christ." He's referring to the conversion experience—the baptism of the Spirit, where we are raised to a new life with Christ. In 4:6 he says, "The gospel was preached even to those who are dead." Most scholars say this refers to believers who were alive in the past and heard the gospel but have since died. Peter says they no longer have a body of flesh but they're alive in the spirit, like God is. Regardless, Peter's point here is that suffering isn't an excuse for disobedience—we can still do good and honor the Keeper of our souls during trials.

TODAY'S GOD SHOT

In Peter's parting words to these suffering Christians, he says, "After you have suffered a little while, the God of all grace, who has called you to his eternal glory in Christ, will himself restore, confirm, strengthen, and establish you" (5:10). He basically reminds them, "None of this suffering is eternal. It's fleeting. And none of it is a sign that God has rejected you or forgotten you. He has called you to His eternal glory, and He'll be the one to rescue you from all of this. Be on the lookout for Him to restore, confirm, strengthen, and establish you." Whether that happens now or in eternity, He will not fail. He's where the joy is!

HEBREWS 1–6

We don't know who wrote this book or whom they wrote it to. Credible theories of authorship include Paul, Luke, Barnabas, and Apollos. It references the Old Testament often and seems to be written to Jewish Christians. It focuses on the supremacy of Christ right from the start: Jesus created the world, He's the radiance of God's glory, He's the exact imprint of the Father, He sustains the universe at all times, He purified us from our sins, He's seated at the Father's right hand, and the earth and the heavens will wear out someday—but Jesus will remain unchanged forever despite both of His homes being done away with and made new.

The author tells his readers not to let all of this escape them. God the Son came down to earth to live as a human, and God the Father made everything subject to the Son, who created it all at the Father's command. It may not look like everything is subject to Him, but someday we'll see His authority and control fully expressed. One of the ways we'll see that is in how He deals with Satan. Jesus died so that "through death he might destroy the one who has the power of death, that is, the devil" (2:14). There are two things worth pointing out here: (1) The word for *destroy* means "render powerless," and it suggests *stopping* more than *annihilating*; and (2) God has ultimate control over life and death but allows Satan certain power when it serves His purposes—but he's always on a leash. And because of Christ's supremacy over it all, we're set free from the fear of death.

The Son has perfectly fulfilled the role the Father appointed to Him, which includes building God's house, His church—and He dwells in us! The author urges us to remain firm in the faith because if we do, it's evidence that He truly lives in us. "We have come to share in Christ, if indeed we hold our original confidence firm to the end." Those who truly know God will continue to believe in Him. Those who fall away

---

For more information on today's reading, see thebiblerecap.com/links.

never truly knew Him—they don't have new hearts; they have hearts of unbelief that have been hardened by the lies sin tells. The author begs his listeners to pay attention to their hearts, to see which direction their hearts are moving. Are they getting softer, or are they becoming hardened by sin? According to 4:2, just because we hear and agree with the truth doesn't mean we've believed and accepted it at a heart level.

At this point in their relationship with God they should be teachers, but they're still working on the basics. They haven't grown in discernment—they can hardly tell good from evil. They need to be trained and practice what they're learning. He says, "Let's start learning how to walk. We've already laid the foundation. You already know about repentance, baptism, resurrection, and eternal judgment—you've got the basics. Now let's build on those basics so you can actually grow up as believers."

Chapter 6 has been a topic of much debate and confusion, because it sounds like he's saying a person can lose their salvation and won't be allowed to repent and return to Christ. However, the person who falls away is a person who *doesn't* know Jesus. He has experienced Jesus, like Judas did, and maybe even affirmed belief in Jesus, but his heart hasn't been transformed. He's like land that got plenty of good rain but still only yielded thorns, not fruit. He doesn't have a new heart. The author says in verse 9, "Though we speak in this way, yet in your case, beloved, we feel sure of better things—things that belong to salvation." He makes a clear distinction that the preceding verses *aren't* about a person losing their salvation; they're about a person who never had it. And for them, there's nowhere else to turn for salvation; Christ has already been sacrificed, and His sacrifice was final—so it's Jesus or nothing. The believer, however, can have full assurance of their hope in Christ—a hope that anchors our souls!

TODAY'S GOD SHOT

God deals gently with the ignorant and the wayward—the uninformed person who doesn't know better and the person who has wandered off by accident. We all fall short sometimes. When we're ignorant and wayward, He's not shocked—He factored that in. He's gentle with us, patiently drawing us in, teaching us, and loving us no less. What a relief! He's where the joy is!

HEBREWS 7–10

The author compares Jesus to the Old Testament priest Melchizedek. Priests during the old covenant were descendants of Levi, but Melchizedek wasn't because he preceded Levi by five hundred years. As a non-Levitical priest, Melchizedek sets a precedent for Jesus as a priest, because Jesus isn't a descendant of Levi either. Jesus gets His priestly authority based on the fact that He's eternal. The old law was great under the old priestly system, but we have a new priest and a new system in place now. Jesus is our high priest, and this new covenant is infinitely better. "He has no need, like those high priests, to offer sacrifices daily, first for His own sins and then for those of the people, since He did this once for all when he offered up Himself." Jesus offered the final sacrifice for our sins; there's no need for a sacrificial system anymore. He finished it—once for all time!

After He finished paying for our sins, He sat down at the right hand of God. Priests don't sit—there's too much work to do. But He's sitting because the work is done. The old covenant also had some major limitations—primarily, it couldn't change hearts. It could reveal sin, but it couldn't make a person stop loving sin. But the new covenant is written on our hearts, reaching us on every level. It makes the old covenant obsolete. You don't need to have laws telling you to do something if your heart *wants* to do it. You do it anyway because you're motivated by love, not by law. "He does away with the first in order to establish the second." This is hard for the Jewish Christians; the law isn't just a preference or a habit or even a belief; it's their entire culture and identity.

The new covenant doesn't do away with blood; sin still has to be atoned for. If blood isn't shed, sins aren't forgiven. But now we have the blood of a perfect sacrifice—the blood of Christ. As the perfect sacrifice, He only has to be sacrificed once. That's why the author keeps repeating the phrase "once for all time." He'll be back again, not to be sacrificed

For more information on today's reading, see thebiblerecap.com/links.

again, but to be *celebrated*. "Christ, having been offered once to bear the sins of many, will appear a second time, not to deal with sin but to save those who are eagerly waiting for him."

The sacrificial system provided a temporary solution to a permanent problem, but Christ's death solved the problem once for all time. The Spirit bears witness that our hearts have changed under the new covenant. And because our sins have been paid for, God is no longer accepting payment. Other solutions don't exist. If we disregard what we know of Christ and look to anyone or anything else to pay for our sins, we heap judgment on ourselves because we're disregarding the truth.

He calls them to endure because endurance is the test of our faith. It's what reveals the state of our hearts, whether we really believe. He encourages them to keep meeting together, prompting each other to walk in love and good works, remembering all the while that Jesus is coming back.

TODAY'S GOD SHOT

Two different aspects of today's reading fit together beautifully. The author describes the place in the temple where God dwelled before He took up residence in His people instead. While God's presence is in all places, His presence was especially concentrated in a room in the temple called the Most Holy Place, which was sectioned off by a curtain. But when Jesus died, the curtain in the temple was split from top to bottom (Matthew 27:51). Those concurrent events signaled a change in station; God's dwelling place wouldn't be in the temple anymore, and not long after that, God's Spirit came to dwell in His people. This is how our hearts can be changed: by the presence of His Spirit in us! We see another layer to this story in 10:19–22: "Since we have confidence to enter the holy places by the blood of Jesus, by the new and living way that he opened for us through the curtain, that is, through his flesh, and since we have a great priest over the house of God, let us draw near with a true heart in full assurance of faith." The curtain was His flesh. His flesh was torn, from heaven to earth, to open the way for us to be united to the Father. He lets us draw near, so let us draw near. He's where the joy is!

HEBREWS 11–13

Hebrews 11 is known as the Faith Hall of Fame, or the Hall of Faith. The author opens by defining faith: "Faith is the assurance of things hoped for and the conviction of things not seen." Faith isn't a vague feeling centered on nothing. Faith isn't good vibes and positive energy. Faith has a definite object. The Christian faith is faith in Christ. He is whom our faith hopes for and is convinced of. He is whom our faith points to and fully rests on. The people in the Old Testament were saved by faith too. "For by it the people of old received their commendation." The former generations were commended because of their faith in Christ, even though they didn't know His name. They knew YHWH, the one true God, and Jesus is God. The next several verses walk us down the hall, starting with Abel and taking us through the stories of the Old Testament. He talks about the incredible things they received and the horrible things they endured. Faith in God isn't just a faith that believes He'll bless us with what we want—it's also what empowers us to endure through trials and denials. Some of these people stopped the mouths of lions, but some of these people were sawn in two.

These great people of faith didn't receive what was promised—they hoped in the Messiah but died before He was born. When He came, the promise was fulfilled for them; they just didn't see it. These people testify to the fact that God is true and Jesus is worth it. They know it fully now, because they're in His presence. With their examples of walking in faith, he calls us to throw off what encumbers us and fix our focus on the finish line. Since God calls us His children, sometimes we'll have to endure His discipline, because every good parent disciplines their kids. His discipline is meant to heal us and train us, not punish us.

He encourages them to walk in unity and holiness, to fight against bitterness, sexual immorality, and impulsivity. In 12:17 he uses Esau as a reference point, saying, "When he desired to inherit the blessing, he was rejected, for he found no chance to repent, though he sought it with tears." This isn't saying Esau wanted to repent but God wouldn't forgive him. After all, Peter committed far graver sins against Jesus, and Jesus *sought him out* to forgive him. So what does this mean? *Repent* means "to turn." Esau couldn't turn things around, even though he really wanted to. He couldn't un-sell his birthright. He couldn't get the blessing back. This section isn't here to say God will never forgive us for our sins—if it were, why would there be all this talk about Jesus paying for our sins? It's here to remind us that sin has consequences. The author implores his readers to take sin seriously, because some of its consequences can mark you for life, even if they don't mark you for eternity.

The things that bring a smile to God's face include loving each other well, being kind to strangers, caring for those in need, honoring the purity of marriage, contentment, honoring our leaders, doing good, sharing, and holding to solid doctrine in our beliefs. But as for the earth, all of this will be shaken someday—both earth and heaven. "Here we have no lasting city, but we seek the city that is to come." This is a reference to the new Jerusalem!

He closes with a beautiful benediction: "Now may the God of peace who brought again from the dead our Lord Jesus, the great shepherd of the sheep, by the blood of the eternal covenant, equip you with everything good that you may do his will, working in us that which is pleasing in his sight, through Jesus Christ, to whom be glory forever and ever. Amen" (13:20–21). He follows that call to do God's will with the reminder that God has not only given us everything we need to do His will, but that He's working in us to accomplish it. What a relief! To God be the glory!

TODAY'S GOD SHOT

"Whoever would draw near to God must believe that he exists and that he rewards those who seek him" (11:6). God is a rewarder of those who seek Him. If you're seeking Him, the best reward you could get is more of Him. Nothing is better and nothing lasts longer and nothing else can't be taken away. He's the Rewarder, and He's the reward, and He's where the joy is!

2 TIMOTHY 1–4

Paul is in a Roman prison, probably for the second time, awaiting trial and expecting execution. He writes to his mentee Timothy to give final instructions, but also possibly because he's lonely. He's been abandoned by many people because he keeps landing in prison. He reminds Timothy that if we don't actively engage in the gift of our faith, we'll default to fear. Because God has granted us faith, we have access to power, love, and self-control through His Spirit. Paul likely worries that Timothy will shrink back from speaking the truth because of the consequences Paul has experienced, so he challenges him: "Don't let this deter you. Don't be ashamed of the gospel or the results of preaching it. It's worth it." He invites Timothy into this suffering—it's what God has planned for them all along.

His repeated use of the word *guard* demonstrates how God works in us. He says, "I am convinced that he is able to guard until that day what has been entrusted to me" (1:12). Then he follows it with, "By the Holy Spirit who dwells within us, guard the good deposit entrusted to you" (1:14). God is at work in us and through us to accomplish what He has promised to us and for us. God is guarding us, and as His Spirit works in us, He engages us in that process too. He encourages Timothy to dig his heels in even more—to do the hard work of spreading the gospel and to not be surprised when it's challenging. He's willing to endure whatever it takes for the gospel to reach those who will believe it, and he wants to impress this same urgency on Timothy: Do not abandon the gospel, no matter what.

False teachers are still lying about the resurrection and gaining influence. Paul has never had a problem correcting them, but he doesn't want Timothy to waste time in fruitless arguments. Perhaps Timothy, who is still young and zealous, is inclined to debate and Paul feels the need to restrain him. He says, "Flee youthful passions and pursue righteousness,

For more information on today's reading, see thebiblerecap.com/links.

faith, love, and peace. . . . Have nothing to do with foolish, ignorant controversies; you know that they breed quarrels" (2:22–23). He doesn't just tell him what to run from, but what to run after: Pursue the things of the Spirit. Be gentle with correction. Don't put speed bumps in the way for people. Our hope isn't that we'll make a great point or win the argument; our hope is that God will grant repentance and free them from Satan's grip! He tells Timothy to avoid certain kinds of people, including those who claim to believe but don't demonstrate a real relationship with Jesus. In Ephesus, some of these people seek out vulnerable women who lack discernment, seduce them, and charge them money to teach them lies.

He tells us what to expect when we follow Jesus: "All who desire to live a godly life in Christ Jesus will be persecuted." But Scripture makes us wise in the midst of trials—it keeps us afloat. He says to preach the Word with patience, because people are increasingly inclined to dismiss it. Paul knows his days are coming to an end, and he wants Timothy to visit. He asks him to bring John Mark with him—the man he had a sharp disagreement with on his first missionary journey (Acts 13:13). God has finally brought restoration. Paul closes by warning Timothy about people who might be a snare to him, but he says no matter what happens, God will rescue him. Sometimes rescue looks like death. "The Lord will rescue me from every evil deed and bring me safely into his heavenly kingdom" (4:18). And He did.

TODAY'S GOD SHOT

"All Scripture is breathed out by God and profitable for teaching, for reproof, for correction, and for training in righteousness, that the man of God may be complete, equipped for every good work" (3:16–17). God breathed out the words we read today. He gave them to us for a variety of reasons: to rebuke us when we're blatantly sinning, to correct us when we're making foolish decisions, and to train us in righteousness so that we can hopefully grow into people who need less reproving and correcting, so that we will be complete, equipped for every good work He has prepared for us. His Word is a gift of grace and wisdom. Knowing His character would be impossible without His Word or His Spirit, who breathed out His Word. He's where the joy is!

2 PETER 1–3; JUDE 1

These two books deal with leaders in the church who are trying to stop false teachers' lies. Peter lives in Rome under the tyranny of Governor Nero; he knows he'll die soon. He writes this letter to be passed from church to church, reminding people to hold tightly to truth. In the midst of persecution, he says God has given them everything they need for life and godliness. Because of this power, their lives should look different from their culture. He wants them to be fruitful and effective in their knowledge of God. But if they aren't, they might be living a lie.

The false teachers accuse the church leaders of lying, so Peter defends the gospel: It's not a myth, no one made it up—not the apostles and not the writers of the Hebrew Scriptures either. Scripture is God's words, written by the guidance of the Spirit. The false teachers are trying to get people to rely on their own words about God instead of Scripture. They claim to know when Jesus will return, even though Jesus said no one knows! Peter says to trust the written Word of God rather than the words of false teachers. Those who lie about God's Word will face judgment. Even the angels brought judgment on themselves when they sinned against God—not to mention the people on earth during the flood and in Sodom and Gomorrah. God brought judgment on them while sparing the righteous.

Peter addresses scoffers who follow their sinful desires and mock the return of Jesus. He says, "Look around—Someone made this. He destroyed it once with water, then restored it. Someday He'll come back, and this time, He'll destroy it with fire. You may wonder why He's not here yet, but His timeline is different than yours. He's taking this long because He's being patient with you. He's giving you time to repent. He'll come when you don't expect it—and all of this will be burned up, heaven and earth. But His kids will be preserved from judgment and will live with Him in the new heaven and new earth."

For more information on today's reading, see thebiblerecap.com/links.

He says Paul's letters are hard to understand sometimes, and ignorant, unstable people twist them and take them out of context. But it's no surprise, because that's what they do with other Scriptures too. Peter, who was in the inner circle of Jesus, refers to Paul's letters as Scripture. It's one reason Paul's letters are in the Bible. Not long after writing this letter, Peter dies by crucifixion, just as Jesus said (John 21:18–19).

Jude is almost certainly written by one of Jesus's brothers (also called Judah and Judas; see Matthew 13:55). He tells the believers that they're called by God and kept in Christ, warns about false teachers, and says none of this surprises God. In fact, even the presence of false teachers is somehow part of God's plan. He recounts the stories of God punishing wicked people and sparing the righteous—the escape from Egypt, the fallen angels, and Sodom and Gomorrah. The false teachers think they won't see God's judgment, but Jude says God will punish them, like all the others, with eternal fire. He references a story from another ancient Jewish book, the Book of Enoch, which says Satan and the archangel Michael fought over Moses' corpse. Some say Satan planned to inhabit Moses' body, like a wolf in sheep's clothing, and damage the message of God. But that side story just illustrates what Jude wants us to know: An archangel didn't pronounce judgment on the enemy; he invoked the Lord's authority to rebuke him. These false teachers were doing the opposite—pronouncing judgment on their own and denying Christ's authority. He tells the church not to be afraid, to keep themselves in the love of God because God is keeping them in His love. As always, He's working in us and through us to do what He has promised to us and for us.

TODAY'S GOD SHOT

Jude says Jesus rescued the Israelites out of Egypt. Even though He hadn't been born as a human at the time, Jesus has always existed. He showed up repeatedly in the Old Testament, doing miraculous things to save His people. He's always been coming to earth and rescuing His people. Then, now, and always, He's where the joy is!

1 JOHN 1–5

Most scholars believe this letter was written by John the apostle, but he's less concerned with his readers knowing who he is and more concerned with them knowing who Jesus is. False teachers are causing division in the church and spreading lies about Jesus. John doesn't waste time with greetings but gets right to the point: Jesus has always existed—He is truly God. We saw Him and touched Him—He was truly human. This God-Man said God is light, completely devoid of darkness, so to walk with Him means we walk in the light. We build community with others who are in the light. We can confess our sins in the light, and it actually enriches our unity, whereas darkness and hiding thwart healthy community. And Jesus brings us freedom in our relationship with the Father, because He paid for our sins and advocates for us. Our relationship with Jesus changes our relationship with sin too—He didn't just set us free from the *penalty* of our sins; He also set us free from the *bondage* to our sins, enabling us to walk in truth. Loving Jesus pushes out our love for worldly things.

There'll be false messiahs, possibly from within the church. There'll be division in the church, and some will abandon the faith, but this serves to reveal that they never truly believed. On the other hand, those who truly believe will persevere in the faith, even amid the presence of false teachers. The presence of the Holy Spirit in their lives is evidence they know and follow the truth, so He calls them to abide in the truth. Despite what the false teachers say, Jesus hasn't returned yet. But when He does, we'll be transformed. We won't be disembodied spirits like the people who are currently in heaven. We'll live in the new heaven and earth in our new bodies. But our focus isn't just about getting to live with Him in eternity; it's about life with Him now and walking in righteousness now.

John knows some readers will be frightened by his words, so he comforts them with reminders that God is greater than any fear or condem-

For more information on today's reading, see thebiblerecap.com/links.

nation they feel in their hearts. As for others, it's hard to know if they're in the truth, so he gives a litmus test: If the Holy Spirit is at work in a person, they'll affirm that Jesus is fully God and fully man. Confessing Jesus as God is a sign of our unity with Him, and our unity with Him is evidence that He loves us; He wouldn't unite Himself to someone He didn't love, so He must love us because He's abiding with us. His abiding with us is how love is made perfect, giving us confidence that we're His. That confidence starts to show up in how we live our lives—we can live fearlessly because He abides in us in perfect love. What do we have to be afraid of? He abides with us now and forever and has taken all our punishment already! Because of Him, we have overcome the world—we can resist sin and temptation, we're no longer in bondage, and we can love like Jesus loves, even when treated with contempt like He was.

Jewish law calls for two witnesses to testify on behalf of a person, but John offers three: the Spirit, the water, and the blood. The Spirit affirms Jesus. The water is almost certainly a reference to the baptism of Jesus—when God the Father said Jesus is His beloved Son. The blood is almost certainly a reference to His death and resurrection. Overcoming the grave speaks for itself. And because He has overcome death, He holds the keys to eternal life; He alone stands as the line of demarcation between life and death. John wants believers to be assured of their faith and know it's real. All this talk about love, obedience, truth, light, and life—it's to help us gain confidence, not just in what we believe but in who He is, and to know we're His.

TODAY'S GOD SHOT

"In this is love, not that we have loved God but that he loved us and sent his Son to be the propitiation for our sins" (4:10). The Father set this all in motion while we were still in rebellion against Him. "We love because he first loved us" (4:19). His love was the catalyst for our love. The only reason we can love Him at all is because all of this was His idea. We never would've sought Him out, but He loved us and made a way for us to abide with Him forever! He's where the joy is!

2 JOHN 1; 3 JOHN 1

Both of these books are written by someone who refers to himself as "the elder," which is a common way to refer to a pastoral leader in the church; most scholars believe this is John the apostle.

Second John is addressed to "the elect lady." Which lady? It could be a person, but when John uses the word *you* in this book, it's typically the plural form. So most scholars conclude that "the elect lady" is likely his way of addressing a specific church, the bride of Christ, God's elect. He starts out by saying he loves the church and its people and that all people who love the truth love the church and its people. This is hard, because the church is made up of sinners. But God continually pours out grace to help us heal wounds, bridge gaps, and restore brokenness, just like with Paul and John Mark. He's committed to the unity of His church, so He sends the Spirit as our Helper in aiming for unity and truth. In fact, those are John's focus: love and truth. Love without truth is foolish, and truth without love is arrogant, but truth and love strike the balance Christ demonstrated. We live those out by doing what Jesus says, obeying His commandments. If we really believe that what Jesus says is truth, then love is living it out. Truth and love fit together beautifully.

Love doesn't mean throwing your doors wide open to anyone. John says to be discerning and to pay attention, because there are some people you should close your doors to. Like 1 John, this letter is written to encourage and direct the church amid the lies of false teachers. This problem is widespread and persistent. John repeats the common theme: (a) the warning to watch out and abide and not be led astray and (b) the encouragement that those who belong to Christ will abide and will not be led astray. This echoes what we read yesterday: "They went out from us, but they were not of us; for if they had been of us, they would have continued with us. But they went out, that it might become plain

---

For more information on today's reading, see thebiblerecap.com/links.

that they all are not of us" (1 John 2:19). Those who are in Christ *will* persevere in the faith.

The enemy loves to set up camp in the church and try to deceive its members and leaders, so John urges the church to stay strong, to be on the lookout for doctrine that's inconsistent with what Christ and Scripture teach. In order to do that, you have to know what Christ and Scripture teach.

Third John is written to a believer named Gaius. We don't know anything about him except that he was probably part of the church John addressed in 2 John. Apparently, all three of these letters arrived at their destination in one packet, which is how and why they were kept together. John encourages Gaius, saying he's hearing good things about him. Some people from his church visited John and told him how Gaius has supported and built them up. John says to keep at it, to support them in a manner worthy of God, because that's kingdom work. Even though he isn't doing the work himself, he's contributing in a way that makes it possible. Then John warns Gaius about Diotrephes, who is trying to call the shots at the church. John will deal with him personally when he gets there, but he wants Gaius to be aware of the problem so things don't get out of control before he arrives. In the meantime, he says to imitate those who display God's character and goodness to the world around them.

TODAY'S GOD SHOT

John says those who don't confess Jesus as Lord are anti-Christs—against Christ. Jesus said, "Whoever is not with me is against me" (Matthew 12:30). In a technical sense, any unbeliever, anyone who denies that Jesus is God, is an anti-Christ. Jesus is the line of demarcation between truth and lies. He's the line of demarcation between life and death. He said, "I am the way, and the truth, and the life. No one comes to the Father except through me" (John 14:6). But the good news and the hope of the gospel is that God reaches across that line into enemy territory and rescues those who oppose Him to bring them into His family. We are evidence of that. There is hope yet for all who are in the other camp. May they come to know and believe that Jesus is the way, the truth, and the life, and that He's where the joy is!

REVELATION 1–5

John—likely the apostle—wrote Revelation from Patmos, a tiny prison island like Alcatraz. Church history tells us Rome tried to burn John alive in oil, but he survived. Since they couldn't figure out how to kill him, they exiled him to Patmos. His letter is a singular revelation—not plural—and it's the revelation of Jesus. Some say that means it reveals *more* of Jesus, and others say Jesus is the one *doing* the revealing; still others say it could be both, because if Jesus is revealing something to His people, it's Himself. There's a blessing promised to those who read this book aloud and pay attention to it. This is the first of seven "blessed are" statements known as the seven beatitudes of Revelation.

Jewish teaching and culture loves numbers and symbols. While this book still has a lot to offer modern readers, most scholars warn against trying to use the numbers to unlock secret information about the future. The stated purpose of this book is to *reveal* something. When you're trying to reveal something to your reader, you don't hide it and bury it in code. That means the pressure is off for us to figure out how and when the world ends. Eschatology (a person's view of the end times) matters, but God-fearing, Christ-exalting, Spirit-filled people have different views. Since eschatology isn't foundational to our understanding of who God is, it's wise to hold it with an open hand. It's actually helpful for some of this to remain a mystery; otherwise it can lead us to fear and control.

John has a vision of Jesus, who says to write a letter to seven churches. Some have fallen into sin, some are undergoing persecution, and some are thriving. He speaks to them regarding their individual circumstances, offering warning, encouragement, and hope. These churches are represented by a seven-candle lampstand—like the temple menorah—and Jesus is in the midst of the lampstands, in the midst of the church. In Judaism and in Scripture, there's a lot of symbolism in the numbers

For more information on today's reading, see thebiblerecap.com/links.

three, seven, ten, and twelve; in their own way, each of these numbers symbolizes perfection and completion. Four times today we encountered the "sevenfold spirit of God." Some say this is a way of symbolizing the wholeness and perfection of God's Spirit, and others say it points to different attributes of God's Spirit—perhaps like we see in Isaiah 11:2: "And the Spirit *of the Lord* shall rest upon him, the Spirit of *wisdom* and *understanding*, the Spirit of *counsel* and *might*, the Spirit of *knowledge* and the *fear of the Lord*."

John gives each church fitting rebukes or encouragement. But to all the churches Jesus mentions listening, obeying, and conquering. Given the context, what do you think He means by "conquering"? This isn't a call to defeat Rome; it's a call to persevere in the faith, to overcome the temptations of the world—whether they're temptations to pursue earthly pleasures or to escape hardship and persecution. To be a conqueror is to love better. To be a conqueror is to keep loving God, regardless of what life throws at us—blessings or challenges.

John gets a glimpse into God's throne room. His throne is surrounded by the twenty-four elders. Some scholars say this is literal, and these are the twelve apostles plus the twelve sons of Jacob; others say it's symbolic and indicates that God is surrounded by *all* His people—with the twelve tribes representing the old covenant family and the twelve apostles representing the new covenant family. God holds a scroll containing His purposes for humankind; it's sealed with seven seals that no one can open. John is despairing until Jesus, the Lamb of God, shows up and takes the scroll. Then everyone falls down to worship Him.

TODAY'S GOD SHOT

Jesus says, "Fear not, I am the first and the last, and the living one. I died, and behold I am alive forevermore, and I have the keys of Death and Hades" (1:17–18). This book can feel scary, but some of Jesus's first words are, "Fear not." Then He tells us who He is. If we first recognize who Christ is, then we can understand and rightly view what He's going to do in this book. Who He is precedes everything, and who He is undergirds everything. We walk through this book with the King of Glory at our side. And He's where the joy is!

REVELATION 6–11

Today Jesus opens the seals of the Father's scroll, one by one. The first four seals give us four horses and four horsemen, commonly referred to as the four horsemen of the apocalypse (*apocalypse* is Greek for our word *revelation*). These are enemies of God; they bring death, disease, and destruction. But they still only operate under His jurisdiction: They come out when His seraphim give the command, and any authority they have is only given temporarily for the purpose of accomplishing God's judgment on earth. They're never in control, and God's reign is never in question. The three final seals pertain to God's people: the martyrs, the great day of the Lord, and the 144,000. This number is probably symbolic, representing a much larger multitude. Some say it's the remnant of the Jews, and others say it represents all believers from all time.

Silence in heaven is followed by the prayers of God's people, then seven angels blow seven trumpets. The first four trumpets bring disaster on earth and in the skies. At the blast of the fifth trumpet, a star falls from heaven; this may reference Satan's fall (Isaiah 14:12; Luke 10:18). He seems to manage a locust attack—which is probably symbolic; locusts often refer to armies. But these locusts aren't allowed to kill any of God's kids. The sixth trumpet brings a plague and more death, but none of it yields repentance. When another angel shows up with another scroll, he plants one foot on earth and one foot on sea, and he reaches his fist to the heavens, then declares God's sovereignty over those three realms. He says the seventh trumpet will sound when the mystery of God is fulfilled, which some say is the return of Jesus and the initiation of His kingdom. Others say it's the gathering of the remnant of Israel after the inclusion of the Gentiles. God has John eat the scroll and prepare to prophesy to the nations.

Here's an important note: In AD 70, Rome destroyed the Second Temple, and it has never been rebuilt. Some Jews say it's impossible to

For more information on today's reading, see thebiblerecap.com/links.

rebuild it, since they've lost the ark of the covenant. Many Christians believe it doesn't need to be rebuilt because God's Spirit dwells in His people now, not in a building. Because of that event, there's debate over the meaning of chapter 11, which includes a vision of the temple and its destruction. Some say this book was written in the mid-60s before the temple was destroyed, and they believe John prophesied what happened in AD 70. Others say this was written in the early 90s and it prophesies about a literal future temple. Still others say it's symbolic and it represents God's current dwelling place—His people. When God says His holy city will be trampled for three and a half years, those same theories apply: It already literally happened in AD 70, it will literally happen someday, or it will symbolically happen to His people.

Two witnesses show up here as well: lampstands and olive branches. Since churches were lampstands earlier in this vision, some believe the lampstands represent the faithful witness of the church in the end times. Some compare them to Moses and Elijah, because they bring blood and fire. Some compare them to Joshua the high priest and Zerubbabel the leader of the people. Either way, God gives His people power in the midst of tragedy. When the enemy appears to be winning, God proves He can't be defeated. He sustains His anointed.

TODAY'S GOD SHOT

When the seventh angel blows his trumpet, things shift. "The kingdom of the world has become the kingdom of our Lord and of his Christ, and he shall reign forever and ever" (11:15). Revelation isn't necessarily happening in chronological order, so we aren't past the death and destruction quite yet. But God lets us catch our breath here with this reminder: Jesus reigns supreme over all of this, and His reign will never end! The end times are just a fraction of the story; they're only the beginning. Many people who talk about Christ's return end up fearing it more than looking forward to it, but the kingdom of God isn't for people who are afraid of hell and pain; the kingdom of God is for people who love God! May we eagerly await His return, knowing and believing that He's where the joy is!

REVELATION 12–18

John's vision is filled with signs and symbols; many of these things aren't literal. John's original audience probably wasn't confused by this. They likely saw this vision through the lens of Israel's history.

A woman gives birth to a child who would rule the nation, but a beast doesn't like this and tries to put a stop to it. She lives in the wilderness, where God takes care of her. Most scholars say the woman is Israel, the dragon is Lucifer, and the stars that are swept down by the dragon's tail are the angels who joined with him. War breaks out in heaven between the elect angels and Satan's angels; the elect angels win, so Lucifer and his angels are evicted. Since they can't stay in heaven, they mount an attack on earth, but God miraculously protects Israel. Thwarted again, Satan's angels go off to attack God's other kids—John's readers would likely see this as a reference to the Gentiles, the church at large, or the remnant of Israel.

A sea beast has seven heads and ten horns, representing nations and leaders. Everyone loves the beast. For John's readers, this is an obvious nod to Rome, which everyone worships except for God's kids. It's also a flashback to when Daniel and his friends lived in Babylon and King Nebuchadnezzar demanded to be worshipped. John reminds them that the way to overcome is to remain faithful despite persecution.

Next, an earth beast makes powerful attempts to counterfeit God and His ways: It looks like a lamb, fakes its own resurrection, and has people mark themselves on the forehead and hand. This is a counterfeit of Jesus, His resurrection, and the phylacteries from Deuteronomy 6:4–8, which the Jews wear on those same spots. The beast counterfeits this with his own name. In Hebrew, each letter has an assigned number. The beast's name is 666, which also spells the name of Nero, the Roman emperor. John's readers likely understand Rome to be Babylon 2.0 (1 Peter 5:13) and the hand and forehead marks to symbolize whom you belong to: Are you marked with God's name or Rome's?

For more information on today's reading, see thebiblerecap.com/links.

Three angels bring three messages: (1) Worship God because judgment is coming, (2) Babylon has fallen, and (3) those who worship the beast instead of God will get God's judgment and everlasting punishment. Despite the beast's attacks, God has the final say. Jesus works out justice and vengeance on earth, aided by angels from the temple in heaven. Some say the earthly temple was a replica of the heavenly temple, and some say the word *temple* just refers to God's dwelling place in general. Seven angels appear carrying seven bowls of God's wrath (plagues). When the world's armies gather in Armageddon, the last angel pours out his bowl of tragedies and God makes Babylon/Rome drink the cup of His wrath. A woman rides a beast—likely a reference to Rome and Nero—and tortures God's people. While this happened with Nero, some say these verses have future implications; regardless, we stand firm on God's goodness, wisdom, and power. The woman and the beast only have power as God allows and only in ways that serve His ultimate purposes. Another angel declares that the rule of Babylon/Rome has ended. God's people rejoice, but those who loved Babylon/Rome and benefited from her evil mourn, because they can't make money from trading things—including human souls, a reference to slaves, who were an estimated 50 percent of Rome's population.

TODAY'S GOD SHOT

Babylon makes war on God and His people, and "the Lamb will conquer them, for he is Lord of lords and King of kings, and those with him are called and chosen and faithful" (17:14). We are called and chosen and faithful. And we are with Him, but He's the one who does the conquering. How does a Lamb defeat a seven-headed beast? By laying down His life. When we first see the Lamb in Revelation 5:6, He's been slain, and His death is what guarantees our victory. "They have conquered him by the blood of the Lamb and by the word of their testimony, for they loved not their lives even unto death" (12:11). We testify of Jesus and His death and resurrection. His victory over death and darkness was His victory over all the enemies of light and life. He's our conqueror, and He's where the joy is!

REVELATION 19–22

After God's massive victory yesterday, heaven erupts in a party today! The multitudes in heaven praise God, then it's time for the marriage of the Lamb and His bride—Christ and the church, who is clothed in purity, in fine white linen. The angel who has been guiding John through these visions has him write down that those who are invited to the marriage supper of the Lamb will be blessed. And this is such a blessing because *they're the bride*. Then John falls down at the angel's feet, but the angel refuses his worship because he's just a servant of God and not worthy of worship.

Jesus appears on a white horse, and He's wearing a robe dipped in blood. He's followed by the armies of heaven—which usually refers to angels, but here it's likely referring to the people of God, because it clarifies that they're wearing the same clothes as before. A sword is coming out of His mouth; this has echoes of the armor of God, where the Word of God is our sword (Ephesians 6:17). His Word is His weapon; He brings justice through His Word and is victorious over His enemies. As for the armies of heaven behind Him, it appears we do nothing. He wins on His own, and quickly.

Chapter 20 has a section known as the Millennium. Opinions vary on whether this is symbolic or if it's a literal, precise number. Opinions also vary on whether it is set in the past, present, or future. In conjunction with the millennium, Satan is bound in the bottomless pit temporarily. Your view on the millennium also determines how you view Satan's binding and the resurrections described here. Satan will eventually suffer total defeat in eternal torment, along with the other members of his counterfeit trinity: the beast and the false prophet. While it appears everyone will be judged by their works, those whose names are in the Lamb's Book of Life will be pardoned because their sins are covered by Christ, the Lamb. He has written our names down on the pages of Life

For more information on today's reading, see thebiblerecap.com/links.

(Luke 10:20; Philippians 4:3). The lake of fire is reserved for anyone whose name isn't in the Book of Life.

After this, heaven and earth pass away. They've both been tarnished by sin—whether by humans or by angels—so they have to be renewed. Scholars disagree on whether heaven and earth will be entirely new material or the old versions will be purged, like with fire, and restored. When He returns and renews them both, the new heaven descends and merges with the new earth. Our disembodied spirits (in the old heaven) will be re-embodied, and we'll live in the new dwelling place of God and His people (1 John 3:2–3). He calls it the new Jerusalem, and it's astonishing. It's a gold cube, each side is roughly 1,400 miles long, and it's decorated with precious jewels. There's no temple, because God Himself is our temple. The gates are never shut, and it's always day, because God is the light. There is free water for the thirsty; this points to Jesus (Isaiah 55:1–3; John 4:13–14; 1 Corinthians 10:4). But those who reject the eternal living water of Jesus will get an eternity of what they long for: complete waterlessness. The river of life flows from the throne and through the city, and the Tree of Life grows on both sides of the river. Its fruit is free for the taking, no longer forbidden.

The angel says to spread the word—people need to know that Jesus is really coming back, judgment is really happening, and the free blessing of knowing God and living with Him for eternity really awaits. The last of the seven beatitudes of Revelation says, "Blessed are those who wash their robes, so that they may have the right to the tree of life and that they may enter the city by the gates" (22:14). Our robes are made pure by the blood of the Lamb. Our needs are met and our unity restored by His death and resurrection!

TODAY'S GOD SHOT

Jesus says three times that He's coming back soon. Knowing the incredible, glorious future that awaits us, John says God's kids will join with the Spirit and beg Christ to return. So when Jesus says, "Surely I am coming soon," John leads the response, "Amen. Come, Lord Jesus!" So we trust Jesus's promise and echo back our prayer, "Amen. Come, Lord Jesus!" You're where the joy is!

(Luke 10:20; Philippians 4:3). The fate of the ungodly and for anyone whose name isn't in the Book of Life.

[illegible] the stories [illegible] knowing the [illegible] God [illegible] with the Spirit [illegible] Christ to return [illegible] Amen. Come, Lord Jesus! He's where the joy is!

Acknowledgments

This book represents the collective love, wisdom, and prayers of some of the best people I know. God has generously surrounded me with family, friends, mentors, and supporters who have given their time to this, and I would be remiss not to tell you about these saints (who would all, of course, humbly point to God as the source of their contributions).

Those who have been formative in my love for God and His Word
My parents: I love you forever. These pages are saturated with your wisdom.
Judy Scheuch, who taught me to study the Bible.
Kemper Crabb, who showed me how much I had (and have) to learn.
Lee McDerment, who taught me to love the Bible and challenged me to read it through for the first time.

TBR Team
Your commitment to this could never receive enough recognition or thanks. You've worked tirelessly to bring this to fruition. God is glorified in you.
Olivia Le, Bonnie Hartwig, Allison King, Emily Pickell, Meg Mitchell, Laura Buchelt, Casey Helmick, Sarah Billings, Jane Long, Jess Wilson, Lindsie Herring, Sarah Yocum, Brooke Stewart, Morgan Young, Landon Wade, Arlette Blackwell, Omar Cardenas

Support Team
Your prayers and encouragement kept me afloat during the fifteen months of solitude while working on this project.

Sonya Higgs, Cherie Duffey, Natalie and Mike McGuire (and Maddy and Sophie), Meg Roe, Candice Romo, Tiffany Clutts, Lauren Swaim, Lauren Gachkar, D-Group, Meredith Land Moore, Dana Crawford, Grant Skeldon, Jon Pendergrass, TBR Patreon Family, Year of the Bible, Nick Hall

Resource Team
Your help working through questions and solving problems extends far beyond me.
Mike West, Chris Crawford, Mark Walz, Chaplain (CPT) Warwick Fuller
A number of other resources were helpful in my research, including the ESV Study Bible, the FaithLife Study Bible, the Blue Letter Bible, and the Bible Project.

Publishing Team
You care about people knowing and loving God's Word. I'm so grateful to be on this team with you!
Lisa Jackson at Alive Literary Agency, for finding me three years too soon (i.e., right on time).
Jeff Braun at Bethany House Publishers, for believing in this from the start.
Hannah Ahlfield, my editor, for "every jot and tittle."
Deirdre Close, Holly Maxwell, Kate Deppe, Stephanie Smith, Rebecca Schriner, Mycah Gavic, Paul Higdon, Kristen Larson, and all the others who worked hard to make this book a reality.

About the Author

Tara-Leigh Cobble's zeal for biblical literacy is at the heart of everything she creates. Her goal is to help people read, understand, and love the Bible. Her daily podcast, The Bible Recap, guides listeners through a chronological one-year reading plan. The podcast has over 500 million downloads and reached number one on the Apple Podcast charts in All Categories. She created and leads D-Group International, which has grown into an international network of more than 500 weekly Bible studies that meet in homes, in churches, and online. A Wall Street Journal bestselling author, she also writes and hosts a daily radio feature called The God Shot, and leads trips to Israel to study the Bible on-site.

Tara-Leigh lives in Dallas, Texas, where she has no pets, children, or anything else that might die if she forgets to feed it.

For more information: TaraLeighCobble.com | TheBibleRecap.com | MyDGroup.org | Israelux.com

Social media: @taraleighcobble | @thebiblerecap | @mydgroup | @israeluxtours

The Bible Recap
Est. 2019 | TheBibleRecap.com
Have you ever closed your Bible and thought, *What did I just read?* In about eight minutes a day, our summary walks you through the one-year chronological plan. Available in podcast, YouTube, and book form. Other supplemental resources available for adults and children.

D-Group International

Est. 2009 | MyDGroup.org

Men's and women's Bible study groups that meet weekly—in homes, online, and in churches around the world. D-Group recently began a series of 40 studies that will cover the entire Bible over the course of a decade.

Israelux

Est. 2014 | Israelux.com

Offering a deluxe tour and life-changing teaching at the sites where Jesus lived, ate, taught, ministered, and made new life possible for us through His death and resurrection. The beauty of Israel is also captured in TLC's book *Israel: Beauty, Light, and Luxury*, a *Wall Street Journal* bestseller.

Books by Tara-Leigh Cobble

The Bible Recap: A One-Year Guide to Reading and Understanding the Entire Bible

The Bible Recap Study Guide: Daily Questions to Deepen Your Understanding of the Entire Bible

The Bible Recap Journal: Your Daily Companion to the Entire Bible

The Bible Recap Discussion Guide: Weekly Questions for Group Conversation on the Entire Bible

The Bible Recap Kids' Devotional: 365 Reflections and Activities for Children and Families

The Bible Recap for Kids: A 365-Day Guide through the Bible for Young Readers

The God Shot: 100 Snapshots of God's Character in Scripture

Israel: Beauty, Light, and Luxury

The Bible Recap 365-Day Chronological Study Bible: English Standard Version

THE BIBLE RECAP KNOWING JESUS SERIES*

Knowing Jesus as King: A 10-Session Study on the Gospel of Matthew

Knowing Jesus as Servant: A 10-Session Study on the Gospel of Mark

Knowing Jesus as Savior: A 10-Session Study on the Gospel of Luke

Knowing Jesus as God: A 10-Session Study on the Gospel of John

* General editor

THE BIBLE RECAP KNOWING GOD SERIES*

Acts: The Spirit and the Bride—
a 10-Week Bible Study on God and His Church

Romans: Dead to Sin and Alive to Christ—
a 10-Week Bible Study

1 & 2 Corinthians: Love Unity, and the Countercultural Power of the Cross—a 10-Week Bible Study

Galatians & Ephesians: The Freedom and Purpose in the Body of Christ—a 10-Week Bible Study

Philippians & Colossians: Humility, Love, and Truth—
a 10-Week Bible Study on the Deity of Christ

1 & 2 Thessalonians: Hope in the Midst of Trials—
a 10-Week Bible Study on Anticipating the Return of Christ

1 & 2 Timothy, Titus & Philemon: Letters to Leaders—
a 10-Week Bible Study on Sound Doctrine and Godly Behavior

* General editor

Also from Tara-Leigh Cobble

Dig deeper into the Word with *The Bible Recap Study Guide*, with daily reflection and research questions specific to each day's reading and space to write your responses and notes.

The Bible Recap Study Guide

Take your study further with *The Bible Recap Journal*, which offers writing prompts and plenty of organized space perfect for responding and tracking each day through the whole Bible.

The Bible Recap Journal

This insightful companion tool to *The Bible Recap* will help you enrich your Scripture reading in community with fellow readers. Whether paired with *The Bible Recap Study Guide* or used on its own, *The Bible Recap Discussion Guide* is thoughtfully written to help you spark meaningful and engaging group conversation.

The Bible Recap Discussion Guide